APA
College
Dictionary
of
Psychology

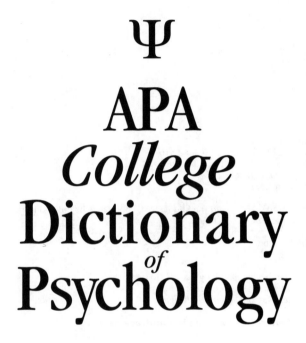

Ψ

APA
College
Dictionary
of
Psychology

American Psychological Association
Washington, DC

Second printing, August 2012.

Published by
American Psychological Association
750 First Street, NE
Washington, DC 20002
www.apa.org

To order
APA Order Department
P.O. Box 92984
Washington, DC 20090-2984
Tel: (800) 374-2721; Direct: (202) 336-5510
Fax: (202) 336-5502; TDD/TTY: (202) 336-6123
Online: www.apa.org/books/
E-mail: order@apa.org

In the U.K., Europe, Africa, and the Middle East, copies may be ordered from
American Psychological Association
3 Henrietta Street
Covent Garden, London
WC2E 8LU England

Typeset in Aylesbury, England, by Market House Books, Ltd.
Printer: Edwards Brothers, Ann Arbor, Michigan
Cover Designer: Naylor Design, Washington, DC

Library of Congress Cataloging-in-Publication Data

APA college dictionary of psychology. — 1st ed.
    p. cm.
ISBN-13: 978-1-4338-0433-5
ISBN-10: 1-4338-0433-6
1. Psychology—Dictionaries. I. American Psychological Association. II. Title: College dictionary of psychology. III. Title: A.P.A. college dictionary of psychology.

  BF31.A68 2009
  150.3—dc22

                              2008048226

British Library Cataloguing-in-Publication Data
A CIP record is available from the British Library.

Printed in the United States of America
First Edition

The citation for this publication is *APA college dictionary of psychology*. (2009). Washington, DC: American Psychological Association.

Contents

Preface

This dictionary is the third in a family of reference works published by the American Psychological Association (APA). The parent reference, the *APA Dictionary of Psychology*—the culmination of some ten years of research and lexicographic activity—was released in 2006, and has since won wide critical endorsement and recognition from both the publishing and reference library communities.

An abridgment of this parent work, the *APA Concise Dictionary of Psychology*, was released two years later. Whereas the original dictionary offered a deeply layered approach to the lexicon of the field in its approximately 25,000 entries, the *Concise*, through an editorial process of reduction and synthesis, offered an equally informative exploration of the fundamental vocabulary, but with broader general appeal, in approximately 10,000 entries. The lexicographical journey undertaken to create both of these works is described in detail for the interested user in their prefaces.

The latest offspring in this reference family, the *APA College Dictionary of Psychology*, naturally carries the same genetic material as its predecessors and bears witness to an ongoing evolutionary process. APA offers it as an even more highly concentrated, easily portable, and economical alternative for the student of psychology—whether he or she is at the advanced placement level in high school, a college undergraduate enrolled in Intro Psych, or an undergraduate considering or making psychology his or her major field of study.

How did we further focus and refine the lexicon so that it answers the needs of this specific population? A brief review of our editorial method and process may be useful here:

In order to delimit an appropriately representative universe of terms for inclusion in a college dictionary, APA reference staff researched psychology texts in use at some three dozen institutions of higher learning in the United States. These schools fell into three broad categories: major public and private universities, small liberal arts colleges, and community colleges. It was important not only to look across these general categories, but also to include predominantly institutions with psychology departments of high repute and with strong programs in the arts and sciences generally. From this spectrum, we sought to pinpoint primary introductory undergraduate texts in general, social, developmental, abnormal, and cognitive psychology, as well as neuroscience and basic methodology and statistics.

Glossaries and indexes from the most popular texts (i.e., those used at several institutions) were then assessed against the corpus of 25,000 entries in the parent dictionary and the 10,000 entries in *Concise,* in order to ascertain overlap (and gaps). Reference staff decided to include the 5,000 most common terms (i.e., those appearing in multiple sources), bearing in mind (a) the abbreviated physical format, (b) our desire to bring out an affordable college dictionary expediently, and (c) coverage at this level easily surpasses that of any similarly focused resource currently available (in a couple instances by almost 3,000 entries). Staff also made use of the APA 2.7-million-records PsycINFO database of citations to the scholarly literature in order to review which of the entries that appeared in only a single source should be considered for inclusion.

As with the method used to create the *APA Concise Dictionary,* our staff of lexicographers then reviewed the text of each selected entry (typically working from the version used in *Concise*), in some cases retaining it and in some cases further cutting or rewording text. Each consideration of a definition has brought opportunities for updating and general textual improvement, and this enhancement is reflected in numerous entries throughout the *APA College Dictionary.* Three excellent examples are *placebo control group, social age,* and *two-factor theory of work motivation.*

Another important gain achieved through vetting our corpus of headwords (i.e., entry terms) with the actual language used in the primary college texts was an accretion of some 200 terms that have not previously appeared in our parent or abridged dictionaries. They range from the relatively broad (e.g., *absolutism, diversity, normal*) to the highly specific (e.g., *acetaldehyde, perseverance effect, skewness*), and their definitions were developed through a careful process of research and successive review by multiple individuals. In addition to appearing in this college context, most of these newly developed entries will be subsumed into second editions of the full and concise versions of the dictionary as well.

We hope that the editorial undertaking described above has resulted in a useful tool for students navigating the sometimes murky waters of the psychology lexicon. Beyond this, we recognize once more the participation of the full editorial board of the *APA Dictionary of Psychology,* whose earlier efforts we gratefully acknowledge as the foundation upon which this college dictionary rests.

We invite the student users of the *APA College Dictionary of Psychology* to participate in the ongoing task of defining the field. Reference staff will appreciate hearing from you with regard to this resource as an entirety or with regard to a particular entry or family of entries. How does the text match your study needs? In what ways can it be improved? Please contact us by post in care of APA Books, 750 First Street, NE, Washington, DC 20002, Attention: Reference; or by e-mail at apadictionary@apa.org.

Gary R. VandenBos, PhD
APA Publisher

Editorial Staff

Editor in Chief

Gary R. VandenBos, PhD

Senior Editors (American Psychological Association)

Theodore J. Baroody
Julia Frank-McNeil
Patricia D. Knowles
Marion Osmun

Senior Editors (Market House Books, Ltd.)

Alan Isaacs
Jonathan Law
Elizabeth Martin

Assistant Editor (American Psychological Association)

Marian E. Haggard

Editorial Board

Mark Appelbaum, PhD
Elizabeth D. Capaldi, PhD
Debra L. Dunivin, PhD
Alan E. Kazdin, PhD
Joseph D. Matarazzo, PhD
Susan H. McDaniel, PhD
Susan K. Nolen-Hoeksema, PhD
Suparna Rajaram, PhD

Editorial Contributors

John G. Albinson, PhD
Mark Appelbaum, PhD
Bernard J. Baars, PhD
Andrew S. Baum, PhD
Roy F. Baumeister, PhD
Daniel S. Beasley, PhD
Leonard Berkowitz, PhD
David F. Bjorklund, PhD

C. Alan Boneau, PhD
Marc N. Branch, PhD
Laura S. Brown, PhD
Joseph J. Campos, PhD
Daniel Cervone, PhD
Stanley H. Cohen, PhD
Deborah J. Coon, PhD
James C. Coyne, PhD

Editorial Contributors (continued)

Editorial Consultants

Quick Guide to Format

Headword

causation *n.* the empirical relation between two events, states, or variables such that one (the cause) is held or known to bring about the other (the effect). See also CAUSALITY. —**causal** *adj.*

Part-of-speech label

Derived word

cautious shift a CHOICE SHIFT in which an individual making a decision as part of a group adopts a more cautious approach than the same individual would have adopted had he or she made the decision alone. Studies suggest that such shifts are rarer than the opposite risky shift. See also GROUP POLARIZATION.

Hidden entry

chronological age (CA) the amount of time elapsed since an individual's birth, typically expressed in terms of months and years.

Abbreviation

client *n.* a person receiving treatment or services, especially in the context of counseling or social work. See PATIENT–CLIENT ISSUE.

Cross-reference

Plural form

crisis *n.* (*pl.* **crises**) **1.** a situation (e.g., a traumatic change) that produces significant cognitive or emotional stress in those involved in it. **2.** a turning point for better or worse in the course of an illness.

Sense number

Sense number

Cronbach's alpha an index of INTERNAL CONSISTENCY reliability, that is, the degree to which a set of items that comprise a measurement instrument tap a single, unidimensional construct. Also called **alpha coefficient.** [Lee J. Cronbach (1916–2001), U.S. psychologist]

Cross-reference

Alternative name

Etymology

APA
College
Dictionary
of
Psychology

Aa

A-B design the simplest SINGLE-CASE DESIGN, in which the DEPENDENT VARIABLE is measured throughout the pretreatment or baseline period (the A phase) and then again following the treatment period (the B phase). Numerous variations of this basic design exist, such as the A-B-A design, A-B-A-B design, A-B-B-A design, and A-B-BC-B design. The latter involves two treatment periods (the B phase and the C phase) and is intended to assess the effect of B both in combination with C and apart from C.

abducens nerve the sixth CRANIAL NERVE, carrying motor fibers for control of the lateral rectus muscle of the eye, which rotates the eyeball outward. Also called **abducent nerve**.

aberration *n.* **1.** any deviation, particularly a significant or undesirable one, from the normal or typical. See also MENTAL ABERRATION. **2.** in vision, the failure of light rays to converge at the same point, due either to distortion by a lens (**spherical aberration**) or to the formation of colored fringes by a lens (**chromatic aberration**).

ability *n.* existing competence or skill to perform a specific physical or mental act. Although ability may be either innate or developed through experience, it is distinct from capacity to acquire competence (see APTITUDE).

ability test any norm-referenced standardized test designed to measure existing competence to perform a physical or mental act. The index

of achievement or performance obtained, reporting the absolute or relative ability of the individual being evaluated, is called an **ability level**.

ablation *n.* the removal or destruction of part of a biological tissue or structure by a surgical procedure or a toxic substance, usually for treatment or to study its function. When the entire tissue or structure is excised, the process is called **extirpation**.

abnormal *adj.* relating to any deviation from what is considered typical, usual, or healthy, particularly if the deviation is considered harmful or maladaptive. In statistics, for example, abnormal scores are those that are outside the usual or expected range. The term, however, is most often applied to behavior that differs from a culturally accepted norm, especially when indicative of a mental disorder. **—abnormality** *n.* **—abnormally** *adv.*

abnormal psychology the branch of psychology devoted to the study, prevention, assessment, and treatment of maladaptive behavior. See also PSYCHOPATHOLOGY.

abortion *n.* the expulsion from the uterus of an embryo or fetus before it is able to survive independently. An abortion may be either spontaneous, in which case it occurs naturally and is also called a **miscarriage**, or induced, in which case it is produced deliberately by artificial means such as drugs or surgery and done for therapeutic reasons or as an elective decision. The practice is controversial and may involve **abortion counseling**, the provision of guidance, advice, information, and support on issues concerning termination of pregnancy and the alternatives of adoption or raising the child.

above-average effect the tendency of a person to hold overly favorable views of his or her intellectual and social abilities. The above-average effect appears to be common and consistent across a variety of judgment domains and occurs because people fail to take into account other peoples' abilities and instead rely on their own abilities when they evaluate themselves relative to others. Compare BELOW-AVERAGE EFFECT.

abreaction *n.* the therapeutic process of bringing forgotten or inhibited material (i.e., experiences, memories) from the unconscious into consciousness, with concurrent emotional release and discharge of tension and anxiety. See also CATHARSIS.

abscissa *n.* the horizontal coordinate in a graph or data plot; that is, the *x*-axis. See also ORDINATE.

absence seizure a type of GENERALIZED SEIZURE, formerly called **petit mal seizure**, in which the individual abruptly ceases activity and cannot afterward remember the event. The absences usually last from 5 to 15 s, during which the individual is unresponsive and motionless, staring blankly. Seizures of this type typically begin between ages 4 and 12 and rarely persist into adulthood.

absolute refractory period see REFRACTORY PERIOD.

absolute threshold the lowest or weakest level of stimulation (e.g., the slightest, most indistinct sound) that can be detected consistently

and accurately on 50% of trials. Although the name suggests a fixed level at which stimuli effectively elicit sensations, the absolute threshold fluctuates according to alterations in receptors and environmental conditions. Also called **absolute limen** (**AL**).

absolute value the numerical value of a figure disregarding its algebraic sign. For example, the absolute value of –1 is 1.

absolutism *n.* the philosophical position that there are absolute ethical, aesthetic, or epistemological values. Phenomena are believed to have a fixed reality; thus, what is regarded as true in one circumstance will be regarded as true in all others as well. For example, a particular action will always be deemed immoral regardless of its outcome or any other individual or subjective consideration. Such a position involves a rejection (in whole or in part) of RELATIVISM.

abstinence *n.* the act of refraining from the use of something, particularly alcohol or drugs, or from participation in sexual or other activity. In most instances, abstinence from drugs or alcohol is the primary goal of substance abuse treatment. See also SUBSTANCE WITHDRAWAL. **—abstinent** *adj.*

abstraction *n.* **1.** the formation of general ideas or concepts by extracting similarities from particular instances. The precise cognitive processes by which this occurs remain a subject of investigation. **2.** such a concept, especially a wholly intangible one, such as "goodness" or "truth." **—abstract** *vb.*

abuse *n.* **1.** interactions in which one person behaves in a cruel, violent, demeaning, or invasive manner toward another person or an animal. The term most commonly implies physical mistreatment but also encompasses sexual and psychological (emotional) mistreatment. **2.** see SUBSTANCE ABUSE. **—abuser** *n.*

acalculia *n.* loss of the ability to perform simple arithmetic operations that results from brain injury or disease, usually to the PARIETAL LOBE. It is an acquired condition, whereas DYSCALCULIA is developmental.

acceleration *n.* **1.** an increase in speed of movement or rate of change. In psychology, the focus is on the range of forces sustained by the human body when it is in a moving vehicle, such as an automobile or aircraft, and the resultant physical, physiological, and psychological consequences (e.g., disturbances of heart rhythm and blood pressure, disorientation and confusion, and loss of consciousness). Compare DECELERATION. **2.** in mathematics and statistics, the rate of change in the SLOPE of a function.

accent *n.* phonetic features of an individual's speech that are associated with geographical region or social class. The standard version of a language is usually considered by native speakers to be unaccented. Compare DIALECT.

acceptance region in SIGNIFICANCE TESTING, the range of values for a test statistic that leads to acceptance of the null hypothesis over the alternative hypothesis. Compare CRITICAL REGION.

accessible *adj.* **1.** in social psychology and psychotherapy, receptive or responsive to personal interaction and other external stimuli. A client in psychotherapy is thought to be accessible if he or she responds to the therapist in a way that facilitates the development of rapport and, ultimately, fosters the examination of cognitive, emotional, and behavioral issues. **2.** retrievable through memory or other cognitive processes, as in ATTITUDE ACCESSIBILITY for example. **—accessibility** *n.*

accessory nerve the 11th CRANIAL NERVE, sometimes so named because one of its functions is that of serving as an accessory to the 10th cranial nerve (the VAGUS NERVE). It innervates the sternomastoid and trapezius muscles in the neck.

accommodation *n.* **1.** adjustment or modification. For example, regarding individuals with disabilities it refers to REASONABLE ACCOMMODATIONS made to meet their needs, whereas in PIAGETIAN THEORY it refers to the adjustment of mental SCHEMAS according to information acquired through experience. **2.** the process by which the focus of the eye is changed to allow near or distant objects to form sharp images on the retina. Accommodation is achieved mainly by contraction or relaxation of the CILIARY MUSCLES but also involves adjustments in the CONVERGENCE of the eyes and the size of the pupils. **—accommodate** *vb.*

acculturation *n.* the processes by which groups or individuals integrate the social and cultural values, ideas, beliefs, and behavioral patterns of their culture of origin with those of a different culture. **Psychological acculturation** is an individual's attitudinal and behavioral adjustment to another culture, which typically varies with regard to degree and type. Compare DECULTURATION; ENCULTURATION. **—acculturate** *vb.*

acetaldehyde *n.* a toxic and volatile initial product of alcohol (ethanol) metabolism that is responsible for the variety of unpleasant effects associated with a hangover, including nausea, vomiting, and headache. It is produced when alcohol is broken down by a liver enzyme called alcohol dehydrogenase and is itself further broken down by another liver enzyme (acetaldehyde dehydrogenase) into acetate and, ultimately, into carbon dioxide and water. Acetaldehyde is widely studied to determine its relationship to and influence upon the development and progression of alcoholism. See also DISULFIRAM.

acetylcholine (**ACh**) *n.* a major, predominantly excitatory but also inhibitory, neurotransmitter in the central nervous system, where it plays an important role in memory formation and learning; and in the peripheral nervous system, where it mediates skeletal, cardiac, and smooth muscle contraction.

acetylcholine receptor (**AChR**) any of certain protein molecules in cell membranes in the central and peripheral nervous systems that are stimulated by acetylcholine or acetylcholine-like substances. There are two main types: MUSCARINIC RECEPTORS and NICOTINIC RECEPTORS.

acetylcholinesterase (**AChE**) *n.* see CHOLINESTERASE.

achievement *n.* **1.** the attainment of some goal, or the goal attained. See also NEED FOR ACHIEVEMENT. **2.** acquired knowledge (especially in a particular subject area such as biology), proficiency, or skill. The term is most often used in this sense to mean academic achievement.

achievement motivation 1. the desire to perform well and be successful. In this sense, the term often is used synonymously with NEED FOR ACHIEVEMENT. **2.** the desire to overcome obstacles and master difficult challenges. High scorers in achievement motivation are likely to set higher standards and work with greater perseverance.

achievement test any norm-referenced standardized test intended to measure an individual's current level of skill or knowledge in a given subject. Often the distinction is made that achievement tests emphasize ability acquired through formal learning or training, whereas APTITUDE TESTS (usually in the form of intelligence tests) emphasize innate potential.

achromatic *adj.* without hue; colorless. **Achromatic stimuli** are black, white, or shades of gray.

achromatism *n.* total color blindness marked by the inability to perceive any color whatsoever: Everything is seen in different shades of gray. It is a congenital condition stemming from a lack of RETINAL CONES. See also DICHROMATISM; MONOCHROMATISM; TRICHROMATISM.

acoustic *adj.* associated with sound. The word is usually used to modify technical terms (e.g., ACOUSTIC REFLEX). **Acoustical** is used as a modifier in all other contexts (e.g., Acoustical Society of America).

acoustic reflex contraction of the middle ear muscles (the tensor tympani and stapedius muscle) elicited by intense sounds. This reflex restricts movement of the OSSICLES, thus reducing the sound energy transmitted to the inner ear and partially protecting it from damage.

acoustic store a component of short-term memory that retains auditory information based on how items sound. Forgetting occurs when words or letters in acoustic store sound alike. Compare ARTICULATORY STORE.

acquiescent response set the tendency of a respondent to agree with statements of opinion regardless of their content. This often reduces the validity of interviews, questionnaires, and other self-reports.

acquired immune deficiency syndrome see AIDS.

acquisition *n.* the attainment by an individual of new behavior, information, or skills or the process by which this occurs. Although often used interchangeably with LEARNING, acquisition tends to be defined somewhat more concretely as the period during which progressive, measurable increases in response strength are seen. —**acquire** *vb.*

ACTH abbreviation for adrenocorticotropic hormone. See CORTICOTROPIN.

actin *n.* see MUSCLE FIBER.

acting out 1. the uncontrolled and inappropriate behavioral expression of denied emotions that serves to relieve tension associated with these emotions or to communicate them in a disguised, or indirect, way to others. Such behaviors may include arguing, fighting, stealing, threatening, or throwing tantrums. **2.** in psychoanalytic theory, reenactment of past events as an expression of unconscious emotional conflicts, feelings, or desires—often sexual or aggressive—with no attempt to understand the origin or meaning of these behaviors.

action *n.* **1.** a self-initiated sequence of movements, usually with respect to some goal. It may consist of an integrated set of component behaviors as opposed to a single response. **2.** the occurrence or performance of a process or function (e.g., the action of an enzyme).

action disorganization syndrome a cognitive deficit resulting from damage to the FRONTAL LOBES of the brain and causing individuals to make errors on multistepped but familiar or routine tasks. Types of errors include omissions or additions of steps, disordered sequencing of steps, and object substitutions or misuse.

action potential the change in electric potential that propagates along a cell during the transmission of a nerve impulse or the contraction of a muscle. It is marked by a rapid, transient DEPOLARIZATION of the cell's plasma membrane, from a RESTING POTENTIAL of about −70 mV (inside negative) to about +30 mV (inside positive), and back again, after a slight HYPERPOLARIZATION, to the resting potential.

action research socially useful and theoretically meaningful research developed and carried out in response to a social issue or problem, results of which are used to improve the situation.

action-specific energy in classical ethology, a hypothetical supply of motivational energy within an organism that is associated with specific unlearned behavioral responses known as FIXED ACTION PATTERNS. Each response has its own energy supply, which builds up until the organism encounters the appropriate RELEASER.

activation *n.* **1.** in many theories of memory, an attribute of the representational units (such as NODES or LOGOGENS) that varies from weaker to stronger, with more strongly activated representations competing to control processing. **2.** the process of alerting an organ or body system for action, particularly arousal of one organ or system by another. —**activate** *vb.* —**activational** *adj.*

activational effect a transient hormonal effect that typically causes a short-term change in behavior or physiological activity in adult animals. For example, increased testosterone in male songbirds in spring leads to increased aggression in territory defense and increased courtship behavior. Compare ORGANIZATIONAL EFFECT.

activation–synthesis hypothesis a hypothesis that explains dreams as a product of cortical interpretation of random activation rising from the lower brain structures, including the PONS.

active euthanasia direct action performed to terminate the life of a person (or animal) who is suffering greatly and is considered to have no chance for recovery. Administering a lethal injection is the most common method of active euthanasia today. This practice is distinguished from PASSIVE EUTHANASIA, in which treatments are withheld but no direct action to terminate the life is taken. See also ASSISTED DEATH.

active listening a psychotherapeutic technique in which the therapist listens to a client closely and attentively, asking questions as needed, in order to fully understand the content of the message and the depth of the client's emotion. The therapist typically restates what has been said to ensure accurate understanding.

activities of daily living (ADLs) activities essential to an individual's personal care, such as getting into and out of bed and chairs, dressing, eating, toileting and bathing, and grooming. A person's ability to perform ADLs is often used as a measure of functional capabilities during the course of a disease or following an injury. See also INSTRUMENTAL ACTIVITIES OF DAILY LIVING.

activity theory 1. a school of thought, developed primarily by Soviet psychologists, that focuses on activity in general—rather than the distinct concepts of behavior or mental states—as the primary unit of analysis. The theory emphasizes a hierarchical structure of activity, object-orientedness, internalization and externalization, mediation (by tools, language, and other cultural artifacts or instruments), and continuous development. Also called **activity psychology. 2.** a theory

proposing that old age is a lively, creative experience characterized by maintaining existing social roles, activities, and relationships or replacing any lost ones with new ones. Compare DISENGAGEMENT THEORY.

actor–observer effect in ATTRIBUTION THEORY, the tendency for individuals acting in a situation to attribute the causes of their behavior to external or situational factors, such as social pressure, but for observers to attribute the same behavior to internal or dispositional factors, such as personality.

actualization *n.* the process of mobilizing one's potentialities and realizing them in concrete form. According to U.S. psychologist Carl Rogers (1902–1987), all humans have an innate **actualizing tendency** to grow and actualize the self fully. See also SELF-ACTUALIZATION. —**actualize** *vb.*

actuarial *adj.* statistical, as opposed to clinical. The use of data about prior instances, in order to estimate the likelihood or risk of a particular outcome, is sometimes cited as an alternative to clinical diagnoses, which are open to human error.

acuity *n.* sharpness of perception. Whereas visual acuity is sharpness of vision and auditory acuity sharpness of hearing, sensory acuity is the precision with which any sensory stimulation is perceived.

acupuncture *n.* a form of COMPLEMENTARY AND ALTERNATIVE MEDICINE in which fine needles are inserted into the body at specific points to relieve pain, induce anesthesia (**acupuncture anesthesia**), or treat disease. It is based on the concept in traditional Chinese medicine that "meridians," or pathways, conduct life-force energy known as chi between places on the skin and the body's organ systems. **—acupuncturist** *n.*

acute *adj.* **1.** denoting conditions or symptoms of sudden onset, short duration, and often great intensity. Compare CHRONIC. **2.** sharp, keen, or very sensitive (e.g., acute hearing).

acute stress disorder a disorder representing the immediate psychological aftermath of exposure to a traumatic stressor. Symptoms are the same as those of POST-TRAUMATIC STRESS DISORDER but do not last longer than 4 weeks. This disorder also includes elements of dissociation, such as DEPERSONALIZATION and DEREALIZATION.

adaptation *n.* **1.** adjustment of a sense organ to the intensity or quality of stimulation, resulting in a temporary change in sensory or perceptual experience, as in visual adaptation when the pupil of the eye adjusts to dim or bright light. **2.** reduced responsiveness in a sensory receptor or sensory system caused by prolonged or repeated stimulation. The adaptation may be specific, for example, to the orientation of a particular stimulus. Also called **sensory adaptation**. **3.** modification to suit different or changing circumstances. In this sense, the term often refers to behavior that enables an individual to adjust to the environment effectively and function optimally in various domains, such as coping with daily stressors. Compare MALADAPTATION. **4.** adjustments to the demands, restrictions, and mores of society, including the ability to live and work harmoniously with others and to engage in satisfying social interactions and relationships. Also called **social adaptation. —adapt** *vb.* **—adaptational** *adj.* **—adaptive** *adj.*

adaptation level the theoretical baseline or zero point, which forms a standard against which new stimuli are evaluated. For example, a person who first lifts a 40 lb weight would then likely judge a 20 lb weight as light, whereas if that person first lifted a 4 lb weight he or she would then likely judge the 20 lb weight as heavy. Although it originated in studies of sensory perception, **adaptation-level theory** has since been applied in other fields, such as aesthetics and attitude change.

ADC abbreviation for AIDS DEMENTIA COMPLEX.

addiction *n.* a state of psychological or physical dependence (or both) on the use of alcohol or other drugs. The equivalent term SUBSTANCE DEPENDENCE is preferred to describe this state because it refers more explicitly to the criteria by which it is diagnosed, which include tolerance, withdrawal, loss of control, and compulsive use of the substance. Chemical substances with significant potential for producing dependence are called **addictive drugs**. They include alcohol, amphetamines and other central nervous system (CNS) stimulants, CNS depressants, cocaine and crack, hallucinogens, inhalants, and opioids. **—addictive** *adj.*

additive effect the joint effect of two or more independent variables on a dependent variable equal to the sum of their individual effects: The value of either independent variable is unconditional upon the value of the other one. Compare INTERACTION EFFECT.

additive task a task or project that a group can complete by aggregating individual members' efforts or contributions (e.g., a five-person group pulling together on a rope to move a heavy object). Groups usually outperform individuals on such tasks, but overall group productivity rarely reaches its maximum potential owing to SOCIAL LOAFING. Compare COMPENSATORY TASK; CONJUNCTIVE TASK; DISJUNCTIVE TASK.

adenosine *n.* a compound in living cells that functions as a neuro-modulator: By binding to special **adenosine receptors**, it influences the release of several neurotrans-mitters in the central nervous system. Combined with three phos-phate units, adenosine becomes ATP (adenosine triphosphate), which functions as an energy source in metabolic activities.

adenosine triphosphate see ATP.

ADH abbreviation for antidiuretic hormone (see VASOPRESSIN).

ADHD abbreviation for ATTENTION-DEFICIT/HYPERACTIVITY DISORDER.

adipose tissue connective tissue consisting largely of fat cells (**adipocytes**), which is found be-neath the skin and around major organs. It provides protection and insulation and functions as an en-ergy reserve.

adjustment *n.* **1.** a change in atti-tude, behavior, or both by an individual on the basis of some rec-ognized need or desire to change, particularly to account for the cur-rent environment or changing, atypical, or unexpected conditions. It may be assessed via a type of sur-vey called an **adjustment inventory**, which compares a person's emo-tional and social adjustment with a representative sample of other indi-viduals. A well-adjusted person is one who satisfies his or her needs in a healthy, beneficial manner and demonstrates appropriate social and psychological responses to situations and demands. **2.** modification to match a standard. See METHOD OF ADJUSTMENT. —**adjust** *vb.*

adjustment disorder impairment in social or occupational function-ing and unexpectedly severe

emotional or behavioral symptoms occurring within three months after an individual experiences a specific identifiable stressful event, such as a divorce, business crisis, or family discord. The event is not as stressful as a traumatic stressor, which can lead to POSTTRAUMATIC STRESS DIS-ORDER. Symptoms may include anxiety, depression, and conduct disturbances and tend to remit fol-lowing elimination of the stressor.

ADLs abbreviation for ACTIVITIES OF DAILY LIVING.

adolescence *n.* the period of human development that starts with puberty (10–12 years of age) and ends with physiological maturity (approximately 19 years of age), al-though the exact age span varies across individuals. During this pe-riod major changes occur at varying rates in physical characteristics, sex-ual characteristics, and sexual interest, resulting in significant ef-fects on body image, self-concept, and self-esteem. Major cognitive and social developments take place as well: Most young people acquire en-hanced abilities to think abstractly, evaluate reality hypothetically, re-consider prior experiences from altered points of view, assess data from multiple dimensions, reflect inwardly, create complex models of understanding, and project compli-cated future scenarios. Adolescents also increase their peer focus and in-volvement in peer-related activities, place greater emphasis on social acceptance, and seek more inde-pendence and autonomy from parents. —**adolescent** *adj., n.*

adoption study a research design that investigates the relationships among genetic and environmental factors in the development of per-sonality, behavior, or disorder by comparing the similarities of biolog-ical parent–child pairs with those of adoptive parent–child pairs.

adrenal gland an endocrine gland adjacent to the kidney. Its outer layer, the **adrenal cortex**, secretes a number of hormones, including AN-DROGENS, GLUCOCORTICOIDS, and MINERALOCORTICOIDS. Its inner core, the **adrenal medulla**, secretes the hormones EPINEPHRINE and NOREPINEPHRINE, both of which are CATECHOLAMINES and also serve as neurotransmitters.

adrenaline *n.* see EPINEPHRINE.

adrenergic *adj.* responding to, re-leasing, or otherwise involving EPINEPHRINE (adrenaline). For ex-ample, an **adrenergic neuron** is one that employs EPINEPHRINE as a neurotransmitter. The term often is used more broadly to include NOREPINEPHRINE as well.

adrenocorticotropic hormone (**ACTH**) see CORTICOTROPIN.

adulthood *n.* the period of human development in which full physical growth and maturity have been achieved and certain biological, cog-nitive, social, personality, and other changes associated with the aging process occur. Beginning after ado-lescence, adulthood is sometimes divided into young adulthood (roughly 20 to 35 years of age); mid-dle adulthood (about 36 to 64 years); and later adulthood (age 65 and beyond). The last is sometimes subdivided into **young-old** (65 to 74), **old-old** (75 to 84), and **oldest old** (85 and beyond). The oldest old group is the fastest growing segment of the population in many devel-oped countries.

advance directive a legal mecha-nism for individuals to specify their wishes and instructions about pro-spective health care in the event they later become unable to make such decisions. This can be achieved by means of a **durable power of at-torney**, a legal document designating someone to make health care decisions on that per-son's behalf, or a **living will**, a legal document clarifying a person's wishes regarding future medical or, increasingly, mental health treat-ment.

advocacy *n.* speaking or acting on behalf of an individual or group to uphold their rights or explain their point of view. For example, health care **advocates** represent consumers to protect their rights to effective treatment, while therapists may act as advocates for clients in court hearings or other situations involv-ing decisions based on the clients' mental health or related issues.

AEP abbreviation for AVERAGE EVOKED POTENTIAL.

aerobic exercise physical activity, typically prolonged and of moderate intensity (e.g., jogging or cycling), that involves the use of oxygen in the muscles to provide the needed energy. Aerobic exercise strengthens the cardiovascular and respiratory systems and is associated with a va-riety of health benefits including increased endurance, reduction of body fat, and decreased depression and anxiety. Compare ANAEROBIC EXERCISE.

aesthesiometry *n.* see ESTHESIOMETRY.

aesthetics *n.* the philosophical study of beauty and art, concerned particularly with the articulation of taste and questions regarding the value of aesthetic experience and the making of aesthetic judgments. —**aesthetic** *adj.*

affect *n.* any feeling or emotion, which may be irreflexive or reflex-ive. Irreflexive affect is the direct experience in consciousness of a particular emotional state (as in a person's feeling of elation upon re-ceiving good news). Reflexive affect occurs when a person makes his or her feelings objects of scrutiny (as when a person wonders why he or she does not feel particularly elated upon receiving good news). A distinction may also be made between NEGATIVE AFFECT and POSITIVE AFFECT. Along with cognition and conation, affect is one of the three traditionally identified components of mind.

affective aggression see AGGRESSION.

affective disorder see MOOD DISORDER.

affective forecasting predicting one's own future emotional states, especially in connection with some event or outcome that one faces. People often "forecast" more extreme and lasting emotional reactions to events than they actually experience.

affective neuroscience a discipline that addresses the brain mechanisms underlying emotions. In seeking to understand the particular roles of major subcortical and cortical structures in the elicitation, experience, and regulation of emotion, affective neuroscience provides an important framework for understanding the neural processes that underlie psychopathology, particularly the mood and substance-related disorders.

afferent *adj.* conducting or conveying from the periphery toward a central point. For example, **afferent nerve fibers** conduct impulses toward the brain or spinal cord. Compare EFFERENT.

affiliation *n.* a social relationship with one or more other individuals, usually based on liking or a personal attachment rather than on perceived material benefits. Affiliation appears to be a basic source of emotional security, given the anxiety, frustration, and loneliness stemming from the absence of such relationships. Some propose that the seeking of cooperative, friendly association with others who resemble or like one or whom one likes is a fundamental human desire, referring to it variously as the **affiliative drive** or **affiliative need**. —**affiliative** *adj.*

affinity *n.* **1.** an inherent attraction to or liking for a particular person, place, or thing, often based on some commonality. **2.** relationship by marriage or adoption rather than blood. This contrasts with **consanguinity**, a biological relationship between individuals who are descended from a common ancestor.

affordance *n.* in the theory of ECOLOGICAL PERCEPTION, any property of the physical environment that is relevant to motor behavior and thus offers or affords an organism the opportunity for a particular action. An example is the orientation of an object's handle. When the handle is closest to the left hand it affords a left-hand reach and grasp movement. This affordance is provided by an intrinsic property, the physical dimensions necessary for grasping it, as well as an extrinsic property, the distance to the nearest hand.

aftercare *n.* a program of outpatient treatment and support services provided for individuals discharged from an institution, such as a hospital or mental health facility, to help maintain improvement, prevent relapse, and aid adjustment of the individual to the community.

afterimage *n.* the image that remains after a stimulus ends or is removed. A positive afterimage occurs rarely, lasts a few seconds, and is caused by a continuation of receptor and neural processes following cessation of the stimulus; it has approximately the color and brightness of the original stimulus. A negative afterimage is more common, often more intense, and lasts longer. It is usually complementary to the original stimulus in color and brightness; for example, if the stimulus was bright yellow, the negative afterimage will be dark blue.

age effect in research, any outcome associated with being a certain age. Such effects may be difficult to separate from COHORT EFFECTS and PERIOD EFFECTS.

ageism *n.* the tendency to be prejudiced against older adults and to negatively stereotype them (for example, as unhealthy, helpless, or incompetent) and the resulting discrimination, especially in employment and in health care. —**ageist** *adj.*

agentic state a psychological state that occurs when individuals, as subordinates to a higher authority in an organized status hierarchy, feel compelled to obey the orders issued by that authority. See BEHAVIORAL STUDY OF OBEDIENCE.

age regression a hypnotic technique in which the therapist helps the client recall a crucial experience by inducing amnesia for the present, then suggesting that he or she return, year by year, to the earlier date when a particular experience took place. This technique is also used in forensic contexts to help eyewitnesses and victims recall their experiences. The use of age regression in either context is controversial, given the potential for FALSE MEMORIES and the debatable legitimacy of RECOVERED MEMORIES.

aggression *n.* behavior that harms others physically or psychologically or destroys property. It can be distinguished from anger in that anger is oriented at overcoming the target but not necessarily through harm or destruction. When such behavior is purposively performed with the primary goal of intentional injury or destruction it is termed **hostile aggression**. Other types of aggression

are less deliberately damaging and may be instrumentally motivated (proactive) or affectively motivated (reactive). **Instrumental aggression** involves an action carried out principally to achieve another goal, such as acquiring a desired resource. **Affective aggression** involves an emotional response to an aversive state of affairs, which tends to be targeted toward the perceived source of the distress but may be displaced onto other people or objects if the disturbing agent cannot be attacked (**displaced aggression**). In the classical psychoanalytic theory of Austrian psychiatrist Sigmund Freud (1856–1939), the aggressive impulse is innate and derived from the DEATH INSTINCT, but most nonpsychoanalytically oriented psychologists view it as socially learned or as a reaction to frustration (see FRUSTRATION–AGGRESSION HYPOTHESIS). —**aggressive** *adj.*

aging *n.* the biological and psychological changes associated with chronological age. A distinction is often made between changes that are due to normal biological processes (see PRIMARY AGING) and changes that are caused by age-related pathologies (see SECONDARY AGING).

agitation *n.* a state of increased but typically purposeless and repetitive activity, as in PSYCHOMOTOR AGITATION.

agnosia *n.* loss or impairment of the ability to recognize or appreciate the nature of sensory stimuli due to brain damage or disorder. Recognition impairment is profound and specific to a particular sensory modality. AUDITORY AGNOSIA, TACTILE AGNOSIA, and VISUAL AGNOSIA are the most common types, and each has a variety of subtypes.

agonist *n.* **1.** a drug or other chemical agent that binds to a particular receptor and produces a physiological effect, typically one similar to that of the body's own neurotransmitter at that receptor. There are **partial agonists**, which stimulate the receptor only somewhat to produce the same physiological effect as the natural neurotransmitter but to a lesser degree, and **inverse agonists**, which act at the receptor to produce a physiological effect opposite to that produced by another agonist at that same receptor. **2.** a contracting muscle whose action generates force in the intended direction. Compare ANTAGONIST. —**agonism** *n.* —**agonistic** *adj.*

agoraphobia *n.* an excessive, irrational fear of being in open or unfamiliar places, resulting in the avoidance of public situations from which escape may be difficult, such as standing in line or being in a crowd. Agoraphobia may accompany PANIC DISORDER, in which an individual experiences unexpected panic attacks, or it may occur in the absence of panic disorder, when an individual experiences paniclike symptoms or limited symptom attacks. —**agoraphobic** *adj.*

agrammatism *n.* a manifestation of APHASIA characterized by loss or impairment of the ability to use speech that conforms to grammatical rules, such as those governing word order, verb tense, and subject–verb agreement.

agranulocytosis *n.* a decline in the number of certain white blood cells (neutrophils), typically as a result of an immune reaction to a drug or other chemical or the toxic effect of this substance on the bone marrow, causing production of white blood cells to fall. The condition results in suppression of the immune response, rendering individuals vulnerable to opportunistic infections.

agraphia *n.* loss or impairment of the ability to write as a result of neu-rological damage or disorder. The specific forms of writing difficulties vary considerably, but may include problems with such things as spelling irregular or ambiguous words, writing numbers or particular letters, or performing the motor movements needed for handwriting. Also called **dysgraphia**. —**agraphic** *adj.*

aha experience the emotional reaction that typically occurs at a moment of sudden insight into a problem or other puzzling issue. For example, in psychotherapy it is a client's sudden insight into his or her motives for cognitions, affects, or behaviors. Also called **aha reaction**.

AI abbreviation for ARTIFICIAL INTELLIGENCE.

AIDS *a*cquired *i*mmune *d*eficiency *s*yndrome: a clinical condition in which the immune system is so severely damaged from infection with human immunodeficiency virus (see HIV) as to result in certain serious opportunistic infections and diseases.

AIDS dementia complex (ADC) neuropsychological dysfunction directly attributable to HIV infection, found most commonly in those who have developed AIDS. It is marked by impairments such as memory loss and inability to concentrate and by disturbances in behavior, motor coordination, and mood. Also called **HIV dementia**.

akathisia (acathisia) *n.* extreme restlessness characterized by an inability to sit or stand still for at least several minutes and by fidgety movements or jitteriness, as well as a subjective report of inner restlessness.

akinesia *n.* loss or reduction of voluntary movement. Also called **akinesis**. —**akinetic** *adj.*

akinetopsia *n.* inability to see objects in motion as a result of damage to the visual cortex. Individuals with akinetopsia perceive moving stimuli as a series of stationary strobelike images and see visual trails behind moving objects. —**akinetopsic** *adj.*

AL abbreviation for absolute limen (see ABSOLUTE THRESHOLD).

alarm reaction see GENERAL ADAPTATION SYNDROME.

alcohol *n.* short for ethyl alcohol (see ETHANOL).

alcohol dependence a pattern of repeated or compulsive use of alcohol despite significant behavioral, physiological, and psychosocial problems, plus indications of physical and psychological dependence—tolerance and characteristic withdrawal symptoms if use is suspended—resulting in impaired control. It is differentiated from **alcohol abuse** by the preoccupation with obtaining alcohol or recovering from its effects, and the overwhelming desire for experiencing alcohol's intoxicating result (i.e., craving). Alcohol dependence is known popularly as **alcoholism**.

aldosterone *n.* the principle MINERALOCORTICOID hormone secreted by the adrenal cortex, the outer layer of the ADRENAL GLAND. It helps to regulate mineral and water metabolism by promoting potassium excretion and sodium retention in the kidneys. Excess secretion of aldosterone results in a pathological condition called **aldosteronism,** marked by headaches, muscle weakness, fatigue, hypertension, and numbness.

alexia *n.* loss or impairment of the ability to comprehend written or printed words as a result of lesions, stroke, or other forms of neurological damage or disorder. It is generally seen in APHASIA but may occur in isolation, in which case it is called **pure alexia** (or **alexia without agraphia**) and characterized by reading impairment with preserved language production and auditory comprehension. See also DYSLEXIA.

alexithymia *n.* an inability to express, describe, or distinguish between one's emotions. It may occur in a variety of disorders (e.g., depression), especially psychosomatic and some substance use disorders, or following repeated exposure to a traumatic stressor.

algorithm *n.* a precisely defined procedure for solving a particular problem or for conducting a series of computations that guarantees a correct outcome. Algorithms are essential to computer programming and information processing. Compare HEURISTIC. —**algorithmic** *adj.*

alias *n.* see CONFOUND.

alienation *n.* **1.** estrangement from others, resulting in the absence of close or friendly relationships with people in one's social group (e.g., family, workplace, community). **2.** estrangement from oneself. An individual experiences life as a search for his or her true personal identity, which has been hidden through socialization and nurturing, and a continuous failure to reach an ideal but unattainable level of personal fulfillment. This creates a deep-seated sense of dissatisfaction with one's personal existence and lack of trust in one's social or physical environment or in oneself. **3.** the experience of being separated from reality or isolated from one's thoughts or feelings, as in DEREALIZATION and DEPERSONALIZATION. —**alienated** *adj.*

alien limb syndrome a motor disorder characterized by involuntary hand, arm, or leg movements in place of or in addition to intended movements (e.g., grabbing objects or throwing things) and the person's feeling that he or she has no control over the limb or that it is "foreign," sometimes to the extent that the person does not recognize the limb as his or her own in the absence of visual clues. The syndrome most often affects the left hand (hence its alternative name **alien hand syndrome**).

allele *n.* an alternate form of a gene that occupies a given position on each of a pair of HOMOLOGOUS chromosomes. Each person typically has two alleles of each gene: One is inherited from the mother and the other from the father. Alleles may be alike (**homozygous**) or different (**heterozygous**), and are responsible for variation in inherited characteristics, such as hair color or blood type. See also DOMINANT ALLELE; RECESSIVE ALLELE. —**allelic** *adj.*

allocentric *adj.* denoting externality to the self, particularly an orientation toward or focus on groups and connections to others. Compare IDIOCENTRIC. See also SOCIOCENTRISM. —**allocentrism** *n.*

allocortex *n.* those regions of the cerebral cortex that are phylogenetically older and have fewer than six main layers of cells. The allocortex is involved primarily in olfactory functions and limbic functions related to memory and emotion, and comprises the three-layered **archicortex** (or **archipallium**), found mostly in the hippocampus, and the four- or five-layered **paleocortex** (or **paleopallium**), found mostly in the pyriform area and parahippocampal gyrus. Compare NEOCORTEX.

allomone *n.* a chemical signal that is released outside the body by members of one species and affects the behavior of members of another species. Compare PHEROMONE.

all-or-none law the principle that the amplitude of the ACTION POTENTIAL in a given neuron is independent of the magnitude of the stimulus. Thus, all stimuli above the neuron's threshold trigger action potentials of identical magnitude. Also called **all-or-none principle**.

all-or-none learning the theory that, in any given learning trial, learning occurs either completely and fully or not at all. This contrasts with a hypothesis of trial-by-trial **incremental learning**.

allostasis *n.* stability through change. Allostasis refers particularly to the idea that parameters of most physiological regulatory systems change to accommodate environmental demands. Although allostatic processes are critical for adaptive functioning, chronic or repeated activation of physiological systems in response to life's challenges are hypothesized to exact a toll on such systems.

alogia *n.* inability to speak because of dysfunction in the central nervous system. In a less severe form, it is sometimes referred to as **dyslogia**.

alpha (symbol: α) *n.* the probability of a TYPE I ERROR.

alpha coefficient see CRONBACH'S ALPHA.

alpha level see SIGNIFICANCE LEVEL.

alpha male the top-ranked or dominant male within a group, with primary access to resources, including food and mates. In many species the alpha male prevents other males from mating or from mating during the peak time of female fertility. There are **alpha females** as well, with primary access to resources within their social groups and who in some species inhibit reproduction among other females.

alpha motor neuron see MOTOR NEURON.

alpha wave in electroencephalography, a type of low-amplitude BRAIN WAVE (frequency 8–12 Hz) that typically occurs when the eyes are unfocused and no active mental processes are taking place, indicating a wakeful but relaxed state. The occurrence of alpha waves may be increased, for example, through meditation or **alpha-wave training**, which involves providing a feedback stimulus (typically an auditory tone) when alpha waves appear on the electroencephalogram (EEG). Also called **alpha rhythm.**

altered state of consciousness a state of psychological functioning that is significantly different from ordinary states of CONSCIOUSNESS, being characterized by altered levels of self-awareness, affect, reality testing, orientation to time and place, wakefulness, responsiveness to external stimuli, or memorability or by a sense of ecstasy, boundlessness, or unity with the universe. Although in some instances altered states of consciousness are symptomatic of mental disorder, in other contexts, such as in certain Eastern philosophies and TRANSPERSONAL PSYCHOLOGY, they are regarded as higher states of consciousness and, often, as indicative of a more profound level of personal and spiritual evolution.

alter ego 1. a second identity or aspect of a person that exists metaphorically as his or her substitute or representative, with different characteristics. **2.** an intimate, supportive friend with whom an individual can share all types of problems and experiences, as if he or she were "another self."

alternate-forms reliability an estimate of the extent to which a test yields consistent reproducible results that is obtained from the correlation of scores on different versions of that test. These **alternate forms** of the test may be of three

types: **comparable forms** have items of similar content and difficulty; **equivalent forms** have items of similar content and difficulty but demonstrate differences in certain statistical characteristics (e.g., standard deviations); and **parallel forms** have items of similar content and difficulty and are similar in all statistical characteristics (e.g., means, standard deviations, correlations with other measures).

alternating treatments design a type of SINGLE-CASE DESIGN in which the researcher changes the experimental conditions or interventions (treatments) applied to the participant from session to session or within sessions. For example, a researcher comparing two methods for eliminating the disruptive classroom behavior of a student might have the teacher use one method throughout the morning and the other method throughout the afternoon and then evaluate the student's behavior with each technique. An alternating treatments design is particularly useful when control of irrelevant variables is especially important.

alternative hypothesis (symbol: H_1) a statement of the position opposite to that of the NULL HYPOTHESIS. It usually outlines the predicted relationship between variables that a researcher is seeking to demonstrate empirically as true. In HYPOTHESIS TESTING, the alternative hypothesis may be considered plausible only when the null hypothesis is rejected at a predetermined SIGNIFICANCE LEVEL.

altruism *n.* an apparently unselfish concern for others or behavior that provides benefit to others at some cost to the individual. In humans, it covers a wide range of behaviors, including volunteerism and martyrdom, but the degree to which such behaviors are legitimately without egotistic motivation is subject to much debate. In animal behavior it is difficult to understand how altruism could evolve since NATURAL SELECTION operates on individuals. However, organisms displaying altruism can benefit if they help their relatives (see KIN SELECTION) or if an altruistic act is subsequently reciprocated (**reciprocal altruism**). **—altruistic** *adj.* **—altruist** *n.*

Alzheimer's disease a progressive neurodegenerative disease characterized by cortical atrophy, neuronal death, synapse loss, and accumulation of SENILE PLAQUES and NEUROFIBRILLARY TANGLES, causing DEMENTIA and a significant decline in functioning. Early features include deficits in memory (e.g., rapid forgetting of new information, impaired recall and recognition), executive dysfunction, and subtle personality changes such as decreased energy, social withdrawal, indifference, and impulsivity. As the disease progresses, there is global deterioration of cognitive capacities with intellectual decline, APHASIA, AGNOSIA, and APRAXIA as well as behavioral features including apathy, emotional blunting, mood-dependent delusions, decreased sleep and appetite, and increased motor activity (e.g., restlessness and wandering). [first described in 1907 by Alois **Alzheimer** (1864–1915), German neurologist]

amacrine cell any of a diverse class of neurons in the retina that connect RETINAL BIPOLAR CELLS and RETINAL GANGLION CELLS. Amacrine cells have no axons and do not contribute directly to the output of the retina.

ambiguity *n.* the property of a behavior, behavior pattern, situation, or other stimulus that might lead to interpretation in more than one way. **—ambiguous** *adj.*

ambiguity tolerance the degree to which one is able to accept, and to function without distress or disorientation in, situations having conflicting or multiple interpretations or outcomes.

ambiguous figure a visual stimulus that can be interpreted in more than one way, such as an EMBEDDED FIGURE or a REVERSIBLE FIGURE. A well-known example is the young girl–old woman image, in which the black-and-white drawing sometimes appears to be of a young girl and sometimes of an old lady. This phenomenon is not restricted to the visual: an **ambiguous stimulus** is one of any sensory modality that can have multiple interpretations.

ambivalence *n.* the simultaneous existence of contradictory feelings and attitudes, such as friendliness and hostility, toward the same person, object, event, or situation. Swiss psychiatrist Eugen Bleuler (1857–1939), who was the first to use this term in a psychological sense, regarded extreme ambivalence as a major symptom of schizophrenia. **—ambivalent** *adj.*

ambivalent attachment see INSECURE ATTACHMENT.

amblyopia *n.* poor vision caused by abnormal visual experience in early life and not any physical defect of the eye. Common predisposing conditions include misalignment of the eyes (strabismus) and differing refractive powers of the eyes (anisometropia). Also called (colloquially) **lazy eye**. **—amblyopic** *adj.*

amenorrhea *n.* the absence of menstruation. When menstruation fails to begin after puberty, the condition is called primary amenorrhea. If menstrual periods stop, in the absence of pregnancy or menopause, after starting, the condition is known as secondary amenorrhea.

American Psychiatric Association (APA) a national medical and professional organization whose physician members specialize in the diagnosis, treatment, and prevention of mental disorders. Founded in 1844, its objectives include the improvement of care for people with mental illnesses, the promotion of research and professional education in psychiatry, and the dissemination of psychological knowledge through nationwide public information, education, and awareness programs and materials. Its extensive publications include the *Diagnostic and Statistical Manual of Mental Disorders* (see DSM–IV–TR), the most widely used psychiatric reference in the world.

American Psychological Association (APA) a scientific and professional organization founded in 1892 that represents psychology in the United States and is the largest association of psychologists worldwide. Its mission is to advance psychology as a science, as a profession, and as a means of promoting health and human welfare. Among its specific goals are the promotion of psychological research and improvement of research methods and conditions; the establishment and maintenance of high standards of professional ethics and conduct of its members; and the increase and diffusion of psychological knowledge through a variety of means, including scholarly journals, the APA *Publication Manual*, books, videotapes, and electronic databases.

Ames room an irregularly shaped but apparently rectangular room in which cues for DEPTH PERCEPTION are used experimentally to distort the viewer's perception of the relative size of objects within the room. Also called **Ames distorted room**. [Adelbert **Ames**, Jr. (1880–1955), U.S. psychologist, inventor, and artist]

amino acid an organic compound that contains an amino group (–NH₂) and a carboxyl group (–COOH), 20 of which are constituents of proteins; 9 of these are essential amino acids, that is, they cannot be synthesized by the body and must be obtained from foods. Other amino acids are neurotransmitters or precursors to neurotransmitters.

amnesia *n.* partial or complete loss of memory. Either temporary or permanent, it may be due to physiological factors such as injury, disease, or substance use, or to psychological factors such as a traumatic experience. A disturbance in memory marked by inability to learn new information is called **anterograde amnesia** and one marked by inability to recall previously learned information or past events is called **retrograde amnesia**. When severe enough to interfere markedly with social or occupational functioning or to represent a significant decline from a previous level of functioning, the memory loss is known as **amnestic disorder**. —**amnesiac** *adj., n.* —**amnesic** or **amnestic** *adj.*

amniocentesis *n.* a method of examining fetal chromosomes for any abnormality or for determination of sex. A hollow needle is inserted through the mother's abdominal wall into the uterus, enabling the collection of amniotic fluid, which contains fetal cells.

amok (amuck) *n.* a CULTURE-BOUND SYNDROME observed among males in Malaysia, the Philippines, and other parts of southeast Asia. The individual experiences a period of social withdrawal and apathy, followed by a violent, unprovoked attack on nearby individuals. If not overpowered or killed, the affected male eventually collapses from exhaustion and afterward has no memory of the event. See also MAL DE PELEA.

AMPA receptor see GLUTAMATE RECEPTOR.

amphetamines *pl. n.* a group of drugs that stimulate the RETICULAR FORMATION and cause a release of stored dopamine and norepinephrine. The effect is a prolonged state of arousal and relief from feelings of fatigue. Introduced in 1932, amphetamines are prone to abuse and dependence, and tolerance develops progressively with continued use. Although widely used in the past for weight loss, relief of depression, and other indications, modern use of amphetamines is more circumscribed because of their adverse effects. They are now used mainly to manage symptoms of attention-deficit/hyperactivity disorder and to treat certain cases of severe depression or narcolepsy.

amplitude *n.* magnitude or extent (e.g., of a stimulus) or peak value (e.g., of a sinusoid wave).

amygdala *n.* an almond-shaped structure in the TEMPORAL LOBE that is a component of the LIMBIC SYSTEM and considered part of the BASAL GANGLIA. It comprises two main groups of nuclei—the corticomedial group and the basolateral group—and through widespread connections with other brain areas has numerous viscerosensory and autonomic functions as well as an important role in memory, emotion, perception of threat, and fear learning. Also called **amygdaloid body**; **amygdaloid complex**; **amygdaloid nuclei. —amygdaloid** *adj.*

amyloid *n.* a chemically diverse protein that accumulates abnormally between neural and other bodily cells, negatively affecting their functioning. There are various types, each associated with different pathological conditions. For example, beta-amyloid has received considerable attention for its detrimental influence upon memory and cognition in ALZHEIMER'S DISEASE. **—amyloidal** *adj.*

amyloid plaque see SENILE PLAQUE.

anabolism *n.* see METABOLISM. **—anabolic** *adj.*

anaclitic depression dependent depression: intense sadness and DYSPHORIA stemming from early disruptions in caring relationships, such as deprivation, inconsistency, or overindulgence, that lead to an indefinite fear of loss of love, abandonment, and impoverishment. The individual expresses a child-like dependency; has little capacity for frustration; and desires to be soothed directly and immediately. Compare INTROJECTIVE DEPRESSION.

anaerobic exercise strength-based physical activity, such as weight training and sprinting, that occurs in short, intense bursts with limited oxygen intake. The **anaerobic threshold** is the point at which energy use by the body is so great as to require the muscles to begin producing energy in the absence of adequate oxygen. Compare AEROBIC EXERCISE.

anaesthesia *n.* see ANESTHESIA.

analgesia *n.* absence of or reduction in the sensation of pain. Drugs and other substances that alleviate pain are called **analgesics.** The former usually are classed as opioid (narcotic) or nonopioid (non-narcotic), depending on their chemical composition and potential for physical dependence. **—analgesic** *adj.*

analogies test a test of the participant's ability to comprehend the relationship between two items and then extend that relationship to a different situation: For example, paintbrush is to paint as pen is to __.

analogue study a research design in which the procedures or participants used are similar but not identical to the situation of interest. For example, if researchers are interested in the effects of therapist gender on client perceptions of therapist trustworthiness, they may use undergraduate students who are not clients and provide simulated counseling dialogues that are typed and identified as offered by a male or female therapist. The results of such studies are assumed to offer a high degree of experimental control and to generalize to actual clinical practice. Also called **analogue model**.

analogy *n.* **1.** in biology, a similarity of function in bodily structures with different evolutionary origins. For example, the hand of a human and the trunk of an elephant are analogous in that both are used for manipulating objects. **2.** a method of argument that relies on an inference that a similarity between two or more entities in some attributes justifies a probable assumption that they will be similar in other attributes. —**analogical** *adj.* —**analogous** *adj.*

anal stage in psychoanalytic theory, the second stage of PSYCHO-SEXUAL DEVELOPMENT, typically occurring during the 2nd year of life, in which the child's interest and sexual pleasure are focused on the expulsion and retention of feces and the sadistic instinct is linked to the desire to both possess and destroy the OBJECT. Also called **anal phase**.

analysand *n.* in psychoanalysis, a patient who is undergoing analysis.

analysis *n.* see PSYCHOANALYSIS. —**analytic** or **analytical** *adj.*

analysis by synthesis any theory of information processing stating

that both data-driven processes and conceptually driven processes interact in the recognition and interpretation of sensory input. According to such theories, which are associated particularly with speech perception and language processing, the person analyzes the original physical stimulus input, hypothesizes what it is based on experience or learning, determines what the input would be like if the hypothesis were correct, and then assesses whether the input is actually like that.

analysis of covariance (ANCOVA) an extension of the ANALYSIS OF VARIANCE that adjusts the dependent variable for the influence of a correlated variable (COVARIATE) that is not being investigated but may influence the study results. An analysis of covariance is appropriate in two types of cases: (a) when experimental groups are suspected to differ on a background-correlated variable in addition to the differences attributed to the experimental treatment and (b) where adjustment on a covariate can increase the precision of the experiment.

analysis of variance (ANOVA) any of several statistical procedures that isolate the joint and separate effects of independent variables upon a dependent variable and test them for statistical significance (i.e., to determine whether they are greater than they would be if obtained by chance alone). See also GENERAL LINEAR MODEL.

analyst *n.* generally, one who practices psychoanalysis. This is usually a PSYCHOANALYST in the tradition of Austrian psychiatrist Sigmund Freud (1856–1939); however, the term is also applied to therapists adhering to the methods of Swiss psychiatrist Carl Jung (1875–1961) (see ANALYTIC PSYCHOLOGY) or Austrian psychiatrist Alfred Adler (1870–1936) (see INDIVIDUAL PSYCHOLOGY).

analytical intelligence in the TRIARCHIC THEORY OF INTELLIGENCE, the skills measured by conventional tests of intelligence, such as analysis, comparison, evaluation, critique, and judgment. Compare CREATIVE INTELLIGENCE; PRACTICAL INTELLIGENCE.

analytic psychology the system of psychoanalysis proposed by Swiss psychiatrist Carl Jung (1875–1961), in which the psyche is interpreted primarily in terms of philosophical values, primordial images and symbols, and a drive for self-fulfillment. Jung's basic concepts are (a) the EGO, which maintains a balance between conscious and unconscious activities and gradually develops a unique self through INDIVIDUATION; (b) the PERSONAL UNCONSCIOUS, made up of memories, thoughts, and feelings based on personal experience; (c) the COLLECTIVE UNCONSCIOUS, made up of ancestral images, or ARCHETYPES, that constitute the inherited foundation of an individual's intellectual life and personality; and (d) dynamic polarities, or tension systems, which derive their psychic energy from the LIBIDO and influence the development and expression of the ego.

anchor *n.* a reference point used when making a series of subjective judgments. For example, in an experiment in which participants gauge distances between objects, the experimenter introduces an anchor by informing the participants that the distance between two of the stimulus objects is a given value. That value then functions as a reference for participants in their subsequent judgments. Also called **anchor point**.

anchoring bias the tendency, in forming perceptions or making

quantitative judgments of some entity under conditions of uncertainty, to give excessive weight to the initial starting value (or ANCHOR), based on the first received information or one's initial judgment, and not to modify this anchor sufficiently in light of later information. For example, estimates of the product of $9 \times 8 \times 7 \times 6 \times 5 \times 4 \times 3 \times 2 \times 1$ tend to be higher than estimates of the product of $1 \times 2 \times 3 \times 4 \times 5 \times 6 \times 7 \times 8 \times 9$. Also called **anchoring effect**.

ANCOVA acronym for ANALYSIS OF COVARIANCE.

androgen *n.* any of a class of steroid hormones that act as the principal male SEX HORMONES, the major one being TESTOSTERONE. Androgens are produced mainly by the testes and influence the development of masculine primary and secondary SEX CHARACTERISTICS. They are also secreted in small quantities by the cortex of the adrenal gland and can be produced synthetically. —**androgenic** *adj.*

androgen-insensitivity syndrome an inherited condition affecting the development of reproductive and genital organs, caused by varying degrees of insensitivity to androgens. There are two forms: complete, in which the insensitivity is total, resulting in external genitalia that are female; and partial, in which some sensitivity to the hormones allows for external genitalia that may be structurally ambiguous. In both forms, however, the internal organs are male (i.e., testes). Also called **testicular feminization syndrome**.

androgyny *n.* **1.** the presence of male and female characteristics in one individual. **2.** the state of being neither distinguishably masculine or feminine in appearance, as in dress. —**androgyne** *n.* —**androgynous** *adj.*

anecdotal method an investigational technique in which informal verbal reports of incidents casually observed (e.g., a particular feat of a particular animal) are accepted as useful information. The anecdotal method is scientifically inadequate but can offer clues as to areas of investigation that warrant more systematic, controlled research.

anencephaly *n.* congenital absence of the cranial vault (the bones forming the rear of the skull), with cerebral hemispheres completely missing or reduced to small masses. Infants born with anencephaly are usually blind, deaf, unconscious, and unable to feel pain. —**anencephalic** *adj.*

anesthesia (anaesthesia) *n.* the loss of sensitivity to stimuli, either in a particular area (local) or throughout the body and accompanied by loss of consciousness (general). It may be produced intentionally, for example via the administration of drugs (called **anesthetics**) or the use of techniques such as ACUPUNCTURE or hypnotic suggestion, or it may occur spontaneously as a result of injury or disease. —**anesthetic** *adj.*

aneurysm (aneurism) *n.* an enlargement (widening) at some point in an artery caused by the pressure of blood on weakened tissues, often at junctions where arteries split off from one another. —**aneurysmal** *adj.*

anger *n.* an emotion characterized by tension and hostility arising from frustration, real or imagined injury by another, or perceived injustice. It can manifest itself in behaviors designed to remove the object of the anger (e.g., determined action) or behaviors designed merely to express the emotion (e.g., swearing). Anger is distinct from, but a significant activator of, AGGRESSION, which is behavior intended to harm someone or something. Despite their mutually influential relationship, anger is neither necessary nor sufficient for aggression to occur.

angioma *n.* a tumor of the vascular system: an abnormal mass of blood vessels or lymph vessels.

angiotensin *n.* one of a family of peptides, including angiotensins I, II, and III, that are produced by the enzymatic action of renin on a precursor protein (**angiotensinogen**) in the bloodstream. Their effects include narrowing of blood vessels (VASOCONSTRICTION), increased blood pressure, thirst, and stimulation of ALDOSTERONE release from the adrenal glands.

angst *n.* in EXISTENTIALISM, a state of anguish or despair in which a person recognizes the fundamental uncertainty of existence and understands the significance of conscious choice and personal responsibility.

angular gyrus a ridge along the lower surface of the PARIETAL LOBE of the brain, formed by a junction of the superior and middle temporal gyri. This region has been proposed as the key area of reading and writing function. Lesions are associated with ALEXIA and AGRAPHIA, and structural abnormalities with DYSLEXIA.

anhedonia *n.* the inability to enjoy experiences or activities that normally would be pleasurable. It is one of two defining symptoms of a MAJOR DEPRESSIVE EPISODE (the other being a persistent depressed mood), but is also seen in other disorders, including schizophrenia. —**anhedonic** *adj.*

animal model characteristics or conditions of an animal that are similar to those of humans, thus making the animal suitable for studying human behavior, processes, disorders or diseases, and so forth.

animism *n.* the belief that natural phenomena or inanimate objects are alive or possess lifelike characteristics, such as intentions, desires, and feelings. Animism was considered by Swiss psychologist Jean Piaget (1896–1980) to be characteristic of the thought of children in the PREOPERATIONAL STAGE, later fading out and being replaced by the strong belief in the universal nature of physical causality. **—animistic** *adj.*

anomaly *n.* anything that is irregular or deviates from the norm, often referring to a congenital or developmental defect. **—anomalous** *adj.*

anomia *n.* loss or impairment of the ability to name objects. All individuals with APHASIA exhibit anomia, and the extent of naming difficulty is a good general measure of aphasia severity. **—anomic** *adj.*

anomie *n.* a sense of alienation and hopelessness in a society or group that is often a response to social upheaval. It may also be accompanied by changes in personal and social values. **—anomic** *adj.*

anorexia *n.* absence or loss of appetite for food or, less commonly, for other desires (e.g., sex), especially when chronic. It may be primarily a psychological disorder, as in ANOREXIA NERVOSA, or it may have physiological causes, such as hypopituitarism. **—anorectic** or **anorexic** *adj., n.*

anorexia nervosa an eating disorder, occurring most frequently in adolescent girls, that involves persistent refusal of food, excessive fear of weight gain, refusal to maintain minimally normal body weight, disturbed perception of body image, and amenorrhea (absence of at least three menstrual periods).

anosmia *n.* absence or loss of the ability to smell, which may be general or limited to certain odors. General or total anosmia implies inability to smell all odorants on both sides of the nose, whereas partial anosmia implies an inability to smell certain odorants. **—anosmic** *adj.*

anosognosia *n.* a neurologically based failure to recognize the existence of a deficit or disorder, such as hearing loss, poor vision, or paralysis.

ANOVA acronym for ANALYSIS OF VARIANCE.

anoxia *n.* total lack of oxygen in the body tissues, including the brain. Consequences depend on the severity of the anoxia and the specific areas of the brain that are affected, but can include generalized cognitive deficits or more focal deficits in memory, perception, or EXECUTIVE FUNCTION. Anoxia sometimes is used as a synonym of HYPOXIA. **—anoxic** *adj.*

ANS abbreviation for AUTONOMIC NERVOUS SYSTEM.

Antabuse *n.* a trade name for DISULFIRAM.

antagonist *n.* **1.** a drug or other chemical agent that inhibits the action of another substance. For example, an antagonist may combine with the substance to alter and thus inactivate it (**chemical antagonism**); an antagonist may reduce the effects of the substance by binding to the same receptor without stimulating it, which decreases the number of available receptors (**pharmacological antagonism**); or an antagonist may bind to a different receptor and produce a physiological effect opposite to that of the substance (**physiological antagonism**). **2.** a contracting muscle whose action generates force opposing the intended direction of movement. This force may serve to slow the movement rapidly as it approaches the target or it may help to define the movement end point.

Compare AGONIST. **—antagonism** *n.* **—antagonistic** *adj.*

antecedent *n.* an event, circumstance, or stimulus that precedes some other event and often elicits, signals, or sets the occasion for a particular behavior or response. See also CONTINGENCY.

anterior *adj.* in front of or toward the front. In reference to two-legged upright animals, this term is sometimes used interchangeably with VENTRAL to mean toward the front surface of the body. Compare POSTERIOR. **—anteriorly** *adv.*

anterior commissure see COMMISSURE.

anterograde amnesia see AMNESIA.

anterograde memory the ability to retain events, experiences, and other information following a particular point in time. When this ability is impaired (i.e., by injury or disease), it becomes very difficult or even impossible to recall what happened from that moment forward, a condition known as anterograde AMNESIA. For example, an individual with deficits of anterograde memory resulting from a stroke might not remember the name of a new person introduced to him or her but would remember the name of a close childhood friend. Compare RETROGRADE MEMORY.

anthropocentrism *n.* the explicit or implicit assumption that human experience is the central reality and, by extension, the idea that all phenomena can be evaluated in the light of their relationship to humans. **—anthropocentric** *adj.*

anthropological linguistics the branch of linguistics that draws connections between the characteristics of a particular language and the cultural practices, social structures, and worldview of the society in which it is spoken (see LINGUISTIC DETERMINISM; LINGUISTIC RELATIVITY).

anthropology *n.* the study of human beings. This typically involves the description and explanation of similarities and differences among human groups in their languages, aesthetic expressions, belief systems, and social structures over the range of human geography and chronology. **—anthropological** *adj.* **—anthropologist** *n.*

anthropometry *n.* **1.** the scientific study of how the size and proportions of the human body are affected by such variables as age, sex, and ethnic and cultural groups. **2.** the taking of measurements of the human body for purposes of comparison and study. **—anthropometric** *adj.* **—anthropometrist** *n.*

anthropomorphism *n.* **1.** the attribution of human characteristics to nonhuman entities such as deities, spirits, animals, plants, or inanimate objects. **2.** in COMPARATIVE PSYCHOLOGY, the tendency to interpret the behavior and mental processes of nonhuman animals in terms of human abilities. A variation is anthropocentrism, which uses human behavior as the standard by which the behavior of nonhuman animals, for example, intelligence, is evaluated. Compare ZOOMORPHISM. **—anthropomorphic** *adj.*

antianxiety medication see ANXIOLYTIC.

antibody *n.* a modified protein molecule, produced by B LYMPHOCYTES, that interacts with an ANTIGEN and renders it harmless. Each type of antibody is designed to interact with a specific antigen and can be mass-produced following previous exposure to an identical antigen. See IMMUNE SYSTEM.

anticholinesterase *n.* see CHOLINESTERASE.

anticonvulsant *n.* any drug used to reduce the frequency or severity of epileptic seizures or to terminate a seizure already underway. Until the advent of the hydantoins in the 1930s, which were developed specifically to control epileptic seizures, anticonvulsants consisted mainly of bromides (largely supplanted due to their toxicity and frequency of adverse side effects) and BARBITURATES. Also effective as antiseizure medications are the BENZODIAZEPINES. Also called **antiepileptic**.

antidepressant *n.* any drug administered in the treatment of depression. Most antidepressants work by increasing the availability of monoamine neurotransmitters such as norepinephrine, serotonin, or dopamine, although they do so by different routes. The MONOAMINE OXIDASE INHIBITORS (MAOIs) work by inhibiting monoamine oxidase, one of the principal enzymes that metabolize these neurotransmitters. Most of the other antidepressants, including the TRICYCLIC ANTIDEPRESSANTS (TCAs) and the selective serotonin reuptake inhibitors (see SSRI), inhibit the reuptake of serotonin or norepinephrine (and to a much lesser degree dopamine) into the presynaptic neuron. Either process leaves more of the neurotransmitter free to bind with postsynaptic receptors, initiating a series of events in the postsynaptic neuron that is thought to produce the actual therapeutic effect.

antidiuretic hormone (ADH) see VASOPRESSIN.

antigen *n.* any substance that is treated by the immune system as foreign and is therefore capable of inducing an immune response, particularly the production of ANTIBODIES that render it harmless.

The antigen may be a virus, a bacterium, a toxin (e.g., bee venom), or tissue (e.g., blood) of another individual with different genetic characteristics. —**antigenic** *adj.*

antimanic see MOOD STABILIZER.

antipsychotic *n.* any pharmacological agent used to control the symptoms of schizophrenia and other disorders characterized by impaired reality testing, as evidenced by severely disorganized thought, speech, and behavior. Formerly called **major tranquilizers** and later **neuroleptics**, antipsychotics are commonly divided into two major classes: **conventional (first-generation) antipsychotics**, and the newer **atypical (second-generation) antipsychotics.** The latter class has fewer adverse side effects than the former, particularly the neurologically based EXTRAPYRAMIDAL SYMPTOMS but also the less serious yet unpleasant autonomic effects, such as dry mouth and blurred vision.

antisocial *adj.* denoting or exhibiting behavior that sharply deviates from social norms and also violates other people's rights. Arson and vandalism are examples of antisocial behavior. Compare PROSOCIAL.

antisocial personality disorder the presence of a chronic and pervasive disposition to disregard and violate the rights of others. Manifestations include repeated violations of the law, exploitation of others, deceitfulness, impulsivity, aggressiveness, reckless disregard for the safety of self and others, and irresponsibility, accompanied by lack of guilt, remorse, and empathy. The disorder has been known by various names, notably **psychopathic personality** and **sociopathic personality**. It is the most heavily researched of the personality disorders and the most difficult to treat.

antithesis *n.* **1.** a THESIS, idea, or proposition that is opposite to or contradicts another. **2.** in philosophy, the second stage of a dialectical process based on proposition, contradiction, and the reconciliation of these (thesis, antithesis, and SYNTHESIS). —**antithetical** *adj.*

anxiety *n.* an emotion characterized by apprehension and somatic symptoms of tension in which an individual anticipates impending danger, catastrophe, or misfortune. The body often mobilizes itself to meet the perceived threat: Muscles become tense, breathing is faster, and the heart beats more rapidly. Anxiety may be distinguished from FEAR both conceptually and physiologically, although the two terms are often used interchangeably. The former is considered a disproportionate response to a vague, unidentifiable threat whereas the latter is an appropriate response to a clearly identifiable and specific threat. —**anxious** *adj.*

anxiety disorder any of a group of disorders that have as their central organizing theme the emotional state of fear, worry, or anxious apprehension. This category includes OBSESSIVE-COMPULSIVE DISORDER, PANIC DISORDER, various PHOBIAS, POSTTRAUMATIC STRESS DISORDER, and GENERALIZED ANXIETY DISORDER. Anxiety disorders have a chronic course, albeit waxing and waning in intensity, and are among the most common mental health problems in the United States.

anxiety sensitivity fear of sensations associated with anxiety because of the belief that they will have harmful consequences. For example, an individual with high anxiety sensitivity is likely to regard feeling lightheaded as a sign of impending illness or fainting, whereas an individual with low anxiety sensitivity would tend to regard this sensation as simply unpleasant. Research indicates that high anxiety sensitivity is a personality risk factor for the development of PANIC ATTACKS and PANIC DISORDER.

anxiolytic *n.* any of a class of drugs used in the control of anxiety, mild behavioral agitation, and insomnia. Formerly called **minor tranquilizers**, they can also be used as adjunctive agents in the treatment of depression and panic disorder. The most widely used anxiolytics are the BENZODIAZEPINES.

anxious–ambivalent attachment style an interpersonal style characterized by worry that a partner will break off a relationship or by hesitancy in forming deeply committed relationships despite a desire to do so.

APA 1. abbreviation for AMERICAN PSYCHIATRIC ASSOCIATION. **2.** abbreviation for AMERICAN PSYCHOLOGICAL ASSOCIATION.

APA style guidelines and standards for writing (e.g., grammar) and formatting (e.g., data display, headings) for students, instructors, researchers, and clinicians in the social and behavioral sciences, as collected in the PUBLICATION MANUAL OF THE AMERICAN PSYCHOLOGICAL ASSOCIATION.

apathy *n.* indifference and lack of response. —**apathetic** *adj.*

Apgar score an evaluation of newborn infants on five factors: skin color, heart rate, respiratory effort, reflexes, and muscle tone. The evaluation is typically performed at 1 min and again at 5 min after birth to assess the physical condition of the infant and to determine quickly if he or she needs immediate medical care. Each factor is scored 0, 1, or 2, with a maximum total of 10 points. [developed in 1952 by Virginia **Apgar** (1909–1974), U.S. anesthesiologist]

aphagia *n.* inability to swallow or eat. Compare HYPERPHAGIA. —**aphagic** *adj.*

aphasia *n.* an acquired language impairment that results from neurological damage to the language areas of the brain, which are typically located in the left hemisphere. Traditionally, a distinction has been made between expressive and receptive forms of aphasia, whereby individuals with the former primarily have difficulty producing spoken and written language and those with the latter primarily have difficulty comprehending spoken and written language. A more contemporary distinction, however, is commonly made between **fluent aphasias**, characterized by plentiful verbal output consisting of well-articulated, easily produced utterances of relatively normal length and prosody (rhythm and intonation), and **nonfluent aphasias**, characterized by sparse, effortful utterances of short phrase length and disrupted prosody. Fluent aphasias are associated with posterior lesions that spare cortical regions critical for motor control of speech, whereas nonfluent aphasias are associated with anterior lesions that compromise motor and premotor cortical regions involved in speech production. Numerous types of aphasia exist, for example BROCA'S APHASIA and WERNICKE'S APHASIA. —**aphasic** *adj.*

apnea (**apnoea**) *n.* temporary suspension of respiration. Apnea can occur during sleep (see SLEEP APNEA) and is also found in many disorders. —**apneic** *adj.*

apoptosis *n.* see PROGRAMMED CELL DEATH. —**apoptotic** *adj.*

a posteriori denoting conclusions derived from observations or other manifest occurrences: reasoning causes from facts. When applied to HYPOTHESIS TESTING, this concept means an **a posteriori test**, which is a statistical test planned after research data have been examined because certain patterns in the data warrant further study. Compare A PRIORI. [Latin, "from the latter"]

apparatus *n.* **1.** any instrument or equipment used during an experiment. **2.** in biology, a group of structures that perform a particular function.

apparent movement an illusion of motion or change in size of a visual stimulus. Several types have been identified and labeled with Greek letters, among them the familiar **beta movement**, in which successive presentations of stationary stimuli across the visual field produce the perception of a single smoothly moving stimulus, and **gamma movement**, the seeming expansion of an object when it is suddenly presented and contraction when withdrawn. Also called **apparent motion**.

appearance–reality distinction the knowledge that the appearance of an object does not necessarily correspond to its reality. For example, a sponge shaped like a rock may look like a rock but it is really a sponge. Children younger than 3 may have difficulty making appearance–reality distinctions.

apperception *n.* **1.** the mental process by which a perception or an idea is assimilated into an individual's existing knowledge, thoughts, and emotions (his or her **apperceptive mass**). **2.** the act or process of perceiving something consciously. —**apperceive** *vb.* —**apperceptive** *adj.*

applied psychology the application of the theories, principles, and techniques of psychology to practical concerns, such as problems of living or coping, education, vocational guidance, industry, ergonomics, consumer affairs, advertising, political campaigns, and environmental issues. It may be contrasted with theoretical psychology or academic psychology, in which the emphasis is on understanding for its own sake rather than the utility of the knowledge.

applied research research conducted for the practical purpose of solving a real-world problem rather than developing a theory or obtaining knowledge for its own sake. Compare BASIC RESEARCH.

applied tension a technique in BEHAVIOR THERAPY that focuses on changing physiological responses (e.g., low blood pressure leading to fainting) by having the client practice muscle tensing and releasing during exposure to increasingly anxiety-evoking stimuli associated with a feared situation. The technique was developed and is still primarily used for blood, injury, and injection phobias.

appraisal *n.* the cognitive evaluation of the nature and significance of a phenomenon or event. In **appraisal theories** of emotion, such evaluations are seen as determinants of emotional experience. See COGNITIVE APPRAISAL THEORY. **—appraise** *vb.*

appraisal motive the desire to gain accurate information about the self. It leads people to seek highly relevant, explicit feedback and to reject flattery or other bias. Compare CONSISTENCY MOTIVE; SELF-ENHANCEMENT MOTIVE.

apprehension *n.* **1.** uneasiness or dread about an upcoming event or the future generally. Also called **apprehensiveness**. **2.** the act or capability of grasping something mentally. For example, the **apprehension span** is the maximum number of distinct objects that can be reported from one glance at an array of items (e.g., specific letters

from a group of words). Compare COMPREHENSION. **—apprehend** *vb.* **—apprehensible** *adj.* **—apprehensive** *adj.*

approach–approach conflict a situation involving a choice between two equally desirable but incompatible alternatives. See also APPROACH–AVOIDANCE CONFLICT; AVOIDANCE–AVOIDANCE CONFLICT.

approach–avoidance conflict a situation involving a single goal or option that has both desirable and undesirable aspects or consequences. The closer an individual comes to the goal, the greater the anxiety, but withdrawal from the goal then increases the desire. See also APPROACH–APPROACH CONFLICT; AVOIDANCE–AVOIDANCE CONFLICT.

apraxia *n.* loss or impairment of the ability to perform purposeful, skilled movements despite intact motor function and comprehension. The condition may be developmental or induced by neurological dysfunction and is believed to represent an impairment of the ability to plan, select, and sequence the motor execution of movements. There are several major types of apraxia, including ideational apraxia, involving difficulty carrying out in the proper order a series of acts that comprise a complex task; ideomotor apraxia, involving difficulty imitating actions or gesturing to command; and speech apraxia, involving difficulty coordinating the movements necessary for speaking. **—apraxic** *adj.*

a priori denoting conclusions derived from premises or principles: deducing effects from prior assumptions. When applied to HYPOTHESIS TESTING, this concept means an **a priori test**, which is a statistical test explicitly planned before research data have been examined and trends observed. Compare A POSTERIORI. [Latin, "prior to"]

A

aptitude *n.* the capacity to acquire competence or skill through training. Specific aptitude is potential in a particular area (e.g., artistic or mathematical aptitude); general aptitude is potential in several fields. Both are distinct from ABILITY, which is an existing competence.

aptitude test any assessment instrument designed to measure potential for acquiring knowledge or skill. Aptitude tests are thought of as providing a basis for making predictions for an individual about future success, particularly in either an educational or occupational situation. In contrast, ACHIEVEMENT TESTS are considered to reflect the amount of learning already obtained.

aqueous humor see EYE.

arachnoid mater see MENINGES.

arachnophobia *n.* a persistent and irrational fear of spiders.

archetype *n.* in ANALYTIC PSYCHOLOGY, a structural component of the mind that derives from the accumulated experience of humankind. These inherited components are stored in the COLLECTIVE UNCONSCIOUS and serve as a frame of reference with which individuals view the world and as one of the major foundations on which the structure of the personality is built. —**archetypal** *adj.*

archicortex *n.* see ALLOCORTEX.

archival research the use of books, journals, historical documents, and other existing records or data available in storage in scientific research. Archival methods provide unobtrusive observation of human activity in natural settings and permit the study of phenomena that otherwise cannot easily be investigated. A persistent drawback, however, is that causal inferences are always more tentative than those provided by laboratory experiments.

arcuate fasciculus a bundle of nerve fibers linking the parts of the brain involved in the interpretation and control of speech (WERNICKE'S AREA and BROCA'S AREA, respectively). Lesions of this tract produce CONDUCTION APHASIA.

arcuate nucleus 1. an arc-shaped collection of neurons in the hypothalamus that produce hormones. **2.** any of various small groups of gray matter on the bulge of the medulla oblongata. They are extensions of neurons in the basal PONS and project to the cerebellum.

argument *n.* a parameter on which the value of a mathematical FUNCTION depends.

arithmetic mean see MEAN.

arousal *n.* **1.** a state of physiological activation or cortical responsiveness, associated with sensory stimulation and activation of fibers from the RETICULAR ACTIVATING SYSTEM. **2.** a state of excitement or energy expenditure linked to an emotion. Usually, arousal is closely related to a person's appraisal of the significance of an event or to the physical intensity of a stimulus. —**arouse** *vb.*

arousal theory the theory that the physical environment can affect arousal levels by stimulation and by stress created when psychological or physical needs are not met. Arousal increases when personal space is diminished or when people are subjected to noise or traffic congestion.

array *n.* any ordered arrangement of data, particularly a two-dimensional grouping of data into rows and columns (i.e., a matrix). The concept may be extended to more than two dimensions.

arrhythmia *n.* any variation from the normal rhythm of the heartbeat. Kinds of arrhythmia include (among others) **tachycardia**, any rate above 100 beats per minute; and **bradycardia**, a rate of less than 60 beats per minute. **—arrhythmic** *adj.*

arteriosclerosis *n.* a group of diseases characterized by hardening and loss of elasticity of the walls of the arteries. A common type is ATHEROSCLEROSIS. **—arteriosclerotic** *adj.*

arthritis *n.* inflammation of a joint, causing pain, swelling, and stiffness. The most severe and disabling form is rheumatoid arthritis, associated with the body attacking its own cells as foreign (see AUTOIMMUNITY). **—arthritic** *adj.*

articulation *n.* **1.** the shaping and production of the sounds required for intelligible speech. It is a complex process involving not only accurate movements of the vocal tract (e.g., lips, tongue, soft palate) but also neural integration of numerous other activities. **2.** a joint between bones, which may be fixed or movable. **—articulate** *vb.*

articulatory loop see WORKING MEMORY.

articulatory store a component of short-term memory that retains auditory information based on the motor systems involved in pronouncing items, rather than how they sound. Compare ACOUSTIC STORE.

artifact *n.* an experimental finding that is not a reflection of the true state of nature but rather the consequent of flawed design or analytic error.

artificial insemination the use of medical techniques to achieve conception by introducing sperm into the female reproductive system through the cervical opening and directly into the uterus. Artificial insemination may need to be done more than once for pregnancy to occur; to maximize success it is usually scheduled to coincide with the days of ovulation.

artificial intelligence (**AI**) a subdiscipline of computer science that aims to produce programs that simulate human intelligence. There are many branches of AI, including robotics, computer vision, machine learning, game playing, and expert systems. AI has also supported research in other related areas, including COGNITIVE SCIENCE and computational linguistics.

artificial selection human intervention in animal or plant reproduction to improve the value or utility of succeeding generations. Compare NATURAL SELECTION.

art therapy the use of artistic activities, such as painting and clay modeling, in psychotherapy and rehabilitation. The process of making art is seen as a means of symbolic communication and a vehicle for developing new insights, resolving conflicts, solving problems, and formulating new perceptions.

asceticism *n.* a character trait or lifestyle characterized by simplicity, renunciation of physical pleasures and worldly goods, social withdrawal, and extreme self-discipline. **—ascetic** *adj.*

Asch situation an experimental paradigm used to study conformity to group opinion. Participants make perceptual judgments as part of a group of confederates who make errors deliberately on certain trials. The extent to which participants publicly agree with the erroneous group judgment or resist the pressure to do so and remain independent provides a measure of conformity. [Solomon **Asch** (1907–1996), Polish-born U.S. psychologist]

ASD abbreviation for AUTISTIC SPECTRUM DISORDER.

Asperger's disorder a pervasive developmental disorder associated with varying degrees of deficits in social and conversational skills, difficulties with transitions from one task to another or with changes in situations or environments, and preference for sameness and predictability of events. Obsessive routines and preoccupation with particular subjects of interest may be present, as may difficulty reading body language and maintaining proper social distance. In contrast to AUTISTIC DISORDER, language skills develop, and there is no clinically significant delay in cognitive or adaptive functioning other than in social interactions. Also called **Asperger's syndrome**. [described in 1944 by Hans **Asperger** (1906–1980), Austrian psychiatrist]

assertiveness training a method of teaching individuals to change verbal and nonverbal signals and behavioral patterns and to enhance interpersonal communication generally through techniques designed to help them express emotions, opinions, and preferences—positive and negative—clearly, directly, and in an appropriate manner. ROLE PLAY or behavior rehearsal is often used to prepare clients to be appropriately assertive in real-life situations.

assessment *n.* see PSYCHOLOGICAL ASSESSMENT.

assimilation *n.* the process of absorbing, incorporating, or making similar. For example, social assimilation is the process by which an immigrant adopts to a new culture adopts the culture's beliefs and practices. —**assimilate** *vb.*

assisted death an action taken by one person to end the life of another, at the request of the latter. This action can take the form of either ASSISTED SUICIDE or ACTIVE EUTHANASIA. Assisted death is sometimes called **physician-assisted suicide**, which assumes a firm determination of the cause of death.

assisted living a form of congregate housing for older adults requiring long-term care services that include meals, personal care, and scheduled nursing care. Typically comprising private rooms or apartments, it encourages a degree of autonomy and independence in residents that is not provided for in nursing homes.

assisted suicide suicide in which the person ending his or her own life is provided the means to do so (e.g., a prescription) by another. See ASSISTED DEATH.

association *n.* **1.** a connection or relationship between items, particularly ideas, events, or feelings. Associations are established by experience and are fundamental to LEARNING THEORY and BEHAVIORISM. **2.** the degree of statistical dependence between two or more phenomena. —**associative** *adj.* —**associational** *adj.*

association cortex any of various areas of the CEREBRAL CORTEX that are not involved principally in sensory or motor representations but may be involved in integrative functions. Also called **association area**.

associative learning the process of acquiring new and enduring information via the formation of bonds between elements. In different types of **associationistic learning theories**, these associated elements may be stimulus and response, mental representations of events, or elements in neural networks. Historically, the associationistic theories of U.S. psychologists Clark L. Hull (1884–1952) and Kenneth W. Spence (1907–1967) are contrasted with the nonassociative and cognitive theory of U.S. psychologist Edward C. Tolman (1886–1959).

assortative mating behavior in which mates are chosen on the basis of a particular trait or group of traits (e.g., attractiveness, similarity of body size). Compare RANDOM MATING.

assumption *n.* one or more conditions that need to be met in order for a statistical procedure to be fully justified from a theoretical perspective. For example, ANALYSIS OF VARIANCE assumes HOMOGENEITY OF VARIANCE and independence of observations, among other criteria. If the assumptions were to be violated to an extreme extent, the results would be invalid. See ROBUSTNESS.

asthma *n.* a chronic disorder in which intermittent inflammation and narrowing of the bronchial passages produces wheezing, gasping, coughing, and chest tightness. Though the precipitating cause is usually an allergen, such as dust or pollen, environmental irritants, respiratory infection, anxiety, stress, and other agents may produce or aggravate symptoms. —**asthmatic** *adj.*

astigmatism *n.* a visual disorder in which the light rays of a visual stimulus do not all focus at a single point on the retina due to uneven curvature of the cornea or lens. The effect is an aberration or distortion of the visual image that makes it difficult to see fine detail. —**astigmatic** *adj.*

astrocyte *n.* a star-shaped nonneuronal central nervous system cell (GLIA) with numerous extensions that run in all directions. They provide structural support for the brain, are responsible for many homeostatic controls, and may iso-late receptive surfaces. Also called **astroglia**.

asylum *n.* originally, a refuge for criminals (from Greek *asylon*, "sanctuary"). From the 19th century, the terms "asylum" or "insane asylum" were applied to mental institutions. These names are now obsolete, discarded because of their emphasis on refuge rather than treatment.

ataxia *n.* inability to perform coordinated voluntary movements. Ataxia may be seen as a symptom of various disorders, such as multiple sclerosis or cerebral palsy, or it can occur in isolation. It can be heritable or acquired from injury or infection affecting the nervous system. When due to damage to the CEREBELLUM it is called **cerebellar ataxia** and when due to loss of sensory feedback from the muscles and joints it is called **sensory ataxia**. —**ataxic** *adj.*

atherosclerosis *n.* a common form of ARTERIOSCLEROSIS resulting from accumulations of lipids such as cholesterol on the inner walls of arteries and their hardening into **atherosclerotic** (or **atheromatous**) **plaques**. —**atherosclerotic** *adj.*

atonia *n.* lack of normal muscle tone. —**atonic** *adj.*

ATP *a*denosine *t*riphosphate: a nucleotide in living cells that is the source of chemical energy for biological processes. A bond between two of its three component phosphate groups is easily split by a particular enzyme, **ATPase** (**adenosine triphosphatase**), yielding energy when a cell requires it.

at risk vulnerable to a disorder or disease. Risk status for an individual is defined by genetic, physical, and behavioral factors or conditions. For example, children of people with schizophrenia may be considered at risk for schizophrenia, and heavy cigarette smokers are at risk for emphysema and lung cancer.

atrophy *n.* a wasting away of the body or a body part, as from lack of nourishment, inactivity, degenerative disease, or normal aging. **—atrophic** *adj.*

attachment *n.* the close emotional bond between a human infant or a young nonhuman animal and its parent figure or caregiver, developed as a step in establishing a feeling of security and demonstrated by calmness while in their presence. Attachment also denotes the tendency to form such strong bonds with certain other individuals in infancy as well as the tendency in adulthood to seek emotionally supportive relationships.

attachment style the characteristic way people relate to others in the context of intimate relationships, which is heavily influenced by SELF-WORTH and INTERPERSONAL TRUST. Theoretically, an adult's degree of attachment security is related directly to how well they bonded to others as children. There are four distinct categories of adult attachment that have been identified: DISMISSIVE ATTACHMENT, FEARFUL ATTACHMENT, PREOCCUPIED ATTACHMENT, and SECURE ATTACHMENT.

attachment theory a theory that (a) postulates an evolutionarily advantageous need, especially in primates, to form close emotional bonds with significant others: specifically, a need for the young to maintain close proximity to and form bonds with their caregivers; and (b) characterizes the different types of relationships between human infants and caregivers. These relationships have been shown to affect the individual's later emotional development and emotional stability. See also STRANGE SITUATION.

attention *n.* a state of awareness in which the senses are focused selectively on aspects of the environment and the central nervous system is in a state of readiness to respond to stimuli. Because human beings do not have an infinite capacity to attend to everything—focusing on certain items at the expense of others—much of the research in this field is devoted to discerning which factors influence attention and to understanding the neural mechanisms involved in the selective processing of information. See also ATTENUATION THEORY; FILTER THEORY.

attention-deficit/hyperactivity disorder (**ADHD**) a behavioral syndrome characterized by the persistent presence of six or more symptoms involving (a) inattention (e.g., failure to complete tasks or listen carefully, difficulty in concentrating, distractibility) or (b) impulsivity or hyperactivity (e.g., restlessness, fidgeting, difficulty taking turns or staying seated, excessive talking, running about). The symptoms, which impair social, academic, or occupational functioning, appear before the age of 7 and are observed in more than one setting. ADHD has been given a variety of names over the years, including the still commonly used **attention-deficit disorder** (**ADD**).

attenuation *n.* in statistics, a reduction in the estimated size of an effect because of errors of measurement.

attenuation theory a version of the FILTER THEORY of attention proposing that unattended messages are attenuated (i.e., processed weakly) but not entirely blocked from further processing. According to the theory, items in unattended channels of information have different thresholds of recognition depending on their significance to the individual. See also COCKTAIL-PARTY EFFECT.

attitude *n.* a relatively enduring

and general evaluation of an object, person, group, issue, or concept on a scale ranging from negative to positive. Attitudes provide summary evaluations of target objects and are often assumed to be derived from specific beliefs, emotions, and past behaviors associated with those objects. **—attitudinal** *adj.*

attitude accessibility the likelihood that an attitude will be automatically activated from memory on encountering the attitude object. Accessibility is assumed to depend on the strength of the associative link in memory between the representation of the object and the evaluation of the object: The stronger the memory link between the object and its evaluation, the more quickly will the attitude come to mind.

attitude strength the extent to which an attitude persists over time, resists change, influences information processing, and guides behavior. Strong attitudes possess all four of these defining features, whereas weak attitudes lack these features.

attraction *n.* **1.** in social psychology, the feeling of being drawn to one or more other individuals and desiring their company, usually but not necessarily because of a personal liking for them. See also INTERPERSONAL ATTRACTION. **2.** in environmental psychology, a quality affecting proximity relationships between individuals, usually reflecting such factors as their liking for each other. Environmental influences, such as noise, heat, and humidity, decrease attraction between pairs of individuals. See PROXEMICS. **—attractive** *adj.*

attribution *n.* an inference regarding the cause of a person's behavior or an interpersonal event. Three dimensions are often used to evaluate people's **attributional styles**, or characteristic tendencies when inferring

such causes: the internal–external dimension (whether they tend to attribute events to the self or to other factors), the stable–unstable dimension (whether they tend to attribute events to enduring or transient causes), and the global–specific dimension (whether they tend to attribute events to causes that affect many events or just a single event).

attribution theory the study of the processes by which people ascribe motives to their own and others' behavior. The motives ascribed may be either internal and personal (DISPOSITIONAL ATTRIBUTION) or external and circumstantial (SITUATIONAL ATTRIBUTION).

attrition *n.* in experimentation and other research, dropout or loss of participants.

atypical antipsychotic see ANTIPSYCHOTIC.

audience effect the influence on behavior of the presence of bystanders. In humans, performance is often improved when the action is simple and well learned (see SOCIAL FACILITATION) but may be inhibited when it is complicated, difficult to perform, or when the person believes the behavior might incur the audience's disapproval (see SOCIAL INHIBITION).

audit *n.* an evaluation or review of the health care services proposed or rendered by a provider.

audition *n.* hearing: the perception of sound.

auditory agnosia loss or impairment of the ability to recognize and understand the nature of verbal or nonverbal sounds. Subtypes are distinguished on the basis of the type of auditory stimulus the person has difficulty recognizing, for example, environmental sounds such as a dog barking or keys jingling (**environmental sounds agnosia**).

auditory canal see EXTERNAL AUDITORY MEATUS.

auditory cortex the sensory area for hearing, located on the upper side of the TEMPORAL LOBE of the cerebral cortex. It receives and processes input from the MEDIAL GENICULATE NUCLEUS in the thalamus.

auditory hallucination the perception of sound in the absence of an auditory stimulus. Hallucinations may, for example, be of accusatory or laudatory voices or of strange noises and other nonverbal sounds. Auditory hallucinations occur frequently in schizophrenia and other psychotic disorders but may be associated with other conditions as well (e.g., delirium, dementia).

auditory localization the ability to identify the position and changes in position of sound sources based on acoustic information. Also called **sound localization**.

auditory masking a reduction in the ability to detect, discriminate, or recognize one sound (the signal or target) due to the presence of another sound (the masker), measured as an increase in the detection threshold caused by the masker. The ability of one sound to mask another has been used extensively to assess the FREQUENCY SELECTIVITY of the auditory system.

auditory nerve the portion of the vestibulocochlear nerve concerned with the sense of hearing. It originates in the cochlea, from which nerve fibers pass through several layers of nuclei in the brainstem to terminate predominantly in the AUDITORY CORTEX.

auditory system the biological structures and processes responsible for hearing. The peripheral auditory system, or auditory periphery, includes the external, middle, and inner ears and the AUDITORY NERVE. Auditory structures of the brain, including the AUDITORY CORTEX, constitute the central auditory system.

aural *adj.* pertaining to or perceived by the ear.

authoritarian parenting see PARENTING.

authoritarian personality a personality pattern characterized by strict adherence to highly simplified conventional values, an attitude of great deference to authority figures while demanding subservience from those regarded as lower in status, and hostility toward people who deviate from conventional moral prescriptions.

authoritative parenting see PARENTING.

autistic disorder a severe neurologically based pervasive developmental disorder characterized by markedly impaired social interactions and verbal and nonverbal communication; narrow interests; and repetitive behavior. Manifestations and features of the disorder appear before age 3 but vary greatly across children according to developmental level, language skills, and chronological age. They may include a lack of awareness of the feelings of others, impaired ability to imitate, absence of social play, abnormal speech, abnormal nonverbal communication, and a preference for maintaining environmental sameness.

autistic spectrum disorder (**ASD**) any one of a group of disorders with an onset typically occurring during the preschool years and characterized by varying but often marked difficulties in communication and social interaction. The group includes the prototype AUTISTIC DISORDER as well as RETT SYNDROME, ASPERGER'S DISORDER, and CHILDHOOD DISINTEGRATIVE

DISORDER. This term is synonymous with PERVASIVE DEVELOPMENTAL DISORDER but is now more commonly used, given its reflection of symptom overlap among the disorders. Also called **autism spectrum disorder**.

autobiographical memory vivid personal memories recalling the time and place of events and factual knowledge about oneself.

autohypnosis *n.* see SELF-HYPNOSIS. —**autohypnotic** *adj.*

autoimmunity *n.* a condition in which the body's immune system fails to recognize its own tissues as "self" and attempts to reject its own cells. It is a primary factor in the development of such diseases as rheumatoid arthritis and systemic lupus erythematosus (called **autoimmune disorders**). —**autoimmune** *adj.*

autokinesis *n.* an illusory perception of movement—often experienced by pilots flying at night—that occurs when fixating on a dim, stationary light source in the dark. Also called **autokinetic effect; autokinetic illusion**.

automaticity *n.* the quality of a mental process that can be carried out rapidly and without effort or intention (an **automatic process**).

automatic thoughts instantaneous, habitual, but unconscious thoughts that affect a person's mood and actions. Helping clients become aware of the presence and impact of negative automatic thoughts and then test their validity is a central task of cognitive therapy.

automatization *n.* the development of a skill or habit to a point at which it becomes routine and requires little if any conscious effort or direction.

autonomic conditioning in PAVLOVIAN CONDITIONING, a procedure in which the unconditioned stimulus is a mildly aversive stimulus such as an electric shock or a loud noise, and the conditioned response measured is an index of physiological arousal, usually an electrodermal measure such as SKIN CONDUCTANCE responses. The conditioned stimulus is usually a simple visual or auditory stimulus presented for 5–10 seconds.

autonomic nervous system (**ANS**) the portion of the nervous system innervating smooth muscle and glands, including the circulatory, digestive, respiratory, and reproductive organs. It is divided into the SYMPATHETIC NERVOUS SYSTEM and PARASYMPATHETIC NERVOUS SYSTEM. **Autonomic responses** typically involve changes in involuntary bodily functions, such as heart rate, salivation, digestion, perspiration, pupil size, hormone secretion, bladder contraction, and engorgement of the penis and clitoris.

autonomous stage in the theory of moral development proposed by Swiss psychologist Jean Piaget (1896–1980), the stage during which the child, typically 10 years of age or older, eventually understands that rules and laws are not permanent, fixed properties of the world but rather are flexible, modifiable entities created by people. The child gradually relies less on parental authority and more on individual and independent morality and learns that intentions, not consequences or the likelihood of punishment, are important in determining the morality of an act. Also called **autonomous morality**. See MORAL RELATIVISM. Compare HETERONOMOUS STAGE; PREMORAL STAGE.

autonomy *n.* a state of independence and self-determination.

autonomy versus shame and doubt the second of ERIKSON'S

EIGHT STAGES OF DEVELOPMENT, between the ages of 1½ and 3 years. During this stage, children acquire a degree of self-reliance and self-confidence if allowed to develop at their own pace but may begin to doubt their ability to control themselves and their world if parents are overcritical, overprotective, or inconsistent.

autoreceptor *n.* a molecule in the membrane of a presynaptic neuron that regulates the synthesis and release of a neurotransmitter by that neuron by monitoring how much transmitter has been released and "telling" the neuron.

autoshaping *n.* a method of establishing OPERANT performance that rewards only elicited responses. It is most commonly used with pigeons. Signals are presented, independently of behavior, on a response device (in the case of pigeons, a pecking disk), which records the response and then immediately presents reinforcement.

autosome *n.* any chromosome that is not a SEX CHROMOSOME. A human normally has a total of 44 autosomes (arranged in 22 HOMOLOGOUS pairs) in the nucleus of each body cell —**autosomal** *adj.*

autosuggestion *n.* the process of making positive suggestions to oneself for such purposes as improving morale, inducing relaxation, or promoting recovery from illness.

autotopagnosia *n.* a type of AGNOSIA involving loss or impairment of the ability to recognize (i.e., point to) parts of one's own or another person's body. Also called **autopagnosia**.

availability heuristic a common strategy for making judgments about likelihood of occurrence in which the individual bases such judgments on the amount of information held in his or her memory about the particular type of event:

The more information there is, the more likely the event is judged to be. Compare REPRESENTATIVENESS HEURISTIC.

average *n.* see MEAN.

average evoked potential (**AEP**) the summated electrical responses of the brain (see EVOKED POTENTIAL) to repeated presentations of the same stimulus. Since any individual potential typically shows considerable random fluctuations, this technique is used to better distinguish the actual response from background "noise." Also called **average evoked response** (**AER**).

aversion *n.* a physiological or emotional response indicating dislike for a stimulus. It is usually accompanied by withdrawal from or avoidance of the objectionable stimulus (an **aversion reaction**). —**aversive** *adj.*

aversive conditioning the process by which a noxious or unpleasant stimulus is paired with an undesired behavior. This technique may be used therapeutically, for example, in the treatment of substance abuse, in which case it is called **aversion** (or **aversive**) **therapy**. Also called **aversion conditioning**.

aversive racism a form of racial PREJUDICE felt by individuals who outwardly endorse egalitarian attitudes and values but nonetheless experience negative emotions in the presence of members of certain racial groups. See also MODERN RACISM.

avoidance *n.* the practice or an instance of keeping away from particular situations, environments, individuals, or things because of either (a) the anticipated negative consequences of such an encounter or (b) anxious or painful feelings associated with those things or events. Psychology brings several theoretical perspectives to the study of avoidance: its use as a means of coping; its use as a response to fear or shame; and its existence as a component in ANXIETY DISORDERS.

avoidance–avoidance conflict a situation involving a choice between two equally objectionable alternatives. See also APPROACH–APPROACH CONFLICT; APPROACH–AVOIDANCE CONFLICT.

avoidance conditioning the establishment of behavior that prevents or postpones aversive stimulation. In a typical conditioning experiment a buzzer is sounded, then a shock is applied to the subject (e.g., a dog) until it performs a particular act (e.g., jumping over a fence). After several trials, the dog jumps as soon as the buzzer sounds, avoiding the shock. Also called **avoidance learning; avoidance training**. See also ESCAPE CONDITIONING.

avoidant attachment see INSECURE ATTACHMENT.

avoidant attachment style an adult interpersonal style characterized by a discomfort in being close to others.

avoidant personality disorder a personality disorder characterized by (a) hypersensitivity to rejection and criticism, (b) a desire for uncritical acceptance, (c) social withdrawal in spite of a desire for affection and acceptance, and (d) low self-esteem. This pattern is long-standing and severe enough to cause objective distress and seriously impair the ability to work and maintain relationships.

awareness *n.* conscious realization, perception, or knowledge. See also SELF-AWARENESS.

axis *n.* (*pl.* **axes**) **1.** in DSM–IV–TR, any of the five dimensions that are helpful for describing individual behavior and thus facilitate clinical

assessment. They are clinical disorders (Axis I), personality disorders and mental retardation (Axis II), general medical conditions (Axis III), psychosocial and environmental problems (Axis IV), and global assessment of functioning (Axis V). **2.** an imaginary line that bisects the body or an organ in a particular plane. For example, the **long** or (**cephalocaudal**) **axis** runs in the median plane, dividing the body into right and left halves. **3.** a system made up of interrelated parts, as in the HYPOTHALAMIC–PITUITARY–ADRENOCORTICAL SYSTEM (or axis). **4.** a fixed reference line in a coordinate system. See also ABSCISSA; ORDINATE.

axon *n.* the long, thin, hollow, cylindrical extension of a NEURON that normally carries a nerve impulse away from the CELL BODY. An axon often branches extensively and may be surrounded by a protective MYELIN SHEATH. Each branch of an axon ends in a **terminal button** from which an impulse is transmitted, through discharge of a NEUROTRANSMITTER, across a SYNAPSE to a neighboring neuron. —**axonal** *adj.*

axonal transport the transportation of materials along the AXON of a neuron via the flow of the jellylike fluid (**axoplasm**) it contains. Transport may be directed away from the CELL BODY (anterograde) or back toward the cell body (retrograde). Also called **axoplasmic transport**.

axon hillock a cone-shaped part of the CELL BODY of a neuron from which the AXON originates. Depolarization must reach a critical threshold at the axon hillock for the axon to propagate a nerve impulse.

axon terminal the bulbous end of an axon or a branch of an axon, which forms a SYNAPSE on a neuron or other target.

Bb

babbling *n.* prespeech sounds, such as *dadada*, made by infants from around 6 months of age. Also called **babble**.

Babinski reflex the reflex occurring in a healthy infant in which the toes are extended upward when the sole of the foot is gently stimulated. In adults, this response is an indication of neurological disorder and called **Babinski's sign**. [Joseph F. Babinski (1857–1932), French neurologist]

baby talk the type of speech used by adults and older children when talking to infants or very young children.

back-translation *n.* see TRANSLATION AND BACK-TRANSLATION.

backward conditioning a procedure in which an UNCONDITIONED STIMULUS is consistently presented before a NEUTRAL STIMULUS. Generally, this arrangement is not thought to produce a change in the effect of a neutral stimulus. Occasionally, however, the neutral stimulus may take on inhibitory functions, presumably because it consistently predicts the absence of the unconditioned stimulus. Also called **backward pairing**. Compare FORWARD CONDITIONING.

backward elimination a technique used in creating MULTIPLE REGRESSION models in which the least important independent (predictor) variables are systematically removed from the REGRESSION EQUATION until a preset criterion is reached. Also called **backward stepwise regression**.

balanced design an experimental design in which the number of observations or measurements obtained in each experimental condition is equal.

balanced scale a scale in which, for each alternative, there is another alternative that means the opposite. An example is a rating scale with the four alternatives very poor, poor, good, and very good.

balance theory a theory specifying that people prefer elements within a cognitive system to be internally consistent with one another (i.e., balanced). Balanced systems are assumed to be more stable and psychologically pleasant than imbalanced ones. These systems are sometimes referred to as **P-O-X triads**, in which P = person (i.e., self), O = other person, and X = some stimulus or event.

Bálint's syndrome a spatial and attentional disorder resulting from lesions in the parieto-occipital region of the brain. It consists of inability to visually guide the hand to an object, inability to change visual gaze, and inability to recognize multiple stimuli in a scene and understand their nature as a whole. [first described in 1909 by Rudolf Bálint (1874–1929), Hungarian physician]

ballismus *n.* involuntary throwing or flinging movements of the limbs, caused by severe muscle contractions due to neurological damage. It may involve both sides of the body or, in the case of hemiballismus, one side only. Also called **ballism**.

ballistic *adj.* describing a movement (or part of a movement) in which the motion, once initiated, is not altered by feedback-based corrections. Ballistic is sometimes also used, incorrectly, to describe any rapid movement.

bandwagon effect the tendency for people in social and sometimes political situations to align themselves with the majority opinion and do or believe things because many other people do or believe the same.

bandwidth *n.* **1.** a range of frequencies, usually expressed in hertz (cycles per second). In INFORMATION THEORY, it is a measure of the amount of information that a communication channel can transmit per unit of time. **2.** the range of information available from measuring instruments. Greater bandwidth is generally associated with lower accuracy (fidelity).

barbiturate *n.* any of a family of drugs derived from barbituric acid that depress activity of the central nervous system. They typically induce profound tolerance and withdrawal symptoms and depress respiration. Use of barbiturates became common in the 1930s, but they were rapidly supplanted in the 1970s by BENZODIAZEPINES, which lack the lethality associated with overdose of the barbiturates. The prototype of the group, **barbital**, was introduced into medical practice in 1903.

bar graph a way of graphically displaying discrete (nonnumerical) data using bars of varying height with spaces between them. For example, to show the political party affiliation of Americans, bars would represent parties along the *x*-axis,

while the heights of the bars would represent numbers of people. Compare HISTOGRAM. Also called **bar chart**.

Barnum effect the tendency of individuals to believe that vague predictions or general personality descriptions, such as those offered by astrology, have specific applications to themselves.

basal age the highest chronological age at which all items on a given standardized test are consistently answered correctly. This concept is less widely used than in the past because it assumes the use of MENTAL AGES, which are declining in popularity.

basal forebrain a region of the ventral FOREBRAIN near the corpus callosum containing CHOLINERGIC neurons that project widely to the cerebral cortex and HIPPOCAMPUS and are thought to be important in aspects of memory, learning, and attention. A particular collection of neurons, the **basal nucleus of Meynert** (or **basal magnocellular nucleus**), is implicated in Alzheimer's disease.

basal ganglia a group of nuclei (neuron cell bodies) deep within the cerebral hemispheres of the brain that includes the CAUDATE NUCLEUS, PUTAMEN, GLOBUS PALLIDUS, SUBSTANTIA NIGRA, and SUBTHALAMIC NUCLEUS. The putamen and globus pallidus are together known as the **lenticular** (or **lentiform**) **nucleus**, the lenticular nucleus and caudate nucleus are together known as the **corpus striatum**, and the caudate nucleus and putamen are together called the **striatum**. The basal ganglia are involved in the generation of goal-directed voluntary movement. Also called **basal nuclei**.

basal metabolism the minimum energy expenditure required to maintain the vital functions of the body while awake but at rest and not expending energy for thermoregulation. **Basal metabolic rate** is measured in kilojoules (or calories) expended per kilogram of body weight or per square meter of body surface per hour.

base rate the naturally occurring frequency of a phenomenon in a population. This rate is often contrasted with the rate of the phenomenon under the influence of some changed condition in order to determine the degree to which the change influences the phenomenon.

base-rate fallacy a decision-making error in which information about rate of occurrence of some trait in a population (the base-rate information) is ignored or not given appropriate weight. For example, people might categorize a man as an engineer, rather than a lawyer, if they heard that he enjoyed physics at school, even if they knew that he was drawn from a population consisting of 90% lawyers and 10% engineers. See REPRESENTATIVENESS HEURISTIC.

basic anxiety in EGO PSYCHOLOGY, a feeling of being helpless, abandoned, and endangered in a hostile world. According to German-born U.S. psychoanalyst Karen D. Horney (1885–1952), it arises from the infant's helplessness and dependence on his or her parents or from parental indifference. Defenses against basic anxiety and hostility may produce NEUROTIC NEEDS.

basic-level category a category formed at the level that people find most natural and appropriate in their normal, everyday experience of the things so categorized. A basic-level category (e.g., "bird," "table") will be broader than the more specific subordinate categories into which it can be divided (e.g., "hawk," "dining table") but less ab-

stract than the superordinate category into which it can be subsumed (e.g., "animals," "furniture"). Also called **basic category**; **natural category**.

basic need see PHYSIOLOGICAL NEED.

basic research research conducted in order to obtain knowledge or to develop or advance a theory. Compare APPLIED RESEARCH.

basic trust versus mistrust the first of ERIKSON'S EIGHT STAGES OF DEVELOPMENT, between birth and 18 months of age. During this stage, the infant either comes to view other people and himself or herself as trustworthy or comes to develop a fundamental distrust of his or her environment. The growth of basic trust, considered essential for the later development of self-esteem and positive interpersonal relationships, is attributed to a primary caregiver who is responsively attuned to the baby's individual needs while conveying the quality of trustworthiness, while the growth of basic distrust is attributed to neglect, lack of love, or inconsistent treatment.

basilar membrane a fibrous membrane within the COCHLEA that supports the ORGAN OF CORTI. In response to sound the basilar membrane vibrates; this leads to stimulation of the HAIR CELLS—the auditory receptors within the organ of Corti.

battered-child syndrome the effects on a child of intentional and repeated physical abuse by parents or other caregivers. In addition to sustaining physical injuries, the child is at increased risk of experiencing longer-term problems, such as depression, POSTTRAUMATIC STRESS DISORDER, substance abuse, decreased self-esteem, and sexual and other behavioral difficulties. See also CHILD ABUSE.

battered-woman syndrome the psychological effects of being physically abused by a spouse or domestic partner. The syndrome includes LEARNED HELPLESSNESS in relation to the abusive spouse, as well as symptoms of posttraumatic stress.

Bayes' theorem a formula derived from probability theory that relates two conditional probabilities: the probability of event A, given that event B has occurred, $p(A|B)$, and the probability of event B, given that event A has occurred, $p(B|A)$. It is expressed as $p(A|B)p(B) = p(B|A)p(A)$ [Thomas **Bayes** (1702–1761), British mathematician and theologian]

Bayley Scales of Infant and Toddler Development scales for assessing the developmental status of infants and young children aged 1 month to 42 months. Test stimuli, such as form boards, blocks, shapes, household objects (e.g., utensils), and other common items, are used to engage the child in specific tasks of increasing difficulty and elicit particular responses. The Bayley scales were originally published in 1969 and subsequently revised in 1993; the most recent version is the **Bayley–III**, published in 2005. [developed by U.S. psychologist Nancy **Bayley** (1899–1994)]

B cell see LYMPHOCYTE.

Bedlam *n.* the popular name for the Hospital of Saint Mary of Bethlehem in London, founded as a monastery in 1247 and converted into a mental institution in 1547. Many of the patients were in a state of frenzy, and as they were shackled, starved, beaten, and exhibited to the public for a penny a look, general turmoil prevailed. The word "bedlam" thus became synonymous with wild confusion or frenzy.

before–after design an experimental design in which one or more groups of participants are measured both prior to and following administration of the treatment or manipulation.

behavior *n.* **1.** an organism's activities in response to external or internal stimuli, including objectively observable activities, introspectively observable activities, and unconscious processes. **2.** more restrictively, any action or function that can be objectively observed or measured in response to controlled stimuli. Historically, objective behavior was contrasted by behaviorists with mental activities, which were considered subjective and thus unsuitable for scientific study. See BEHAVIORISM. —**behavioral** *adj.*

behavioral approach system a brain system theorized to underlie incentive motivation by activating approach behaviors in response to stimuli related to positive reinforcement. It has been suggested that the system is associated as well with the generation of positive affective responses, and that a strong or chronically active behavioral approach system tends to result in extraversion. Also called **behavioral activation system**. Compare BEHAVIORAL INHIBITION SYSTEM.

behavioral assessment the systematic study and evaluation of an individual's behavior using a wide variety of techniques, including direct observation, interviews, and self-monitoring. When used to identify patterns indicative of disorder, the procedure is called **behavioral diagnosis** and is essential in deciding upon the use of specific behavioral or cognitive-behavioral interventions.

behavioral contract an agreement between therapist and client in which the client agrees to carry out certain behaviors, usually between sessions but sometimes during the session as well.

behavioral couples therapy a COUPLES THERAPY that focuses on interrupting negative interaction patterns through instruction, modeling, rehearsal, feedback, positive behavior exchange, and structured problem solving. When practiced with legally married partners, it is called **behavioral marital therapy**. See also INTEGRATIVE BEHAVIORAL COUPLES THERAPY.

behavioral endocrinology the study of the relationships between behavior and the functioning of the endocrine glands and neuroendocrine cells. For example, gonadal secretion of sex hormones affects sexual behavior, and secretion of corticosteroids by the adrenal glands affects physiological and behavioral responses to stress.

behavioral genetics the study of familial or hereditary behavior patterns and of the genetic mechanisms of behavior traits. Also called **behavior genetics**.

behavioral inhibition a temperamental predisposition characterized by restraint in engaging with the world combined with a tendency to scrutinize the environment for potential threats and to avoid or withdraw from unfamiliar situations or people.

behavioral inhibition system a brain system theorized to underlie behavioral inhibition by activating avoidance behaviors in response to perceived threats. It has been suggested that the system is associated as well with the generation of negative affective responses, and that a strong or chronically active system tends to result in introversion. Compare BEHAVIORAL APPROACH SYSTEM.

behavioral medicine a multidisciplinary field that applies behavioral theories and methods to the prevention and treatment of medical and psychological disorders. Areas of application include chronic illness, lifestyle issues (e.g., tobacco, drugs, alcohol, obesity), SOMATOFORM DISORDERS, and the like.

behavioral model a conceptualization of psychological disorders in terms of overt behavior patterns produced by learning and the influence of REINFORCEMENT CONTINGENCIES. Treatment techniques, including SYSTEMATIC DESENSITIZATION and MODELING, focus on modifying ineffective or maladaptive patterns.

behavioral neuroscience a branch of NEUROSCIENCE and BIOLOGICAL PSYCHOLOGY that seeks to understand and characterize the specific neural circuitry and mechanisms underlying behavioral propensities or capacities.

behavioral psychotherapy see BEHAVIOR THERAPY.

behavioral science any of a number of disciplines, including psychology, psychiatry, sociology, and anthropology, that study the behavior of humans and nonhuman animals from a scientific and research perspective.

behavioral study of obedience the experimental analysis, especially as carried out by U.S. social psychologist Stanley Milgram (1933–1984) in the 1960s, of individuals' willingness to obey the orders of an authority. In Milgram's experiment, each participant played the role of a teacher who was instructed to deliver painful electric shocks to another "participant" for each failure to answer a question correctly. The latter were in fact CONFEDERATES who did not actually receive shocks for their many deliberate errors. Milgram found that a substantial number of participants (65%) were completely obedient, delivering what they believed were shocks of increasing intensity despite the protestations and apparent suffering of the victim. See also AGENTIC STATE.

behavior analysis the decomposition of behavior into its component parts or processes. This approach to psychology emphasizes interactions between behavior and the environment.

behavior disorder any persistent and repetitive pattern of behavior that violates societal norms or rules or that seriously impairs a person's functioning. The term is used in a very general sense to cover a wide range of disorders or other syndromes.

behaviorism *n.* an approach to psychology, formulated in 1913 by U.S. psychologist John B. Watson (1878–1958), based on the study of objective, observable facts rather than subjective, qualitative processes, such as feelings, motives, and consciousness. To make psychology a naturalistic science, Watson proposed to limit it to quantitative events, such as stimulus–response relationships, effects of conditioning, physiological processes, and a study of human and animal behavior, all of which can best be investigated through laboratory experiments that yield objective measures under controlled conditions. Historically, behaviorists held that mind was not a proper topic for scientific study since mental events are subjective and not independently verifiable. See METHODOLOGICAL BEHAVIORISM; NEOBEHAVIORISM; RADICAL BEHAVIORISM.

behavior modification the use of OPERANT CONDITIONING, BIOFEEDBACK, MODELING, AVERSIVE CONDITIONING, RECIPROCAL INHIBI-

TION, or other learning techniques as a means of changing human behavior. For example, behavioral modification is used in clinical contexts to improve adaptation and alleviate symptoms and in industrial and organizational contexts to encourage employees to adopt safe work practices. The term is often used synonymously with BEHAVIOR THERAPY.

behavior observation a recording or evaluation (or both) of the ongoing behavior of one or more research participants by one or more observers. Observations may be made—using charts, checklists, rating scales, etc.—either directly as the behavior occurs or from such media as film, videotape, or audiotape.

behavior shaping see SHAPING.

behavior theory the assumption that behavior, including its acquisition, development, and maintenance, can be adequately explained by principles of learning. Behavior theory attempts to describe environmental influences on behavior, often using controlled studies of animals.

behavior therapy a form of psychotherapy that applies the principles of learning, OPERANT CONDITIONING, and PAVLOVIAN CONDITIONING to eliminate symptoms and modify ineffective or maladaptive patterns of behavior. The focus of this therapy is upon the behavior itself and the CONTINGENCIES and environmental factors that reinforce it, rather than exploration of the underlying psychological causes of the behavior. A wide variety of techniques are used in behavior therapy, such as BIOFEEDBACK, MODELING, and SYSTEMATIC DESENSITIZATION. Also called **behavioral psychotherapy**.

belief *n.* **1.** acceptance of the truth, reality, or validity of something (e.g., a phenomenon, a person's veracity), particularly in the absence of substantiation. **2.** an association of some characteristic or attribute, usually evaluative in nature, with an attitude object (e.g., this car is reliable).

belief bias the tendency to be influenced by one's knowledge about the world in evaluating conclusions and to accept them as true because they are believable rather than because they are logically valid. Belief bias is most often assessed with syllogistic reasoning tasks in which the believability of the conclusion conflicts with logical validity. For example, given the syllogisms *All flowers have petals; roses have petals; therefore, roses are flowers* and *All fish can swim; tuna are fish; therefore, tuna can swim* an individual is more likely to rely upon prior knowledge and personal beliefs and to accept both conclusions as valid when in fact only the second is actually logically valid.

belief in a just world the idea that people get what they deserve, and that the world is orderly and fair. In other words, bad things happen to bad people, and good things happen to good people. There is a large body of evidence that belief in a just world affects people's behaviors and attitudes, often through secondary victimization of innocent victims or the promotion of helping behavior.

belief perseverance the tendency to maintain a belief even after the information that originally gave rise to it has been refuted or otherwise shown to be inaccurate.

belief system a set of two or more beliefs, attitudes, or both that are associated with one another in memory.

bell curve the characteristic curve obtained by plotting a graph of a NORMAL DISTRIBUTION. With a large rounded peak tapering off on either side, it resembles a cross-sectional representation of a bell. Also called **bell-shaped curve**.

Bell–Magendie law the principle that the VENTRAL ROOTS of the spinal cord are motor in function and DORSAL ROOTS are sensory. [Charles **Bell** (1774–1842), British surgeon and anatomist; François **Magendie** (1783–1855), French physiologist]

below-average effect the tendency of a person to underestimate his or her intellectual and social abilities relative to others. The below-average effect is common when the skill in question is relatively hard (e.g., sculpting human figures from clay), whereas the opposite ABOVE-AVERAGE EFFECT generally occurs when the skill in question is relatively easy (e.g., operating a computer mouse).

Bender Visual–Motor Gestalt Test a visuoconstructive test used to assess visual–motor functioning and perceptual ability as well as to diagnose neurological impairment. The participant copies line drawings of geometric figures onto blank pieces of paper, and these reproductions are scored on a 5-point scale, ranging from 0 (no resemblance) to 4 (nearly perfect). Originally developed in 1938, the test (often shortened to **Bender–Gestalt**) is now in its second edition (published in 2003). [Lauretta **Bender** (1897–1987), U.S. psychiatrist]

benign *adj.* **1.** in mental health, denoting a disorder or illness that is not serious and has a favorable prognosis. **2.** denoting a condition that is relatively mild, transient, or not associated with serious pathology. See also NEOPLASM. Compare MALIGNANT.

benzodiazepine *n.* any of a family of drugs that depress central nervous system activity and also produce sedation and relaxation of skeletal muscles. Benzodiazepines are commonly used in the treatment of generalized anxiety and insomnia and are useful in the management of acute withdrawal from alcohol and in seizure disorders. Clinically introduced in the 1960s, they rapidly supplanted the barbiturates, largely due to their significantly lower toxicity in overdose. Prolonged use can lead to tolerance and psychological and physical dependence.

bereavement *n.* a feeling of loss, especially over the death of a friend or loved one. The bereaved person may experience emotional pain and distress (see GRIEF) and may or may not express this distress to others (see MOURNING; DISENFRANCHISED GRIEF). —**bereaved** *adj.*

Bernoulli trial see BINOMIAL DISTRIBUTION. [Jacques **Bernoulli** (1654–1705), Swiss mathematician and scientist]

beta (symbol: β) *n.* the probability of a TYPE II ERROR.

beta movement see APPARENT MOVEMENT.

beta wave in electroencephalography, the type of BRAIN WAVE (frequency 13–30 Hz) associated with alert wakefulness and intense mental activity. Also called **beta rhythm**.

beta weight (symbol: β) in REGRESSION ANALYSIS, the multiplicative constant that reflects a variable's contribution to the prediction of a criterion, given the other variables in the prediction equation (e.g., b in $y = a + bx$). Also called **beta coefficient**.

between-groups variance the variation in experimental scores that is attributable only to membership in different groups and exposure to different experimental conditions. It is reflected in the ANALYSIS OF VARIANCE by the degree to which the several group means differ from one another and is compared with WITHIN-GROUP VARIANCE to obtain an F RATIO.

between-subjects design any of a large number of experimental designs in which each participant experiences only one experimental condition (treatment). Also called **between-groups design**; **independent-groups design**. Compare WITHIN-SUBJECTS DESIGN.

bias *n.* **1.** partiality: an inclination or predisposition for or against something. See also PREJUDICE. **2.** a tendency or preference, such as a RESPONSE BIAS. **3.** in research, systematic and directional error arising during SAMPLING, data collection, data analysis, or data interpretation. **4.** in statistics, the difference between the expected value of a statistic and the actual value that is obtained. —**biased** *adj.*

Big Five personality model a model of the primary dimensions of individual differences in personality. The dimensions are usually labeled EXTRAVERSION, NEUROTICISM, agreeableness (denoting the tendency to act in a cooperative, unselfish manner), conscientiousness (denoting the tendency to be responsible and hardworking), and openness to experience (denoting a willingness to participate in new aesthetic, cultural, or intellectual experiences), though the labels vary somewhat among researchers. See also FIVE-FACTOR PERSONALITY MODEL.

bigram *n.* any two-letter combination. In PSYCHOLINGUISTICS research, the term typically refers to a within-word consecutive character sequence (e.g., "paper" contains the bigrams pa, ap, pe, and er), whereas in learning and memory research it generally refers to a freestanding nonword (e.g., TL, KE).

bilateral *adj.* denoting or relating to both sides of the body or an organ. For example, **bilateral symmetry** is the symmetrical arrangement of an organism's body such that the right and left halves are approximately mirror images of one another; **bilateral transfer** is the TRANSFER OF TRAINING or patterns of performance for a skill from one side of the body, where the skill (e.g., handwriting) was originally learned and primarily used, to the other side of the body. —**bilaterally** *adv.*

bilingual education instruction in two languages, typically in one's native language and in the dominant language of the country in which one is educated. In the 1970s, the United States adopted a bilingual education program to help immigrant children learn English. By providing the ability to perform equivalent academic work in two languages, this kind of education enables children to do regular schoolwork with their English-speaking classmates, thus receiving an equal educational opportunity.

bilingualism *n.* the regular use of two or more languages by a person or within a group of people. —**bilingual** *adj.*

bimodal distribution a set of scores that has two modes (represented by two peaks in their graphical distribution), reflecting a tendency for scores to cluster around two separate values. See also UNIMODAL DISTRIBUTION.

binaural cue any difference in the sound arriving at the two ears from a given sound source (interaural difference) that acts as a cue to permit AUDITORY LOCALIZATION. The common cues are interaural level differences, interaural time differences, and interaural phase differences.

binding problem the difficulty of perceiving and representing different features, or conjunctions of properties, as one object or event. This problem arises because different attributes of a stimulus (e.g., hue, form, spatial location, motion) are analyzed by different areas of the cerebral cortex; it is relevant in all areas of knowledge representation, including such complex cognitive representations as THEORY OF MIND.

binge-eating disorder a disorder marked by recurring episodes of binge eating (i.e., discrete periods of uncontrolled consumption of abnormally large quantities of food) and distress associated with this behavior. There is an absence of inappropriate compensatory behaviors (e.g., vomiting, laxative misuse, excessive exercise, fasting).

binocular cue any cue to the perception of distance or depth that requires the use of both eyes, such as BINOCULAR DISPARITY and CONVERGENCE. Compare MONOCULAR CUE.

binocular disparity the slight difference between the right and left retinal images. When both eyes focus on an object, the different position of the eyes produces a disparity of visual angle, and a slightly different image is received by each retina. The two images are automatically compared and fused, providing an important cue to depth perception. Also called **retinal disparity**.

binocular rivalry the failure of the eyes to fuse stimuli. For example, if horizontal bars are viewed through the left eye and vertical bars through the right eye, the perception is a patchy and fluctuating alternation of the two patterns, rather than a superimposition of the patterns to form a stable checker-board. Also called **retinal rivalry**.

binomial distribution the distribution of the outcomes in a sequence of **Bernoulli trials**, experiments of chance that are independent of one another and each have one of two possible outcomes (0 or 1; success or failure), with a fixed probability of each outcome on each trial.

bioecological model a paradigm that treats human development as a process that continues both through the life span and across successive generations, thus according importance to historical continuity and change as forces indirectly affecting human development through their impact on proximal processes.

biofeedback *n.* the use of an external monitoring device to provide an individual with information regarding his or her physiological state. When used to help a person obtain voluntary control over autonomic body functions, such as heart rate or blood pressure, the technique is called **biofeedback training**. It may be applied therapeutically to treat various conditions, including chronic pain and hypertension.

biogenic *adj.* **1.** produced by living organisms or biological processes. **2.** necessary for the maintenance of life.

biogenic amine any of a group of amines (chemical compounds that contain one or more amino groups [–NH2]) that affect bodily processes and nervous system functioning. Biogenic amines are divided into subgroups (e.g., CATECHOLAMINES, INDOLEAMINES) and include the neurotransmitters dopamine, epinephrine, histamine, norepinephrine, and serotonin.

biological clock the mechanism within an organism that controls the periodicity of BIOLOGICAL RHYTHMS, even in the absence of any external cues. A biological clock in mammals is located in the SUPRACHIASMATIC NUCLEUS of the hypothalamus.

biological determinism the concept that psychological and behavioral characteristics are entirely the result of constitutional and biological factors. Environmental conditions serve only as occasions for the manifestation of such characteristics. Compare ENVIRONMENTAL DETERMINISM.

biological marker a variation in the physiological processes of an organism that accompanies a disorder, irrespective of whether it directly causes the disorder. Also called **biomarker.**

biological perspective an approach to abnormal psychology that emphasizes physiologically based causative factors, such as the SENILE PLAQUES in Alzheimer's disease, and consequently tends to focus primarily upon BIOLOGICAL THERAPIES.

biological psychology the science that deals with the area of overlap between psychology and biology and with the reciprocal relations between biological and psychological processes. It includes such fields as BEHAVIORAL NEUROSCIENCE, COGNITIVE NEUROSCIENCE, BEHAVIORAL ENDOCRINOLOGY, and PSYCHONEUROIMMUNOLOGY. Also called **biopsychology**.

biological rhythm any periodic variation in a living organism's physiological or psychological function, such as energy level, sexual desire, or menstruation. Such rhythms are usually linked to cyclical changes in environmental cues, such as daylength or passing of the seasons, and tend to be daily (**circadian rhythm**) or annual (**circannual rhythm**). See also INFRADIAN RHYTHM; ULTRADIAN RHYTHM.

biological therapy any form of treatment for mental disorders that attempts to alter physiological functioning, including various drug therapies, ELECTROCONVULSIVE THERAPY, and PSYCHOSURGERY. Also called **biomedical therapy**.

biopsychology *n.* see BIOLOGICAL PSYCHOLOGY.

biopsychosocial *adj.* denoting a systematic integration of biological, psychological, and social approaches to the study of mental health and specific mental disorders.

biorhythm *n.* **1.** a synonym of BIOLOGICAL RHYTHM. **2.** according to pseudoscientific belief, any one of three basic cycles (physical, emotional, and intellectual) with which every individual is programmed at birth. It is maintained that these rhythms continue unaltered until death and that good and bad days for various activities can be calculated accordingly.

biosocial *adj.* pertaining to the interplay or mingling of biological and social factors, as with human behavior that is influenced simultaneously by complex neurophysiological processes and social interactions.

bipolar *adj.* denoting something with two opposites or extremities, such as a BIPOLAR NEURON or the BIPOLAR DISORDERS. —**bipolarity** *n.*

bipolar disorder any of a group of MOOD DISORDERS in which symptoms of mania and depression alternate. A distinction is made between **bipolar I disorder**, involving one or more MANIC EPISODES and one or more MAJOR DEPRESSIVE EPISODES, and **bipolar II disorder**, characterized by one or more major depressive episodes and at least one HYPOMANIC EPISODE. In certain diagnostic classifications CYCLO-THYMIC DISORDER is also categorized as a bipolar disorder. The former official name for bipolar disorders, manic-depressive illness, is still in frequent use.

bipolar neuron a neuron with only two processes—an AXON and a DENDRITE—that extend from opposite sides of the CELL BODY. Also called **bipolar cell**. Compare MULTIPOLAR NEURON; UNIPOLAR NEURON.

birth order the ordinal position of a child in the family (firstborn, second-born, youngest, etc.). There has been much psychological research into how birth order affects personal adjustment and family status, but the notion that it has strong and consistent effects on psychological outcomes is not supported. Current family-structure research sees birth order not so much as a causal factor but rather as an indirect variable that follows more process-oriented variables (e.g., parental discipline, sibling interaction, and genetic and hormonal makeup) in importance.

birth trauma the psychological shock of being born, due to the sudden change from the security of the womb to being bombarded with stimuli from the external world. Though first proposed by Austrian psychoanalyst Otto Rank (1884–1939), the concept of the birth trauma incorporates many of the ideas of Austrian psychiatrist Sigmund Freud (1856–1939), who viewed birth as the child's first anxiety experience and the prototype of separation anxiety.

bisection *n.* the act of splitting something into two equal parts. In psychophysics it refers to a scaling method in which a participant adjusts a stimulus until it is perceived as halfway between two other stimuli with respect to a particular dimension.

biserial correlation a measure of the association between a CONTINU-

OUS VARIABLE and a DICHOTOMOUS VARIABLE.

bisexuality *n.* **1.** sexual attraction to or sexual behavior with both men and women. **2.** the existence of both male and female genitals in the same organism. Such anatomical (structural) bisexuality is more properly termed HERMAPHRODITISM. —**bisexual** *adj., n.*

bit *n.* in information theory, the quantity of information that decreases uncertainty or the germane alternatives of a problem by one half. For example, if a dollar bill has been placed in one of 16 identical books standing side by side on a shelf, and one were to ask if the book is to the right (or to the left) of center, the answer would provide one bit of information. [bi(nary) + (digi)t]

bivariate *adj.* characterized by two variables or attributes. See also MULTIVARIATE; UNIVARIATE.

black box a model for a device, system, or other complex entity—humans and nonhuman animals included—whose internal properties and processes must be hypothesized on the basis of observed empirical relationships between external factors (input) and the resulting effects (output).

blackout *n.* **1.** total but temporary loss of consciousness. **2.** amnesia produced by alcoholic intoxication.

black sheep effect the tendency of an individual to evaluate a poorly performing or deviant INGROUP member less positively than an equally poorly performing or deviant OUTGROUP member. Although an apparent contradiction of INGROUP BIAS, the black sheep effect is explained by SOCIAL IDENTITY THEORY as an individual protection strategy: people favor their ingroup because of the importance of group membership for SELF-IDENTITY.

blaming the victim a social psychological phenomenon in which individuals or groups attempt to cope with the bad things that have happened to others by holding the victim responsible for the trauma or tragedy.

blastocyst *n.* the mammalian EMBRYO at a very early stage of development. It consists of a tiny hollow sphere containing an inner cell mass, enclosed in a thin layer of cells that help implant the blastocyst in the uterine lining.

blended family see STEPFAMILY.

blind *adj.* **1.** denoting a lack of sight. See BLINDNESS. **2.** denoting a lack of awareness. In research, a blind procedure may be employed deliberately to enhance experimental control: A **single blind** is a procedure in which participants are unaware of the experimental conditions under which they are operating; a **double blind** is a procedure in which both the participants and the experimenters interacting with them are unaware of the particular experimental conditions; and a **triple blind** is a procedure in which the participants, experimenters, and data analysts are all unaware of the particular experimental conditions.

blindness *n.* profound, near-total, or total impairment of the ability to perceive visual stimuli, defined in the United States as ACUITY of 20/200 or worse in the better eye with best correction or a VISUAL FIELD of 20° or less in the widest meridian of the better eye. Major causes include CATARACT, GLAUCOMA, age-related MACULAR DEGENERATION, and diabetes. —**blind** *adj.*

blindsight *n.* the capacity of some individuals with blindness in parts or all of the visual field to detect and localize visual stimuli presented within the blind field region. Discrimination of movement, flicker, wavelength, and orientation may also be present. However, these visual capacities are not accompanied by awareness: They have been demonstrated only in experimental conditions, when participants are forced to guess.

blind spot the area of the monocular visual field in which stimulation cannot be perceived because the image falls on the site of the OPTIC DISK in the eye.

blob *n.* see CYTOCHROME OXIDASE BLOB.

block design an experimental design that divides participants into relatively homogeneous subsets or blocks. The greater the homogeneity of each of the blocks, the greater the statistical power of the analysis. See also RANDOMIZED BLOCK DESIGN.

blocking *n.* **1.** a process in which one's flow of thought or speech is suddenly interrupted. The individual is suddenly aware of not being able to perform a particular mental act, such as finding the words to express something he or she wishes to say. Also called **thought deprivation; thought obstruction. 2.** a phenomenon of STIMULUS CONTROL in which previous learning restricts or prevents conditioning of a response to a new stimulus. For example, a light paired with an unconditioned stimulus for several trials results in some conditioning for the light. Adding a tone at this point would result in the tone being less effective as an elicitor than it would if it had been present from the beginning. Also called **blocking effect; Kamin effect**.

blood–brain barrier a semipermeable barrier formed by cells lining the blood capillaries that supply the brain and that helps maintain a constant environment in which the brain can function. It prevents large molecules, including many drugs, passing from the blood to the fluid surrounding brain cells and to the cerebrospinal fluid, and thus protects the brain from potentially harmful substances. Ions and small molecules, such as water, oxygen, carbon dioxide, and alcohol, can cross relatively freely.

blood phobia a persistent and irrational fear of blood, specifically of seeing blood. An individual confronting blood experiences a subjective feeling of disgust and fears the consequences of the situation, such as fainting. In certain diagnostic classifications, such as DSM–IV–TR, the broader term **blood-injection-injury phobia** is used instead.

blood pressure the pressure exerted by the blood against the walls of the blood vessels, especially the arteries. It varies with the strength of the heartbeat, the elasticity of the artery walls and resistance of the arterioles, and the person's health, age, and state of activity. See also HYPERTENSION.

BMI abbreviation for BODY MASS INDEX.

bodily-kinesthetic intelligence in the MULTIPLE-INTELLIGENCES THEORY, the skills involved in forming and coordinating bodily movements, such as dancing, playing a violin, or playing basketball.

body *n.* **1.** the entire physical structure of an organism, such as the human body. See also MIND–BODY PROBLEM. **2.** the main part of a structure or organ, such as the body of the penis. **3.** a discrete anatomical or cytological structure, such as the MAMMILLARY BODY.

body dysmorphic disorder a SOMATOFORM DISORDER characterized by excessive preoccupation with an imagined defect in physical appearance or markedly excessive concern with a slight physical anomaly.

body image the mental picture one forms of one's body as a whole, including both its physical and functional characteristics (**body percept**) and one's attitudes toward these characteristics (**body concept**).

body language the expression of feelings and thoughts, which may or may not be verbalized, through posture, gesture, facial expression, or other movements. Although body language is often called NONVERBAL COMMUNICATION, such movements may be unintentional, and many investigators therefore believe the term "communication" is often inappropriate in this context.

body mass index (**BMI**) a widely used measure of adiposity or obesity based on the following formula: weight (kg) divided by height squared (m^2).

bonding *n.* the process in which ATTACHMENTS or other close relationships are formed between individuals, especially between mother and infant. An early, positive relationship between a mother and a newborn child is considered to be essential in establishing unconditional love on the part of the parent, as well as security and trust on the part of the child. In subsequent development, bonding establishes friendship and trust.

Bonferroni correction a procedure for adjusting the *p*-value (see SIGNIFICANCE LEVEL) of individual related T TESTS. It involves dividing the usual significance level value by the number of comparisons being made, so as to avoid the increased risk of TYPE I ERROR that comes with multiple comparisons. Also called **Bonferroni adjustment**; **Bonferroni test**.

boomerang effect a situation in which a persuasive message produces attitude change in the direction opposite to that intended. Boomerang effects occur when recipients generate counterarguments substantially stronger than the arguments contained in the original message.

bootstrapping *n.* any process or operation in which a system uses its initial resources to develop more powerful and complex processing routines, which are then used in the same fashion, and so on cumulatively. In LANGUAGE ACQUISITION, the term is used of children's ability to learn complex linguistic rules, which can be endlessly reapplied, from extremely limited data. In statistics, it denotes a method for estimating the variability of a parameter associated with a batch of data, such as the standard error. A number of samples of equal size are obtained from the original data by sampling with replacement, the parameter is calculated for each, and the individual parameters are combined to provide an estimate of the overall parameter for the entire sample. —**bootstrap** *vb.*

borderline 1. *adj.* pertaining to any phenomenon difficult to categorize because it straddles two distinct classes, showing characteristics of both. Thus, **borderline intelligence** is supposed to show characteristics of both the average and subaverage categories. **2.** *n.* an inappropriate designation for someone with BORDERLINE PERSONALITY DISORDER or its symptoms.

borderline personality disorder a personality disorder characterized by a long-standing pattern of instability in mood, interpersonal relationships, and self-image that is severe enough to cause extreme distress or interfere with social and occupational functioning. Symptoms include impulsive behavior in such areas as gambling, sex, spending, overeating, and substance use; intense but unstable relationships; uncontrollable temper outbursts; self-injurious behavior, such as fights, suicidal gestures, or self-mutilation; and chronic feelings of emptiness.

bottom-up processing information processing that proceeds from the data in the stimulus input to higher level processes, such as recognition, interpretation, and categorization. Typically, perceptual or cognitive mechanisms use bottom-up processing when information is unfamiliar or highly complex. Compare TOP-DOWN PROCESSING. See also SHALLOW PROCESSING.

box-and-whisker plot a graphical display of a batch of data involving rectangular boxes with lines or "whiskers" extending outwards from them. The ends of the box indicate the upper and lower HINGES, a dividing line within the box indicates the MEDIAN, and the whiskers extending from both ends indicate the smallest and largest scores. Also called **box plot**.

bradycardia *n.* see ARRHYTHMIA.

bradykinesia *n.* abnormal slowness in the execution of voluntary movements. Also called **bradykinesis**. Compare HYPOKINESIS. —**bradykinetic** *adj.*

brain *n.* the enlarged, anterior part of the CENTRAL NERVOUS SYSTEM within the skull. The brain develops by differentiation of the embryonic NEURAL TUBE along an anterior-posterior axis to form three main regions—the FOREBRAIN, MIDBRAIN, and HINDBRAIN—that can be further subdivided on the basis of anatomical and functional criteria. The cortical tissue is concentrated in the forebrain, and the midbrain and hindbrain structures are often considered together as the BRAINSTEM.

brain damage injury to the brain,

manifested by impairment of cognitive, motor, or sensory skills mediated by the brain.

brain localization theory any of various theories that different areas of the brain serve different functions. Since the early 19th century, opinion has varied between notions of highly precise localization and a belief that the brain, or large portions of it, functions as a whole. For many investigators, however, the concept of extreme parcellation of functions has given way to concepts of distributed control by collective activity of different regions.

brainstem *n.* the part of the brain that connects the cerebrum with the spinal cord. It includes the MIDBRAIN, PONS, and MEDULLA OBLONGATA and is involved in the autonomic control of visceral activity, such as salivation, respiration, heartbeat, and digestion.

brain stimulation stimulation of specific areas of the brain, for example by ELECTRICAL STIMULATION or TRANSCRANIAL MAGNETIC STIMULATION, as a means of determining their functions and their effects on behavior and as a therapeutic technique.

brainstorming *n.* a problem-solving strategy in which ideas are generated spontaneously and uninhibitedly, usually in a group setting, without any immediate critical judgment about their potential value. —**brainstorm** *vb.*

brainwashing *n.* a broad class of intense and often coercive tactics intended to produce profound changes in attitudes, beliefs, and emotions.

brain waves spontaneous, rhythmic electrical impulses emanating from different areas of the brain. According to their frequencies, brain waves are classified as ALPHA WAVES (8–12 Hz), BETA WAVES (13–30 Hz),

DELTA WAVES (1–3 Hz), GAMMA WAVES (31–80 Hz), or THETA WAVES (4–7 Hz).

breakthrough *n.* a significant, sometimes sudden, forward step in therapy, especially after an unproductive plateau.

Brief Psychiatric Rating Scale a system of evaluating the presence and severity of clinical psychiatric signs on the basis of 24 factors, such as bizarre behavior, hostility, emotional withdrawal, and disorientation. Each factor is rated on a 7-point scale ranging from "not present" to "extremely severe," based on the judgments of trained observers.

brief psychodynamic psychotherapy a collection of time-limited PSYCHODYNAMIC PSYCHOTHERAPY approaches intended to enhance client self-awareness and understanding of the influence of the past on present behavior. One particularly important issue is identified as the central focus for the treatment, thus creating a structure and establishing a goal for the sessions. Rather than allowing the client to associate freely and discuss unconnected issues, as occurs in more traditional psychoanalytic practice, the brief psychodynamic therapist is expected to be fairly active in keeping the session focused on the main issue. The number of sessions varies from one approach to another, but brief psychodynamic therapy is typically considered to be no more than 20–25 sessions. Also called **short-term psychodynamic psychotherapy**.

brief psychotherapy any form of psychotherapy intended to achieve change during a short period (generally 10–20 sessions). Brief psychotherapies rely on active techniques of inquiry, focus, and goal setting and tend to be symptom specific. They may be applied on an individual or group level and are used in the treatment of a variety of behavioral and emotional problems. There are numerous different types, such as brief COGNITIVE BEHAVIOR THERAPY, brief PLAY THERAPY, BRIEF PSYCHODYNAMIC PSYCHOTHERAPY, FOCAL PSYCHOTHERAPY, and INTERPERSONAL PSYCHOTHERAPY. Also called **short-term psychotherapy**.

brief psychotic disorder a disturbance involving the sudden onset of incoherence or loosening of associations, delusions, hallucinations, or grossly disorganized or catatonic behavior. The condition lasts no longer than 1 month, with complete remission of all symptoms and a full return to previous levels of functioning.

brightness *n.* the perceptual correlate of light intensity. The brightness of a stimulus depends on its amplitude (energy), wavelength, the ADAPTATION state of the observer, and the nature of any surrounding or intervening stimuli.

brightness constancy the tendency to perceive a familiar object as having the same brightness under different conditions of illumination. Brightness constancy is one of the PERCEPTUAL CONSTANCIES. Also called **lightness constancy**.

Broca's aphasia one of eight classically identified APHASIAS, characterized by nonfluent conversational speech and slow, halting speech production. Auditory comprehension is relatively good for everyday conversation, but there is considerable difficulty with complex syntax or multistep commands. It is associated with injury to BROCA'S AREA of the brain. [Pierre Paul **Broca** (1824–1880), French physician]

Broca's area a region of the posterior portion of the inferior frontal convolution of the left CEREBRAL HEMISPHERE that is associated with

B

the motor control of speech. [discovered in 1861 by Pierre Paul **Broca**]

Brodmann's area any of more than 200 distinctive areas of cerebral cortex characterized by variation in the occurrence and arrangement of cells (see CYTOARCHITECTURE) from that of neighboring areas. These areas are identified by numbers and in many cases have been associated with specific brain functions, such as area 17 (STRIATE CORTEX, or primary visual cortex), areas 18 and 19 (PRESTRIATE CORTEX), area 4 (motor area, or primary MOTOR CORTEX), and area 6 (PREMOTOR AREA). [Korbinian **Brodmann** (1868–1918), German neurologist]

brood parasitism a practice in which female birds of some species lay their eggs in the nest of another species, leaving the other parents to rear the chicks.

BuChE abbreviation for butyrylcholinesterase. See CHOLINESTERASE.

buffering *n.* the protection against stressful experiences that is afforded by an individual's social support. **—buffer** *vb.*

bulimia *n.* insatiable hunger for food. It may have physiological causes or be primarily a psychological disorder. **—bulimic** *adj.*, *n.*

bulimia nervosa an EATING DISORDER involving recurrent episodes of binge eating (i.e., discrete periods of uncontrolled consumption of abnormally large quantities of food) followed by inappropriate compensatory behaviors (e.g., self-induced vomiting, misuse of laxatives, fasting, excessive exercise).

bullying *n.* persistent threatening and aggressive physical behavior or verbal abuse directed toward other people, especially those who are younger, smaller, weaker, or in some other situation of relative disadvantage.

burnout *n.* physical, emotional, or mental exhaustion, especially in one's job or career, accompanied by decreased motivation, lowered performance, and negative attitudes towards oneself and others. It results from performing at a high level until stress and tension, especially from extreme and prolonged physical or mental exertion or an overburdening workload, take their toll. Burnout is most often observed in professionals who work closely with people (e.g., social workers, teachers, correctional officers) in service-oriented vocations and experience chronic high levels of STRESS.

buspirone *n.* an anxiolytic that produces relief of subjective symptoms of anxiety without the sedation, behavioral disinhibition, and risk of dependence associated with the benzodiazepines. Its use has been limited due to its relative lack of efficacy compared with benzodiazepines. U.S. trade name: **BuSpar**.

butyrophenone *n.* any of a class of ANTIPSYCHOTICS used primarily in the treatment of schizophrenia, mania, and severe agitation. They are associated with TARDIVE DYSKINESIA and numerous EXTRAPYRAMIDAL SYMPTOMS.

butyrylcholinesterase (BuChE) *n.* see CHOLINESTERASE.

bystander effect the tendency for people not to offer help when they know that others are present and capable of helping. Research suggests that a number of cognitive and social processes contribute to the effect, including misinterpreting other people's lack of response as an indication that help is not needed, CONFUSION OF RESPONSIBILITY, and DIFFUSION OF RESPONSIBILITY.

Cc

CA abbreviation for CHRONOLOGICAL AGE.

caffeine *n.* a central nervous system STIMULANT found in coffee, tea, cola, cocoa, chocolate, and certain prescribed and over-the-counter medications. Its effects include rapid breathing, increased pulse rate and blood pressure, and diminished fatigue. Precise effects vary with the amount ingested and the tolerance of the individual. Moderate doses produce an improved flow of thought and clearness of ideas, together with increased respiratory and vasomotor activity; large doses may make concentration or continued attention difficult and cause insomnia, headaches, and confusion in some individuals.

CAI abbreviation for COMPUTER-ASSISTED INSTRUCTION.

calcium-channel blocker any of a class of drugs used in the treatment of hypertension and abnormal heart rhythms (arrhythmias). Calcium-channel blockers inhibit the flow of calcium ions into the smooth-muscle cells of blood vessels and the cells of heart muscle, which need calcium to contract, thus inducing prolonged relaxation of the muscles.

CAM abbreviation for COMPLEMENTARY AND ALTERNATIVE MEDICINE.

cAMP abbreviation for CYCLIC AMP.

canalization *n.* **1.** the containment of variation of certain characters within narrow bounds so that expression of underlying genetic variation is repressed. It is a developmental mechanism that maintains a constant PHENOTYPE over a range of different environments in which the organism might normally occur. **2.** the hypothetical process by which repeated use of a neural pathway leads to greater ease of transmission of impulses and hence its establishment as permanent.

cancer *n.* any one of a group of diseases characterized by the unregulated, abnormal growth of cells to form malignant tumors (see NEOPLASM), which invade neighboring tissues. Causes of cancer are numerous but commonly include viruses, environmental toxins, diet, and inherited genetic variations. Cancers are generally classified as carcinomas if they involve the epithelium (e.g., cancers of the lungs, stomach, or skin) and sarcomas if the affected tissues are connective (e.g., bone, muscle, or fat). **—cancerous** *adj.*

cannabinoid *n.* any of a class of about 60 substances in the CANNABIS plant that includes those responsible for the psychoactive properties of the plant. The most important cannabinoid is TETRAHYDROCANNABINOL.

cannabis *n.* any of three related plant species (*Cannabis sativa*, *C. indica*, or *C. ruderalis*) whose dried flowering or fruiting tops or leaves are widely used as a recreational drug, known as **marijuana**. When smoked, the principal psychoactive agent in these plants, delta-9-TETRAHYDROCANNABINOL (THC), is rapidly absorbed into the blood and almost immediately distributed to the brain, causing the rapid onset of subjective effects that last 2–3 hours. These effects include a sense of euphoria or well-being, perceptual distortions, and impairment of concentration and short-term memory. Tolerance to the effects of THC develops with repeated use, but reports of cannabis DEPENDENCE are rare.

Cannon–Bard theory the theory that emotional states result from the influence of lower brain centers (the hypothalamus and thalamus) on higher ones (the cortex), rather than from sensory feedback to the brain produced by peripheral internal organs and voluntary musculature. According to this theory, the thalamus controls the experience of emotion, and the hypothalamus controls the expression of emotion. [proposed in the 1920s and early 1930s by Walter B. **Cannon** (1871–1945) and Philip **Bard** (1898–1977), U.S. psychologists]

canonical analysis a class of statistical analyses that assess the degree of relationship between two or more sets of measurements. Examples are DISCRIMINANT ANALYSIS and MULTIPLE REGRESSION analysis, among others.

capacity *n.* the maximum ability of an individual to receive or retain information and hence his or her potential for intellectual or creative development or accomplishment.

carcinogen *n.* any substance that initiates the development of CANCER (**carcinogenesis**) when exposed to living tissue. Tobacco smoke, which induces lung cancer, is an example. **—carcinogenic** *adj.*

cardiac muscle the specialized muscle tissue of the heart. It consists of striated fibers that branch and interlock and are in electrical continuity with each other. This ar-

rangement permits ACTION POTENTIALS to spread rapidly from cell to cell, allowing large groups of cells to contract in unison.

cardiovascular *adj.* relating to the heart and blood vessels or to blood circulation. For example, **cardiovascular reactivity** is the degree of change in blood pressure, heart rate, and related responses to a psychological or physical challenge or stressor.

cardiovascular disease any disease, congenital or acquired, that affects the heart and blood vessels. Cardiovascular diseases include HYPERTENSION, ARTERIOSCLEROSIS, and CORONARY HEART DISEASE.

caregiver *n.* a person who attends to the needs of and provides assistance to someone else who is not fully independent, such as an infant or an ill adult. **—caregiving** *adj.*

caregiver burden the stress and other psychological symptoms experienced by family members and other nonprofessional caregivers in response to looking after individuals with mental or physical disabilities, disorders, or diseases.

carrier *n.* an individual who has a mutation in a gene that conveys either increased susceptibility to a disease or other condition or the certainty that the condition will develop.

carryover effect the effect on the current performance of a research participant of the experimental conditions that preceded the current conditions.

Cartesian dualism the position taken by French philosopher, mathematician, and scientist René Descartes (1596–1650) that the world comprises two distinct and incompatible classes of substance: res extensa, or extended substance, which extends through space; and res cogitans, or thinking substance, which has no extension in space. The body (including the brain) is composed of extended and divisible substance, whereas the mind is not. Descartes accepted that there is interaction between mind and body, holding that in some activities the mind operates independently of bodily influences, whereas in others the body exerts an influence. Similarly, in some bodily activities there is influence from the mind, while in others there is not. However, to the question of how such incompatible substances can interact at all, Descartes had no answer. See DUALISM; MIND–BODY PROBLEM.

case history a record of information relating to a person's psychological or medical condition used as an aid to diagnosis and treatment. It usually contains test results, interviews, professional evaluations, and sociological, occupational, and educational data.

case study an in-depth investigation of a single individual, family, or other social unit. Multiple types of data (psychological, physiological, biographical, environmental) are assembled in order to understand the subject's background, relationships, and behavior.

castration anxiety fear of injury to or loss of the genitals. As posited by psychoanalytic theory, the various losses and deprivations experienced by the infant boy may give rise to the fear that he will also lose his penis. See also CASTRATION COMPLEX.

castration complex in psychoanalytic theory, the whole combination of the child's unconscious feelings and fantasies associated with being deprived of the PHALLUS, which in boys means the loss of the penis and in girls the belief that it has already been removed. It derives from the discovery

that girls have no penis and is closely tied to the OEDIPUS COMPLEX.

CAT acronym for computerized axial tomography (see COMPUTED TOMOGRAPHY).

catabolism *n.* see METABOLISM. **—catabolic** *adj.*

catalepsy *n.* a state of sustained unresponsiveness in which a fixed body posture or physical attitude is maintained over a long period of time. It is seen in cases of CATATONIC SCHIZOPHRENIA, EPILEPSY, and other disorders. **—cataleptic** *adj.*

cataplexy *n.* a sudden loss of muscle tone that may be localized, causing (for example) loss of grasp or head nodding, or generalized, resulting in collapse of the entire body. It is a temporary condition usually precipitated by an extreme emotional stimulus. **—cataplectic** *adj.*

cataract *n.* a progressive clouding (opacification) of the lens of the eye that eventually results in severe visual impairment if untreated. Central vision in particular is impaired, with symptoms including dim or fuzzy vision, sensitivity to glare, and difficulty seeing at night. Cataract is frequently associated with the degenerative processes of aging, but it may also be congenital or due to disease or injury.

catastrophe theory a mathematical theory regarding discontinuous changes in one variable as a function of continuous change in some other variable or variables. It proposes that a small change in one factor may cause an abrupt and large change in another, for example, the dramatic change in the physical properties of water as the temperature reaches 0 °C or 100 °C (32 or 212 °F).

C

catatonia *n.* a state of muscular rigidity or other disturbance of motor behavior, such as CATALEPSY. —**catatonic** *adj.*

catatonic schizophrenia a relatively rare subtype of schizophrenia characterized by abnormal motor activity, specifically long periods of motor immobility (posturing) interspersed with excessive motor activity. Other common features include extreme NEGATIVISM (apparently motiveless resistance to all instructions) or MUTISM and ECHOLALIA or ECHOPRAXIA.

catecholamine *n.* any of a class of BIOGENIC AMINES formed by a catechol molecule and an amine group. Derived from tyrosine, catecholamines include dopamine, epinephrine and norepinephrine, which are the predominant neurotransmitters in the SYMPATHETIC NERVOUS SYSTEM.

categorical data numerical values that indicate counts or observations in specific categories, for example, the number of people in a particular town who are male and the number who are female. Categorical data are similar to NOMINAL DATA, and the two terms are often used interchangeably.

categorical perception in speech perception, the phenomenon in which a continuous acoustic dimension, such as VOICE-ONSET TIME, is perceived as having distinct categories with sharp discontinuities at certain points. Whereas discrimination is much more accurate between categories, individuals tested are often unable to discriminate between acoustically different stimuli that fall within the same categorical boundaries. Categorical perception is crucial in the identification of PHONEMES.

categorical scale see NOMINAL SCALE.

categorical variable a variable defined by membership in a group, class, or category, rather than by rank or by scores on more continuous scales of measurement.

categorization *n.* the process by which objects, events, people, or experiences are grouped into classes on the basis of (a) characteristics shared by members of the same class and (b) features distinguishing the members of one class from those of another. Theories of categorization are numerous and include the prototype model, proposing that people form an average of the members of a category and then use the average as a prototype for making judgments about category membership, and instance theory, hypothesizing that categorization depends on specific remembered instances of the category. Also called **classification**. —**categorize** *vb.*

catharsis *n.* in psychoanalytic theory, the discharge of affects connected to traumatic events that had previously been repressed by bringing these events back into consciousness and reexperiencing them. See also ABREACTION. [from Greek, literally: "purgation, purification"] —**cathartic** *adj.*

cathexis *n.* in psychoanalytic theory, the investment of PSYCHIC ENERGY in an OBJECT of any kind, such as a wish, fantasy, person, goal, idea, social group, or the self. Such objects are said to be **cathected** when an individual attaches emotional significance (positive or negative affect) to them.

caudal *adj.* **1.** pertaining to a tail. **2.** situated at or toward the tail end of an organism. Compare ROSTRAL.

caudate nucleus one of the BASAL GANGLIA, so named because it has a long extension, or tail.

causal attribution see ATTRIBUTION.

causality *n.* in philosophy, the position that all events have causes, that is, that they are consequences of antecedent events. Traditionally, causality has been seen as an essential assumption of NATURALISM and all scientific explanation, although some have questioned whether causality is a necessary assumption of science. See also CAUSATION; DETERMINISM. —**causal** *adj.*

causation *n.* the empirical relation between two events, states, or variables such that one (the cause) is held or known to bring about the other (the effect). See also CAUSALITY. —**causal** *adj.*

cautious shift a CHOICE SHIFT in which an individual making a decision as part of a group adopts a more cautious approach than the same individual would have adopted had he or she made the decision alone. Studies suggest that such shifts are rarer than the opposite **risky shift**. See also GROUP POLARIZATION.

CBT abbreviation for COGNITIVE BEHAVIOR THERAPY.

ceiling age the lowest chronological age at which all items on a given standardized test are consistently answered incorrectly. This concept is less widely used than in the past because it assumes the use of MENTAL AGES, which are declining in popularity. Compare BASAL AGE.

ceiling effect a situation in which a large proportion of participants perform as well as, or nearly as well as, possible on a task or other evaluative measure, thus skewing the distribution of scores and making it impossible to discriminate differences among the many individuals at that high level. For example, a test whose items are too easy for those taking it would show a ceiling effect because most people would obtain or be close to the highest possible score of 100. Compare FLOOR EFFECT.

cell *n.* **1.** the basic unit of organized tissue, consisting of an outer plasma membrane, the NUCLEUS, and various organelles (specialized, membrane-bound structures) in a watery fluid together comprising the **cytoplasm. 2.** the space formed at the intersection of a row and a column in a table. For example, a tabular display of a study of handedness in men and women would consist of four cells: left-handed females, left-handed males, right-handed females, and right-handed males.

cell assembly a group of neurons that are repeatedly active at the same time and develop as a single functional unit, which may become active when any of its constituent neurons is stimulated. This enables, for example, a person to form a complete mental image of an object when only a portion is visible or to recall a memory from a partial cue. Cell assembly is influential in biological theories of memory.

cell body the part of a NEURON (nerve cell) that contains the nucleus and most organelles. Also called **soma**.

cell death see PROGRAMMED CELL DEATH.

censor *n.* in psychoanalytic theory, the mental agency, located in the PRECONSCIOUS, that is responsible for REPRESSION. The censor is posited to determine which of one's wishes, thoughts, and ideas may enter consciousness and which must be kept unconscious because they violate one's conscience or society's standards. The idea was introduced in the early writings of Austrian psychiatrist Sigmund Freud (1856–1939), who later developed it into the concept of the SUPEREGO. —**censorship** *n.*

center–surround receptive field a type of RECEPTIVE FIELD, common in the visual and somatosensory systems, that exhibits **center–surround antagonism**, a characteristic in which stimulation in the center evokes opposite responses to stimulation in the periphery. Most center–surround receptive fields consist of a circular center area and an annular surrounding area.

centile *n.* another name for PERCENTILE, often used in statistics.

central canal the channel in the center of the SPINAL CORD, which contains CEREBROSPINAL FLUID.

central dyslexia any form of acquired dyslexia characterized by difficulties with the pronunciation and comprehension of written words. Unlike PERIPHERAL DYSLEXIA, the visual analysis system is intact, and the damage is to other, higher level pathways and systems involved in reading (e.g., the semantic system).

central executive see WORKING MEMORY.

central fissure see CENTRAL SULCUS.

central gray see PERIAQUEDUCTAL GRAY.

central limit theorem the statistical principle that a linear combination of values (including the mean of those values) tends to be normally distributed over repeated samples as the sample sizes increase, whether or not the population from which the observations are drawn is normal in distribution.

central nervous system (CNS) the entire complex of NEURONS, AXONS, and supporting tissue that constitute the brain and spinal cord. The CNS is primarily involved in mental activities and in coordinating and integrating incoming sensory messages and outgoing

motor messages. Compare PERIPHERAL NERVOUS SYSTEM.

central pattern generator any of the sets of neurons in the spinal cord capable of producing oscillatory behavior and thought to be involved in the control of locomotion and other tasks.

central route to persuasion the process by which attitudes are formed or changed as a result of carefully scrutinizing and thinking about the central merits of attitude-relevant information. See also ELABORATION; ELABORATION-LIKELIHOOD MODEL. Compare PERIPHERAL ROUTE TO PERSUASION.

central sulcus a major cleft (see SULCUS) that passes roughly vertically along the lateral surface of each CEREBRAL HEMISPHERE from a point beginning near the top of the cerebrum. It marks the border between the FRONTAL LOBE and the PARIETAL LOBE. Also called **central fissure**.

central tendency the middle or center point of a DISTRIBUTION, estimated by a number of different statistics (e.g., MEAN and MEDIAN).

centration *n.* in PIAGETIAN THEORY, the tendency of children in the PREOPERATIONAL STAGE to attend to one aspect of a problem, object, or situation at a time, to the exclusion of others. Compare DECENTRATION.

cephalocaudal *adj.* from head to tail, as in the long axis of the body. The term typically refers to the maturation of an embryo or infant, where the greatest development takes place at the top of the body (i.e., the head) before the lower parts (i.e., the arms, trunk, legs, etc.). Compare PROXIMODISTAL.

cerebellar ataxia see ATAXIA.

cerebellar cortex the GRAY MATTER, or unmyelinated nerve cells, covering the surface of the CEREBEL-LUM.

cerebellum *n.* (*pl.* **cerebella**) a portion of the HINDBRAIN dorsal to the rest of the brainstem, to which it is connected by the cerebellar peduncles. The cerebellum modulates muscular contractions to produce smooth, accurately timed BALLISTIC movements and it helps maintain equilibrium by predicting body positions ahead of actual body movements.

cerebral aqueduct a passage containing CEREBROSPINAL FLUID that extends through the MIDBRAIN to link the third and fourth cerebral VENTRICLES of the brain.

cerebral cortex the layer of GRAY MATTER that covers the outside of the CEREBRAL HEMISPHERES in the brain and is associated with higher cognitive functions, such as language, learning, perception, and planning. It consists mostly of NEO-CORTEX, which has six main layers of cells; regions of cerebral cortex that do not have six layers are known as ALLOCORTEX. Differences in the CYTOARCHITECTURE of the layers led to the recognition of distinct areas, called BRODMANN'S AREAS, many of which are known to serve different functions.

cerebral dominance the controlling or disproportionate influence on certain aspects of behavior by one CEREBRAL HEMISPHERE (e.g., language is typically left-lateralized in right-handed people). See DOMINANCE.

cerebral hemisphere either half (left or right) of the cerebrum. The hemispheres are separated by a deep LONGITUDINAL FISSURE but they are connected by commissural, projection, and association fibers so that each side of the brain normally is linked to functions of tissues on either side of the body. See also HEMISPHERIC LATERALIZATION.

cerebral lateralization see HEMISPHERIC LATERALIZATION.

cerebral palsy (**CP**) a set of nonprogressive movement disorders that results from trauma to the brain occurring prenatally or during the birth process. Symptoms include SPASTICITY, paralysis, unsteady gait, and speech abnormalities.

cerebrospinal fluid (**CSF**) the fluid within the CENTRAL CANAL of the spinal cord, the four VENTRICLES of the brain, and the subarachnoid space beneath the middle of the three MENINGES of the brain. It serves as a watery cushion to protect vital tissues of the central nervous system from damage by shock pressure, and it mediates between blood vessels and brain tissue in exchange of materials, including nutrients.

cerebrovascular accident (**CVA**) a disorder of the brain arising from CEREBROVASCULAR DISEASE, such as cerebral HEMORRHAGE, EMBOLISM, or THROMBOSIS, resulting in temporary or permanent alterations in cognition, motor and sensory skills, or levels of consciousness. This term is often used interchangeably with STROKE.

cerebrovascular disease a pathological condition of the blood vessels of the brain. It may manifest itself as symptoms of STROKE or a TRANSIENT ISCHEMIC ATTACK.

cerebrum *n.* the largest part of the brain, forming most of the FORE-BRAIN and lying in front of and above the cerebellum. It consists of two CEREBRAL HEMISPHERES bridged by the CORPUS CALLOSUM. Each hemisphere is divided into four main lobes: the FRONTAL LOBE, OCCIPITAL LOBE, PARIETAL LOBE, and TEMPORAL LOBE. The outer layer of the cerebrum—the CEREBRAL COR-TEX—is intricately folded and composed of GRAY MATTER. Also called **telencephalon**.

cesarean section (caesarean section; C-section) a surgical procedure in which incisions are made through a woman's abdominal and uterine walls to deliver a baby under circumstances in which vaginal delivery is inadvisable.

CFF abbreviation for CRITICAL FLICKER FREQUENCY.

CFS abbreviation for CHRONIC FATIGUE SYNDROME.

cGMP abbreviation for CYCLIC GMP.

change agent a specific causative factor or element or an entire process that results in change, particularly in the sense of improvement. In psychotherapy research, a change agent may be a component or process in therapy that results in improvement in the behavior or psychological adaptation of a patient or client.

change blindness an inability to notice changes in the visual array between one scene and another. For example, when a picture of an airplane is shown, followed by a blank screen, participants have surprising difficulty detecting a missing engine in a second picture of the airplane.

charisma *n.* the special quality of personality that enables an individual to gain the confidence of large numbers of people. It is exemplified in outstanding political, social, and religious leaders. —**charismatic** *adj.*

ChE abbreviation for CHOLINESTERASE.

chemical antagonism see ANTAGONIST.

chemical synapse a type of specialized junction through which a signal is transmitted from one neuron to another across the narrow gap (SYNAPTIC CLEFT) separating them through the release and diffusion of NEUROTRANSMITTER. Though slower than ELECTRICAL SYNAPSES, chemical synapses are more flexible and comprise the majority of neuronal junctions within the body. Because of this prevalence, the qualifier generally is omitted and SYNAPSE used alone to denote a chemical junction.

chemoaffinity hypothesis the notion that each neuron has a chemical identity that directs it to synapse on the proper target cell during development.

chemoreceptor *n.* a sensory nerve ending, such as any of those in the TASTE BUDS or OLFACTORY EPITHELIUM, that is capable of reacting to certain chemical stimuli. In humans, there are hundreds of different taste receptor proteins and a total of about 300,000 TASTE CELLS. Humans also have about 1,000 types of OLFACTORY RECEPTORS and about 1,000 receptors of each type, giving a total of one million olfactory receptors; other mammals (e.g., dogs) may have ten times that number.

chemotherapy *n.* the use of chemical agents to treat diseases, particularly cancer. —**chemotherapeutic** *adj.* —**chemotherapist** *n.*

child abuse harm to a child caused by a parent or other caregiver. The harm may be physical (violence), sexual (violation or exploitation), psychological (causing emotional distress), or neglect (failure to provide needed care). See also BATTERED-CHILD SYNDROME.

child advocacy any organized and structured interventions on behalf of children by professionals or institutions, often in relation to such issues as special parenting needs, child abuse, and adoption or foster care.

child development the sequential changes in the behavior, cognition, and physiology of children as they grow and mature from birth to adolescence. See DEVELOPMENTAL TASK.

child-directed speech the specialized REGISTER of speech that adults and older children use when talking to young children. It is simplified and often more grammatically correct than adult-directed speech. See also INFANT-DIRECTED SPEECH.

childhood *n.* the period between the end of infancy (about 2 years of age) and the onset of puberty, marking the beginning of ADOLESCENCE (10–12 years of age). This period is sometimes divided into (a) early childhood, from 2 years through the preschool age of 5 or 6 years; (b) middle childhood, from 6 to 8–10 years of age; and (c) late childhood or preadolescence, which is identified as the 2-year period before the onset of puberty.

childhood amnesia the inability to recall events from the first years of life (from infancy through about 5 years of age). Childhood amnesia has been attributed to the facts that (a) cognitive abilities necessary for encoding events for the long term have not yet been fully developed and (b) parts of the brain responsible for remembering personal events have not yet matured. Also called **infantile amnesia**.

childhood disintegrative disorder a PERVASIVE DEVELOPMENTAL DISORDER characterized by a significant loss of previously acquired language skills, social skills or adaptive behavior, bowel or bladder control, play, or motor skills. This regression in functioning follows a period of normal development and occurs between the ages of 2 and 10.

child neglect see CHILD ABUSE.

chi-square distribution (χ^2 **distribution**) the distribution of the sum of a set of independent squared normal random deviates. If p independent variables are involved, the distribution is said to have p DEGREES OF FREEDOM.

chi-square test a measure of how well a theoretical probability distribution fits a set of data. If values x_1, x_2, ... x_p are observed o_1, o_2, ... o_p times and are expected by theory to occur e_1, e_2, ... e_p times, then chi-square is calculated as $(o_1 - e_1)^2/e_1 + (o_2 - e_2)^2/e_2 + ...$ Tables of chi-square for different DEGREES OF FREEDOM can be used to indicate the probability that the theory is correct. Also called **chi-square procedure**.

chlorpromazine *n.* the first synthesized ANTIPSYCHOTIC agent, effective in managing the acute symptoms of schizophrenia, acute mania, and other psychoses. Associated with a number of unwanted adverse effects, including TARDIVE DYSKINESIA, chlorpromazine has been largely supplanted by newer antipsychotic agents but is still used as a referent for dose equivalency of other antipsychotics. U.S. trade name: **Thorazine**.

choice reaction time the total time that elapses between the presentation of a stimulus and the occurrence of a response in a task that requires a participant to make one of several different responses depending on which one of several different stimuli is presented. In other words, the participant must make a conscious decision before responding. Also called **complex reaction time; compound reaction time**. Compare SIMPLE REACTION TIME.

choice shift any shift in an individual's choices or decisions that occurs as a result of group discussion, as measured by comparing his or her prediscussion and postdiscussion responses. In many cases the result of such shifts is a **choice-**

shift effect within the group as a whole. See also CAUTIOUS SHIFT.

cholecystokinin *n.* a PEPTIDE HORMONE that is released from the duodenum and may be involved in the satiation of hunger. It also serves as a NEUROTRANSMITTER at some locations in the nervous system.

cholinergic *adj.* responding to, releasing, or otherwise involving ACETYLCHOLINE. For example, a **cholinergic neuron** is one that employs acetylcholine as a neurotransmitter.

cholinesterase (ChE) *n.* an enzyme that splits ACETYLCHOLINE into choline and acetic acid, thus inactivating the neurotransmitter after its release at a synaptic junction. Cholinesterase occurs in two forms: **acetylcholinesterase (AChE)**, found in nerve tissue and red blood cells; and **butyrylcholinesterase (BuChE)**, found in blood plasma and other tissues. Drugs that block the ability of this enzyme to degrade acetylcholine are called **cholinesterase inhibitors (ChEIs, or acetylcholinesterase inhibitors [AChEIs],** or **anticholinesterases**).

chorea *n.* irregular and involuntary jerky movements of the limbs and facial muscles. Chorea is associated with various disorders, including HUNTINGTON'S DISEASE. —**choreal** *adj.* —**choreic** *adj.*

chromatic *adj.* in vision, relating to the attribute of color.

chromatic aberration see ABERRATION.

chromosome *n.* a strand or filament in the cell nucleus composed of nucleic acid (mainly DNA in humans) and proteins that carries the genetic, or hereditary, traits of an individual. The normal human complement of chromosomes totals 46, or 23 pairs (44 AUTOSOMES and 2 SEX CHROMOSOMES), which contain an estimated 20,000–25,000 genes. Each parent contributes one chromosome to each pair, so a child receives half its chromosomes from its mother and half from its father. —**chromosomal** *adj.*

chronic *adj.* denoting conditions or symptoms that persist or progress over a long period of time and are resistant to cure. Compare ACUTE.

chronic fatigue syndrome (CFS) an illness characterized by often disabling fatigue, decrease in physical activity, and flulike symptoms, such as muscle weakness, swelling of the lymph nodes, headache, sore throat, and sometimes depression. The condition is typically not diagnosed until symptoms have been ongoing for several months and it can last for years. The cause is unknown, although certain viral infections can set off the illness.

chronobiology *n.* the branch of biology concerned with BIOLOGICAL RHYTHMS, such as the sleep–wake cycle.

chronological age (CA) the amount of time elapsed since an individual's birth, typically expressed in terms of months and years.

chunking *n.* the process by which the mind sorts information into small, easily digestible units (chunks) that can be retained in SHORT-TERM MEMORY. As a result of this recoding, one item in memory (e.g., a keyword or key idea) can stand for multiple other items (e.g., a short list of associated points). The capacity of short-term memory is believed to be constant for the number of individual units it can store (seven plus or minus two), but the units themselves can range from simple chunks (e.g., individual letters or numbers) to complex chunks (e.g., words or phrases).

ciliary muscle smooth muscle behind the iris of the eye that changes the shape of the lens to bring objects into focus on the retina. The ciliary muscle regulates the tension of the zonules, delicate elastic fibers that are connected to the lens and cause it to flatten (which lessens the power of the lens and allows focus of distant objects) or become more curved (which increases the power of the lens and allows focus of near objects). The action of the ciliary muscle is a large component of AC-COMMODATION.

cingulate gyrus a long strip of CE-REBRAL CORTEX on the medial surface of each cerebral hemisphere. The cingulate gyrus arches over and generally outlines the location of the CORPUS CALLOSUM, from which it is separated by a groove called the **callosal sulcus**. It is a component of the LIMBIC SYSTEM.

circadian rhythm see BIOLOGI-CAL RHYTHM.

circannual rhythm see BIOLOGI-CAL RHYTHM.

circular reaction in PIAGETIAN THEORY, repetitive behavior observed in children during the SENSORIMOTOR STAGE, characterized as primary, secondary, or tertiary circular reactions. The primary phase involves ineffective repetitive behaviors; the secondary phase involves repetition of actions that are followed by reinforcement, typically without understanding causation; and the tertiary phase involves repetitive object manipulation, typically with slight variations among subsequent behaviors.

civil commitment a legal procedure that permits a person who is not charged with criminal conduct to be certified as mentally ill and to be institutionalized involuntarily.

CJD abbreviation for CREUTZFELDT–JAKOB DISEASE.

clairvoyance *n.* in parapsychol-ogy, the alleged ability to "see" things beyond the normal range of sight, such as distant or hidden objects or events in the past or future. See also EXTRASENSORY PERCEPTION. —**clairvoyant** *n., adj.*

classical conditioning see PAV-LOVIAN CONDITIONING.

classical psychoanalysis 1. psychoanalytic theory in which major emphasis is placed on the LIBIDO, the stages of PSYCHOSEXUAL DEVEL-OPMENT, and the ID instincts or drives. The prototypical theory of this kind is that of Austrian psychiatrist Sigmund Freud (1856–1939). **2.** psychoanalytic treatment that adheres to Sigmund Freud's basic procedures, using dream interpretation, free association, and analysis of RESISTANCE, and to his basic aim of developing insight into the patient's unconscious life as a way to restructure personality.

classical test theory (**CTT**) a body of psychometric theory of measurement that partitions observed scores into two components—true scores and error scores—and estimates error variance by calculating INTERNAL CONSIS-TENCY reliability, RETEST RELIA-BILITY, and ALTERNATE-FORMS RELIABILITY. The principal framework for test development prior to the 1970s, CTT is applicable to a broad range of measurement situations but has several major limitations, notably that examinee characteristics cannot be separated from test characteristics and that the measurement statistics derived from it are fundamentally concerned with how people perform on a given test as opposed to any single item on that test.

classification *n.* see CATEGORIZA-TION. —**classify** *vb.*

class inclusion the concept that a subordinate class (e.g., dogs) must always be smaller than the superordinate class in which it is contained (e.g., animals). According to PIAGETIAN THEORY, understanding the concept of class inclusion represents an important developmental step.

class interval the range of scores or numerical values that constitute one segment or class in a frequency distribution; for example, weights might be grouped in class intervals of 5 kg each. Also called **class size**.

claustrophobia *n.* a persistent and irrational fear of enclosed places (e.g., elevators, closets, tunnels) or of being confined (e.g., in an airplane or the backseat of a car). The focus of fear is typically on panic symptoms triggered in these situations, such as feelings of being unable to breathe, choking, sweating, and fears of losing control or going crazy. —**claustrophobic** *adj.*

claustrum *n.* (*pl.* **claustra**) a thin layer of gray matter in the brain that separates the white matter of the lenticular nucleus from the INSULA (from Latin: "barrier"). The claustrum forms part of the BASAL GANGLIA and its function is unknown. —**claustral** *adj.*

Clever Hans the "thinking horse," reputed to be able to solve mathematical problems, spell words, distinguish colors, and identify coins, that became famous in Berlin around 1900. It signaled its answers by tapping its foot. However, German psychologist Oskar Pfungst (1874–1932), using experimental methods, demonstrated that the horse was responding to minimal cues in the form of involuntary movements on the part of its owner.

client *n.* a person receiving treatment or services, especially in the context of counseling or social work. See PATIENT–CLIENT ISSUE.

client-centered therapy a form

of psychotherapy developed by U.S. psychologist Carl Rogers (1902–1987) in which client self-discovery and actualization occurs in response to the therapist's consistent empathic understanding of, acceptance of, and respect for the client's FRAME OF REFERENCE. The therapist reflects and clarifies the ideas of the client, who is able to see himself or herself more clearly, learn how to interpret his or her thoughts and feelings, reorganize values and approaches to life, and resolve problems or change behavior. It was originally known as **nondirective therapy,** although this term is now used more broadly to denote any approach to psychotherapy in which the therapist establishes an encouraging atmosphere but avoids giving advice, offering interpretations, or engaging in other actions to actively direct the therapeutic process. Also called **person-centered therapy.**

climacteric *n.* the biological stage of life in which reproductive capacity declines and finally ceases. In women this period, which results from changes in the levels of estrogens and progesterone and is known as **menopause,** occurs between 45 and 55 years of age. During this time, menstrual flow gradually decreases and finally ceases altogether, and various physical and potentially psychological changes occur, typically manifest as hot flashes, night sweats, and emotional lability. Men undergo a similar period of hormonal change (**male climacteric**), manifest as reduced energy, sexual drive, and fertility.

clinical *adj.* of or relating to the diagnosis and treatment of psychological, medical, or other disorders. Originally involving only direct observation of patients, clinical methods have now broadened to take into account biological and statistical factors in treating patients and diagnosing disorders.

clinical interview a type of directed conversation initially used with children but now applied in a variety of contexts, including HUMAN FACTORS research and diagnostic evaluation and treatment planning of patients by mental health professionals. In a clinical interview, the investigator may utilize certain standard material but essentially determines which questions to ask based on the responses given by the participant to previous ones. This technique is largely spontaneous and enables the interviewer to adapt questions to the patient's understanding and ask additional questions to clarify ambiguities and enhance understanding.

clinical method the process by which a clinical psychologist, psychiatrist, or other mental health or medical professional arrives at a conclusion, judgment, or diagnosis about a client or patient.

clinical neuropsychology an applied specialty in NEURO-PSYCHOLOGY that comprises neuropsychological assessment and rehabilitation, which are critical in cases of neuropsychological injury that results in a range of impairments that disrupt an individual's ability to function.

clinical psychology the branch of psychology that specializes in the research, assessment, diagnosis, evaluation, prevention, and treatment of emotional and behavioral disorders. The **clinical psychologist** is a doctorate-level professional who has received training in research methods and techniques for the diagnosis and treatment of various psychological disorders (see also PSYCHOLOGIST). Clinical psychologists work primarily in health and mental health clinics, in research, or in group and independent practices.

They also serve as consultants to other professionals in the medical, legal, social-work, and community-relations fields.

clique *n.* a status- or friendship-based subgroup within a larger group or organization. Cliques are particularly common during adolescence, when they are often used to raise social standing, strengthen friendship ties, and reduce feelings of isolation and exclusion.

clone *n.* an organism that is genetically identical to another. This may be because both organisms originate naturally from a single common parent as a result of asexual reproduction or because one is derived from genetic material taken from the other. —**clonal** *adj.*

clonic *adj.* of, relating to, or characterized by **clonus**, a type of involuntary movement caused by a rapid succession of alternate muscular contractions and relaxations. Although some forms of clonus, such as hiccups, are considered normal, most such movements are abnormal; for example, clonus occurs as part of a TONIC–CLONIC SEIZURE.

closure *n.* **1.** the act, achievement, or sense of completing or resolving something. In psychotherapy, for example, a client achieves closure with the recognition that he or she has reached a resolution to a particular psychological issue or relationship problem. **2.** one of the GESTALT PRINCIPLES OF ORGANIZATION. It states that people tend to perceive incomplete forms (e.g., images, sounds) as complete, synthesizing the missing units so as to perceive the image or sound as a whole. Also called **law of closure**; **principle of closure**.

cluster analysis a method of data analysis in which individuals (cases) are grouped together into clusters based on their strong similarity with regard to specific attributes.

clustering *n.* the tendency for items to be consistently grouped together in the course of recall. This grouping typically occurs for related items. It is readily apparent in memory tasks in which items from the same category, such as animals, are recalled together. —**cluster** *n.*, *vb.*

cluster suicides a statistically high occurrence of suicides within a circumscribed geographic area, social group, or time period. Such clusters typically occur among adolescents who imitate the suicide of a high-status peer or among dispersed individuals who imitate the suicide of a widely admired role model.

CNS abbreviation for CENTRAL NERVOUS SYSTEM.

coacting group a group consisting of two or more individuals working in one another's presence on tasks and activities that require little or no interaction or communication (**coaction tasks**), such as clerical staff working at individual desks in an open-design office. Researchers often create coacting groups in laboratory studies to determine the impact of the mere presence of others on performance.

coarticulation *n.* a phenomenon in which the performance of one or more actions in a sequence of actions varies according to the other actions in the sequence. This is particularly important in speech, where the formation of certain PHONEMES varies according to the speech sounds that immediately precede or follow: So, for example, the aspirated [p] sound in *pin* differs slightly from the unaspirated [p] in *spin*.

cocaine *n.* a drug, obtained from leaves of the coca shrub (*Erythroxylum coca*), that stimulates the central nervous system, with the effects of reducing fatigue and in-creasing well-being. These are followed by a period of depression as the initial effects diminish. The drug acts by blocking the reuptake of the neurotransmitters DOPAMINE, SEROTONIN, and NOREPINEPHRINE.

cochlea *n.* the bony fluid-filled part of the inner ear that is concerned with hearing. Shaped like a snail shell, it forms part of the bony LABYRINTH. Along its length run three canals: the SCALA VESTIBULI, SCALA TYMPANI, and SCALA MEDIA, or cochlear duct. The floor of the scala media is formed by the BASILAR MEMBRANE; the ORGAN OF CORTI, which rests on the basilar membrane, contains the HAIR CELLS that act as auditory receptor organs. —**cochlear** *adj.*

cochlear implant an electronic device designed to enable individuals with complete deafness to hear and interpret some sounds, particularly those associated with speech. It consists of a microphone to detect sound, a headpiece to transmit sound, a processor to digitize sound, and a receiver to signal electrodes that are surgically implanted in the cochlea to stimulate the auditory nerve.

cochlear nucleus a mass of cell bodies of second-order auditory neurons in the brainstem. The principal subdivisions are the ventral, dorsal, and anterior cochlear nuclei.

cocktail-party effect the ability to attend to one of several speech streams while ignoring others, as when one is at a cocktail party. Research in this area in the early 1950s suggested that the unattended messages are not processed, but later findings indicated that meaning is identified in at least some cases. For example, the mention of one's name is processed even if it occurs in an unattended speech stream. See also ATTENUATION THEORY.

C

codeine *n.* an OPIATE derived from morphine, with which it shares many properties—it is a potent analgesic (used alone or in combination with other analgesics, e.g., aspirin) and it induces euphoria.

code of ethics a set of standards and principles of professional conduct, such as the *Ethical Principles of Psychologists and Code of Conduct* of the American Psychological Association. See ETHICS.

coefficient *n.* **1.** a number that functions as a measure of some property. For example, the CORRELATION COEFFICIENT is a measure of the degree of linear relatedness. **2.** in algebra, a scalar that multiplies a variable in an equation. For example, in the equation $y = bx$, the scalar quantity b is said to be a coefficient.

coefficient of determination (symbol: r^2) a numerical index that reflects the degree to which variation in the DEPENDENT VARIABLE is accounted for by one INDEPENDENT VARIABLE.

coefficient of multiple determination (symbol: R^2) a numerical index that reflects the degree to which variation in the DEPENDENT VARIABLE is accounted for by two or more INDEPENDENT VARIABLES.

coevolution *n.* the concurrent evolution of two or more species that mutually affect each other's evolution.

cognition *n.* all forms of knowing and awareness, such as perceiving, conceiving, remembering, reasoning, judging, imagining, and problem solving. Along with affect and conation, it is one of the three traditionally identified components of mind. **—cognitional** *adj.* **—cognitive** *adj.*

cognitive appraisal theory the theory that cognitive evaluation is involved in the generation of each and every emotion. This concept is more appropriately expressed in the **cognitive–motivational–relational theory**, as the latter recognizes that cognition is only one of three simultaneously operating processes that contribute to the generation of any emotion.

cognitive behavior therapy (**CBT**) a form of psychotherapy that integrates theories of cognition and learning with treatment techniques derived from BEHAVIOR THERAPY. CBT assumes that cognitive, emotional, and behavioral variables are functionally interrelated. Treatment is aimed at identifying and modifying the client's maladaptive thought processes and problematic behaviors through COGNITIVE RESTRUCTURING and behavioral techniques to achieve change.

cognitive coping strategy any COPING STRATEGY in which mental activity is used to counter the problem or situation. Examples include thinking out the cause of the problem, working out how others might handle it, diverting one's attention to something less stressful or anxiety-provoking (e.g., remembering happy times, solving mathematical problems), and meditation or prayer.

cognitive development the growth and maturation of thinking processes of all kinds, including perceiving, remembering, concept formation, problem solving, imagining, and reasoning.

cognitive developmental theory any theory that attempts to explain the mechanisms underlying the growth and maturation of thinking processes. Explanations may be in terms of stages of development in which the changes in thinking are relatively abrupt and discontinuous, or the changes may be viewed as occurring gradually and continuously over time.

cognitive disorder any disorder that involves impairment of the EXECUTIVE FUNCTIONS, affecting performance in many areas, including reasoning, planning, judgment, decision making, emotional engagement, perseveration, awareness, attention, language, learning, memory, and timing.

cognitive dissonance an unpleasant psychological state resulting from inconsistency between two or more elements in a cognitive system. It is presumed to involve a state of heightened arousal and to have characteristics similar to physiological drives (e.g., hunger).

cognitive dissonance theory a theory proposing that people have a fundamental motivation to maintain consistency among elements in their cognitive systems. When inconsistency occurs, people experience an unpleasant psychological state that motivates them to reduce the dissonance in a variety of ways.

cognitive ergonomics a specialty area of ERGONOMICS that seeks to understand the cognitive processes and representations involved in human performance. Cognitive ergonomics studies the combined effect of information-processing characteristics, task constraints, and task environment on human performance and applies the results of such studies to the design and evaluation of work systems.

cognitive learning theory any theory postulating that learning requires central constructs and new ways of perceiving events. Cognitive theory is usually contrasted with behavioral learning theories, which suggest that behaviors or responses are acquired through experience.

cognitive map a mental understanding of an environment, formed through trial and error as well as observation. Human beings and other animals have well-developed cognitive maps that contain spatial information enabling them to orient themselves and find their way in the real world.

cognitive model a theoretical view of thought and mental operations, which provides explanations for observed phenomena and makes predictions about an unknown future. People are continually creating and accessing internal representations (models) of what they are experiencing in the world for the purposes of perception, comprehension, and behavior selection (action).

cognitive neuropsychology the study of the structure and function of the brain as it relates to perception, reasoning, remembering, and all other forms of knowing and awareness. Cognitive neuropsychology focuses on examining the effects of brain damage on thought processes—typically through the use of in-depth SINGLE-CASE DESIGNS—so as to construct models of normal cognitive functioning.

cognitive neuroscience a branch of NEUROSCIENCE and BIOLOGICAL PSYCHOLOGY that focuses on the neural mechanisms of cognition. Although overlapping with the study of the mind in COGNITIVE PSYCHOLOGY, cognitive neuroscience, with its grounding in such areas as experimental psychology, neurobiology, physics, and mathematics, specifically examines how mental processes occur in the brain.

cognitive overload the situation in which the demands placed on a person by mental work (the **cognitive load**) are greater than the person's mental abilities can cope with.

cognitive process any of the

mental functions assumed to be involved in the acquisition, storage, interpretation, manipulation, transformation, and use of knowledge. These processes encompass such areas as attention, perception, learning, and problem solving and are commonly understood through several basic theories, including the SERIAL PROCESSING approach, the PARALLEL PROCESSING approach, and a combination theory, which assumes that cognitive processes are both serial and parallel, depending on the demands of the task.

cognitive psychology the branch of psychology that explores the operation of mental processes related to perceiving, attending, thinking, language, and memory, mainly through inferences from behavior. The cognitive approach, which developed in the 1940s and 1950s, diverged sharply from contemporary BEHAVIORISM in (a) emphasizing unseen knowledge processes instead of directly observable behaviors and (b) arguing that the relationship between stimulus and response was complex and mediated rather than simple and direct. Its concentration on the higher mental processes also contrasted with the focus on the instincts and other unconscious forces typical of psychoanalysis. More recently, cognitive psychology has been influenced by approaches to INFORMATION PROCESSING and INFORMATION THEORY developed in computer science and ARTIFICIAL INTELLIGENCE. See also COGNITIVE SCIENCE.

cognitive restructuring a technique used in COGNITIVE THERAPY and COGNITIVE BEHAVIOR THERAPY to help the client identify his or her self-defeating beliefs or cognitive distortions, refute them, and then modify them so that they are adaptive and reasonable.

cognitive science an interdisciplinary approach to understanding the mind and mental processes that combines aspects of cognitive psychology, the philosophy of mind, epistemology, neuroscience, anthropology, psycholinguistics, and computer science.

cognitive style a person's characteristic mode of perceiving, thinking, remembering, and problem solving. Cognitive styles might differ in preferred elements or activities, such as visual versus verbal ENCODING, and along various dimensions, such as FIELD DEPENDENCE/field independence. Many use the term **learning style** interchangeably with cognitive style, whereas others use the former more specifically to mean a person's characteristic cognitive, affective, and psychological behaviors that influence his or her preferred instructional methods and interactions with the learning environment.

cognitive theory any theory of mind that focuses on mental activities, such as perceiving, attending, thinking, remembering, evaluating, planning, language, and creativity, especially one that suggests a model for the various processes involved.

cognitive therapy (**CT**) a form of psychotherapy based on the concept that emotional and behavioral problems in an individual are, at least in part, the result of maladaptive or faulty ways of thinking and distorted attitudes toward oneself and others. The objective of the therapy is to identify these faulty cognitions and replace them with more adaptive ones, a process known as COGNITIVE RESTRUCTURING. The therapist takes the role of an active guide who attempts to make the client aware of these distorted thinking patterns and who helps the client correct and revise his or her perceptions and attitudes by citing evidence to the contrary or by eliciting it from the client. See also COGNITIVE BEHAVIOR THERAPY.

cognitive triad a set of three beliefs thought to characterize MAJOR DEPRESSIVE EPISODES. These are negative beliefs about the self, the world, and the future.

cognitive unconscious unreportable mental processes, collectively. There are many sources of evidence for a cognitive unconscious, including regularities of behavior due to habit or AUTOMATICITY, inferred grammatical rules, the details of sensorimotor control, and implicit knowledge after brain damage. It is often contrasted with the psychoanalytically derived notion of the dynamic UNCONSCIOUS, which involves material that is kept out of consciousness to avoid anxiety, shame, or guilt.

cohabitation *n.* the state or condition of living together as sexual and domestic partners without being married. —**cohabit** *vb.* —**cohabitee** *n.*

Cohen's kappa (symbol: κ) a numerical index that reflects the degree of agreement between two raters or rating systems classifying data into mutually exclusive categories, corrected for the level of agreement expected by chance alone. [Jacob **Cohen** (1923–1998), U.S. psychologist and statistician]

cohesion *n.* the unity or solidarity of a group, as indicated by the strength of the bonds that link group members to the group as a whole, the sense of belongingness and community within the group, the feelings of attraction for specific group members and the group itself experienced by individuals, and the degree to which members coordinate their efforts to achieve goals. Group cohesion is frequently con-

sidered essential to effective GROUP THERAPY. —**cohesive** *adj.*

cohesiveness *n.* a tendency of acts, either successive or simultaneous, to become connected or affiliated so as to form a unified whole.

cohort *n.* a group of people who have experienced a significant life event (e.g., marriage) during the same period of time. The term usually refers to a birth cohort, or generation.

cohort effect any outcome associated with being a member of a group born at a particular time and therefore influenced by the events and practices at that time. Cohort effects may be difficult to separate from AGE EFFECTS and PERIOD EFFECTS in research.

collective monologue a form of speech in which 2- or 3-year-old children talk among themselves without apparently communicating with each other in a meaningful way, such that the statements of one child seem unrelated to the statements of the others.

collective unconscious the part of the UNCONSCIOUS that, according to Swiss psychiatrist Carl Jung (1875–1961), is common to all humankind and contains the inherited accumulation of primitive human experiences in the form of ideas and images called ARCHETYPES. It is the deepest and least accessible part of the unconscious mind. See also PERSONAL UNCONSCIOUS.

collectivism *n.* a social or cultural tradition, ideology, or personal outlook that emphasizes the unity of the group or community rather than each person's individuality. Collectivist societies tend to stress cooperation, communalism, constructive interdependence, and conformity to cultural roles and mores. Compare INDIVIDUALISM. —**collectivist** *adj.*

colliculus *n.* (*pl.* **colliculi**) a small elevation. Two pairs of colliculi are found on the dorsal surface of the MIDBRAIN. The rostral pair, the **superior colliculi**, receive and process visual information and help control eye movements. The caudal pair, the **inferior colliculi**, receive and process auditory information.

color *n.* the subjective quality of light that corresponds to wavelength as perceived by retinal receptors. Color can be characterized by its HUE, SATURATION, and BRIGHTNESS.

color blindness the inability to discriminate between colors and to perceive color hues. Color blindness may be caused by disease, drugs, or brain injury (acquired color blindness), but most often is an inherited trait (congenital color blindness) that affects about 10% of men (it is rare in women). The most common form of the disorder involves the green or red receptors of the cone cells in the retina, causing a red–green confusion. Total color blindness is called ACHROMATISM and is rare. See also DICHROMATISM; MONOCHROMATISM; TRICHROMATISM.

color constancy the tendency to perceive a familiar object as having the same color under different conditions of illumination. Color constancy is an example of PERCEPTUAL CONSTANCY.

color contrast the effect of one color upon another when they are viewed in close proximity. In simultaneous contrast, complementary colors, such as yellow and blue, are enhanced by each other: The yellow appears yellower, and the blue appears bluer. In successive contrast, the complement of a color is seen after shifting focus to a neutral surface.

color vision the ability to distinguish visual stimuli on the basis of the wavelengths of light they emit or reflect.

column *n.* in anatomy, a structure that resembles an architectural pillar. An example is the SPINAL COLUMN. —**columnar** *adj.*

coma *n.* a profound state of unconsciousness resulting from disease, injury, or poisoning and characterized by little or no response to stimuli, absence of reflexes, and suspension of voluntary activity.

combination *n.* in statistics, the selection of *r* objects from among *n* objects without regard to the order in which the objects are selected. The number of combinations of *n* objects taken *r* at a time is often denoted as $_nC_r$. A combination is similar to a PERMUTATION but distinguished by its irrelevance of order.

commissure *n.* a structure that forms a bridge or junction between two anatomical areas, particularly the two cerebral hemispheres or the halves of the spinal cord. Examples include the two key landmarks in brain mapping: the **anterior commissure**, a bundle of myelinated fibers that joins the TEMPORAL LOBES; and the **posterior commissure**, a bundle of myelinated fibers that connects regions in the midbrain and DIENCEPHALON. See also CORPUS CALLOSUM. —**commissural** *adj.*

commissurotomy *n.* surgical transection or severing of a COMMISSURE, especially surgical separation of the cerebral hemispheres of the brain by severing the CORPUS CALLOSUM and often the anterior commissure. This procedure is used clinically to treat severe epilepsy and has been used experimentally in animals to study the functions of each hemisphere. See also SPLIT BRAIN.

commitment *n.* confinement to a

mental institution by court order following certification by appropriate psychiatric or other mental health authorities. The process may be voluntary but is generally involuntary.

common fate one of the GESTALT PRINCIPLES OF ORGANIZATION, stating that objects functioning or moving in the same direction appear to belong together, that is, they are perceived as a single unit (e.g., a flock of birds). Also called **law of common fate**; **principle of common fate**.

communal relationship a relationship in which interaction is governed primarily by consideration of the other's needs and wishes. This contrasts with an **exchange relationship**, in which the people involved are concerned mainly with receiving as much as they give.

communication *n.* the transmission of information, which may be by verbal (oral or written) or nonverbal means (see NONVERBAL COMMUNICATION). Humans communicate to relate and exchange ideas, knowledge, feelings, and experiences and for many other interpersonal and social purposes. Nonhuman animals likewise communicate vocally or nonvocally for a variety of purposes. **Communication disorders** are treated by mental and behavioral health therapists and by speech and language therapists.

community mental health activities undertaken in the community, rather than in institutional settings, to promote mental health. The community approach focuses primarily on the total population of a single catchment area and involves overall planning and demographic analyses. It emphasizes preventive services as distinguished from therapeutic services (e.g., by identifying sources of stress within the community) and seeks to pro-

vide a continuous, comprehensive system of services designed to meet all mental health-related needs in the community.

community mental health center a community-based facility providing a full range of prevention, treatment, and rehabilitation services, including full diagnostic evaluation, outpatient individual and group therapy, emergency inpatient treatment, substance abuse treatment, and vocational, educational, and social rehabilitation programs.

community psychology the branch of psychology that focuses on social issues, social institutions, and other settings that influence individuals, groups, and organizations. Community researchers examine the ways that individuals interact with each other, social groups (e.g., clubs, churches, schools, families), and the larger culture and environment.

comorbidity *n.* the simultaneous presence in an individual of two or more mental or physical illnesses, diseases, or disorders. —**comorbid** *adj.*

companionate love a type of love characterized by strong feelings of intimacy and affection for another person but not accompanied by strong passion or emotional arousal in the other's presence. In these respects, companionate love is distinguished from PASSIONATE LOVE. See also TRIANGULAR THEORY OF LOVE.

comparable forms see ALTERNATE-FORMS RELIABILITY.

comparative psychology the study of animal behavior with the dual objective of understanding the behavior of nonhuman animals for its own sake as well as furthering the understanding of human behavior. Comparative psychology usually involves laboratory studies (compare ETHOLOGY) and typically refers to any study involving nonhuman species, whether or not the comparative method is used.

comparison level in SOCIAL EXCHANGE THEORY, the standard by which an individual evaluates the quality of any social relationship in which he or she is currently engaged. The comparison level derives from the average of all outcomes experienced by the individual in previous similar relationships or observed by the individual in similar relationships of others.

compensation n. **1.** substitution or development of strength or capability in one area to offset real or imagined lack or deficiency in another. This may be referred to as **overcompensation** when the substitute behavior exceeds what might actually be necessary in terms of level of compensation for the lack or deficiency. In his classical psychoanalytic theory, Austrian psychiatrist Sigmund Freud (1856–1939) described compensation as a DEFENSE MECHANISM that protects the individual against the conscious realization of such lacks or deficiencies. The idea of compensation also is central to the personality theory of Austrian psychiatrist Alfred Adler (1870–1937), which sees all human striving as a response to feelings of inferiority (see also INFERIORITY COMPLEX). **—compensate** vb. **—compensatory** adj.

compensatory task a task or project that a group can complete by averaging together individual members' solutions or recommendations. Groups outperform individuals on such tasks when the members are equally proficient at the task and do not share common biases that produce systematic tendencies toward overestimation or underestimation.

Compare ADDITIVE TASK; CONJUNCTIVE TASK; DISJUNCTIVE TASK.

competence n. **1.** the ability to exert control over one's life, to cope with specific problems effectively, and to make changes to one's behavior and one's environment. Affirming, strengthening, or achieving a client's competence is often a basic goal in psychotherapy. **2.** one's developed repertoire of skills, especially as applied to a particular task. **3.** in linguistics, the unconscious knowledge of the underlying rules of a language that enables individuals to speak and understand it. In this sense, competence is distinct from the actual linguistic **performance** of any particular speaker, which may be constrained by such nonlinguistic factors as memory, attention, or fatigue. **4.** in law, the capacity to comprehend the nature of a transaction and to assume legal responsibility for one's actions. See also INCOMPETENCE. Also called **competency**. **—competent** adj.

competition n. any performance situation structured in such a way that success depends on performing better than others. **Interpersonal competition** involves individuals striving to outperform each other; **intergroup competition** involves groups competing against other groups; **intragroup competition** involves individuals within a group trying to best each other. Compare COOPERATION. **—compete** vb. **—competitive** adj.

complementary and alternative medicine (CAM) a group of therapies and health care systems that fall outside the realm of conventional Western medical practice. Examples include ACUPUNCTURE, MEDITATION, and the use of certain dietary supplements. Complementary medicine is used as an adjunct to conventional treatment; alternative medicine stands alone and replaces conventional treatment.

completion test a type of test in which the participant is required to supply a missing item, such as a word, number, or symbol.

complex *n*. a group or system of related ideas or impulses that have a common emotional tone and exert a strong but usually unconscious influence on the individual's attitudes and behavior. The term, introduced by Swiss psychoanalyst Carl Jung (1875–1961) to denote the contents of the PERSONAL UNCONSCIOUS, has taken on an almost purely pathological connotation in popular usage, which does not necessarily reflect usage in psychology.

complex cell a neuron in the cerebral cortex that responds to visual stimulation of appropriate contrast, orientation, and direction anywhere in the receptive field. Compare SIMPLE CELL.

complex reaction time see CHOICE REACTION TIME.

compliance *n*. submission to the desires of others, often involving a change in a person's behavior in response to a direct request. A variety of techniques have been developed to enhance compliance with requests. Although some techniques may enhance compliance by producing attitude change, behavioral change is the primary goal of these techniques. —**compliant** *adj*. —**comply** *vb*.

compound reaction time see CHOICE REACTION TIME.

comprehension *n*. the act or capability of understanding something, especially the meaning of a communication. Compare APPREHENSION. —**comprehend** *vb*.

compulsion *n*. a type of behavior (e.g., hand washing, checking) or a mental act (e.g., counting, praying)

engaged in to reduce anxiety or distress. Typically the individual feels driven or compelled to perform the compulsion to reduce the distress associated with an OBSESSION or to prevent a dreaded event or situation. Compulsions may also take the form of rigid or stereotyped acts based on idiosyncratic rules that do not have a rational basis (e.g., having to perform a task in a certain way). Compulsions do not provide pleasure or gratification and are disproportionate or irrelevant to the feared situation they are used to neutralize. See OBSESSIVE-COMPULSIVE DISORDER. —**compulsive** *adj*.

compulsive personality disorder see OBSESSIVE-COMPULSIVE PERSONALITY DISORDER.

computational model any account of cognitive or psychobiological processes that assumes that the human mind functions like a digital computer, specifically in its ability to form representations of events and objects and to carry out complex sequences of operations on these representations.

computed tomography (**CT**) a radiographic technique for quickly producing detailed, three-dimensional images of the brain or other soft tissues. An X-ray beam is passed through the tissue from many different locations, and the different patterns of radiation absorption are analyzed and synthesized by a computer. Also called **computerized axial tomography** (**CAT**); **computerized tomography**. See also MAGNETIC RESONANCE IMAGING.

computer addiction see INTERNET ADDICTION.

computer-assisted instruction (**CAI**) a sophisticated offshoot of programmed learning, in which a computer is used to provide drill and practice, problem solving, simulation, and gaming forms of instruction. It is also useful for relatively individualized tutorial instruction. Also called **computer-assisted learning**.

computerized assessment the process of using a computer to obtain and evaluate psychological information about a person. The computer presents questions or tasks and then makes diagnoses and prognoses based on a comparison of the participant's responses or performance to databases of previously acquired information on many other individuals.

conation *n.* the proactive (as opposed to habitual) part of motivation that connects knowledge, affect, drives, desires, and instincts to behavior. Along with cognition and affect, conation is one of the three traditionally identified components of mind.

concentration *n.* the act of bringing together or focusing, as, for example, bringing one's thought processes to bear on a central problem or subject (see ATTENTION). —**concentrate** *vb.*

concept *n.* an idea that represents a class of objects or events or their properties, such as "cats," "walking," "honesty," "blue," or "fast." —**conceptual** *adj.*

concept formation the process by which a person abstracts a common idea or concept from particular examples, such as learning what dogs are by experience of various different dogs.

concept hierarchy a collection of objects, events, or other items with common properties arranged in a multilevel structure. Concepts on the higher levels have broad meanings, while those at lower levels are more specific. For example, a concept hierarchy of ANXIETY

DISORDERS would place that term on top, with PHOBIAS lower, and specific types of phobia (e.g., CLAUSTROPHOBIA) on the bottom.

conceptual replication see REPLICATION.

concordance *n.* in TWIN STUDIES, the probability that a given trait or disorder in one twin will appear in the other. Evidence for genetic factors in the production of the trait or disorder comes from the comparison of concordance rates between identical and fraternal twins. Compare DISCORDANCE.

concrete operational stage in PIAGETIAN THEORY, the third major stage of cognitive development, occurring approximately from 7 to 12 years of age, in which children can decenter their perception (see DECENTRATION), are less egocentric, and can think logically about physical objects and about specific situations or experiences involving those objects.

concurrent validity the extent of correspondence between two measurements at about the same point in time: specifically, the assessment of one test's validity by comparison of its results with a separate but related measurement, such as a standardized test, at the same point in time.

concussion *n.* mild injury to the brain due to trauma or jarring that temporarily disrupts function and usually involves at least brief unconsciousness.

conditional positive regard an attitude of acceptance and esteem expressed by others that depends on the acceptability of the individual's behavior and the other's personal standards. Conditional regard works against sound psychological development and adjustment in the recipient. Compare UNCONDITIONAL POSITIVE REGARD.

conditional probability the probability that an event will occur given that another event is known to have occurred.

conditioned reinforcement see SECONDARY REINFORCEMENT.

conditioned response (CR) in PAVLOVIAN CONDITIONING, the learned or acquired response to a conditioned stimulus.

conditioned stimulus (CS) a neutral stimulus that is repeatedly presented with an UNCONDITIONED STIMULUS until it acquires the ability to elicit a response that it previously did not. In many (but not all) cases, the response elicited by the conditioned stimulus is similar to that elicited by the unconditioned stimulus. A light, for example, by being repeatedly paired with food (the unconditioned stimulus), eventually comes to elicit the same response as food (i.e., salivation) when presented alone.

conditioned taste aversion the association of the taste of a food or fluid with an aversive stimulus (usually gastrointestinal discomfort or illness) and subsequent avoidance of that particular taste. Conditioned taste aversion challenges traditional theories of associative learning, since very few pairings between the food and illness are needed to produce the effect (often one pairing will suffice), the delay between experiencing the taste and then feeling ill can be relatively long, and the aversion is highly resistant to EXTINCTION.

conditioning *n.* the process by which certain kinds of experience make particular actions more or less likely. See INSTRUMENTAL CONDITIONING; OPERANT CONDITIONING; PAVLOVIAN CONDITIONING.

conditions of worth the state in which an individual considers love and respect to be conditional on meeting the approval of others. This belief derives from the child's sense of being worthy of love on the basis of parental approval: As the individual matures, he or she may continue to feel worthy of affection and respect only when expressing desirable behaviors.

conduct disorder a persistent pattern of behavior that involves violating the basic rights of others and ignoring age-appropriate social standards. Specific behaviors include lying, theft, arson, running away from home, aggression, truancy, burglary, cruelty to animals, and fighting. This disorder is distinguished from OPPOSITIONAL DEFIANT DISORDER by the increased severity of the behaviors and their occurrence independently of an event occasioning opposition.

conduction aphasia a form of APHASIA characterized by difficulty in differentiating speech sounds and repeating them accurately, even though spontaneous articulation may be intact. It is associated with lesions in the ARCUATE FASCICULUS, the tract linking the areas of the brain involved in the interpretation and control of speech.

conduction deafness see DEAFNESS.

cone *n.* see RETINAL CONE.

confabulation *n.* the falsification of memory in which gaps in recall are filled by fabrications that the individual accepts as fact. It is not typically considered to be a conscious attempt to deceive others. Confabulation occurs most frequently in KORSAKOFF'S SYNDROME and to a lesser extent in other conditions associated with organically derived amnesia. —**confabulate** *vb.*

confederate *n.* in an experimental situation, an aide of the experimenter who poses as a participant but whose behavior is rehearsed prior to the experiment. The real participants are sometimes referred to as NAIVE PARTICIPANTS.

confidence interval a range of values (an interval) used for estimating the value of a population parameter from data obtained in a SAMPLE, with a preset, fixed probability that the interval will include the true value of the population parameter being estimated. Most research is done on samples, but it is done in order to draw inferences about the entire relevant population.

confidence level the probability that a CONFIDENCE INTERVAL contains the true value of an experimental variable under investigation. It is expressed as a percentage that indicates the statistical likelihood that the value of the variable obtained using a SAMPLE is an accurate reflection of the actual value in the entire POPULATION. For example, a survey of 100 individuals in a small town of 1,000 people might indicate that 20% of respondents intend to enroll in a distance learning class within the next month. If the confidence level for this research is 95%, this indicates that if the entire town were surveyed then the results obtained would be within 5% of the value obtained with the sample (i.e., anywhere between 16 and 24% of respondents would enroll in a class). In other words, the researcher is 95% certain that his or her results for the sample are accurate for the entire population and thus would be obtained were the research to be repeated with additional samples.

confidentiality *n.* a principle of professional ETHICS requiring providers of mental health care or medical care to limit the disclosure of a patient's identity, his or her condition or treatment, and any data entrusted to professionals during assessment, diagnosis, and treatment. Similar protection is given to research participants and survey respondents against unauthorized access to information they reveal in confidence. **—confidential** *adj.*

configural learning learning to respond to a combination of two or more stimuli paired with an outcome when none of the stimuli presented alone is paired with that outcome. For example, if neither a tone nor a light presented separately is followed by food, but a tone–light combination is followed by food, configural learning has occurred when a conditioned response is elicited by the tone–light combination.

confirmation bias the tendency to gather evidence that confirms preexisting expectations, typically by emphasizing or pursuing supporting evidence while dismissing or failing to seek contradictory evidence.

confirmatory factor analysis one of a set of procedures used in FACTOR ANALYSIS to demonstrate that a group of variables possess a theoretically expected factor structure. In other words, confirmatory factor analysis provides formal statistical tests of a priori hypotheses about the specific underlying (latent) variables thought to explain the data obtained on a set of observed (manifest) variables. Unlike EXPLORATORY FACTOR ANALYSIS, in which all measured variables relate to all latent factors, confirmatory factor analysis imposes explicit restrictions so that the measured variables relate with some (or usually just one) latent factors but do not relate with others.

conflict *n.* the occurrence of mutually antagonistic or opposing forces, including events, behaviors, desires, attitudes, and emotions.

This general term has more specific meanings within different areas of psychology. For example, in psychoanalytic theory it refers to the opposition between incompatible instinctual impulses or between incompatible aspects of the mental structure (i.e., the ID, EGO, and SUPEREGO) that may be a source of NEUROSIS if it results in the use of defense mechanisms other than SUBLIMATION. In interpersonal relations conflict denotes the disagreement, discord, and friction that occur when the actions or beliefs of one or more individuals are unacceptable to and resisted by others.

conformity *n.* the adjustment of one's opinions, judgments, or actions so that they match either (a) the opinions, judgments, or actions of other people or (b) the normative standards of a social group or situation. Conformity includes the temporary COMPLIANCE of individuals, who agree publicly with the group but do not accept its position as their own, as well as the CONVERSION of individuals, who fully adopt the group position.

confound *n.* in an experiment using a FACTORIAL DESIGN, a variable that is conceptually distinct but empirically inseparable from one or more other variables. **Confounding** makes it impossible to differentiate that variable's effects in isolation from its effects in conjunction with other variables. These indistinguishable effects are themselves called **aliases**.

confusion of responsibility the tendency for bystanders to refrain from helping in both emergencies and nonemergencies in order to avoid being blamed by others for causing the problem. This is a contributing factor in the BYSTANDER EFFECT. See also DIFFUSION OF RESPONSIBILITY.

congenital *adj.* denoting a condition or disorder that is present at birth.

congenital adrenal hyperplasia an inherited disorder caused by mutations that encode for enzymes involved in one of the various steps of steroid hormone synthesis in the adrenal gland. These defects result in the absence or decreased synthesis of CORTISOL from its cholesterol precursor and a concomitant abnormal increase in the production of androgens.

congenital defect any abnormality present at birth, regardless of the cause. It may be caused by faulty fetal development (e.g., spina bifida, cleft palate), hereditary factors (e.g., Huntington's disease), chromosomal aberration (e.g., Down syndrome), maternal conditions affecting the developing fetus (e.g., fetal alcohol syndrome), metabolic defects (e.g., phenylketonuria), or injury to the brain before or during birth (e.g., some cases of cerebral palsy).

congruence *n.* in phenomenological personality theory, (a) the need for a therapist to act in accordance with his or her true feelings rather than with a stylized image of a therapist or (b) the conscious integration of an experience into the self. —**congruent** *adj.*

conjunctive task a group task or project that cannot be completed successfully until all members of the group have completed their portion of the job (e.g., a factory assembly line). This means that the speed and quality of the work are determined by the least skilled member. Compare ADDITIVE TASK; COMPENSATORY TASK; DISJUNCTIVE TASK.

connectionism *n.* **1.** an approach that views human cognitive processes in terms of massively parallel cooperative and competitive interactions among large numbers of simple neuronlike computational units. Although each unit exhibits nonlinear spatial and temporal summation, units and connections are not generally to be taken as corresponding directly to individual neurons and synapses. **2.** as used by U.S. psychologist Edward L. Thorndike (1874–1949), the concept that learning involves the acquisition of neural links, or connections, between stimulus and response. **—connectionist** *adj.*

connectionist model any of a class of theories hypothesizing that knowledge is encoded by the connections among representations stored in the brain rather than in the representations themselves. Connectionist models suggest that knowledge is distributed rather than being localized and that it is retrieved through SPREADING ACTIVATION among connections. The connectionist model concept has been extended to artificial intelligence, particularly to its NEURAL NETWORK models of problem solving.

connector neuron see INTERNEURON.

connotative meaning see DENOTATIVE MEANING.

consanguinity *n.* see AFFINITY.

conscience *n.* an individual's sense of right and wrong or of transgression against moral values. In psychoanalysis, conscience is the SUPEREGO, or ethical component of personality, which acts as judge and critic of one's actions and attitudes. More recent biopsychological approaches suggest that the capacity of conscience may be genetically determined, and research on brain damage connects behavioral inhibitions to specific brain regions (e.g., the PREFRONTAL CORTEX). Psychosocial approaches emphasize the

role of conscience in the formation of groups and societies.

conscious 1. (Cs) *n.* in the classical psychoanalytic theory of Austrian psychiatrist Sigmund Freud (1856–1939), the region of the psyche that contains thoughts, feelings, perceptions, and other aspects of mental life currently present in awareness. The content of the conscious is thus inherently transitory and continuously changing. Compare PRECONSCIOUS; UNCONSCIOUS. **2.** *adj.* relating to or marked by awareness or consciousness.

consciousness *n.* any of various subjective states of awareness in which mental contents and activities can be reported. The phenomena that humans report experiencing range from sensory and somatic perception to images, ideas, inner speech, intentions to act, recalled memories, semantics, dreams, hallucinations, emotional feelings, "fringe" feelings (e.g., a sense of knowing), and aspects of cognitive and motor control. Consciousness most often refers to the ordinary waking state, but it may also refer to the state of sleeping or to an ALTERED STATE OF CONSCIOUSNESS.

consensual validation the process by which a therapist helps a client check the accuracy of his or her perception or the results of his or her experience by comparing it with those of others, often in the context of GROUP THERAPY.

consensus *n.* general agreement among the members of a group, especially when making an appraisal or decision.

consent *n.* voluntary assent or approval given by an individual: specifically, permission granted by an individual for medical or psychological treatment, participation in research, or both. Individuals should be fully informed about the treatment or study and its risks and potential benefits (see INFORMED CONSENT).

conservation *n.* the awareness that physical quantities do not change in amount when they are altered in appearance, such as when water is poured from a wide, short beaker into a thin, tall one. According to PIAGETIAN THEORY, children become capable of this mental operation in the CONCRETE OPERATIONAL STAGE. See also REVERSIBILITY.

conservation psychology a relatively new subfield of psychology that seeks to understand the attitudes and behavior of individuals and groups toward the natural environment so as to promote their use of environmentally sustainable practices. Because of the highly diverse categories of behavior being studied, conservation psychologists generally focus on specific actions, such as paper recycling, rather than general tendencies. Although related to ENVIRONMENTAL PSYCHOLOGY, conservation psychology is distinct in its orientation toward protecting ecosystems and preserving resources while ensuring quality of life for humans and other species.

consistency motive the desire to get feedback that confirms what one already believes about one's self. This contributes to maintaining a stable, unchanging SELF-CONCEPT, whether positive or negative. Compare APPRAISAL MOTIVE; SELF-ENHANCEMENT MOTIVE.

consolidation *n.* the biological processes by which a permanent memory is formed following a learning experience. See PERSEVERATION–CONSOLIDATION HYPOTHESIS.

conspecific 1. *adj.* belonging to the same species. **2.** *n.* a member of the same species.

constancy *n.* see PERCEPTUAL CONSTANCY.

constant 1. *n.* a mathematically fixed value: a quantity that is unchangeable under specified conditions. **2.** *adj.* unvarying or continual.

constitution *n.* the basic psychological and physical makeup of an individual, due partly to heredity and partly to life experience and environmental factors. —**constitutional** *adj.*

construal *n.* a person's perception and interpretation of attributes and behavior of the self or others. See also INDEPENDENT SELF-CONSTRUAL; INTERDEPENDENT SELF-CONSTRUAL.

construct *n.* an explanatory model based on empirically verifiable and measurable events or processes—an empirical construct—or on processes inferred from data of this kind but not themselves directly observable—a hypothetical construct. Many of the models used in psychology are hypothetical constructs.

constructionism *n.* see CONSTRUCTIVISM.

constructive memory a form of remembering marked by the use of general knowledge stored in one's memory to construct a more complete and detailed account of an event or experience.

constructive play a form of play in which children manipulate materials in order to create or build objects, for example, making a sand castle or using blocks to build a house.

constructivism *n.* the theoretical perspective that people actively build their perception of the world and interpret objects and events that surround them in terms of what they already know. Thus, their current state of knowledge guides processing, substantially influencing how (and what) new information is acquired. Also called **constructionism**. See also SOCIAL CONSTRUCTIVISM.

construct validity the degree to which a test or instrument is capable of measuring a theoretical construct, trait, or ability (e.g., intelligence).

consultant *n.* a mental health care or medical specialist called upon to provide professional advice or services in terms of diagnosis, treatment, or rehabilitation.

consumer psychology the branch of psychology that specializes in the behavior of individuals as consumers and in the techniques of communicating information to influence consumer decisions to purchase a manufacturer's product. **Consumer psychologists** investigate the reasons and psychological processes underlying behavior in for-profit as well as not-for-profit marketing.

contact comfort the positive effects experienced by infants or young animals when in close contact with soft materials. The term originates from experiments in which young rhesus monkeys exposed both to an artificial cloth mother without a bottle for feeding and to an artificial wire mother with a bottle for feeding spent more time on the cloth mother and, when frightened, were more readily soothed by the presence of the cloth mother than the wire mother.

contact hypothesis the theory that people belonging to one group can become less prejudiced against (and perhaps more favorably disposed toward) members of other groups merely through increased contact with them. It is now thought that greater contact is unlikely to reduce intergroup prejudice unless the people from the different groups are of equal status, are not in

competition with each other, and do not readily categorize the others as very different from themselves.

contagion *n.* in social theory, the spread of behaviors, attitudes, and affect through crowds and other types of social aggregation from one member to another. Early analyses of contagion suggested that it resulted from the heightened suggestibility of members, but subsequent studies have argued that contagion is sustained by relatively mundane interpersonal processes, such as comparison, imitation, SOCIAL FACILITATION, CONFORMITY, and UNIVERSALITY.

contamination *n.* in testing and experimentation, the process of permitting knowledge, expectations, or other factors about the variable under study to influence the collection and interpretation of data about that variable.

content analysis a systematic, quantitative procedure for coding the themes in qualitative material, such as projective-test responses, propaganda, or fiction. For example, content analysis of verbally communicated material (e.g., articles, speeches, films) is done by determining the frequency of specific ideas, concepts, or terms.

content validity the extent to which a test measures a representative sample of the subject matter or behavior under investigation. For example, if a test is designed to survey arithmetic skills at a third-grade level, content validity will indicate how well it represents the range of arithmetic operations possible at that level.

content word in linguistics, a word with an independent lexical meaning, that is, one that can be defined with reference to the physical world or abstract concepts and without reference to any sentence in which the word may appear. Nouns, verbs, adjectives, and many adverbs are considered to be content words. Compare FUNCTION WORD.

context *n.* the conditions or circumstances in which a particular phenomenon occurs, especially as this influences memory, learning, judgment, or other cognitive processes. —**contextual** *adj.*

contiguity *n.* the co-occurrence of stimuli in time or space. Learning an association between two stimuli is generally thought to depend at least partly on the contiguity of those stimuli. —**contiguous** *adj.*

contingencies of self-worth particular areas of life in which people invest their SELF-ESTEEM, such that feedback regarding their standing or abilities in these domains has a crucial impact on their SELF-CONCEPT. Research indicates that people choose to stake their self-esteem in different domains, so that for some people material or professional success is vital to their sense of self-worth, whereas for others this is much less important than being well liked or sexually attractive.

contingency *n.* a conditional, probabilistic relation between two events. When the probability of Event B given Event A is 1.0, a perfect positive contingency is said to exist. When Event A predicts with certainty the absence of Event B, a perfect negative contingency is said to exist. Contingencies may be arranged via dependencies or they may emerge by accident. See also REINFORCEMENT CONTINGENCY.

contingency management in BE-HAVIOR THERAPY, a technique in which a reinforcement, or reward, is given each time the desired behavior is performed. This technique is particularly common in substance abuse treatment.

contingency table a two-dimensional table in which the number of cases that are simultaneously in a given spot in a given row and column of the table are specified. For example, the ages and geographical locations of a sample of individuals applying for a particular job may be displayed in a contingency table, such that there are X number of individuals under 25 from New York City, Y number of individuals under 25 from Los Angeles, Z number of individuals between the ages of 25 and 35 from New York City, and so on.

continuity *n.* the quality or state of being unending or connected into a continuous whole. For example, the traditional concept of continuity of care implies the provision of a full range of uninterrupted medical and mental health care services to a person throughout his or her lifespan, from birth to death, as needed.

continuity hypothesis the assumption that successful DIS-CRIMINATION learning or problem solving results from a progressive, incremental, continuous process of trial and error. Responses that prove unproductive are extinguished, whereas every reinforced response results in an increase in associative strength, thus producing the gradual rise of the learning curve. Problem solving is conceived as a step-by-step learning process in which the correct response is discovered, practiced, and reinforced. Compare DISCONTINUITY HYPOTHESIS.

continuity theory see DISEN-GAGEMENT THEORY.

continuous reinforcement in operant and instrumental conditioning, the REINFORCEMENT of every correct (desired) response.

continuous variable a RANDOM VARIABLE that can take on an infinite number of values; that is, a variable measured on a continuous scale, as opposed to a CATEGORICAL VARIABLE.

contraction *n.* a shortening or tensing of a group of MUSCLE FIBERS.

contralateral *adj.* situated on or affecting the opposite side of the body. For example, motor paralysis occurs on the side of the body contralateral to the side on which a brain lesion is found. Compare IPSILATERAL. —**contralaterally** *adv.*

contrast *n.* **1.** that state in which the differences between one thing, event, or idea and another are emphasized by a comparison of their qualities. This may occur when the stimuli are juxtaposed (simultaneous contrast) or when one immediately follows the other (successive contrast). **2.** in the ANALYSIS OF VARIANCE, a comparison among group means using one DEGREE OF FREEDOM.

contrast sensitivity a measure of spatial RESOLUTION based on an individual's ability to detect subtle differences in light and dark coloring or shading in an object of a fixed size. Detection is affected by the size of contrasting elements and is usually tested using a grating of alternating light and dark bars, being defined by the minimum contrast required to distinguish that there is a bar pattern rather than a uniform screen.

contributing cause a cause that is not sufficient to bring about an end or event but that helps in some way to bring about that end or event. A contributing cause may be a necessary condition or it may influence events more indirectly by affecting other conditions that make the event more likely.

control *n.* **1.** authority, power, or influence over events, behaviors, situations, or people. **2.** the regulation

of all extraneous conditions and variables in an experiment so that any change in the DEPENDENT VARIABLE can be attributed solely to manipulation of the INDEPENDENT VARIABLE. In other words, the results obtained will be due solely to the experimental condition or conditions and not to any other factors.

control group a group of participants in an experiment that are exposed to the **control conditions**, that is, the conditions of the experiment not involving a treatment or exposure to the INDEPENDENT VARIABLE. Compare EXPERIMENTAL GROUP.

control processes those processes that organize the flow of information in an INFORMATION-PROCESSING system.

control theory the idea that behavior is caused by what a person wants and that each person takes actions to achieve those wants, independent of the influence of outside stimuli. This implies responsibility toward and direct determination of one's behavior.

control variable a variable that is purposely not changed during an experiment in order to minimize its effects on the outcome. Because control variables are outside factors related in some way to the other variables under investigation, their influence may potentially distort research results.

conventional antipsychotic see ANTIPSYCHOTIC.

conventional level in KOHLBERG'S THEORY OF MORAL DEVELOPMENT, the intermediate level of moral reasoning, characterized by an individual's identification with and conformity to the expectations and rules of family and society: The individual evaluates actions and determines right and wrong in terms of other people's opinions. This level is divided into two stages: the earlier interpersonal concordance orientation, in which moral behavior is that which obtains approval and pleases others; and the later law-and-order orientation, in which moral behavior is that which respects authority, allows the person to do his or her duty, and maintains the existing social order. Also called **conventional morality**. See also PRECONVENTIONAL LEVEL; POSTCONVENTIONAL LEVEL.

convergence *n.* the rotation of the two eyes inward toward a light source so that the image falls on corresponding points on the foveas. Convergence enables the slightly different images of an object seen by each eye to come together and form a single image.

convergent thinking critical thinking in which an individual uses linear, logical steps to analyze a number of already formulated solutions to a problem to determine the correct one or the one that is most likely to be successful. Compare DIVERGENT THINKING.

conversation analysis in linguistics, see DISCOURSE ANALYSIS.

conversion *n.* **1.** an unconscious process in which anxiety generated by psychological conflicts is transformed into physical symptoms. **2.** actual change in an individual's beliefs, attitudes, or behaviors that occurs as a result of SOCIAL INFLUENCE. Unlike COMPLIANCE, which is outward and temporary, conversion occurs when the targeted individual is personally convinced by a persuasive message or internalizes and accepts as his or her own the beliefs expressed by other group members. Also called **private acceptance**. See also CONFORMITY. **—convert** *vb.*

conversion disorder a SOMATOFORM DISORDER characterized by one or more symptoms or deficits affecting voluntary motor and sensory functioning that suggest a physical disorder but for which there is instead evidence of psychological involvement. These **conversion symptoms** are not intentionally produced or feigned and are not under voluntary control. They include paralysis, loss of voice, blindness, seizures, disturbance in coordination and balance, and loss of pain and touch sensations.

convolution *n.* a folding or twisting, especially of the surface of the brain.

convulsion *n.* an involuntary, generalized, violent muscular contraction, in some cases tonic (contractions without relaxation), in others clonic (alternating contractions and relaxations of skeletal muscles).

Cook's D an index used in REGRESSION ANALYSIS to show the influence of a particular case on the complete set of fitted values. [R. Denis **Cook** (1944–), U.S. statistician]

Coolidge effect increased sexual vigor when an animal or human being mates with multiple partners. The phenomenon is named for U.S. President Calvin Coolidge, alluding to a visit that he and his wife made to a farm where Mrs. Coolidge observed a rooster mating frequently.

cooperation *n.* the process of working together toward the attainment of a goal. This contrasts with COMPETITION, in which an individual's actions in working toward a goal lessen the likelihood of others achieving the same goal. Studies of animals often suggest cooperation, but whether nonhuman animals understand that individuals must act together to reach a common solution or whether they act randomly and occasionally appear to cooperate by chance is still unclear.

—**cooperate** *vb.* —**cooperative** *adj.*

coping *n.* the use of cognitive and behavioral strategies to manage the demands of a situation when these are appraised as taxing or exceeding one's resources or to reduce the negative emotions and conflict caused by stress. See also COPING STRATEGY. —**cope** *vb.*

coping strategy an action, a series of actions, or a thought process used in meeting a stressful or unpleasant situation or in modifying one's reaction to such a situation. Coping strategies typically involve a conscious and direct approach to problems, in contrast to DEFENSE MECHANISMS. See also EMOTION-FOCUSED COPING; PROBLEM-FOCUSED COPING.

coping style the characteristic manner in which an individual confronts and deals with stress, anxiety-provoking situations, or emergencies.

coprolalia *n.* spontaneous, unprovoked, and uncontrollable use of obscene or profane words and expressions. It is a symptom that may be observed in individuals with a variety of neurological disorders, particularly TOURETTE'S DISORDER.

cornea *n.* the transparent part of the outer covering of the eye, through which light first passes. It is continuous laterally with the SCLERA. The cornea provides the primary refractive power of the eye. —**corneal** *adj.*

coronal plane the plane that divides the front (anterior) half of the body or brain from the back (posterior) half.

coronary heart disease a cardiovascular disorder characterized by restricted flow of blood through the coronary arteries supplying the heart muscle. The cause is usually ATHEROSCLEROSIS of the coronary arteries and often leads to fatal myocardial infarction (i.e., death of a section of heart muscle). Also called **coronary artery disease**.

corpus callosum a large tract of nerve fibers running across the LONGITUDINAL FISSURE of the brain and connecting the cerebral hemispheres: It is the principal connection between the two sides of the brain and the largest of the interhemispheric COMMISSURES.

corpus striatum see BASAL GANGLIA.

correlation *n.* the degree of a relationship (usually linear) between two attributes. See NEGATIVE CORRELATION; POSITIVE CORRELATION.

correlational design a research method that attempts to identify and describe the relationship between two variables without directly manipulating them. Correlational designs are often used in clinical and other applied areas of psychology and do not allow for inferences regarding cause and effect; that is, a change in one particular variable employed in the research cannot be said with any certainty to result in a change in the other.

correlation coefficient (symbol: r) a numerical index reflecting the degree of relationship (usually linear) between two attributes scaled so that the value of +1 indicates a perfect positive relationship, −1 a perfect negative relationship, and 0 no relationship. The most commonly used type of correlation coefficient is the PRODUCT–MOMENT CORRELATION.

correlation matrix a square symmetric ARRAY in which the correlation coefficient between the ith and jth variables in a set of variables is displayed in the intersection of the ith row and the jth column of the matrix.

correspondence bias see FUNDA-MENTAL ATTRIBUTION ERROR.

correspondent inference theory a model describing how people form inferences about other people's stable personality characteristics from observing their behaviors. Correspondence between behaviors and traits is more likely to be inferred if the actor is judged to have acted (a) freely, (b) intentionally, (c) in a way that is unusual for someone in the situation, and (d) in a way that does not usually bring rewards or social approval. See also ATTRIBUTION THEORY.

cortex *n.* (*pl.* **cortices**) the outer or superficial layer or layers of a structure, as distinguished from the central core. In mammals, the cortex of a structure is identified with the name of the gland or organ, for example, the CEREBELLAR CORTEX or CEREBRAL CORTEX. Compare MEDULLA. —**cortical** *adj.*

cortical blindness blindness with normal pupillary responses due to complete destruction of the OPTIC RADIATIONS or the STRIATE CORTEX. Typically caused by a stroke affecting the occipital lobe of the brain, cortical blindness can also result from traumatic injury or HYPOXIA.

cortical deafness deafness that is caused by damage to auditory centers in the cerebral cortex of the brain. The peripheral auditory system (which includes the retrocochlear neural pathways terminating in the brainstem) can be intact in this condition.

corticospinal tract see VENTROMEDIAL PATHWAY.

corticosteroid *n.* any of the steroid hormones produced by the adrenal cortex, the outer layer of the ADRENAL GLAND. They include the GLUCOCORTICOIDS (e.g., CORTISOL), which are involved in carbohydrate metabolism; and the MINERALO-CORTICOIDS (e.g., ALDOSTERONE), which have a role in electrolyte balance and sodium retention.

corticotropin *n.* a hormone secreted by the anterior pituitary gland, particularly when a person experiences stress. It stimulates the release of various other hormones (primarily CORTICOSTEROIDS) from the adrenal cortex, the outer layer of the adrenal gland. Also called **adrenocorticotropic hormone (ACTH)**; **adrenocorticotropin**.

cortisol *n.* a major GLUCO-CORTICOID hormone whose activity increases blood sugar levels. Blood levels of cortisol in humans vary according to sleep–wake cycles (being highest around 9:00 a.m. and lowest at midnight) and other factors; for example, they increase with stress and during pregnancy but decrease during diseases of the liver and kidneys.

counseling *n.* professional assistance in coping with personal problems, including emotional, behavioral, vocational, marital, educational, rehabilitation, and life-stage (e.g., retirement) problems. The **counselor** makes use of such techniques as ACTIVE LISTENING, guidance, advice, discussion, clarification, and the administration of tests.

counseling psychology the branch of psychology that specializes in facilitating personal and interpersonal functioning across the life span to improve well-being. The **counseling psychologist** has received professional education and training in one or more areas, such as educational, vocational, employee, aging, personal, marriage, or rehabilitation counseling. In contrast to a clinical psychologist (see CLINICAL PSYCHOLOGY), who usually emphasizes origins of maladaptations, a counseling psychologist emphasizes adaptation, adjustment, and more efficient use of the individual's available resources.

counterbalancing *n.* the process of arranging a series of experimental conditions or treatments in such a way as to minimize the influence of other factors, such as practice or fatigue, on experimental effects. A simple form of counterbalancing would be to administer experimental conditions in the order AB to half the participants and in the order BA to the other half.

counterconditioning *n.* an experimental procedure in which an animal, already conditioned to respond to a stimulus in a particular way, is trained to produce a different response to the same stimulus that is incompatible with the original response. This same principle underlies many of the techniques used in BEHAVIOR THERAPY to eliminate unwanted behavior.

counterculture *n.* a social movement that maintains its own alternative mores and values in opposition to prevailing cultural norms. The term is historically associated with the hippie movement and attendant drug culture of the late 1960s and early 1970s, which rejected such societal norms as the work ethic and the traditional family unit. See also SUBCULTURE.
—**countercultural** *adj.*

counterfactual thinking imagining ways in which events in one's life might have turned out differently. This often involves feelings of regret or disappointment (e.g., *If only I hadn't been so hasty*) but may also involve a sense of relief, as at a narrow escape (e.g., *If I had been standing three feet to the left* …).

countertransference *n.* the therapist's unconscious reactions to the patient and to the patient's TRANSFERENCE. These thoughts and feelings are based on the therapist's own psychological needs and conflicts and may be either unexpressed or revealed through conscious responses to patient behavior. The term was originally used to describe this process in psychoanalysis but has since become part of the common lexicon in other forms of psychodynamic psychotherapy and in other therapies. In CLASSICAL PSYCHOANALYSIS, countertransference is viewed as a hindrance to the analyst's understanding of the patient, but to some modern analysts and therapists it may serve as a source of insight into the patient's impact on other people.

couples therapy therapy in which both partners in a committed relationship are treated at the same time by the same therapist or therapists. Couples therapy is concerned with problems within and between the individuals that affect the relationship. For example, one partner may have an undiagnosed, physiologically based depression that is affecting the relationship, and both partners may have trouble communicating effectively with one another. Couples therapy for married couples is known as **marital therapy**.

covariance *n.* a scale-dependent measure of the relationship between two variables.

covariate *n.* a correlated variable that is often controlled or held constant through the ANALYSIS OF COVARIANCE.

covariation *n.* a relationship between two phenomena (objects or events) such that there is a systematic correlation between variation of the one and variation of the other. Unlike mere co-occurrence, covariation carries a strong presumption that there is a causal link between the covarying phenomena.
—**covary** *vb.*

covert *adj.* **1.** denoting anything that is not directly observable, open to view, or publicly known, either by happenstance or by deliberate design. **2.** hidden. Compare OVERT.

covert sensitization a BEHAVIOR THERAPY technique for reducing an undesired behavior in which the client imagines performing the undesired behavior (e.g., overeating) and then imagines an unpleasant consequence (e.g., vomiting).

CP abbreviation for CEREBRAL PALSY.

CR abbreviation for CONDITIONED RESPONSE.

Cramér's V coefficient (symbol: *V*) a correlation-like index that reflects the ASSOCIATION between two CATEGORICAL VARIABLES. [Carl Harald **Cramér** (1893–1985), Swedish statistician]

cranial nerve any of the 12 pairs of nerves that arise directly from the brain and are distributed mainly to structures in the head and neck. Some of the cranial nerves are sensory, some are motor, and some are mixed (i.e., both sensory and motor). Cranial nerves are designated by Roman numerals, as follows: I, OLFACTORY NERVE; II, OPTIC NERVE; III, OCULOMOTOR NERVE; IV, TROCHLEAR NERVE; V, TRIGEMINAL NERVE; VI, ABDUCENS NERVE; VII, FACIAL NERVE; VIII, VESTIBULOCOCHLEAR NERVE; IX, GLOSSOPHARYNGEAL NERVE; X, VAGUS NERVE; XI, ACCESSORY NERVE; XII, HYPOGLOSSAL NERVE.

creative intelligence in the TRIARCHIC THEORY OF INTELLI-GENCE, the set of skills used to create, invent, discover, explore, imagine, and suppose. This set of skills is alleged to be relatively (although not wholly) distinctive with respect to analytical and practical skills. Compare ANALYTICAL INTELLI-GENCE; PRACTICAL INTELLIGENCE.

creativity *n.* the ability to produce or develop original work, theories, techniques, or thoughts. A creative individual typically displays originality, imagination, and expressiveness, but analyses have failed to ascertain why one individual is more creative than another. See also DIVERGENT THINKING. —**creative** *adj.*

creole *n.* a language that has evolved from profound and prolonged contact between two or more languages and both shares features of the parent languages and evolves altogether novel features. Although typically developing from a PIDGIN, a creole becomes stable over time and will usually have a fully developed grammatical system.

Creutzfeldt–Jakob disease (CJD) a rapidly progressive neurological disease caused by abnormal prion proteins and characterized by DEMENTIA, involuntary muscle movements, muscular incoordination (ataxia), visual disturbances, and seizures. Vacuoles form in the gray matter of the brain and spinal cord, giving it a spongy appearance; the prion is thought to cause misfolding of other proteins, leading to the cellular pathology. Classical CJD occurs sporadically worldwide and typically affects individuals who are middle-aged or older. Variant CJD (vCJD) typically affects younger people, who are believed to have acquired the disease by eating meat or meat products from cattle infected with bovine spongiform encephalopathy. [Hans Gerhard **Creutzfeldt** (1885–1964) and Alfons **Jakob** (1884–1931), German neuropathologists]

criminal responsibility a defendant's ability to formulate a criminal intent at the time of the crime with which he or she is charged, which must be proved in court before the person can be convicted. Criminal responsibility may be excluded for reason of INSANITY or mitigated for a number of other reasons.

crisis *n.* (*pl.* **crises**) **1.** a situation (e.g., a traumatic change) that produces significant cognitive or emotional stress in those involved in it. **2.** a turning point for better or worse in the course of an illness.

crisis intervention 1. the brief ameliorative, rather than specifically curative, use of psychotherapy or counseling to aid individuals, families, and groups who have undergone a highly disruptive experience, such as an unexpected bereavement or a disaster. **2.** psychological intervention provided on a short-term, emergency basis for individuals experiencing mental health crises, such as attempted suicide.

crista (**crysta**) *n.* the structure within the ampulla at the end of each SEMICIRCULAR CANAL that contains hair cells sensitive to the direction and rate of movements of the head.

criterion *n.* (*pl.* **criteria**) a standard against which a judgment, evaluation, or comparisons can be made. An example is a test score or item against which other tests or items can be validated.

criterion group a group tested for traits its members are already known to possess, usually for the purpose of validating a test. For example, a group of children with diagnosed visual disabilities may be given a visual test to assess its VALIDITY as a means of evaluating the presence of visual disabilities.

criterion-referenced testing an approach to testing based on the comparison of a person's performance with an established standard or criterion. The criterion is fixed, that is, each person's score is measured against the same criterion and is not influenced by the performance of others. See NORM-REFERENCED TESTING.

criterion validity an index of how well a test correlates with a criterion, that is, an established standard of comparison. Criterion validity is divided into two types: CONCURRENT VALIDITY and PREDICTIVE VALIDITY.

criterion variable in statistical analysis, a variable to be predicted; that is, a DEPENDENT VARIABLE.

critical flicker frequency (**CFF**) the rate at which a periodic change, or flicker, in an intense visual stimulus fuses into a smooth, continuous stimulus. A similar phenomenon can occur with rapidly changing auditory stimuli. Also called **flicker fusion frequency**.

critical period 1. an early stage in life when an organism is especially open to specific learning, emotional, or socializing experiences that occur as part of normal development and will not recur at a later stage. For example, the first 3 days of life are thought to constitute a critical period for IMPRINTING in ducks, and there may be a critical period for language acquisition in human infants. **2.** in vision, the period of time after birth, varying from weeks (in cats) to months (in humans), in which full, binocular visual stimulation is necessary for the structural and functional maturation of the VISUAL SYSTEM.

critical region in SIGNIFICANCE TESTING, the range of values for a test statistic that leads to rejection of the null hypothesis in favor of the alternative hypothesis. Compare ACCEPTANCE REGION.

critical thinking a form of directed, problem-focused thinking in which the individual tests ideas or possible solutions for errors or drawbacks. It is essential to such activities as examining the validity of a hypothesis or interpreting the meaning of research results.

critical value the value of either end point of the CRITICAL REGION; that is, either of the values of the test statistic above and below which the NULL HYPOTHESIS will be rejected.

Cronbach's alpha an index of INTERNAL CONSISTENCY reliability, that is, the degree to which a set of items that comprise a measurement instrument tap a single, unidimensional construct. Also called **alpha coefficient.** [Lee J. Cronbach (1916–2001), U.S. psychologist]

cross-adaptation *n.* the change in sensitivity to one stimulus caused by adaptation to another.

cross-correlation *n.* a statistical measure of the association between corresponding values from a series of values for two or more variables. A cross-correlation analysis generally is applied to TIME SERIES information and indicates how similar the data sets are to one another.

cross-cultural psychology a branch of psychology that studies similarities and variances in human behavior across different cultures and identifies the different psychological constructs and explanatory models used by these cultures. It may be contrasted with CULTURAL PSYCHOLOGY, which tends to adopt a systemic, within-culture approach.

crossing over in genetics, see RECOMBINATION.

cross-lagged panel design a longitudinal experimental design used to increase the plausibility of causal inference in which two variables, *A* and *B*, are measured at time 1 (A_1, B_1) and at time 2 (A_2, B_2). Comparison of **cross-lagged panel correlations** between A_1B_2 and B_1A_2

may suggest a preponderance of causal influence of *A* over *B* or of *B* over *A*.

cross-modal matching see INTERMODAL MATCHING.

cross-modal perception see INTERSENSORY PERCEPTION.

cross-modal transfer recognition of an object through a sense that differs from the sense through which it was originally encountered.

cross-sectional design an experimental design in which individuals of different ages or developmental levels are directly compared, for example, in a **cross-sectional study** comparing 5-year-olds with 10-year-olds. Compare LONGITUDINAL DESIGN.

cross-sequential design an experimental design in which two or more groups of individuals of different ages are directly compared over a period of time. It is thus a combination of a CROSS-SECTIONAL DESIGN and a LONGITUDINAL DESIGN. For example, a **cross-sequential study** of children's mathematical skills initially might compare a group of 5-year-olds to a group of 10-year-olds, and then subsequently reassess the same children every 6 months for the next 5 years.

cross-tolerance *n.* the potential for a drug to produce the diminished effects of another drug of the same type when tissue tolerance for the effects of the latter substance has developed. Thus, a person with alcohol dependence can substitute a barbiturate or another sedative to prevent withdrawal symptoms, and vice versa. Similarly, cross-tolerance exists among most of the hallucinogens, except marijuana.

cross-validation *n.* a model-evaluation approach in which the VALIDITY of a model is assessed by applying it to new data (i.e., data that were not used in developing the model). For example, a test's validity may be confirmed by administering the same test to a new sample in order to check the correctness of the initial validation. Cross-validation is necessary because chance and other factors may have inflated or biased the original validation.

crowding *n.* psychological tension produced in environments of high population density, especially when individuals feel that the amount of space available to them is insufficient for their needs. Crowding may have a damaging effect on mental health and may result in poor performance of complex tasks, stressor aftereffects, and increased physiological stress. Two key mechanisms underlying crowding are lack of control over social interaction (i.e., privacy) and the deterioration of socially supportive relationships.

crowd psychology 1. the mental and emotional states and processes unique to individuals when they are members of street crowds, mobs, and other such collectives. **2.** the scientific study of these phenomena.

crystallized intelligence the form of intelligence that comprises those abilities, such as vocabulary and cultural knowledge, that are a function of learning and experience in a specific culture. Crystallized intelligence is believed to depend on physiological condition somewhat less than does FLUID INTELLIGENCE and thus may be better sustained in old age.

Cs abbreviation for CONSCIOUS.

CS abbreviation for CONDITIONED STIMULUS.

CSF abbreviation for CEREBRO-SPINAL FLUID.

CT 1. abbreviation for COGNITIVE THERAPY. **2.** abbreviation for COMPUTED TOMOGRAPHY.

CTT abbreviation for CLASSICAL TEST THEORY.

cue *n.* a stimulus that serves to guide behavior, such as a RETRIEVAL CUE.

cue-dependent forgetting forgetting caused by the absence at testing of a stimulus (or cue) that was present when the learning occurred. See also MOOD-DEPENDENT MEMORY; STATE-DEPENDENT LEARNING.

cultural bias the tendency to interpret and judge phenomena in terms of the distinctive values, beliefs, and other characteristics of the society or community to which one belongs. This sometimes leads people to form opinions and make decisions about others in advance of any actual experience with those others (see PREJUDICE). Cultural bias has become a significant concern in many areas, including PSYCHO-METRICS, ERGONOMICS, and CLINICAL PSYCHOLOGY. See also CULTURE-FAIR TEST; CULTURE-FREE TEST.

cultural determinism the theory or premise that individual and group character patterns are produced largely by a given society's economic, social, political, and religious organization. See also DETERMINISM; SOCIAL DETERMIN-ISM.

cultural psychology an interdisciplinary extension of general psychology concerned with those psychological processes that are inherently organized by culture. It is a heterogeneous class of perspectives that focus on explaining how human psychological functions are culturally constituted through various forms of relations between people and their social contexts. It may be contrasted with CROSS-CULTURAL PSYCHOLOGY, which tends to examine multiple cultures in order to identify the similarities and variances among them.

cultural relativism the view that attitudes, behaviors, values, concepts, and achievements must be understood in the light of their own cultural milieu and not judged according to the standards of a different culture. In psychology, the relativist position questions the universal application of psychological theory, research, therapeutic techniques, and clinical approaches, since those used or developed in one culture may not be appropriate or applicable to another. See also RELATIVISM. Compare CULTURAL UNIVERSALISM.

cultural universalism the view that the values, concepts, and behaviors characteristic of diverse cultures can be viewed, understood, and judged according to universal standards. Such a view involves the rejection, at least in part, of CULTURAL RELATIVISM. Also called **cultural absolutism**.

culture *n.* the distinctive customs, values, beliefs, language, and other characteristics of a society or a community. See also COUNTERCULTURE; SUBCULTURE. —**cultural** *adj.*

culture-bound syndrome a pattern of mental illness and abnormal behavior that is unique to a small ethnic or cultural population and does not conform to Western classifications of psychiatric disorders. Culture-bound syndromes include, among others, AMOK, IMU, KORO, LATAH, MAL DE PELEA, MYRIACHIT, PIBLOKTO, SUSTO, VOODOO DEATH, and WINDIGO. Also called **culture-specific syndrome**.

culture-fair test an intelligence test based on common human experience designed to apply across social lines and to permit fair comparisons among people from different cultures. Nonverbal, nonacademic items are used, such as matching identical forms, selecting a design that completes a given series, or drawing human figures. Studies have shown, however, that any test reflects certain cultural norms in some degree, and hence may tend to favor members of certain cultures over members of others.

culture-free test an intelligence test designed to eliminate cultural bias completely by constructing questions that contain either no environmental influences or no environmental influences that reflect any specific culture. However, the creation of such a test is probably impossible, and psychometricians instead generally seek to develop CULTURE-FAIR TESTS.

culture of honor a cultural NORM in a region, nation, or ethnic group prescribing violence as the preferred reaction to an insult or other threat to a person's honor. It has been held to account for regional and national differences in violent crime rates. A related concept is **subculture of violence**, used to explain the relatively high rates of violent crime in certain minority populations in poverty-stricken urban areas.

cumulative record a continuous record to which new data are added. In CONDITIONING, for example, a cumulative record is a graph showing the number of responses over a continuous period of time. It is often used in such contexts to display freely occurring behavior under SCHEDULES OF REINFORCEMENT and provides a direct and continuous indicator of the rate of response.

curvilinear correlation a functional relationship between variables that is not of a straight-line form when depicted graphically.

cutaneous *adj.* relating to or affecting the skin. For example, a cutaneous receptor, such as PACINIAN CORPUSCLE, is a specialized cell in the skin that detects and responds to specific external stimuli.

CVA abbreviation for CEREBROVASCULAR ACCIDENT.

cybernetics *n.* the scientific study of communication and control as applied to machines and living organisms. It includes the study of self-regulation mechanisms, as in thermostats or feedback circuits in the nervous system, as well as transmission and self-correction of information in both computers and human communications. Cybernetics was formerly used to describe research in ARTIFICIAL INTELLIGENCE. —**cybernetic** *adj.*

cyclic AMP (cAMP; cyclic adenosine monophosphate) a SECOND MESSENGER that is involved in the activities of DOPAMINE, NOREPINEPHRINE, and SEROTONIN in transmitting signals at nerve synapses.

cyclic GMP (cGMP; cyclic guanosine monophosphate) a SECOND MESSENGER that is common in neurons receiving signals at synapses.

cyclothymic disorder a MOOD DISORDER characterized by periods of hypomanic symptoms and periods of depressive symptoms that occur over the course of at least 2 years. The number, duration, and severity of these symptoms do not meet the full criteria for a MAJOR DEPRESSIVE EPISODE or a HYPOMANIC EPISODE. It often is considered to be a mild BIPOLAR DISORDER. Also called **cyclothymia**.

cytoarchitecture *n.* the arrangement of cells in organs and tissues, particularly those in the NEOCOR-

TEX. The different types of cortical cells are organized in layers and zones; the number of layers varies in different brain areas, but a typical section of neocortex shows six distinct layers. Differences in cytoarchitecture have been used to divide the neocortex into 50 or more regions, many of which differ in function. The scientific study of the cytoarchitecture of an organ is called **cytoarchitectonics**. See also BRODMANN'S AREA. —**cytoarchitectural** *adj.*

cytochrome oxidase blob a small patch of neurons in the STRIATE CORTEX with greater than background levels of activity of **cytochrome oxidase**, an enzyme in the inner membrane of MITOCHONDRIA that is important in aerobic respiration. Neurons in cytochrome oxidase blobs are sensitive to the wavelength of a visual stimulus. Also called **blob**.

cytokine *n.* any of a variety of small proteins or peptides that are released by cells as signals to those or other cells. Each type stimulates a target cell that has a specific receptor for that cytokine. Cytokines mediate many responses of the IMMUNE SYSTEM, including proliferation and differentiation of lymphocytes, inflammation, allergies, and fever.

cytoplasm *n.* see CELL. —**cytoplasmic** *adj.*

cytoskeleton *n.* an internal framework or "scaffolding" present in all CELLS. Composed of a network of filaments and MICROTUBULES, it maintains the cell shape and plays an important role in cell movement, growth, division, and differentiation, as well as in intracellular transport (e.g., the movement of VESICLES).

Dd

d′ symbol for D PRIME.

DA abbreviation for DOPAMINE.

DALYs acronym for DISABILITY ADJUSTED LIFE YEARS.

dark adaptation the ability of the eye to adjust to conditions of low ilumination by means of an increased sensitivity to light. The bulk of the process takes 30 min and involves expansion of the pupils and retinal alterations, specifically the regeneration of RHODOPSIN and IODOPSIN. Compare LIGHT ADAPTATION.

data *pl. n.* (*sing.* **datum**) observations or measurements, usually quantified and obtained in the course of research.

data analysis the process of applying graphical, statistical, or quantitative techniques to a set of data (observations or measurements) in order to summarize it or to find general patterns.

data collection a systematic gathering of information for research or practical purposes. Examples include mail surveys, interviews, laboratory experiments, and psychological testing.

data mining the automated (computerized) examination of a large set of observations or measurements, particularly as collected in a complex database, in order to discover patterns, correlations, and other regularities that can be used for predictive purposes. Although a relatively new discipline, data mining has become a widely utilized technique within commercial and scientific research. For example, retailers often use data mining to predict the future buying trends of customers or design targeted marketing strategies, while clinicians may use it to determine variables predicting hospitalization in psychological disorders. Data mining incorporates methods from statistics, logic, and ARTIFICIAL INTELLIGENCE.

data set a collection of individual but related observations or measurements considered as a single entity. For example, the entire range of scores obtained from a class of students taking a particular test would constitute a data set.

daydream *n.* a waking fantasy or reverie, in which wishes, expectations, and other potentialities are played out in imagination. Part of the stream of thoughts and images that occupy most of a person's waking hours, daydreams may be unbidden and apparently purposeless or simply fanciful thoughts, whether spontaneous or intentional. Researchers have identified at least three ways in which individuals' daydreaming styles differ: positiveconstructive daydreaming, guilty and fearful daydreaming, and poor attentional control. These styles are posited to reflect the daydreamer's overall tendencies toward positive emotion, negative emotion, and other personality traits.

day hospital a nonresidential facility where individuals with mental disorders receive a full range of treatment and support services dur ing the day and return to their homes at night. Specific service offerings vary across facilities but generally include psychological evaluation, individual and group psychotherapy, social and occupational rehabilitation, and SOMATIC THERAPY. Staff members are multidisciplinary, comprising psychiatrists, psychologists, social workers, vocational counselors, and others.

dB symbol for DECIBEL.

deafferentation *n.* the cutting or removal of sensory neurons or axons that convey information toward a particular nervous system structure (e.g., the olfactory bulb).

deafness *n.* the partial or complete loss of the sense of hearing. The condition may be hereditary or acquired by injury or disease. The major kinds are **conduction deafness**, due to a disruption in sound vibrations before they reach the nerve endings of the inner ear; and **sensorineural deafness**, caused by a failure of the nerves or brain centers associated with the sense of hearing to transmit or interpret properly the impulses from the inner ear. **—deaf** *adj.*

death education learning activities or programs designed to educate people about death, dying, coping with grief, and the various emotional effects of bereavement. Death education is typically provided by certified thanatologists from a wide array of mental and medical health personnel, educators, clergy, and volunteers.

death instinct in psychoanalytic theory, a drive whose aim is the reduction of psychical tension to the lowest possible point, that is, death. It is first directed inward as a self-destructive tendency and is later turned outward in the form of the aggressive instinct. In the dual instinct theory of Austrian psychiatrist Sigmund Freud (1856–1939), the death instinct, or THANATOS, stands opposed to the LIFE INSTINCT, or EROS, and is believed to underlie such behaviors as aggressiveness, sadism, and masochism.

debriefing *n.* the process of giving participants in a completed research project a fuller explanation of the study in which they participated than was possible before or during the research.

decay theory a theory of FORGETTING stating that learned material leaves in the brain a trace or impression that autonomously recedes and disappears unless the material is practiced and used.

deceleration *n.* a decrease in speed of movement or rate of change. Compare ACCELERATION.

decentration *n.* in PIAGETIAN THEORY, the gradual progression of a child away from egocentrism toward a reality shared with others. Decentration includes understanding how others perceive the world, knowing in what ways one's own perceptions differ, and recognizing that people have motivations and feelings different from one's own. It can also be extended to the ability to consider many aspects of a situation, problem, or object, as reflected, for example, in the child's grasp of the concept of CONSERVATION. Also called **decentering**. Compare CENTRATION. **—decenter** *vb.*

deception *n.* any distortion of fact or withholding of fact with the purpose of misleading others. For example, a researcher who has not disclosed the true purpose of an experiment to a participant has engaged in deception, as has an animal that has given a false alarm call that disperses competitors and thus allows him or her to gain more food. **—deceive** *vb.* **—deceptive** *adj.*

decibel (symbol: dB) *n.* a logarithmic unit used to express the ratio of acoustic or electric power (intensity). An increase of 1 bel is a 10-fold increase in intensity; a decibel is one tenth of a bel and is the more commonly used unit, partly because a 1-dB change in intensity is just detectable (approximately and under laboratory conditions).

decision making the cognitive process of choosing between two or more alternatives. Psychologists have adopted two converging strategies to understand decision making: (a) statistical analysis of multiple decisions involving complex tasks and (b) experimental manipulation of simple decisions, looking at elements that recur within these decisions.

decision rule in hypothesis testing, the formal statement of the set of values of the test statistic that will lead to rejection of the NULL HYPOTHESIS.

decision theory a broad class of theories in the quantitative, social, and behavioral sciences that aim to explain the decision-making process and identify optimal ways of arriving at decisions (e.g., under conditions of uncertainty) in such a way that prespecified criteria are met.

declarative memory memory that can be consciously recalled in response to a request to remember. In some theories, declarative memory includes EPISODIC MEMORY and SEMANTIC MEMORY. See also EXPLICIT MEMORY. Compare PROCEDURAL MEMORY.

decoding *n.* in information theory, the process in which a receiver (e.g., the brain or a device, such as a cell phone) translates signals (sounds, writing, gestures, electrical impulses) into meaningful messages. Compare ENCODING. **—decode** *vb.*

decompensation *n.* a breakdown in an individual's DEFENSE MECHANISMS, resulting in progressive loss of normal functioning or worsening of psychiatric symptoms.

deconditioning *n.* a technique in BEHAVIOR THERAPY in which learned responses, such as phobias, are "unlearned" (deconditioned). For example, a person with a phobic reaction to flying might be deconditioned initially by practicing going to the airport when not actually taking a flight and using breathing techniques to control anxiety. See also DESENSITIZATION.

decortication *n.* surgical removal of the outer layer (cortex) of an anatomical structure, especially the outer layer of the CEREBRUM of the brain (i.e., the CEREBRAL CORTEX).

deculturation *n.* the processes, intentional or unintentional, by which traditional cultural beliefs or practices are suppressed or otherwise eliminated as a result of contact with a different, dominant culture. Compare ACCULTURATION. **—deculturate** *vb.*

deduction *n.* **1.** a conclusion derived from formal premises by a valid process of DEDUCTIVE REASONING. **2.** the process of deductive reasoning itself. Compare INDUCTION. **—deductive** *adj.*

deductive reasoning the form of logical reasoning in which a conclusion is shown to follow necessarily from a sequence of premises, the first of which stands for a self-evident truth or agreed-upon data. In the empirical sciences, deductive reasoning underlies the process of deriving predictions from general laws or theories. Compare INDUCTIVE REASONING. See also LOGIC.

deep dyslexia a form of acquired dyslexia characterized by semantic errors (e.g., reading *parrot* as *canary*), difficulties in reading abstract words (e.g., *idea, usual*) and function words (e.g., *the, and*), and an inability to read pronounceable nonwords.

deep processing cognitive processing of a stimulus that focuses on its meaningful properties rather than its perceptual characteristics. It is considered that processing at this semantic level, which usually involves a degree of ELABORATION, produces stronger, longer-lasting memories than SHALLOW PROCESSING.

deep structure in TRANSFORMATIONAL GENERATIVE GRAMMAR, an abstract base form of a sentence in which the logical and grammatical relations between the constituents are made explicit. The deep structure generates the SURFACE STRUCTURE of a sentence through transformations, such as changes in word order or addition or deletion of elements.

Deese paradigm a laboratory memory task used to study false recall. It is based on the report in 1959 that, after presentation of a list of related words (e.g., *snore, rest, dream, awake*), participants mistakenly recalled an unpresented but strongly associated item (e.g., *sleep*). Following renewed research into the technique, it is now generally referred to as the **Deese–Roediger–McDermott paradigm**. [James **Deese** (1921–1999), U.S. psychologist; Henry L. **Roediger** III (1947–) and Kathleen B. **McDermott** (1968–), U.S. cognitive psychologists]

defense mechanism in classical psychoanalytic theory, an unconscious reaction pattern employed by the EGO to protect itself from the anxiety that arises from psychic conflict. Such mechanisms range from mature to immature, depending on how much they distort reality. In more recent psychological theories, defense mechanisms are seen as normal means of coping with everyday problems, but excessive use of any

one, or the use of immature defenses (e.g., DISPLACEMENT or REPRESSION), is still considered pathological. See also AVOIDANCE; DENIAL; PROJECTION; REGRESSION; SUBLIMATION; SUBSTITUTION.

defensive attribution a bias or error in attributing cause for some event such that a perceived threat to oneself is minimized. For example, people might blame an automobile accident on the driver's mistake rather than on a chance occurrence because this attribution lessens their perception that they themselves could be victimized by chance.

deferred imitation imitation of an act minutes, hours, or days after viewing the behavior. Recent research indicates that deferred imitation of simple tasks can be observed in infants late in their 1st year.

deficiency motivation in the HUMANISTIC PSYCHOLOGY of U.S. psychologist Abraham Maslow (1908–1970), the type of motivation operating on the lower four levels of his hierarchy of needs (see MASLOW'S MOTIVATIONAL HIERARCHY). Deficiency motivation is characterized by the striving to correct a deficit that may be physiological or psychological in nature. Compare METAMOTIVATION.

degeneration *n.* deterioration or decline of organs or tissues, especially of neural tissue, to a less functional form. —**degenerate** *vb.*

degradation *n.* in neurophysiology, the process by which neurotransmitter molecules are broken down into inactive metabolites.

degrees of freedom (symbol: *df*; v) the number of elements that are free to vary in a statistical calculation, or the number of scores minus the number of mathematical restrictions. For example, if four individuals have a mean IQ of 100, then there are three degrees of freedom, because knowing three of the IQs determines the fourth IQ.

dehumanization *n.* any process or practice that is thought to reduce human beings to the level of nonhuman animals or mechanisms, especially by denying them autonomy, individuality, and a sense of dignity. —**dehumanize** *vb.*

deindividuation *n.* an experiential state characterized by loss of self-awareness, altered perceptions, and a reduction of inner restraints that results in the performance of unusual, atypical behavior. It can be caused by a number of factors, such as a sense of anonymity or of submersion in a group.

deinstitutionalization *n.* the joint process of moving people with developmental or psychiatric disabilities from structured institutional facilities to their home communities and developing comprehensive community-based residential, day, vocational, clinical, and supportive services to address their needs. —**deinstitutionalize** *vb.*

déjà vu the feeling that a new event has already been experienced or that the same scene has been witnessed before. [French: "already seen"]

delay conditioning in PAVLOVIAN CONDITIONING, a procedure in which the CONDITIONED STIMULUS is presented, and remains present, for a fixed period (the delay) before the UNCONDITIONED STIMULUS is introduced. Compare SIMULTANEOUS CONDITIONING.

delayed matching to sample a procedure in which the participant is shown initially one stimulus as a sample (the study phase) and subsequently, after a variable interval, a pair of stimuli (the test phase), the task being to choose the stimulus in

the test phase that matches the sample presented in the study phase. In **delayed nonmatching to sample**, the participant must choose the stimulus that was not presented in the study phase.

delayed response a response that occurs some time after its DISCRIMINATIVE STIMULUS has been removed. The most common **delayed response task** for nonhuman animals is one in which the animal is required to recall the location of a reward after a delay period has elapsed.

delinquency *n.* behavior violating social rules or conventions. The term is often used to denote the misbehavior of children or adolescents. —**delinquent** *adj., n.*

delirium *n.* a state of disturbed consciousness in which attention cannot be sustained, the environment is misperceived, and the stream of thought is disordered. The individual may experience such symptoms as disorientation, memory impairment, disturbance in language, hallucinations, illusions, and misinterpretation of sounds or sights. Delirium may be caused by a variety of conditions, including infections, cerebral tumors, substance intoxication and withdrawal, head trauma, and seizures.

delirium tremens (DTs) a potentially fatal alcohol withdrawal syndrome involving extreme agitation and anxiety, fearfulness, paranoia, visual and tactile hallucinations, tremors, sweating, and increased heart rate, body temperature, and blood pressure.

delta wave the lowest frequency BRAIN WAVE recorded in electroencephalography. Delta waves are large, regular-shaped waves that have a frequency of 1–3 Hz. They are associated with deep, often dreamless, sleep (**delta-wave sleep**). Also called **delta rhythm**.

delusion *n.* an improbable, often highly personal, idea or belief system, not endorsed by one's culture or subculture, that is maintained with conviction in spite of irrationality or evidence to the contrary. Common types include DELUSIONS OF GRANDEUR, DELUSIONS OF PERSECUTION, and DELUSIONS OF REFERENCE.

delusional disorder any one of a group of psychotic disorders with the essential feature of one or more delusions regarding situations that could conceivably occur in real life (e.g., being followed, poisoned, infected, deceived by one's government, etc.).

delusion of grandeur the false attribution to the self of great ability, knowledge, importance or worth, identity, prestige, power, accomplishment, or the like.

delusion of persecution the false conviction that others are threatening or conspiring against one.

delusion of reference the false conviction of a person that the actions of others and events occurring in the external world have some special meaning or significance (typically negative) to him or her.

demand characteristics in an experiment or research project, cues that may influence or bias participants' behavior, for example, by suggesting the outcome or response that the experimenter expects or desires.

dementia *n.* a generalized, pervasive deterioration of cognitive functions, such as memory, language, and EXECUTIVE FUNCTIONS, due to any of various causes but commonly including Alzheimer's disease, Pick's disease, and cerebrovascular disease. The loss of

intellectual abilities is severe enough to interfere with an individual's daily functioning and social and occupational activity. When occurring after the age of 65 it is termed **senile dementia** and when appearing before 65 it is called **presenile dementia**. However, dementia should not be confused with age-associated memory impairment, which has a much less deleterious impact on day-to-day functioning.

dementia of the Alzheimer's type another name for ALZHEIMER'S DISEASE.

dementia praecox the original, now obsolete, name for SCHIZOPHRENIA, first used in 1896 by German psychiatrist Emil Kraepelin (1856–1926) and reflecting the belief that the symptoms of the disorder arose in adolescence or before and involved incurable degeneration. Swiss psychiatrist Eugen Bleuler (1857–1939) questioned both of these views and in 1911 renamed the disorder schizophrenia.

demography *n.* the statistical study of human populations in regard to various factors and characteristics, including geographical distribution, sex and age distribution, size, structure, and growth trends. —**demographer** *n.* —**demographic** *adj.*

dendrite *n.* a branching, threadlike extension of the CELL BODY that increases the receptive surface of a neuron. —**dendritic** *adj.*

dendritic spine a mushroom-shaped outgrowth along the DENDRITE of a neuron, which forms a SYNAPSE with the axon terminals of neighboring neurons.

denial *n.* a DEFENSE MECHANISM in which unpleasant thoughts, feelings, wishes, or events are ignored or excluded from conscious awareness. It may take such forms as refusal to acknowledge the reality of a terminal illness, a financial problem, an addiction, or a partner's infidelity. Denial is an unconscious process that functions to resolve emotional conflict or reduce anxiety. —**deny** *vb.*

denotative meaning the objective or literal meaning of a word or phrase as opposed to its **connotative meaning**, which includes the various ideas and emotions that it suggests within a particular culture. So, for example, the word *father* denotes "male parent" but may connote a range of ideas involving protection, authority, and love.

density *n.* a measure of the amount of physical space per individual. High density can produce crowding, a psychological state of needing more space. Interior indices of density (e.g., people per room) are consistently related to negative psychological consequences, whereas external indices (e.g., people per square mile) are not. —**dense** *adj.*

dentate gyrus a strip of gray matter that connects the HIPPOCAMPUS with the ENTORHINAL CORTEX.

deoxyribonucleic acid see DNA.

dependence *n.* **1.** a state in which assistance from others is intuitively expected or actively sought for emotional or financial support, protection, security, or daily care. The dependent person leans on others for guidance, decision making, and nurturance. Whereas some degree of dependence is natural in interpersonal relations, excessive, inappropriate, or misdirected reliance on others is often a focus of psychological treatment. **2.** see SUBSTANCE DEPENDENCE. **3.** in OPERANT CONDITIONING, a causal relation between a response and a consequence, which results in a CONTINGENCY. Also called **dependency.** —**dependent** *adj.*

dependency ratio the percentage of a population that is not working for pay: a measure of the portion of a population that is composed of people who are too young to work or who have retired. The dependency ratio is often defined as the number of individuals aged below 15 or above 64 divided by the number of individuals aged 15 to 64.

dependent personality disorder a personality disorder manifested in a long-term pattern of passively allowing others to take responsibility for major areas of life and of subordinating personal needs to the needs of others.

dependent variable (**DV**) the "outcome" variable in an experiment that is observed to occur or change after the occurrence or variation of the INDEPENDENT VARIABLE.

depersonalization *n.* a state of mind in which the self appears unreal. Individuals feel estranged from themselves and usually from the external world, and thoughts and experiences have a distant, dreamlike character.

depersonalization disorder a DISSOCIATIVE DISORDER characterized by one or more episodes of DEPERSONALIZATION severe enough to impair social and occupational functioning. Onset of depersonalization is rapid and accompanied by a feeling that one's extremities are changed in size and, in some cases, a feeling that the external world is unreal (DEREALIZATION).

depolarization *n.* a reduction in the electric potential across the plasma membrane of a cell, especially a neuron, such that the inner surface of the membrane becomes less negative in relation to the outer surface. Depolarization occurs when the membrane is stimulated and sodium ions (Na^+) flow into the cell. If the stimulus intensity exceeds the excitatory threshold of the neuron an ACTION POTENTIAL is created and a nerve impulse propagated. Compare HYPERPOLARIZATION.

depressant *n.* any agent that diminishes or retards any function or activity of a body system or organ, especially a CENTRAL NERVOUS SYSTEM depressant.

depression *n.* **1.** a fluctuation in normal mood ranging from unhappiness and discontent to an extreme feeling of sadness, pessimism, and despondency. **2.** in psychiatry, any of the DEPRESSIVE DISORDERS. **—depressed** *adj.*

depressive disorder any of the MOOD DISORDERS that typically have sadness as one of their symptoms, such as DYSTHYMIC DISORDER and MAJOR DEPRESSIVE DISORDER.

depressive personality disorder a recently classified and still controversial personality disorder characterized by glumness, pessimism, a lack of joy, the inability to experience pleasure, and a low sense of self-worth and self-esteem.

deprivation *n.* the removal, denial, or unavailability of something needed or desired. In CONDITIONING, for example, deprivation refers to a reduction of access to or intake of a REINFORCER. **—deprive** *vb.*

depth cue any of a variety of means used to inform the visual system about the depth of a target or its distance from the observer. MONOCULAR CUES require only one eye whereas BINOCULAR CUES require integration of information from the two eyes.

depth interview an interview designed to reveal deep-seated feelings, attitudes, opinions, and motives by encouraging the individual to express himself or herself freely without fear of disapproval or concern about the interviewer's reactions. Such interviews may be

conducted, for example, in counseling and as part of qualitative market research. They tend to be relatively lengthy, unstructured, one-on-one conversations.

depth-of-processing hypothesis the theory that the strength of memory is dependent on the degree of cognitive processing the material receives. Depth has been defined variously as ELABORATION, amount of cognitive effort expended, and the distinctiveness of the MEMORY TRACE formed. This theory is an expanded empirical investigation of the LEVELS-OF-PROCESSING MODEL OF MEMORY.

depth perception awareness of three-dimensionality, solidity, and the distance between the observer and the object. Depth perception is achieved through such cues as visual ACCOMMODATION, BINOCULAR DISPARITY, and CONVERGENCE. See also VISUAL CLIFF.

depth psychology a general approach to psychology and psychotherapy that focuses on unconscious mental processes as the source of emotional disturbance and symptoms, as well as personality, attitudes, creativity, and lifestyle. A typical example is CLASSICAL PSYCHOANALYSIS, but others include the ANALYTIC PSYCHOLOGY of Swiss psychiatrist and psychoanalyst Carl Jung (1875–1961) and the INDIVIDUAL PSYCHOLOGY of Austrian psychiatrist Alfred Adler (1870–1937).

depth therapy any form of psychotherapy, brief or extended, that involves identifying and working through unconscious conflicts and experiences that underlie and interfere with behavior and adjustment. Compare SURFACE THERAPY.

derealization *n.* a state characterized by a sense of unreality; that is, an alteration in the perception of external reality so that it seems strange or unreal ("This can't be happening"), often due to trauma or stress. It may also occur as a feature of SCHIZOPHRENIA or of certain DISSOCIATIVE DISORDERS. See also DEPERSONALIZATION.

dermatome *n.* an area of skin that is innervated primarily by fibers from the dorsal root of a particular SPINAL NERVE.

descriptive norm see SOCIAL NORM.

descriptive statistic a numerical index used to describe (summarize) a particular feature of the data, such as a MEAN or STANDARD DEVIATION.

descriptive study a research method in which the primary goal is to reveal patterns and illustrate connections in the phenomena under investigation, without manipulating variables or seeking to establish cause and effect. For example, a survey undertaken to ascertain the political party preferences of a group of voters would be a descriptive study because it is intended simply to identify attitudes rather than systematically analyze influencing factors.

desensitization *n.* a reduction in emotional or physical reactivity to stimuli that is achieved by such means as gaining insight into its nature or origin or the use of DECONDITIONING techniques.

determinism *n.* the philosophical position that all events, physical or mental, are the necessary results of antecedent causes or other entities or forces. Determinism, which requires that both the past and the future are fixed, manifests itself in psychology as the position that all human behaviors result from specific efficient causal antecedents, such as biological structures or processes, environmental conditions, or past experience. The relationships

between these antecedents and the behaviors they produce can be described by generalizations much like the laws that describe regularities in nature. Determinism contrasts with belief in FREE WILL, which implies that individuals can choose to act in some ways independent of antecedent events and conditions. Those who advocate free-will positions often adopt a position of SOFT DETERMINISM, which holds that free will and responsibility are compatible with determinism. Others hold that free will is illusory, a position known as HARD DETERMINISM. Of contemporary psychological theories, BEHAVIORISM takes most clearly a hard determinist position. Compare INDETERMINISM. See also CAUSALITY. **—determinist** *adj., n.* **—deterministic** *adj.*

detoxification *n.* a therapeutic procedure, popularly known as **detox**, that reduces or eliminates toxic substances in the body, particularly as related to intoxication by or withdrawal from drugs or alcohol.

development *n.* the progressive series of changes in structure, function, and behavior patterns that occur over the life span of a human being or other organism. **—developmental** *adj.*

developmental coordination disorder a motor skills disorder characterized by performance in activities that require motor coordination substantially below that expected given the child's chronological age and measured intelligence. Significant impairment of academic performance or daily living activities is also observed. However, the difficulties are not due to mental retardation or a physical deficit.

developmental disability a developmental level or status that is attributable to a cognitive or physical impairment, or both, originating before the age of 22. Such an impairment is likely to continue indefinitely and results in substantial functional or adaptive limitations. Examples of developmental disabilities include mental retardation, autistic disorder, and learning disorders. Also called **developmental disorder**.

developmental norm the typical skills and expected level of achievement associated with a particular stage of development.

developmental psychology the branch of psychology that studies the changes—physical, mental, and behavioral—that occur from conception to old age.

developmental psychopathology the scientific study of the origins and progression of psychological disorders as related to the typical processes of human growth and maturation. Central to this field is the belief that studying departures from developmental NORMS will enhance understanding of those norms, which will in turn enhance the conceptualization and treatment of mental illness.

developmental systems approach the view that development is the result of bidirectional interaction between all levels of biological and experiential variables, from the genetic through the cultural.

developmental task any of the fundamental physical, social, intellectual, and emotional achievements and abilities that must be acquired at each stage of life for normal and healthy development.

developmental theory any theory based on the continuity of human development and the importance of early experiences in shaping the personality. Examples are the psychoanalytic theory of PSYCHOSEXUAL DEVELOPMENT,

ERIKSON'S EIGHT STAGES OF DEVELOPMENT, learning theories that stress early conditioning, and role theories that focus on the gradual acquisition of different roles in life.

deviation *n.* a significant departure or difference. This conceptually broad term has a variety of applications in psychology and related fields but most commonly refers to behavior that is significantly different from the accepted standard or norm, or to the arithmetical difference between one of a set of values and some fixed amount, generally the mean of the set (see STANDARD DEVIATION) or the value predicted by a model.

deviation IQ see IQ.

deviation score a RAW SCORE subtracted from the mean, indicating the value of the score relative to the mean.

df symbol for DEGREES OF FREEDOM.

diagnosis (Dx) *n.* (*pl.* **diagnoses**) **1.** the process of identifying and determining the nature of a disease or disorder by its signs and symptoms, through the use of assessment techniques (e.g., tests and examinations) and other available evidence. **2.** the classification of individuals on the basis of a disease, disorder, abnormality, or set of characteristics. Psychological diagnoses have been codified for professional use, notably in the DSM–IV–TR. —**diagnostic** *adj.*

Diagnostic and Statistical Manual of Mental Disorders see DSM–IV–TR.

diagnostic test any examination or assessment measure that may help reveal the nature and source of an individual's physical, mental, or behavioral problems or anomalies.

dialect *n.* a variety of a language that is associated with a particular geographical region, social class, or ethnic group and has its own characteristic words, grammatical forms, and pronunciation. Dialects of a language are generally mutually intelligible. Compare ACCENT; REGISTER. —**dialectal** *adj.*

dialectical behavior therapy a flexible, stage-based therapy that combines principles of BEHAVIOR THERAPY, COGNITIVE BEHAVIOR THERAPY, and MINDFULNESS. Dialectical behavior therapy concurrently promotes acceptance and change, especially with difficult-to-treat patients.

diary method a technique for compiling detailed data about an individual who is being observed or studied by having the individual record his or her daily behavior and activities.

diaschisis *n.* a loss or deficiency of function in brain regions surrounding or connected to an area of localized damage.

diathesis *n.* a susceptibility to acquiring (not inheriting) certain diseases or disorders.

diathesis–stress model the theory that mental and physical disorders develop from a predisposition for that illness (diathesis) combined with stressful conditions that play a precipitating or facilitating role.

dichotic listening the process of receiving different auditory messages presented simultaneously to each ear. Listeners experience two streams of sound, each localized at the ear to which it is presented, and are able to focus on the message from one ear while ignoring the message from the other ear.

dichotomous thinking the tendency to think in terms of bipolar opposites, that is, in terms of the best and worst, without accepting the possibilities that lie between these two extremes. This is sometimes thought to be a risk factor for MAJOR DEPRESSIVE DISORDER.

dichotomous variable a variable that can have only two values to designate membership in one of two possible categories, for example, female versus male.

dichromatism *n.* partial color blindness in which the eye contains only two types of cone PHOTOPIGMENT instead of the typical three: Lack of the third pigment leads to confusion between certain colors. Red–green color blindness is the most common, whereas the blue–green variety is relatively rare. Another type, yellow–blue, has been proposed but its existence has yet to be firmly established. See also ACHROMATISM; MONOCHROMATISM; TRICHROMATISM. —**dichromatic** *adj.*

diencephalon *n.* the posterior part of the FOREBRAIN that includes the THALAMUS, EPITHALAMUS, and HYPOTHALAMUS. —**diencephalic** *adj.*

difference score an index of dissimilarity or change over time, reflecting the degree of discrepancy in the measurement of a construct or attribute on two separate occasions.

difference threshold the smallest difference between two stimuli that can be consistently and accurately detected on 50% of trials. Also called **difference limen (DL); just noticeable difference (JND; jnd)**. See also WEBER'S LAW.

differential diagnosis 1. the process of determining which of two or more diseases or disorders with overlapping symptoms a particular patient has. **2.** the distinction between two or more similar conditions by identifying critical symptoms present in one but not the other.

differential psychology the

branch of psychology that studies the nature, magnitude, causes, and consequences of psychological differences between individuals and groups, as well as the methods for assessing these differences.

differentiation *n.* **1.** sensory discrimination of differences among stimuli. For example, wines that at first taste identical may, with experience, be readily distinguished. **2.** a conditioning process in which a limited range of behavior types is achieved through selective REINFORCEMENT of only some forms of behavior. **3.** in embryology, the process whereby cells of a developing embryo undergo the changes necessary to become specialized in structure and function.

diffusion of responsibility the lessening of responsibility often experienced by individuals in groups and social collectives. This has been proposed as one reason for the BYSTANDER EFFECT; in groups the obligation to intervene is shared by all onlookers rather than focused on any specific individual. See also CONFUSION OF RESPONSIBILITY.

digit span the number of random digits from a series that a person can recall following a single auditory presentation. A span of 5-9 digits is considered typical for an adult.

diglossia *n.* the situation in which two varieties of a language coexist and have distinct social functions within a community; these are usually characterized by high (H) and low (L) uses, H being associated with formality and literacy, and L with everyday colloquial usage.

dimorphism *n.* the existence among members of the same species of two distinct forms that differ in one or more characteristics, such as size, shape, or color. **—dimorphic** *adj.*

diploid *adj.* denoting or possessing the normal number of chromosomes, which in humans is 46: 22 HOMOLOGOUS pairs of AUTOSOMES plus the male or female set of XY or XX SEX CHROMOSOMES. Compare HAPLOID.

directional hypothesis a prediction regarding the direction in which one experimental group will differ from another.

directional test see ONE-TAILED TEST.

directive therapy an approach to psychotherapy in which the therapeutic process is directed along lines considered relevant by the therapist. Directive therapy is based on the assumption that the professional training and experience of the therapist equip him or her to manage the therapeutic process and to guide the client's behavior. Therapy is considered to progress along primarily intellectual lines in contrast to the approaches of PSYCHODYNAMIC PSYCHOTHERAPY, which emphasizes unconscious motivation and affective dynamics.

direct replication see REPLICATION.

disability *n.* a lasting physical or mental impairment that significantly interferes with an individual's ability to function in one or more central life activities, such as self-care, ambulation, communication, social interaction, sexual expression, or employment. For example, an individual who cannot see has visual disability. See also HANDICAP. **—disabled** *adj.*

disability adjusted life years (DALYs) a measure of the impact of disease or injury on the length and quality of a person's life. It takes into account the potential loss of years due to premature mortality and the value of years lived with disability. One DALY represents one lost year of "healthy" life.

D

discontinuity effect the markedly greater competitiveness of intergroup interactions relative to the competitiveness of interactions involving individuals.

discontinuity hypothesis the viewpoint that emphasizes the role of sudden insight and perceptual reorganization in successful DISCRIMINATION learning and problem solving. According to this view, a correct answer is only recognized when its relation to the issue as a whole is discovered. Compare CONTINUITY HYPOTHESIS.

discordance *n.* in TWIN STUDIES, dissimilarity between a pair of twins with respect to a particular trait or disease. Compare CONCORDANCE. **—discordant** *adj.*

discourse *n.* the areas of written, spoken, and signed communication, whether formal (debate) or informal (conversation). The term is most often used in LINGUISTICS, where **discourse analysts** focus on both the study of LANGUAGE (sentences, speech acts, and lexicons) as well as the rhetoric, meanings, and strategies that underlie social interactions.

discourse analysis the study of linguistic structures that extend beyond the single sentence, such as conversations, narratives, or written arguments. Discourse analysis is particularly concerned with the ways in which a sequence of two or more sentences can produce meanings that are different from or additional to any found in the sentences considered separately. The norms and expectations that govern conversation are a major concern of discourse analysis, as is the structure of conversational language generally.

discovery learning learning that occurs through solving problems, by formulating and testing hypotheses, and in actual experience and manipulation in attempting solutions.

discrete variable a variable that takes on only a relatively small number of distinct values. Compare CONTINUOUS VARIABLE.

discriminant analysis a MULTIVARIATE statistical method that combines information from a set of predictor variables in order to allow maximal discrimination among a set of predefined groups.

discriminant function any of a range of statistical techniques to situate an item that could belong to any of two or more variables in the correct set, with minimal probability of error.

discrimination *n.* **1.** the ability to distinguish between stimuli or objects that differ quantitatively or qualitatively from one another. In conditioning, this meaning is extended to include as well the ability to respond in different ways in the presence of such different stimuli. **2.** differential treatment of the members of different ethnic, religious, national, or other groups. Discrimination is usually the behavioral manifestation of PREJUDICE and therefore involves negative, hostile, and injurious treatment of the members of rejected groups. **—discriminate** *vb.*

discrimination training a procedure in which an OPERANT RESPONSE is reinforced in the presence of a particular stimulus but not in the absence of that stimulus. For example, a rat's lever-press response might be reinforced when a stimulus light is on but not when the light is off. This rat will eventually learn to press the lever only when the light is on.

discriminative stimulus (symbol: S^D) in OPERANT CONDITIONING, a stimulus that increases the probability of a response because of a previous history of differential REINFORCEMENT in the presence of that stimulus. For example, if a pigeon's key pecks are reinforced when the key is illuminated red, but not when the key is green, the red stimulus will come to serve as an S^D and the pigeon will learn to peck only when the key is red.

disease model any of several theories concerning the causes and course of a pathological condition or process.

disenfranchised grief grief that society limits, does not expect, or may not allow a person to express. Examples include the grief of parents for stillborn babies and of teachers for the death of students. Disenfranchised grief may isolate the bereaved individual from others and thus impede recovery. See also GRIEF COUNSELING; GRIEFWORK; MOURNING.

disengagement *n.* the act of withdrawing from an attachment or relationship or, more generally, from an unpleasant situation. —**disengaged** *adj.*

disengagement theory a theory proposing that old age involves a gradual withdrawal of the individual from society and of society from the individual. According to this theory, those happiest in old age have turned their attention inward toward the self and away from involvement in the outside world. Empirical research has shown, however, that this mutual withdrawal is not an inevitable component of old age and that a **continuity theory** of aging is most likely, in which older people are happiest when they are able to maintain their preferred level of social involvement. Compare ACTIVITY THEORY.

disgust *n.* a strong aversion, for example, to the taste, smell, or touch of something deemed revolting, or toward a person or behavior deemed morally repugnant. —**disgusting** *adj.*

dishabituation *n.* the reappearance or enhancement of a habituated response (i.e., one that has been weakened following repeated exposure to the evoking stimulus) due to the presentation of a new stimulus. It is a useful method for investigating perception in nonverbal individuals or animals. Compare HABITUATION.

disinhibition *n.* diminution or loss of the normal control exerted by the cerebral cortex, resulting in poorly controlled or poorly restrained emotions or actions.

disintegration *n.* a breakup or severe disorganization of some structure or system of functioning.

disjunctive task a group task or project, such as solving a complex problem, that is completed when a single solution, decision, or group member's recommendation is adopted by the group. This means that the group's performance tends to be determined by the most skilled member. Compare ADDITIVE TASK; COMPENSATORY TASK; CONJUNCTIVE TASK.

dismissive attachment an adult attachment style that combines a positive INTERNAL WORKING MODEL OF ATTACHMENT of oneself, characterized by a view of oneself as competent and worthy of love, and a negative internal working model of attachment of others, characterized by one's view that others are untrustworthy or undependable. Individuals with dismissive attachment are presumed to discount the importance of close relationships and to maintain rigid self-sufficiency. Compare FEARFUL ATTACHMENT; PREOCCUPIED ATTACHMENT; SECURE ATTACHMENT.

disorder of written expression a LEARNING DISORDER in which writing skills are substantially below those expected, given the person's chronological age, formal education experience, and measured intelligence. The writing difficulties significantly interfere with academic achievement and activities of daily living that require writing skills.

disorganization *n.* loss or disruption of orderly or systematic structure or functioning.

disorganized attachment a form of INSECURE ATTACHMENT in which infants show no coherent or consistent behavior during separation from and reunion with their parent.

disorganized schizophrenia a subtype of schizophrenia characterized primarily by random and fragmented speech and behavior and by flat or inappropriate affect. Also called **hebephrenia.**

disorientation *n.* a state of impaired ability to identify oneself or to locate oneself in relation to time, place, or other aspects of one's surroundings. Long-term disorientation can be characteristic of disorders; temporary disorientation can be caused by alcohol or drugs or can occur in situations of acute stress. —**disoriented** *adj.*

dispersion *n.* the degree to which a batch of scores deviate from the mean. Also called **spread**.

displaced aggression see AGGRESSION.

displacement *n.* the transfer of feelings or behavior from their original object to another person or thing. In psychoanalytic theory, displacement is considered to be a DEFENSE MECHANISM in which the individual discharges tensions associated with, for example, hostility and fear by taking them out on a neutral, nonthreatening or less threatening target. Thus, an angry child might hurt a sibling instead of

attacking the father; a frustrated employee might criticize his or her spouse instead of the boss; or a person who fears his or her own hostile impulses might transfer that fear to knives, guns, or other objects that might be used as a weapon. —**displace** *vb.*

display *n.* more or less stereotyped actions (i.e., actions repeated with little variation) that bring about a response in another individual: an integral part of animal communication. Display behavior may be verbal or nonverbal, usually involving stimulation of the visual or auditory senses. It may include body language that would convey a message of courtship to a member of the opposite sex (e.g., a show of plumage or color) or a suggestion that would be interpreted by an opponent as threatening (e.g., bared teeth or hissing noises).

display rule a socially learned standard that regulates the expression of emotion. Display rules vary from culture to culture; for example, the expression of anger may be considered appropriate in some cultures but not in others.

disposition *n.* a recurrent behavioral or affective tendency that distinguishes an individual from others.

dispositional attribution the ascription of one's own or another's actions, an event, or an outcome to internal or psychological causes specific to the person concerned, such as moods, attitudes, decisions and judgments, abilities, or effort. Also called **internal attribution**. Compare SITUATIONAL ATTRIBUTION.

dissociation *n.* an unconscious DEFENSE MECHANISM in which conflicting impulses are kept apart or threatening ideas and feelings are separated from the rest of the psyche.

dissociative amnesia a DISSOCIATIVE DISORDER characterized by failure to recall important information about one's personal experiences, usually of a traumatic or stressful nature, that is too extensive to be explained by normal forgetfulness. Recovery of memory often occurs spontaneously within a few hours and is usually connected with removal from the traumatic circumstances with which the amnesia was associated.

dissociative disorder any of a group of disorders characterized by a sudden, gradual, transient, or chronic disruption in the normal integrative functions of consciousness, memory, or perception of the environment. Such disruption may last for minutes or years, depending on the type of disorder. Included in this category are DISSOCIATIVE AMNESIA, DISSOCIATIVE FUGUE, DISSOCIATIVE IDENTITY DISORDER, and DEPERSONALIZATION DISORDER.

dissociative fugue a DISSOCIATIVE DISORDER in which the individual suddenly and unexpectedly travels away from home or a customary place of daily activities and is unable to recall some or all of his or her past. Symptoms also include either confusion about personal identity or assumption of a new identity. The fugue state can last from hours to months, and there may be no memory of travel once the individual is brought back to the prefugue state.

dissociative identity disorder a DISSOCIATIVE DISORDER characterized by the presence in one individual of two or more distinct identities or personality states that each recurrently take control of the individual's behavior. It is typically associated with severe physical and sexual abuse, especially during childhood. Research suggests that there may be a hereditary component.

dissonance *n.* see COGNITIVE DISSONANCE.

distal *adj.* **1.** situated or directed toward the periphery of the body or toward the end of a limb. **2.** remote from or mostly distantly related to the point of reference or origin. Compare PROXIMAL.

distal stimulus in perception, the actual object in the environment that stimulates or acts on a sense organ. Compare PROXIMAL STIMULUS.

distance cue any of the auditory or visual cues that enable an individual to judge the distance of the source of a stimulus. Auditory distance cues include intensity of familiar sounds (e.g., voices), intensity differences between the ears, and changes in spectral content. In vision, distance cues include the size of familiar objects and ACCOMMODATION.

distress *n.* the negative stress response, involving excessive levels of stimulation: a type of stress that results from being overwhelmed by demands, losses, or perceived threats. It has a detrimental effect by generating physical and psychological maladaptation and posing serious health risks for individuals. This generally is the intended meaning of the word STRESS. Compare EUSTRESS. —**distressing** *adj.*

distributed cognition a model for intelligent problem solving in which either the input information comes from separated and independent sources or the processing of this input information takes place across autonomous computational devices.

distributed practice a learning procedure in which practice periods for a particular activity or to improve recall of specific material are separated by regular, lengthy rest periods or periods of practicing

D

different activities or studying other material. In many learning situations, distributed practice is found to be more effective than MASSED PRACTICE.

distribution *n.* the relation between the values that a variable may take and the relative number of cases taking on each value. A distribution may be simply an empirical description of that relationship or a mathematical (probabilistic) specification of the relationship.

distribution-free test a test of statistical significance that makes relatively few, if any, assumptions about the underlying distribution of scores. See NONPARAMETRIC STATISTICS.

distributive justice the belief that rules can be changed and punishments and rewards distributed according to relative standards, specifically according to equality and equity. Distributive justice makes allowances for subjective considerations, personal circumstances, and motive. Compare IMMANENT JUSTICE.

disulfiram *n.* a drug used as an aversive agent in managing alcohol abuse or dependence. Disulfiram inhibits the activity of acetaldehyde dehydrogenase, an enzyme responsible for the metabolism of alcohol (ethanol) in the liver. Consumption of alcohol following administration of disulfiram results in accumulation of acetaldehyde, a toxic metabolic product of ethanol, with such unpleasant effects as nausea, vomiting, sweating, headache, a fast heart rate, and palpitations. U.S. trade name: Antabuse.

diurnal *adj.* **1.** daily; that is, recurring every 24 hours. **2.** occurring or active during daylight hours. Compare NOCTURNAL. **—diurnality** *n.*

divergence *n.* the rotation of the two eyes outward when shifting fixation from a nearby target object to one that is far away. **—divergent** *adj.*

divergent thinking creative thinking in which an individual solves a problem or reaches a decision using strategies that deviate from commonly used or previously taught strategies. This term is often used synonymously with LATERAL THINKING. Compare CONVERGENT THINKING.

diversity *n.* the wide range of variation of living organisms in an ecosystem. When describing people and population groups, diversity can include such factors as age, gender, sexual orientation, race, ethnicity, and religion, as well as education, livelihood, and marital status. Many organizations have **diversity training** programs to help employees appreciate and deal effectively with cultural and other differences among people.

divided attention attention to two or more channels of information at the same time, so that two or more tasks may be performed concurrently. Divided attention can occur through just one sense (e.g., hearing), or two or more senses (e.g., hearing and vision) may be engaged in the process.

dizygotic twins (DZ twins) twins, of the same or different sexes, that have developed from two separate ova fertilized by two separate sperm. DZ twins are genetically as much alike as ordinary full siblings born separately. On average, DZ twins are approximately half as genetically similar to one another as MONOZYGOTIC TWINS. Also called **fraternal twins**.

DNA *d*eoxyribo*n*ucleic *a*cid: one of the two types of nucleic acid found in living organisms, which is the principal carrier of genetic information in chromosomes. Certain segments of the DNA molecules constitute the organism's genes, with each gene specifying the manufacture of a particular protein or ribosome. Structurally, DNA consists of two intertwined, helically coiled strands of nucleotides—the double helix. The nucleotides each contain one of four bases: adenine, guanine, cytosine, or thymine. Each base forms hydrogen bonds with the adjacent base on the other, sister strand, producing consecutive base pairs arranged rather like the "rungs" on a helical ladder. Because of DNA's ability to conserve its base sequence when replicating, the genetic instructions it carries are also conserved. See also RNA.

DNR abbreviation for do not resuscitate. See INFORMED CONSENT.

dogmatism *n.* a personality trait characterized by the tendency to act in a blindly certain, assertive, and authoritative manner in accord with a strongly held set of beliefs that are presumed to be resistant to change. These belief systems contain elements that are isolated from one another and thus may contradict one another. Dogmatic people tend to be intolerant of those who hold different beliefs. —**dogmatic** *adj.*

domestic violence any action by a person that causes physical harm to one or more members of his or her family unit. For example, it can involve battering of one partner by another, violence against children by a parent, or violence against elders by younger family members.

dominance *n.* **1.** the exercise of major influence or control over others. In nonhuman animals, dominance ranks are often thought to be linear, with a clear ordering from most to least dominant, but may also be dependent (i.e., based on kin or age relationships) or governed by coalitions in which some subordinate individuals can outrank more dominant ones by acting to-

gether. **2.** the tendency for one hemisphere of the brain to exert greater influence than the other over certain functions, such as language or handedness. The two hemispheres contribute differently to many functions; researchers therefore use the term HEMISPHERIC LATERALIZATION in preference to dominance. **3.** in genetics, the ability of one allele to determine the PHENOTYPE of a HETEROZYGOUS individual. See DOMINANT ALLELE. —**dominant** *adj.*

dominance hierarchy 1. in social psychology, a system of stable linear variations in prestige, status, and authority among group members. It defines who gives orders and who carries them out. **2.** any ordering of motives, needs, or other psychological or physical responses based on priority or importance. An example is MASLOW'S MOTIVATIONAL HIERARCHY.

dominant allele the version of a gene (see ALLELE) whose effects are manifest in preference to another version of the same gene (the RECESSIVE ALLELE) when both are present in the same cell. Hence, the trait determined by a dominant allele (the **dominant trait**) is apparent even when the allele is carried on only one of a pair of HOMOLOGOUS chromosomes.

door-in-the-face technique a two-step procedure for enhancing COMPLIANCE in which an extreme initial request is presented immediately before the more moderate target request. Rejection of the initial request makes people more likely to accept the target request than would have been the case if the latter had been presented on its own. See also FOOT-IN-THE-DOOR TECHNIQUE; LOW-BALL TECHNIQUE; THAT'S-NOT-ALL TECHNIQUE.

dopa (DOPA) *n.* 3,4-*d*ihydroxy-*p*henyl*a*lanine: an amino acid that is

D

a precursor to DOPAMINE and other catecholamines.

dopamine (DA) *n.* a CATECHOL-AMINE neurotransmitter that has an important role in motor behavior and is implicated in numerous mental conditions. For example, destruction of the DOPAMINERGIC neurons in the SUBSTANTIA NIGRA is responsible for the symptoms of Parkinson's disease (e.g., rigidity, tremor), and blockade of the actions of dopamine in other brain regions accounts for the therapeutic activities of antischizophrenic drugs. Dopamine is synthesized from the dietary amino acid tyrosine and may be further metabolized to form norepinephrine and epinephrine, respectively.

dopamine hypothesis the influential theory that schizophrenia is caused by an excess of dopamine in the brain, due either to an overproduction of dopamine or a deficiency of the enzyme needed to convert dopamine to norepinephrine (adrenaline). There is some supporting pharmacological and biochemical evidence for this hypothesis, and it is still widely discussed and promoted, particularly in a revised form that postulates the involvement in schizophrenia of both an increased mesolimbic and a decreased prefrontal dopaminergic activity. See also GLUTAMATE HYPOTHESIS.

dopaminergic *adj.* responding to, releasing, or otherwise involving dopamine. For example, a **dopaminergic neuron** is any neuron in the brain or other parts of the central nervous system for which dopamine serves as the principal neurotransmitter. Three major tracts of dopamine-containing neurons are classically described: the mesolimbic–mesocortical tract, in which excess dopamine activity is hypothesized to be associated with positive and negative symptoms of schizophrenia; the nigrostriatal tract, which is involved in motor functions and Parkinson's disease; and the tuberoinfundibular pathway, a local circuit in the hypothalamus that is involved in the regulation of the pituitary hormone prolactin.

Doppler effect the apparent increase or decrease in wavelength or frequency observed when a source of electromagnetic radiation or sound approaches or recedes from the observer or listener, producing a change in hue or pitch. The **total Doppler effect** may result from motion of both the observer or listener and the source. [Christian Andreas **Doppler** (1803–1853), Austrian mathematician]

dorsal *adj.* denoting the hind region or the back surface of the body. In reference to the latter, this term sometimes is used interchangeably with POSTERIOR. Compare VENTRAL. —**dorsally** *adv.*

dorsal column any of various tracts of sensory nerve fibers that run through the white matter of the SPINAL CORD on its dorsal (back) side.

dorsal horn either of the upper regions of the H-shaped pattern formed by the GRAY MATTER in the central portion of the spinal cord. The dorsal horns extend toward the dorsal roots and mainly serve sensory mechanisms. Compare VENTRAL HORN.

dorsal root any of the SPINAL ROOTS that convey sensory nerve fibers and enter the spinal cord on the back surface of each side. Compare VENTRAL ROOT.

dorsal stream a series of specialized visual regions in the cerebral cortex of the brain that originate in the STRIATE CORTEX (primary visual cortex) of the occipital lobe and project forward and upward into the parietal lobe. Known informally as the "where" or "how" pathway, it is involved in processing object motion and location in space. Compare VENTRAL STREAM.

dorsolateral *adj.* located both dorsally (toward the back) and laterally (toward the side). —**dorsolaterally** *adv.*

dorsolateral prefrontal cortex a region of the PREFRONTAL CORTEX involved in WORKING MEMORY and attentional control. Damage to this region in humans results in an inability to select task-relevant information and to shift attention based on external cues.

dorsoventral *adj.* oriented or directed from the back (dorsal) region of the body to the front (ventral) region. Compare VENTRODORSAL. —**dorsoventrally** *adv.*

dose–response relationship a principle relating the potency of a drug to the efficacy of that drug in affecting a target symptom or organ system. **Potency** refers to the amount of a drug necessary to produce the desired effect; **efficacy** refers to the drug's ability to act at a target receptor or organ to produce the desired effect. Dose–response curves may be graded, suggesting a continuous relationship between dose and effect, or quantal, where the desired effect is an either–or phenomenon, such as prevention of arrhythmias.

double bind a situation in which an individual receives contradictory messages from another person or from two different people. For example, a parent may respond negatively when his or her child approaches or attempts to engage in affectionate behavior, but then, when the child turns away or tries to leave, reaches out to encourage the child to return. Double-binding

communication was once considered a causative factor in schizophrenia.

double blind see BLIND.

double dissociation a research process for demonstrating the action of two separable psychological or biological systems, such as differentiating between types of memory or the function of brain areas. One experimental variable is found to affect one of the systems, whereas a second variable affects the other. The differentiating variables may be task-related, pharmacological, neurological, or individual differences.

double standard the hypocritical belief that a code of behavior is permissible for one group or individual but not for another.

Down syndrome a disorder characterized by an extra chromosome 21 and by particular facial features and below-average brain size and weight. Affected individuals usually have mild to severe mental retardation, and muscular movements tend to be slow, clumsy, and uncoordinated. Lifespan is reduced compared to the general population, and affected individuals typically show early onset of ALZHEIMER'S DISEASE. Down syndrome is one of the most common organic causes of mental retardation. [described in 1866 by John Langdon Haydon **Down** (1828–1896), British physician]

d prime (symbol: d′) a measure of an individual's ability to detect signals; more specifically, a measure of sensitivity or discriminability derived from SIGNAL DETECTION THEORY that is unaffected by response biases. It is the difference (in standard deviation units) between the means of the NOISE and signal+noise distributions. A value of d′ = 3 is close to perfect performance; a value of d′ = 0 is chance ("guessing") performance.

dream *n.* a mental state that occurs in sleep and is characterized by a rich array of sensory, motor, emotional, and cognitive experiences. Dreams occur most often, but not exclusively, during periods of REM SLEEP. They are characterized by (a) vivid imagery, especially visual imagery, and a strong sense of movement; (b) intense emotion, especially fear, elation, or anger; (c) delusional acceptance of the dream as a waking reality; and (d) discontinuity in time and space and incongruity of character and plot. Despite the vivid intensity of dreams, it can be difficult to remember them to any extent unless promptly awakened from REM sleep, but even then much content cannot be accurately retrieved. Diverse theories about the significance of dreams and the process of dream production have arisen from varied sources throughout history. These range from the suggestion of Greek physician Hippocrates (c. 460–c. 377 BCE) that dreams provide early evidence of disease, to the interpretation by Austrian psychiatrist Sigmund Freud (1856–1939) of dreams as a struggle in which the part of the mind representing social strictures (the SUPEREGO) plays out a conflict with the sexual impulses (the LIBIDO) while the rational part of the mind (the EGO) is at rest, and scientific study of dreaming as a neurocognitive process, a recent product of which is the ACTIVATION–SYNTHESIS HYPOTHESIS. —**dreamlike** *adj.* —**dreamy** *adj.*

dream analysis a technique in which the content of dreams is interpreted to reveal underlying motivations or symbolic meanings and representations (i.e., LATENT CONTENT). Also called **dream interpretation**.

dream-work *n.* in psychoanalytic theory, the transformation of the LATENT CONTENT of a dream into the MANIFEST CONTENT experienced by the dreamer. This transformation is effected by such processes as SYMBOLISM and DISPLACEMENT.

drive *n.* **1.** a generalized state of readiness precipitating or motivating an activity or course of action. Drive is hypothetical in nature, usually created by deprivation of a needed substance (e.g., food), the presence of negative stimuli (e.g., pain, cold), or the occurrence of negative events. **2.** in the psychoanalytic theory of Austrian psychiatrist Sigmund Freud (1856–1939), a concept used to understand the relationship between the psyche and the soma (mind and body); drive is conceived as having a somatic source but creating a psychic effect. Freud identified two separate drives as emerging from somatic sources: LIBIDO and AGGRESSION. See also MOTIVATION.

drive-reduction theory a theory of learning in which the goal of motivated behavior is a reduction of a drive state. It is assumed that all motivated behavior arises from drives, stemming from a disruption in homeostasis, and that responses that lead to reduction of those drives tend to be reinforced or strengthened.

drug *n.* any substance, other than food, that influences motor, sensory, cognitive, or other bodily processes. Drugs generally are administered for experimental, diagnostic, or treatment purposes but also tend to be used recreationally to achieve particular effects.

drug abuse see SUBSTANCE ABUSE.

drug addiction see SUBSTANCE DEPENDENCE.

drug dependence see SUBSTANCE DEPENDENCE.

drug therapy see PHARMA-COTHERAPY.

drug tolerance see TOLERANCE.

drug withdrawal see SUBSTANCE WITHDRAWAL.

DSM–IV–TR the text revision of the fourth edition of the *Diagnostic and Statistical Manual of Mental Disorders*, prepared by the American Psychiatric Association and published in 2000. The classification presents descriptions of diagnostic categories without favoring any particular theory of etiology. It is largely modeled on the INTERNATIONAL CLASSIFICATION OF DISEASES (9th edition, 1978), developed by the World Health Organization, but contains greater detail and recent changes, as well as a method of coding on different AXES.

DTs abbreviation for DELIRIUM TREMENS.

dual coding theory the theory that linguistic input can be represented in memory in both verbal and visual formats. Concrete words that readily call to mind a picture, such as *table* or *horse*, are remembered better than abstract words, such as *honesty* or *conscience*, which do not readily call to mind a picture, because the concrete words are stored in two codes rather than one.

dualism *n.* the position that reality consists of two separate substances, defined by French philosopher René Descartes (1596–1650) as thinking substance (mind) and extended substance (matter). In the context of the MIND–BODY PROBLEM, dualism is the position that the mind and the body constitute two separate realms or substances. Dualistic positions raise the question of how mind and body interact in thought and behavior. Compare MONISM. See also CARTESIAN DUALISM. **—dualist** *adj., n.* **—dualistic** *adj.*

dual process theory of color vision see OPPONENT PROCESS THEORY OF COLOR VISION.

dual-store model of memory the concept that memory is a two-stage process, comprising SHORT-TERM MEMORY, in which information is retained for a few seconds, and LONG-TERM MEMORY, which permits the retention of information for hours to many years. Also called **dual memory theory**.

dual trace hypothesis a restatement of the PERSEVERATION–CONSOLIDATION HYPOTHESIS of memory formation specifying that short-term memory is represented neurally by activity in reverberating circuits and that stabilization of these circuits leads to permanent synaptic change, reflecting the formation of long-term memory. See HEBBIAN SYNAPSE.

dummy variable coding a method of assigning numerical values (often 0 and 1) to a CATEGORICAL VARIABLE in such a way that the variable reflects class membership.

Dunnett's multiple comparison test a method for comparing all groups with a single control group mean in such a way that the SIGNIFICANCE LEVEL for the set of comparisons is controlled at α (the criterion value). [Charles W. **Dunnett** (1921–   ), Canadian statistician]

Dunn's multiple comparison test a method for comparing the means of samples from *k* populations that is based on the BONFERRONI CORRECTION.

durable power of attorney see ADVANCE DIRECTIVE.

dura mater see MENINGES.

DV abbreviation for DEPENDENT VARIABLE.

dwarfism *n.* a condition of under-developed body structure due to a developmental defect, hormonal or nutritional deficiencies, or diseases. Some forms of dwarfism, such as that due to thyroid-hormone deficiency, are associated with mental retardation.

Dx abbreviation for DIAGNOSIS.

dyad (diad) *n.* a pair of individuals in an interpersonal situation. **—dyadic** *adj.*

dynamic formulation the ongoing attempt to organize the clinical material elicited about a client's behavior, traits, attitudes, and symptoms into a structure that helps the therapist understand the client and plan his or her treatment more effectively.

dynamic psychology a theory of psychology emphasizing causation and motivation in relation to behavior, specifically the stimulus–organism–response chain in which the stimulus–response relationship is regarded as the mechanism of behavior and the drives of the organism are the mediating variable.

dynamic psychotherapy see PSYCHODYNAMIC PSYCHOTHERAPY.

dynamic systems theory a theory that attempts to explain behavior and personality in terms of constantly changing, self-organizing interactions among multiple organismic and environmental factors that operate on multiple timescales and multiple levels of analysis.

dynamometry *n.* the measurement of force expended or power, especially muscular effort or strength of humans or animals. A **dynamometer** usually consists of a spring that can be compressed by the force applied. **—dynamometric** *adj.*

dysarthria *n.* any of a group of motor speech disorders caused by

muscular impairment originating in the central or peripheral nervous system. Respiration, articulation, phonation, resonance, and prosody may be affected. There are four main types: dyskinetic, spastic, peripheral, and mixed. **—dysarthric** *adj.*

dyscalculia *n.* an impaired ability to perform simple arithmetic operations that results from a congenital deficit. It is a developmental condition, whereas ACALCULIA is acquired.

dysexecutive syndrome a collection of symptoms that involve impaired executive control of actions, caused by damage to the frontal lobes of the brain. Individuals have difficulty in initiating and switching actions and organizing behavior.

dysfunction *n.* any impairment, disturbance, or deficiency in behavior or operation. **—dysfunctional** *adj.*

dysgraphia *n.* see AGRAPHIA. **—dysgraphic** *adj.*

dyslexia *n.* a neurologically based disorder manifested as severe difficulties in reading, resulting from impairment in the ability to make connections between written letters and their sounds. It can be either acquired (in which case it often is referred to as ALEXIA) or developmental, is independent of intellectual ability, and is unrelated to disorders of speech and vision that may also be present. Investigators have proposed various subtypes of dyslexia but there is no universally accepted system of classification. **—dyslexic** *adj.*

dyslogia *n.* see ALOGIA.

dysmenorrhea *n.* difficult or painful menstruation. **—dysmenorrheic** *adj.*

dyspareunia *n.* painful sexual intercourse.

dysphoria *n.* a mood characterized by generalized discontent and agitation. **—dysphoric** *adj.*

dysrhythmia *n.* any rhythmic abnormality, as might be detected in speech or in brain waves.

dyssomnia *n.* any of various sleep disorders marked by abnormalities in the amount, quality, or timing of sleep.

dysthymia *n.* any depressed mood

that is mild or moderate in severity. **—dysthymic** *adj.*

dysthymic disorder a DEPRESSIVE DISORDER characterized by a depressed mood for most of the day, occurring more days than not, that persists for at least 2 years. It is distinguished from MAJOR DEPRESSIVE DISORDER in that the symptoms are less severe but more enduring.

DZ twins abbreviation for DIZYGOTIC TWINS.

Ee

ear *n.* the organ of hearing and balance. In humans and other mammals the ear is divided into external, middle, and inner sections. The PINNA of the EXTERNAL EAR collects sounds that are then funneled through the EXTERNAL AUDITORY MEATUS to the TYMPANIC MEMBRANE. The sounds are vibrations of air molecules that cause the tympanic membrane to vibrate, which in turn vibrates the OSSICLES, three tiny bones in the MIDDLE EAR. The motion of the last of these bones produces pressure waves in the fluid-filled COCHLEA of the INNER EAR. The motion of the fluid in the cochlea is converted by specialized receptors called HAIR CELLS into neural signals that are sent to the brain by the AUDITORY NERVE.

eardrum *n.* see TYMPANIC MEMBRANE.

early intervention a collection of specialized services provided to children from birth to 3 years of age with identified conditions placing them at risk of developmental disability or with evident signs of developmental delay. Services are designed to minimize the impact of the infant's or toddler's condition, and in addition to stimulatory, social, therapeutic, and treatment programs may include family training, screening, assessment, or health care.

early-selection theory any theory of attention proposing that selection of stimuli for in-depth analysis occurs early in the processing stream, prior to stimulus identification. According to early-selection theory, unattended stimuli receive only a slight degree of processing that does not encompass meaning, whereas attended stimuli proceed through a significant degree of deep, meaningful analysis. Compare LATE-SELECTION THEORY.

eating disorder any disorder characterized primarily by a pathological disturbance of attitudes and behaviors related to food, such as ANOREXIA NERVOSA, BULIMIA NERVOSA, and BINGE-EATING DISORDER.

EBP abbreviation for EVIDENCE-BASED PRACTICE.

ECG abbreviation for ELECTROCARDIOGRAM.

echoic memory the retention of auditory information for a brief period (2–3 s) after the end of the stimulus.

echolalia *n.* mechanical repetition of words and phrases uttered by another individual. It is often a symptom of a neurological or developmental disorder, particular catatonic schizophrenia or autism.

echolocation *n.* the ability to judge the direction and distance of objects from reflected echoes made by acoustic signals. For example, both bats and marine mammals (e.g., dolphins) can locate objects by emitting high-pitched sounds that are reflected from features of the physical environment and prey objects.

echopraxia *n.* mechanical repetition of another person's movements or gestures. It is often a symptom of a neurological disorder, particularly catatonic schizophrenia.

eclecticism *n.* a theoretical or practical approach that blends, or attempts to blend, diverse conceptual formulations or techniques into an integrated approach. —**eclectic** *adj.*

ecological niche the function or position of an organism or a population within a physical and biological environment.

ecological perception an organism's detection of the AFFORDANCES and INVARIANCES within its natural, real-world environment, as mediated and guided by the organism's immersion in and movement through that environment.

ecological systems theory an evolving body of theory and research concerned with the processes and conditions that govern the course of human development in the actual environments in which human beings live. Generally, ecological systems theory accords equal importance to the concept of environment as a context for development and to the role of biopsychological characteristics of the individual person. The current paradigm is now referred to as the BIOECOLOGICAL MODEL.

ecological validity the degree to which research results are representative of conditions in the wider world. For example, psychological research carried out exclusively among university students might have a low ecological validity when applied to the population as a whole.

ecology *n.* the study of relationships between organisms and their physical and social environments. —**ecological** *adj.* —**ecologist** *n.*

Ecstasy *n.* the popular name for MDMA.

ECT abbreviation for ELECTRO-CONVULSIVE THERAPY.

edema *n.* an excess accumulation of fluid in body cells, organs, or cavities. —**edematous** *adj.*

educational psychology a branch of psychology dealing with the application of psychological principles and theories to a broad spectrum of teaching, training, and learning issues in educational settings.

EE abbreviation for EXPRESSED EMOTION.

EEG abbreviation for ELECTRO-ENCEPHALOGRAPHY or electro-encephalogram.

effective stimulus see FUNCTIONAL STIMULUS.

effect size the magnitude of an effect (influence of independent variables) in a study. It is often an indicator of the strength of a relationship, the magnitude of mean differences among several groups, or the like.

efferent *adj.* conducting or conveying away from a central point. For example, **efferent nerve fibers** conduct impulses away from the brain or spinal cord. Compare AFFERENT.

efficacy *n.* in pharmacology, see DOSE–RESPONSE RELATIONSHIP.

effortful processing mental activity that requires deliberation and control and involves a sense of effort, or overcoming resistance. Compare AUTOMATICITY.

effort justification a phenomenon whereby people come to evaluate a particular task or activity more favorably when it involves something that is difficult or unpleasant. Because expending effort to perform a useless or unenjoyable

E

task, or experiencing unpleasant consequences in doing this, is cognitively inconsistent (see COGNITIVE DISSONANCE), people are assumed to shift their evaluations of the task in a positive direction to restore consistency.

ego *n.* **1.** the SELF, particularly the conscious sense of self (Latin, "I"). In its popular and quasi-technical sense, ego refers to all the psychological phenomena and processes that are related to the self and that comprise the individual's attitudes, values, and concerns. **2.** in psychoanalytic theory, the component of the personality that deals with the external world and its practical demands. More specifically, the ego enables the individual to perceive, reason, solve problems, test reality, and adjust the instinctual impulses of the ID to the behests of the SUPEREGO.

ego analysis psychoanalytic techniques directed toward discovering the strengths and weaknesses of the EGO and uncovering its defenses against unacceptable impulses. Ego analysis is a short form of psychoanalysis: It does not attempt to penetrate to the ultimate origin of impulses and repressions. See also EGO STRENGTH; EGO WEAKNESS.

egocentric speech speech in which there is no attempt to exchange thoughts or take into account another person's point of view.

egocentrism *n.* **1.** the tendency to emphasize one's personal needs and focus on one's individual concerns. Also called **egocentricity**. See also IDIOCENTRIC. Compare SOCIOCENTRISM. **2.** in PIAGETIAN THEORY, the tendency to perceive the situation from one's own perspective, believing that others see things from the same point of view as oneself. —**egocentric** *adj.*

ego defense in psychoanalytic theory, protection of the EGO from anxiety arising from threatening impulses and conflicts as well as external threats through the use of DEFENSE MECHANISMS.

ego-ideal *n.* in psychoanalytic theory, the part of the EGO that is the repository of positive identifications with parental goals and values that the individual genuinely admires and wishes to emulate, such as integrity and loyalty, and which acts as a model of how he or she wishes to be. In his later theorizing, Austrian psychoanalyst Sigmund Freud (1856–1939) incorporated the ego-ideal into the concept of the SUPEREGO.

egoism *n.* a personality characteristic marked by selfishness and behavior based on self-interest with disregard for the needs of others. See also EGOTISM. —**egoistic** *adj.*

egoistic suicide a type of suicide associated with an extreme sense of alienation. Lacking significant attachments to family members and others, the person withdraws from society and comes to feel his or her life is meaningless.

ego psychology in psychoanalysis, an approach that emphasizes the functions of the EGO in controlling impulses and dealing with the external environment. This is in contrast to ID PSYCHOLOGY, which focuses on the primitive instincts of sex and hostility.

ego strength in psychoanalytic theory, the ability of the EGO to maintain an effective balance between the inner impulses of the ID, the SUPEREGO, and outer reality. An individual with a strong ego is thus one who is able to tolerate frustration and stress, postpone gratification, modify selfish desires when necessary, and resolve internal conflicts and emotional problems before they lead to NEUROSIS. Compare EGO WEAKNESS.

egotism *n.* excessive conceit or excessive preoccupation with one's own importance. See also EGOISM. **—egotistic** *adj.*

ego weakness in psychoanalytic theory, the inability of the EGO to control impulses and tolerate frustration, disappointment, or stress. The individual with a weak ego is thus one who suffers from anxiety and conflicts, makes excessive use of DEFENSE MECHANISMS or uses immature defense mechanisms, and is likely to develop neurotic symptoms. Compare EGO STRENGTH.

eidetic image a clear, specific, high-quality mental image of a visual scene that is retained for a period (seconds to minutes) after the event. As with a real-time image, an eidetic image can be reviewed to report on its details and their relation to one another. Essentially, people with eidetic imagery continue to see the stimulus even though they know it is no longer there. This type of imagery is more common in children than in adults.

eigenvalue (symbol: λ) *n.* a numerical index, commonly used in FACTOR ANALYSIS and PRINCIPAL COMPONENT ANALYSIS, that indicates the portion of the total variance among several correlated variables that is accounted for by a more basic, underlying variable. Eigenvalues are of central importance in linear algebra (i.e., matrix algebra).

Einstellung *n.* an expectation or readiness associated with particular stimuli. It may foster a degree of mental inflexibility by instilling a tendency to respond to a situation in a certain way. For example, a person who successfully solves a series of problems using one formula may apply that same formula to a new problem solvable by a simpler method. The contemporary term for this concept is MENTAL SET. [German: "attitude"]

ejaculation *n.* see ORGASM. **—ejaculatory** *adj.*

EKG abbreviation for ELECTROCARDIOGRAM.

elaborated code a linguistic REGISTER typically used in formal situations (e.g., academic discourse), characterized by a wide vocabulary, complex constructions, and unpredictable collocations of word and idea. This contrasts with the **restricted code** used in much informal conversation, which is characterized by a narrow vocabulary, simple constructions, and predictable ritualized forms, with much reliance on context and nonverbal communication to convey meaning.

elaboration *n.* **1.** the process of interpreting or embellishing information to be remembered or of relating it to other material already known and in memory. The LEVELS-OF-PROCESSING MODEL OF MEMORY holds that the level of elaboration applied to information as it is processed affects both the length of time that it can be retained in memory and the ease with which it can be retrieved. See also DEEP PROCESSING. **2.** the process of scrutinizing and thinking about the central merits of attitude-relevant information. This process includes generating inferences about the information, assessing its validity, and considering the implications of evaluative responses to the information. **—elaborate** *vb.*

elaboration-likelihood model (ELM) a theory of persuasion postulating that attitude change occurs on a continuum of elaboration and thus, under certain conditions, may be a result of relatively extensive (see CENTRAL ROUTE TO PERSUASION)

E

or relatively little (see PERIPHERAL ROUTE TO PERSUASION) scrutiny of attitude-relevant information. The theory postulates that the strength of an attitude depends on the amount of elaboration on which the attitude is based.

elaborative rehearsal an ENCODING strategy to facilitate the formation of memory by repeatedly reviewing new information and linking it to what one already knows. See DEPTH-OF-PROCESSING HYPOTHESIS.

elder abuse harm to an older adult caused by another individual. The harm can be physical (violence), sexual (nonconsensual sex), psychological (causing emotional distress), material (improper use of belongings or finances), or neglect (failure to provide needed care).

elderspeak *n.* adjustments to speech patterns, such as speaking more slowly, shortening sentences, or using limited or less complex vocabulary, that are sometimes made by younger people when communicating with older adults.

Electra complex in the writings of Swiss psychoanalyst Carl Jung (1875–1961), the female counterpart of Sigmund Freud's OEDIPUS COMPLEX, involving the daughter's love for her father, jealousy toward the mother, and blame of the mother for depriving her of a penis. Although Freud rejected the phrase, using the term Oedipus complex to refer to both boys and girls, many modern textbooks of psychology propagate the mistaken belief that Electra complex is a Freudian term.

electrical potential see POTENTIAL.

electrical stimulation the stimulation of brain cells or sensory or motor neurons by electrical or electronic devices.

electrical synapse a type of connection in which neurons are not separated by a cleft but instead are joined by a GAP JUNCTION so that the nerve impulse is transmitted across without first being translated into a chemical message.

electrocardiogram (ECG; EKG) *n.* a wavelike tracing, either printed or displayed on a monitor, that represents the electrical impulses of the conduction system of the heart muscle as it passes through a typical cycle of contraction and relaxation. The electrical currents are detected by electrodes attached to specific sites on the patient's chest, legs, and arms and recorded by an instrument, the **electrocardiograph**. In the procedure, which is called **electrocardiography**, the wave patterns of the electrocardiogram reveal the condition of the heart chambers and valves to provide an indication of cardiac problems.

electroconvulsive therapy (ECT) a controversial treatment in which a seizure is induced by passing a controlled, low-dose electric current (an **electroconvulsive shock; ECS**) through one or both temples. The patient is prepared by administration of an anesthetic and injection of a muscle relaxant. Now a somewhat rare procedure, it is sometimes used with patients with severe endogenous depression who fail to respond to antidepressant drugs. Benefits are temporary, and the mechanisms of therapeutic action are unknown. Also called **electroconvulsive shock therapy (EST); electroshock therapy (EST)**.

electrode *n.* an instrument with a positive-pole cathode and a negative-pole anode used to electrically stimulate biological tissues or record electrical activity in these tissues. See also MICROELECTRODE.

electroencephalography (EEG) *n.* a method of studying BRAIN

WAVES using an instrument (**electro-encephalograph**) that amplifies and records the electrical activity of the brain through electrodes placed at various points on the scalp. The resulting record (**electroencephalo-gram [EEG]**) of the brain-wave patterns is primarily used in diagnosing epilepsy and other neurological disorders.

electromyography (EMG) *n*. the recording (via an instrument called an **electromyograph**) of the electrical activity of muscles through electrodes placed in or on different muscle groups. This procedure is used in the diagnosis of neuromuscular diseases, such as myasthenia gravis or amyotrophic lateral sclerosis. A record of the electric potentials is called an **electromyogram (EMG)**.

electroshock therapy (EST) see ELECTROCONVULSIVE THERAPY.

ELM abbreviation for ELABORATION-LIKELIHOOD MODEL.

embarrassment *n*. a SELF-CONSCIOUS EMOTION in which a person feels awkward or flustered in other people's company or because of the attention of others, as, for example, when being observed engaging in actions that are subject to mild disapproval from others. —**embarrassed** *adj*.

embedded figure a type of AMBIGUOUS FIGURE in which one or more images blend into a larger pattern and so are not immediately obvious.

emblem *n*. a bodily GESTURE that substitutes for a spoken word or phrase and that can be readily comprehended by most individuals in a culture. Examples are shaking the head back and forth to signify *no* and nodding the head up and down to indicate *yes*. —**emblematic** *adj*.

embolism *n*. the interruption of blood flow due to blockage of a ves-

sel by an **embolus**, material formed elsewhere and carried by the bloodstream to become lodged at the site of obstruction. The embolus may be a blood clot, air bubble, fat globule, or other substance.

embryo *n*. an animal in the stages of development between cleavage of the fertilized egg and birth or hatching. In human prenatal development, the embryo comprises the products of conception during the first 8 weeks of pregnancy; thereafter it is called a FETUS. —**embryonic** *adj*.

EMDR abbreviation for EYE-MOVEMENT DESENSITIZATION AND REPROCESSING.

emergent property a characteristic of a complex system that is not implicit in or predictable from an analysis of the components or elements that make it up and that, thus, often arises unexpectedly. For example, it has been said that conscious experience is not predictable by analysis of the neurophysiological and biochemical complexity of the brain.

emerging adulthood a developmental stage that is neither adolescence nor young adulthood but is theoretically and empirically distinct from them both, spanning the late teens through the twenties, with a focus on ages 18–25. Emerging adulthood is distinguished by relative independence from social roles and from normative expectations. Having left the dependency of childhood and adolescence, and having not yet entered the enduring responsibilities that are normative in adulthood, emerging adults engage in identity exploration, a process of trying out various life possibilities (e.g., in love, work, and worldviews) and gradually moving toward making enduring decisions.

EMG abbreviation for ELECTROMYOGRAPHY.

emic *adj.* denoting an approach to the study of human cultures that interprets behaviors and practices in terms of the system of meanings created by and operative within a particular cultural context. Such an approach would generally be of the kind associated with ETHNOGRAPHY rather than ETHNOLOGY. Compare ETIC.

emitted behavior a natural response that is not influenced by, or dependent on, any external stimuli. Compare RESPONDENT BEHAVIOR.

emotion *n.* a complex reaction pattern, involving experiential, behavioral, and physiological elements, by which the individual attempts to deal with a personally significant matter or event. The specific quality of the emotion (e.g., FEAR, SHAME) is determined by the specific significance of the event. For example, if the significance involves threat, fear is likely to be generated; if the significance involves disapproval from another, shame is likely to be generated. Emotion typically involves FEELING but differs from feeling in having an overt or implicit engagement with the world. —**emotional** *adj.*

emotional abuse nonphysical abuse: a pattern of behavior in which one person deliberately and repeatedly subjects another to acts that are detrimental to behavioral and affective functioning and overall mental well-being. Researchers have yet to formulate a universally agreed upon definition of the concept, but have identified a variety of forms emotional abuse may take, including verbal abuse, intimidation and terrorization, humiliation and degradation, exploitation, harassment, rejection and withholding of affection, isolation, and excessive control. Also called **psychological abuse**.

emotional disorder 1. any psychological disorder characterized primarily by maladjustive emotional reactions that are inappropriate or disproportionate to reality. **2.** loosely, any mental disorder.

emotional intelligence the ability to process emotional information and use it in reasoning and other cognitive activities. It comprises four abilities: to perceive and appraise emotions accurately; to access and evoke emotions when they facilitate cognition; to comprehend emotional language and make use of emotional information; and to regulate one's own and others' emotions to promote growth and well-being.

emotional regulation the ability of an individual to modulate an emotion or set of emotions. Techniques of conscious emotional regulation can include learning to construe situations differently in order to manage them better and recognizing how different behaviors can be used in the service of a given emotional state.

emotion-focused coping a type of COPING STRATEGY that focuses on regulating negative emotional reactions to a stressor, as opposed to taking actions to change the stressor. Emotion-focused coping may include social withdrawal, disengagement, and acceptance of the situation. Compare PROBLEM-FOCUSED COPING.

emotive *adj.* related to or arousing emotion.

empathy *n.* understanding a person from his or her frame of reference rather than one's own, so that one vicariously experiences the person's feelings, perceptions, and thoughts. In psychotherapy, therapist empathy for the client can be a path to comprehension of the client's cognitions, affects, or behaviors. **—empathic** or **—empathetic** *adj.* **—empathize** *vb.*

empirical *adj.* derived from or denoting experimentation or systematic observation.

empirically derived test a test developed using content, criterion, or construct validation procedures or a combination of these.

empiricism *n.* **1.** an approach to EPISTEMOLOGY holding that all knowledge of matters of fact either arises from experience or requires experience for its validation. In particular, empiricism denies the possibility of ideas present in the mind prior to any experience, arguing that the mind at birth is like a blank sheet of paper. Although there is a strong emphasis on empiricism in psychology, this can take different forms. Some approaches to psychology hold that sensory experience is the origin of all knowledge and thus, ultimately, of personality, character, beliefs, emotions, and behavior. BEHAVIORISM is the purest example of empiricism in this sense. Advocates of other theoretical approaches to psychology, such as PHENOMENOLOGY, argue that the definition of experience as only sensory experience is too narrow. **2.** the view that experimentation is the most important, if not the only, foundation of scientific knowledge and the means by which individuals evaluate truth claims or the adequacy of theories and models. **—empiricist** *adj., n.*

empowerment *n.* the promotion of the skills, knowledge, and confidence necessary to take greater control of one's life, as in certain educational or social schemes. In psychotherapy, the process involves helping clients become more active in meeting their needs and fulfilling their desires. **—empower** *vb.*

empty nest the family home after the children have reached maturity and left, often creating an emotional void (**empty nest syndrome**) in the lives of the parents (**empty nesters**).

encapsulation *n.* **1.** the process of separating or keeping separate, particularly the ability of some people experiencing delusions to maintain high levels of functioning and prevent their delusions from pervading everyday behavior and cognitive states. **2.** enclosure, as in a sheath or other covering.

encephalitis *n.* inflammation of the brain, typically caused by viral infection. The symptoms, which may be potentially fatal, include fever, vomiting, confusion or disorientation, drowsiness, seizures, and loss of consciousness or coma. **—encephalitic** *adj.*

encoding *n.* the conversion of a sensory input into a form capable of being processed and deposited in memory. Encoding is the first stage of memory processing, followed by RETENTION and then RETRIEVAL.

encoding specificity the principle that RETRIEVAL of memory is optimal when the retrieval conditions (such as context or cues present at the time of retrieval) duplicate the conditions that were present when the memory was formed.

encopresis *n.* repeated defecation in inappropriate places (clothing, floor, etc.) that occurs after the age of 4 and is not due to a substance (e.g., a laxative) or to a general medical condition. Encopresis may or may not be accompanied by constipation and is often associated with poor toilet training and stressful situations.

encounter group a group of individuals in which constructive insight, sensitivity to others, and personal growth are promoted through direct interactions on an

E

emotional and social level. The leader functions as a catalyst and facilitator rather than as a therapist and focuses on here-and-now feelings and interaction, rather than on theory or individual motivation.

enculturation *n.* the processes, beginning in early childhood, by which particular cultural values, ideas, beliefs, and behavioral patterns are instilled in the members of a society. Compare ACCULTURATION. —**enculturate** *vb.*

endocrine gland any ductless gland that secretes hormones directly into the bloodstream to act on distant targets. Such glands include the PITUITARY GLAND, ADRENAL GLAND, THYROID GLAND, gonads (TESTIS and OVARY), and ISLETS OF LANGERHANS. Compare EXOCRINE GLAND.

endocrine system the set of ENDOCRINE GLANDS, which synthesize and secrete HORMONES into the bloodstream.

endogamy *n.* the custom or practice of marrying within one's KINSHIP NETWORK, caste, or other religious or social group. Compare EXOGAMY. —**endogamous** *adj.*

endogenous *adj.* originating within the body as a result of normal biochemical or physiological processes (e.g., endogenous OPIOIDS) or of predisposing biological or genetic influences (e.g., ENDOGENOUS DEPRESSION). Compare EXOGENOUS. —**endogenously** *adv.*

endogenous depression depression that occurs in the absence of an obvious psychological stressor and in which a biological or genetic cause is implied. Compare REACTIVE DEPRESSION.

endolymph *n.* the fluid contained in the membranous labyrinth of the inner ear, that is, within the SCALA MEDIA, SEMICIRCULAR CANALS, SACCULE, and UTRICLE. —**endolymphatic** *adj.*

endophenotype *n.* a type of BIOLOGICAL MARKER that is simpler to detect than genetic sequences and that may be useful in researching vulnerability to a wide range of psychological and neurological disorders. Endophenotypes may be a useful link between genetic sequences and their external emotional, cognitive, or behavioral manifestations.

endoplasmic reticulum a network of membranous tubules and sacs extending from the nucleus to the outer membrane of a typical animal or plant cell. It is responsible for the processing and modification of proteins and lipids, both for distribution within the cell and for secretion.

endorphin *n.* any of a class of NEUROPEPTIDES, found mainly in the pituitary gland, that function as endogenous OPIOIDS. The best known is beta-endorphin; the others are alpha-endorphin and gamma-endorphin. The production of endorphins during intense physical activity is one explanation for the runner's high or exercise high.

endowment effect the tendency of people to place a higher value on items once they own them or once these have been associated with the self in some other way. The endowment effect is characterized by increased positive emotions toward the object.

end plate a specialized region of a muscle-cell membrane that faces the terminus of a motor neuron within a **neuromuscular junction**. The depolarization that is induced in this muscular region when stimulated by neurotransmitter released from the adjacent motor neuron terminus is called the **end-plate potential**.

engineering psychology see HUMAN FACTORS PSYCHOLOGY.

engram *n.* the hypothetical MEMORY TRACE that is stored in the brain. The nature of the engram, in terms of the exact physiological changes that occur to encode a memory, is as yet unknown.

enmeshment *n.* a condition in which two or more people, typically family members, are involved in each other's activities and personal relationships to an excessive degree, thus limiting or precluding healthy interaction and compromising individual AUTONOMY and IDENTITY.

enrichment *n.* **1.** enhancement or improvement by the addition or augmentation of some desirable property, quality, or component. For example, job enrichment policies are designed to enhance quality of worklife and thus employees' interest in and attitude toward work tasks; marriage-enrichment groups are intended to enhance the interpersonal relationships of married couples. **2.** the provision of opportunities to increase levels of behavioral or intellectual activity in an otherwise unstimulating (i.e., impoverished) environment. For example, the provision of play materials and opportunities for social contacts has been shown to enhance the development of young children. In laboratory studies of animal behavior, the addition of physical features or task requirements to an environment elicits a more natural behavioral repertoire from the animals.

entitativity *n.* the extent to which a group or collective is considered by others to be a real entity rather than a set of independent individuals. In general, groups whose members share a common fate, are similar to one another, and are located close together are more likely to be considered a group rather than a mere aggregation. Also called **entitivity**.

entity theory the belief that psychological attributes, such as level of intelligence, are fixed, essential qualities rather than attributes that develop gradually.

entorhinal cortex a region of cerebral cortex in the ventromedial portion of the temporal lobe. It has reciprocal connections with various other cortical and subcortical structures and is an integral component of the medial temporal lobe memory system.

entrainment *n.* in CHRONOBIOLOGY, the process of activating or providing a timing cue for a BIOLOGICAL RHYTHM. For example, the production of gonadal hormones in seasonally breeding animals can be a result of entrainment to increasing day length.

entrapment *n.* **1.** a process in which one makes increasing commitments to a failing course of action or an unattainable goal in order to justify the amount of time and effort already invested, feeling helpless to do otherwise. An example is provided by a company that proceeds with the design and construction of a new building for its employees after economic and other changes significantly reduce profits, halt business growth, and result in staff layoffs that make the new space not only financially burdensome but no longer necessary. **2.** a pathological condition in which swelling of surrounding tissue places excessive pressure on a nerve. Fibers located on the surface of the nerve usually bear the brunt of the compression, while interior fibers tend to be less affected. Repeated or longterm entrapment can cause nerve damage and muscle weakness.

enuresis *n.* repeated involuntary urination in inappropriate places

E

(clothing, floor, etc.) that occurs after the chronological age when continence is expected (generally 5 years old) and is not due to a substance (e.g., a diuretic) or to a general medical condition. Enuresis is frequently associated with delayed bladder development, poor toilet training, and stressful situations.

envelope *n.* in acoustics, a slowly varying or "smoothed" change in amplitude. Usually it refers to temporal changes, such as those produced by amplitude MODULATION, but it can also refer to the shape of a spectrum or to spatial changes. Temporal and spectral envelopes are important in auditory perception.

environment *n.* the aggregate of external agents or conditions—physical, biological, social, and cultural—that influence the functions of an organism. See also ECOLOGY. **—environmental** *adj.*

environmental determinism the view that psychological and behavioral characteristics are largely or completely the result of environmental conditions. Biological factors are considered to be of minor importance, exerting little if any influence. Compare BIOLOGICAL DETERMINISM.

environmentalism *n.* **1.** the concept that the environment and learning are the chief determinants of behavior. They are, therefore, the major cause of interpersonal variations in ability and adjustment; accordingly, behavior is largely modifiable. Compare HEREDITARIANISM. See also NATURE–NURTURE. **2.** a social movement and position that emphasizes the ecological relationship between humans and the natural environment and strives to protect the environment as an essential resource. **—environmentalist** *n.*

environmental press–competence model a model of stress and adaptation in which adaptive functioning in the environment depends on the interaction between stimuli in a person's physical and social environment that interact with needs and place demands on that individual (**environmental press**) and the individual's competence in meeting these demands, which is shaped by such personal characteristics as physical health and cognitive and perceptual abilities.

environmental psychology a multidisciplinary field that emphasizes the reciprocal effects of the physical environment on human behavior and welfare. Influences may include environmental stressors (e.g., noise, crowding, air pollution, temperature), design variables (e.g., lighting and illumination), the design of technology (see ERGONOMICS), and larger, more ambient qualities of the physical environment, such as floorplan layouts, symbolic elements, the size and location of buildings, and proximity to nature.

environmental sounds agnosia see AUDITORY AGNOSIA.

environmental stress theory the concept that autonomic and cognitive factors combine to form an individual's appraisal of stressors in the environment as threatening or nonthreatening.

enzyme *n.* a protein that acts as a biological catalyst, accelerating the rate of a biochemical reaction without itself becoming permanently altered. Many enzymes require other organic molecules (coenzymes) or inorganic ions (cofactors) to function normally.

EP abbreviation for EVOKED POTENTIAL.

ependyma *n.* the membrane lining the brain VENTRICLES and the CEN-

TRAL CANAL of the spinal cord. **—ependymal** *adj.*

EPI abbreviation for EYSENCK PERSONALITY INVENTORY.

epidemiology *n.* the study of the incidence and distribution of specific diseases and disorders. The **epidemiologist** also seeks to establish relationships to such factors as heredity, environment, nutrition, or age at onset. Results of epidemiological studies are intended to find clues and associations rather than necessarily to show causal relationships. See also INCIDENCE; PREVALENCE. **—epidemiologic** or **epidemiological** *adj.*

epigenesis *n.* **1.** the theory that characteristics of an organism, both physical and behavioral, arise from an interaction between genetic and environmental influences rather than from one or the other. See also NATURE–NURTURE. **2.** in genetics, the occurrence of a heritable change in gene function that is not the result of a change in the base sequence of the organism's DNA. **—epigenetic** *adj.*

epilepsy *n.* a common neurological disorder associated with disturbances in the electrical discharges of brain cells and characterized by recurrent seizures that may be manifested as alterations in sensation, motor functions, and consciousness. Many forms of epilepsy have been linked to viral, fungal, or parasitic infections of the central nervous system; known metabolic disturbances; the ingestion of toxic agents; brain lesions; tumors or congenital defects; or cerebral trauma. Types of seizure vary depending on the nature of the abnormal electrical discharge and the area of the brain affected. **—epileptic** *adj.*

epinephrine *n.* a CATECHOLAMINE neurotransmitter and adrenal hormone that is the end product of the metabolism of the dietary amino acid tyrosine. It is synthesized primarily in the adrenal medulla by methylation of norepinephrine, which itself is formed from dopamine. As a hormone, it is secreted in large amounts when an individual is stimulated by fear, anxiety, or a similar stressful situation. As a neurotransmitter, it increases the heart rate and force of heart contractions, relaxes bronchial and intestinal smooth muscle, and produces varying effects on blood pressure as it acts both as a vasodilator and vasoconstrictor. Also called **adrenaline**.

epiphenomenon *n.* (*pl.* **epiphenomena**) a mere byproduct of a process that has no effect on the process itself. The term is used most frequently to refer to mental events considered as products of brain processes. Thus, while mental events are real in some sense, they are not real in the same way that biological states and events are real, and not necessary to the explanation of mental events themselves. Epiphenomena are conceived of as having no causal power. **—epiphenomenal** *adj.*

episodic memory memory for specific, personally experienced events that happened at a particular time or place. Episodic memory supplements SEMANTIC MEMORY and may decline with normal aging. See also DECLARATIVE MEMORY.

epistemology *n.* the branch of philosophy concerned with the nature, origin, and limitations of knowledge. It is also concerned with the justification of truth claims. In psychology, interest in epistemology arises from two principal sources. First, as the study of the behavior of human beings, psychology has long had interest in the processes of knowledge acquisition and learning of all sorts. Second, as a science, psychology has an interest in the justification of its knowledge claims. In connection with this concern, most work on epistemology in psychology has concentrated on scientific method and on the justification of scientifically derived knowledge claims. In general, the guiding epistemology of psychology has been EMPIRICISM, although some approaches to the subject, such as PSYCHOANALYSIS, the developmental psychology of Swiss epistemologist and psychologist Jean Piaget (1896–1980), and the HUMANISTIC PSYCHOLOGY of U.S. psychologist Carl Rogers (1902–1987), are heavily influenced by RATIONALISM. —**epistemological** adj.

epithalamus n. a portion of the DIENCEPHALON that is immediately above and behind the THALAMUS. It includes the PINEAL GLAND and the posterior COMMISSURE.

EPS abbreviation for EXTRA-PYRAMIDAL SYMPTOMS.

EPSP abbreviation for EXCITATORY POSTSYNAPTIC POTENTIAL.

equal-interval scale see INTERVAL SCALE.

equilibration n. in PIAGETIAN THEORY, the process by which an individual uses assimilation and accommodation to restore or maintain a psychological equilibrium, that is, a cognitive state devoid of conflicting SCHEMAS.

equilibrium n. balance, particularly in reference to posture (see VESTIBULAR SENSE) or physiological processes (see HOMEOSTASIS).

equilibrium potential the state in which the tendency of ions (electrically charged particles) to flow across a cell membrane from regions of high concentration is exactly balanced by the opposing potential

difference (electric charge) across the membrane.

equipotentiality n. the generalization by U.S. psychologist Karl S. Lashley (1890–1958) that large areas of cerebral cortex have equal potential to perform particular functions, being equally involved in learning and certain other complex processes, such that intact cortical areas can assume to some extent the functions of damaged or destroyed areas. Proposed in 1929 following experimental observations of the effects of different brain lesions on rats' ability to learn a complex maze, the concept has been challenged by subsequent research showing that areas of cortex have relatively specific functions. See also MASS ACTION.

equity theory a theory of justice regarding what individuals are likely to view as a fair return from activities involving themselves and a number of other people. The theory posits that people compare the ratio of the outcome of the activity (i.e., the benefits they receive from it) to their input with the outcome-to-input ratios of those engaged in a comparable activity.

equivalent forms see ALTERNATE-FORMS RELIABILITY.

ER abbreviation for evoked response (see EVOKED POTENTIAL).

erectile dysfunction see IMPO-TENCE.

ergonomics n. the discipline that applies a knowledge of human abilities and limitations drawn from physiology, biomechanics, anthropometry, and other areas to the design of systems, equipment, and processes for safe and efficient performance. —**ergonomic** adj.

Erikson's eight stages of development the theory of psychosocial development proposed by German-born U.S psychologist Erik Erikson

(1902–1994), in which ego identity (a sense of continuity, worth, and integration) is gradually achieved by facing positive goals and negative risks during eight stages of development across the lifespan. The stages are: (a) infancy: BASIC TRUST VERSUS MISTRUST; (b) toddler: AUTONOMY VERSUS SHAME AND DOUBT; (c) preschool age: INITIATIVE VERSUS GUILT; (d) school age: INDUSTRY VERSUS INFERIORITY; (e) adolescence: IDENTITY VERSUS IDENTITY CONFUSION; (f) young adulthood: INTIMACY VERSUS ISOLATION; (g) middle age: GENERATIVITY VERSUS STAGNATION; and (h) older adulthood: INTEGRITY VERSUS DESPAIR.

erogenous zone an area or part of the body sensitive to stimulation that is a source of erotic or sexual feeling or pleasure. Among the primary zones are the genitals, buttocks and anus, the breasts (especially the nipples), and the mouth.

Eros *n.* the god of love in Greek mythology (equivalent to the Roman Cupid), whose name was chosen by Austrian psychoanalyst Sigmund Freud (1856–1939) to designate a theoretical set of strivings oriented toward sexuality, development, and increased life activity (see LIFE INSTINCT). In Freud's dual instinct theory, Eros is seen as involved in a dialectic process with THANATOS, the striving toward reduced psychical tension and life activity (see DEATH INSTINCT). See also LIBIDO.

ERP abbreviation for EVENT-RELATED POTENTIAL.

error *n.* **1.** in experimentation, any change in a DEPENDENT VARIABLE not attributable to the manipulation of an INDEPENDENT VARIABLE. **2.** in statistics, a deviation of an observed score from a true score, where true score is often defined by the mean (average) of the particular group or condition in which the score being assessed for error occurs, or from the score predicted by a model.

error term the element of a statistical equation that indicates what is unexplained by the INDEPENDENT VARIABLES.

error variance unexplained variability in a score that is produced by extraneous factors, such as measurement imprecision, and is not attributable to the INDEPENDENT VARIABLE or other controlled experimental manipulations.

escape conditioning the process in which a subject acquires a response that results in the termination of an aversive stimulus. For example, if a monkey learns that pulling a string frequently results in the elimination of a loud noise, escape conditioning has occurred. Also called **escape learning; escape training**. See also AVOIDANCE CONDITIONING.

ESP abbreviation for EXTRASENSORY PERCEPTION.

essentialism *n.* in philosophy, the position that things (or some things) have "essences"; that is, they have certain necessary properties without which they could not be the things they are. In Marxism, POSTMODERNISM, POST-STRUCTURALISM, and certain feminist perspectives, essentialism is the rejected position that human beings have an essential nature that transcends such factors as social class, gender, and ethnicity. See also UNIVERSALISM.

EST abbreviation for electroshock therapy or electroconvulsive shock therapy. See ELECTROCONVULSIVE THERAPY.

esteem need any desire for achievement, reputation, or prestige that is necessary for a sense of personal value and the development of SELF-ESTEEM. Comprising the fourth level of MASLOW'S MOTIVATIONAL HIERARCHY, esteem needs thus are dependent upon the admiration and approval of others.

esthesiometry (aesthesiometry) *n.* the measurement of sensitivity to touch. Classically, two different versions of an instrument called an **esthesiometer** have been used. One consists of bristles of different lengths and thicknesses that are applied to determine the minimum pressure intensity required to produce a sensation. The other is a compasslike device to determine the smallest separation distance at which two points of stimulation on the skin are perceived as one. More sophisticated techniques have now been developed, such as those involving electrodes.

estimator *n.* a quantity calculated from the values in a sample according to some rule and used to give an estimate of the value in a population. For example, the sample mean is an estimator for the population mean; the value of the sample mean is the estimate.

estrogen *n.* any of a class of STEROID HORMONES that are produced mainly by the ovaries and act as the principal female SEX HORMONES, inducing estrus in female mammals and secondary female sexual characteristics in humans. The estrogens occurring naturally in humans are **estradiol** (the most potent), **estrone**, and **estriol**, secreted by the ovarian follicle, corpus luteum, placenta, testes, and adrenal cortex. —**estrogenic** *adj.*

estrous cycle the cyclical sequence of reproductive activity shown by most female mammals (except humans and other primates; see MENSTRUAL CYCLE). Animals that experience one estrous cycle per year are called monestrous; those that have multiple estrous cycles annually are polyestrous.

ethanol *n.* a substance formed by the fermentation of glucose and found in beverages such as beers, wines, and distilled liquors. It is the most frequently used and abused DEPRESSANT in many cultures. When consumed its primary effects are on the central nervous system, mood, and cognitive functions. In small doses, it can produce feelings of warmth, well-being, and confidence. As more is consumed, there is a gradual loss of self-control, and speech and control of limbs become difficult; at high consumption levels, nausea and vomiting, loss of consciousness, and even fatal respiratory arrest may occur. Ethanol has been mistakenly identified as a stimulant, since its stimulating effect derives from an associated loss of cortical inhibition. Also called **alcohol**; **ethyl alcohol**.

ethical code see CODE OF ETHICS.

ethics *n.* **1.** the branch of philosophy that investigates both the content of moral judgments (i.e., what is right and what is wrong) and their nature (i.e., whether such judgments should be considered objective or subjective). **2.** the principles of morally right conduct accepted by a person or a group or considered appropriate to a specific field (e.g., medical ethics, ethics of animal research). —**ethical** *adj.*

ethnic *adj.* denoting or referring to a group of people having a shared social, cultural, linguistic, religious, and usually racial background.

ethnic group any major social group that possesses a common ethnic identity based on history, culture, language, and, often, religion. Members are likely to be biologically related, but an ethnic group is not equivalent to a RACE.

ethnic identity an individual's sense of being a person who is defined, in part, by membership in a specific ethnic group. This sense is usually considered to be a complex construct involving shared social, cultural, linguistic, religious, and often racial factors but identical with none of them.

ethnocentrism *n.* the tendency to reject and malign other ethnic groups and their members while glorifying one's own group and its members. Just as EGOCENTRISM is the tendency to judge oneself as superior to others, so ethnocentrism is the parallel tendency to judge one's group as superior to other groups. Also called **ethnocentricity**. —**ethnocentric** *adj.*

ethnography *n.* the descriptive study of cultures or societies based on direct observation and (ideally) some degree of participation. Compare ETHNOLOGY. See also EMIC. —**ethnographer** *n.* **ethnographic** *adj.*

ethnology *n.* the comparative, analytical, or historical study of human cultures or societies. Compare ETHNOGRAPHY. See also ETIC. —**ethnological** *adj.* —**ethnologist** *n.*

ethnomethodology *n.* the analysis of the underlying conventions and systems of meaning that people use to make sense of commonplace social interactions and experiences. —**ethnomethodological** *adj.* —**ethnomethodologist** *n.*

ethogram *n.* a detailed listing and description of the behavior patterns of an animal in its natural habitat. The description is objective rather than interpretative. For example, a vocalization given in response to a predator would be described in terms of its acoustic properties rather than its apparent function of alarm call.

ethology *n.* the comparative study of the behavior of animals, typically in their natural habitat but also involving experiments both in the field and in captivity. Ethology is often associated with connotations of innate or species-specific behavior patterns, in contrast with COMPARATIVE PSYCHOLOGY. —**ethological** *adj.* —**ethologist** *n.*

etic *adj.* denoting an approach to the study of human cultures based on concepts or constructs that are held to be universal and applicable cross-culturally. Such an approach would generally be of the kind associated with ETHNOLOGY rather than ETHNOGRAPHY. Compare EMIC.

etiology *n.* **1.** the causes and progress of a disease or disorder. **2.** the branch of medical and psychological science concerned with the systematic study of the causes of physical and mental disorders. —**etiological** *adj.*

eugenics *n.* a social and political philosophy that seeks to eradicate genetic defects and improve the genetic makeup of populations through selective human breeding. The eugenic position is groundless and scientifically naive, in that many conditions associated with disability or disorder are inherited recessively and occur unpredictably.

euphoria *n.* an elevated mood of well-being and happiness. An exaggerated degree of euphoria that does not reflect the reality of one's situation is a frequent symptom of MANIC EPISODES and HYPOMANIC EPISODES. —**euphoric** *adj.*

eustachian tube a slender tube extending from the middle ear to the pharynx (connecting the mouth and nostrils to the esophagus), with the primary function of equalizing air pressure on both sides of the tympanic membrane (eardrum). [Bartolommeo **Eustachio** (1524–1574), Italian anatomist]

eustress *n.* the positive stress response, involving optimal levels of stimulation: a type of stress that results from challenging but attainable and enjoyable or worthwhile tasks (e.g., participating in an athletic event, giving a speech). It has a beneficial effect by generating a sense of fulfillment or achievement and facilitating growth, development, mastery, and high levels of performance. Compare DISTRESS.

euthanasia *n.* the act or process of terminating a life to prevent further suffering. Euthanasia is distinguished from the much more widely accepted practice of forgoing invasive treatments, as permitted under natural-death laws throughout the United States. Traditionally, a distinction between PASSIVE EUTHANASIA (withholding treatment) and ACTIVE EUTHANASIA (taking directly lethal action) has been made. In current practice, however, the term euthanasia typically is used to mean active euthanasia only. See also ASSISTED DEATH.

evaluation *n.* a careful examination or overall appraisal of something, particularly to determine its worth, value, or desirability. For example, the evaluation of a particular therapeutic technique refers to a determination of its success in achieving defined goals.

evaluation apprehension uneasiness or worry about being judged by others, especially feelings of worry experienced by participants in an experiment as a result of their desire to be evaluated favorably by the experimenter.

event-related potential (ERP) a specific pattern of electrical activity produced in the brain when a person is engaged in a cognitive act, such as discriminating one stimulus from another. There are a number of different ERP components, and different cognitive operations have been associated with the amplitude and latency of each. Because ERPs

provide specific information about the precise timing and (given appropriate caveats) location of mental events, they serve as an important bridge between psychological function and neural structures. Although the terms are sometimes used synonymously, ERPs are distinct from EVOKED POTENTIALS, which are associated with more elementary sensory stimulation.

event sampling a strategy commonly used in direct observation that involves noting and recording the occurrence of a carefully specified behavior whenever it is seen. For example, a researcher may record each episode of apnea that occurs within a 9-hour period overnight while a person sleeps.

evidence-based practice (EBP) the integration of the best available scientific research from laboratory and field settings with clinical expertise so as to provide effective psychological services that are responsive to a patient's culture, preferences, and characteristics (e.g., functional status, level of social support, strengths). In uniting researchers and practitioners, EBP ensures that the research on psychological assessment, case formulation, intervention strategies, therapeutic relationships and outcomes, and specific problems and patient populations is both clinically relevant and internally valid. Clinical decisions should be made in collaboration with the patient, based on relevant data, and with consideration for the probable costs, benefits, and available resources and options. The ultimate goal of EBP is to promote empirically supported principles that can be used to enhance public health.

evoked potential (EP) a specific pattern of electrical activity produced in a particular part of the nervous system, especially the brain, in response to external stimulation, such as a flash of light or a brief tone. Different modalities and types of stimuli produce different types of sensory potentials, and these are labeled according to their electrical polarity (positive- or negative-going) and timing (by serial order or in milliseconds). Although the terms are sometimes used synonymously, EPs are distinct from EVENT-RELATED POTENTIALS, which are associated with higher level cognitive processes. Also called **evoked response (ER)**.

evolution *n.* the process of gradual change in the appearance of populations of organisms that has taken place over generations. Such changes are widely held to account for the present diversity of living organisms originating from relatively few ancestors since the emergence of life on Earth. —**evolutionary** *adj.*

evolutionary psychology an approach to psychological inquiry that views human cognition and behavior in a broadly Darwinian context of adaptation to evolving physical and social environments and new intellectual challenges. It differs from SOCIOBIOLOGY mainly in its emphasis on the effects of NATURAL SELECTION on INFORMATION PROCESSING and the structure of the human mind.

exacerbation *n.* an increase in the severity of a disease or disorder or of its symptoms.

exchange relationship see COMMUNAL RELATIONSHIP.

exchange theory see SOCIAL EXCHANGE THEORY.

excitation *n.* the electrical activity elicited in a neuron or muscle cell in response to an external stimulus, specifically the propagation of an ACTION POTENTIAL.

excitation-transfer theory the theory that emotional responses can be intensified by AROUSAL from other stimuli not directly related to the stimulus that originally provoked the response. According to this theory, when a person becomes aroused physiologically, there is a subsequent period of time when the person will experience a state of residual arousal yet be unaware of it. If additional arousing stimuli are presented during this time, the individual will experience more arousal, and thus greater response, to those succeeding stimuli than if there had been no residual arousal.

excitatory postsynaptic potential (EPSP) a brief decrease in the difference in electrical charge across the membrane of a neuron that is caused by the transmission of a signal from a neighboring neuron across the synapse (specialized junction) separating them. EPSPs increase the probability that the postsynaptic neuron will initiate an ACTION POTENTIAL and hence fire a nerve impulse. Compare INHIBITORY POSTSYNAPTIC POTENTIAL.

excitatory synapse a specialized type of junction at which activity from one neuron (in the form of an ACTION POTENTIAL) facilitates activity in an adjacent neuron by initiating an EXCITATORY POSTSYNAPTIC POTENTIAL. Compare INHIBITORY SYNAPSE.

executive functions higher level cognitive processes that organize and order behavior, such as judgment, abstraction and concept formation, logic and reasoning, problem solving, planning, and sequencing of actions. Deficits in executive functioning are seen in various disorders, including Alzheimer's disease and schizophrenia. In the latter, for example, major deficits in such cognitive abilities as selecting goals or task-relevant information and eliminating extraneous information are apparent and are a focus of neurorehabilitative treatment.

exercise psychology see SPORT AND EXERCISE PSYCHOLOGY.

exhaustion stage see GENERAL ADAPTATION SYNDROME.

exhibitionism *n.* a PARAPHILIA in which a person repeatedly exposes his or her genitals to unsuspecting strangers as a means of achieving sexual satisfaction. **—exhibitionist** *n.*

existential anxiety a general sense of anguish or despair associated with an individual's recognition of the inevitability of death and associated search for purpose and meaning in life, in light of the finitude of past choices and the unknowns inherent to future choices.

existential–humanistic therapy a form of psychotherapy that focuses on the entire person, rather than just behavior, cognition, or underlying motivations. Emphasis is placed on the client's subjective experiences, free will, and ability to decide the course of his or her own life. Also called **humanistic–existential therapy**.

existentialism *n.* a philosophical and literary movement that emerged in Europe in the period between the two World Wars and became the dominant trend in Continental thought during the 1940s and 1950s. In the immediate postwar years French philosopher and author Jean-Paul Sartre (1905–1980), who is usually seen as the existentialist thinker *par excellence,* popularized both the term "existentialism" and most of the ideas now associated with it. Existentialism represents a turning away from systematic philosophy, with its emphasis on metaphysical absolutes and principles of rational certainty, toward an emphasis on the concrete existence of a human being "thrown" into a world that is merely "given" and contingent. Such a being encounters the world as a subjective consciousness, "condemned" to create its own meanings and values in an "absurd" and purposeless universe. The human being must perform this task in the absence of any possibility of rational certainty. Various forms of EXISTENTIAL PSYCHOLOGY have taken up the task of providing explanations, understandings of human behavior, and therapies based on existentialist assumptions about human existence. **—existential** *adj.* **—existentialist** *n., adj.*

existential neurosis a pathological condition characterized by feelings of despair and anxiety that arise from living inauthentically, that is, from failing to take responsibility for one's own life and to make choices and find meaning in living.

existential psychology a general approach to psychological theory and practice that derives from EXISTENTIALISM. It emphasizes the subjective meaning of human experience, the uniqueness of the individual, and personal responsibility reflected in choice.

existential psychotherapy a form of psychotherapy that deals with the here and now of the client's total situation rather than with the client's past or underlying dynamics. It emphasizes the exploration and development of meaning in life, focuses on emotional experiences and decision making, and stresses a person's responsibility for his or her own existence.

exocrine gland any gland that secretes a product onto the outer body surface or into body cavities through a duct, for example, the tear-producing lacrimal gland or the salivary gland. Compare ENDOCRINE GLAND.

exogamy *n.* the custom or practice of marrying outside one's KINSHIP NETWORK (such as a clan) or other religious or social group. Compare ENDOGAMY. **—exogamous** *adj.*

exogenous *adj.* originating outside the body: referring, for example, to drugs (exogenous chemicals) or to phenomena, conditions, or disorders resulting from the influence of external factors (e.g., exogenous stress). Compare ENDOGENOUS. **—exogenously** *adv.*

exogenous depression see REACTIVE DEPRESSION.

exosystem *n.* in ECOLOGICAL SYSTEMS THEORY, those societal structures that function largely independently of the individual but which nevertheless affect the immediate context within which he or she develops. They include the government, the legal system, and the media. Compare MACROSYSTEM; MESOSYSTEM.

expectancy effect the effect of one person's expectation about the behavior of another person on the actual behavior of that other person (interpersonal expectancy effect) or the effect of a person's expectation about his or her own behavior on that person's actual subsequent behavior (intrapersonal expectancy effect).

expectancy-value model the concept that motivation for an outcome depends on the significance of that outcome and the probability of achieving it.

experience-dependent synaptogenesis a process whereby SYNAPSES are formed and maintained as a result of the unique experiences of an individual.

experience-expectant synaptogenesis a process whereby SYNAPSES

are formed and maintained when an organism has species-typical experiences. As a result, such functions as vision will develop for all members of a species, given species-typical environmental stimulation (e.g., light).

experiment *n.* a series of observations conducted under controlled conditions to study a relationship with the purpose of drawing causal inferences about that relationship. Experiments involve the manipulation of an INDEPENDENT VARIABLE, the measurement of a DEPENDENT VARIABLE, and the exposure of various participants to one or more of the conditions being studied. **—experimental** *adj.*

experimental control see CONTROL.

experimental design an outline or plan of the procedures to be followed in scientific experimentation in order to reach valid conclusions, with consideration of such factors as participant selection, variable manipulation, data collection and analysis, and minimization of external influences.

experimental group a group of participants in an experiment who are exposed to a particular manipulation of the INDEPENDENT VARIABLE (i.e., a particular treatment). Compare CONTROL GROUP.

experimental hypothesis a premise that describes what a researcher in a scientific study hopes to demonstrate if certain experimental conditions are met.

experimental method a system of scientific investigation, usually based on a design to be carried out under controlled conditions, that is intended to test a hypothesis and establish a causal relationship between independent and dependent variables.

experimental neurosis a patho-

E

logical condition induced in an animal during conditioning experiments requiring discriminations between nearly indistinguishable stimuli or involving punishment for necessary activities (e.g., eating). Experimental neurosis may be characterized by any of a range of behavioral abnormalities, including agitation, irritability, aggression, regressive behavior, escape and avoidance, and disturbances in physiological activity, such as pulse, heart, and respiration rates.

experimental philosophy 1. in the late 17th and 18th centuries, a name for the new discipline of experimental science then emerging. Use of the term often went with an optimism about the ability of experimental science to answer the questions that had been posed but unsolved by "natural philosophy." The systematic work of British physicist Isaac Newton (1642–1727) is often given as a defining example of the experimental philosophy. **2.** a late 20th-century movement holding that modern experimental science, particularly neuroscience, will ultimately uncover the biological foundations of thought and thereby provide a material answer to the questions of EPISTEMOLOGY. In other words, experimental philosophy holds that answers to philosophical questions regarding the mind and its activities can, and likely will, be reduced to questions of how the brain functions. See REDUCTIONISM.

experimental psychology the scientific study of behavior, motives, or cognition in a laboratory or other experimental setting in order to predict, explain, or control behavior or other psychological phenomena. Experimental psychology aims at establishing quantified relationships and explanatory theory through the analysis of responses under various

controlled conditions and the synthesis of adequate theoretical accounts from the results of these observations.

experimental realism the extent to which an experimental situation is meaningful and engaging to participants, eliciting responses that are spontaneous and natural. See also MUNDANE REALISM.

experimental research research utilizing randomized assignment of participants to conditions and systematic manipulation of variables with the objective of drawing causal inference. It is generally conducted within a laboratory or other controlled environment, which in reducing the potential influence of extraneous factors increases INTERNAL VALIDITY but decreases EXTERNAL VALIDITY.

experimental treatment an intervention or regimen that has shown some promise as a cure or ameliorative for a disease or condition but is still being evaluated for efficacy, safety, and acceptability.

experimental variable an INDEPENDENT VARIABLE: a variable under investigation that is manipulated by the experimenter to determine its relationship to or influence upon some DEPENDENT VARIABLE.

experimenter bias any unintended errors in the experimental process or the interpretation of its results that are attributable to an experimenter's preconceived beliefs about results.

experimenter effect any influence an experimenter may have on the results of his or her research, derived from either interaction with participants or unintentional errors of observation, measurement, analysis, or interpretation. In the former, the experimenter's personal characteristics (e.g., age, sex, race), attitudes, and expectations directly affect the behavior of participants. In the latter, the experimenter's procedural errors (arising from his or her predictions about results) have no effect on participant responses but indirectly distort the experimental findings.

explanation *n.* an account that provides a meaning for some phenomenon or event in terms of causal conditions, a set of beliefs or assumptions, or a metaphor that relates it to something already understood. —**explanatory** *adj.*

explicit attitude a relatively enduring and general evaluative response of which a person is consciously aware. Compare IMPLICIT ATTITUDE.

explicit memory long-term memory that can be consciously recalled: general knowledge or information about personal experiences that an individual retrieves in response to a specific need or request to do so. This term is used interchangeably with DECLARATIVE MEMORY but typically with a performance-based orientation—that is, a person is aware that he or she possesses certain knowledge and specifically retrieves it to complete successfully a task overtly eliciting that knowledge (e.g., a multiple-choice exam). Compare IMPLICIT MEMORY.

exploratory factor analysis one of a set of techniques used in FACTOR ANALYSIS when strong theory is lacking and the observed data are freely explored in search of meaningful patterns among the observations. That is, the data are examined in order to discover the underlying (latent) variables that explain the interrelationships among a larger set of observable (manifest) variables. Compare CONFIRMATORY FACTOR ANALYSIS.

exposure therapy a form of BEHAVIOR THERAPY that is effective in treating anxiety disorders. Exposure therapy involves systematic confrontation with a feared stimulus, either in vivo (live) or in the imagination, and may encompass any of a number of behavioral interventions, including DESENSITIZATION, FLOODING, IMPLOSIVE THERAPY, and extinction-based techniques. It works by (a) HABITUATION, in which repeated exposure reduces anxiety over time by a process of EXTINCTION; (b) disconfirming fearful predictions; (c) deeper processing of the feared stimulus; and (d) increasing feelings of SELF-EFFICACY and mastery.

expressed emotion (**EE**) negative attitudes, in the form of criticism, hostility, and emotional overinvolvement, demonstrated by family members toward a person with a mental disorder. High levels of expressed emotion have been shown to be associated with poorer outcomes in mood, anxiety, and schizophrenic disorders and increased likelihood of relapse.

expressive language disorder a developmental disorder characterized by impairment in acquiring the ability to use language effectively for communicating with others despite normal language comprehension. Manifestations include below-average vocabulary skills, difficulty producing complete sentences, and problems recalling words.

extended family 1. a family unit consisting of parents and children living in one household with certain other individuals united by kinship (e.g., grandparents, cousins). **2.** in modern Western societies, the NUCLEAR FAMILY together with various other relatives who live nearby and keep in regular touch.

extension *n.* the straightening of a joint in a limb (e.g., the elbow joint) so that two parts of the limb (e.g., the forearm and upper arm) are drawn away from each other.

extensor a muscle whose contraction extends a part of the body; for example, the triceps muscle group extends, or straightens, the arm. Compare FLEXOR.

external attribution see SITUATIONAL ATTRIBUTION.

external auditory meatus the canal that conducts sound through the external ear, from the pinna to the tympanic membrane (eardrum). Also called **auditory canal**.

external capsule a thin layer of myelinated nerve fibers separating the CLAUSTRUM from the PUTAMEN. See also INTERNAL CAPSULE.

external ear the part of the ear consisting of the PINNA, the EXTERNAL AUDITORY MEATUS, and the outer surface of the eardrum (see TYMPANIC MEMBRANE). Also called **outer ear**.

externalization n. **1.** a DEFENSE MECHANISM in which one's thoughts, feelings, or perceptions are attributed to the external world and perceived as independent of oneself or one's own experiences. A common expression of this is PROJECTION. **2.** the process of learning to distinguish between the self and the environment during childhood.

external locus of control see LOCUS OF CONTROL.

external validity the extent to which the results of research or testing can be generalized beyond the sample that generated the results to other individuals or situations. The more specialized the sample, the less likely it will be that the results are highly generalizable.

exteroception n. sensitivity to stimuli that are outside the body, resulting from the response of specialized sensory cells called **exteroceptors** to objects and occurrences in the external environment. Exteroception includes the five senses of sight, smell, hearing, touch, and taste, and exteroceptors thus take a variety of forms (e.g., photoreceptors—retinal rods and cones—for sight; cutaneous receptors—Pacinian corpuscles, Meissner's corpuscles, Merkel's tactile disks—for touch). Compare INTEROCEPTION.

extinction n. **1.** in PAVLOVIAN CONDITIONING: (a) a procedure in which pairing of stimulus events is discontinued, either by presenting the CONDITIONED STIMULUS alone or by presenting the conditioned stimulus and the UNCONDITIONED STIMULUS independently of one another; or (b) the result of this procedure, which is a gradual decline in the probability and magnitude of the CONDITIONED RESPONSE. **2.** in OPERANT CONDITIONING: (a) a procedure in which reinforcement is discontinued, that is, the reinforcing stimulus is no longer presented; or (b) the result of this procedure, which is a decline in the rate of the formerly reinforced response. **—extinguish** vb.

extirpation n. see ABLATION.

extraneous variable a variable that is not under investigation in an experiment but may potentially affect the DEPENDENT VARIABLE and thus influence results.

extrapsychic adj. pertaining to that which originates outside the mind or that which occurs between the mind and the environment. Compare INTRAPSYCHIC.

extrapunitive adj. referring to the punishment of others: tending to direct anger, blame, or hostility away from the self toward the external factors, such as situations and other people, perceived to be the source of one's frustrations. Compare INTRO-PUNITIVE.

extrapyramidal symptoms (EPS) a group of adverse drug reactions attributable to dysfunction of the extrapyramidal tract of the central nervous system, which regulates muscle tone and body posture and coordinates opposing sets of skeletal muscles and movement of their associated skeletal parts. Manifestations include rigidity of the limbs, tremor, and other Parkinson-like signs; dystonia (abnormal facial and body movements); and akathisia (restlessness). Extrapyramidal symptoms are among the most common side effects of the high-potency ANTIPSYCHOTICS.

extrasensory perception (ESP) alleged awareness of external events by other means than the known sensory channels. It includes TELEPATHY, CLAIRVOYANCE, PRECOGNITION, and, more loosely, PSYCHOKINESIS. Despite considerable research, the existence of any of these modalities remains highly controversial. See PARAPSYCHOLOGY.

extrastriate cortex see PRE-STRIATE CORTEX.

extraversion (extroversion) *n.* one of the elements of the BIG FIVE PERSONALITY MODEL and the FIVE-FACTOR PERSONALITY MODEL, characterized by an orientation of one's interests and energies toward the outer world of people and things rather than the inner world of subjective experience. Extraversion is a broad personality trait and, like IN-TROVERSION, exists on a continuum of attitudes and behaviors. Extroverts are relatively more outgoing, gregarious, sociable, and openly expressive. **—extraversive** *adj.* **—extraverted** *adj.* **—extravert** *n.*

extrinsic motivation an external incentive to engage in a specific ac-tivity, especially motivation arising from the expectation of punishment or reward (e.g., studying to avoid failing an examination). Compare INTRINSIC MOTIVATION.

eye *n.* the organ of sight. The human eye has three layers: (a) the outer corneoscleral coat, which includes the transparent CORNEA and the fibrous SCLERA; (b) the middle layer, called the uveal tract, which includes the IRIS, the ciliary body, and the choroid layer; and (c) the innermost layer, the RETINA, which is sensitive to light. RETINAL GANGLION CELLS within the retina communicate with the central nervous system through the OPTIC NERVE, which leaves the retina at the OPTIC DISK. The eye also has three chambers. The anterior chamber, between the cornea and the iris, and the posterior chamber, between the ciliary body, LENS, and posterior aspect of the iris, are filled with a clear, watery fluid, the **aqueous humor**, and connected by the PUPIL. The third chamber, the vitreous body, is the large cavity between the lens and the retina filled with thick, transparent fluid called **vitreous humor**.

eye contact a direct look exchanged between two people who are interacting. Social-psychological studies of eye contact generally find that people typically look more at the other person when listening to that person than when they themselves are talking, that they tend to avoid eye contact when they are embarrassed, that women are apt to maintain more eye contact than are men, and that the more intimate the relationship, the greater is the eye contact.

eye-movement desensitization and reprocessing (EMDR) a treatment methodology used to reduce the emotional impact of trauma-based symptomatology associated

E

with anxiety, nightmares, flashbacks, or intrusive thought processes. The therapy incorporates simultaneous visualization of the traumatic event while concentrating on the rapid lateral movements of a therapist's finger.

eye movements movements of the eyes within the eye socket caused by contraction of the extrinsic eye muscles. These include movements that allow or maintain the visual FIXATION of stationary targets; SMOOTH-PURSUIT MOVEMENTS; VERGENCE movements; and reflexive movements of the eyes, such as the OPTOKINETIC REFLEX and VESTIBULO-OCULAR REFLEX.

eyewitness memory an individual's recollection of an event, often a crime or accident of some kind, that he or she personally saw or experienced. The reliability of eyewitness testimony is a major issue in FORENSIC PSYCHOLOGY.

Eysenck Personality Inventory (EPI) a self-report test comprising 57 yes–no questions designed to measure two major personality dimensions: introversion–extraversion and neuroticism. The EPI has been revised and expanded since its initial publication in 1963 to become the **Eysenck Personality Questionnaire (EPQ)**, the most recent version of which (the **EPQ–R**) includes 90 questions and measures the additional personality dimension of psychoticism. [Hans **Eysenck** (1916–1997), German-born British psychologist; Sybil B. G. **Eysenck**, British psychologist]

Ff

fabulation *n.* random speech that includes the recounting of imaginary incidents by a person who believes these incidents are real. See also DELUSION.

face validity apparent validity: the extent to which the items or content of a test or other assessment instrument appear to be appropriate for measuring something, regardless of whether they really are.

facework *n.* in social interactions, a set of strategic behaviors by which people maintain both their own dignity ("face") and that of the people with whom they are dealing. Facework strategies include politeness, deference, tact, avoidance of difficult subjects, and the use of half-truths and "white lies." The conventions governing facework differ widely between cultures.

facial affect program a hypothetical set of central nervous system structures that accounts for the patterning of universal, basic facial expressions of emotion in humans. Such a program could provide the link between a specific emotion and a given pattern of facial muscular activity.

facial electromyography a technique for measuring the endogenous electrical activity of any muscle or muscle group in the face by the appropriate placement of electrodes (see ELECTROMYOGRAPHY). This procedure is usually carried out to detect implicit, invisible facial movements related to emotion or speech.

facial expression a form of nonverbal signaling using the movement of facial muscles. As well as being an integral part of communication, facial expression also reflects an individual's emotional state. Cross-cultural research and studies of blind children indicate that certain facial expressions are spontaneous and universally correlated with such primary emotions as surprise, fear, anger, sadness, and happiness; DISPLAY RULES, however, can modify or even inhibit these expressions.

facial feedback hypothesis the hypothesis that sensory information provided to the brain from facial muscle movements is a major determinant of intrapsychic feeling states, such as fear, anger, joy, contempt, and so on.

facial nerve the seventh CRANIAL NERVE, which innervates facial musculature and some sensory receptors, including those of the external ear and the tongue.

facilitation *n.* in neuroscience, the phenomenon in which the threshold for propagation of the action potential of a neuron is lowered due to repeated signals at a SYNAPSE or the SUMMATION of subthreshold impulses. —**facilitate** *vb.*

facilitator *n.* a professionally trained or lay member of a group who fulfills some or all of the functions of a group leader. The facilitator encourages discussion among all group members, without necessarily entering into the discussion.

factitious disorder any of a group of disorders in which the patient intentionally produces or feigns symptoms solely so that he or she may assume the SICK ROLE. It is distinct from MALINGERING, which involves a specific external factor as motivation. See also MUNCHAUSEN SYNDROME.

factitious disorder by proxy see MUNCHAUSEN SYNDROME BY PROXY.

factor *n.* **1.** anything that contributes to a result or has a causal relationship to a phenomenon, event, or action. In ANALYSIS OF VARIANCE, for example, a factor is an independent variable, whereas in FACTOR ANALYSIS it is an underlying, unobservable LATENT VARIABLE thought (together with other factors) to be responsible for the interrelations among a set of variables.

factor analysis a broad family of mathematical procedures for reducing a set of intercorrelations among MANIFEST VARIABLES to a smaller set of unobserved LATENT VARIABLES (factors). For example, a number of tests of mechanical ability might be intercorrelated to enable factor analysis to reduce them to a few factors, such as fine motor coordination, speed, and attention. This technique is often used to examine the common influences believed to give rise to a set of observed measures (measurement structure) or to reduce a larger set of measures to a smaller set of linear composites for use in subsequent analysis (data reduction).

factorial design an experimental design in which two or more independent variables are simultaneously manipulated or observed in order to study their joint and separate influences on a dependent variable.

factor rotation in FACTOR ANALY-SIS, the repositioning of factors (latent variables) to a new, more interpretable configuration by a set of mathematically specifiable TRANSFORMATIONS. Rotations can be orthogonal (e.g., varimax, quartimax), in which the rotated factors are uncorrelated, or oblique, in which the rotated factors are correlated.

fading *n.* in conditioning, the gradual changing of one stimulus to another, which is often used to transfer STIMULUS CONTROL. Stimuli can be faded out (gradually removed) or faded in (gradually introduced).

failure to thrive (**FTT**) significantly inadequate gain in weight and height by an infant. It reflects a degree of growth failure due to inadequate release of growth hormone and, despite an initial focus on parental neglect and emotional deprivation, is currently believed to have multifactorial etiology, including biological, nutritional, and environmental contributors. The condition is associated with poor long-term developmental, growth, health, and socioemotional outcomes.

faith healing 1. the treatment of physical or psychological illness by means of religious practices, such as prayer or "laying on of hands." **2.** any form of unorthodox medical treatment whose efficacy is said to depend upon the patient's faith in the healer or the healing process (see PLACEBO EFFECT). In such cases any beneficial effects may be attributed to a psychosomatic process rather than a paranormal or supernatural one.

faking *n.* the practice of some participants in an evaluation or psychological test who either "fake good" by choosing answers that create a favorable impression or "fake bad" by choosing answers that make them appear disturbed or incompetent. —**fake** *vb.*

fallopian tube either of the slender fleshy tubes in mammals that convey ova (egg cells) from each ovary to the uterus and where fertilization may occur. [Gabriele **Fallopius** (1523–1562), Italian anatomist]

false-consensus effect the tendency to assume that one's own opinions, beliefs, attributes, or behaviors are more widely shared than is actually the case. A robustly demonstrated phenomenon, the false-consensus effect is often attributed to a desire to view one's thoughts and actions as appropriate, normal, and correct. Compare FALSE-UNIQUENESS EFFECT.

false memory a distorted recollection of an event or, most severely, recollection of an event that never happened at all. False memories are errors of commission, because details, facts, or events come to mind, often vividly, but the remembrances fail to correspond to prior events. Even when people are highly confident that they are remembering "the truth" of the original situation, experimental evidence shows that they can be wrong. The phenomenon is of particular interest in legal cases, specifically those involving eyewitness memories and **false memory syndrome** (**FMS**), in which adults seem to recover memories of having been physically or sexually abused as children, with such recoveries often occurring during therapy. The label is controversial, as is the evidence for and against recovery of abuse memories; false memory syndrome is not an accepted diagnostic term, and some have suggested using the more neutral phrase RE-COVERED MEMORY. Also called **paramnesia**.

false-uniqueness effect the tendency to underestimate the extent to which others possess the same beliefs and attributes as oneself or engage in the same behaviors, particularly when these characteristics or behaviors are positive or socially desirable. It is often attributed to a desire to view one's thoughts and actions as unusual, arising from personal, internal causes. Compare FALSE-CONSENSUS EFFECT.

falsifiability *n.* the condition of admitting falsification: the logical possibility that an assertion, hypothesis, or theory can be shown to be false. The most important properties that make a statement falsifiable in this way are (a) that it makes a prediction about an outcome or a universal claim of the type "All Xs have property Y" and (b) that what is predicted or claimed is observable. Austrian-born British philosopher Karl Popper (1902–1994) argued that falsifiability is an essential characteristic of any genuinely scientific hypothesis. —**falsifiable** *adj.*

familial study a study in which some measure or measures of an attribute or condition (e.g., a disorder, intelligence, suicidal behavior) among people of a known genetic relationship are correlated. The extent to which performance on a given measure varies as a function of genetic similarity is used as an indication of the HERITABILITY of that measure.

familiarity *n.* a form of remembering in which a situation, event, place, person, or the like provokes a subjective feeling of recognition and is therefore believed to be in memory, although it is not specifically recalled.

familism *n.* a cultural value common in collectivist or traditional societies that emphasizes strong interpersonal relationships within the EXTENDED FAMILY together with interdependence, collaboration, and the placing of group interests ahead

F

of individual interests. **—familistic** *adj.*

family systems theory a broad conceptual model that focuses on the relationships between and among interacting individuals in the family. Combining core concepts from such areas as GENERAL SYSTEMS THEORY, OBJECT RELATIONS THEORY, and SOCIAL LEARNING THEORY, family systems theory stresses that therapists cannot work only with individual family members to create constructive family changes but must see the whole family to effect systemic and lasting changes.

family therapy a form of PSYCHO-THERAPY that focuses on the improvement of interfamilial relationships and behavioral patterns of the family unit as a whole, as well as among individual members and groupings, or subsystems, within the family. Family therapy includes a large number of treatment forms with diverse conceptual principles, processes and structures, and clinical foci. Some family therapy approaches (e.g., that based on OBJECT RELATIONS THEORY) reflect extensions of models of psychotherapy with individuals in the interpersonal realm, whereas others (e.g., STRUC-TURAL FAMILY THERAPY) evolved in less traditional contexts.

fantasy *n.* **1.** any of a range of mental experiences and processes marked by vivid imagery, intensity of emotion, and relaxation or absence of logic. Fantasizing is normal and common and often serves a healthy purpose of releasing tension, giving pleasure and amusement, or stimulating creativity. It can also be indicative of pathology, as in delusional thinking or significant disconnection from reality. **2.** in psychoanalytic theories, a figment of the imagination: a mental image, night DREAM, or DAYDREAM in which a person's conscious or unconscious wishes and impulses are fulfilled (see WISH-FULFILLMENT). **—fantasize** *vb.*

FAP abbreviation for FIXED ACTION PATTERN.

farsightedness *n.* see HYPEROPIA.

FAS abbreviation for FETAL ALCOHOL SYNDROME.

fast mapping the ability of young children to learn new words quickly on the basis of only one or two exposures to these words.

father surrogate a substitute for a person's biological father, who performs typical paternal functions and serves as an object of identification and attachment. Father surrogates may include such individuals as adoptive fathers, stepfathers, older brothers, teachers, and others. Also called **father figure**; **surrogate father**.

fatigue effect a decline in performance on a prolonged or physically demanding research task that is generally attributed to the participant becoming tired or bored with the task.

F distribution a theoretical PROBABILITY DISTRIBUTION widely used in the ANALYSIS OF VARIANCE and other statistical tests of hypotheses about population variances. It is the ratio of the variances of two independent random variables each divided by its DEGREES OF FREEDOM.

fear *n.* an intense emotion aroused by the detection of imminent threat, involving an immediate alarm reaction that mobilizes the organism by triggering a set of physiological changes. These include rapid heartbeat, redirection of blood flow away from the periphery toward the gut, tensing of the muscles, and a general mobilization of the organism to take action (see FIGHT-OR-FLIGHT RESPONSE). According to some theorists, fear

F

differs from ANXIETY in that it has an object (e.g., a predator, financial ruin) and is a proportionate response to the objective threat, whereas anxiety typically lacks an object or is a more intense response than is warranted by the perceived threat.

fearful attachment an adult attachment style characterized by a negative INTERNAL WORKING MODEL OF ATTACHMENT of oneself and of others. Individuals with fearful attachment doubt both their own and others' competence and efficacy and are presumed not to seek help from others when distressed. Compare DISMISSIVE ATTACHMENT; PREOCCUPIED ATTACHMENT; SECURE ATTACHMENT.

fear of failure persistent and irrational anxiety about failing to measure up to the standards and goals set by oneself or others. Fear of failure may be associated with perfectionism and is implicated in a number of psychological disorders, including some ANXIETY DISORDERS and EATING DISORDERS.

fear of success a fear of accomplishing one's goals or succeeding in society, or a tendency to avoid doing so. Fear of success was originally thought to be experienced primarily by women, because striving for success was held to place a woman in conflict between a general need for achievement and social values that tell her not to achieve "too much." It is now thought that men and women are equally likely to experience fear of success.

feature detector any of various hypothetical or actual mechanisms within the human information-processing system that respond selectively to specific distinguishing features. For example, the visual system has feature detectors for lines and angles of different orientations or even for more complex stimuli,

such as faces. Feature detectors are also thought to play an important role in speech perception, where their function would be to detect those features that distinguish one PHONEME from another.

feature-integration theory a two-stage theory of visual ATTENTION. In the first (preattentive) stage, basic features (e.g., color, shape) are processed automatically, independently, and in parallel. In the second (attentive) stage, other properties, including relations between features of an object, are processed in series, one object (or group) at a time, and "bound" together to create a single object that is perceived.

Fechner's law a mathematical formula relating subjective experience to changes in physical stimulus intensity: specifically, the sensation experienced is proportional to the logarithm of the stimulus magnitude. It is derived from WEBER'S LAW and expressed as $\Psi = k \log S$, where Ψ is the sensation, k is a constant, and S is the physical intensity of the stimulus. See also STEVENS LAW. [Gustav Theodor **Fechner** (1801–1887), German physician and philosopher]

feedback *n.* information about a process or interaction provided to the governing system or agent and used to make adjustments that eliminate problems or otherwise optimize functioning. It may be stabilizing NEGATIVE FEEDBACK or amplifying POSITIVE FEEDBACK. The term's origins in engineering and cybernetics lend it a distinct connotation of input–output models that is not as strictly applicable to the wide variety of usages found in psychology, such as BIOFEEDBACK, information feedback, and social feedback.

feedback loop in cybernetic theory, a self-regulatory model that determines whether the current operation of a system is acceptable and, if not, attempts to make the necessary changes. Its operation is summarized by the acronym TOTE (*t*est, *o*perate, *t*est, *e*xit). The two test phases compare the current reality against the goal or standard. Operate refers to any processes or interventions designed to resolve unacceptable discrepancies between the reality and the standard. Exit refers to the closing down of the supervisory feedback loop because the circumstances have been brought into agreement with the standard. Also called **TOTE model**.

feeling *n.* **1.** a self-contained phenomenal experience. Feelings are subjective, evaluative, and independent of the sensory modality of the sensations, thoughts, or images evoking them. They are inevitably evaluated as pleasant or unpleasant but they can have more specific intrapsychic qualities as well. The core characteristic that differentiates feelings from cognitive, sensory, or perceptual intrapsychic experiences is the link of AFFECT to APPRAISAL. Feelings differ from EMOTIONS in being purely mental, whereas emotions are designed to engage with the world. **2.** any experienced sensation, particularly a tactile or temperature sensation (e.g., pain or coldness).

female orgasmic disorder a condition in which a woman recurrently or persistently has difficulty obtaining orgasm or is unable to reach orgasm at all following sexual stimulation and excitement, causing marked distress or interpersonal difficulty. Female orgasmic disorder is the second most frequently reported women's sexual problem.

female sexual arousal disorder a condition in which a woman recurrently or persistently is unable to attain or maintain adequate vaginal lubrication and swelling during sexual excitement, causing marked distress or interpersonal difficulty. It is a prevalent sexual problem for women and has a complex etiology involving a variety of physiological and psychological factors.

feminism *n.* any of a number of perspectives that take as their subject matter the problems and perspectives of women, or the nature of biological and social phenomena related to GENDER. Although some feminist perspectives focus on issues of fairness and equal rights, other approaches emphasize what are taken to be inherent and systematic gender inequities in Western society (see PATRIARCHY). In psychology, feminism has focused attention on the nature and origin of gender differences in psychological processes. **—feminist** *adj., n.*

fertilization *n.* the fusion of a sperm and an egg cell to produce a ZYGOTE. In humans, fertilization occurs in a FALLOPIAN TUBE.

fetal alcohol syndrome (FAS) a group of adverse fetal and infant health effects associated with heavy maternal alcohol intake during pregnancy. It is characterized by low birth weight and retarded growth, craniofacial anomalies (e.g., microcephaly), neurobehavioral problems (e.g., hyperactivity), and cognitive abnormalities (e.g., language acquisition deficits); mental retardation may be present. Children showing some (but not all) features of this syndrome are described as having **fetal alcohol effects (FAE)**.

fetishism *n.* a type of PARAPHILIA in which inanimate objects—commonly undergarments, stockings, rubber items, shoes, or boots—are repeatedly or exclusively used in achieving sexual excitement. Fetishism occurs primarily among males and may compete or interfere with sexual contact with a partner. **—fetishistic** *adj.*

fetus *n.* an animal EMBRYO in the later stages of development. In humans, the fetal period is from the end of the eighth week after fertilization until birth. **—fetal** *adj.*

field *n.* **1.** a defined area or region of space, such as the VISUAL FIELD. **2.** a complex of personal, physical, and social factors within which a psychological event takes place. See FIELD THEORY. **3.** somewhere other than a laboratory, library, or academic setting in which experimental work is carried out or data collected. See FIELD EXPERIMENT.

field dependence a COGNITIVE STYLE in which the individual consistently relies more on external referents (environmental cues) than on internal referents (bodily sensation cues). The opposite tendency, relying more on internal than external referents, is called **field independence**. Both were discovered during experiments conducted in the 1950s to understand the factors that determine perception of the upright in space.

field experiment an experiment that is conducted outside the laboratory in a "real-world" setting. Participants are exposed to one of two or more levels of an independent variable and observed for their reactions; they are likely to be unaware of the experiment.

field research research conducted outside the laboratory, in a natural, real-world setting. Field research has the advantages of ECOLOGICAL VALIDITY and the opportunity to understand how and why behavior occurs in a natural social environment. Compare LABORATORY RESEARCH.

field theory a systematic approach describing behavior in terms of patterns of dynamic interrelationships between individuals and the psychological, social, and physical situation in which they exist. This situation is known as the **field space** or LIFE SPACE, and the dynamic interactions are conceived as forces with positive or negative valences (subjective values).

field work a less common name for FIELD RESEARCH.

fight-or-flight response a pattern of physiological changes elicited by activity of the SYMPATHETIC NERVOUS SYSTEM in response to threatening or otherwise stressful situations that leads to mobilization of energy for physical activity (e.g., attacking or avoiding the offending stimulus), either directly or by inhibiting physiological activity that does not contribute to energy mobilization. Specific sympathetic responses involved in the reaction include increased heart rate, respiratory rate, and sweat gland activity; elevated blood pressure; decreased digestive activity; pupil dilation; and a routing of blood flow to skeletal muscles.

figure–ground *adj.* relating to the principle that perceptions have two parts: a figure that stands out in good contour and an indistinct, homogeneous background.

file-drawer problem the fact that a large proportion of all studies actually conducted are not available for review because they remain unpublished in "file drawers," having failed to obtain positive results.

filter theory an early theory of attention proposing that unattended channels of information are filtered prior to identification. This theory continues to be influential in the form of its successor, the ATTENUATION THEORY.

fine motor describing activities or skills that require coordination of small muscles to control small, precise movements, particularly in the hands and face. Examples of **fine motor skills** include handwriting, drawing, cutting, and manipulating small objects. Compare GROSS MOTOR.

first-generation antipsychotic see ANTIPSYCHOTIC.

first-impression bias see PRIMACY EFFECT.

Fisher's r to Z transformation a mathematical transformation of the PRODUCT–MOMENT CORRELATION coefficient (r) to a new statistic (Z) whose sampling distribution is the normal distribution. It is used for testing hypotheses about correlations and constructing CONFIDENCE INTERVALS on correlations. [Sir Ronald Aylmer **Fisher** (1890–1962), British statistician and geneticist]

fissure *n.* a cleft, groove, or indentation in a surface, especially any of the deep grooves in the cerebral cortex. See also SULCUS.

fitness *n.* **1.** a set of attributes that people have or are able to achieve relating to their ability to perform physical work and to carry out daily tasks with vigor and alertness, without undue fatigue, and with ample energy to enjoy leisure pursuits. **2.** in biology, the extent to which an organism or population is able to produce viable offspring in a given environment, which is a measure of that organism's or population's adaptation to that environment. See also INCLUSIVE FITNESS. —**fit** *adj.*

five-factor personality model a model of personality in which five dimensions of individual difference—EXTRAVERSION, NEUROTICISM, conscientiousness (being responsible and hardworking), agreeableness (acting in a cooperative, unselfish manner), and openness to experience (participating in new aesthetic, cultural, or intellectual experiences)—are viewed as core personality structures. Unlike the BIG FIVE PERSONALITY MODEL, which views the five personality dimensions as descriptions of behavior and treats the five-dimensional structure as a taxonomy of individual differences, the five-factor personality model also views the factors as psychological entities with causal force. The two models are frequently and incorrectly conflated in the scientific literature, without regard for their distinctly different emphases.

fixation *n.* **1.** an obsessive preoccupation: excessive interest in or focus upon something, such as a particular idea or approach to solving a problem. **2.** in psychoanalytic theory, either the persistence of an early stage of PSYCHOSEXUAL DEVELOPMENT or an inappropriate attachment to an early OBJECT (especially the mother or father). **3.** the orientation of the eyes so that the image of a viewed object falls on the FOVEA CENTRALIS, in the central part of the retina. —**fixate** *vb.*

fixed action pattern (FAP) in classical ethology, a stereotyped, genetically preprogrammed, species-specific behavioral sequence that is evoked by a RELEASER stimulus and is carried out without sensory feedback. In contemporary ethology the term MODAL ACTION PATTERN is more often used.

fixed-interval schedule (FI schedule) in conditioning, an arrangement in which the first response after a set interval has elapsed is reinforced. "FI 3 min" means that reinforcement is given to the first response occurring at least 3 min after a previous reinforcement. Often, experience with FI schedules results in a temporal pattern of responding, characterized by little or no responding at the beginning of the interval, followed by an increased rate later on as reinforcement becomes more imminent. This pattern is often referred to as the **fixed-interval scallop**.

fixed-ratio schedule (FR schedule) in conditioning, an arrangement in which reinforcement is given after a specified number of responses. "FR 1" means that reinforcement is given after each response; "FR 50" means that reinforcement is given after 50 responses.

flashback *n.* **1.** the reliving of a traumatic event after the initial adjustment to the trauma appears to have been made. Flashbacks are part of POSTTRAUMATIC STRESS DISORDER: Forgotten memories are reawakened by words, sounds, smells, or scenes that are reminiscent of the original trauma (e.g., when a backfiring car elicits the kind of anxiety that a combat veteran experienced when he or she was the target of enemy fire). **2.** the spontaneous recurrence of the perceptual distortions and disorientation to time and place experienced during a previous period of hallucinogen intoxication. Flashbacks may occur months or even years after the last use of the drug and are associated particularly with LSD.

flashbulb memory a vivid, enduring memory associated with a personally significant and emotional event. Such memories have the quality of a photograph taken the moment the individual experienced the emotion, including such details as where the individual was or what he or she was doing.

flat affect total or near absence of appropriate emotional responses to situations and events. See also SHALLOW AFFECT.

flexion *n.* the bending of a joint in a limb (e.g., the elbow joint) so that two parts of the limb (e.g., the fore-

arm and upper arm) are brought toward each other.

flexor *n.* a muscle whose contraction bends a part of the body, such as the biceps muscle of the upper arm. Compare EXTENSOR.

flicker fusion frequency see CRITICAL FLICKER FREQUENCY.

flight into health in psychotherapy, an abrupt "recuperation" by a prospective client after or during intake interviews and before entry into therapy proper or, more commonly, by a client in ongoing therapy. Psychoanalytic theory interprets the flight into health as an unconscious DEFENSE MECHANISM.

flight into illness in psychotherapy, the sudden development of physical or other symptoms by a client or prospective client. Psychoanalytic theory interprets this as an unconscious DEFENSE MECHANISM that is used to avoid examination of a deeper underlying conflict.

flooding *n.* a technique in BEHAVIOR THERAPY in which the individual is exposed directly to a maximum-intensity anxiety-producing situation or stimulus, either in the imagination but most often in reality, without any attempt made to lessen or avoid anxiety or fear during the exposure. For an individual with claustrophobia, for example, this would entail spending extended periods of time in a small room. Flooding techniques aim to diminish or extinguish the undesired behavior and are used primarily in the treatment of individuals with phobias and similar disorders. It is distinct from SYSTEMATIC DESENSITIZATION, which involves a gradual, step-by-step approach to encountering the feared situation or stimulus while attempting throughout to maintain a nonanxious state. See also IMPLOSIVE THERAPY.

F

floor effect a situation in which a large proportion of participants perform as poorly as, or nearly as poorly as, possible on a task or other evaluative measure, thus skewing the distribution of scores and making it impossible to discriminate differences among the many individuals at that low level. For example, a test whose items are too difficult for those taking it would show a floor effect because most people would obtain or be close to the lowest possible score of 0. Compare CEILING EFFECT.

flow *n.* a state of optimal experience arising from intense involvement in an activity that is enjoyable, such as playing a sport, performing a musical passage, or writing a creative piece. Flow arises when one's skills are fully utilized yet equal to the demands of the task, intrinsic motivation is at a peak, one loses self-consciousness and temporal awareness, and one has a sense of total control, effortlessness, and complete concentration on the immediate situation (the here and now).

fluent aphasia see APHASIA.

fluid intelligence the form of intelligence that comprises those abilities, such as memory span and mental quickness, that are functionally related to physiological condition and maturation. Fluid intelligence appears to increase during childhood and to deteriorate, to some extent, in old age. Compare CRYSTALLIZED INTELLIGENCE.

fluoxetine *n.* an antidepressant that is the prototype of the SSRIS (selective serotonin reuptake inhibitors). Fluoxetine differs from other SSRIs in that it and its biologically active metabolic product, norfluoxetine, have a prolonged HALF-LIFE of 5–7 days after a single dose. U.S. trade name: **Prozac**.

Flynn effect the gradual cross-cultural rise in raw scores obtained on measures of general intelligence. These increases have been roughly 9 points per generation (i.e., 30 years). [James **Flynn** (1934–), New Zealand philosopher who first documented its occurrence]

fMRI abbreviation for FUNCTIONAL MAGNETIC RESONANCE IMAGING.

focal psychotherapy a form of BRIEF PSYCHOTHERAPY in which a single problematic area (e.g., excessive anxiety) is made the target of the entire course of treatment. The therapist continually redirects the process so as to avoid deviations from this specifically identified aim, for example, by preventing discussion of material he or she deems irrelevant to the intended therapeutic goal.

focal seizure see PARTIAL SEIZURE.

focus group a small group of people who share common characteristics and are selected to discuss a topic of which they have personal experience. Originally used in marketing to determine consumer response to particular products, focus groups are now used for determining typical reactions, adaptations, and solutions to any number of issues, events, or topics.

folie à deux see SHARED PSYCHOTIC DISORDER. [French, "double insanity"]

follicle *n.* a cluster of cells enclosing, protecting, and nourishing a cell or structure within. —**follicular** *adj.*

follicle-stimulating hormone (**FSH**) a GONADOTROPIN released by the anterior pituitary gland that, in females, stimulates the development in the ovary of graafian follicles (see MENSTRUAL CYCLE). The same hormone in males stimulates Sertoli cells in the testis to produce spermatozoa. Also called **follitropin**.

follow-up study a long-term study designed to examine the degree to which effects seen shortly after the imposition of a therapeutic intervention persist over time.

foot-in-the-door technique a two-step procedure for enhancing compliance in which a minor initial request is presented immediately before the more substantial target request. Agreement to the initial request makes people more likely to agree to the target request than would have been the case if the latter had been presented on its own. See also DOOR-IN-THE-FACE TECHNIQUE; LOW-BALL TECHNIQUE; THAT'S-NOT-ALL TECHNIQUE.

forced-choice *adj.* describing any procedural format or assessment instrument in which participants are provided with a predetermined set of alternatives from which they must choose a response. For example, a forced-choice test in signal detection tasks is a test in which two or more intervals are presented, one of which contains the signal. The observer must choose the interval in which the signal was presented. Compare FREE-RESPONSE.

forced compliance effect the tendency of a person who has behaved in a way that contradicts his or her attitude to subsequently alter the attitude to be consistent with the behavior. It is one way of reducing COGNITIVE DISSONANCE. Also called **induced compliance effect**.

forebrain *n.* the part of the brain that develops from the anterior section of the NEURAL TUBE in the embryo, containing the TELENCEPHALON and the DIENCEPHALON. The former comprises the cerebral hemispheres with their various regions (e.g., BASAL GANGLIA, AMYGDALA, HIPPOCAMPUS); the latter comprises the THALAMUS and HYPOTHALAMUS. Also called **prosencephalon**.

foreclosure *n.* in development, see IDENTITY FORECLOSURE.

forensic psychology the application of psychological principles and techniques to situations involving the civil and criminal legal systems. Its functions include assessment and treatment services, provision of advocacy and expert testimony, and research and policy analysis.

forgetting *n.* the failure to remember material previously learned. Numerous processes and theories have been proposed throughout its long history of study to account for forgetting, including DECAY THEORY and INTERFERENCE THEORY. Forgetting typically is a normal phenomenon that plays an important adaptive role in restricting access to information that is likely to be needed in current interactions with the environment, but may also be pathological, as, for example, in amnesia.

forgiveness *n.* willfully putting aside feelings of resentment toward an individual who has committed a wrong, been unfair or hurtful, or otherwise harmed one in some way. Forgiveness is not equated with reconciliation or excusing another, and it is not merely accepting what happened or ceasing to be angry. Rather, it involves a voluntary transformation of one's feelings, attitudes, and behavior toward the individual, so that one is no longer dominated by resentment and can express compassion, generosity, or the like toward the individual. Forgiveness is often considered an important process in psychotherapy or counseling.

formal operational stage the fourth and final stage in the

PIAGETIAN THEORY of cognitive development, beginning around age 12, during which complex intellectual functions, such as abstract thinking, logical processes, conceptualization, and judgment, develop.

formal thought disorder disruptions in the form or structure of thinking. Examples include derailment, frequent interruptions and jumps from one idea to another, and tangentiality, constant digressions to irrelevant topics. It is distinct from THOUGHT DISORDER, in which the disturbance relates to thought content.

formants *pl. n.* the frequency bands of sounds produced by the vocal cords and other physical features of the head and throat in speaking. A simple sound, such as the vowel /a/, may span several kilohertz of frequencies.

fornix *n.* (*pl.* **fornices**) any arch-shaped structure, especially the long tract of white matter in the brain arching between the HIPPOCAMPUS and the HYPOTHALAMUS.

forward conditioning in PAVLOVIAN CONDITIONING, the pairing of two stimuli such that the conditioned stimulus is presented before the unconditioned stimulus. Also called **forward pairing**. Compare BACKWARD CONDITIONING.

forward selection a technique used in creating MULTIPLE REGRESSION models in which independent variables are added to the REGRESSION EQUATION in the order of their predictive power until a preset criterion is reached. Also called **forward stepwise regression**.

foster care temporary care provided to children in settings outside their family of origin and by individuals other than their natural or adoptive parents, under the supervision of a public child welfare agency. Foster care is intended to keep children whose parents are unavailable or incapable of proper care safe from harm, with the ultimate goal being to find a secure and permanent home. Typically, a child is placed with a family approved for foster care and paid a fee for such by a public child welfare agency. Although these **foster home** arrangements are most common, children may also be placed in group homes or other institutions.

four-card problem see WASON SELECTION TASK.

Fourier analysis the mathematical analysis of complex waveforms using the fact that they can be expressed as an infinite sum of sine and cosine functions (a **Fourier series**). It is accomplished via a **Fourier transform**, a mathematical operation that analyzes any waveform into a set of simple waveforms with different frequencies and amplitudes. Fourier analysis is particularly important in the study of sound and the theoretical understanding of visual analysis. [Jean Baptiste Joseph **Fourier** (1768–1830), French mathematician and physicist]

fourth ventricle see VENTRICLE.

fovea centralis a small depression in the central portion of the retina in which RETINAL CONE cells are most concentrated and an image is focused most clearly. Also called **fovea**. —**foveal** *adj.*

fractionation *n.* a psychophysical procedure to scale the magnitude of sensations in which an observer adjusts a variable stimulus to be half that of a standard stimulus.

fragile X syndrome a genetic condition that differentially affects males and causes a range of developmental problems including learning disabilities and mental retardation. The disorder is so named because of alterations in the *FMR1* gene, on the arm of the X chromosome, that abnormally expand and destabilize it. Males with fragile X syndrome have characteristic physical features that become more apparent with age, such as large ears, prominent jaw and forehead, a long and narrow face, and enlarged testicles. Both males and females with fragile X may exhibit hyperactivity and attention deficits, while some males also show autistic behavior.

frame of reference in social psychology, the set of assumptions or criteria by which a person judges ideas, actions, and experiences. A frame of reference can often limit or distort perception, as in the case of prejudice and stereotypes.

framing *n.* the process of defining the context or issues surrounding a question, problem, or event in a way that serves to influence how the context or issues are perceived and evaluated. See also REFRAMING.

fraternal twins see DIZYGOTIC TWINS.

F ratio (symbol: *F*) in an ANALYSIS OF VARIANCE or a MULTIVARIATE ANALYSIS OF VARIANCE, the ratio of explained to unexplained variance; that is, the ratio of BETWEEN-GROUPS VARIANCE to WITHIN-GROUP VARIANCE.

free association a basic process in PSYCHOANALYSIS and other forms of PSYCHODYNAMIC PSYCHOTHERAPY, in which the patient is encouraged to verbalize without censorship or selection whatever thoughts come to mind, no matter how embarrassing, illogical, or irrelevant. The object is to allow unconscious material, such as traumatic experiences or threatening impulses, and otherwise inhibited thoughts and emotions to come to the surface where they can be interpreted.

freedom to withdraw the right of a research participant to drop out of an experiment at any time.

free-floating anxiety a diffuse, chronic sense of uneasiness and apprehension not directed toward any specific situation or object. It may be a characteristic of a number of anxiety disorders, in particular GENERALIZED ANXIETY DISORDER.

free nerve ending a highly branched terminal portion of a sensory neuron. Found particularly in the different layers of skin, free nerve endings are the most common type of nerve ending and act as pain and temperature receptors.

free radical an atom or molecule that has at least one "unpaired" electron in its outer shell. This makes it highly reactive and able to engage in rapid chain reactions that destabilize the molecules around it, thus causing the formation of more free radicals. Free radicals can damage cells and have been implicated in aging, inflammation, and the progression of various pathological conditions, including cancer.

free recall a type of memory task in which a list of items is presented one at a time and participants attempt to remember them in any order.

free-response *adj.* describing any procedural format or assessment instrument in which participants construct their own responses to items rather than choosing from a list of alternatives as in FORCED-CHOICE techniques. An essay test is an example of a free-response method.

free-running rhythm a cycle of behavior or physiological activity that occurs if external stimuli do not provide ENTRAINMENT.

free will the power or capacity of a human being for self-direction. The concept of free will thus suggests that inclinations, dispositions, thoughts, and actions are not determined entirely by forces over which people have no independent directing influence. Free will is generally seen as necessary for moral action and responsibility and is implied by much of our everyday experience, in which we are conscious of having the power to do or forbear. However, it has often been dismissed as illusory by advocates of DETERMINISM, who hold that all occurrences, including human actions, are predetermined.

frequency *n.* the number of occurrences of a particular phenomenon in a given period. More specifically, frequency is the number of repetitions of a periodic waveform in a given unit of time. The standard measure of frequency is the hertz (Hz); this replaces, and is equivalent to, cycles per second (cps).

frequency distribution a plot of the frequency of occurrence of scores of various sizes, arranged from lowest to highest score.

frequency polygon a graph depicting a statistical distribution, made up of lines connecting the peaks of adjacent intervals.

frequency selectivity the property of a system that enables it to be "tuned" to respond better to certain frequencies than to others. The frequency selectivity of the auditory system is a fundamental aspect of hearing and has been a major research theme for many decades.

frequency theory a late 19th-century theory specifying that pitch is coded by the rate at which ACTION POTENTIALS are generated by auditory neurons within the BASILAR MEMBRANE of the ear. According to this theory, the wavelength (frequency) of a tone is precisely replicated in the electrical impulses transmitted through the AUDITORY NERVE. For example, a 100 Hz tone would be signaled by 100 impulses per second in the auditory nerve.

However, frequency theory cannot explain the perception of sounds above 500 Hz because the REFRACTORY PERIOD of a neuron renders it incapable of firing at a rate greater than 500 impulses per second. This discrepancy was accounted for by the later VOLLEY THEORY.

Freudian slip in the popular understanding of psychoanalytic theory, an unconscious error or oversight in writing, speech, or action that is held to be caused by unacceptable impulses breaking through the EGO's defenses and exposing the individual's true wishes or feelings. See PARAPRAXIS; SLIP OF THE TONGUE. [Sigmund **Freud** (1856–1939), Austrian psychiatrist]

Friedman test a nonparametric test of the equality of medians in *J* repeated measures of a matched group. [Herbert **Friedman** (1933–1996), U.S. psychologist and statistician]

friendship *n.* a voluntary relationship between two or more people that is relatively long-lasting and in which those involved tend to be concerned with meeting the others' needs and interests as well as satisfying their own desires.

frontal cortex the CEREBRAL CORTEX of the frontal lobe. See also PREFRONTAL CORTEX.

frontal lobe one of the four main lobes of each cerebral hemisphere of the brain, lying in front of the CENTRAL SULCUS. It is concerned with motor and higher order EXECUTIVE FUNCTIONS. See also PREFRONTAL LOBE.

frontal lobe syndrome deterioration in personality and behavior resulting from lesions in the frontal lobe. Typical symptoms include loss of initiative, inability to plan activities, difficulty with abstract thinking, perseveration, impairments in social judgment and impulse control, and mood disturbances such as apathy or mania.

frotteurism *n.* a PARAPHILIA in which an individual deliberately and persistently seeks sexual excitement by rubbing against other people. This may occur as apparently accidental contact in crowded public settings, such as elevators or lines.

frustration *n.* **1.** the thwarting of impulses or actions that prevents individuals from obtaining something they have been led to expect based on past experience, as when a hungry animal is prevented from obtaining food that it can see or smell or when a child is prevented from playing with a visible toy. **2.** the emotional state an individual experiences when such thwarting occurs. —**frustrate** *vb.*

frustration–aggression hypothesis the theory that (a) frustration always produces an aggressive urge and (b) aggression is always the result of prior frustrations.

frustration tolerance the ability of an individual to delay gratification or to preserve relative equanimity on encountering obstacles. The growth of adequate frustration tolerance generally occurs as part of a child's cognitive and affective development but may also be strengthened to more adaptive levels later in life through therapeutic intervention.

FSH abbreviation for FOLLICLE-STIMULATING HORMONE.

F test any of a class of statistical tests, notably including the widely used ANALYSIS OF VARIANCE, that rely on the assumption that the test statistic—the F RATIO—follows the F DISTRIBUTION when the null hypothesis is true. F tests are tests of hypotheses about population variances.

FTT abbreviation for FAILURE TO THRIVE.

fugue *n.* see DISSOCIATIVE FUGUE.

fully functioning person in CLIENT-CENTERED THERAPY, a person with a healthy personality, who experiences freedom of choice and action, is creative, and is able to live fully in the present and respond freely and flexibly to new experience without fear.

function *n.* **1.** in biology, an activity of an organ or an organism that contributes to the organism's FITNESS, such as the secretion of a sex hormone by a gonad to prepare for reproduction or the defensive behavior of a female with young toward an intruder. **2.** (symbol: f) a mathematical procedure that relates one number, quantity, or entity to another according to a defined rule. For example, if $y = 2x + 1$, y is said to be a function of x. This is often written $y = f(x)$.

functional *adj.* **1.** denoting or referring to a disorder for which there is no known organic or structural basis. In psychology and psychiatry, functional disorders are improperly considered equivalent to PSYCHOGENIC disorders. **2.** based on or relating to use rather than structure.

functional age an individual's age as determined by measures of functional capability indexed by age-normed standards. Functional age is distinct from CHRONOLOGICAL AGE and represents a combination of physiological, psychological, and social age. In adults it is calculated by measuring a range of variables, such as eyesight, hearing, mobility, cardiopulmonary function, concentration, and memory. The functional age of a child is measured in terms of the developmental level he or she has reached.

functional analysis the detailed analysis of a behavior to identify contingencies that sustain the behavior.

functional autonomy the ability of a person to perform independently the various tasks required in daily life, a core concept in such areas as rehabilitation and successful aging. For example, decline in functional autonomy is a major component of symptoms in severe dementia. Very few INSTRUMENTAL ACTIVITIES OF DAILY LIVING remain, and there is a gradual loss of self-care, or basic ACTIVITIES OF DAILY LIVING.

functional fixedness the tendency to perceive an object only in terms of its most common use. For example, people generally perceive cardboard boxes as containers, thus hindering them from potentially flipping the boxes over for use as platforms upon which to place objects (e.g., books).

functionalism *n.* a general psychological approach that views mental life and behavior in terms of active adaptation to environmental challenges and opportunities. Functionalism was developed at the beginning of the 20th century as a revolt against the atomistic point of view of STRUCTURALISM, which limited psychology to the dissection of states of consciousness and the study of mental content rather than mental activities. Functionalism emphasizes the causes and consequences of human behavior; the union of the physiological with the psychological; the need for objective testing of theories; and the applications of psychological knowledge to the solution of practical problems, the evolutionary continuity between animals and humans, and the improvement of human life.

functional magnetic resonance imaging (fMRI; functional MRI)
a form of MAGNETIC RESONANCE IMAGING that detects changes in blood flow and therefore identifies regions of the brain that are particularly active during a given task.

functional stimulus in stimulus–response experiments, the characteristic of the stimulus that actually produces a particular effect on the organism and governs its behavior. This may be different from the NOMINAL STIMULUS as defined by the experimenter. For example, if an experimenter presents a blue square to a pigeon as a nominal stimulus, the functional stimulus may simply be the color blue. Also called **effective stimulus**.

function word in linguistics, a word that has little or no meaning of its own but plays an important grammatical role: Examples include the articles (*a*, *the*, etc.), prepositions (*in*, *of*, etc.), and conjunctions (*and*, *but*, etc.). The distinction between function words and CONTENT WORDS is of great interest to the study of language disorders, LANGUAGE ACQUISITION, and psycholinguistic processing.

fundamental attribution error in ATTRIBUTION THEORY, the tendency to overestimate the degree to which an individual's behavior is determined by his or her abiding personal characteristics, attitudes, or beliefs and, correspondingly, to minimize the influence of the surrounding situation on that behavior (e.g., financial or social pressures). Also called **correspondence bias**.

fusiform gyrus a spindle-shaped ridge on the inferior (lower) surface of each TEMPORAL LOBE in the brain. It lies between the inferior temporal gyrus and the PARAHIPPOCAMPAL GYRUS and is involved in high-level visual processing, including color perception and face recognition.

Gg

g symbol for GENERAL FACTOR.

GABA abbreviation for GAMMA-AMINOBUTYRIC ACID.

GABA_A receptor one of the two main types of receptor protein that bind the neurotransmitter GAMMA-AMINOBUTYRIC ACID (GABA), the other being the GABA_B RECEPTOR. It is located at most synapses of most neurons that use GABA as a neurotransmitter. The predominant inhibitory receptor in the central nervous system (CNS), it functions as a chloride channel (see ION CHANNEL).

GABA_B receptor one of the two main types of receptor protein that bind the neurotransmitter GAMMA-AMINOBUTYRIC ACID (GABA), the other being the GABA_A RECEPTOR. GABA_B receptors, which are G PROTEIN-coupled receptors, are less plentiful in the brain than GABA_A receptors and their activation results in relatively long-lasting neuronal inhibition.

GAD abbreviation for GENERALIZED ANXIETY DISORDER.

galvanic skin response (GSR) a change in the electrical properties (conductance or resistance) of the skin in reaction to stimuli, owing to the activity of sweat glands located in the fingers and palms. Though strictly an indication of physiological arousal, the galvanic skin response is widely considered a reflection of emotional arousal and stress as well.

gambler's fallacy a failure to rec-ognize the independence of chance events, leading to the mistaken belief that one can predict the outcome of a chance event on the basis of the outcomes of past chance events.

gambling *n.* see PATHOLOGICAL GAMBLING.

game *n.* a social interaction, transaction, or other organized activity with formal rules. In psychotherapy, for example, a game is a situation in which members of a group take part in some activity designed to elicit emotions, increase self-awareness, or stimulate revealing interactions and interrelationships. In PLAY THERAPY games are often used as a projective or observational technique. See also ZERO-SUM GAME.

gamete *n.* either of the female or male reproductive cells that take part in fertilization to produce a zygote. In humans and other animals, the female gamete is the OVUM and the male gamete is the SPERMATOZOON. Gametes contain the HAPLOID number of chromosomes rather than the DIPLOID number found in body (somatic) cells. See also GERM CELL.

game theory a branch of mathematics concerned with the analysis of the behavior of decision makers (called players) whose choices affect one another. Game theory is often used in both theoretical modeling and empirical studies of conflict, cooperation, and competition, and has helped to structure interactive decision-making situations in numerous disciplines, including economics, political science, social psychology, and ethics.

gamma-aminobutyric acid (GABA) a major inhibitory NEURO-TRANSMITTER in the mammalian nervous system that is synthesized from the amino acid glutamic acid.

gamma motor neuron see MOTOR NEURON.

gamma movement see APPARENT MOVEMENT.

gamma wave in electroencepha-lography, a type of low-amplitude BRAIN WAVE ranging from 31 to 80 Hz (with power peaking near 40 Hz) and associated with higher-level cognitive activities, such as memory storage. Also called **gamma rhythm**.

ganglion *n.* (*pl.* **ganglia**) a collec-tion of CELL BODIES of neurons that lies outside the central nervous sys-tem (the BASAL GANGLIA, however, are an exception). Many inverte-brates have only distributed ganglia and no centralized nervous system. Compare NUCLEUS. —**ganglionic** *adj.*

ganglion cell see RETINAL GAN-GLION CELL.

gap junction a type of inter-cellular junction consisting of a gap of about 2–4 nm between the plasma membranes of two cells, spanned by protein channels that allow passage of electrical signals. See ELECTRICAL SYNAPSE.

GAS abbreviation for GENERAL AD-APTATION SYNDROME.

gate-control theory the hypothe-sis that the subjective experience of pain is modulated by large nerve fi-bers in the spinal cord that act as gates, such that pain is not the prod-uct of a simple transmission of stimulation from the skin or some internal organ to the brain. Rather, sensations from noxious stimulation

impinging on pain receptors have to pass through these spinal gates to the brain in order to emerge as pain perceptions. The status of the gates, however, is subject to a variety of influences (e.g., drugs, injury, emo-tions, possibly even instructions coming down from the brain itself), which can operate to shut them, thus inhibiting pain transmission, or cause them to be fully open, thus facilitating transmission.

gatekeeper *n.* a health care profes-sional, usually a PRIMARY CARE provider associated with a MANAGED CARE organization, who determines a patient's access to health care ser-vices and whose approval is required for referrals to specialists.

gateway drug any chemical sub-stance whose chronic use leads to the subsequent use of more harmful substances that have significant po-tential for abuse and dependence. For example, alcohol, tobacco, and MARIJUANA are often considered a gateway to such drugs as HEROIN, COCAINE, LSD, and PCP. Introduced in the 1950s, the concept has be-come the most popular framework for understanding drug use among adolescent populations, guiding pre-vention efforts and even shaping governmental policy.

gating *n.* the inhibition or exclu-sion from attention of certain sensory stimuli when attention is focused on other stimuli. That is, while attending to specific informa-tion in the environment, other information does not reach aware-ness.

Gaussian distribution see NOR-MAL DISTRIBUTION. [Karl Friedrich **Gauss** (1777–1855), German mathe-matician]

gender *n.* the condition of being male, female, or neuter. In a human context, the distinction between gender and sex reflects usage of these terms: Sex usually refers to the biological aspects of maleness or femaleness, whereas gender implies the psychological, behavioral, social, and cultural aspects of being male or female (i.e., masculinity or femininity).

gender bias any one of a variety of stereotypical beliefs about individuals on the basis of their sex, particularly as related to the differential treatment of females and males. These biases often are expressed linguistically, as in use of the phrase *physicians and their wives* (instead of *physicians and their spouses*, which avoids the implication that physicians must be male) or of the term *he* when people of both sexes are under discussion.

gender consistency the understanding that one's own and other people's sex is fixed across situations, regardless of superficial changes in appearance or activities. See GENDER CONSTANCY.

gender constancy a child's emerging sense of the permanence of being a boy or a girl, an understanding that occurs in a series of stages: GENDER IDENTITY, GENDER STABILITY, and GENDER CONSISTENCY.

gender differences typical differences between men and women that are specific to a particular culture and influenced by its attitudes and practices. Gender differences emerge in a variety of domains, such as careers, communication, and interpersonal relationships.

gender dysphoria discontent with the physical or social aspects of one's own sex. See also DYSPHORIA.

gender identity a recognition that one is male or female and the internalization of this knowledge into one's self-concept. Although the dominant approach in psychology for many years had been to regard gender identity as residing in indi-

viduals, the importance of societal structures, cultural expectations, and personal interactions in its development is now recognized as well. Indeed, significant evidence now exists to support the conceptualization of gender identity as influenced by both environmental and biological factors. See GENDER CONSTANCY. See also GENDER ROLE.

gender identity disorder a disorder characterized by clinically significant distress or impairment of functioning due to cross-gender identification (i.e., a desire to be or actual insistence that one is of the opposite sex) and persistent discomfort arising from the belief that one's sex or gender is inappropriate to one's true self. The disorder is distinguished from simple dissatisfaction or nonconformity with gender roles.

gender role the pattern of behavior, personality traits, and attitudes that define masculinity or femininity in a particular culture. It frequently is considered the external manifestation of the internalized GENDER IDENTITY, although the two are not necessarily consistent with one another.

gender schema the organized set of beliefs and expectations that guides one's understanding of maleness and femaleness.

gender stability the understanding that one's own or other people's sex does not change over time. See GENDER CONSTANCY.

gender stereotype a relatively fixed, overly simplified concept of the attitudes and behaviors considered normal and appropriate for a person in a particular culture, based on his or her biological sex. Research indicates that these STEREOTYPES are prescriptive as well as descriptive. Gender stereotypes often support the social conditioning of gender roles.

gender typing expectations about people's behavior that are based on their biological sex or the process through which children acquire and internalize such expectations.

gene *n.* the basic unit of heredity, responsible for storing genetic information and transmitting it to subsequent generations. The observable characteristics of an organism (i.e., its PHENOTYPE) are determined by numerous genes, which contain the instructions necessary for the functioning of the organism's constituent cells. Each gene consists of a section of DNA, a large and complex molecule that, in higher organisms, is arranged to form the CHROMOSOMES of the cell nucleus. Instructions are embodied in the chemical composition of the DNA, according to the GENETIC CODE. In classical genetics, a gene is described in terms of the trait that it determines and is investigated largely by virtue of the variations brought about by its different forms, or ALLELES. At the molecular level, most genes encode proteins, which carry out the functions of the cell or act to regulate the expression of other genes.

gene mapping the creation of a schematic representation of the arrangement of genes, genetic markers, or both as they occur in the genetic material of an organism.

general adaptation syndrome (**GAS**) the physiological consequences of severe stress. The syndrome has three stages: alarm, resistance, and exhaustion. The first stage, the **alarm reaction** (or **alarm stage**), comprises two substages: the **shock phase**, marked by a decrease in body temperature, blood pressure, and muscle tone and loss of fluid from body tissues; and the **countershock phase**, during which

the sympathetic nervous system is aroused and there is an increase in adrenocortical hormones, triggering a defensive reaction, such as the FIGHT-OR-FLIGHT RESPONSE. The **resistance stage** consists of stabilization at the increased physiological levels. Resources may be depleted, and permanent organ changes produced. The **exhaustion stage** is characterized by breakdown of acquired adaptations to a prolonged stressful situation; it is evidenced by such signs as sleep disturbances, irritability, severe loss of concentration, restlessness, trembling that disturbs motor coordination, fatigue, and depressed mood.

general factor (symbol: *g*) a basic ability that underlies the performance of different varieties of intellectual tasks, in contrast to SPECIFIC FACTORS, which are alleged each to be unique to a single task. The general factor represents individuals' abilities to perceive relationships and to derive conclusions from them.

general intelligence intelligence that is applicable to a very wide variety of tasks. See GENERAL FACTOR.

generalizability *n.* the accuracy with which results or findings can be transferred to situations or people other than those originally studied.

generalization *n.* **1.** the process of deriving a concept, judgment, principle, or theory from a limited number of specific cases and applying it more widely, often to an entire class of objects, events, or people. **2.** in conditioning, see STIMULUS GENERALIZATION. —**generalize** *vb.*

generalized anxiety disorder (**GAD**) excessive anxiety and worry about a range of events and activities (e.g., finances, health, work) accompanied by such symptoms as restlessness, fatigue, impaired concentration, irritability, muscle tension, and disturbed sleep.

generalized other in SYMBOLIC INTERACTIONISM, the aggregation of other people's viewpoints. It is distinguished from specific other people and their individual views.

generalized seizure a seizure in which abnormal electrical activity involves the entire brain rather than a specific focal area. The two most common forms are ABSENCE SEIZURES and some TONIC–CLONIC SEIZURES.

general linear model a large class of statistical techniques, including REGRESSION ANALYSIS, ANALYSIS OF VARIANCE, and correlational analysis, that describe the relationship between a DEPENDENT VARIABLE and one or more INDEPENDENT VARIABLES. Most statistical techniques employed in the behavioral sciences can be subsumed under the general linear model.

General Problem Solver a computer program so named because its approach to problem solving using MEANS–ENDS ANALYSIS was intended to address many different problems and problem types.

general systems theory an interdisciplinary conceptual framework that views an entity or phenomenon holistically as a set of elements interacting with one another (i.e., as a system), with the ultimate goal being to identify and understand the principles applicable to all systems. The impact of each element in a system depends on the role played by other elements in the system and order arises from interaction among these elements. General systems theory was designed to move beyond the reductionistic and mechanistic tradition in science (see REDUCTIONISM) and integrate the fragmented approaches and different classes of phenomena studied. Also called **systems theory**.

generation gap the differences in values, morals, attitudes, and behavior apparent between younger and older people in a society. The term was first used with reference to the burgeoning youth culture of the late 1960s. See also COHORT EFFECT.

generative grammar an approach to linguistics whose goal is to account for the infinite set of possible grammatical sentences in a language using a finite set of generative rules. Unlike earlier inductive approaches that set out to describe and draw inferences about grammar on the basis of a corpus of natural language, the theories of generative grammar developed by U.S. linguist Noam Chomsky (1928–   ) in the 1950s and 1960s took for their basic data the intuitions of native speakers about what is and is not grammatical. In taking this approach, Chomsky revolutionized the whole field of linguistics, effectively redefining it as a branch of COGNITIVE PSYCHOLOGY. Much research in PSYCHOLINGUISTICS has since focused on whether the various models suggested by generative grammar have psychological reality in the production and reception of language. See also PHRASE-STRUCTURE GRAMMAR; TRANSFORMATIONAL GENERATIVE GRAMMAR.

generativity versus stagnation the seventh stage of ERIKSON'S EIGHT STAGES OF DEVELOPMENT. Generativity is the positive goal of middle adulthood, interpreted in terms not only of procreation but also of creativity and fulfilling one's full parental and social responsibilities toward the next generation, in contrast to a narrow interest in the self, or self-absorption. Also called **generativity versus self-absorption**.

gene therapy the insertion of segments of healthy DNA into human body cells to correct defective segments responsible for disease development. A carrier molecule called a vector is used to deliver the therapeutic gene to the patient's target cells, restoring them to a normal state of producing properly functioning proteins. Though experimental, current gene therapy holds significant promise as an effective treatment for a variety of pathological conditions, including neurodegenerative disorders. It is, however, not without its share of problems: (a) difficulties integrating therapeutic DNA into the genome and the rapidly dividing nature of many cells have prevented any long-term benefits; (b) avoiding the stimulation of the immune system response to foreign objects; and (c) conditions that arise from mutations in a single gene are the best candidates for gene therapy, yet some the most commonly occurring disorders (e.g., heart disease, high blood pressure, Alzheimer's disease, arthritis, diabetes) are caused by the combined effects of variations in many genes. Additionally, there are ethical, legal, and social concerns associated with the practice. See also GENETIC ENGINEERING.

genetic code the instructions in genes that "tell" the cell how to make specific proteins. The code resides in the sequence of bases occurring as constituents of DNA or RNA. These bases are represented by the letters A, T, G, and C (which stand for adenine, thymine, guanine, and cytosine, respectively). In messenger RNA, uracil (U) replaces thymine. Each unit of the code consists of three consecutive bases.

genetic counseling an interactive method of educating a prospective parent about genetic risks, benefits and limitations of genetic testing, reproductive risks, and options for surveillance and screening related to diseases with potentially inherited causes.

genetic determinism the doctrine that human and nonhuman animal behavior and mental activity are largely (or completely) controlled by the genetic constitution of the individual and that responses to environmental influences are for the most part innately determined. See BIOLOGICAL DETERMINISM.

genetic engineering techniques by which the genetic contents of living cells or viruses can be deliberately altered, either by modifying the existing genes or by introducing novel material (e.g., a gene from another species). This is undertaken for many different reasons; for example, there have been attempts to modify defective human body cells in the hope of treating certain genetic diseases. However, considerable public concern focuses on the effects and limits of genetic engineering.

genetic epistemology a term used by Swiss child psychologist Jean Piaget (1896–1980) to denote his theoretical approach to and experimental study of the development of knowledge.

genetic psychology the study of the development of mental functions in children and their transformation across the life span. In the 19th and early 20th centuries, the term was preferred over the synonymous DEVELOPMENTAL PSYCHOLOGY, although currently the reverse is true.

genetics *n.* the branch of biology that is concerned with the mechanisms and phenomena of heredity.

genitalia *pl. n.* the reproductive organs of the male or female. The male genitalia include the penis, testes and related structures, prostate gland, seminal vesicles, and bulbourethral glands. The female genitalia consist of the vagina, uterus, ovaries, fallopian tubes, and related structures. The external genitalia comprise the vulva in females and the penis and testicles in males. Also called **genitals**.

genital stage in psychoanalytic theory, the final stage of PSYCHOSEXUAL DEVELOPMENT, ideally reached in puberty, when the OEDIPUS COMPLEX has been fully resolved and erotic interest and activity are focused on intercourse with a sexual partner. Also called **genital phase**.

genius *n*. an extreme degree of intellectual or creative ability, or any person who possesses such ability. Genius may be demonstrated by exceptional achievement, particularly the creation of literary, artistic, or scientific masterpieces of extraordinary power or inventiveness, or the production of insights or ideas of great originality. Although a frustratingly vague definition, it is virtually impossible to provide a more precise one, or even a definitive list of attributes, given that the term essentially is an acknowledgment of what a person has done rather than a description of what a person is like. Additionally, genius is seen to emerge as a joint product of heredity and environment and to require a great deal of very hard and dedicated work to achieve.

genome *n*. all of the genetic material contained in an organism or cell. Mapping of the estimated 20,000–25,000 genes in human DNA was one of several goals of the HUMAN GENOME PROJECT.

genotype *n*. the genetic composition of an individual organism as a whole or at one or more specific positions on a chromosome. Compare PHENOTYPE. —**genotypic** *adj*.

genotype–environment effects the proposal that an individual's GENOTYPE influences which environments he or she encounters and the type of experiences he or she has.

geometric illusion any misinterpretation by the visual system of a figure made of straight or curved lines. Examples of such illusions are the MÜLLER-LYER ILLUSION and the ZÖLLNER ILLUSION.

geon *n*. see RECOGNITION BY COMPONENTS THEORY.

G

geriatrics *n*. the branch of medicine that deals with the diagnosis and treatment of disorders in older adults. —**geriatric** *adj*.

germ cell any of the cells in the gonads that give rise to the GAMETES by a process involving growth and MEIOSIS. See OOGENESIS; SPERMATOGENESIS.

gerontology *n*. the scientific interdisciplinary study of old age and the aging process. —**gerontological** *adj*. —**gerontologist** *n*.

Gerstmann's syndrome a set of four symptoms associated with lesions of a specific area of the (usually left) PARIETAL LOBE. They are inability to recognize one's individual fingers, inability to distinguish between the right and left sides of one's body, inability to perform mathematical calculations, and inability to write. The existence of Gerstmann's syndrome as a true independent entity is subject to debate. [Josef G. **Gerstmann** (1887–1969), Austrian neurologist]

gestalt *n*. an entire perceptual configuration (from German: "shape," "form"), made up of elements that are integrated and interactive in such a way as to confer properties on the whole configuration that are not possessed by the individual elements.

gestalt principles of organization principles of perception, derived by the Gestalt psychologists, that describe the tendency to perceive and interpret certain configurations at the level of the whole, rather than in terms of their component features. Examples include GOOD CONTINUATION, CLOSURE, and PRÄGNANZ. Also called **gestalt laws of organization**.

Gestalt psychology a psychological approach that focuses on the dynamic organization of experience into patterns or configurations. This view was espoused in the early 20th century as a revolt against STRUCTURALISM, which analyzed experience into static, atomistic sensations, and also against the equally atomistic approach of BEHAVIORISM, which attempted to dissect complex behavior into elementary conditioned reflexes. Gestalt psychology holds, instead, that experience is an organized whole of which the pieces are an integral part. Later experimentation in this approach gave rise to principles of perceptual organization (including CLOSURE, PRÄGNANZ, and PROXIMITY), which were then applied to the study of learning, insight, memory, social psychology, and art.

gestalt therapy a form of PSYCHOTHERAPY in which the central focus is on the totality of the client's functioning and relationships in the here and now, rather than on investigation of past experiences and developmental history. One of the themes is that growth occurs by assimilation of what is needed from the environment and that psychopathology arises as a disturbance of contact with the environment. Gestalt techniques, which can be applied in either a group or an individual setting, are designed to bring out spontaneous feelings and self-awareness and promote personality growth.

gestation *n.* the development of the embryo and fetus in the uterus until birth. —**gestational** *adj.*

gesture *n.* **1.** a movement, such as the waving of a hand, that communicates a particular meaning or indicates the individual's emotional state or attitude. **2.** a statement or act, usually symbolic, that is intended to influence the attitudes of others (as in a *gesture of goodwill*). —**gestural** *adj.*

ghrelin *n.* a peptide secreted by endocrine cells in the stomach that binds to growth hormone receptors in the hypothalamus and anterior pituitary, stimulating appetite and the release of growth hormone.

giftedness *n.* the state of possessing a great amount of natural ability, talent, or intelligence, which usually becomes evident at a very young age. Giftedness in intelligence is often categorized as an IQ of two standard deviations above the mean or higher (130 for most IQ tests). Many schools and service organizations now use a combination of attributes as the basis for assessing giftedness, including one or more of the following: high intellectual capacity, academic achievement, demonstrable real-world achievement, creativity, task commitment, proven talent, leadership skills, and physical or athletic prowess. —**gifted** *adj.*

gland *n.* an organ that secretes a substance for use by or discharge from the body. EXOCRINE GLANDS release their products through a duct onto internal or external bodily surfaces, whereas ENDOCRINE GLANDS are ductless and secrete their products directly into the bloodstream.

glass ceiling an unofficial, intangible barrier that prevents able and ambitious individuals, particularly women and members of minority groups, from rising to positions of authority in many organizations.

glaucoma *n.* a common eye disease marked by raised pressure inside one or both eyes, causing progressive peripheral visual field loss. If untreated, glaucoma results in severe visual impairment and ultimately blindness.

glia *n.* nonneuronal tissue in the nervous system that provides structural, nutritional, and other kinds of support to neurons. It may consist of very small cells (MICROGLIA) or relatively large ones (MACROGLIA). The latter include ASTROCYTES, cells of the EPENDYMA, and the two types of cells that form the MYELIN SHEATH around axons: OLIGODENDROCYTES in the central nervous system and SCHWANN CELLS in the peripheral nervous system. Also called **neuroglia**. —**glial** *adj.*

glioma *n.* a form of brain tumor that develops from support cells (GLIA) of the central nervous system. There are three main types, grouped according to the form of support cell involved: astrocytoma (from ASTROCYTES), ependymoma (from EPENDYMA), and oligodendroglioma (from OLIGODENDROCYTES). Glioma is the most common type of brain cancer and accounts for about a quarter of spinal cord tumors. Also called **neuroglioma**.

globus pallidus one of the BASAL GANGLIA. It is the main output region of the basal ganglia: Its output neurons terminate on thalamic neurons, which in turn project to the cerebral cortex.

glossolalia *n.* unintelligible utterances that simulate coherent speech, which may have meaning to the utterer but do not to the listener. Glossolalia is found in religious ecstasy ("speaking in tongues"), hypnotic or mediumistic trances,

and occasionally in schizophrenia. See also NEOLOGISM.

glossopharyngeal nerve the ninth CRANIAL NERVE, which supplies the pharynx, soft palate, and posterior third of the tongue, including the taste buds of that portion. It contains both motor and sensory fibers and is involved in swallowing and conveying taste information.

glucagon *n.* a polypeptide hormone, secreted by the A cells of the ISLETS OF LANGERHANS, that increases the concentration of glucose in the blood. It opposes the effects of INSULIN by promoting the breakdown of glycogen and fat reserves to yield glucose.

glucocorticoid *n.* any CORTICOSTEROID hormone that acts chiefly on carbohydrate metabolism. An example is CORTISOL.

glucoreceptor *n.* any of certain cells in the HYPOTHALAMUS that bind glucose. Glucoreceptors are a putative mechanism for detecting levels of circulating glucose and conveying this information to brain areas.

glucose *n.* a soluble sugar, abundant in nature, that is a major source of energy for body tissues. The brain relies almost exclusively on glucose for its energy needs. Glucose is derived from the breakdown of carbohydrates, proteins, and—to a much lesser extent—fats. Its concentration in the bloodstream is tightly controlled by the opposing actions of the hormones INSULIN and GLUCAGON.

glucostatic theory the theory that short-term regulation of food intake is governed by the rate of glucose metabolism (i.e., utilization), rather than by overall blood levels of glucose. See also LIPOSTATIC HYPOTHESIS.

G

glutamate *n.* a salt or ester of the amino acid glutamic acid that serves as the predominant excitatory NEUROTRANSMITTER in the brain. Glutamate exerts its effects by binding to GLUTAMATE RECEPTORS on neurons and plays a critical role in cognitive, motor, and sensory functions.

glutamate hypothesis the theory that decreased activity of the excitatory neurotransmitter glutamate is responsible for the clinical expression of schizophrenia. The hypothesis developed from observations that administration of NMDA receptor antagonists, such as PCP (phencyclidine), produce psychotic symptoms in humans and is supported by a number of recent studies. See also DOPAMINE HYPOTHESIS.

glutamate receptor any of various receptors that bind and respond to the excitatory neurotransmitter glutamate. There are two main divisions of glutamate receptors: the IONOTROPIC RECEPTORS and the METABOTROPIC RECEPTORS. Ionotropic glutamate receptors are further divided into three classes: **NMDA receptors** (binding NMDA as well as glutamate), **AMPA receptors** (binding AMPA as well as glutamate), and **kainate receptors** (binding kainic acid as well as glutamate). Metabotropic glutamate receptors (mGlu or mGluR) are subdivided into several classes denoted by subscript numbers (i.e., $mGlu_1$, $mGlu_2$, etc.).

glutamatergic *adj.* responding to, releasing, or otherwise involving GLUTAMATE. For example, a **glutamatergic neuron** is one that uses glutamate as a neurotransmitter. Also called **glutaminergic**.

glycine *n.* an AMINO ACID that serves as one of the two major inhibitory neurotransmitters in the central nervous system (particularly the spinal cord), the other being GAMMA-AMINOBUTYRIC ACID (GABA).

GnRH abbreviation for GONADOTROPIN-RELEASING HORMONE.

goal setting a process that establishes specific, time-based behavior targets that are measurable, achievable, and realistic. In work-related settings, for example, this practice usually provides employees with both (a) a basis for motivation, in terms of effort expended, and (b) guidelines or cues to behavior that will be required if the goal is to be met.

Golgi apparatus an irregular network of membranes and vesicles within a cell that is responsible for modifying, sorting, and packaging proteins produced within the cell. [Camillo **Golgi** (1843–1926), Italian histologist]

Golgi tendon organ a receptor in muscle tendons that sends impulses to the central nervous system when a muscle contracts. [Camillo **Golgi**]

gonad *n.* either of the primary male and female sex organs, that is, the TESTIS or the OVARY. —**gonadal** *adj.*

gonadotropin *n.* any of several hormones produced primarily by the anterior pituitary gland that stimulate functions of the gonads, particularly FOLLICLE-STIMULATING HORMONE and LUTEINIZING HORMONE. —**gonadotropic** *adj.*

gonadotropin-releasing hormone (GnRH) a hormone secreted by neurons of the hypothalamus that controls the release of LUTEINIZING HORMONE and FOLLICLE-STIMULATING HORMONE from the anterior pituitary gland.

good continuation one of the GESTALT PRINCIPLES OF ORGANIZATION. It states that people tend to perceive objects in alignment as forming smooth, unbroken contours. For example, when two lines meet in a figure the preferred interpretation is of two continuous lines: a cross is interpreted as a vertical line and a horizontal line, rather than two right angles meeting at their vertices. Also called **law of continuity**; **law of good continuation**; **principle of continuity**; **principle of good continuation**.

goodness of fit any index that reflects the degree to which values predicted by a model agree with empirically observed values.

G protein any of a class of proteins that are coupled to the intracellular portion of a type of membrane RECEPTOR (**G-protein-coupled receptors**) and are activated when the receptor binds an appropriate ligand (e.g., a neurotransmitter) on the extracellular surface. G proteins thus have a role in signal transduction, serving to transmit the signal from the receptor to other cell components (e.g., ion channels) in various ways, for example by controlling the synthesis of SECOND MESSENGERS within the cell.

graded potential any change in electric potential of a neuron that is not propagated along the cell (as is an ACTION POTENTIAL) but declines with distance from the source. RECEPTOR POTENTIALS are an example.

gradient *n.* **1.** the slope of a line or surface. **2.** a measure of the change of a physical quantity (e.g., temperature) or other property (e.g., strength of a DRIVE).

graduated and reciprocated initiatives in tension reduction (**GRIT**) an approach to intergroup conflict reduction that encourages the parties to communicate cooperative intentions, engage in behaviors that are consistent with these intentions, and initiate cooperative responses even in the face of competition. GRIT is usually recommended when disputants have a prolonged history of conflict, misunderstanding, misperception, and hostility.

grammar *n.* in linguistics, an abstract system of rules that describes how a language works. Although it is traditionally held to consist of SYNTAX (rules for arranging words in sentences) and MORPHOLOGY (rules affecting the form taken by individual words), PHONOLOGY and SEMANTICS are also included in some modern systems of grammar. —**grammatical** *adj.*

grand mal see TONIC–CLONIC SEIZURE.

grand mean a mean (numerical average) of a group of means.

grandmother cell any hypothetical neuron in the visual system that is stimulated only by a single highly complex and meaningful stimulus, such as a particular individual (e.g., one's grandmother) or a particular well-known object (e.g., the Sydney Opera House). It is an extension of the FEATURE DETECTOR concept to a degree that has been dismissed by many as overly simplistic and untenable, although recent research has provided support for the concept by revealing a much higher degree of neuronal specificity than previously believed.

granule cell a type of small, grainlike neuron found in certain layers of the cerebral cortex and cerebellar cortex.

granulocyte see LEUKOCYTE.

graph *n.* a visual representation of the relationship between numbers or quantities, which are plotted on a drawing with reference to axes at right angles (the horizontal x-axis and the vertical y-axis) and linked by lines, dots, or the like.

grapheme *n.* a minimal meaningful unit in the writing system of a particular language. It is usually a letter or fixed combination of letters corresponding to a PHONEME in that language. —**graphemic** *adj.*

graphology *n.* the study of the physical characteristics of handwriting, particularly as a means of inferring the writer's psychological state or personality characteristics. For example, it is sometimes used in personnel selection as a predictor of job performance. Graphology is based on the premise that writing is a form of expressive behavior, although there is little empirical evidence for its validity. Also called **handwriting analysis**. —**graphological** *adj.* —**graphologist** *n.*

grasp reflex an involuntary grasping by an individual of anything that touches the palm. This reflex is typical of infants but in older individuals it may be a sign of FRONTAL LOBE damage.

gray matter any area of neural tissue that is dominated by CELL BODIES and is devoid of myelin, such as the CEREBRAL CORTEX. Compare WHITE MATTER.

great man theory a view of political leadership and historical causation that assumes that history is driven by a small number of exceptional individuals with certain innate characteristics that predispose them for greatness. A ZEITGEIST (spirit of the times) view of history, in contrast, supposes that history is largely determined by economics, technological development, and a broad spectrum of social influences.

grief *n.* the anguish experienced after significant loss, usually the death of a beloved person. Grief is distinguished from, but a common component of, the process of BEREAVEMENT and MOURNING. Not all bereavements result in a strong grief response; nor is all grief given public expression (see DISENFRANCHISED GRIEF). Grief often includes physiological distress, anxiety about being separated from the person, confusion, yearning, obsessive dwelling on the past, and apprehension about the future.

grief counseling the provision of advice, information, and psychological support to help individuals whose ability to function has been impaired by someone's death, particularly that of a loved one or friend. It includes counseling for the grieving process and practical advice concerning arrangements for the funeral and burial of the loved one. Grief counseling is sometimes offered by staff in specialized agencies (e.g., hospices) or it may be carried out in the context of other counseling.

griefwork *n.* the theoretical process through which bereaved people gradually reduce or transform their emotional connection to the person who has died and thereby refocus appropriately on their own ongoing lives. It is not necessary to sever all emotional connections with the dead person. Instead, adaptive griefwork will help transform the relationship symbolically, as a continuing bond that provides a sense of meaning and value conducive to forming new relationships.

GRIT acronym for GRADUATED AND RECIPROCATED INITIATIVES IN TENSION REDUCTION.

gross motor describing activities or skills that use large muscles to move the trunk or limbs and control posture to maintain balance. Examples of **gross motor skills** include waving an arm, walking, hopping, and running. Compare FINE MOTOR.

ground *n.* the relatively homogeneous and indistinct background of FIGURE–GROUND perceptions.

grounded theory a set of procedures for the systematic analysis of unstructured qualitative data so as to derive by INDUCTION a theory that explains the observed phenomena.

group *n.* any collection or assemblage, particularly of items or individuals. For example, in social psychology the term refers to two or more interdependent individuals who influence one another through social interactions that commonly include structures involving roles and norms, a degree of cohesiveness, and shared goals; in animal behavior it refers to an organized collection of individuals that moves together or otherwise acts to achieve some common goal (e.g., protection against predators) that would be less effectively achieved by individual action; and in research it denotes a collection of participants who all experience the same experimental conditions and whose responses are to be compared to the responses of one or more other collections of research participants.

group dynamics 1. the dynamic rather than static processes, operations, and changes that occur within social groups, which affect patterns of affiliation, communication, conflict, conformity, decision making, influence, leadership, norm formation, and power. **2.** the field of psychology devoted to the study of groups and group processes.

grouping *n.* in statistics, the process of arranging scores in categories, intervals, classes, or ranks.

group interview a conference or meeting in which one or more questioners elicit information from two or more respondents. This method encourages the interviewees to interact with one other in responding to the interviewer.

group mind a hypothetical, transcendent consciousness created by the fusion of the individual minds in a collective, such as a nation or race. This controversial idea assumes that the group mind is greater than the sum of the psychological experiences of the individuals and that it can become so powerful that it can overwhelm the will of the individual.

group norm see SOCIAL NORM.

group polarization the tendency for members of a group discussing an issue to move toward a more extreme version of the positions they held before the discussion began. As a result, the group as a whole tends to respond in more extreme ways than one would expect given the sentiments of the individual members prior to deliberation.

group process the interpersonal component of a group session, in contrast to the content (such as decisions or information) generated during the session.

group-serving bias any one of a number of cognitive tendencies that contribute to an overvaluing of one's group, particularly the tendency to credit the group for its successes but to blame external factors for its failures (the **ultimate attribution error**). Compare SELF-SERVING BIAS.

group socialization theory a theory of personality development proposing that children are primarily socialized by their peers and that the influences of parents and teachers are filtered through children's peer groups. According to this theory, children seek to be like their peers rather than like their parents.

group test a test designed to be administered to several individuals simultaneously. Compare INDIVIDUAL TEST.

group therapy treatment of psychological problems in which two or more participants interact with each other on both an emotional and a cognitive level, in the presence of one or more psychotherapists who serve as catalysts, facilitators, or interpreters. The approaches of groups vary, but in general they aim to provide an environment in which problems and concerns can be shared in an atmosphere of mutual respect and understanding. Group therapy seeks to enhance self-respect, deepen self-understanding, and improve interpersonal relationships. Also called **group psychotherapy**. Compare INDIVIDUAL THERAPY.

groupthink *n.* a strong concurrence-seeking tendency that interferes with effective group decision making. Symptoms include apparent unanimity, illusions of invulnerability and moral correctness, biased perceptions of the OUTGROUP, interpersonal pressure, self-censorship, and defective decision-making strategies.

growth spurt any period of accelerated physical development, especially the pubescent growth spurt.

GSR abbreviation for GALVANIC SKIN RESPONSE.

guided participation a process in which the influences of social partners and sociocultural practices combine in various ways to provide children and other learners with direction and support, while the learners themselves also shape their learning engagements. It occurs not only during explicit instruction but also during routine activities and communication of everyday life. See SOCIOCULTURAL PERSPECTIVE.

guiding fiction a personal principle that serves as a guideline by which an individual can understand and evaluate his or her experiences and determine his or her lifestyle. In individuals considered to be in good or reasonable mental health, the guiding fiction is assumed to approach reality and be adaptive. In those who are not, it is assumed to be largely unconscious, unrealistic, and nonadaptive.

guilt *n.* a SELF-CONSCIOUS EMOTION characterized by a painful sense of having done (or thought) something that is wrong and often by a readiness to take action designed to undo or mitigate this wrong. —**guilty** *adj.*

guilty but mentally ill a court judgment that may be made in some states when defendants plead INSANITY. Defendants found guilty but mentally ill are treated in a mental hospital until their mental health is restored; they then serve the remainder of their sentence in the appropriate correctional facility.

gustation *n.* the sense of taste. —**gustatory** *adj.*

gustatory system the primary structures and processes involved in an organism's detection of and responses to taste stimuli. The gustatory system includes lingual PAPILLAE, TASTE BUDS and TASTE CELLS, taste TRANSDUCTION, neural impulses and pathways, and associated brain areas and their functions (see PRIMARY TASTE CORTEX; SECONDARY TASTE CORTEX; SOLITARY NUCLEUS).

gyrus *n.* (*pl.* **gyri**) a ridged or raised portion of the cerebral cortex, bounded on either side by a SULCUS.

Hh

H₀ symbol for NULL HYPOTHESIS.

H₁ symbol for ALTERNATIVE HYPOTHESIS.

habilitation *n.* the process of enhancing the independence, well-being, and level of functioning of an individual with a disability or disorder by providing appropriate resources, such as treatment or training, to enable that person to develop skills and abilities he or she had not had the opportunity to acquire previously. Compare REHABILITATION.

habit *n.* a well-learned behavior that is relatively situation-specific and over time has become motorically reflexive and independent of motivational or cognitive influence, that is, it is performed with little or no conscious intent. —**habitual** *adj.*

habituation *n.* **1.** the weakening of a response to a stimulus, or the diminished effectiveness of a stimulus, following repeated exposure to the stimulus. Compare DISHABITUATION. **2.** the process of becoming psychologically dependent on the use of a particular drug, such as cocaine, but without the increasing tolerance and physiological dependence that are characteristic of addiction.

hair cell 1. any of the sensory receptors for hearing, located in the ORGAN OF CORTI within the cochlea of the inner ear. They respond to vibrations of the BASILAR MEMBRANE via movement of fine hairlike processes (**stereocilia**) that protrude from the cells. **2.** any of the sensory receptors for balance, similar in structure to the cochlear hair cells. They are located in the inner ear within the ampullae of the SEMICIRCULAR CANALS (forming part of the CRISTA) and within the SACCULE and UTRICLE (forming part of the MACULA).

half-life (symbol: $t_{1/2}$) *n.* in pharmacokinetics, the time necessary for the concentration in the blood of an administered drug to fall by 50%. Clinically, half-life varies among individuals as a result of age, disease states, or concurrent administration of other drugs.

halfway house a transitional living arrangement for people, such as individuals recovering from alcohol or substance abuse, who have completed treatment at a hospital or rehabilitation center but still require support to assist them in restructuring their lives.

hallucination *n.* a false sensory perception that has a compelling sense of reality despite the absence of an external stimulus. It may affect any of the senses, but AUDITORY HALLUCINATIONS and VISUAL HALLUCINATIONS are most common. Hallucination is typically a symptom of a PSYCHOTIC DISORDER, particularly schizophrenia, but also may result from substance use, neurological abnormalities, and other conditions. It is important to distinguish hallucinations from ILLUSIONS, which are misinterpretations of real sensory stimuli.

hallucinogen *n.* a substance capable of producing a sensory effect (visual, auditory, olfactory, gustatory, or tactile) in the absence of an actual stimulus. Because they produce alterations in perception, cognition, and mood, hallucinogens are also called **psychedelic drugs** (from the Greek, meaning "mind-manifesting"). **—hallucinogenic** *adj.*

hallucinosis *n.* a pathological condition characterized by prominent and persistent hallucinations without alterations of consciousness, particularly when due to the direct physiological effects of a substance or associated with neurological factors.

halo effect the tendency for a general evaluation of a person, or an evaluation of a person on a specific dimension, to be used as a basis for judgments of that person on other specific dimensions. For example, a person who is generally liked might be judged as more intelligent, competent, and honest than a person who is generally disliked.

handedness *n.* the consistent use of one hand rather than the other in performing certain tasks.

handicap *n.* any disadvantage or characteristic that limits or prevents a person from performing various physical, cognitive, or social tasks or from fulfilling particular roles within society. For example, a nonaccessible building entry or exit for a person in a wheelchair would be considered a handicap, as would the person's inability to walk. The term generally is considered pejorative nowadays and its use has fallen into disfavor. See also DISABILITY. **—handicapped** *adj.*

handwriting analysis see GRAPHOLOGY.

haploid *adj.* describing a nucleus, cell, or organism that possesses only one representative of each chromosome, as in a sperm or egg cell. In most organisms, including humans,

fusion of the haploid sex cells following fertilization restores the normal DIPLOID condition of body cells, in which the chromosomes occur in pairs. Hence for humans, the **haploid number** is 23 chromosomes, that is, half the full complement of 46 chromosomes.

happiness *n.* an emotion of joy, gladness, satisfaction, and well-being. **—happy** *adj.*

haptic *adj.* relating to the sense of touch or contact and the cutaneous sensory system in general. It typically refers to active touch, in which the individual intentionally seeks sensory stimulation, moving the limbs to gain information about an object or surface.

hard determinism the doctrine that human actions and choices are causally determined by forces and influences over which a person exercises no meaningful influence. The term can also be applied to nonhuman events, implying that all things must be as they are and could not possibly be otherwise. Compare SOFT DETERMINISM. See DETERMINISM.

hardiness *n.* an ability to adapt easily to unexpected changes combined with a sense of purpose in daily life and of personal control over what occurs in one's life. Hardiness dampens the effects of a stressful situation through information gathering, decisive actions, and learning from the experience. **—hardy** *adj.*

harmonic mean a measure of CENTRAL TENDENCY. It is computed for *n* scores as $n/\Sigma(1/x_i)$, that is, *n* divided by $1/x_1 + 1/x_2 + ...1/x_n$.

harm reduction a theoretical approach in programs designed to reduce the adverse effects of risky behaviors (e.g., alcohol use, drug use, indiscriminate sexual activity), rather than to eliminate the behaviors altogether. Programs focused on alcohol use, for example, do not advocate abstinence but attempt instead to teach people to anticipate the hazards of heavy drinking and learn to drink safely.

hashish *n.* the most potent CANNA-BIS preparation. It contains the highest concentration of delta-9-TETRAHYDROCANNABINOL (THC) because it consists largely of pure resin from one of the species of the *Cannabis* plant from which it is derived.

Hawthorne effect the effect on the behavior of individuals of knowing that they are being observed or are taking part in research. The Hawthorne effect is typically positive and is named after the Western Electric Company's Hawthorne Works plant in Cicero, Illinois, where the phenomenon was first observed during a series of studies on worker productivity conducted from 1924 to 1932. These **Hawthorne Studies** began as an investigation of the effects of illumination conditions, monetary incentives, and rest breaks on productivity, but evolved into a much wider consideration of the role of worker attitudes, supervisory style, and GROUP DYNAMICS.

HD abbreviation for HUNTINGTON'S DISEASE.

health–belief model a model that identifies the relationships of the following to the likelihood of taking preventive health action: (a) individual perceptions about susceptibility to and seriousness of a disease, (b) sociodemographic variables, (c) environmental cues, and (d) perceptions of the benefits and costs.

health maintenance organization see HMO.

health psychology the subfield of psychology that focuses on (a) the examination of the relations be-

tween behavioral, cognitive, psychophysiological, and social and environmental factors and the establishment, maintenance, and detriment of health; (b) the integration of psychological and biological research findings in the design of empirically based interventions for the prevention and treatment of illness; and (c) the evaluation of physical and psychological status before, during, and after medical and psychological treatment.

hearing loss the inability to hear a normal range of tone frequencies, a normally perceived level of sound intensity, or both.

Hebbian synapse a junction between neurons that is strengthened when activity in the axon of the presynaptic (transmitting) neuron results in simultaneous activity in the postsynaptic (receiving) neuron. See DUAL TRACE HYPOTHESIS. [Donald O. **Hebb** (1904–1985), Canadian psychologist]

hebephrenia *n.* see DISORGANIZED SCHIZOPHRENIA.

hedonics *n.* the branch of psychology concerned with the study of pleasant and unpleasant sensations and thoughts, especially in terms of their role in human motivation.

hedonism *n.* **1.** in philosophy, the doctrine that pleasure is an intrinsic good and the proper goal of all human action. One of the fundamental questions of ethics has been whether pleasure can or should be equated with the good in this way. **2.** in psychology, any theory that suggests that pleasure and the avoidance of pain are the only or the major motivating forces in human behavior. Hedonism is a foundational principle in psychoanalysis, in behaviorism, and even in theories that stress self-actualization and need-fulfillment. —**hedonistic** *adj.*

helping a type of PROSOCIAL behavior that involves one or more individuals acting to improve the status or well-being of another or others. Although typically in response to a small request that involves little individual risk, all helping incurs some cost to the individual providing it.

helplessness theory the theory that LEARNED HELPLESSNESS explains the development of or vulnerability to depression. According to this theory, people repeatedly exposed to stressful situations beyond their control develop an inability to make decisions or engage effectively in purposeful behavior.

hemianopia *n.* loss of vision in half of the visual field. Also called **hemianopsia**. —**hemianopic** *adj.* —**hemianoptic** *adj.*

hemiplegia *n.* complete paralysis that affects one side of the body. —**hemiplegic** *adj.*

hemisphere *n.* either of the symmetrical halves of the cerebrum (see CEREBRAL HEMISPHERE) or the CEREBELLUM. —**hemispheric** or **hemispherical** *adj.*

hemispherectomy *n.* surgical removal of either one of the cerebral hemispheres of the brain.

hemispheric asymmetry the idea that the two cerebral hemispheres of the brain are not identical but differ in size, shape, and function. The functions that display the most pronounced asymmetry are language processing in the left hemisphere and visuospatial processing in the right hemisphere.

hemispheric lateralization the processes whereby some functions, such as HANDEDNESS or language, are controlled or influenced more by one cerebral hemisphere than the other and each hemisphere is specialized for particular ways of working, managing information in a unique fashion and, in some cases, being structurally asymmetrical. Researchers now prefer to speak of hemispheric lateralization or **hemispheric specialization** for particular functions, rather than hemispheric or lateral DOMINANCE.

hemorrhage *n.* bleeding; any loss of blood from an artery or vein. A hemorrhage may be external, internal, or within a tissue, such as the skin. —**hemorrhagic** *adj.*

hereditarianism *n.* the view that genetic inheritance is the major influence on behavior. Opposed to this view is the belief that environment and learning account for the major differences between people. The question of heredity versus environment or "nature versus nurture" continues to be controversial, especially as it applies to human intelligence. See GENETIC DETERMINISM; NATURE–NURTURE. —**hereditarian** *adj.*

heredity *n.* the transmission of traits from parents to their offspring. Study of the mechanisms and laws of heredity is the basis of the science of GENETICS. Heredity depends upon the character of the genes contained in the parents' CHROMOSOMES, which in turn depends on the particular GENETIC CODE carried by the DNA of which the chromosomes are composed.

Hering theory of color vision a theory of color vision postulating that there are three sets of receptors, one of which is sensitive to white and black, another to red and green, and the third to yellow and blue. The breaking down (catabolism) of these substances is supposed to yield one member of these pairs (white, red, or yellow), while the building up (anabolism) of the same substances yields the other (black, green, or blue). See OPPONENT PROCESS THEORY OF COLOR VISION. [proposed in 1875 by German physiologist and psychologist Ewald **Hering** (1834–1918)]

heritability *n.* an estimate of the contribution of inheritance to a given trait or function. Heritabilities can range from 0, indicating no contribution of heritable factors, to 1, indicating total contribution of heritable factors. The heritability of intelligence is believed to be roughly .5, for example. Heritability is not the same as genetic contribution, because heritability is sensitive only to sources of individual differences. Moreover, a trait can be heritable and yet modifiable.

heritage *n.* any traditions or other immaterial attributes passed from preceding to successive generations. Heritage may be cultural, encompassing the customs, language, values, and skills that help to maintain a particular group's sense of identity, or social, encompassing learned interpersonal behaviors (e.g., shaking hands when greeting others, giving gifts on particular occasions).

hermaphroditism *n.* the condition of possessing both male and female sex organs (in humans, for example, possessing both ovarian and testicular tissue). Hermaphroditism is very rare and should not be confused with the more common pseudohermaphroditism, in which the gonads are of one sex but the external genitalia are either ambiguous or of the opposite sex. See also INTERSEXUALITY. **—hermaphrodite** *n.*

hermeneutics *n.* the theory or science of interpretation. Hermeneutics is concerned with the ways in which humans derive meaning from language or other symbolic expression. Two main strains of hermeneutic thought have developed. In the first, a key concept is the need to gain insight into the mind of the person or people whose ex-

pression is the subject of interpretation. In the second, more radical, strain of hermeneutics, the project of interpretation was expanded to include the human being itself. This suggests that all human behavior can be understood as meaningful expression, much as one would understand a written text. This move has given rise to a broad movement within philosophy, psychology, and literary criticism in which richness of interpretation is considered more valuable than consistent methodology or arriving at the "correct" interpretation. This type of hermeneutics has informed other contemporary movements, notably EXISTENTIALISM, POSTMODERNISM, and POSTSTRUCTURALISM. **—hermeneutic** *adj.*

heroin *n.* a highly addictive OPIOID that is a synthetic analog of MORPHINE and three times more potent. Its rapid onset of action leads to an intense initial high, followed by a period of euphoria and a sense of well-being.

hertz (symbol: Hz) *n.* the unit of FREQUENCY equal to one cycle per second. [Heinrich Rudolf **Hertz** (1857–1894), German physicist]

Heschl's gyrus one of several transverse ridges on the upper side of the TEMPORAL LOBE of the brain that are associated with the sense of hearing. [Richard **Heschl** (1824–1881), Austrian pathologist who first traced the auditory pathways of humans to this convolution]

heterogeneity of variance the situation in which populations or CELLS in a experimental design have unequal variances. Compare HOMOGENEITY OF VARIANCE.

heterogeneous *adj.* composed of diverse elements. Compare HOMOGENEOUS.

heteronomous stage in the theory of moral development expounded by Swiss psychologist Jean Piaget (1896–1980), the stage at which the child, approximately 6 to 10 years of age, equates morality with the rules and principles of his or her parents and other authority figures. That is, the child evaluates the rightness or wrongness of an act only in terms of adult sanctions for or against it and of the consequences or possible punishment it may bring. Also called **heteronomous morality**. See also IMMANENT JUSTICE; MORAL ABSOLUTISM; MORAL REALISM. Compare AUTONOMOUS STAGE; PREMORAL STAGE.

heterophily *n.* any tendency for individuals who differ from one another in some way to make social connections. It is less common than HOMOPHILY.

heteroscedasticity *n.* the situation in which Var($Y|X$) is not the same for all values of X, that is, the variance in Y is a function of the variable X. Compare HOMOSCEDASTICITY. —**heteroscedastic** *adj.*

heterosexuality *n.* sexual attraction to or activity between members of the opposite sex. Compare HOMOSEXUALITY. —**heterosexual** *adj.*

heterozygous *adj.* see ALLELE. —**heterozygote** *n.*

heuristic *n.* a strategy for solving a problem or making a decision that provides an efficient means of finding an answer but cannot guarantee a correct outcome. By contrast, an ALGORITHM guarantees a solution to a problem (if there is one) but may be much less efficient. See also AVAILABILITY HEURISTIC; REPRESENTATIVENESS HEURISTIC.

heuristic-systematic model a theory of persuasion postulating that the validity of a persuasive message can be assessed in two different ways. **Systematic processing** involves the careful scrutiny of the merits of attitude-relevant information in the message. **Heuristic processing** involves the use of a subset of information in the message as a basis for implementing a simple decision rule to determine if the message should be accepted (e.g., judging a message to be valid because its source is highly credible).

hidden observer the phenomenon whereby highly hypnotizable people (see HYPNOTIC SUSCEPTIBILITY) who are asked to block certain stimuli (e.g., pain) can sometimes register the blocked pain or other sensation via hand signals, as if a dissociated observer is simultaneously taking part in events that are disavowed by the dominant observer. Such individuals can later recall auditory, visual, or tactile stimuli to which they appeared oblivious at the time.

hierarchy *n.* a clear ordering of phenomena on some dimension, such as a DOMINANCE HIERARCHY.

hierarchy of motives (hierarchy of needs) see MASLOW'S MOTIVATIONAL HIERARCHY.

higher mental process any of the more complex types of cognition, such as thinking, judgment, imagination, memory, and language.

higher order conditioning in PAVLOVIAN CONDITIONING, a procedure in which the CONDITIONED STIMULUS of one experiment acts as the UNCONDITIONED STIMULUS of another, for the purpose of conditioning a NEUTRAL STIMULUS. For example, after pairing a tone with food, and establishing the tone as a conditioned stimulus that elicits salivation, a light could be paired with the tone. If the light alone comes to elicit salivation, then higher order conditioning has occurred.

higher order interaction in the ANALYSIS OF VARIANCE, the joint effect of three or more independent variables on the dependent variable.

high risk significantly heightened vulnerability to a disorder or disease. An individual's risk status is influenced by genetic, physical, and behavioral factors or conditions. For example, children of a parent with bipolar disorder have a much greater risk of developing the disorder than other children, and individuals who engage in unprotected sex are at high risk of contracting HIV and other sexually transmitted diseases.

hindbrain *n.* the posterior of three bulges that appear in the embryonic brain as it develops from the NEURAL TUBE. The bulge eventually becomes the MEDULLA OBLONGATA, PONS, and CEREBELLUM. Also called **rhombencephalon**.

hindsight bias the tendency, after an event has occurred, to overestimate the extent to which the outcome could have been foreseen.

hinge *n.* either of the scores in a batch of data that divide the lower 25% of cases (the lower hinge) and the upper 25% of cases (the upper hinge) from the remainder of the cases.

hippocampus *n.* (*pl.* **hippocampi**) a seahorse-shaped part of the forebrain, in the basal medial region of the TEMPORAL LOBE, that is important for DECLARATIVE MEMORY and learning. —**hippocampal** *adj.*

histogram *n.* a graphical depiction of continuous data using bars of varying height, similar to a BAR GRAPH but with blocks on the *x*-axis adjoining one another so as to denote their continuous nature. For example, to show the average credit card debt of individuals by age, bars along the *x*-axis would represent age and would be connected to one another, while the heights of the bars

would represent the dollar amount of debt.

histology *n.* the scientific study of the structure and function of tissues. —**histological** *adj.* —**histologist** *n.*

histrionic personality disorder a personality disorder characterized by a pattern of long-term (rather than episodic) self-dramatization in which individuals draw attention to themselves, crave activity and excitement, overreact to minor events, experience angry outbursts, and are prone to manipulative suicide threats and gestures.

HIV *h*uman *i*mmunodeficiency *v*irus: a parasitic agent in blood, semen, and vaginal fluid that destroys a class of lymphocytes with a crucial role in the immune response. HIV infection can occur by various routes—unprotected sexual intercourse, administration of contaminated blood products, sharing of contaminated needles and syringes by intravenous drug users, or transmission from an infected mother to her child *in utero* or through breast feeding—and is characterized by a gradual deterioration of immune function that can progress to AIDS.

HIV dementia see AIDS DEMENTIA COMPLEX.

HMO *h*ealth *m*aintenance *o*rganization: a health plan that offers a range of services through a specified network of health professionals and facilities to subscribing members for a fixed fee. Members select a PRIMARY CARE provider who coordinates all care and is required to use approved providers for all services. The HMO is reimbursed through fixed, periodic prepayments (capitated rates) by, or on behalf of, each member for a specified period of time.

holism *n.* any approach or theory

H

holding that a system or organism is a coherent, unified whole that cannot be fully explained in terms of individual parts or characteristics. The system or organism may have properties, as a complete entity or phenomenon, in addition to those of its parts. Thus, an analysis or understanding of the parts does not provide an understanding of the whole. —**holistic** *adj.*

holophrase *n.* one of the single-word utterances characteristic of children in the early stages of LANGUAGE ACQUISITION, such as *dada* or *yes*. These are considered to involve a SPEECH ACT going beyond the literal meaning of the single word so that, for example, *biscuit* means *I want a biscuit now.* —**holophrastic** *adj.*

holophrastic stage see ONE-WORD STAGE.

homeostasis *n.* the regulation by an organism of all aspects of its internal environment, including body temperature, salt–water balance, acid–base balance, and blood sugar level. This involves monitoring changes in the external and internal environments by means of RECEPTORS and adjusting bodily processes accordingly. —**homeostatic** *adj.*

homeostatic model in social psychology, a model that assumes that all people are motivated by the **homeostatic principle**, that is, the need to maintain or restore their optimal level of environmental, interpersonal, and psychological stimulation. According to this theory, insufficient or excessive stimulation causes tension and often prompts the behavior required to achieve optimal stimulation levels.

home range the entire space through which an animal moves during its normal activities. The part of the home range in which the

greatest activity occurs is known as the core area.

homing *n.* the ability of organisms to return to an original home after traveling or being transported to a point that is a considerable distance from the home and that lacks most visual clues as to its location.

homogeneity of variance the condition in which multiple populations, or CELLS in an experimental design, have the same variance: a basic assumption of many statistical procedures. Compare HETEROGENEITY OF VARIANCE.

homogeneous *adj.* having the same, or relatively similar, composition throughout. Compare HETEROGENEOUS.

homologous *adj.* exhibiting resemblance in terms of structure, location, or origin. For example, DIPLOID organisms, such as humans, possess homologous pairs of chromosomes in the nuclei of their body cells.

homophily *n.* the tendency for individuals who are socially connected in some way to display certain affinities, such as similarities in demographic background, attitudes, values, and so on. Compare HETEROPHILY.

homophobia *n.* dread or fear of gay men and lesbians.

homoscedasticity *n.* the situation in which $Var(Y|X) = Var(Y)$, that is, the variance of variable Y is unrelated to the value of another variable X. Homoscedasticity is a basic assumption in some forms of REGRESSION ANALYSIS. Compare HETEROSCEDASTICITY. —**homoscedastic** *adj.*

homosexuality *n.* sexual attraction or activity between members of the same sex. Although the term can refer to such sexual orientation in both men and women, current practice distinguishes between gay men and lesbians, and homosexuality itself is now commonly referred to as same-sex sexual orientation or activity. Compare HETEROSEXUALITY. **—homosexual** *adj., n.*

homozygous *adj.* see ALLELE. **—homozygote** *n.*

homunculus *n.* (*pl.* **homunculi**) **1.** a putative process or entity in the mind or the nervous system whose operations are invoked to explain some aspect of human behavior or experience. The problem with such theories is that the behavior or experience of the homunculus usually requires explanation in exactly the same way as that of the person as a whole. As a result, homunculus theories tend to end in circular reasoning or to involve an infinite regression of homunculi. For example, to explain its theory that certain ideas are kept from conscious awareness because they are threatening to the person, psychoanalysis must posit some specialized part of the person that is aware of the ideas, and knows that they are threatening. **2.** in neuroanatomy, a figurative representation, in distorted human form, of the relative sizes of motor and sensory areas in the brain that correspond to particular parts of the body. For example, the brain area devoted to the tongue is much larger than the area for the forearm, so the homunculus has a correspondingly larger tongue. **—homuncular** *adj.*

honestly significant difference (**HSD**) see TUKEY'S HONESTLY SIGNIFICANT DIFFERENCE TEST.

hopelessness *n.* the feeling that one will not experience positive emotions or an improvement in one's condition. Hopelessness is common in DEPRESSIVE DISORDERS and is often implicated in attempted and completed suicides. **—hopeless** *adj.*

horizontal cell see RETINAL HORIZONTAL CELL.

horizontal décalage in PIAGETIAN THEORY, the invariant order in which accomplishments occur within a particular stage of development. For example, an understanding of CONSERVATION of quantity is always achieved before understanding conservation of weight. Compare VERTICAL DÉCALAGE.

horizontal plane an imaginary flat surface that divides the body or brain into upper and lower parts.

horizontal–vertical illusion the misperception that vertical lines are longer than horizontal lines when both are actually the same length. The vertical element of an upper case letter T, for example, looks longer than the cross bar, even when the lengths are identical.

hormone *n.* a substance secreted into the bloodstream by an ENDOCRINE GLAND or other tissue or organ to regulate processes in distant target organs and tissues. **—hormonal** *adj.*

hormone replacement therapy (**HRT**) the administration of female sex hormones, typically estrogen and progesterone, to postmenopausal women to relieve menopausal symptoms. Long-term use, however, may increase the risk of breast cancer, cardiovascular disease, stroke, and other conditions associated with the aging process.

horopter *n.* the location in space occupied by points that fall on corresponding locations on the two retinas.

hospice *n.* a place or form of care for terminally ill individuals, often those with life expectancies of less than a year as determined by medical personnel. Instead of curing disease and prolonging life, the emphases of the hospice concept are patient comfort, psychological well-being, and pain management.

hostile aggression see AGGRESSION.

hostility *n.* the overt expression of intense animosity or antagonism in action, feeling, or attitude. —**hostile** *adj.*

HPA system abbreviation for HYPOTHALAMIC–PITUITARY–ADRENOCORTICAL SYSTEM.

HRT abbreviation for HORMONE REPLACEMENT THERAPY.

HSD abbreviation for honestly significant difference. See TUKEY'S HONESTLY SIGNIFICANT DIFFERENCE TEST.

5-HT abbreviation for 5-hydroxytryptamine. See SEROTONIN.

hue *n.* the subjective quality of color, which is determined primarily by wavelength and secondarily by amplitude.

human engineering the design of environments and equipment that promote optimum use of human capabilities and optimum safety, efficiency, and comfort.

human factors 1. in ERGONOMICS, the impact of human beings, with their characteristic needs, abilities, and limitations, on system function and the considerations to be made when designing, evaluating, or optimizing systems for human use, especially with regard to safety, efficiency, and comfort. **2.** the field of ERGONOMICS itself.

human factors psychology a branch of psychology that studies the role of HUMAN FACTORS in operating systems, with the aim of redesigning environments, equipment, and processes to fit human abilities and characteristics. Also called **engineering psychology**.

Human Genome Project an international project to map each human gene and determine the complete sequence of base pairs in human DNA. The project began in 1990 and was completed in 2003. It has yielded vast amounts of valuable information about the genes responsible for various diseases.

human immunodeficiency virus see HIV.

humanism *n.* a perspective that begins with a presumption of the inherent dignity and worth of humankind and focuses attention on the study and representation of human beings and human experiences. This position is in opposition to religious belief or other forms of supernaturalism. Within psychology, the term humanism is often applied to any perspective that seeks to uphold human values and to resist the reduction of human beings and behaviors to merely natural objects and events. In this spirit, HUMANISTIC PSYCHOLOGIES, particularly those in the tradition of U.S. psychologists Carl Rogers (1902–1987) and Abraham Maslow (1908–1970), have resisted not only natural scientific psychology, but also theories that emphasize the negative and pathological aspects of human nature. —**humanist** *adj., n.* —**humanistic** *adj.*

humanistic–existential therapy see EXISTENTIAL–HUMANISTIC THERAPY.

humanistic perspective the assumption in psychology that people are essentially good and constructive, that the tendency toward SELF-ACTUALIZATION is inherent, and that, given the proper environment, human beings will develop to their maximum potential. The humanistic perspective arose from the contributions of U.S. psychologists Gordon Allport(1897–1967), Abraham Maslow (1908–1970), and Carl

Rogers (1902–1987), who advocated a personality theory based on the study of healthy individuals as opposed to people with mental disorders.

humanistic psychology an approach to psychology that flourished particularly in academia between the 1940s and the early 1970s and that is most visible today as a family of widely used approaches to psychotherapy and counseling. It derives largely from ideas associated with EXISTENTIAL-ISM and PHENOMENOLOGY and focuses on individuals' capacity to make their own choices, create their own style of life, and actualize themselves in their own way. Its approach is holistic, and its emphasis is on the development of human potential through experiential means rather than analysis of the unconscious or behavior modification. Leading figures associated with this approach include U.S. psychologists Abraham Maslow (1908–1970), Carl Rogers (1902–1987), and Rollo May (1909–1994).

humanistic therapy any of a variety of psychotherapeutic approaches that seek to foster personal growth through direct experience and focus on the development of human potential, the here and now, concrete personality change, responsibility for oneself, and trust in natural processes and spontaneous feeling. Some examples of humanistic therapy are CLIENT-CENTERED THERAPY, GESTALT THERAPY, and EXISTENTIAL PSYCHOTHERAPY.

humiliation *n.* a feeling of shame due to being disgraced or deprecated.

humor *n.* **1.** the capacity to perceive or express the amusing aspects of a situation. There is little agreement about the essence of humor and the reasons one laughs or smiles

at jokes or anecdotes. For example, some have claimed that individuals laugh at people and situations that make them feel superior, some have emphasized surprise and anticlimax, and still others have seen humor as "playful pain," a way of taking serious things lightly and thereby triumphing over them. **2.** the semifluid substance that occupies the spaces in the eyeball. **3.** anciently, one of four bodily fluids (blood, black bile, yellow bile, and phlegm) that were thought to be responsible for a person's physical and psychological characteristics. **—humoral** *adj.* **—humorous** *adj.*

Huntington's disease (HD) a progressive hereditary disease associated with degeneration of nerve cells in the BASAL GANGLIA and CEREBRAL CORTEX. It is characterized by abnormalities of gait and posture, motor incoordination, and involuntary jerking motions (CHOREA) as well as DEMENTIA, mood disturbances, and personality and behavioral changes. The age of onset is usually between 30 and 50, but there is a juvenile form of the disease in which symptoms first appear before the age of 20. Also called **Huntington's chorea**. [George Huntington (1850–1916), U.S. physician]

hydrocephalus *n.* a condition caused by excessive accumulation of cerebrospinal fluid in the ventricles of the brain, resulting in raised pressure within the skull, with such symptoms as headache, vomiting, poor coordination, lethargy, drowsiness, or irritability or other changes in personality or cognition. **—hydrocephalic** *adj.*

hydrophobia *n.* a persistent and irrational fear of water, resulting in avoidance of activities involving water, such as swimming, drinking, or washing one's hands. **—hydrophobic** *adj.*

H

hydrotherapy *n.* the therapeutic use of water to promote recovery from disease or injury. Hydrotherapy includes such treatments as baths, streams of water (douches), and aquatic sports or exercise.

5-hydroxytryptamine (5-HT) *n.* see SEROTONIN.

hygiene factors in the TWO-FACTOR THEORY OF WORK MOTIVATION, certain aspects of the working situation that can produce discontent if they are poor or lacking but that cannot by themselves motivate employees to improve their job performance. These include pay, relations with peers and supervisors, working conditions, and benefits. Compare MOTIVATORS.

hyperactivity *n.* spontaneous, excessive motor or other activity. —**hyperactive** *adj.*

hyperalgesia *n.* an abnormal sensitivity to pain.

hypercomplex cell a neuron in the visual cortex for which the optimal stimulus is a moving line of specific length or a moving corner.

hyperkinesis *n.* **1.** excessive involuntary movement. **2.** restlessness or HYPERACTIVITY. Also called **hyperkinesia**. —**hyperkinetic** *adj.*

hyperlexia *n.* the development of extremely good reading skills at a very early age, well ahead of word comprehension or cognitive ability. Children with hyperlexia often start to recognize words without instruction and before any expressive language develops. —**hyperlexic** *adj.*

hypermnesia *n.* an extreme degree of retentiveness and recall, with unusual clarity of memory images.

hyperopia *n.* farsightedness. Hyperopia is a refractive error due to an abnormally short eyeball, in which the image of close objects is blurred because the focal point of one or both eyes lies behind, rather than on, the retina. Compare MYOPIA.

hyperphagia *n.* pathological overeating, particularly when due to a metabolic disorder or to a brain lesion. Compare APHAGIA; HYPOPHAGIA. —**hyperphagic** *adj.*

hyperpolarization *n.* an increase in the electric potential across the plasma membrane of a cell, especially a neuron, such that the inner surface of the membrane becomes more negative in relation to the outer surface. It occurs during the final portion of an ACTION POTENTIAL or in response to inhibitory neural messages. Compare DEPOLARIZATION.

hypersomnia *n.* excessive sleepiness during daytime hours or abnormally prolonged episodes of nighttime sleep. This can be a feature of certain disorders, or it can be associated with neurological dysfunction or damage, with a general medical condition, or with substance use. Compare HYPOSOMNIA.

hypertension *n.* high blood pressure: a circulatory disorder characterized by persistent arterial blood pressure that exceeds readings higher than an arbitrary standard, which usually is 140/90. Compare HYPOTENSION. —**hypertensive** *adj.*

hyperthyroidism *n.* overactivity of the thyroid gland, resulting in excessive production of thyroid-hormones and a consequent increase in metabolic rate. Manifestations include nervousness, excessive activity, and weight loss and other physical problems. Compare HYPOTHYROIDISM.

hyperventilation *n.* abnormally rapid and deep breathing, usually due to anxiety or emotional stress. This lowers the carbon dioxide level of the blood and produces such symptoms as light-headedness and numbness and tingling in the extremities.

hypesthesia *n.* severely diminished sensitivity in any of the senses, especially the touch sense. Also called **hypoesthesia**.

hypnagogic *adj.* describing or relating to a state of drowsiness or light sleep that occurs just before falling fully asleep.

hypnogenic *adj.* **1.** sleep-producing. **2.** hypnosis-inducing.

hypnosis *n.* (*pl.* **hypnoses**) the procedure, or the state induced by that procedure, whereby a hypnotist suggests that a subject experience various changes in sensation, perception, cognition, emotion, or control over motor behavior. Subjects appear to be receptive, to varying degrees, to suggestions to act, feel, and behave differently than in a normal waking state. As a specifically psychotherapeutic intervention, hypnosis is referred to as HYPNOTHERAPY.

hypnotherapy *n.* the use of hypnosis in psychological treatment, either for alleviation of symptoms and modification of behavior patterns or for more long-term personality adaptation or change. Hypnotherapy may use one or a combination of techniques, typically involving the administration by a properly trained professional of therapeutic suggestions to patients or clients. Although discussions of its clinical applications engender controversy, there has been scientific evidence that hypnotherapy can be applied with some success to a wide range of clinical problems (e.g., hypertension, asthma, insomnia); chronic and acute pain management; habit modification (e.g., smoking); mood and anxiety disorders (e.g., some phobias); and personality disorders.

hypnotic 1. *n.* a drug that helps induce and sustain sleep by increasing drowsiness and reducing motor activity. In general, hypnotics differ from SEDATIVES only in terms of the dose administered, with higher doses used to produce sleep or anesthesia and lower doses to produce sedation or relieve anxiety. **2.** *adj.* pertaining to hypnosis or sleep.

hypnotic susceptibility the degree to which an individual is able to enter into hypnosis. Although many individuals can enter at least a light trance, people vary greatly in their ability to achieve a moderate or deep trance. Also called **hypnotizability**.

hypoactive sexual desire disorder persistent and distressing deficiency or absence of sexual interest and desire to engage in sexual activity. This may be global, involving all forms of sexual activity, or situational, limited to one partner or one type of sexual activity.

hypoactivity *n.* abnormally slowed or deficient motor or other activity.

hypochondriasis *n.* a SOMATOFORM DISORDER characterized by a preoccupation with the fear or belief that one has a serious physical disease based on the incorrect and unrealistic interpretation of bodily symptoms. This fear or belief persists for at least 6 months and interferes with social and occupational functioning in spite of medical reassurance that no physical disorder exists.

hypoglossal nerve the 12th CRANIAL NERVE, a motor nerve that innervates the muscles of the tongue.

hypokinesis *n.* abnormal slowness in the initiation of voluntary movement. Compare BRADYKINESIA. Also called **hypokinesia**. —**hypokinetic** *adj.*

hypomanic episode a period of elevated, expansive, or irritable mood lasting at least 4 days and accompanied by at least three of the following (four if the mood is irritable): inflated self-esteem, a decreased need for sleep, increased speech, racing thoughts, distractibility, increase in activity or PSYCHOMOTOR AGITATION, and increased involvement in risky activities (e.g., foolish investments, sexual indiscretions), all of which affect functioning and are noticeable by others but do not cause marked impairment. Also called **hypomania**.

hypophagia *n.* pathologically reduced food intake. Compare HYPERPHAGIA.

hyposomnia *n.* a reduction in a person's sleep time, often as a result of INSOMNIA or some other sleep disturbance. Compare HYPERSOMNIA.

hypotension *n.* abnormally low blood pressure, causing dizziness and fainting. Compare HYPERTENSION. —**hypotensive** *adj.*

hypothalamic–pituitary–adrenocortical system (**HPA system**) a neuroendocrine system that is involved in the physiological response to stress. Outputs from the amygdala to the hypothalamus stimulate the release of corticotropin-releasing factor (CRF). CRF elicits the release from the anterior pituitary of CORTICOTROPIN, which in turn regulates the production and release of stress hormones (e.g., cortisol) from the adrenal cortex into the bloodstream.

hypothalamus *n.* (*pl.* **hypothalami**) part of the DIENCEPHALON of the brain, lying ventral to the THALAMUS, that contains nuclei with primary control of the autonomic (involuntary) functions of the body. It also helps integrate autonomic activity into appropriate responses to internal and external stimuli. —**hypothalamic** *adj.*

hypothesis *n.* (*pl.* **hypotheses**) an empirically testable proposition about some fact, behavior, relationship, or the like, usually based on theory, that states an expected outcome resulting from specific conditions or assumptions.

hypothesis testing the process of using any of a collection of statistical tests to assess the likelihood that an experimental result might have been the result of a chance or random process.

hypothetico-deductive method a method of examining the accuracy of predictions made on the basis of some theory, in which the theory gains credibility as more predictions are found to be accurate.

hypothetico-deductive reasoning the abstract logical reasoning that, according to the PIAGETIAN THEORY of cognitive development, emerges in early adolescence and marks the FORMAL OPERATIONAL STAGE. Hypothetico-deductive reasoning is distinguished by the capacity for abstract thinking and hypothesis testing.

hypothyroidism *n.* underactivity of the thyroid gland, resulting in underproduction of thyroid hormones and a consequent decrease in metabolic rate. Manifestations include fatigue, weakness, and weight gain and other physical problems. Compare HYPERTHYROIDISM.

hypovolemic thirst thirst caused by blood loss and other conditions (e.g., severe vomiting) that result in depletion of the volume of extracellular fluid. Also called **volumetric thirst**. Compare OSMOMETRIC THIRST.

hypoxia *n.* reduced oxygen in the body tissues, including the brain. This can result in widespread brain injury depending on the degree of oxygen deficiency and its duration. Signs and symptoms of hypoxia vary according to its cause, but generally include shortness of breath, rapid pulse, fainting, and mental disturbances (e.g., delirium, euphoria). See also ANOXIA. **—hypoxic** *adj.*

hysterectomy *n.* the surgical removal of the uterus.

hysteria *n.* the historical name for the condition now classified as SOMATIZATION DISORDER. Although technically outdated, it is often used as a lay term for any psychogenic disorder characterized by such symptoms as paralysis, blindness, loss of sensation, and hallucinations and often accompanied by suggestibility, emotional outbursts, and histrionic behavior. Austrian psychiatrist Sigmund Freud (1856–1939) interpreted hysterical symptoms as defenses against guilty sexual impulses (e.g., a paralyzed hand cannot masturbate), but other conflicts are now recognized. Freud also included dissociative conditions in his concept of hysteria, but these are now regarded as separate disorders. **—hysterical** *adj.*

Hz symbol for HERTZ.

H

Ii

IADLs abbreviation for INSTRUMENTAL ACTIVITIES OF DAILY LIVING.

iatrogenic *adj.* denoting or relating to a pathological condition that is caused inadvertently by treatment, particularly the actions of a health care professional. For example, an **iatrogenic addiction** is a dependence on a substance, most often a painkiller, originally prescribed by a physician to treat a physical or psychological disorder.

ICD abbreviation for INTERNATIONAL CLASSIFICATION OF DISEASES.

iconic memory the brief retention of an image of a visual stimulus beyond cessation of the stimulus. This iconic image usually lasts less than a second. In a MULTISTORE MODEL OF MEMORY, iconic memory precedes SHORT-TERM MEMORY.

id *n.* in psychoanalytic theory, the component of the personality that contains the instinctual, biological drives that supply the psyche with its basic energy or LIBIDO. Austrian psychiatrist Sigmund Freud (1856–1939) conceived of the id as the most primitive component of the personality, located in the deepest level of the unconscious; it has no inner organization and operates in obedience to the PLEASURE PRINCIPLE. Thus the infant's life is dominated by the desire for immediate gratification of instincts, such as hunger and sex, until the EGO begins to develop and operate in accordance with reality. See also PRIMARY PROCESS; STRUCTURAL MODEL.

idea *n.* in cognitive psychology, a mental image or cognition that is ultimately derived from experience but that may occur without direct reference to perception or sensory processes.

idealism *n.* in philosophy, the position that reality, including the natural world, is not independent of mind. Positions range from strong forms, holding that mind constitutes the things of reality, to weaker forms holding that reality is correlated with the workings of the mind. There is also a range of positions as to the nature of mind, from those holding that mind must be conceived of as absolute, universal, and apart from nature itself to those holding that mind may be conceived of as individual minds. See also MIND–BODY PROBLEM. Compare MATERIALISM. **—idealist** *n.* **—idealistic** *adj.*

ideal self in models of self-concept, a mental representation of an exemplary set of psychological attributes that one strives or wishes to possess.

idée fixe a firmly held, irrational idea or belief that is maintained despite evidence to the contrary. It may take the form of a delusion and become an obsession.

identical twins see MONOZYGOTIC TWINS.

identification *n.* **1.** the process of associating the self closely with other individuals and their characteristics or views. Identification operates largely on an unconscious or semiconscious level. **2.** in psychoanalytic theory, a DEFENSE MECHANISM in which the individual incorporates aspects of his or her OBJECTS inside the EGO in order to alleviate the anxiety associated with OBJECT LOSS or to reduce hostility between himself or herself and the object.

identity *n.* **1.** an individual's sense of self defined by (a) a set of physical and psychological characteristics that is not wholly shared with any other person and (b) a range of social and interpersonal affiliations (e.g., ethnicity) and social roles. Identity involves a sense of continuity: the feeling that one is the same person today that one was yesterday or last year (despite physical or other changes). Also called **personal identity. 2.** in cognitive development, awareness that an object remains the same even though it may undergo many transformations. For example, a piece of clay may be made to assume various forms but is still the same piece of clay.

identity crisis a phase of life marked by role experimentation, changing, conflicting, or newly emerging values, and a lack of understanding of oneself or one's roles in society.

identity diffusion in the EGO PSYCHOLOGY of German-born U.S. psychologist Erik Erikson (1902–1994), a possible outcome of the IDENTITY VERSUS IDENTITY CONFUSION stage in which the individual emerges with an uncertain sense of identity and confusion about his or her wishes, attitudes, and goals.

identity foreclosure premature commitment to an identity: the unquestioning acceptance by individuals (usually adolescents) of the role, values, and goals that others (e.g., parents, close friends, teachers, athletic coaches) have chosen for them.

identity style an adolescent's characteristic mode of approaching problems and decisions that are relevant to his or her personal identity

or sense of self. Differences in style reflect differences in the social-cognitive processes that individuals use to construct a sense of identity. Three basic identity styles are recognized: informational, normative, and diffuse-avoidant. Information-oriented individuals actively seek out, evaluate, and use self-relevant information. They are skeptical about their self-constructions and willing to test and revise aspects of their self-identity when confronted with discrepant feedback. Normative individuals deal with identity questions and decisional situations by conforming to the prescriptions and expectations of significant others. Diffuse-avoidant-oriented individuals are reluctant to face up to and confront personal problems and decisions.

identity versus identity confusion the fifth of ERIKSON'S EIGHT STAGES OF DEVELOPMENT, occurring during adolescence, in which the individual experiences a psychosocial MORATORIUM, a period of time that permits experimentation with social roles. The individual may "try on" different roles and identify with different groups before forming a cohesive, positive identity that allows him or her to contribute to society; alternatively, the individual may remain confused about his or her sense of identity, a state Erikson calls IDENTITY DIFFUSION.

ideology *n.* a systematic ordering of ideas with associated doctrines, attitudes, beliefs, and symbols that together form a more or less coherent philosophy for a person, group, or sociopolitical movement. **—ideological** *adj.*

idiocentric *adj.* denoting internality to the self, particularly an orientation toward or focus on personal needs and interests. See also EGOCENTRISM. Compare ALLOCENTRIC. **—idiocentrism** *n.*

idiographic *adj.* relating to the description and understanding of an individual case, as opposed to the formulation of NOMOTHETIC general laws describing the average case. An **idiographic approach** involves the thorough, intensive study of a single person or case in order to obtain an in-depth understanding of that person or case, as contrasted with a study of the universal aspects of groups of people or cases.

idiolect *n.* a DIALECT spoken at the level of an individual. The term is typically reserved for the most idiosyncratic forms of personal language use, especially those involving eccentricities of construction or vocabulary. —**idiolectal** *adj.*

idiosyncrasy *n.* a peculiarity of an individual, such as a habit or abnormal susceptibility to something (e.g., a drug). —**idiosyncratic** *adj.*

idiosyncrasy-credit model an explanation of the leniency that groups sometimes display when high-status members violate group norms. This model assumes that such individuals, by contributing to the group in significant ways and expressing loyalty to it, build up **idiosyncrasy credits**, which they "spend" whenever they make errors or deviate from the group's norms.

idiot savant (*pl.* **idiots savants** or, less often, **idiot savants**) see SAVANT. [French, "learned idiot"]

id psychology in psychoanalysis, an approach that focuses on the unorganized, instinctual impulses contained in the ID that seek immediate pleasurable gratification of primitive needs. The id is believed to dominate the lives of infants and is frequently described as blind and irrational until it is disciplined by the other two major components of the personality: the EGO and the SUPEREGO. Compare EGO PSYCHOLOGY.

IEP abbreviation for INDIVIDUALIZED EDUCATION PROGRAM.

illusion *n.* a false perception. Illusions result from the misinterpretation of sensory stimuli and are normal occurrences. Visual (or optical) illusions are particularly common and include the well-known MÜLLER-LYER ILLUSION. —**illusory** *adj.*

illusory conjunction the attribution of a characteristic of one stimulus to another stimulus when the stimuli are presented only briefly. Illusory conjunctions are most common with visual stimuli when, for example, the color of one form can be attributed to a different form.

illusory correlation the appearance of a relationship that in reality does not exist or an overestimation of the degree of relationship (i.e., correlation) between two variables.

image *n.* **1.** a likeness or cognitive representation of an earlier sensory experience recalled without external stimulation. For example, remembering the shape of a horse or the sound of a jet airplane brings to mind an image derived from earlier experiences with these stimuli. **2.** a representation of an object produced by an optical system. See also RETINAL IMAGE.

imagery *n.* **1.** the generation of mental images. **2.** such images considered collectively.

imaginal exposure a type of EXPOSURE THERAPY used for treating individuals with anxiety disorders (e.g., PHOBIAS, OBSESSIVE-COMPULSIVE DISORDER) or posttraumatic stress disorder. Vivid imagery evoked through speech is used by the therapist to expose the client mentally to an anxiety-evoking stimulus. Compare IN VIVO EXPOSURE.

imaginary audience the belief of an adolescent that others are constantly focusing attention on him or her, scrutinizing behaviors, appearance, and the like. The adolescent feels as though he or she is continually the central topic of interest to a group of spectators (i.e., an audience) when in fact this is not the case (i.e., an imaginary audience). It is reflective of acute self-consciousness and is considered an expression of adolescent EGOCENTRISM.

imaging *n.* **1.** the process of scanning the brain or other organs or tissues to obtain an optical image. Techniques used include COMPUTED TOMOGRAPHY, POSITRON EMISSION TOMOGRAPHY (PET), anatomical MAGNETIC RESONANCE IMAGING (aMRI), and FUNCTIONAL MAGNETIC RESONANCE IMAGING (fMRI). **2.** in therapy, the use of suggested mental images to control body function, including the easing of pain.

imago *n.* an unconscious mental image of another person, especially the mother or father, that influences the way in which an individual relates to others. The imago is typically formed in infancy and childhood and is generally an idealized or otherwise not completely accurate representation. The term was originally used by Austrian psychiatrist Sigmund Freud (1856–1939) and the early psychoanalysts, and its meaning has carried over into other schools of psychology and psychotherapy.

imitation *n.* the process of copying the behavior of another person, group, or object, intentionally or unintentionally. Some theorists propose that true imitation requires that an observer be able to take the perspective of the model. This contrasts with other forms of SOCIAL LEARNING, such as emulation (engaging in similar behavior that does not necessarily replicate the specific actions of the model) and MIMICRY. —**imitate** *vb.*

immanent justice the belief that rules are fixed and immutable and that punishment automatically follows misdeeds regardless of extenuating circumstances. Children up to the age of 8 equate the morality of an act only with its consequences; not until later do they develop the capacity to judge motive and subjective considerations. See MORAL ABSOLUTISM; MORAL REALISM. Compare DISTRIBUTIVE JUSTICE.

immaterialism *n.* the philosophical position that denies the independent existence of matter as a substance in which qualities might inhere. Sensible objects are held to exist as the sum of the qualities they produce in the perceiving mind, with no material substratum. It is difficult to distinguish such a position from IDEALISM, which holds that mind is essential to all reality and that things and qualities exist only as perceived. Compare MATERIALISM.

immaturity *n.* a state of incomplete growth or development (e.g., neural immaturity). The term, however, is often used to describe childish, maladaptive, or otherwise inappropriate behaviors, particularly when indicative of a lack of age-relevant skills.

immediate memory another name for SHORT-TERM MEMORY.

immune system a complex system in vertebrates that helps protect the body against pathological effects of foreign substances (ANTIGENS), such as viruses and bacteria. The organs involved include the bone marrow and thymus, in which LYMPHOCYTES—the principal agents responsible for specific **immune responses**—are produced, together with the spleen, lymph nodes, and other lymphoid tissues and various chemicals (e.g., CYTOKINES) that mediate the immune response.

impairment *n.* any departure from the body's typical physiological or psychological functioning.

implicit association test an IM-PLICIT ATTITUDE measure in which participants perform a series of categorization tasks on computer for a set of words representing an attitude object (e.g., words such as *ant*, *fly*, and *grasshopper* representing the attitude object of insects) and for a second set of intermixed words, selected to be highly evaluative in nature. If attitudes are positive, judging the target words should be faster when the same response key is used for category membership and positive words than when the same response key is used for category membership and negative words. Negative attitudes produce the opposite pattern.

implicit attitude a relatively enduring and general evaluative response of which a person has little or no conscious awareness. Compare EXPLICIT ATTITUDE.

implicit learning learning of a cognitive or behavioral task that occurs without intention to learn or awareness of what has been learned. Implicit learning is evidenced by improved task performance rather than as a response to an explicit request to remember.

implicit memory memory for a previous event or experience that is produced indirectly, without an explicit request to recall the event and without awareness that memory is involved. For instance, after seeing the word *store* in one context, a person would complete the word fragment *st_r_* as *store* rather than *stare*, even without remembering that *store* had been recently encoun-

tered. This term is used interchangeably with NONDECLARATIVE MEMORY. Compare EXPLICIT MEMORY.

implicit personality theory any set of tacit assumptions about the interrelations of personality traits, used in everyday life when people infer the presence of one trait on the basis of observing another.

implosive therapy a technique in BEHAVIOR THERAPY that is similar to FLOODING but distinct in generally involving imagined stimuli and in attempting to enhance anxiety arousal by adding imaginary exposure cues believed by the therapist to be relevant to the client's fear. Also called **implosion therapy**.

impotence *n.* the inability of a man to complete the sex act due to partial or complete failure to achieve or maintain erection. This condition is called **male erectile disorder** in DSM–IV–TR and **erectile dysfunction** in clinical contexts. —**impotent** *adj.*

impression formation the process in which an individual develops a perceptual SCHEMA of some object, person, or group. Early research on impression formation demonstrated that the accuracy of impressions was frequently poor; more recent studies have focused on the roles played in the process by such factors as the perceiver's cognitive processes (e.g., how readily some types of ideas come to mind) and feelings (e.g., anger can predispose the perceiver to stereotype an individual).

impression management behaviors that are designed to control how others perceive one's self, especially by guiding them to attribute desirable traits to the self. Impression management has been offered as an alternative explanation for some phenomena that have traditionally been interpreted in terms of

COGNITIVE DISSONANCE theory. Some psychologists distinguish impression management from SELF-PRESENTATION by proposing that impression management involves only deliberate, conscious strategies.

imprinting *n.* a simple yet profound and highly effective learning process that occurs during a CRITICAL PERIOD in the life of some animals. A well-known example is that of newly hatched chicks following the first moving object, human or animal, they see. Some investigators believe that such processes are instinctual; others regard them as a form of PREPARED LEARNING.

impulsive *adj.* describing or displaying behavior characterized by little or no forethought, reflection, or consideration of the consequences. Compare REFLECTIVE. —**impulsiveness** or **impulsivity** *n.*

imu *n.* a CULTURE-BOUND SYNDROME resembling LATAH, observed among the Ainu and Sakhalin women of Japan. It is characterized by an extreme STARTLE RESPONSE involving automatic movements, imitative behavior, infantile reactions, and obedience to command. See also MYRIACHIT.

inappropriate affect emotional responses that are not in keeping with the situation or are incompatible with expressed thoughts or wishes, for example, smiling when told about the death of a friend.

inattentional blindness failure to notice and remember otherwise perceptible stimuli in the visual background while the focus of attention is elsewhere. Research into inattentional blindness has led some to conclude that there is no conscious perception of the world without attention.

incentive *n.* an external stimulus, such as a condition or an object, that enhances or serves as a motive for behavior.

incentive theory the theory that motivation arousal depends on the interaction between environmental incentives (i.e., stimulus objects)—both positive and negative—and an organism's psychological and physiological states (e.g., drive states).

incest *n.* sexual activity between people of close blood relationship (e.g., brother and sister) that is prohibited by law or custom. Incest taboos of some kind are found in practically every society. —**incestuous** *adj.*

incidence *n.* the rate of occurrence of new cases of a given event or condition, such as a disorder, disease, symptom, or injury, in a particular population in a given period. An **incidence rate** is normally expressed as the number of cases per some standard proportion (1,000 or 100,000 are commonly used) of the entire population at risk per year. See also PREVALENCE.

incidental learning learning that is not premeditated, deliberate, or intentional and that is acquired as a result of some other, possibly unrelated, mental activity. Some theorists believe that much learning takes place without any intention to learn, occurring incidentally to other cognitive processing of information. See also LATENT LEARNING.

inclusion *n.* the practice of teaching students with disabilities in the same classroom as other students to the fullest extent possible, via the provision of appropriate supportive services.

inclusive fitness the REPRODUCTIVE SUCCESS not only of an individual but of all that individual's relatives in proportion to their coefficient of relatedness (mean number of genes shared). In calculating estimates of reproductive

I

success, it is assumed that parents, offspring, and siblings have an average of 50% of their genes in common, grandparents and grand-offspring, and uncles and nieces, share 25% of genes, and so forth.

incompetence *n.* **1.** the inability to carry out a required task or activity adequately. **2.** in law, the inability to make sound judgments regarding one's transactions or personal affairs. With regard to the criminal justice system, incompetence is the inability of a defendant to participate meaningfully in criminal proceedings. See also COMPETENCE. **—incompetent** *adj.*

incongruence *n.* lack of consistency or appropriateness, as in INAPPROPRIATE AFFECT or as when one's subjective evaluation of a situation is at odds with reality. **—incongruent** *adj.*

incremental learning see ALL-OR-NONE LEARNING.

incus *n.* see OSSICLES.

independence *n.* **1.** freedom from the influence or control of other individuals or groups. **2.** complete lack of relationship between two or more events, sampling units, or variables such that none is influenced by any other and that changes in any one have no implication for changes in any other. **—independent** *adj., n.*

independent-groups design see BETWEEN-SUBJECTS DESIGN.

independent living 1. the ability of an individual to perform—without assistance from others—all or most of the daily functions typically required to be self-sufficient, including those tasks essential to personal care (see ACTIVITIES OF DAILY LIVING) and to maintaining a home and job. **2.** a philosophy and civil reform movement promoting the rights of people with disabilities to determine the course of their lives

and be full, productive members of society with access to the same social and political freedoms and opportunities as individuals without disabilities.

independent self-construal a view of the self that emphasizes one's unique traits and accomplishments and downplays one's embeddedness in a network of social relationships. Compare INTERDEPENDENT SELF-CONSTRUAL.

independent variable (IV) the variable in an experiment that is specifically manipulated. Independent variables may or may not be causally related to the DEPENDENT VARIABLE. In statistical analysis, an independent variable is likely to be referred to as a **predictor variable**.

indeterminism *n.* the philosophical position that events do not have necessary and sufficient causes. Indeterminism manifests itself in psychology as the doctrine that humans have FREE WILL and are able to act independently of antecedent or current situations, as in making choices. Compare DETERMINISM. **—indeterminist** *adj.*

index case see PROBAND.

individual differences traits or other characteristics by which individuals may be distinguished from one another. This is the focus of DIFFERENTIAL PSYCHOLOGY, for which the term **individual differences psychology** increasingly is used.

individualism *n.* a social or cultural tradition, ideology, or personal outlook that emphasizes the individual and his or her rights and independence. Compare COLLECTIVISM. **—individualist** *n.* **—individualistic** *adj.*

individualized education program (IEP) a plan for providing specialized educational services and procedures that meet the unique needs of a child with a disability. Each IEP must be documented in writing, tailored to a particular child, and implemented in accordance with the requirements of U.S. federal law.

individual psychology the psychological theory of Austrian psychologist Alfred Adler (1870–1937), which is based on the idea that throughout life individuals strive for a sense of mastery, completeness, and belonging and are governed by a conscious drive to overcome their sense of inferiority by developing to their fullest potential, obtaining their life goals, and creating their own styles of life.

individual test a test designed to be administered to a single examinee at a time. Compare GROUP TEST.

individual therapy treatment of psychological problems that is conducted on a one-to-one basis. One therapist sees one client at a time, tailoring the process to his or her unique needs in the exploration of contributory factors and alleviation of symptoms. Also called **individual psychotherapy**. Compare GROUP THERAPY.

individuation *n.* **1.** the physiological, psychological, and sociocultural processes by which a person attains status as an individual human being and exerts himself or herself as such in the world. **2.** in the psychoanalytic theory of Swiss psychiatrist Carl Jung (1875–1961), the gradual development of a unified, integrated personality that incorporates greater and greater amounts of the UNCONSCIOUS, both personal and collective, and resolves any conflicts that exist, such as those between introverted and extraverted tendencies.

indoleamine *n.* any of a class of BIOGENIC AMINES formed by an indole molecule, which is produced as a breakdown metabolite of tryptophan, and an amine group. Indoleamines include the neurotransmitter serotonin and the hormone melatonin.

induced abortion see ABORTION.

induced compliance effect see FORCED COMPLIANCE EFFECT.

induction *n.* **1.** a general conclusion, principle, or explanation derived by reasoning from particular instances or observations. See INDUCTIVE REASONING. Compare DEDUCTION. **2.** the process of inductive reasoning itself. **3.** in conditioning, the phenomenon in which REINFORCEMENT of some forms of behavior results in an increased probability not only of these forms but also of similar but nonreinforced forms. For example, if lever presses with forces between 0.2 and 0.3 N are reinforced, presses with forces less than 0.2 N or greater than 0.3 N will increase in frequency although they are never explicitly reinforced. Also called **response generalization**. —**inductive** *adj.*

inductive reasoning the form of reasoning in which inferences and general principles are drawn from specific observations and cases. Inductive reasoning is a cornerstone of the scientific method in that it underlies the process of developing hypotheses from particular facts and observations. Compare DEDUCTIVE REASONING.

industrial and organizational psychology (**I/O psychology**) the branch of psychology that studies human behavior in the work environment and applies general psychological principles to work-related issues and problems, notably in such areas as personnel selection and training, employee evaluation, working conditions, accident prevention, job analysis, job satisfaction, leadership, team effectiveness, organizational effectiveness, work motivation, and the welfare of employees. Also called **occupational psychology**; **work psychology**.

industry versus inferiority the fourth of ERIKSON'S EIGHT STAGES OF DEVELOPMENT, occurring from ages 6 to 11 years, during which the child learns to be productive and to accept evaluation of his or her efforts or becomes discouraged and feels inferior or incompetent.

infancy *n.* the earliest period of postnatal life, in humans generally denoting the time from birth through the first year. —**infant** *n.*

infant-directed speech the specialized style of speech that adults and older children use when talking specifically to infants, which usually includes much inflection and repetition. See also CHILD-DIRECTED SPEECH.

infantile amnesia see CHILD-HOOD AMNESIA.

infantile sexuality in psychoanalytic theory, the concept that PSYCHIC ENERGY or LIBIDO concentrated in various organs of the body throughout infancy gives rise to erotic pleasure. This is manifested in sucking the mother's breast during the ORAL STAGE of development, in defecating during the ANAL STAGE, and in self-stimulating activities during the early GENITAL STAGE. The term and concept, first enunciated by Austrian psychiatrist Sigmund Freud (1856–1939), proved highly controversial from the start, and it is more in line with subsequent thought to emphasize the sensual nature of breast feeding, defecation, and discovery of the body in childhood and the role of the pleasurable feelings so obtained in the origin and development of sexual feelings.

infantilism *n.* behavior, physical

characteristics, or mental functioning in older children or adults that is characteristic of that of infants or young children. See REGRESSION.

inferential statistics a broad class of statistical techniques that allows inferences about characteristics of a population to be drawn from a sample of data from that population while controlling (at least partially) the extent to which errors of inference may be made. These techniques include approaches for testing hypotheses and estimating the value of parameters.

inferior *adj.* in anatomy, lower, below, or toward the feet. Compare SUPERIOR.

inferior colliculus see COLLICULUS.

inferiority complex a basic feeling of inadequacy and insecurity, deriving from actual or imagined physical or psychological deficiency, that may result in behavioral expression ranging from the "withdrawal" of immobilizing timidity to the overcompensation of excessive competition and aggression. See also SUPERIORITY COMPLEX.

inferotemporal cortex a region of the brain on the inferior (lower) portion of the outer layer (cortex) of the temporal lobe that is particularly involved in the perception of form.

infertility *n.* inability to produce offspring. —**infertile** *adj.*

informational influence see SOCIAL PRESSURE.

information overload the state that occurs when the amount or intensity of environmental stimuli exceeds the individual's processing capacity, thus leading to an unconscious or subliminal disregard for some environmental information.

information processing in cognitive psychology, the flow of knowledge through the human nervous system, involving the operation of perceptual systems, memory stores, decision processes, and response mechanisms. **Information processing psychology** is the approach that concentrates on understanding these operations.

information theory the principles relating to the communication or transmission of information, which is defined as any message that reduces uncertainty. These principles deal with such areas as the encoding and decoding of messages, types of channels of communication and their capacity to throughput information, the application of mathematical methods to the process, the problem of noise (distortion), and the relative effectiveness of various kinds of FEEDBACK.

informed consent voluntary agreement to participate in a research or therapeutic procedure on the basis of the participant's or patient's understanding of its nature, its potential benefits and possible risks, and available alternatives.

infradian rhythm any periodic variation in physiological or psychological function recurring in a cycle of less than 24 hours. Compare ULTRADIAN RHYTHM.

infrasound *n*. sound whose frequency is too low to be detected by human hearing, generally encompassing the range of 20 Hz to .001 Hz. The scientific study of infrasound is known as **infrasonics**. Able to cover long distances and circumvent or penetrate obstacles without dispersing, infrasonic waves are used by many animals to communicate and have a variety of applications in geological monitoring (e.g., prediction of volcanic eruptions, detection of earthquakes). Compare ULTRASOUND.

ingratiation *n*. efforts to win the liking and approval of other people, especially by deliberate IMPRESSION MANAGEMENT. Ingratiation is usually regarded as consisting of illicit or objectionable strategies, especially for manipulative purposes, which distinguishes it from sincere efforts to be likable. —**ingratiate** *vb*.

ingroup *n*. any group to which one belongs or with which one identifies, but particularly a group judged to be different from, and often superior to, other groups (OUTGROUPS).

ingroup bias the tendency to favor one's own group, its members, its characteristics, and its products, particularly in reference to other groups. The favoring of the ingroup tends to be more pronounced than the rejection of the OUTGROUP, but both tendencies become more pronounced during periods of intergroup contact. At the regional, cultural, or national level, this bias is often termed ETHNOCENTRISM.

inhalant *n*. any of a variety of volatile substances that can be inhaled to produce intoxicating effects. Anesthetic gases (e.g., ether, chloroform, nitrous oxide), industrial solvents (e.g., toluene, gasoline, trichloroethylene, various aerosol propellants), and organic nitrites (e.g., amyl nitrite) are common inhalants.

inhibition *n*. the process of restraining or prohibiting, particularly one's impulses or behavior. The term is applied to a variety of contexts and occurrences, but is associated especially with psychoanalysis, referring to an unconscious mechanism in which the SUPEREGO controls instinctive impulses that would threaten the EGO if allowed conscious expression. —**inhibit** *vb*. —**inhibited** *adj*.

inhibition of return difficulty in

returning attention to a previously attended location. When attention has been directed to a location for a period of time, it is more difficult to redirect attention to that location than to direct it to another location.

inhibitory postsynaptic potential (IPSP) a brief increase in the difference in electrical charge across the membrane of a neuron that is caused by the transmission of a signal from a neighboring neuron across the synapse (specialized junction) separating them. IPSPs decrease the probability that the postsynaptic neuron will initiate an ACTION POTENTIAL and hence fire a nerve impulse. Compare EXCITATORY POSTSYNAPTIC POTENTIAL.

inhibitory synapse a specialized type of junction at which activity from one neuron (in the form of an ACTION POTENTIAL) reduces the probability of activity in an adjacent neuron by initiating an INHIBITORY POSTSYNAPTIC POTENTIAL. Compare EXCITATORY SYNAPSE.

initiative versus guilt the third of ERIKSON'S EIGHT STAGES OF DEVELOPMENT, which occurs during the child's 3rd through 5th years. In planning, launching, and initiating all forms of fantasy, play, and other activity, the child learns to believe in his or her ability to successfully pursue goals. However, should these pursuits often fail or be criticized, the child may develop instead a feeling of self-doubt and guilt.

injunctive norm see SOCIAL NORM.

inkblot test see RORSCHACH INKBLOT TEST.

innate *adj.* inborn, native, or natural: denoting a capability or characteristic existing in an organism from birth, that is, belonging to the original or essential constitution of the body or mind. Innate processes should be distinguished from those that develop later under maturational control or through experience.

innate releasing mechanism (IRM) in ethology, the hypothesized neurological means by which organisms exhibit a FIXED ACTION PATTERN given a particular RELEASER, suggesting that there is a direct correspondence between a specific elicitor and a specific behavioral event.

inner ear the part of the ear that comprises the bony and membranous LABYRINTHS and contains the sense organs responsible for hearing and balance. For hearing the major structure is the COCHLEA. For the sense of balance, the major structures are the SEMICIRCULAR CANALS, SACCULE, and UTRICLE.

inner nuclear layer the layer of retinal cell bodies interposed between the photoreceptors and the RETINAL GANGLION CELLS. The inner nuclear layer contains AMACRINE CELLS, RETINAL HORIZONTAL CELLS, RETINAL BIPOLAR CELLS, and MÜLLER CELLS.

inner plexiform layer the synaptic layer in the retina in which contacts are made between the dendrites of RETINAL GANGLION CELLS, BIPOLAR NEURONS, and AMACRINE CELLS.

innervation *n.* the supply of nerves to an organ (e.g., muscle or gland) or a body region. —**innervate** *vb.*

inpatient *n.* a person who has been formally admitted to a hospital for a period of at least 24 hours for observation, care, diagnosis, or treatment, as distinguished from an OUTPATIENT or an emergency-room patient.

insanity *n.* in law, a condition of the mind that renders a person incapable of being responsible for his or her criminal acts. Whether a person is insane, in this legal sense, is determined by judges and juries, not psychologists or psychiatrists. —**insane** *adj.*

insecure attachment in the STRANGE SITUATION, one of several patterns of generally negative parent–child relationship in which the child fails to display confidence when the parent is present, sometimes shows distress when the parent leaves, and reacts to the returning parent by not seeking close contact (**avoidant attachment**) or by simultaneously seeking and avoiding close contact (**ambivalent attachment**). See also DISORGANIZED ATTACHMENT.

insight *n.* **1.** the clear and often sudden discernment of a solution to a problem by means that are not obvious and may never become so, even after one has tried hard to work out how one has arrived at the solution. There are many different theories of how insights are formed and of the kinds of insights that exist. **2.** in psychotherapy, an awareness of underlying sources of emotional, cognitive, or behavioral difficulty in oneself or another person.

insight learning a form of learning involving the mental rearrangement or restructuring of the elements in a problem to achieve a sudden understanding of the problem and arrive at a solution. Originally described around 1917 by German experimental psychologist Wolfgang Köhler (1887–1967), based on observations of apes stacking boxes or using sticks to retrieve food, insight learning was offered as an alternative to TRIAL-AND-ERROR LEARNING.

insight therapy any form of psychotherapy based on the theory that a client's problems cannot be resolved without his or her gaining self-understanding and thus becoming aware of their origins. This approach (characteristic, for example, of PSYCHOANALYSIS and PSYCHODYNAMIC PSYCHOTHERAPY) contrasts with therapies directed toward removal of symptoms or behavior modification.

insomnia *n.* difficulty in initiating or maintaining a restorative sleep that results in fatigue, the severity or persistence of which causes clinically significant distress or impairment in functioning. —**insomniac** *n.*

instinct *n.* **1.** an innate, species-specific biological force that impels an organism to do something, particularly to perform a certain act or respond in a certain manner to specific stimuli. **2.** in psychoanalytic theory, a basic biological drive (e.g., hunger, thirst, sex, or aggression) that must be fulfilled in order to maintain physical and psychological equilibrium. Austrian psychiatrist Sigmund Freud (1856–1939) classified instincts into two types: those derived from the LIFE INSTINCT and those derived from the DEATH INSTINCT. **3.** in popular usage, any inherent or unlearned predisposition (behavioral or otherwise) or motivational force. —**instinctive** or **instinctual** *adj.*

institutionalization *n.* **1.** placement of an individual in an institution for therapeutic or correctional purposes. **2.** an individual's gradual adaptation to institutional life over a long period, especially when this is seen as rendering him or her passive, dependent, and generally unsuited to life outside the institution. —**institutionalize** *vb.*

institutionalized racism differential treatment of individuals on the basis of their racial group by social institutions, including religious organizations, governments, businesses, the media, and educational institutions. Examples include DIS-CRIMINATION in hiring, promotion, and advancement at work, restrictive housing regulations that promote segregation, unfair portrayal of minority members in newspapers and magazines, and legal statutes that restrict the civil liberties of the members of specific racial categories. A parallel phenomenon exists for SEXISM.

institutional review board (IRB) a committee named by an agency or institution to review research proposals originating within that agency for ethical acceptability.

instrumental activities of daily living (IADLs) activities essential to an individual's ability to function autonomously, including cooking, doing laundry, using the telephone, managing money, shopping, getting to places beyond walking distance, and the like. See also ACTIVITIES OF DAILY LIVING.

instrumental aggression see AGGRESSION.

instrumental conditioning any form of CONDITIONING in which the correct response is essential for REINFORCEMENT. Instrumental conditioning is similar to OPERANT CONDITIONING and usually involves complex activities in order to reach a goal, such as when a rat is trained to navigate a maze to obtain food. It contrasts with PAVLOVIAN CONDITIONING, in which reinforcement is given regardless of the response.

instrumentalism *n.* a theory of knowledge that emphasizes the pragmatic value, rather than the truth value, of ideas. In this view, the value of an idea, concept, or judgment lies in its ability to explain, predict, and control one's concrete functional interactions with the experienced world. For example, a theory should not be considered as either true or false but

as an instrument that allows observations of the world to be meaningfully ordered. This view is related to PRAGMATISM. —**instrumentalist** *adj., n.*

insula *n.* (*pl.* **insulae**) a region of the cerebral cortex of primate brains that is buried in a cleft near the lower end of the LATERAL SULCUS.

insulin *n.* a hormone, secreted by the B cells of the ISLETS OF LANGERHANS in the pancreas, that facilitates the transfer of glucose molecules through cell membranes. Together with GLUCAGON, it plays a key role in regulating blood sugar and carbohydrate metabolism.

intake interview 1. the initial interview with a client by a therapist or counselor to obtain both information regarding the issues or problems that have brought the client into therapy or counseling and preliminary information regarding personal and family history. **2.** the initial interview with a patient who is being admitted into a psychiatric hospital, day treatment, or inpatient substance abuse facility to determine the best course of treatment and the appropriate therapist to provide it.

integration *n.* the coordination or unification of parts into a totality. This general meaning has been incorporated into a wide variety of psychological contexts and topics. For example, the integration of personality denotes the gradual bringing together of constituent traits, behavioral patterns, motives, and so forth to form an organized whole that functions effectively and with minimal effort or without conflict.

integrative behavioral couples therapy couples therapy that uses techniques of BEHAVIORAL COUPLES THERAPY but also focuses on each person's emotional acceptance of his

I

or her partner's genuine incompatibilities, which may or may not be amenable to change. It is based on the conviction that focusing on changing incompatibilities leads to a resistance to change when change is possible or that this focus results in unnecessary frustration for both partners when change is not possible.

integrative psychotherapy psychotherapy that selects models or techniques from various therapeutic schools to suit the client's particular problems. For example, PSYCHODYNAMIC PSYCHOTHERAPY and GESTALT THERAPY may be combined through the practice of INTERPRETATION of material in the here and now. There is growing interest in and use of such combined therapeutic techniques.

integrity versus despair the eighth and final stage of ERIKSON'S EIGHT STAGES OF DEVELOPMENT, which occurs during old age. In this stage the individual reflects on the life he or she has lived and may develop either integrity—a sense of satisfaction in having lived a good life and the ability to approach death with equanimity—or despair—a feeling of bitterness about opportunities missed and time wasted, and a dread of approaching death.

intelligence *n.* the ability to derive information, learn from experience, adapt to the environment, understand, and correctly utilize thought and reason. There are many different definitions of intelligence, and there is currently much debate, as there has been in the past, over the exact nature of intelligence. **—intelligent** *adj.*

intelligence quotient see IQ.

intelligence test an individually administered test measuring a person's ability to solve problems, form concepts, reason, acquire detail, and perform other intellectual tasks. It comprises mental, verbal, and performance tasks of graded difficulty that have been standardized by use on a representative sample of the population.

intensity *n.* the strength or quantitative value of a stimulus (e.g., intensity of a sound) or sensation (e.g., intensity of an emotion). **—intense** *adj.*

intention *n.* a conscious decision to perform a behavior. In experiments, intention is often equated with the goals defined by the task instructions. **—intentional** *adj.*

interaction *n.* a relationship between two or more systems, people, or groups that results in mutual or reciprocal influence. See also SOCIAL INTERACTION. **—interact** *vb.*

interaction effect the joint effect of two or more independent variables on a dependent variable above and beyond the sum of their individual effects: The independent variables combine to have a different (and multiplicative) effect, such that the value of one is contingent upon the value of another. This indicates that the relationship between the independent variables changes as their values change. Interaction effects contrast with—and may obscure—MAIN EFFECTS. Compare ADDITIVE EFFECT.

interactionism *n.* **1.** the position that mind and body are distinct, incompatible substances that nevertheless interact, so that each has a causal influence on the other. This position is particularly associated with French philosopher René Descartes (1596–1650). See MIND–BODY PROBLEM. **2.** a set of approaches, particularly in personality psychology, in which behavior is explained not in terms of personality attributes or situational influences but by references to interactions that typify the behavior of a certain type of person in a certain type of setting. —**interactionist** *adj.*

interaction-process analysis a technique used to study the emotional, intellectual, and behavioral interactions among members of a group, for example, during GROUP THERAPY. It requires observers to classify every behavior displayed by a member of a group into one of 12 mutually exclusive categories, such as "asks for information" or "shows tension."

intercorrelation *n.* the correlation between each variable and every other variable in a group of variables.

interdependence *n.* a state in which factors rely on or react with one another such that one cannot change without affecting the other. —**interdependent** *adj., n.*

interdependent self-construal a view of the self that emphasizes one's embeddedness in a network of social relationships and downplays one's unique traits or accomplishments. Compare INDEPENDENT SELF-CONSTRUAL.

interdisciplinary approach a manner of dealing with psychological, medical, or other scientific questions in which individuals from different disciplines or professions collaborate to obtain a more thorough, detailed understanding of the nature of the questions and consequently develop more comprehensive answers. Also called **multidisciplinary approach**.

interference *n.* **1.** the blocking of learning or recall by the learning or remembering of other, conflicting material. Interference has many sources, including prior learning (**proactive interference**), subsequent learning (**retroactive interference**), competition during recall (**output**

interference), and presentation of other material. **2.** the mutual effect on meeting of two or more light, sound, or any other waves, the overlap of which produces a new pattern of waves.

interference theory the hypothesis that forgetting is due to competition from other learning or other memories.

interjudge reliability see INTERRATER RELIABILITY.

intermittent explosive disorder an impulse-control disorder consisting of multiple episodes in which the individual commits assaultive acts or destroys property. These aggressive acts are significantly out of proportion to any precipitating factors, are not caused by any other mental disorder or a general medical condition, and are not substance-induced. Compare ISOLATED EXPLOSIVE DISORDER.

intermittent reinforcement in operant or instrumental conditioning, any pattern of REINFORCEMENT in which only some responses are reinforced. Also called **partial reinforcement**.

intermodal matching the ability to recognize an object initially inspected with one modality (e.g., touch) via another modality (e.g., vision). Also called **cross-modal matching**.

intermodal perception the coordination or integration of information from two or more senses, such as touch and vision.

internal attribution see DISPOSITIONAL ATTRIBUTION.

internal capsule a large band of nerve fibers in the corpus striatum (see BASAL GANGLIA) that extends between the CAUDATE NUCLEUS on its medial side and the GLOBUS PALLIDUS and PUTAMEN on its lateral side. It contains afferent and efferent fibers from all parts of the cerebral cortex as they converge near the brainstem. See also EXTERNAL CAPSULE.

internal consistency the degree to which all the items on a test measure the same thing.

internalization *n.* **1.** the unconscious mental process by which the characteristics, beliefs, feelings, or attitudes of other individuals or groups are assimilated into the self and adopted as one's own. **2.** in psychoanalytic theory, the process of incorporating an OBJECT relationship inside the psyche, which reproduces the external relationship as an intrapsychic phenomenon. For example, through internalization the relationship between father and child is reproduced in the relationship between SUPEREGO and EGO. Internalization is often mistakenly used as a synonym for INTROJECTION. —**internalize** *vb.*

internal locus of control see LOCUS OF CONTROL.

internal validity the degree to which a study or experiment is free from flaws in its internal structure and its results can therefore be taken to represent the true nature of the phenomenon.

internal working model of attachment a cognitive construction or set of assumptions about the workings of relationships, such as expectations of support or affection. The earliest relationships may form the template for this internal model, which may be positive or negative.

International Classification of Diseases (**ICD**) a system of categories of disease conditions compiled by the World Health Organization (WHO) in conjunction with 10 WHO collaborating centers worldwide. The **ICD-10** (10th revision), published in 1992 as the *International Statistical Classification of Diseases and Related Health Problems*, uses a four-character alphanumeric coding system to classify diseases and disorders and their subtypes. See also DSM–IV–TR.

Internet addiction a behavioral pattern characterized by excessive or obsessive online and offline computer use that leads to distress and impairment. The condition, though controversial, has attracted increasing attention in the popular media and among healthcare professionals; it has been proposed for inclusion in the next edition of the *Diagnostic and Statistical Manual of Mental Disorders* (see DSM–IV–TR). Expanding research has identified various subtypes, including those involving excessive gaming, sexual preoccupations, and e-mail and text messaging.

interneuron *n.* any neuron that is neither sensory nor motor but connects other neurons within the central nervous system.

interobserver reliability see INTERRATER RELIABILITY.

interoception *n.* sensitivity to stimuli that are inside the body, resulting from the response of specialized sensory cells called **interoceptors** to occurrences within the body (e.g., from the viscera). Compare EXTEROCEPTION.

interpersonal *adj.* pertaining to actions, events, and feelings between two or more individuals. For example, **interpersonal skill** is an aptitude enabling a person to carry on effective relationships with others, such as an ability to communicate thought and feeling or to assume appropriate social responsibilities.

interpersonal attraction the interest in and liking of one individual by another, or the mutual interest and liking between two or more individuals. Interpersonal attraction may be based on shared experiences,

I

physical appearances, internal motivation (e.g., loneliness), or some combination of these.

interpersonal influence see SOCIAL PRESSURE.

interpersonal psychotherapy a time-limited form of psychotherapy in which the central feature is the clarification of the client's interpersonal interactions with significant others. The therapist helps the client explore current and past experiences in detail, relating not only to interpersonal reaction but also to environmental influences generally on personal adaptive and maladaptive thinking and behavior.

interpersonal theory the theory of personality developed by U.S. psychoanalyst Harry Stack Sullivan (1892–1949), which is based on the belief that people's interactions with other people, especially SIGNIFICANT OTHERS, determine their sense of security, sense of self, and the dynamisms that motivate their behavior.

interpersonal trust the confidence a person has in the honesty and reliability of others.

interposition *n.* a monocular DEPTH CUE occurring when two objects are in the same line of vision and the closer object, which is fully in view, partly conceals the farther object.

interpretation *n.* in psychotherapy, explanation by the therapist in terms that are meaningful to the client of the client's issues, behaviors, or feelings. Interpretation typically is made along the lines of the particular conceptual framework or dynamic model of the form of therapy. In psychoanalysis, for example, the analyst uses the constructs of psychoanalytic theory to interpret the patient's early experiences, dreams, character defenses, and resistance. Although interpretation

exists to some extent in almost any form of therapy, it is a critical procedural step in psychoanalysis and in other forms of PSYCHODYNAMIC PSYCHOTHERAPY.

interpretivism *n.* in EPISTEMOLOGY, the assertion that knowledge is deeply tied to the act of interpretation; there are multiple apprehendable and equally valid realities as opposed to a single objective reality. Interpretivism thus represents a form of RELATIVISM. See also CONSTRUCTIVISM.

interquartile range an index of the dispersion within a batch of scores: the difference between the 75th and 25th percentile scores within a distribution.

interrater reliability the consistency with which different examiners produce similar ratings in judging the same abilities or characteristics in the same target person or object. It usually refers to continuous measurement assignments. Also called **interjudge reliability**; **interobserver reliability**.

interrupted-time-series design an experimental design in which the effects of an intervention are evaluated by comparing outcome measures obtained at several time intervals before, and several time intervals after, the intervention was introduced.

intersensory perception the coordination of information presented through separate modalities into an integrated experience. Information from one sensory source is transmitted to the ASSOCIATION CORTEX, where it can be integrated with information from another sensory source. Also called **cross-modal perception**.

intersexuality *n.* a modern term for HERMAPHRODITISM and pseudohermaphroditism: the condition of possessing the sexual characteristics of both sexes. —**inter-sexual** *adj.*

intersubjectivity *n.* the property of being accessible in some way to more than one mind, implying a communication and understanding among different minds and the possibility of converting subjective, private experiences into objective, public ones. —**intersubjective** *adj.*

interval data numerical values that indicate magnitude but lack a "natural," meaningful zero point. Interval data represent exact quantities of the variables under consideration, and when arranged consecutively have equal differences among adjacent values (regardless of the specific values selected) that correspond to genuine differences between the physical quantities being measured. Temperature is an example of interval data: the difference between 50 °F and 49 °F is the same as the difference between 40 °F and 39 °F, but a temperature of 0 °F does not indicate that there is no temperature. See also RATIO DATA.

interval estimate an estimated range of likely values for a given population parameter. Compare POINT ESTIMATE.

interval reinforcement the REINFORCEMENT of the first response to a stimulus after a predetermined interval has lapsed. Reinforcement may be given at uniform or variable intervals; the number of responses during the interval is irrelevant. Compare RATIO REINFORCEMENT.

interval scale a scale marked in equal intervals so that the difference between any two consecutive values on the scale is equivalent regardless of the two values selected. Interval scales lack a true, meaningful zero point, which is what distinguishes them from RATIO SCALES.

intervening variable 1. a hypothetical entity that is influenced by an INDEPENDENT VARIABLE and that in turn influences a DEPENDENT VARIABLE. **2.** more specifically, an unseen process or event, inferred to occur within the organism between a stimulus event and the time of response, that affects the relationship between the stimulus and response.

intervention *n.* **1.** action on the part of a therapist to deal with the issues and problems of a client. The selection of the intervention is guided by the nature of the problem, the orientation of the therapist, the setting, and the willingness and ability of the client to proceed with the treatment. **2.** a technique in addictions counseling in which significant individuals in a client's life meet with him or her, in the presence of a trained counselor, to express their observations and feelings about the client's addiction and related problems. The session, typically a surprise to the client, may last several hours, after which the client has a choice of seeking a recommended treatment immediately (e.g., as an inpatient) or ignoring the intervention. If the client chooses not to seek treatment, participants state the interpersonal consequences.

interview *n.* a directed conversation intended to elicit specific information from an individual for purposes of research, diagnosis, treatment, or employment. Interviews may be either highly structured, including set questions, or unstructured, varying with material introduced by the interviewee.

interviewer effects the influence of an interviewer's attributes and behaviors on a respondent's answers. The interviewer's appearance, demeanor, training, age, sex, and ethnicity may all produce effects of this kind. The term **interviewer bias** refers more specifically to an interviewer's expectations, beliefs, and prejudices as they influence the interview process and the interpretation of the data it provides.

intimacy *n.* an interpersonal state of extreme emotional closeness that usually characterizes affectionate or loving personal relationships and requires the parties to have a detailed knowledge or deep understanding of each other. **—intimate** *adj.*

intimacy versus isolation the sixth of ERIKSON'S EIGHT STAGES OF DEVELOPMENT, which extends from late adolescence through courtship and early family life to early middle age. During this period, individuals must learn to share and care without losing themselves; if they fail, they will feel alone and isolated. The development of a cohesive identity in the previous stage provides the opportunity to achieve true intimacy.

intoxication *n.* see SUBSTANCE INTOXICATION.

intraclass correlation 1. an index of the homogeneity of members (people, items, etc.) within a group. **2.** the average intercorrelation among randomly formed pairs of cases within a group.

intrapersonal *adj.* describing factors operating or constructs occurring within the person, such as attitudes, decisions, self-concept, self-esteem, or self-regulation.

intrapsychic *adj.* pertaining to phenomena that arise or occur within the psyche or mind. An **intrapsychic** (or **inner**) **conflict**, for example, is the clash of opposing forces within the psyche, such as conflicting drives, wishes, or agencies. Compare EXTRAPSYCHIC.

intrinsic motivation an incentive to engage in a specific activity that derives from the activity itself (e.g., a genuine interest in a subject studied), rather than because of any external benefits that might be ob-tained (e.g., course credits). Compare EXTRINSIC MOTIVATION.

introjection *n.* **1.** a process in which an individual unconsciously incorporates aspects of the external environment into the self, particularly the attitudes, values, and qualities of another person. Introjection may occur, for example, in the mourning process for a loved one. **2.** in psychoanalytic theory, the process of internalizing the qualities of an external OBJECT into the psyche in the form of an internal object or mental REPRESENTATION, which then has an influence on behavior. This process is posited to be a normal part of development, as when introjection of parental values and attitudes forms the SUPEREGO, but may also be used as a DEFENSE MECHANISM in situations that arouse anxiety. **—introject** *vb.* **—introjective** *adj.*

introjective depression self-critical depression: intense sadness and DYSPHORIA stemming from punitive, relentless feelings of self-doubt, self-criticism, and self-loathing that often are related to the internalization of the attitudes and values of harsh and critical parental figures. The individual with introjective depression becomes involved in numerous activities in an attempt to compensate for his or her excessively high standards, constant drive to perform and achieve, and feelings of guilt and shame over not having lived up to expectations. Compare ANACLITIC DEPRESSION.

intromission *n.* the act of sending or putting in something, especially the insertion of the penis into the vagina. **—intromissive** *adj.*

intropunitive *adj.* referring to the punishment of oneself: tending to turn anger, blame, or hostility internally, against the self, in response to frustration. Compare

EXTRAPUNITIVE. —**intropunitive-ness** *n.*

introspection *n.* the process of attempting to access directly one's own internal psychological processes, judgments, perceptions, or states. —**introspective** *adj.*

introspectionism *n.* the doctrine that the basic method of psychological investigation is or should be INTROSPECTION. Historically, such an approach is associated with the school of psychological STRUCTURALISM. —**introspectionist** *adj.*

introversion *n.* orientation toward the internal private world of one's self and one's inner thoughts and feelings, rather than toward the outer world of people and things. Introversion is a broad personality trait and, like EXTRAVERSION, exists on a continuum of attitudes and behaviors. Introverts are relatively more withdrawn, retiring, reserved, quiet, and deliberate; they may tend to mute or guard expression of positive affect, adopt more skeptical views or positions, and prefer to work independently. —**introversive** *adj.* —**introvert** *n.* —**introverted** *adj.*

intrusion error in a memory test, the recall of an item that was not among the material presented for remembering. Intrusion errors can be informative about the nature of forgetting, for instance, if the intrusion is a synonym, rhyme, or associate of a correct item.

invariance *n.* **1.** in the theory of ECOLOGICAL PERCEPTION, any property of an object that remains constant although the point of observation or surrounding conditions may change. **2.** in statistics, the property of being unchanged by a TRANSFORMATION. —**invariant** *adj.*

invasive *adj.* **1.** denoting procedures or tests that require puncture

or incision of the skin or insertion of an instrument or foreign material into the body. **2.** able to spread from one tissue to another, or having the capacity to spread, as in the case of an infection or a malignant tumor. Compare NONINVASIVE.

inverse agonist see AGONIST.

inverted-U hypothesis a proposed correlation between motivation (or AROUSAL) and performance such that performance is poorest when motivation or arousal is at very low or very high states. This function is typically referred to as the YERKES–DODSON LAW. Emotional intensity (motivation) increases from a zero point to an optimal point, increasing the quality of performance; increase in intensity after this optimal point leads to performance deterioration and disorganization, forming an inverted U-shaped curve. The optimal point is reached sooner (i.e., at lower intensities) the less well learned or more complex the performance.

investment model a theory explaining commitment to a relationship in terms of one's satisfaction with, alternatives to, and investments in the relationship. According to the model, commitment is a function not only of a comparison of the relationship to the individual's expectations, but also the quality of the best available alternative and the magnitude of the individual's investment in the relationship; the investment of resources serves to increase commitment by increasing the costs of leaving the relationship. Although originally developed in the context of romantic associations and friendships, the investment model has since been extended to a variety of other areas, including employment and education.

in vitro fertilization (IVF) a procedure in which an ovum (egg) is removed from a woman's body, fertilized externally with sperm, and then returned to the uterus. It is used to treat the most difficult cases of INFERTILITY, but success rates for the procedure are not high.

in vivo desensitization a technique used in BEHAVIOR THERAPY, usually to reduce or eliminate phobias, in which the client is exposed to the stimuli that induce anxiety. The therapist, in discussion with the client, produces a hierarchy of anxiety-invoking events or items relating to the anxiety-producing stimulus or phobia. The client is then exposed to the actual stimuli in the hierarchy, rather than being asked to imagine them. Success depends on the client overcoming anxiety as the events or items are encountered. See also SYSTEMATIC DESENSITIZATION.

in vivo exposure a type of EXPOSURE THERAPY, generally used for treating individuals with PHOBIAS, OBSESSIVE-COMPULSIVE DISORDER, and other anxiety disorders, in which the client directly experiences anxiety-provoking situations or stimuli in real-world conditions. For example, a client who fears flying could be accompanied by a therapist to the airport to simulate boarding a plane while practicing anxiety-decreasing techniques, such as deep breathing. Compare IMAGINAL EXPOSURE.

involuntary *adj.* describing activity, movement, behavior, or other processes that occur without choice or intention (i.e., they are not under the control of the will). See also AUTONOMIC NERVOUS SYSTEM. Compare VOLUNTARY.

involuntary hospitalization the confinement of a person with a serious mental disorder or illness to a mental hospital by medical authorization and legal direction. Individuals so hospitalized may be considered dangerous to themselves or others, may fail to recognize the severity of their illness and the need for treatment, or may be unable to have their daily living and treatment needs otherwise met in the community or survive without medical attention.

involutional *adj.* describing the decline of the body or any of its parts from an optimal level of functioning as a result of increasing age. —**involution** *n.*

iodopsin *n.* see PHOTOPIGMENT.

ion *n.* an atom or molecule that has acquired an electrical charge by gaining or losing one or more electrons. —**ionic** *adj.*

ion channel a group of proteins forming a channel that spans a cell membrane, allowing the passage of ions between the extracellular environment and the cytoplasm of the cell. Ion channels are selective; allow passage of ions of a particular chemical nature, size, or electrostatic charge; and may be ungated (i.e., always open) or gated, opening and closing in response to chemical, electrical, or mechanical signals. Ion channels are important in the transmission of neural signals between neurons at a SYNAPSE.

ionotropic receptor a RECEPTOR protein that includes an ION CHANNEL that is opened when the receptor is activated. Compare METABOTROPIC RECEPTOR.

I/O psychology abbreviation for INDUSTRIAL AND ORGANIZATIONAL PSYCHOLOGY.

ipsative *adj.* referring back to the self. For example, ipsative analyses of personal characteristics involve assessing multiple psychological attributes and conducting within-person analyses of the degree to which an individual possesses one attribute versus another.

ipsilateral *adj.* situated on or affecting the same side of the body. Compare CONTRALATERAL. —**ipsilaterally** *adv.*

IPSP abbreviation for INHIBITORY POSTSYNAPTIC POTENTIAL.

IQ *i*ntelligence *q*uotient: a standard measure of an individual's intelligence level based on psychological tests. In the early years of intelligence testing, IQ was calculated by dividing the MENTAL AGE by the CHRONOLOGICAL AGE and multiplying by 100 to produce a **ratio IQ**. This concept has now mostly been replaced by the **deviation IQ**, computed as a function of the discrepancy of an individual score from the mean (or average) score. The mean IQ is customarily 100, with slightly more than two thirds of all scores falling within plus or minus 15 points of the mean (usually one standard deviation). Some tests yield more specific IQ scores, such as a verbal IQ and performance IQ. Discrepancies between the two can be used diagnostically to detect learning disabilities or specific cognitive deficiencies. There are critics who consider the concept of IQ (and other intelligence scales) to be flawed. They point out that the IQ test is more a measure of previously learned skills and knowledge and also refer to cases of misrepresentation of facts in the history of IQ research.

IRB abbreviation for INSTITUTIONAL REVIEW BOARD.

iris *n.* a muscular disk that surrounds the pupil of the eye and controls the amount of light entering the eye by contraction or relaxation. The stroma of the iris, which faces the cornea, contains a pigment that gives the eye its coloration; the back of the iris is lined with a dark pigment that restricts light entry to the pupil, regardless of the apparent color of the iris.

IRM abbreviation for INNATE RE-LEASING MECHANISM.

irrational *adj.* lacking in reason or sound judgment: illogical or unreasonable.

IRT abbreviation for ITEM RESPONSE THEORY.

ischemia *n.* deficiency of blood in an organ or tissue, due to functional constriction or actual obstruction of a blood vessel. —**ischemic** *adj.*

islets of Langerhans small clusters of cells that function as an ENDOCRINE GLAND within the pancreas, an abdominal organ near the stomach. The A (or alpha) cells secrete GLUCAGON, the B (or beta) cells secrete INSULIN, and the D (or delta) cells secrete SOMATOSTATIN. Together these hormones play a key role in regulating blood sugar and carbohydrate metabolism. [Paul **Langerhans** (1847–1888), German anatomist]

isolated explosive disorder an impulse-control disorder characterized by a single, discrete episode in which the individual commits a violent, catastrophic act, such as shooting a group of strangers. The episode is out of all proportion to any precipitating stress, is not due to any other mental disorder or to a general medical condition, and is not substance-induced. Compare INTERMITTENT EXPLOSIVE DISORDER.

isolation *n.* **1.** the condition of being separated from other individuals. See LONELINESS. **2.** in psychoanalytic theory, a DEFENSE MECHANISM that relies on keeping unwelcome thoughts and feelings from forming associative links with other thoughts and feelings, with the result that the unwelcome thought is rarely activated. —**isolate** *vb.*

item analysis a set of procedures used to evaluate the statistical merits of individual items comprising a psychological measure or test. These procedures may be used to select items for a test from a larger pool of initial items or to evaluate items on an established test.

item response theory (IRT) a psychometric theory of measurement based on the concept that the probability that an item will be correctly answered is a function of an underlying (latent) trait or ability that is not directly observable. Item response theory models differ in terms of the number of parameters contained in the model (as in the RASCH MODEL).

iteration *n.* the repetition of a certain computational step until further repetition no longer changes the outcome or until the repetition meets some other predefined criterion.

IV abbreviation for INDEPENDENT VARIABLE.

IVF abbreviation for IN VITRO FERTILIZATION.

Jj

James–Lange theory the theory that different feeling states stem from the feedback from the viscera and voluntary musculature to the brain: that is, the physiological response precedes rather than follows the feeling. [William **James** (1842–1910), U.S. psychologist and philosopher; Carl Georg **Lange** (1834–1900), Danish physiologist]

jargon *n.* the specialized words and forms of language used within a particular profession or field of activity. Although jargon is often unavoidable in dealing with technical or specialist subjects, inappropriate or unnecessary use can alienate outsiders, who find it unintelligible.

jealousy *n.* a negative EMOTION in which an individual resents a third party for appearing to take away the affections of a loved one. Jealousy requires a triangle of social relationships between three individuals: the one who is jealous, the partner with whom the jealous individual has or desires a relationship, and the rival who represents a preemptive threat to that relationship. Romantic relationships are the prototypic source of jealousy, but any significant relationship (with parents, friends, and so on) is capable of producing it. It differs from envy in that three people are always involved. —**jealous** *adj.*

jet lag a maladjustment of circadian rhythms (see BIOLOGICAL RHYTHM) that results from traveling through several global time zones within a short span of time. Rest, work, eating, body temperature, and adrenocortical-secretion cycles may require several days to adjust to local time.

jigsaw classroom a team-learning technique used to foster a cooperative learning environment that reduces prejudice and social isolation and improves academic achievement. Students work in groups on a content unit. The teacher assigns specific topics in the unit to each group member and allows students with the same topics to leave their group to study the topic with others who have that same assignment. The students then return to their original groups and teach their topics to the other members.

JND (jnd) abbreviation for just noticeable difference (see DIFFERENCE THRESHOLD).

job analysis the collection and study of information about the behaviors, tools, working conditions, skills, and other characteristics of a specific job. Job analysis is the first step in developing effective personnel selection, employee evaluation, job evaluation, and personnel training programs.

job satisfaction the attitude of a worker toward his or her job, often expressed as a hedonic response of liking or disliking the work itself, the rewards (pay, promotions, recognition), or the context (working conditions, colleagues).

joint attention attention overtly

focused by two or more people on the same object, person, or action at the same time, with each being aware of the other's interest. Joint attention is an important developmental tool; by focusing attention on an object as well as on the adult's reaction to it, children can learn about the world. This technique is also used in primate studies.

joy *n.* a feeling of extreme gladness, delight, or exultation of the spirit arising from a sense of well-being or satisfaction. Joy promotes confidence and an increase in energy, which in turn tend to promote positive feelings about the self.

just noticeable difference (JND; jnd) see DIFFERENCE THRESHOLD.

just-world hypothesis the need to believe that the environment is a just and orderly place where what happens to people generally is what they deserve. This belief in a just world enables an individual to confront his or her physical and social environment as though they were stable and orderly but may, for example, result in the belief that the innocent victim of an accident must somehow be responsible for, or deserve, it. Also called **just-world bias; just-world phenomenon**.

juvenile delinquency illegal behavior by a minor (usually identified as a person under age 18) that would be considered criminal in an adult. Examples are vandalism, theft, rape, arson, and aggravated assault.

Kk

kainate receptor see GLUTAMATE RECEPTOR.

kappa *n.* an index of the degree to which a group of judges, tests, or instruments rate an attribute in the same way, corrected for chance association. See COHEN'S KAPPA.

K complex a characteristic brief, high-amplitude pattern of electrical activity recorded from the brain during the early stages of sleep.

kindness *n.* benevolent and helpful action intentionally directed toward another person. Kindness is motivated by the desire to help another, not to gain explicit reward or to avoid explicit punishment. See ALTRUISM. **—kind** *adj.*

kinesics *n.* the study of the part played by body movements, such as hand gestures, eye movements, and so on, in communicating meaning. See BODY LANGUAGE.

kinesthesis *n.* the sense that provides information about the position, movement, tension, and so forth of body parts via specialized **kinesthetic receptors** in the muscles, tendons, and joints. This information, called **kinesthetic feedback**, enables humans and other animals to control and coordinate their movements. Also called **kinesthesia**. See PROPRIOCEPTION. **—kinesthetic** *adj.*

kin selection a variation of natural selection that favors behavior by an individual that increases the chances of its relatives surviving and reproducing successfully (see ALTRUISM). If an individual risks its own ability to reproduce or survive but helps its parents or more than two siblings to survive or reproduce, the sacrificing individual will benefit indirectly by gaining INCLUSIVE FITNESS.

kinship network the system of formal and informal relationships that make up an EXTENDED FAMILY in a given culture or society, typically based on blood ties, marriage, or adoption. The analysis of kinship networks in preindustrial societies has been a major concern of cultural anthropology. Also called **kinship system**.

kleptomania *n.* an impulse-control disorder characterized by repeated stealing of objects that have no immediate use or intrinsic value to the individual, accompanied by feelings of increased tension before committing the theft and either pleasure or relief during the act. **—kleptomaniac** *n.*

Klinefelter's syndrome a disorder in which males are born with an extra X chromosome, resulting in small testes, absence of sperm, enlarged breasts, mental retardation, and abnormal behavior. Also called **XXY syndrome**. [Harry F. Klinefelter (1912–), U.S. physician]

Klüver–Bucy syndrome a condition resulting from damage to both medial temporal lobes and marked by hypersexuality, a tendency to examine all objects by placing them in the mouth, visual AGNOSIA, and decreased emotional responsivity (including loss of normal fear and anger responses). [Heinrich **Klüver** (1897–1975), German-born U.S. neurologist; Paul **Bucy** (1904–1992), U.S. neurosurgeon]

knowledge base an individual's general background knowledge, which influences his or her performance on most cognitive tasks.

knowledge function of an attitude the role an attitude can play in helping to interpret ambiguous information or to organize information. For example, a positive attitude toward a friend may assist in attributing that person's negative behavior to situational factors rather than personal characteristics.

Kohlberg's theory of moral development as proposed by U.S. psychologist Lawrence Kohlberg (1927–1987), the theory that the cognitive processes associated with moral judgment develop through a number of universal, invariant stages. According to the theory, there are three main levels: the PRECONVENTIONAL LEVEL, the CONVENTIONAL LEVEL, and the POSTCONVENTIONAL LEVEL.

Kolmogorov–Smirnov test a nonparametric test of the distributional equivalence of two samples or of the fit of a sample to a theoretical distribution. [Andrei Nikolaevich **Kolmogorov** and Nikolai Vasilevich **Smirnov**, 20th-century Soviet mathematicians]

koro *n.* a CULTURE-BOUND SYNDROME observed primarily in males in China and southeast Asia. It is an acute anxiety reaction in which the male suddenly fears that his penis is shrinking and will disappear into his abdomen, bringing death. In females, the fear is focused on the vulva and nipples.

Korsakoff's syndrome amnesia caused by thiamine (vitamin B$_1$) deficiency. Individuals have a severe, enduring difficulty in learning new information and often cannot recall memories of events from recent years, although general intellectual functioning and SEMANTIC MEMORY are unimpaired. Korsakoff's syndrome frequently is associated with alcoholism and often follows an episode of WERNICKE'S ENCEPHALOPATHY. [first described in 1887 by Sergei **Korsakoff** (1853–1900), Russian neurologist]

Kruskal–Wallis test a nonparametric method for determining statistical significance of the equality of centrality with ranked data. It is analogous to ONE-WAY ANALYSIS OF VARIANCE. [William **Kruskal** and Wilson Allen **Wallis** (1912–1998), U.S. statisticians]

kurtosis *n.* the fourth central MOMENT of a probability distribution. It is a statistical description of the degree of peakedness of that distribution.

kwashiorkor *n.* a form of malnutrition caused by inadequate intake of protein, usually observed in children in impoverished countries. The symptoms include impaired growth, distention of the abdomen, and pigment changes in the skin and hair. Normal cerebral development also may be impaired. See also MARASMUS.

Ll

labeled-line theory of taste coding a theory postulating that each gustatory neuron type comprises a private circuit (labeled line) through which is signaled the presence of its associated primary taste quality. The taste is perceived exclusively as a product of activity in that labeled line; activity in neurons outside the labeled line contributes only noise. Compare PATTERN THEORY OF TASTE CODING.

labeling *n.* in psychological assessment, classifying a patient according to a certain diagnostic category. Patient labeling may be incomplete or misleading, because not all cases conform to the sharply defined characteristics of the standard diagnostic categories.

labeling theory the sociological hypothesis that describing an individual in terms of particular behavioral characteristics (i.e., labeling) may have a significant effect on his or her behavior, as a form of SELF-FULFILLING PROPHECY.

la belle indifférence inappropriate lack of concern about the seriousness or implications of one's physical symptoms, often seen in CONVERSION DISORDER.

labile *adj.* liable to change or disruption. **Labile affect**, for example, is highly variable, suddenly shifting emotional expression. —**lability** *n.*

laboratory research scientific study conducted in a laboratory or other such workplace, where the investigator has some degree of direct control over the environment and can manipulate variables. Compare FIELD RESEARCH.

labyrinth *n.* in anatomy, the complex system of cavities, ducts, and canals within the temporal bone of the skull that comprises the inner ear. The bony (or osseous) labyrinth is a system of bony cavities that houses the membranous labyrinth, a membrane-lined system of ducts containing the receptors for hearing and balance.

laceration *n.* a jagged tear or cut: a wound with rough, irregular edges.

laddering *n.* a knowledge elicitation technique that is used in interviewing to impose a systematic framework upon questioning so as to reveal complex themes across answers. In laddering, a respondent replies to a series of "why?" probes, thus requiring him or her to expose and explain choices or preferences and justify behavior in terms of goals, values, and PERSONAL CONSTRUCTS. Laddering is concerned with linkages between concepts elicited from the participant (e.g., attitudes and beliefs associated with a particular consumer product), and provides greater scope for probing salient issues while optimizing the often limited time available with respondents.

Lamarckism *n.* the theory that changes acquired by an organism during its lifetime, for example, through use or disuse of particular parts, can be inherited by its offspring. Evidence for such inheritance of acquired characteristics, however, is lacking. [Jean-Baptiste

Lamarck (1744–1829), French natural historian] —**Lamarckian** *adj.*

language *n.* **1.** a system for expressing or communicating thoughts and feelings through speech sounds or written symbols, comprising a distinctive vocabulary, grammar, and phonology. **2.** any comparable nonverbal means of communication, such as SIGN LANGUAGE or the languages used in computer programming.

language acquisition the process by which children learn language. Although often used interchangeably with **language development**, this term is preferred by those who emphasize the active role of the child as a learner with considerable innate linguistic knowledge.

language acquisition device a hypothetical faculty used to explain a child's ability to acquire language. In the early model proposed by U.S. linguist Benjamin Lee Whorf (1897–1941), it is an inherited mechanism that enables children to develop a language structure from linguistic data supplied by parents and others. As reinterpreted by U.S. linguist Noam Chomsky (1928–   ), however, the language acquisition device contains significant innate knowledge that actively interprets the input: Only this can explain how a highly abstract COMPETENCE in language results from a relatively deprived input.

language acquisition support system the adults and older children who help a young child to acquire language. Children learn language in and from conversation: Family members talk to them, tailoring their language to the children's level of comprehension and often using higher pitch and exaggerated intonation. The language acquisition support system is conceptualized as essential to language learning and may interact with the LANGUAGE ACQUISITION DEVICE of the younger child.

language disorder see SPEECH AND LANGUAGE DISORDER.

language therapy see SPEECH AND LANGUAGE THERAPY.

latah (**lattah**) *n.* a CULTURE-BOUND SYNDROME in Malaysia and Indonesia characterized by an exaggerated startle reaction, imitative behavior in speech (see ECHOLALIA) and body movements (see ECHOPRAXIA), a compulsion to utter profanities and obscenities (see COPROLALIA), command obedience, and disorganization. See also IMU; MYRIACHIT.

latency stage in psychoanalytic theory, the stage of PSYCHOSEXUAL DEVELOPMENT in which overt sexual interest is sublimated and the child's attention is focused on skills and peer activities with members of his or her own sex. This stage is posited to last from about the resolution of the OEDIPUS COMPLEX, at about age 6, to the onset of puberty during the 11th or 12th year. Also called **latency phase**.

latent content in psychoanalytic theory, the unconscious wishes seeking expression in dreams or fantasies. This unconscious material is posited to encounter censorship and to be distorted by the DREAM-WORK into symbolic representations in order to protect the EGO. Through DREAM ANALYSIS, the latent content may be uncovered.

latent learning learning that is not manifested as a change in performance until a specific need for it arises. For example, a rat allowed to explore a maze without reward will later learn to find the goal more rapidly than a rat without prior exposure to the maze. See also INCIDENTAL LEARNING.

latent variable a hypothetical,

unobservable characteristic that is thought to underlie and explain observed, manifest attributes that are directly measurable. The values of latent variables are inferred from patterns of interrelationships among the MANIFEST VARIABLES.

lateral *adj.* toward the side of the body or of an organ. Compare MEDIAL. —**laterally** *adv.*

lateral geniculate nucleus either of two small oval clusters of nerve cell bodies on the underside of the THALAMUS in the brain that relay information from cone-rich areas of the retina to the VISUAL CORTEX via OPTIC RADIATIONS.

lateral hypothalamic syndrome a four-stage pattern of recovery from lesions of the LATERAL HYPOTHALAMUS induced in nonhuman animals. The stages are marked by: (a) an initial inability to eat and drink (aphagia and adipsia); (b) continued inability to drink and poor appetite for food (adipsia-anorexia); (c) improving appetite but continued avoidance of water; and (d) the establishment of new, altered feeding and drinking habits and a stable, albeit lower, body weight. Compare VENTROMEDIAL HYPOTHALAMIC SYNDROME.

lateral hypothalamus the region of the HYPOTHALAMUS that may be involved in the regulation of eating. Lesions of the lateral hypothalamus in animals result in fasting and weight loss. Stimulation of that part of the brain increases food intake.

lateral inhibition in perception, a mechanism for detecting contrast in which a sensory neuron is excited by one particular receptor but inhibited by neighboring (lateral) receptors. In vision, for example, lateral inhibition is seen in neurons that respond to light at one position but are inhibited by light at surrounding positions.

laterality *n.* the preferential use of one side of the body for certain functions, such as eating, writing, and kicking. See also HANDEDNESS.

lateralization *n.* see HEMISPHERIC LATERALIZATION.

lateral lemniscus a bundle of nerve fibers running from the auditory nuclei in the brainstem (i.e., the COCHLEAR NUCLEI) upward through the PONS and terminating in the inferior COLLICULUS and in the THALAMUS. It is primarily concerned with hearing.

lateral sulcus a prominent groove that runs along the lateral surface of each CEREBRAL HEMISPHERE, separating the TEMPORAL LOBE from the FRONTAL LOBE and PARIETAL LOBE. Also called **lateral fissure**; **Sylvian fissure**.

lateral thinking creative thinking that deliberately attempts to reexamine basic assumptions and change perspective or direction in order to provide a fresh approach to solving a problem. This term is often used synonymously with DIVERGENT THINKING.

lateral ventricle see VENTRICLE.

late-selection theory any theory of attention proposing that selection occurs after stimulus identification. According to late-selection theory, within sensory limits, all stimuli—both attended and unattended—are processed to the same deep level of analysis until stimulus identification occurs; subsequently, only the most important stimuli are selected for further processing. Compare EARLY-SELECTION THEORY.

Latin square an experimental design in which treatments, denoted by Latin letters, are administered in sequences that are systematically varied such that each treatment occurs equally often in each position of the sequence (e.g., first, second,

L

third, etc.). The number of treatments administered must be the same as the number of groups or individual participants receiving them. For example, one group might receive treatments A, then B, and then C, while a second group receives them in sequence B, C, A, and a third group in sequence C, A, B.

law of closure see CLOSURE.

law of common fate see COMMON FATE.

law of continuity see GOOD CONTINUATION.

law of effect broadly, the principle that consequences of behavior act to modify the future probability of occurrence of that behavior. As originally postulated by U.S. psychologist Edward L. Thorndike (1874–1949), the law of effect stated that responses followed by a satisfying state of affairs are strengthened and responses followed by an unpleasant or annoying state of affairs are weakened. Thorndike later revised the law to include only the response-strengthening effect of reinforcement.

law of good continuation see GOOD CONTINUATION.

law of parsimony the principle that the simplest explanation of an event or observation is the preferred explanation. Simplicity is understood in various ways, including the requirement that an explanation should (a) make the smallest number of unsupported assumptions, (b) postulate the existence of the fewest entities, and (c) invoke the fewest unobservable constructs. Also called **principle of parsimony**. See OCCAM'S RAZOR.

law of Prägnanz see PRÄGNANZ.

law of proximity see PROXIMITY.

law of similarity 1. a principle of association stating that like produces like: Encountering or thinking about something (e.g., one's birthday month) tends to bring to mind other similar things (e.g., other people one knows with the same birthday month). **2.** see SIMILARITY.

lay analysis psychoanalytic therapy performed by a person who has been trained in psychoanalytic theory and practice but is not a physician (i.e., a layperson). This is to be distinguished from psychoanalysis performed by a fully accredited psychiatrist.

lazy eye see AMBLYOPIA.

LD 1. abbreviation for LEARNING DISABILITY. **2.** abbreviation for LEARNING DISORDER.

leadership *n.* the processes involved in leading others, including organizing, directing, coordinating, and motivating their efforts toward achievement of certain group or organizational goals.

leadership style the stable behavioral tendencies and methods displayed by a particular leader when guiding a group. Some common leadership styles are autocratic, in which the leader exercises unrestricted authority; bureaucratic, in which the leader rigidly adheres to prescribed routine; charismatic, in which the leader articulates distal goals and visions; democratic, in which the leader establishes and maintains an egalitarian group climate; and laissez-faire, in which the leader provides little guidance.

learned helplessness a phenomenon in which repeated exposure to uncontrollable stressors results in individuals failing to use any control options that may later become available. Essentially, individuals learn that they lack behavioral control over environmental events, which, in turn, undermines the motivation to make changes or attempt to alter situations. Learned helplessness was first described in 1967 by U.S. psychologists J. Bruce Overmier (1938–) and Martin E. P. Seligman (1942–) following experiments in which animals exposed to a series of unavoidable electric shocks later failed to learn to escape these shocks when tested in a different apparatus, whereas animals exposed to shocks that could be terminated by a response did not show interference with escape learning in another apparatus. In the 1970s, Seligman extended the concept from nonhuman animal research to clinical depression in humans. Subsequent researchers have noted a robust fit between the concept and POST-TRAUMATIC STRESS DISORDER.

learned optimism an acquired explanatory style that attributes causes for negative events to factors that are more external, unstable, and specific: that is, problems are believed to be caused by other people or situational factors, the causes are seen as fleeting in nature, and are localized to one or a few situations in one's life. According to LEARNED HELPLESSNESS theory, the manner in which individuals routinely explain the events in their lives can drain or enhance motivation, reduce or increase persistence, and enhance vulnerability to depression or protect against it, making learned optimism a putative mechanism by which therapy ameliorates depression.

learning *n.* the process of acquiring new and relatively enduring information, behavior patterns, or abilities, characterized by modification of behavior as a result of practice, study, or experience.

learning curve a graphic representation of the course of learning of an individual or a group. A measure of performance (e.g., gains, errors) is plotted along the vertical axis; the horizontal axis plots trials or time.

learning disability (**LD**) any of various conditions with a neurological basis that are marked by substantial deficits in acquiring certain scholastic or academic skills, particularly those associated with written or expressive language. Learning disabilities include learning problems that result from perceptual disabilities, brain injury, and MINIMAL BRAIN DYSFUNCTION but exclude those that result from visual impairment or hearing loss, mental retardation, emotional disturbance, or environmental, cultural, or economic factors.

learning disorder (**LD**) any neurologically based information-processing disorder characterized by achievement that is substantially below that expected for the age, education, and intelligence of the individual, as measured by standardized tests in reading, mathematics, and written material. Major types of learning disorders are DISORDER OF WRITTEN EXPRESSION, MATHEMATICS DISORDER, NONVERBAL LEARNING DISORDER, and READING DISORDER. This term essentially is synonymous with LEARNING DISABILITY.

learning set a phenomenon observed when a participant is given a succession of discriminations to learn, such as learning that one object contains a food reward and a different object does not. After a large number of such problems the participant acquires a rule or MENTAL SET for solving them, and successive discriminations are learned faster.

learning style see COGNITIVE STYLE.

learning theory a body of concepts and principles that seeks to explain the learning process. Learning theory encompasses a number of specific theories whose common interest is the description of the basic laws of learning, statements describing the circumstances under which learning is generally known to occur (i.e., the LAW OF EFFECT).

least restrictive environment in the United States, an educational setting that gives a student with disabilities the opportunity to receive instruction within a classroom that meets his or her learning needs and physical requirements. See also MAINSTREAMING.

least significant difference (**LSD**) a value representing the point at which a difference between the means of experimental groups being compared can be considered not to have been caused by chance. It is a method of controlling for TYPE I ERROR and must be calculated for each experiment according to specific criteria.

left hemisphere the left half of the cerebrum, the part of the brain concerned with sensation and perception, motor control, and higher level cognitive processes. The two CEREBRAL HEMISPHERES differ somewhat in function; for example, in most people the left hemisphere has greater responsibility for speech. Some have proposed that, given this involvement in speech, the left hemisphere is the seat of consciousness, an idea known as **left-hemisphere consciousness**. See HEMISPHERIC LATERALIZATION. Compare RIGHT HEMISPHERE.

lens *n.* in vision, a transparent, biconvex structure in the anterior portion of the eyeball (just behind the IRIS) that provides the fine, adjustable focus of the optical system. It is composed of tiny hexagonal prism-shaped cells, called lens fibers, fitted together in concentric layers.

lenticular nucleus see BASAL GANGLIA.

leptin *n.* a protein, manufactured and secreted by fat cells, that may communicate to the brain the amount of body fat stored and may help to regulate food intake. Leptin receptors have been found in the hypothalamus, and when they are stimulated food intake is reduced.

leptokurtic *adj.* describing a frequency distribution that is more peaked than the normal distribution, that is, having more scores in the center and fewer at the extremes than in a normal distribution. See also PLATYKURTIC; MESOKURTIC.

lesbianism *n.* female–female sexual orientation or behavior. See also HOMOSEXUALITY. —**lesbian** *adj., n.*

lesion *n.* any disruption of or damage to the normal structure or function of a tissue or organ.

less-is-more hypothesis the proposition that the cognitive limitations of infants and young children may serve to simplify the body of language they process, thus making it easier for them to learn the complicated syntactical system of any human language.

lethality scale a set of criteria used to predict the probability of a suicide or attempted suicide occurring. A variety of such scales exist, most including gender, prior suicide attempts, and psychiatric diagnosis and history.

leukocyte (leucocyte) *n.* a type of blood cell that plays a key role in the body's defense against infection. Leukocytes include **granulocytes**, which ingest foreign particles; and LYMPHOCYTES, which are involved in the production of antibodies and other specific immune responses.

leukotomy (leucotomy) *n.* see LOBOTOMY.

level *n.* in experimental design, the quantity, magnitude, or category of the independent variable (or variables).

level-of-aspiration theory a conceptual approach to group and individual performance that assumes that the emotional, motivational, and behavioral consequences of any particular performance will be determined not only by the absolute degree of success attained but also by the ideal outcome or goal envisioned prior to undertaking the task.

level of significance see SIGNIFICANCE LEVEL.

levels-of-processing model of memory the theory that ENCODING into memory, and therefore subsequent retention, depends on the depth of cognitive ELABORATION that the information receives and that deeper encoding improves memory.

lexical access in psycholinguistics, the process by which an individual produces a specific word from his or her MENTAL LEXICON or recognizes it when used by others.

lexical decision a task in which the participant is presented with strings of letters, such as HOUSE or HOUPE, and is required to determine whether each string spells a word.

lexicon *n.* the vocabulary of a language and, in psychology, the lexical knowledge of an individual. See MENTAL LEXICON.

LH abbreviation for LUTEINIZING HORMONE.

libido *n.* in psychoanalytic theory, either the PSYCHIC ENERGY of the LIFE INSTINCT in general, or the energy of the SEXUAL INSTINCT in particular. In his first formulation, Austrian psychiatrist Sigmund Freud (1856–1939) conceived of this energy as narrowly sexual, but subsequently he broadened the concept to include all expressions of love, pleasure, and self-preservation. See also EROS. **—libidinal** *adj.* **—libidinize** *vb.* **—libidinous** *adj.*

lie detector see POLYGRAPH.

lie scale a group of items on a test (e.g., the MINNESOTA MULTIPHASIC PERSONALITY INVENTORY) used to help evaluate the general truthfulness of a person's responses on the test.

life crisis a period of distress and major adjustment associated with a significant life experience, such as divorce or death of a family member.

life cycle the sequence of developmental stages through which an organism passes between a specified stage of one generation (e.g., fertilization, birth) and the same stage in the next generation.

life events important occasions throughout the life span that are either age-related and thus expected (e.g., marriage, retirement) or unrelated to age and unexpected (e.g., accidents, relocation).

life expectancy the number of years that a person can, on average, expect to live. Life expectancy is based on statistical probabilities and increases with improvements in medical care and hygiene.

life-history method a STRUCTURED INTERVIEW that attempts to summarize historical data about events that are relevant to evaluating the person's current functioning.

life instinct in psychoanalytic theory, the drive comprising the instinct of self-preservation, which is aimed at individual survival, and the SEXUAL INSTINCT, which is aimed at the survival of the species. In the dual instinct theory of Austrian psychiatrist Sigmund Freud (1856–1939), the life instinct, or EROS, stands opposed to the DEATH INSTINCT, or THANATOS.

life review the tendency of individuals, especially older adults, to reflect upon and analyze past life experiences. Life review is often made use of in counseling older adults showing symptoms of mild depression or people with terminal illness, sometimes as an adjunct to psychotherapy.

life satisfaction the extent to which a person finds life rich, meaningful, full, or of high quality. Improved life satisfaction is often a goal of treatment, especially with older people. See also QUALITY OF LIFE.

life space in the FIELD THEORY of German-born U.S. psychologist Kurt Lewin (1890–1947), the "totality of possible events" for one person at a particular time, that is, a person's possible options together with the environment that contains them. The life space is a representation of the environmental, biological, social, and psychological influences that define one person's unique reality at a given moment in time. Contained within the life space are positive and negative valences, that is, forces or pressures on the individual to approach a goal or move away from a perceived danger.

life span 1. the maximum age that can be obtained by any given individual within a particular species. **2** the precise length of an individual's life.

life-span developmental psychology the study of psychological and behavioral change across and within individuals from birth through death. Such an approach assumes that human developmental processes are complex, interactive, and fully understood only in the

context of influencing events. It also assumes that there is no end state of maturity, that no specific period of the life course is more important or influential than another in subsequent development, and that not all developmental change is related to chronological age.

lifestyle *n.* the typical way of life or manner of living that is characteristic of an individual or group, as expressed by behaviors, attitudes, interests, and other factors.

light adaptation the process by which the eye adjusts to conditions of high illumination, such as occurs when exiting a dark theater into a sunny parking lot. It takes less than 10 min and involves constriction of the pupil and a shift in the sensitivity of the retina so that the RETINAL CONES become active in place of the RETINAL RODS. Compare DARK ADAPTATION.

lightness constancy see BRIGHTNESS CONSTANCY.

light therapy see PHOTOTHERAPY.

likelihood ratio the ratio of two probabilities, a/b, where a is the probability of obtaining the data observed if a particular research hypothesis (A) is true and b is the probability of obtaining the data observed when a different hypothesis (B) is true.

Likert scale a type of direct attitude measure that consists of statements reflecting strong positive or negative evaluations of an attitude object. Respondents indicate their reaction to each statement on a response scale ranging from "strongly agree" to "strongly disagree," and these ratings are summed to provide a total attitude score. [Rensis **Likert** (1903–1981), U.S. psychologist]

limbic lobe a fifth subdivision of each cerebral hemisphere that is often distinguished in addition to the four main lobes (see CEREBRUM). It comprises the CINGULATE GYRUS, PARAHIPPOCAMPAL GYRUS, and HIPPOCAMPUS.

limbic system a loosely defined, widespread group of brain nuclei that innervate each other to form a network that is involved in autonomic and visceral processes and mechanisms of emotion, memory, and learning. It includes portions of the cerebral cortex, THALAMUS, and certain subcortical structures, such as the AMYGDALA and HIPPOCAMPUS.

limen *n.* see THRESHOLD.

limited-capacity system a conceptualization of WORKING MEMORY in which resource constraints restrict the processing of sensory information to only what is directly relevant. When pertinent new information is encountered, older, less relevant information is either relegated to long-term memory or eliminated, providing the resources to retain the newer data. For example, a person drafting a sentence in an e-mail who is asked a question may ignore the question and finish typing or may answer the question and subsequently be unable to remember what he or she intended to write. ATTENTION and CONSCIOUSNESS are often similarly conceived of as limited-capacity systems. See also CHUNKING.

linear *adj.* describing any relationship between two variables (X and Y) that can be expressed in the form $Y = a + bX$, where a and b are numerical constants. No COEFFICIENT can be raised to a power greater than 1 or be the denominator of a fraction. When depicted graphically, the relationship is a straight line.

linear model any model for empirical data that attempts to relate the values of the dependent variable to linear functions of the independent variables. Most commonly used statistical techniques (analysis of variance, regression analysis, etc.) can be represented as linear models.

linear perspective one of the monocular DEPTH CUES, arising from the principle that the size of an object's visual image is a function of its distance from the eye. Thus, two objects appear closer together as the distance from them increases, as seen in the tracks of a railroad that appear to converge on the horizon.

linear regression a REGRESSION ANALYSIS that assumes that the predictor (independent) variable is related to the criterion (dependent) variable through a linear function.

linear transformation a transformation of X to Y by means of the equation $Y = a + bX$, where a and b are numerical constants.

linguistic determinism the hypothesis that the semantic structure of a particular language determines the structure of mental categories among its speakers. Because languages differ in how they refer to basic categories and dimensions, such as time, space, and duration, native speakers of these languages are assumed to show corresponding differences in their ways of thinking. Also called **Sapir–Whorf hypothesis**. Compare LINGUISTIC RELATIVITY.

linguistic relativity the observation that languages differ in the ways in which semantic space is identified and categorized. For example, the Native American language Hopi uses a completely different word for water in a natural setting and water in a vessel but has only one word for flying objects, which is applied to birds, insects, airplanes, and the like. Linguistic relativity is not to be equated with LINGUISTIC DETERMINISM, which is a

L

theoretical commitment to the idea that these differences have cognitive consequences. See ANTHROPOLOGICAL LINGUISTICS.

linguistics *n.* the scientific study of the physical, structural, functional, psychological, and social characteristics of human language. See also PSYCHOLINGUISTICS; SOCIOLINGUISTICS.

link analysis in ergonomics, the analysis of operational sequences and the movements of workers or objects that these entail in order to determine the design of tools, equipment, jobs, and facilities that will best serve worker efficiency and safety.

lipostatic hypothesis a hypothesis stating that the long-term regulation of food intake is governed by the concentration in the blood of free fatty acids, which result from the metabolism of fat. See also GLUCOSTATIC THEORY.

literacy *n.* the ability to read and write in a language. —**literate** *adj.*

lithium *n.* an element of the alkali metal group whose salts are used in psychopharmacotherapy as MOOD STABILIZERS, particularly in managing acute manic phases of bipolar disorder. Its mechanism of action remains unclear and it has a narrow therapeutic margin of safety, making close monitoring of blood levels necessary. U.S. trade names (among others): **Lithobid.**

Little Albert the name of a boy used by U.S. psychologist John B. Watson (1878–1958) and his graduate student Rosalie Rayner (1899–1935) to demonstrate Pavlovian fear conditioning in humans.

Little Hans a landmark case of Austrian psychiatrist Sigmund Freud (1856–1939), illustrating the OEDIPUS COMPLEX. Freud traced a child's phobia for horses to CASTRATION ANXIETY stemming from masturbation, to repressed death wishes toward the father, and to fear of retaliation owing to rivalry with the mother, with DISPLACEMENT of these emotions onto horses.

living will see ADVANCE DIRECTIVE.

Lloyd Morgan's canon the principle that the behavior of an animal should not be interpreted in complex psychological terms if it can instead be interpreted with simpler concepts. Some recent authors have argued that its application oversimplifies the abilities of animals. [Conway **Lloyd Morgan** (1852–1936), British comparative psychologist]

lobe *n.* a subdivision of an organ, such as the brain or the lungs, particularly when rounded and surrounded by distinct structural boundaries, such as fissures. —**lobar** *adj.* —**lobate** *adj.*

lobotomy *n.* incision into various nerve tracts in the FRONTAL LOBE of the brain. The original surgical procedure, called **prefrontal** (or **frontal**) **lobotomy**, was introduced in 1936. Connections between the frontal lobe and other brain structures—notably the thalamus—were severed by manipulating a narrow blade known as a leukotome inserted into brain tissue through several small holes drilled in the skull. A second procedure, called **transorbital lobotomy**, was devised in 1945 and involved the manipulation of a pointed instrument resembling an ice pick driven with a mallet through the thin bony wall of the eye socket and into the prefrontal brain. Both procedures were widely used to relieve the symptoms of severe mental disorder (including depression and schizophrenia) until the advent of ANTIPSYCHOTIC drugs in the 1950s. These operations have been replaced by more sophisticated, stereotactic forms of neurosurgery that are less invasive and whose effects are more certain and less damaging. Also called **leukotomy**.

LOC abbreviation for LOSS OF CONSCIOUSNESS.

localization *n.* the ability to determine the physical position or spatial location of a stimulus in any sensory modality.

localization of function the concept that specific parts of the cerebral cortex are relatively specialized for particular types of cognitive and behavioral processes.

location constancy the tendency for a resting object and its setting to appear to have the same position even if the relationship between setting and observer is altered as the observer shifts position. See also OBJECT CONSTANCY.

locomotor play play that involves exaggerated, repetitive movement and is physically vigorous, such as chasing, climbing, and wrestling. Locomotor play is one of three traditionally identified basic types of play, the others being OBJECT PLAY and SOCIAL PLAY.

locus *n.* (*pl.* **loci**) **1.** the place or position of an anatomical entity. **2.** the position of a gene on a chromosome.

locus ceruleus (locus coeruleus; locus caeruleus) a small bluish-tinted NUCLEUS in the brainstem whose neurons produce NOREPINEPHRINE and modulate large areas of the forebrain.

locus of control a construct that is used to categorize people's basic motivational orientations and perceptions of how much control they have over the conditions of their lives. People with an **external locus of control** tend to behave in response to external circumstances and to perceive their life outcomes

as arising from factors out of their control. People with an **internal locus of control** tend to behave in response to internal states and intentions and to perceive their life outcomes as arising from the exercise of their own agency and abilities.

logic *n.* **1.** the branch of EPISTEMOLOGY that is concerned with the forms of argument by which a valid conclusion may be drawn from accepted premises. As such it is also concerned with distinguishing correct from fallacious reasoning. **2.** a particular rule-governed form of symbolic expression used to analyze the relations between propositions. —**logical** *adj.*

logistic regression a statistical technique for the prediction of a binary DEPENDENT VARIABLE from one or more continuous variables.

log–linear model a class of statistical techniques used to study the relationship among several CATEGORICAL VARIABLES. As compared with CHI-SQUARE TESTS, log–linear models use odds, rather than proportions, and they can be used to examine the relationship among several nominal variables in the manner of ANALYSES OF COVARIANCE.

logogen *n.* a theoretical memory unit corresponding to a word, letter, or digit, which when excited results in the output (recognition) of the unit and recall of characteristics and information associated with that unit. For example, the logogen for *table* is activated by hearing the component sounds or seeing the typographical features of the word, bringing to mind such knowledge as the typical structure and shape of a table and its general function.

loneliness *n.* affective and cognitive discomfort or uneasiness from being or perceiving oneself to be

L

alone or otherwise solitary. Psychological theory and research offer multiple perspectives: For example, social psychology emphasizes the emotional distress that results when inherent needs for intimacy and companionship are not met, while cognitive psychology emphasizes the unpleasant and unsettling experience that results from a perceived discrepancy between an individual's desired and actual social relationships.

longevity *n.* **1.** long life. **2.** the actual length of an individual's life.

longitudinal design the study of a variable or group of variables in the same cases or participants over a period of time, sometimes of several years. Compare CROSS-SECTIONAL DESIGN.

longitudinal fissure a deep groove that marks the division between the left and right cerebral hemispheres of the brain. At the bottom of the groove the hemispheres are connected by the CORPUS CALLOSUM.

long-term depression (LTD) a long-lasting decrease in the amplitude of neuronal response due to persistent weak synaptic stimulation (in the case of the hippocampus) or strong synaptic stimulation (in the case of the cerebellum). Compare LONG-TERM POTENTIATION.

long-term memory (LTM) a relatively permanent information storage system, enabling one to retain, retrieve, and make use of skills and knowledge hours, weeks, or even years after they were originally learned. Various theories have been proposed to explain the biological processes by which this occurs (e.g., the PERSEVERATION–CONSOLIDATION HYPOTHESIS) and a major distinction is made between LTM and SHORT-TERM MEMORY. Additionally, LTM is divided into several categories, including DECLARATIVE MEMORY and PROCEDURAL MEMORY.

long-term potentiation (LTP) a long-lasting enhancement of synaptic efficiency caused by repeated brief stimulations of one nerve cell that trigger stimulation of a succeeding cell. The capacity for potentiation has been best shown in hippocampal tissue. LTP is studied as a model of the neural changes that underlie memory formation and it may be a mechanism involved in some kinds of learning. Compare LONG-TERM DEPRESSION.

looking-glass self a SELF-CONCEPT formed by learning how other people perceive and evaluate one. The term suggests a self that is a reflection of other people's impressions, reactions, and opinions. See SYMBOLIC INTERACTIONISM.

loss of consciousness (LOC) a state in which an organism capable of consciousness can no longer experience events or exert voluntary control. Examples of conditions associated with loss of consciousness include fainting (syncope), deep sleep, coma, general anesthesia, narcolepsy, and epileptic absence.

loudness *n.* the subjective magnitude of sound. It is determined primarily by intensity but is also affected by other physical properties, such as frequency, spectral configuration, and duration. The unit of loudness is the sone: One sone is the loudness of a 1-kHz tone presented at 40 dB SPL (sound-pressure level).

love *n.* a complex emotion involving strong feelings of affection and tenderness for a person, pleasurable sensations in his or her presence, devotion to his or her well-being, and sensitivity to his or her reactions to oneself. Although love takes many forms, the TRIANGULAR THEORY OF

LOVE proposes three essential components: passion, intimacy, and commitment. Social psychological research in this area has focused largely on PASSIONATE LOVE, in which passion (sexual desire and excitement) is predominant, and COMPANIONATE LOVE, in which passion is relatively weak and commitment is strong.

love need in MASLOW'S MOTIVATIONAL HIERARCHY, the third level of the hierarchy of needs, characterized by the striving for affiliation and acceptance. Also called **social need**.

low-ball technique a procedure for enhancing compliance by first obtaining agreement to a request and then revealing the hidden costs of this request. Compliance to the target request is greater than would have been the case if these costs had been made clear at the time of the initial request. See also DOOR-IN-THE-FACE TECHNIQUE; FOOT-IN-THE-DOOR TECHNIQUE; THAT'S-NOT-ALL TECHNIQUE.

lower motor neuron see MOTOR NEURON.

LSD 1. *ly*sergic acid *d*iethylamide: a highly potent HALLUCINOGEN that structurally resembles the neurotransmitter SEROTONIN and is capable of producing visual distortions or frank hallucinations, together with feelings of euphoria or arousal; it became a widely used and controversial recreational drug during the mid-1960s and early 1970s. The effects of LSD were the subject of research during the 1950s as a possible model for psychosis, and various attempts were made to use LSD as an aid to psychotherapy although they did not prove effec-

tive. **2.** abbreviation for LEAST SIGNIFICANT DIFFERENCE.

LTD abbreviation for LONG-TERM DEPRESSION.

LTM abbreviation for LONG-TERM MEMORY.

LTP abbreviation for LONG-TERM POTENTIATION.

lucid dream a dream in which the sleeper is aware that he or she is dreaming.

lunacy *n.* **1.** an obsolete name for any mental illness. **2.** in legal use, an obsolete name for mental incompetence or legal INSANITY. —**lunatic** *adj., n.*

luteinizing hormone (**LH**) a GONADOTROPIN secreted by the anterior pituitary gland that, in females, stimulates the rapid growth of a graafian follicle (small, pouchlike cavity) in the ovary until it ruptures and releases an ovum (see MENSTRUAL CYCLE). In males it stimulates the interstitial cells of the TESTIS to secrete androgens.

lymphocyte *n.* a type of blood cell (see LEUKOCYTE) that plays a key role in specific immune responses. **B lymphocytes** (or **B cells**), which develop and mature in the bone marrow, are responsible for humoral immunity: They produce circulating antibodies when they bind to an appropriate antigen and are costimulated by certain T cells. **T lymphocytes** (or **T cells**), which mature in the thymus, are responsible for cell-mediated immunity: They are characterized by the presence of particular cell-surface molecules and are capable of antigen recognition. —**lymphocytic** *adj.*

lysergic acid diethylamide see LSD.

L

Mm

MA abbreviation for MENTAL AGE.

mAChR abbreviation for MUSCARINIC RECEPTOR.

macrocephaly *n.* a condition in which the head is abnormally large in relation to the rest of the body. Compare MICROCEPHALY. —**macrocephalic** *adj.*

macroglia *n.* a relatively large type of nonneuronal central nervous system cell (GLIA), including ASTROCYTES, cells of the EPENDYMA, and OLIGODENDROCYTES. —**macroglial** *adj.*

macrosystem *n.* in ECOLOGICAL SYSTEMS THEORY, the level of environmental influence that is most distal to the developing individual and that affects all other systems. It includes the values, traditions, and sociocultural characteristics of the larger society. See also EXOSYSTEM; MESOSYSTEM.

macula *n.* (*pl.* **maculae**) in hearing, a patch of sensory tissue in the UTRICLE and SACCULE of the inner ear that provides information about the position of the body in relation to gravity. The macula contains sensory HAIR CELLS whose processes (stereocilia) are embedded in a gelatinous matrix (cupula) containing calcareous particles (OTOLITHS). When the orientation of the head changes, the relatively dense otoliths respond to gravity, causing the gelatinous mass to shift and the stereocilia to flex, which triggers nerve impulses in the hair-cell fibers.

macula lutea a small spot in the retina that is in direct alignment with the optics of the eye. It contains a yellow pigment and a central depression, the FOVEA CENTRALIS.

macular degeneration dystrophy of the MACULA LUTEA, which affects both eyes and causes progressive loss of central vision.

madness *n.* an obsolete name for mental illness or for legal INSANITY.

magical thinking the belief that events or the behavior of others can be influenced by one's thoughts, wishes, or rituals. Magical thinking is typical of children up to 4 or 5 years of age, after which reality thinking begins to predominate.

magnetic resonance imaging (**MRI**) a noninvasive diagnostic technique that uses the responses of hydrogen in tissue molecules to strong magnetic impulses to form a three-dimensional picture of body organs and tissues, particularly the brain, with more accuracy than COMPUTED TOMOGRAPHY. See also FUNCTIONAL MAGNETIC RESONANCE IMAGING.

magnetoencephalography (**MEG**) *n.* the measurement of the magnetic fields arising from the electrical activity of the brain, using a device called a **magnetoencephalograph** (**MEG**).

magnitude estimation a psychophysical procedure in which the participant makes subjective judgments of the magnitude of stimuli by assigning them numerical values along a scale.

magnitude of effect see EFFECT SIZE.

magnocellular system the part of the visual system that projects to or originates from large neurons in the two most ventral layers (the **magnocellular layers**) of the LATERAL GENICULATE NUCLEUS. It allows the rapid perception of movement, form, and changes in brightness but is relatively insensitive to stimulus location and color. See also M-CELL. Compare PARVOCELLULAR SYSTEM.

main effect the consistent total effect of a particular independent variable on a dependent variable over all other independent variables in an experimental design. It is separate from, but may be obscured by, an INTERACTION EFFECT.

mainstreaming *n.* the placement of children with disabilities into regular classroom environments on a part-time basis, such that they attend only some regular education classes during the school day and spend the remaining time in special education classes. The aim is to offer each child the opportunity to learn in an environment that has the highest probability of facilitating rehabilitation efforts and supporting academic growth. See also LEAST RESTRICTIVE ENVIRONMENT.

maintenance rehearsal repeating items over and over to maintain them in SHORT-TERM MEMORY, as in repeating a telephone number until it has been dialed (see REHEARSAL). According to the LEVELS-OF-PROCESSING MODEL OF MEMORY, maintenance rehearsal does not effectively promote long-term retention because it involves little ELABORATION of the information to be remembered.

major depressive disorder a DEPRESSIVE DISORDER in which the individual has experienced at least one MAJOR DEPRESSIVE EPISODE but has never experienced a MANIC EPISODE, MIXED EPISODE, or HYPOMANIC EPISODE. Also called **major depression**.

major depressive episode an episode of a MOOD DISORDER in which, for at least 2 weeks, the individual has either persistent depressed mood or ANHEDONIA as well as at least four other symptoms. These other symptoms include: poor or increased appetite with significant weight loss or gain; insomnia or excessive sleep; PSYCHOMOTOR AGITATION or PSYCHOMOTOR RETARDATION; loss of energy with fatigue; feelings of worthlessness or inappropriate guilt; reduced ability to concentrate or make decisions; and recurrent thoughts of death, SUICIDAL IDEATION, or attempted suicide. All of these symptoms cause significant distress or impair normal functioning (social, occupational, etc.).

major tranquilizer see ANTIPSYCHOTIC.

maladaptation *n.* a condition in which biological traits or behavior patterns are detrimental, counterproductive, or otherwise interfere with optimal functioning in various domains, such as successful interaction with the environment and effectual coping with the challenges and stresses of daily life. Compare ADAPTATION. —**maladaptive** *adj.*

maladjustment *n.* inability to maintain effective relationships, function successfully in various domains, or cope with difficulties and stresses. —**maladjusted** *adj.*

malapropism *n.* a linguistic error in which one word is mistakenly used for another having a similar sound, often to ludicrous effect, as in *She was wearing a cream casserole* (for *camisole*).

mal de pelea a CULTURE-BOUND

SYNDROME found in Puerto Rico that is similar to AMOK.

male erectile disorder see IMPOTENCE.

male orgasmic disorder persistent or recurrent delay in, or absence of, male orgasm during sexual stimulation that produces arousal.

malignant *adj.* describing a condition that gets progressively worse or is resistant to treatment, particularly a tumor that spreads to other sites by invading and destroying neighboring tissues. Compare BENIGN.

malingering *n.* the deliberate feigning of an illness or disability to achieve a particular desired outcome. For example, it may take the form of faking mental illness as a defense in a trial or faking physical illness to win compensation. Malingering is distinguished from FACTITIOUS DISORDER in that it involves a specific external factor as the motivating force. **—malingerer** *n.*

malleus *n.* see OSSICLES.

maltreatment *n.* ABUSE or NEGLECT of another person, which may involve emotional, sexual, or physical action or inaction, the severity or chronicity of which can result in significant harm or injury. Maltreatment also includes such actions as exploitation and denial of basic needs (e.g., food, shelter, medical attention).

mammillary body either of a pair of small, spherical NUCLEI at the base of the brain, slightly posterior to the infundibulum (pituitary stalk), that are components of the LIMBIC SYSTEM.

mammography *n.* a diagnostic procedure that uses low-dose x-ray photography to detect breast tumors or other abnormalities, either noncancerous (BENIGN) or cancerous

(MALIGNANT). The x-ray negative produced is called a **mammogram**.

managed care any system of health care delivery that regulates the use of member benefits to contain expenses. The term is also used to denote the organization of health care services and facilities into groups to increase cost-effectiveness. **Managed care organizations** (**MCOs**) include HMOs (health maintenance organizations), PPOs (preferred provider organizations), point of service plans (POSs), exclusive provider organizations (EPOs), physician–hospital organizations (PHOs), integrated delivery systems (IDSs), and independent practice associations (IPAs).

mand *n.* in linguistics, a category of UTTERANCES in which the speaker makes demands on the hearer, as in *Listen to me* or *Pass the salt, please.* According to the behaviorist analysis of language, this form of verbal behavior is reinforced by the compliance of the listener. See BEHAVIORISM.

mania *n.* excitement, overactivity, and PSYCHOMOTOR AGITATION, often accompanied by impaired judgment.

manic *adj.* relating to MANIA.

manic-depressive illness see BIPOLAR DISORDER.

manic episode a period lasting at least 1 week characterized by elevated, expansive, or irritable mood with three or more of the following symptoms: an increase in activity or PSYCHOMOTOR AGITATION; talkativeness; racing thoughts; inflated self-esteem or grandiosity; a decreased need for sleep; extreme distractibility; and involvement in pleasurable activities that are likely to have unfortunate consequences, such as buying sprees or sexual indiscretions. All of these symptoms

M

impair normal functioning and relationships with others.

manifest content in psychoanalytic theory, the images and events of a DREAM or FANTASY as experienced and recalled by the dreamer or fantasist, as opposed to the LATENT CONTENT, which is posited to contain the hidden meaning. See also DREAM ANALYSIS; DREAM-WORK.

manifest variable a variable that is directly observed or measured, as opposed to one whose value is inferred (see LATENT VARIABLE).

manipulation *n.* conscious behavior designed to exploit, control, or otherwise influence others to one's advantage.

manipulation check any means by which an experimenter evaluates the efficacy of the experimental manipulation, that is, verifies that the manipulation affected the participants as intended.

Mann–Whitney U test a nonparametric statistical test of centrality for ranked data that contrasts scores from two independent samples in terms of the probabilities of obtaining the ranking distributions. [Henry Berthold **Mann** (1905–2000), Austrian-born U.S. mathematician; Donald Ransom **Whitney** (1915–2001), U.S. statistician]

MANOVA acronym for MULTI-VARIATE ANALYSIS OF VARIANCE.

mantra *n.* any verbal formula used for spiritual, religious, or meditative purposes to help block out extraneous thoughts and induce a state of relaxation that enables the individual to reach a deeper level of consciousness.

manualized therapy interventions that are performed according to specific guidelines for administration, maximizing the probability of therapy being conducted consistently across settings, therapists, and clients.

MAOI (MAO inhibitor) abbreviation for MONOAMINE OXIDASE INHIBITOR.

MAP abbreviation for MODAL ACTION PATTERN.

marasmus *n.* a condition of extreme emaciation in infancy, resulting from severe protein–energy malnutrition and leading to delayed physical and cognitive development and potentially death. Marasmus tends to occur mostly in developing countries, often as a result of famine. See also KWASHIORKOR.

marginalization *n.* a reciprocal process through which an individual or group with relatively distinctive qualities, such as idiosyncratic values or customs, becomes identified as one that is not accepted fully into the larger group. **—marginalize** *vb.*

margin of error a statistic expressing the CONFIDENCE INTERVAL associated with a given measurement; it is an allowance for a slight miscalculation or an acceptable deviation. The larger the margin of error for the sample data, the less confidence one has that the results obtained are accurate for the entire population of interest.

marijuana (marihuana) *n.* see CANNABIS.

marital therapy see COUPLES THERAPY.

market research research undertaken to understand the competitive challenges in a particular market by assessing the relative positions of various suppliers in the minds of consumers.

masking *n.* in perception, the partial or complete obscuring of one stimulus (the target) by another (the masker). The stimuli may be sounds

M

(AUDITORY MASKING), visual images (**visual masking**), tastes, odorants, or tactile stimuli. Forward masking occurs when the masker is presented a short time before the target stimulus, backward masking occurs when it is presented shortly afterward, and simultaneous masking occurs when the two stimuli are presented at the same instant. —**mask** *vb.*

Maslow's motivational hierarchy the hierarchy of human motives, or needs, as described by U.S. psychologist Abraham Maslow (1908–1970). PHYSIOLOGICAL NEEDS (air, water, food, sleep, sex, etc.) are at the base; followed by safety and security (the SAFETY NEEDS); then love, affection, and gregariousness (the LOVE NEEDS); then prestige, competence, and power (the ESTEEM NEEDS); and, at the highest level, aesthetic needs, the need for knowing, and SELF-ACTUALIZATION (the METANEEDS).

masochism *n.* the derivation of pleasure from experiencing pain and humiliation. The term generally denotes SEXUAL MASOCHISM but is also applied to other experiences not involving sex, such as martyrdom, religious flagellation, or asceticism. In psychoanalytic theory, masochism is interpreted as resulting from the DEATH INSTINCT or from aggression turned inward because of excessive guilt feelings. [Leopold Sacher **Masoch** (1835–1895), Austrian writer] —**masochist** *n.* —**masochistic** *adj.*

mass action the generalization of U.S. psychologist Karl S. Lashley (1890–1958) that the size of a cortical lesion, rather than its specific location, determines the extent of any resulting performance decrement. Proposed in 1929 following experimental observations of the effects of different brain lesions on rats' ability to learn a complex maze, the concept reflects Lashley's belief

that large areas of the cortex function together in learning and other complex processes. See also EQUIPOTENTIALITY.

massed practice a learning procedure in which material is studied either in a single lengthy session or in sessions separated by short intervals. Massed practice is often found to be less effective than DISTRIBUTED PRACTICE.

mastery orientation an adaptive pattern of achievement behavior in which individuals enjoy and seek challenge, persist in the face of obstacles, and tend to view their failings as due to lack of effort or poor use of strategy rather than to lack of ability.

masturbation *n.* manipulation of one's own genital organs for purposes of sexual gratification. —**masturbate** *vb.*

matched-group design an experimental design in which experimental and control groups are matched on one or more background variables before being exposed to the experimental or control conditions. Compare RANDOMIZED-GROUP DESIGN.

matching *n.* a research technique for ensuring comparability of participants by making sure that they all have similar background variables. The individuals in a CONTROL GROUP and in an EXPERIMENTAL GROUP might be matched, for example, on years of education, income, and marital status.

matching hypothesis the proposition that people tend to form relationships with individuals who have a similar level of physical attractiveness to their own. Research indicates that this similarity tends to be greater for couples having a romantic relationship than for friends.

materialism *n.* the philosophical

position that everything, including mental events, is composed of physical matter and is thus subject to the laws of physics. From this perspective, the mind is considered to exist solely as a set of brain processes (see MIND–BODY PROBLEM). Compare IDEALISM; IMMATERIALISM. **—materialist** *adj., n.* **—materialistic** *adj.*

maternal deprivation lack of adequate nurturing for a young animal or child due to the absence or premature loss of, or neglect by, its mother or primary caregiver, postulated to negatively impact a child's emotional development by disrupting ATTACHMENT formation.

mathematics disorder a LEARNING DISORDER in which mathematical ability is substantially below what is expected given the person's chronological age, formal education experience, and measured intelligence. It may involve difficulties, for example, in counting, learning multiplication tables, or performing mathematical operations.

matriarchy *n.* **1.** a society in which descent and inheritance is **matrilineal**, that is, traced through the female only. **2.** more loosely, a family, group, or society in which women are dominant. Compare PATRIARCHY. **—matriarchal** *adj.*

maturation *n.* the biological processes involved in an organism's becoming functional or fully developed.

maturity *n.* a state of completed growth or development, as in adulthood.

maze *n.* a complex system of intersecting paths and blind alleys that must be navigated from an entrance to an exit. Various types of mazes are used in learning experiments for animals and humans.

MBTI abbreviation for MYERS–BRIGGS TYPE INDICATOR.

M-cell *n.* any of various large neurons in the two most ventral layers of the LATERAL GENICULATE NUCLEUS. M-cells are the origin of the MAGNOCELLULAR SYSTEM. The large RETINAL GANGLION CELLS that provide input to the M-cells of the lateral geniculate nucleus are called **M-ganglion cells**. See also P-CELL.

MDMA *n.* 3,4-methylenedioxymethamphetamine: a catecholamine-like HALLUCINOGEN with amphetamine-like stimulant properties that is among the most commonly used illicit drugs, generally sold under the name **Ecstasy**. Taken orally, onset of effects is rapid; the high lasts several hours, and residual effects can be experienced for several days. Intoxication is characterized by euphoria, feelings of closeness and spirituality, and diverse symptoms of autonomic arousal.

mean (symbol: $\bar{X}$; M) *n.* the numerical average of a batch of scores (X_i): the most widely used statistic for describing CENTRAL TENDENCY. It is computed as:

$$\bar{X} = (\sum_i X_i)/n,$$

where n is the number of scores; that is, the scores are added up, and the total is divided by the number of scores. Also called **arithmetic mean**.

mean deviation for a set of numbers, a measure of dispersion or spread equal to the average of the differences between each number and the mean value. It is given by $(\sum|x_i - \mu|)/n$, where μ is the mean value and n the number of values.

mean length of utterance a measure of language development in young children based on the mean length of UTTERANCES in their spontaneous speech. It is usually calculated by counting MORPHEMES

M

rather than words, and is based on at least 100 successive utterances.

means–ends analysis a technique to solve problems that sets up subgoals as means to achieve the goals (ends) and compares subgoals and goals using a recursive goal-reduction search procedure. Means-ends analysis originated in artificial intelligence and expanded into human cognition as a general problem-solving strategy.

mean square a SUM OF SQUARES divided by its DEGREES OF FREEDOM. The mean square is a variance ESTIMATOR.

measurement *n.* the act of appraising the extent of some amount, dimension, or criterion—or the resultant descriptive or quantified appraisal itself—often, but not always, expressed as a numerical value.

measurement error a difference between an observed measurement and the true value of the parameter being measured that is attributable to flaws or biases in the measurement process.

measurement level the degree of specificity, accuracy, and precision reflected in a particular set of observations or measurements. Examples of common levels of measurement include NOMINAL SCALES, ORDINAL SCALES, INTERVAL SCALES, and RATIO SCALES.

measurement model a statistical modeling technique that quantifies the association between observations obtained during research (observed indicators) and theoretical underlying constructs. In contrast with a structural equation model (see STRUCTURAL EQUATION MODELING), a measurement model specifies the relationships between observed indicators and the LATENT VARIABLES that support or affect them.

measurement scale any of four methods for quantifying attributes of variables during the course of research, listed in order of increasing power and complexity: NOMINAL SCALE, ORDINAL SCALE, INTERVAL SCALE, and RATIO SCALE.

mechanistic theory the assumption that psychological processes and behaviors can ultimately be understood in the same way that mechanical or physiological processes are understood. Its explanations of human behavior are based on the model or metaphor of a machine, reducing complex psychological phenomena to simpler physical phenomena. See REDUCTIONISM.

mechanoreceptor *n.* a receptor that is sensitive to mechanical forms of stimuli. Examples of mechanoreceptors are the receptors in the ear that translate sound waves into nerve impulses, the touch receptors in the skin, and the receptors in the joints and muscles.

medial *adj.* toward or at the middle of the body or of an organ. Compare LATERAL. **—medially** *adv.*

medial forebrain bundle a collection of nerve fibers passing through the midline of the forebrain to the hypothalamus. It provides the chief pathway for reciprocal connections between the hypothalamus and the BIOGENIC AMINE systems of the brainstem.

medial geniculate nucleus either of two small oval clusters of nerve cell bodies in the THALAMUS, just medial to the LATERAL GENICULATE NUCLEUS, that receive information from the inferior COLLICULUS and relay it to the AUDITORY CORTEX.

medial lemniscus either of a pair of somatosensory tracts in the midbrain carrying fibers from the spinal cord that communicate with the thalamus.

median *n.* the score that divides a DISTRIBUTION into two equal-sized halves.

median test a nonparametric statistical procedure that tests the equality of the medians in two or more samples.

mediation *n.* in dispute resolution, use of a neutral outside person—the mediator—to help the contending parties communicate and reach a compromise. The process of mediation has gained popularity, for example for couples involved in separation or divorce proceedings.

mediational deficiency in problem solving, inability to make use of a particular strategy to benefit task performance even if it is taught to a person. Compare PRODUCTION DEFICIENCY; UTILIZATION DEFICIENCY.

medical model the concept that mental and emotional problems are analogous to biological problems, that is, they have detectable, specific, physiological causes (e.g., an abnormal gene or damaged cell) and are amenable to cure or improvement by specific treatment.

meditation *n.* profound and extended contemplation or reflection, sometimes in order to attain an ALTERED STATE OF CONSCIOUSNESS. Traditionally associated with spiritual and religious exercises, it is now increasingly also used to provide relaxation and relief from stress. See also TRANSCENDENTAL MEDITATION.

medulla *n.* the central or innermost region of an organ, such as the adrenal medulla. Compare CORTEX. —**medullary** *adj.*

medulla oblongata the most inferior (lowest), or caudal (tailward), part of the HINDBRAIN. It contains many nerve tracts that conduct impulses between the spinal cord and higher brain centers, as well as autonomic nuclei involved in the control of breathing, heartbeat, and blood pressure.

MEG abbreviation for MAGNETO-ENCEPHALOGRAPHY or magnetoencephalograph.

megalomania *n.* a highly inflated conception of one's importance, power, or capabilities.

meiosis *n.* a special type of division of the cell nucleus that occurs during the formation of the sex cells—ova and spermatozoa. During meiosis, a parental cell in the gonad produces four daughter cells that are all HAPLOID, that is, they possess only one of each chromosome, instead of the normal DIPLOID complement of homologous pairs of chromosomes. During the process of fertilization, the ova and spermatozoa undergo fusion, which restores the double set of chromosomes within the nucleus of the zygote thus formed.

melancholia *n.* an archaic name for depression. —**melancholic** *adj.*

melatonin *n.* a hormone, produced mainly by the PINEAL GLAND as a metabolic product of the neurotransmitter SEROTONIN, that helps to regulate seasonal changes in physiology and may also influence puberty. It is implicated in the initiation of sleep and in the regulation of the sleep–wake cycle.

membrane *n.* a thin layer of tissue that covers a surface, lines a cavity, or connects or divides anatomical spaces or organs. One of the fundamental functions of a membrane is to contain the components within it. In cells, the membrane surrounds the cytoplasm and is composed of proteins and lipids. It is semipermeable, and acts to control the passage of substances in and out of the cell (e.g., see ION CHANNEL).

M

membrane potential a difference in electric potential across a membrane, especially the plasma membrane of a cell. See also RESTING POTENTIAL.

meme *n.* a unit of practice or belief through which a society or culture evolves and that passes from one generation to the next. In this sense the term (derived from the Greek word for "imitation") is a kind of metaphorical parallel to the term GENE.

memory *n.* **1.** the ability to retain information or a representation of past experience, based on the mental processes of learning or ENCODING, RETENTION across some interval of time, and RETRIEVAL or reactivation of the memory. **2.** specific information or a specific past experience that is recalled. **3.** the hypothesized part of the brain where traces of information and past experiences are stored.

memory consolidation see CONSOLIDATION.

memory span the number of items that can be recalled immediately after one presentation. Usually, the items consist of letters, words, numbers, or syllables that the participant must reproduce in order. A distinction may be drawn between visual memory span and auditory memory span, depending on the nature of the presentation.

memory trace a hypothetical modification of the nervous system that encodes a representation of information or experience. See ENGRAM.

menarche *n.* the first incidence of MENSTRUATION in a female, marking the onset of puberty. The age at which menarche occurs varies among individuals and cultures. —**menarcheal** *adj.*

Mendelian inheritance a type of inheritance that conforms to the basic principles developed around 1865 by Austrian monk Gregor Mendel (1822–1884), regarded as the founder of genetics. Mendelian inheritance is essentially determined by genes located on chromosomes, which are transmitted from both parents to their offspring. It includes autosomal dominant (see DOMINANT ALLELE), autosomal recessive (see RECESSIVE ALLELE), and SEX-LINKED inheritance.

meninges *pl. n.* (*sing.* **meninx**) the three membranous layers that provide a protective cover for the brain and spinal cord. They consist of a tough outer **dura mater**, a middle **arachnoid mater**, and a thin, transparent **pia mater**, which fits over the various contours and fissures of the cerebral cortex.

meningioma *n.* a benign brain tumor that develops in the arachnoid layer of the MENINGES. Meningiomas are typically slow growing and cause damage mainly by pressure against the brain.

menopause *n.* see CLIMACTERIC. —**menopausal** *adj.*

menstrual cycle a modified ESTROUS CYCLE that occurs in most primates, including humans (in which it averages about 28 days). The events of the cycle are dependent on cyclical changes in the concentrations of GONADOTROPINS secreted by the anterior pituitary gland, under the control of GONADOTROPIN-RELEASING HORMONE, and can be divided into two phases. In the follicular phase, FOLLICLE-STIMULATING HORMONE (FSH) and LUTEINIZING HORMONE (LH) stimulate development of an ovum and secretion of estrogen within the ovary, culminating in OVULATION. The estrogen stimulates thickening of the endometrium (lining) of the uterus in preparation to receive a fertilized ovum. The luteal phase begins immediately after ovulation and is characterized by the formation of the corpus luteum, a yellowish glandular mass that inhibits further secretion of releasing hormone (and hence of FSH and LH). If fertilization does not occur, this phase ends with menstruation and a repeat of the follicular phase.

menstruation *n.* a periodic discharge of blood and endometrial tissue from the uterus through the vagina that occurs in fertile women as part of the MENSTRUAL CYCLE.

mental *adj.* **1.** of or referring to the MIND or to processes of the mind, such as thinking, feeling, sensing, and the like. **2.** phenomenal or consciously experienced. In contrast to physiological or physical, which refer to objective events or processes, mental denotes events known only privately and subjectively; it may refer to the COGNITIVE PROCESSES involved in these events, to differentiate them from physiological processes.

mental aberration a pathological deviation from normal thinking, particularly as a symptom of a mental or emotional disorder.

mental age (MA) a numerical scale unit derived by dividing an individual's results in an intelligence test by the average score for other people of the same age. Thus, a 4-year-old child who scored 150 on an IQ test would have a mental age of 6 (the age-appropriate average score is 100; therefore, MA = $(150/100) \times 4 = 6$). The MA measure of performance is not effective beyond the age of 14.

mental disorder any condition characterized by cognitive and emotional disturbances, abnormal behaviors, impaired functioning, or any combination of these. Such disorders cannot be accounted for solely by environmental circumstances and may involve physiological, genetic, chemical, social, and other factors. Specific classifications of mental disorders are elaborated in the American Psychiatric Association's *Diagnostic and Statistical Manual of Mental Disorders* (see DSM–IV–TR) and the World Health Organization's INTERNATIONAL CLASSIFICATION OF DISEASES. Also called **mental illness.**

mental handicap the condition of being unable to function independently in the community because of arrested or delayed cognitive development. Its use is generally discouraged nowadays in preference to MENTAL RETARDATION and other terms considered more objective and less offensive.

mental health a state characterized by emotional well-being, good behavioral adjustment, and a capacity to establish constructive relationships and cope with the ordinary demands and stresses of life.

mental hospital see PSYCHIATRIC HOSPITAL.

mental hygiene a general approach aimed at maintaining mental health and preventing mental disorder through such means as educational programs, promotion of a stable emotional and family life, prophylactic and early treatment services (see PRIMARY PREVENTION), and public health measures. The term itself is now less widely used than formerly.

mental illness see MENTAL DISORDER.

mental imagery see IMAGERY.

mentalism *n.* a position that insists on the reality of explicitly mental phenomena, such as thinking and feeling. It holds that mental phenomena cannot be reduced to physical or physiological phenomena (see REDUCTIONISM). The term is often used as a synonym for IDE-

M

ALISM, although some forms of mentalism may hold that mental events, while not reducible to physical substances, are nonetheless grounded in physical processes. Most modern cognitive theories are examples of this latter type of mentalism. —**mentalist** *adj.*

mental lexicon the set of words that a person uses regularly (productive vocabulary) or recognizes when used by others (receptive vocabulary). Psycholinguistics has proposed various models for such a lexicon, in which words are mentally organized with respect to such features as meaning, lexical category (e.g., noun, verb, etc.), frequency, length, and sound.

mental model any internal representation of the relations between a set of elements, as, for example, between workers in an office or the configuration of objects in a space. Such models may contain perceptual qualities and may be abstract in nature. They can be manipulated to provide dynamic simulations of possible scenarios and are thought to be key components in decision making.

mental representation a hypothetical entity that is presumed to stand for a perception, thought, memory, or the like in the mind during cognitive operations. For example, when doing mental arithmetic, one presumably operates on mental representations that correspond to the digits and numerical operators; when one imagines looking at the reverse side of an object, one presumably operates on a mental representation of that object.

mental retardation a disorder characterized by intellectual function that is significantly below average: specifically that of an individual with a measured IQ of 70 or below, whose level of performance of tasks required to fulfill typical roles in society—including maintaining independence and meeting cultural expectations of personal and social responsibility—is impaired, and in whom the condition is manifested during the developmental period, defined variously as below the ages of 18 or 22. Mental retardation may be the result of brain injury, disease, or genetic causes.

mental set a temporary readiness to perform certain psychological functions that influences response to a situation or stimulus, such as the tendency to apply a previously successful technique in solving a new problem. It is often determined by instructions but need not be.

mentoring *n.* the provision of instruction, encouragement, and other support to an individual (e.g., a student, youth, or colleague) to aid his or her overall growth and development or the pursuit of greater learning skills, a career, or other educational or work-related goals. Numerous **mentoring programs** exist today within occupational, educational, and other settings; they use frequent communication and contact between **mentors** and their respective protégés as well as a variety of other techniques and procedures to develop positive productive relationships.

mere-exposure effect the finding that individuals show an increased preference (or liking) for a stimulus (e.g., a name, sound, or picture) as a consequence of repeated exposure to that stimulus. Research indicates that this effect is most likely to occur when there is no preexisting negative attitude toward the stimulus object, and that it tends to be strongest when the person is not consciously aware of the stimulus presentations.

mescaline *n.* a HALLUCINOGEN derived from the peyote cactus. Its effects often include nausea and vomiting as well as visual hallucinations involving lights and colors; they have a slower onset than those of LSD and usually last 1–2 hours.

mesencephalon *n.* see MIDBRAIN. —**mesencephalic** *adj.*

mesmerism *n.* an old name, used in the mid-18th through the mid-19th centuries, for HYPNOSIS. [Franz Anton **Mesmer** (1733–1815), Austrian physician and an early proponent of hypnosis] —**mesmerist** *n.* —**mesmeric** *adj.*

mesokurtic *adj.* describing a statistical distribution that is neither flatter nor more peaked than a comparison, such as the normal distribution. See also PLATYKURTIC; LEPTOKURTIC.

mesosystem *n.* in ECOLOGICAL SYSTEMS THEORY, the groups and institutions outside the home (e.g., day care, school, or a child's peer group) that influence the child's development and interact with aspects of the **microsystem** (e.g., relations in the home). See also EXOSYSTEM; MACROSYSTEM.

messenger RNA (mRNA) a type of RNA that carries instructions from a cell's genetic material (usually DNA) to the protein-manufacturing apparatus elsewhere in the cell and directs the assembly of protein components in precise accord with those instructions. The instructions are embodied in the sequence of bases in the mRNA, according to the GENETIC CODE.

meta-analysis *n.* a quantitative technique for synthesizing the results of multiple studies of a phenomenon into a single result by combining the EFFECT SIZE estimates from each study into a single estimate of the combined effect size or into a distribution of effect sizes.

metabolism *n.* the physical and chemical processes within a living cell or organism that are necessary to maintain life. It includes **catabolism**, the breaking down of complex molecules into simpler ones, often with the release of energy; and **anabolism**, the synthesis of complex molecules from simple ones. —**metabolic** *adj.*

metabotropic receptor a neurotransmitter RECEPTOR that does not itself contain an ION CHANNEL but may use a G PROTEIN to open a nearby ion channel. Compare IONOTROPIC RECEPTOR.

metacognition *n.* awareness of one's own cognitive processes, often involving a conscious attempt to control them. The so-called TIP-OF-THE-TONGUE PHENOMENON, in which one struggles to "know" something that one knows one knows, provides an interesting example of metacognition. —**metacognitional** *adj.*

metalinguistic awareness a conscious awareness of the formal properties of language as well as its functional and semantic properties. It is associated with a mature stage in language and metacognitive development (see METACOGNITION) and does not usually develop until around age 8.

metamemory *n.* awareness of one's own memory processes, often involving a conscious attempt to direct or control them. It is an aspect of METACOGNITION.

metamotivation *n.* in the HUMANISTIC PSYCHOLOGY of U.S. psychologist Abraham Maslow (1908–1970), those motives that impel an individual toward SELF-ACTUALIZATION and transcendence. Metamotivation is distinct from the motivation operating in the lower level needs, which he calls DEFICIENCY MOTIVATION, and it emerges

M

after the lower needs are satisfied. See METANEED.

metaneed *n.* in the HUMANISTIC PSYCHOLOGY of U.S. psychologist Abraham Maslow (1908–1970), any need for knowledge, beauty, and creativity. Metaneeds, which are involved in SELF-ACTUALIZATION, comprise the highest level of needs and come into play primarily after the lower level needs have been met. See METAMOTIVATION.

metapsychology *n.* the study of, or a concern for, the fundamental underlying principles of any psychology. The term was used by Austrian psychiatrist Sigmund Freud (1856–1939) to denote his own psychological theory, emphasizing its ability to offer comprehensive explanations of psychological phenomena on a fundamental level. —**metapsychological** *adj.*

metatheory *n.* a higher order theory about theories, allowing one to analyze, compare, and evaluate competing theories. The concept of a metatheory suggests that theories derive from other theories such that there are always prior theoretical assumptions and commitments behind any theoretical formulation. These prior assumptions and commitments are worthy of study in their own right, and an understanding of them is essential to a full understanding of derivative theories. —**metatheoretical** *adj.*

methadone *n.* a synthetic OPIOID analgesic that is used for pain relief and as a substitute for heroin in METHADONE MAINTENANCE THERAPY. It is quite effective when orally ingested and has a long duration of action.

methadone maintenance therapy a drug-rehabilitation therapy in which those with heroin DEPENDENCE are prescribed a daily oral dose of METHADONE to blunt craving for opioid drugs. A controversial treatment, it is nonetheless widely considered the most effective approach to heroin addiction.

methamphetamine *n.* a STIMULANT whose chemical structure is similar to that of amphetamine but that has a more pronounced effect on the CENTRAL NERVOUS SYSTEM. It is used for treating attention-deficit/hyperactivity disorder in children and as a short-term aid to obesity treatment in adults. Like all AMPHETAMINES, methamphetamine is prone to abuse and dependence.

method *n.* the procedures and system of analysis used in scientific investigation in general or in a particular research project.

method of adjustment a psychophysical technique in which the participant adjusts a variable stimulus to match a constant or standard. For example, the observer is shown a standard visual stimulus of a specific intensity and is asked to adjust a comparison stimulus to match the brightness of the standard.

method of constant stimuli a psychophysical procedure for determining the sensory threshold by randomly presenting several stimuli known to be close to the threshold. The threshold is the stimulus value that was detected 50% of the time.

method of limits a psychophysical procedure for determining the sensory threshold by gradually increasing or decreasing the magnitude of the stimulus presented in discrete steps. That is, a stimulus of a given intensity is presented to a participant; if it is perceived, a stimulus of lower intensity is presented on the next trial, until the stimulus can no longer be detected. If it is not perceived, a stimulus of higher intensity is presented, until the stimulus is detected.

method of loci a MNEMONIC in which the items to be remembered are converted into mental images and associated with specific positions or locations. For instance, to remember a shopping list, each product could be imagined at a different location along a familiar street.

methodological behaviorism a form of BEHAVIORISM that concedes the existence and reality of conscious events but contends that the only suitable means of studying them scientifically is via their expression in behavior. Compare RADICAL BEHAVIORISM. See NEO-BEHAVIORISM.

methodology *n*. **1.** the science of method or orderly arrangement; specifically, the branch of logic concerned with the application of the principles of reasoning to scientific and philosophical inquiry. **2.** the system of methods, principles, and rules of procedure used within a particular discipline.

methylphenidate *n*. a stimulant related to the AMPHETAMINES and with a similar mechanism of action. It blocks the reuptake of catecholamines from the synaptic cleft and stimulates presynaptic release of catecholamines. Methylphenidate is used for the treatment of attention-deficit/hyperactivity disorder (ADHD) and narcolepsy and as an adjunct to antidepressant therapy and to increase concentration and alertness in patients with brain injuries, brain cancer, or dementia. U.S. trade name (among others): **Ritalin**.

microcephaly *n*. a condition in which the head is abnormally small in relation to the rest of the body. Compare MACROCEPHALY. —**microcephalic** *adj*.

microelectrode *n*. an electrode with a tip no larger than a few micrometers in diameter, sometimes less than 1 μm, that can be inserted into a single cell. In the **microelectrode technique**, used in studies of neurophysiology and disorders of the nervous system, intracellular microelectrodes with tips less than 1 μm in diameter are able to stimulate and record activity within a single neuron (single-cell or single-unit recording).

microgenetic method a research methodology that looks at developmental change within a single set of individuals over relatively brief periods of time, usually days or weeks.

microglia *n*. an extremely small type of nonneuronal central nervous system cell (GLIA) that removes cellular debris from injured or dead cells. —**microglial** *adj*.

micrographia *n*. a disorder characterized by very small, often unreadable writing and associated most often with PARKINSON'S DISEASE.

microsleep *n*. a brief interval of dozing or loss of awareness that occurs during periods when a person is fatigued and trying to stay awake while doing monotonous tasks, such as driving a car, looking at a computer screen, or monitoring controls. Such periods of "nodding off" typically last for 2–30 s and are more likely to occur in the predawn and mid-afternoon hours.

microsystem *n*. see MESOSYSTEM.

microtubule *n*. a small, hollow, cylindrical structure (typically 20–26 nm in diameter), numbers of which occur in various types of cell. Microtubules are part of the cell's internal scaffolding (cytoskeleton) and form the spindle during cell division. In neurons, microtubules are involved in AXONAL TRANSPORT.

midbrain *n*. a relatively small region of the upper brainstem that connects the FOREBRAIN and

M

HINDBRAIN. It contains the TECTUM (and associated inferior and superior COLLICULI), TEGMENTUM, and SUBSTANTIA NIGRA. Also called **mesencephalon**.

middle ear a membrane-lined cavity in the temporal bone of the skull. It is filled with air and communicates with the nasopharynx through the EUSTACHIAN TUBE. It contains the OSSICLES, which transmit sound vibrations from the outer ear and the tympanic membrane (eardrum) to the OVAL WINDOW of the inner ear.

midlife crisis a period of psychological distress occurring in some individuals during the middle years of adulthood, roughly from ages 35 to 65. Causes may include significant life events and health or occupational problems and concerns.

midline *n.* a bisecting or median line, especially in reference to an imaginary median line or plane through the body or a part of the body.

midpoint *n.* the point or value halfway between the highest and lowest values in a FREQUENCY DISTRIBUTION.

migraine *n.* a headache that is recurrent, usually severe, usually limited to one side of the head, and likely to be accompanied by nausea, vomiting, and extreme sensitivity to light (photophobia). Migraine headaches may be preceded by a subjective sensation of flickering or flashing light, blacking out of part of the visual field, or illusions of colors or patterns.

migration *n.* **1.** in animal behavior, travel over relatively long distances to or from breeding areas. Migration is observed in birds, fish, and some mammals and insects (among others). In some species it is seasonal, involving movement from a breeding area to an overwintering area; in others, particularly the salmon, it is observed only once in the lifetime of an individual. **2.** in the development of the nervous system, the movement of nerve cells from their origin in the ventricular zone to establish distinctive cell populations, such as brain nuclei and layers of the cerebral cortex.

milieu *n.* (*pl.* **milieux**) the environment in general or, more typically, the social environment.

milieu therapy psychotherapeutic treatment based on modification or manipulation of the client's life circumstances or immediate environment. Milieu therapy attempts to organize the social and physical setting in which the client lives or is being treated in such a way as to promote healthier, more adaptive cognitions, emotions, and behavior. See also THERAPEUTIC COMMUNITY.

mimicry *n.* **1.** the presence of physical or behavioral traits in one species that so closely resemble those of another species that they confuse observers. This serves either to evade predators or to attract prey. **2.** a form of SOCIAL LEARNING that involves duplication of a behavior without any understanding of the goal of that behavior.

mind *n.* **1.** most broadly, all intellectual and psychological phenomena of an organism, encompassing motivational, affective, behavioral, perceptual, and cognitive systems; in other words, the organized totality of the MENTAL and PSYCHIC processes of an organism and the structural and functional cognitive components on which they depend. The term, however, is often used more narrowly to denote only cognitive activities and functions, such as perceiving, attending, thinking, problem solving, language, learning, and memory. The nature of the relationship between the mind and the body, including the brain and its mechanisms or activities, has been, and continues to be, the subject of much debate. See MIND–BODY PROBLEM. **2.** a set of EMERGENT PROPERTIES automatically derived from a brain that has achieved sufficient biological sophistication. In this sense, the mind is considered more the province of humans and of human consciousness than of organisms in general. **3.** human consciousness regarded as an immaterial entity distinct from the brain. **4.** the brain itself and its activities: in this view, the mind essentially is both the anatomical organ and what it does.

mind–body problem the problem of accounting for and describing the relationship between mental and physical processes (psyche and soma). Solutions to this problem fall into six broad categories: (a) INTERACTIONISM, in which mind and body are separate processes that nevertheless exert mutual influence; (b) parallelism, in which mind and body are separate processes with a point-to-point correspondence but no causal connection; (c) IDEALISM, in which only mind exists and the soma is a function of the psyche; (d) double-aspect theory, in which body and mind are both functions of a common entity; (e) epiphenomenalism, in which mind is a byproduct of bodily processes; and (f) MATERIALISM, in which body is the only reality and the psyche is nonexistent. Categories (a) and (b) are varieties of DUALISM; the remainder are varieties of MONISM. Also called **body–mind problem**.

mindfulness *n.* full awareness of one's internal states and surroundings: the opposite of absent-mindedness. The concept has been applied to various therapeutic interventions—for example, mindfulness-based COGNITIVE

BEHAVIOR THERAPY, mindfulness-based stress reduction, mindfulness for addictions, and mindfulness MEDITATION—to help people avoid destructive or automatic habits and responses by learning to observe their thoughts, emotions, and other present-moment experiences without judging or reacting to them. **—mindful** *adj.*

mineralocorticoid *n.* any CORTICOSTEROID hormone that affects ion concentrations in body tissues and helps to regulate the excretion of salt and water. In humans the principal mineralocorticoid is ALDOSTERONE.

minimal brain dysfunction a relatively mild impairment of brain function that is presumed to account for a variety of subtle and nonspecific clinical, behavioral, or neurological disturbances seen in certain learning or behavioral disabilities. These disturbances include hyperactivity, impulsivity, emotional lability, and distractibility.

minimal group a temporary group of anonymous people lacking interdependence, COHESION, structure, and other characteristics typically found in social groups. An example is a group of people disembarking from a bus. Minimal groups are an essential component of a particular research procedure, used mainly in studies of intergroup conflict, called the **minimal intergroup situation** or the **minimal group paradigm**. It has been found that individuals in such groups respond in biased ways when allocating resources to INGROUP and OUTGROUP members, even though the groups are not psychologically or interpersonally meaningful.

Minnesota Multiphasic Personality Inventory (MMPI) a PERSONALITY INVENTORY first published in 1940 and now one of the most widely used SELF-REPORT

M

methods for assessing personality and psychological maladjustment across a range of mental health, medical, substance abuse, forensic, and personnel screening settings. It features 567 true–false questions that assess symptoms, attitudes, and beliefs that relate to emotional and behavioral problems.

minority influence social pressure exerted on the majority faction of a group by a smaller faction of the group. Studies suggest that minorities who argue consistently for change prompt the group to reconsider even long-held or previously unquestioned assumptions and procedures.

minor tranquilizer see ANXIO-LYTIC.

mirror neuron a type of cell in the brains of primates that responds in the same way to a given action (e.g., reaching out to grasp an object) whether it is performed by the primate itself or whether the primate has merely observed another primate perform the same action.

misandry *n.* hatred or contempt for men. Compare MISOGYNY. —**misandrist** *n., adj.*

misanthropy *n.* a hatred, aversion, or distrust of human beings and human nature. —**misanthrope** *n.* —**misanthropic** *adj.*

misattribution *n.* an incorrect inference as to the cause of an individual's or group's behavior or of an interpersonal event. For example, **misattribution of arousal** is an effect in which the physiological stimulation generated by one stimulus is mistakenly ascribed to another source. See also ATTRIBUTION THE-ORY.

miscarriage *n.* see ABORTION.

misinformation effect a phenomenon in which a person mistakenly recalls misleading infor-mation that an experimenter has provided, instead of accurately recalling the correct information that had been presented earlier. The misinformation effect is studied in the context of EYEWITNESS MEMORY.

misogyny *n.* hatred or contempt for women. Compare MISANDRY. —**misogynist** *n.* —**misogynistic** *adj.*

mitochondrion *n.* (*pl.* **mitochondria**) a specialized, membrane-bound structure (organelle) that is the main site of energy production in cells. Mitochondria are most numerous in cells with a high level of metabolism. They also have their own DNA (mitochondrial DNA). —**mitochondrial** *adj.*

mitosis *n.* (*pl.* **mitoses**) the type of division of a cell nucleus that produces two identical daughter nuclei, each possessing the same number and type of chromosomes as the parent nucleus. It is usually accompanied by division of the cytoplasm, leading to the formation of two identical daughter cells. Compare MEIOSIS. —**mitotic** *adj.*

mixed design an experimental design that combines features of both a BETWEEN-SUBJECTS DESIGN and a WITHIN-SUBJECTS DESIGN. For example, a researcher studying the influence of different types of music on relaxation might use a mixed design. He or she divides participants into a CONTROL GROUP (listening to no music) and two EXPERIMENTAL GROUPS (one listening to classical music and one listening to rock music). The researcher then gives participants in all groups a PRETEST to determine the baseline level of physiological arousal prior to hearing any music, introduces the music, and then gives a POSTTEST to determine what specific reduction in arousal may have occurred. In this situation, music type is a between-subjects factor (each participant hears only a single genre of music) and physiological arousal is a within-subjects factor (each participant is evaluated on this variable on multiple occasions and the different assessments compared).

mixed episode an episode of a MOOD DISORDER lasting at least 1 week in which symptoms meeting criteria for both a MAJOR DEPRESSIVE EPISODE and a MANIC EPISODE are prominent over the course of the disturbance.

mixed receptive-expressive language disorder a communication disorder characterized by levels of language comprehension and production substantially below those expected for intellectual ability and developmental level.

MMPI abbreviation for MINNESOTA MULTIPHASIC PERSONALITY INVENTORY.

mnemonic *n.* any device or technique used to assist memory, usually by forging a link or association between the new information to be remembered and information previously encoded. For instance, one might remember the numbers in a password by associating them with familiar birth dates, addresses, or room numbers. See also METHOD OF LOCI.

mob psychology CROWD PSYCHOLOGY, as applied to disorderly, unruly, and emotionally charged gatherings of people.

modal *n.* pertaining to a particular MODE, model, technique, or process. In LINGUISTICS, modal refers to the mood of a verb; that is, for example, whether it is *indicative* (states a fact), *imperative* (expresses an order or command), or *subjunctive* (expressing a wish or a state of possibility).

modal action pattern (MAP) the typical or most common behavioral pattern expressed in response to a

RELEASER. In classical ethology the term FIXED ACTION PATTERN was used to describe behavioral responses, but this term obscures the variation in behavior typically seen within and between individuals.

modality *n.* **1.** a particular therapeutic technique or process. **2.** a medium of sensation, such as vision or hearing. See SENSE.

mode *n.* the most frequently occurring score in a batch of data, which is sometimes used as a measure of CENTRAL TENDENCY.

model *n.* a graphic, theoretical, or other type of representation of a concept (e.g., a disorder) or of basic behavioral or bodily processes that can be used for various investigative and demonstrative purposes, such as enhancing understanding of the concept, proposing hypotheses, showing relationships, or identifying epidemiological patterns.

modeling *n.* **1.** a technique used in COGNITIVE BEHAVIOR THERAPY and BEHAVIOR THERAPY in which learning occurs through observation and imitation alone, without comment or reinforcement by the therapist. **2.** in DEVELOPMENTAL PSYCHOLOGY, the process in which one or more individuals or other entities serve as examples (models) that a child will emulate. Models are often parents, other adults, or other children, but may also be symbolic, for example, a book or television character. See also SOCIAL LEARNING THEORY.

moderator variable in statistics, a variable that alters the relationship between other variables. In REGRESSION ANALYSIS, for example, it is a variable that is unrelated to a criterion variable but is retained in the REGRESSION EQUATION because of its significant relationship to other predictor variables.

modernism *n.* a philosophical position whose defining characteristics include a sense that religious dogma and classical metaphysics can no longer provide a sure foundation in intellectual matters and a quest for certain knowledge from other sources. Traditional psychology can be seen to be the product of modernism to the extent that it is characterized by faith in scientific method, pursuit of control and prediction of behavior, explanation in terms of laws and principles, and the assumption that human behavior is ultimately rational as opposed to irrational. See also POSTMODERNISM. —**modernist** *adj.*, *n.*

modern racism a contemporary form of PREJUDICE against members of other racial groups that is expressed indirectly and covertly, typically by condemning the cultural values of the OUTGROUP or by experiencing aversive emotions when interacting with its members but not acting on those negative emotions (see AVERSIVE RACISM).

modularity *n.* a theory of the human mind in which the various components of cognition are characterized as independent modules, hypothetical centers of information processing each with its own specific domain and particular properties. More recently, evolutionary psychologists have shown interest in the idea that the various modules may be adaptive specializations.

modulation *n.* changes in some parameter of a waveform so that the information contained by the variations of this parameter can be transmitted by the wave, which is known as the carrier wave. Amplitude modulation (AM) refers to changes in amplitude that are relatively slow compared to the usually sinusoidal variations in the carrier. In frequency modulation (FM) the frequency of the carrier is varied but its amplitude remains constant. In phase modulation the relative phase

of the carrier wave is varied in accordance with the amplitude of the signal variations.

molar *adj.* characterized by or pertaining to units, masses, and systems in their entirety. **Molar analysis** in psychology is a way of examining behavioral processes as holistic units, extended through time. This approach stresses comprehensive concepts or overall frameworks or structures. Compare MOLECULAR.

molecular *adj.* characterized by or pertaining to the component parts of a phenomenon, process, or system. **Molecular analysis** in psychology is a way of examining behavioral processes in terms of elemental units, sometimes analyzing them in a moment-by-moment or phase-by-phase manner. Compare MOLAR.

molecular genetics the branch of biology that is concerned with the structure and processes of genetic material at the molecular level.

moment *n.* the power to which the expected value of a RANDOM VARIABLE is raised. Thus, $E(x^k)$ is the kth moment of x. Moments are used for computing distribution measures, such as the MEAN, VARIANCE, SKEWNESS, and KURTOSIS.

monism *n.* the position that reality consists of a single substance, whether this is identified as mind, matter, or God. In the context of the MIND–BODY PROBLEM, monism is any position that avoids DUALISM. —**monist** *adj.*, *n.* —**monistic** *adj.*

monitoring *n.* the process of watching or overseeing individuals and their behavior, often for the purpose of collecting information (e.g., as in a study) or influencing function (e.g., as in a therapeutic intervention).

monoamine *n.* a chemical compound that contains only one amine group, $-NH_2$. Monoamines include neurotransmitters, such as the CATE-CHOLAMINES norepinephrine and dopamine and the INDOLEAMINE serotonin.

monoamine hypothesis the theory that depression is caused by a deficit in the production or uptake of monoamines (serotonin, norepinephrine, and dopamine). This theory has been used to explain the effects of MONOAMINE OXIDASE INHIBITORS, but is now regarded as too simplistic.

monoamine oxidase inhibitor (MAOI; MAO inhibitor) any of a group of antidepressant drugs that function by inhibiting the activity of the enzyme **monoamine oxidase** in presynaptic neurons, thereby increasing the amounts of monoamine neurotransmitters (serotonin, norepinephrine, and dopamine) available for release at the presynaptic terminal. There are two categories of MAOIs: irreversible and reversible inhibitors. Irreversible MAOIs bind tightly to the enzyme and permanently inhibit its ability to metabolize any monoamine. This may lead to dangerous interactions with foods and beverages containing the amino acid tryptophan or the amine tyramine. Reversible inhibitors of monoamine oxidase do not bind irreversibly to the enzyme, thereby freeing it to take part in the metabolism of amino acids and other amines.

monochromatism *n.* a partial color blindness in which the eye contains only one type of cone PHOTOPIGMENT instead of the typical three: Everything appears in various shades of a single color. See also ACHROMATISM; DICHROMATISM; TRICHROMATISM.

monocular cue a cue to the perception of distance or depth that involves only one eye, such as LIN-EAR PERSPECTIVE, relative position, relative movement, and ACCOMMODATION. Compare BINOCULAR CUE.

monogamy *n.* **1.** an animal mating system in which two individuals mate exclusively with each other. Many species display serial monogamy, in which there is an exclusive social bond with each of a series of sexual partners at different times during the individual's life. Compare POLYANDRY; POLYGYNANDRY; POLYGYNY. **2.** traditionally, marriage to only one spouse at a time. Compare POLYGAMY. —**monogamous** *adj.*

monotonic *adj.* denoting a variable that progressively either increases or decreases as a second variable increases or decreases but that does not change its direction. For example, a monotonically increasing variable is one that rises as a second variable increases.

monozygotic twins (MZ twins) twins, always of the same sex, that develop from a single fertilized ovum (zygote) that splits in the early stages of MITOSIS to produce two individuals who carry exactly the same complement of genes; that is, they are clones, with identical DNA. Also called **identical twins**. Compare DIZYGOTIC TWINS.

mood *n.* a disposition to respond emotionally in a particular way that may last for hours, days, or even weeks, perhaps at a low level and without the person knowing what prompted the state. Moods differ from EMOTIONS in lacking an object; for example, the emotion of anger can be aroused by an insult, but an angry mood may arise when one does not know what one is angry about or what elicited the anger. Disturbances in mood are characteristic of MOOD DISORDERS.

mood congruent relating to a consistency or agreement between a particular expressed feeling and the general emotional context within which it occurs. Thus, crying at a time of sadness or personal distress is viewed as mood congruent. Similarly, in psychiatric diagnosis, the term relates to a consistency between the expression of a particular symptom or behavior with those characteristics or patterns of ideation or action used to classify a particular mental disorder. In both instances, inconsistencies are described as **mood incongruent**.

mood-dependent memory a condition in which memory for some event can be recalled more readily when one is in the same emotional mood (e.g., happy or sad) as when the memory was initially formed. See also STATE-DEPENDENT MEMORY.

mood disorder a psychiatric disorder in which the principal feature is a prolonged, pervasive mood disturbance, such as a DEPRESSIVE DISORDER (e.g., MAJOR DEPRESSIVE DISORDER, DYSTHYMIC DISORDER) or BIPOLAR DISORDER. A mood disorder is less commonly called an **affective disorder**.

mood incongruent see MOOD CONGRUENT.

mood stabilizer any of various drugs used in the treatment of cyclic mood disorders (BIPOLAR DISORDERS and CYCLOTHYMIC DISORDER). Because they reduce the symptoms of mania or manic episodes, mood stabilizers are sometimes known as **antimanics**.

moon illusion see SIZE–DISTANCE PARADOX.

moral *adj.* relating to the distinction between right and wrong or to behavior that is considered ethical or proper.

moral absolutism the belief that the morality or immorality of an action can be judged according to fixed standards of right and wrong. According to Swiss psychologist Jean Piaget (1896–1980), moral absolutism is characteristic of young children in the HETERONOMOUS STAGE of moral development, who interpret laws and rules as absolute. See MORAL REALISM. Compare MORAL RELATIVISM.

moral development the gradual formation of an individual's concepts of right and wrong, conscience, ethical and religious values, social attitudes, and behavior. Some of the major theorists in the area of moral development are Austrian psychiatrist Sigmund Freud (1856–1939), Swiss psychologist Jean Piaget (1896–1980), German-born U.S. psychologist Erik Erikson (1902–1994), and U.S. psychologist Lawrence Kohlberg (1927–1987).

morality *n.* a system of beliefs or set of values relating to right conduct, against which behavior is judged to be acceptable or unacceptable.

moral realism the type of thinking characteristic of younger children, who equate good behavior with obedience just as they equate the morality of an act only with its consequences. For example, 15 cups broken accidentally would be judged to be a far worse transgression than 1 cup broken mischievously, because more cups are broken. Moral realism shapes the child's thinking until the age of about 8, when the concepts of intention, motive, and extenuating circumstances begin to modify the child's early MORAL ABSOLUTISM. Compare MORAL RELATIVISM.

moral relativism the belief that the morality or immorality of an action is determined by social custom rather than by universal or fixed standards of right and wrong. According to Swiss psychologist Jean Piaget (1896–1980), moral relativism is characteristic of children in the AUTONOMOUS STAGE of moral development, who consider the intention behind an act along with possible extenuating circumstances when judging its rightness or wrongness. Compare MORAL ABSOLUTISM; MORAL REALISM.

moral therapy a form of psychotherapy from the 19th century based on the belief that a person with a mental disorder could be helped by being treated with compassion, kindness, and dignity in a clean, comfortable environment that provided freedom of movement, opportunities for occupational and social activity, and reassuring talks with physicians and attendants. This approach advocating humane and ethical treatment was a radical departure from the prevailing practice at that time of viewing the "insane" with suspicion and hostility, confining them in unsanitary conditions, and routinely abusing them through the use of such practices as mechanical restraint, physical punishment, and bloodletting. Moral therapy originated in the family-care program established in the Gheel colony, Belgium, during the 13th century, but came to fruition in the 19th century through the efforts of Philippe Pinel and Jean Esquirol (1772–1840) in France, William Tuke (1732–1822) in England, and Benjamin Rush (1745–1813), Isaac Ray (1807–1881), and Thomas Kirkbride (1809–1883) in the United States. The THERAPEUTIC COMMUNITY of today has its roots in this movement. Also called **moral treatment.**

moratorium *n.* in ERIKSON'S EIGHT STAGES OF DEVELOPMENT, the experimental period of adolescence in which, during the task of discovering who one is as an individual separate from family of origin and as part of the broader social context,

young people try out alternative roles before making permanent commitments to an IDENTITY. See IDENTITY VERSUS IDENTITY CONFUSION.

morbid *adj.* unhealthy, diseased, or otherwise abnormal.

morbidity *n.* a pathological (diseased) condition or state, either organic or functional.

Moro reflex a reflex in which a newborn infant, when startled, throws out the arms, extends the fingers, and quickly brings the arms back together as if clutching or embracing. In normal, healthy babies, the Moro reflex disappears during the 1st year. See also STARTLE RESPONSE. [Ernst **Moro** (1874–1951), German physician]

morpheme *n.* in linguistic analysis, a unit of meaning that cannot be analyzed into smaller such units. For example, the word *books* is composed of two morphemes, *book* and the suffix *-s* signifying a plural noun. **—morphemic** *adj.*

morphine *n.* the primary active ingredient in OPIUM, first synthesized in 1806 and widely used as an analgesic and sedative. Prolonged administration or abuse can lead to dependence and to withdrawal symptoms on cessation.

morphology *n.* **1.** the branch of biology concerned with the forms and structures of organisms. **2.** the branch of linguistics that investigates the form and structure of words. It is particularly concerned with the regular patterns of word formation in a language. With SYNTAX, morphology is one of the two traditional subdivisions of GRAMMAR. **—morphological** *adj.*

Morris water maze a device used to test animal spatial learning, consisting of a water-filled tank with a platform hidden underwater. An an-

M

imal is placed in the water and can escape only by finding and climbing on the hidden platform. Typically a variety of external cues are provided for spatial reference. [devised in 1981 by Richard G. M. **Morris**, British neuroscientist]

mortality *n.* the death rate in a population.

motherese *n.* the distinctive form of speech used by parents and other caregivers when speaking to infants and young children. It is characterized by grammatically simple and phonologically clear utterances, often delivered in a high-pitched sing-song intonation.

mother surrogate a substitute for an individual's biological mother (e.g., a sister, grandmother, stepmother, or adoptive mother), who assumes the responsibilities of that person and may function as a role model and significant attachment figure. Also called **mother figure**; **surrogate mother**.

motion aftereffect the perception that a stationary object or scene moves following prolonged fixation of a moving stimulus. The illusory movement is in the opposite direction to the movement of the stimulus that induced the effect. The best known example is the **waterfall illusion**, produced by watching a waterfall for a period and then shifting one's gaze to the stationary surrounding scenery; the stationary objects appear to move upward.

motion parallax the interrelated movements of elements in a scene that can occur when the observer moves relative to the scene. Motion parallax is a DEPTH CUE.

motivated forgetting a memory lapse motivated by a desire to avoid a disagreeable recollection. It is one of the cognitive mechanisms that has been suggested as a cause of de-

layed memories of childhood trauma.

motivation *n.* the impetus that gives purpose or direction to human or animal behavior and operates at a conscious or unconscious level. Motives are frequently divided into (a) physiological, primary, or organic motives, such as hunger, thirst, and need for sleep, and (b) personal, social, or secondary motives, such as affiliation, competition, and individual interests and goals. An important distinction must also be drawn between internal motivating forces and external factors, such as rewards or punishments, that can encourage or discourage certain behaviors. See EXTRINSIC MOTIVATION; INTRINSIC MOTIVATION. —**motivate** *vb.* —**motivated** *adj.* —**motivational** *adj.*

motivators *pl. n.* in the TWO-FACTOR THEORY OF WORK MOTIVATION, those aspects of the working situation that can increase satisfaction and motivation. Motivators involve the work itself rather than the work context and are increased by means of job ENRICHMENT and expansion of responsibilities. Compare HYGIENE FACTORS.

motive *n.* **1.** a specific physiological or psychological state of arousal that directs an organism's energies toward a goal. See MOTIVATION. **2.** a reason offered as an explanation for or cause of an individual's behavior.

motor *adj.* involving, producing, or referring to muscular movements.

motor aphasia another name for BROCA'S APHASIA.

motor cortex the region of the frontal lobe of the brain responsible for the control of voluntary movement. It is divided into two parts. The **primary motor cortex**, or **motor area**, is the main source of neurons in the corticospinal tract (see VENTROMEDIAL PATHWAY). The **sec-**

ondary (or **nonprimary**) **motor cortex**, made up of the PREMOTOR AREA and the SUPPLEMENTARY MOTOR AREA, is specialized for planning upcoming movements and learning new movements. Also called **motor strip**.

motor development the changes in motor skills that occur over an entire life span, which reflect the development of muscular coordination and control and are also affected by personal characteristics, the environment, and interactions of these two factors.

motor neuron a neuron whose axon connects directly to muscle fibers. There are two types: **lower motor neurons** (or **alpha motor neurons**), which are responsible for muscle contraction; and **upper motor neurons** (or **gamma motor neurons**), which modulate the sensitivity of MUSCLE SPINDLES, thus influencing activity of the lower motor neurons. Also called **motoneuron**.

motor program a stored representation, resulting from motor planning and refined through practice, that is used to produce a coordinated movement. Motor programs store the accumulated experience underlying skill at a task.

motor strip see MOTOR CORTEX.

motor system the complex of skeletal muscles, neural connections with muscle tissues, and structures of the central nervous system associated with motor functions.

motor unit a group of muscle fibers that respond collectively and simultaneously because they are connected by nerve endings to a single motor neuron.

mourning *n.* the process of feeling or expressing grief following the death of a loved one, or the period during which this occurs. It typically involves feelings of apathy and dejection, loss of interest in the outside world, and diminution in activity and initiative. These reactions are similar to depression, but are less persistent and are not considered pathological. See also BEREAVEMENT.

Mozart effect a temporary increase in the performance of research participants on tasks involving SPATIAL-TEMPORAL REASONING after listening to the music of Austrian composer Wolfgang Amadeus Mozart (1756-1791). More generally, the term refers to the possibility that listening to music enhances inherent cognitive functioning. Apart from the neurological research on this effect, some experts propose an AROUSAL THEORY perspective, such that listening to music heightens emotional levels that correspond to higher performance on intelligence tests. The notion of the Mozart effect has entered into popular culture to carry the as-yet-unsupported suggestion that early childhood exposure to certain types of music has a beneficial effect on mental development.

MRI abbreviation for MAGNETIC RESONANCE IMAGING.

mRNA abbreviation for MESSENGER RNA.

MS abbreviation for MULTIPLE SCLEROSIS.

Müller cell an elongated nonneuronal central nervous system cell (GLIA) that traverses and supports all the layers of the retina, collecting light and directing it toward the PHOTORECEPTORS. A component of the INNER NUCLEAR LAYER, these cells were originally called **Müller fibers** because of their thin, stretched shape. [Heinrich **Müller** (1820–1864), German anatomist]

Müllerian duct either of a pair of

ducts that occur in a mammalian embryo and develop into female reproductive structures (fallopian tubes, uterus, and upper vagina) if testes are not present in the embryo. Compare WOLFFIAN DUCT. [Johannes **Müller** (1801–1858), German anatomist]

Müller-Lyer illusion a GEOMETRIC ILLUSION in which a difference is perceived in the length of a line depending upon whether arrowheads at either end are pointing toward each other or away from each other. [first described in 1889 by Franz **Müller-Lyer** (1857–1916), German psychiatrist]

multicollinearity *n.* in MULTIPLE REGRESSION, a state that occurs when the INDEPENDENT (PREDICTOR) VARIABLES are extremely highly interrelated, making it difficult to determine separate effects on the DEPENDENT VARIABLE.

multicultural therapy any form of psychotherapy that takes into account not only the increasing racial and ethnic diversity of clients in many countries but also diversity in spirituality, sexual orientation, ability and disability, and social class and economics; the potential cultural bias (e.g., racism, sexism) of the practitioner; the history of oppressed and marginalized groups; diversity within diversity; acculturation and issues involving living in two worlds; and the politics of power as they affect clients. **2.** any form of therapy that assesses, understands, and evaluates a client's behavior in the multiplicity of cultural contexts (e.g., ethnic, national, demographic, social, and economic) in which that behavior was learned and is displayed.

multidimensional *adj.* having a number of different dimensions or composed of many aspects: complex. Compare UNIDIMENSIONAL.

multidimensional scaling a scaling method that represents perceived similarities among stimuli by arranging similar stimuli in spatial proximity to one another, while disparate stimuli are represented far apart from one another. Multidimensional scaling is an alternative to FACTOR ANALYSIS for dealing with large multidimensional matrices of data or stimuli.

multidisciplinary approach see INTERDISCIPLINARY APPROACH.

multifactorial *adj.* consisting or arising out of several factors, variables, or causes.

multifactorial inheritance inheritance of a trait, such as height or predisposition to a certain disease, that is determined not by a single gene but by many different genes acting cumulatively. Such traits show continuous, rather than discrete, variation among the members of a given population and are often significantly influenced by environmental factors, such as nutritional status. Also called **polygenic inheritance.**

multi-infarct dementia see VASCULAR DEMENTIA.

multinomial distribution a theoretical probability distribution that describes the distribution of *n* objects sampled at random from a population of *k* kinds of things with regard to the number of each of the kinds that appears in the sample.

multiple baseline design an experimental design in which two or more behaviors are assessed to determine their naturally occurring expression (baseline) and then an intervention or manipulation is applied to one of the behaviors while the others are unaffected. After a period, the manipulation is then applied to the next behavior while the remaining behaviors are unaltered, and so forth until the experimental manipulation has been applied in sequential fashion to all of the behaviors in the design.

multiple correlation coefficient (symbol: R) a numerical index of the degree of relationship between a particular variable (e.g., a dependent variable) and two or more other variables (e.g., independent variables).

multiple-intelligences theory the idea that intelligence is made up of eight distinct categories: linguistic, musical, bodily-kinesthetic, logical-mathematical, spatial, naturalist, intrapersonal, and interpersonal.

multiple personality disorder a former name for DISSOCIATIVE IDENTITY DISORDER.

multiple regression a statistical technique for examining the linear relationship between a continuous DEPENDENT VARIABLE and a set of two or more INDEPENDENT VARIABLES. It is often used to predict the score of individuals on a criterion variable from multiple predictor variables.

multiple sclerosis (MS) a chronic disease of the central nervous system characterized by inflammation and multifocal scarring of the protective MYELIN SHEATH of nerves, which damages and destroys the sheath and the underlying nerve, disrupting neural transmission. Symptoms include visual disturbances, fatigue, weakness, numbness, tremors, difficulties with coordination and balance, and difficulties with speaking. The cause of MS is unknown, but the destruction of myelin may be due to an autoimmune response (see AUTOIMMUNITY).

multipolar neuron a neuron that has many dendrites and a single axon extending from the CELL BODY. Also called **multipolar cell**.

Compare BIPOLAR NEURON; UNIPOLAR NEURON.

multistore model of memory any theory hypothesizing that information can move through and be retained in any of several memory storage systems, usually of a short-term and a long-term variety.

multivariate *adj.* consisting of or otherwise involving two or more variables. For example, a **multivariate analysis** is any statistical technique that simultaneously assesses multiple dependent variables; examples include the MULTIVARIATE ANALYSIS OF VARIANCE and FACTOR ANALYSIS. Compare UNIVARIATE. See also BIVARIATE.

multivariate analysis any of several types of statistical analysis that simultaneously model multiple DEPENDENT VARIABLES.

multivariate analysis of variance (MANOVA) an extension of the ANALYSIS OF VARIANCE (ANOVA) model that identifies the simultaneous effects of the independent variables upon a set of dependent variables.

Munchausen syndrome a severe and chronic form of FACTITIOUS DISORDER characterized by repeated and elaborate fabrication of clinically convincing physical symptoms and a false medical and social history. Other features are recurrent hospitalization and widespread or excessive traveling from place to place (peregrination), and there may be multiple scars from previous (unnecessary) investigative surgery. [Baron Karl Friedrich Hieronymus von **Münchhausen** (1720–1797), German soldier-adventurer famous for his tall tales]

Munchausen syndrome by proxy a psychological disorder in which caregivers fabricate or intentionally cause symptoms in those they are caring for in order to seek

M

and obtain medical investigation or treatment. Typically, the caregiver is a parent, who behaves as if distressed about the child's illness and denies knowing what caused it. Also called **factitious disorder by proxy**.

mundane realism the extent to which an experimental situation resembles a real-life situation or event. This is related to EXPERIMENTAL REALISM, the degree to which experimental procedures elicit valid responses even if the events of the experiment do not resemble ordinary occurrences.

muscarinic receptor (**mAChR**) a type of ACETYLCHOLINE RECEPTOR that responds to the alkaloid muscarine as well as to acetylcholine. Muscarinic receptors are found in smooth muscle, cardiac muscle, endocrine glands, and the central nervous system and mediate chiefly the inhibitory activities of acetylcholine. Compare NICOTINIC RECEPTOR.

muscle fiber a microscopic strand of muscle tissue that functions as a molecular machine converting chemical energy into force. Thousands of muscle fibers are linked by connective tissue into a muscle. Each fiber is, in turn, composed of millions of longitudinally aligned protein filaments. It is the interaction of **actin** and **myosin** protein molecules (sometimes together referred to as **actomyosin**) in these filaments that creates muscle CONTRACTION.

muscle spindle a receptor that lies within skeletal muscle, parallel to the main contractile MUSCLE FIBERS, and sends impulses to the central nervous system when the muscle is stretched.

music therapy the use of music as an adjunct to the treatment or rehabilitation of individuals to enhance their psychological, physical, cognitive, or social functioning.

mutation *n.* a permanent change in the genetic material of an organism. It may consist of an alteration to the number or arrangement of chromosomes (a chromosomal mutation) or a change in the composition of DNA, generally affecting only one or a few bases in a particular gene (a point mutation). A mutation occurring in a body cell (i.e., a somatic mutation) cannot be inherited, whereas a mutation in a reproductive cell producing ova or spermatozoa (i.e., a germ-line mutation) can be transmitted to that individual's offspring.

mutism *n.* lack or absence of speaking. The condition may result from neurological damage or disorder, a structural defect in the organs necessary for speech, congenital or early deafness in which an individual's failure to hear spoken words inhibits the development of speech, psychological disorders (e.g., CONVERSION DISORDER, CATATONIC SCHIZOPHRENIA), or severe emotional disturbance (e.g., extreme anger). The condition may also be voluntary, as in monastic vows of silence.

mutualism *n.* an interaction in which two species live together in close association, to the mutual benefit of both species. See also SYMBIOSIS.

myasthenia gravis an autoimmune disorder (see AUTOIMMUNITY) in which the body produces antibodies against ACETYLCHOLINE RECEPTORS, causing faulty transmission of nerve impulses at neuromuscular junctions. Affected muscles—initially those of the face and neck—are easily fatigued and may become paralyzed temporarily (e.g., muscles involved in eating may fail to function normally toward the end of a meal, or speech may become slurred after a period of talking). The disease is progressive, eventually affecting muscles throughout the body.

myelin *n.* the substance that forms the insulating MYELIN SHEATH around the axons of many neurons. It consists mainly of phospholipids, with additional **myelin proteins**, and accounts for the whitish color of WHITE MATTER. **Myelinated fibers** conduct nerve impulses much faster than nonmyelinated fibers (see SALTATION).

myelin sheath the insulating layer around many axons that increases the speed of conduction of nerve impulses. It consists of MYELIN and is laid down by GLIA, which wrap themselves around adjacent axons in a process called **myelination**. The myelin sheath is interrupted by small gaps, called NODES OF RANVIER, which are spaced about every millimeter along the axon.

Myers–Briggs Type Indicator (**MBTI**) a personality test designed to classify individuals according to their expressed choices between contrasting alternatives in certain categories of traits. The categories are (a) Extraversion–Introversion, (b) Sensing–Intuition, (c) Thinking–Feeling, and (d) Judging–Perceiving. The participant is assigned a type (e.g., INTJ or ESFP) according to the pattern of choices made. The test has little credibility among research psychologists but is widely used in educational counseling and human resource management to help improve work and personal relationships, increase productivity, and identify interpersonal communication preferences and skills. [Isabel Briggs **Myers** (1897–1980), U.S. personologist, and her mother Katharine Cook **Briggs** (1875–1968)]

myopia *n.* nearsightedness, a refractive error due to an abnormally long eye: The retinal image of distant objects is blurred because the focal point of one or both eyes lies in front of, rather than on, the retina. Compare HYPEROPIA.

myosin *n.* see MUSCLE FIBER.

myotonia *n.* increased tone and contractility of a muscle, with slow or delayed relaxation. —**myotonic** *adj.*

myriachit *n.* a CULTURE-BOUND SYNDROME found in Siberian populations. Similar to LATAH, it is characterized by indiscriminate, apparently uncontrolled imitations of the actions of other people encountered by the individual. See also IMU.

MZ twins abbreviation for MONOZYGOTIC TWINS.

M

Nn

n-Ach abbreviation for NEED FOR ACHIEVEMENT.

nAchR abbreviation for NICOTINIC RECEPTOR.

n-Aff abbreviation for NEED FOR AFFILIATION.

naive participant a participant who has not previously participated in a particular research study and has not been made aware of the experimenter's hypothesis. Compare CONFEDERATE.

naloxone *n.* a morphine-derived opioid ANTAGONIST that prevents the binding of opioids to OPIOID RECEPTORS. Like other opioid antagonists, it can quickly reverse the effects of opioid overdose and is useful in emergency settings to reverse respiratory depression. U.S. trade name: **Narcan**.

naltrexone *n.* an opioid ANTAGONIST that, like the shorter acting naloxone, prevents the binding of opioid agonists to OPIOID RECEPTORS. If naltrexone is taken prior to use of opiate drugs, it will prevent their reinforcing effects, and can therefore be used for the management of opioid dependence in individuals desiring abstinence. Naltrexone is also appropriate as an adjunctive treatment in the management of alcoholism. U.S. trade name: **ReVia**.

narcissism *n.* excessive self-love or egocentrism. See NARCISSISTIC PERSONALITY DISORDER. **—narcissist** *n.* **—narcissistic** *adj.*

narcissistic personality disor-

der a personality disorder with the following characteristics: (a) a long-standing pattern of grandiose self-importance and exaggerated sense of talent and achievements; (b) fantasies of unlimited sex, power, brilliance, or beauty; (c) an exhibitionistic need for attention and admiration; (d) either cool indifference or feelings of rage, humiliation, or emptiness as a response to criticism, indifference, or defeat; and (e) various interpersonal disturbances, such as feeling entitled to special favors, taking advantage of others, and inability to empathize with the feelings of others.

narcolepsy *n.* a disorder consisting of excessive daytime sleepiness accompanied by brief "attacks" of sleep during waking hours. These sleep attacks may occur at any time or during any activity, including in potentially dangerous situations, such as driving an automobile. The attacks are marked by immediate entry into REM SLEEP without going through the usual initial stages of sleep. **—narcoleptic** *adj.*

narcotic 1. *n.* originally, any drug that induces a state of stupor or insensibility (narcosis). More recently, the term referred to strong OPIOIDS used clinically for pain relief but this usage is now considered imprecise and pejorative; the term is still sometimes used in legal contexts to refer to a wide variety of abused substances. **2.** *adj.* of or relating to narcotics or narcosis.

narrative therapy treatment for individuals, couples, or families that helps clients reinterpret and rewrite their life events into true but more life-enhancing narratives or stories. Narrative therapy posits that individuals are primarily meaning-making beings who are the linguistic authors of their lives and who can reauthor these stories by learning to deconstruct them, by seeing patterns in their ways of interpreting life events or problems, and by reconstruing problems or events in a more helpful light. See also CONSTRUCTIVISM.

nativism *n.* **1.** the doctrine that the mind has certain innate structures and that experience plays a limited role in the creation of knowledge. Compare CONSTRUCTIVISM; EMPIRICISM. **2.** the doctrine that mental and behavioral traits are largely determined by hereditary, rather than environmental, factors. See NATURE–NURTURE. **—nativist** *adj., n.* **—nativistic** *adj.*

natural category see BASIC-LEVEL CATEGORY.

natural childbirth a method of labor and child delivery that does not include (or is designed to eliminate) the need for medical interventions, such as anesthetics. The mother receives preparatory education in such areas as breathing and relaxation coordination, exercise of the muscles involved in labor and delivery, and postural positions that make labor more comfortable and allow for conscious participation in delivery.

natural experiment a natural event, often a natural disaster (e.g., a flood, tornado, or volcanic eruption), that is treated as an experimental condition to be compared to some control condition. However, since natural events cannot be manipulated or prearranged, natural experiments are in fact not true experiments at all but rather a type of NONEXPERIMENTAL RESEARCH.

naturalism *n.* in philosophy, the doctrine that reality consists solely of natural objects and that therefore the methods of natural science offer the only reliable means to knowledge and understanding of reality. Naturalism is closely related to MATERIALISM and explicitly opposes any form of supernaturalism positing the existence of realities beyond the natural and material world. See also POSITIVISM. **—naturalistic** *adj.*

naturalistic observation data collection in a field setting, usually without laboratory controls or manipulation of variables. These procedures are usually carried out by a trained observer, who watches and records the everyday behavior of participants in their natural environments. Examples of naturalistic observation include an ethologist's study of the behavior of chimpanzees and an anthropologist's observation of playing children. See OBSERVATIONAL STUDY.

natural killer cell a type of LYMPHOCYTE that destroys infected or cancerous cells. Unlike the B lymphocytes and T lymphocytes, natural killer cells do not require the target cells to display on their surface foreign ANTIGENS combined with host histocompatibility proteins.

natural selection the process by which such forces as competition, disease, and climate tend to eliminate individuals who are less well adapted to a particular environment and favor the survival and reproduction of better adapted individuals. Hence, over successive generations, the nature of the population changes. This is the fundamental mechanism driving the evolution of living organisms and the emergence of new species, as originally pro-

N

posed independently by British naturalists Charles Darwin (1809–1882) and Alfred Russel Wallace (1823–1913). See EVOLUTION. Compare ARTIFICIAL SELECTION.

nature *n.* **1.** the phenomena of the natural world, including plants, animals, and physical features, as opposed to human beings and their creations. **2.** the innate, presumably genetically determined, characteristics and behaviors of an individual. In psychology, those characteristics most often and traditionally associated with nature are temperament, body type, and personality. Compare NURTURE. —**natural** *adj.*

nature–nurture the dispute over the relative contributions of hereditary and constitutional factors (NATURE) and environmental factors (NURTURE) to the development of the individual. Nativists emphasize the role of heredity, whereas environmentalists emphasize sociocultural and ecological factors, including family attitudes, child-rearing practices, and economic status. Most scientists now accept that there is a close interaction between hereditary and environmental factors in the ontogeny of behavior (see EPIGENESIS).

navigation *n.* the mechanisms used by an organism to find its way through the environment, for example, to a MIGRATION site or to its home site. A variety of cues have been documented in nonhuman animals, including using the sun or stars as a compass, magnetic lines, olfactory cues, visual cues (e.g., rivers or coastlines), and wind-sheer effects from air masses crossing mountain ranges. See also HOMING.

nay-saying *n.* answering questions negatively regardless of their content, which can distort the results of surveys, questionnaires, and similar instruments. Compare YEA-SAYING.

NE abbreviation for NOREPINE-PHRINE.

near-death experience (NDE) an image, perception, event, interaction, or feeling (or a combination of any of these) reported by some people after a life-threatening episode. Typical features include a sense of separation from the body, often accompanied by the ability to look down on the situation; a peaceful and pleasant state of mind; and an entering into the light, sometimes following an interaction with a spiritual being. There is continuing controversy regarding the existence, cause, and nature of NDEs.

nearsightedness *n.* see MYOPIA.

Necker cube a line drawing of a cube in which all angles and sides can be seen, as if it were transparent. It is an AMBIGUOUS FIGURE whose three-dimensionality fluctuates when viewed for a prolonged period of time. [Louis Albert **Necker** (1730–1804), Swiss crystallographer]

need *n.* a condition of tension in an organism resulting from deprivation of something required for survival, well-being, or personal fulfillment.

need for achievement (n-Ach) a strong desire to accomplish goals and attain a high standard of performance and personal fulfillment. People with a high need for achievement often undertake tasks in which there is a reasonable probability of success and avoid tasks that are either too easy (because of lack of challenge) or too difficult (because of fear of failure).

need for affiliation (n-Aff) a strong desire to socialize and be part of a group. People with a high need for affiliation often seek the approval and acceptance of others.

need for cognition a personality trait reflecting a person's tendency to enjoy engaging in extensive cognitive activity. This trait primarily reflects a person's motivation to engage in cognitive activity rather than his or her actual ability to do so. Individuals high in need for cognition tend to develop attitudes or take action based on thoughtful evaluation of information.

need to belong the motivation to be a part of relationships, belong to groups, and to be viewed positively by others.

negative affect the internal feeling state (AFFECT) that occurs when one has failed to achieve a goal or to avoid a threat or when one is not satisfied with the current state of affairs. The tendency to experience such states is known as **negative affectivity**.

negative correlation a relationship between two variables in which the value of one variable increases while the value of the other variable decreases. For example, in a study about babies crying and being held, the discovery that those who are held more tend to cry less is a negative correlation. See also CORRELATION COEFFICIENT.

negative feedback 1. an arrangement whereby some of the output of a system, whether mechanical or biological, is fed back to reduce the effect of input signals. Such systems, which measure the deviation from a desired state and apply a correction, are important in achieving HOMEOSTASIS, whereas systems employing POSITIVE FEEDBACK tend to amplify small deviations and become highly unstable. **2.** in social psychology, nonconstructive criticism, disapproval, and other negative information received by a person in response to his or her performance.

negative priming the ability of a preceding stimulus to inhibit the response to a subsequent stimulus. This is measured by the detectability

of the second stimulus or the time taken to make a response to the second stimulus. The most striking examples occur when the participant is instructed to ignore a feature of the first stimulus (e.g., its color) and then to attend to that same feature in the second stimulus. PRIMING effects are usually facilitative.

negative punishment punishment that results because some stimulus or circumstance is removed as a consequence of a response. For example, if a response results in a subtraction of money from an accumulating account, and the response becomes less likely as a result of this experience, then negative punishment has occurred. Compare POSITIVE PUNISHMENT.

negative reinforcement the removal, prevention, or postponement of an aversive stimulus as a consequence of a response, which, in turn, increases the probability of that response. Compare POSITIVE REINFORCEMENT.

negative schizophrenia a form of schizophrenia characterized by a predomination of NEGATIVE SYMPTOMS, suggesting deficiency or absence of behavior normally present in a person's repertoire, as shown in apathy, blunted affect, emotional withdrawal, poor rapport, and lack of spontaneity. Compare POSITIVE SCHIZOPHRENIA.

negative skew see SKEWNESS.

negative-state-relief model the hypothesis that helping behavior is used by some people in stressful situations and periods of boredom and inactivity to avoid or escape negative moods.

negative symptom a deficit in the ability to perform the normal functions of living—logical thinking, self-care, social interaction, planning, initiating, and carrying

N

through constructive actions, and so forth—as shown in apathy, blunted affect, emotional withdrawal, poor rapport, and lack of spontaneity. In schizophrenia, a predominance of negative symptoms is often associated with a poor prognosis. Compare POSITIVE SYMPTOM. See NEGATIVE SCHIZOPHRENIA.

negative transfer a process in which previous learning obstructs or interferes with present learning. For instance, tennis players who learn racquetball must often unlearn their tendency to take huge, muscular swings with the shoulder and upper arm. See also TRANSFER OF TRAINING. Compare POSITIVE TRANSFER.

negative triad see COGNITIVE TRIAD.

negativism *n.* an attitude characterized by persistent resistance to the suggestions of others (passive negativism) or the tendency to act in ways that are contrary to the expectations, requests, or commands of others (active negativism), typically without any identifiable reason for opposition. In young children and adolescents, such reactions may be considered a healthy expression of self-assertion. Negativism may also be associated with a number of disorders (extreme negativism is a feature of CATATONIC SCHIZOPHRENIA). See also OPPOSITIONAL DEFIANT DISORDER; PASSIVE-AGGRESSIVE PERSONALITY DISORDER. —**negativistic** *adj.*

neglect *n.* **1.** failure to provide for the basic needs of a person in one's care. The neglect may be emotional (e.g., rejection or apathy), material (e.g., withholding food or clothing), or service-oriented (e.g., depriving of education or medical attention). See also MALTREATMENT. **2.** a syndrome characterized by lack of awareness of a specific area or side of the body caused by a brain injury. It may involve failure to recognize the area as

belonging to oneself or ignoring the existence of one side of the body or one side of the visual field. Neglect has also been found in auditory, tactile, and proprioceptive tasks.

negotiation *n.* a reciprocal communication process in which two or more parties to a dispute examine specific issues, explain their positions, and exchange offers and counteroffers in an attempt to identify a solution or outcome that is acceptable to all parties. —**negotiate** *vb.*

neobehaviorism *n.* an approach to psychology that emphasized the development of comprehensive theories and frameworks of behavior, such as those of U.S. psychologists Clark L. Hull (1884–1952) and Edward C. Tolman (1886–1959), through empirical observation of behavior and the use of consciousness and mental events as explanatory devices. It thus contrasts with classical BEHAVIORISM, which was concerned with freeing psychology of mentalistic concepts and explanations. See also RADICAL BEHAVIORISM. —**neobehaviorist** *adj., n.*

neocortex *n.* regions of the CEREBRAL CORTEX that are the most recently evolved and contain six main layers of cells. Neocortex, which comprises the majority of human cerebral cortex, includes the primary sensory and motor cortex and association cortex. Compare ALLOCORTEX. —**neocortical** *adj.*

neodissociative theory a theory that explains the paradoxical phenomena of hypnosis as a result of divided consciousness. For example, hypnotic analgesia can produce subjectively reported relief from pain while physiological measures indicate that pain is still being registered.

neo-Freudian 1. *adj.* denoting an approach that derives from the

CLASSICAL PSYCHOANALYSIS of Austrian psychiatrist Sigmund Freud (1856–1939), but with modifications and revisions that typically emphasize social and interpersonal elements over biological instincts. The term is not usually applied to the approaches of Freud's contemporaries, such as Austrian psychiatrist Alfred Adler (1870–1937) and Swiss psychiatrist Carl Jung (1875–1961), who broke away from his school quite early. German-born U.S. psychologist Erik Erikson (1902–1994), German-born U.S. psychoanalyst Erich Fromm (1900–1980), German-born U.S. psychoanalyst Karen Horney (1885–1952), and U.S. psychiatrist Harry Stack Sullivan (1892–1949) are considered to be among the most influential neo-Freudian theorists and practitioners. **2.** *n.* an analyst or theoretician who adopts such an approach.

neologism *n.* a recently coined word or expression. In a psychopathological context neologisms, whose origins and meanings are usually nonsensical and unrecognizable (e.g., "klipno" for watch), are typically associated with APHASIA or SCHIZOPHRENIA. —**neologistic** *adj.*

neonate *n.* a newborn human or nonhuman animal. Human infants born after the normal gestational period of 36 weeks are known as full-term neonates; infants born prematurely before the end of this period are known as preterm neonates (or, colloquially, as "preemies").

neonativism *n.* the belief that much cognitive knowledge, such as OBJECT PERMANENCE and certain aspects of language, is innate, requiring little in the way of specific experiences to be expressed. Neonativists hold that cognitive development is influenced by biological constraints and that individuals are predisposed to process certain types of information. —**neonativist** *adj.*, *n.*

neoplasm *n.* a new, abnormal growth, that is, a benign or malignant tumor. The term is generally used to specify a malignant tumor (see CANCER). A neoplasm usually grows rapidly by cellular proliferation but generally lacks structural organization. —**neoplastic** *adj.*

nerve *n.* a bundle of AXONS outside the central nervous system (CNS), enclosed in a sheath of connective tissue to form a cordlike structure. Nerves serve to connect the CNS with the tissues and organs of the body. They may be motor, sensory, or mixed (containing axons of both motor and sensory neurons). See CRANIAL NERVE; SPINAL NERVE. Compare TRACT.

nerve cell see NEURON.

nerve growth factor (NGF) an endogenous polypeptide that stimulates the growth and development of neurons in the DORSAL ROOT of each SPINAL NERVE and in the ganglia of the SYMPATHETIC NERVOUS SYSTEM.

nervous breakdown a lay term for an emotional illness or other mental disorder that has a sudden onset, produces acute distress, and significantly interferes with one's functioning.

nervous system the system of NEURONS, NERVES, TRACTS, and associated tissues that, together with the endocrine system, coordinates activities of the organism in response to signals received from the internal and external environments. The nervous system of higher vertebrates is often considered in terms of its divisions, principally the CENTRAL NERVOUS SYSTEM, the PERIPHERAL NERVOUS SYSTEM, and the AUTONOMIC NERVOUS SYSTEM.

N

nesting *n.* in an experimental design, the appearance of the levels of one factor (the **nested factor**) only within a single level of another factor. For example, classrooms are nested within a school because each specific classroom is found only within a single school; similarly, schools are nested within school districts.

neural correlate an association between a physical occurrence in the nervous system and a mental state or event. In the cerebellum, for example, the neural correlate of fear memory is provided by a LONG-TERM POTENTIATION of the excitatory synapses between the PARALLEL FIBERS and the PURKINJE CELLS. The existence of neural correlates suggests potential biological bases for a variety of complex cognitive, emotional, and behavioral phenomena, including consciousness (awareness), perception, learning and memory, judgments and decisions, attitudes, and motivation.

neural Darwinism a biological theory of mind that attempts to explain specific cognitive functions, such as learning or memory, in terms of the selection of particular groups of neuronal structures inside individual brains. This selection of the best adapted structures is placed within the general framework of the Darwinian theory of NATURAL SELECTION. Critics of the theory argue that natural selection cannot apply without reproduction.

neural network 1. a technique for modeling the neural changes in the brain that underlie cognition and perception in which a large number of simple hypothetical neural units are connected to one another. **2.** a form of ARTIFICIAL INTELLIGENCE system used for learning and classifying data. Neural networks are usually abstract structures modeled on a computer and consist of a number of interconnected processing elements (**nodes**), each with a finite number of inputs and outputs. The elements in the network can have a "weight" determining how they process data, which can be adjusted according to experience. In this way, the network can be "trained" to recognize patterns in input data by optimizing the output of the network. The analogy is with the supposed action of neurons in the brain.

neural pathway any route followed by a nerve impulse through central or peripheral nerve fibers of the nervous system. A neural pathway may consist of a simple REFLEX ARC or a complex but specific routing, such as that followed by impulses transmitting a specific wavelength of sound from the CO-CHLEA to the auditory cortex.

neural plasticity the ability of the nervous system to change in response to experience or environmental stimulation. For example, following an injury remaining neurons may adopt certain functions previously performed by those that were damaged, or a change in reactivity of the nervous system and its components may result from constant, successive activations. Also called **neuroplasticity**.

neural quantum theory a theory to explain linear psychophysical functions, which are sometimes obtained instead of the ogival (S-shaped) form, whereby changes in sensation are assumed to occur in discrete steps and not along a continuum, based on the all-or-none law of neural activity. In this context, quantum refers to a functionally distinct unit in the neural mechanisms that mediate sensory experience—that is, a perceptual rather than a physical unit. Also called **quantal hypothesis**; **quantal theory**.

neural synchrony the simultaneous firing or activation of neurons in multiple areas of the brain, particularly in response to the same stimulus. Many motor and higher level cognitive processes (see EXECUTIVE FUNCTIONS) appear to be based on the coordinated interactions of large numbers of neurons that are distributed within and across different specialized brain areas. Additionally, recent research suggests dysfunctions in neural synchrony may be associated with several psychological disorders, including AUTISTIC SPECTRUM DISORDERS.

neural tube a structure formed during early development of an embryo, when folds of the neural plate curl over and fuse. Cells of the neural tube differentiate along its length on the anterior–posterior axis to form swellings that correspond to the future FOREBRAIN, MIDBRAIN, and HINDBRAIN; the posterior part of the tube develops into the spinal cord. See also NEURULATION.

neurite *n.* a projection from the neuronal cell body: an AXON or a DENDRITE. This general term is used especially in relation to developing neurons whose axons and dendrites often are difficult to distinguish from one another.

neuritic plaque see SENILE PLAQUE.

neuroanatomy *n.* the study of the structures and relationships among the various parts of the nervous system. —**neuroanatomist** *n.*

neuroblast *n.* an undifferentiated cell that is capable of developing into a neuron.

neurochemistry *n.* the branch of NEUROSCIENCE that deals with the roles of atoms, molecules, and ions in the functioning of nervous systems.

neurodevelopmental hypothe-
sis a prominent theory stating schizophrenia results from an early brain LESION, either fetal or neonatal, that disrupts normal neurological development and leads to abnormalities and later psychotic symptoms. Consequences of this early disruption appear in childhood and adolescence, prior to the actual onset of schizophrenic symptoms, as subtle differences in motor coordination, cognitive and social functioning, and temperament. Much evidence supports this hypothesis and risk factors operating in early life (e.g., obstetric complications) have been shown to be associated with the later development of schizophrenia.

neurofibrillary tangles twisted strands of abnormal filaments within neurons that are associated with Alzheimer's disease. The filaments form microscopically visible knots or tangles consisting of tau protein, which normally is associated with MICROTUBULES. If the structure of tau is rendered abnormal, the microtubule structure collapses, and the tau protein collects in neurofibrillary tangles.

neurogenesis *n.* the division of nonneuronal cells to produce neurons.

neuroglia *n.* see GLIA. —**neuroglial** *adj.*

neuroglioma *n.* see GLIOMA.

neurohormone *n.* a hormone produced by neural tissue and released into the general circulation

neuroleptic *n.* see ANTIPSYCHOTIC.

neurological evaluation analysis of the data gathered by an examining physician of an individual's mental status and sensory and motor functioning. The examination typically includes assessment of cognition, speech and behavior, orientation and level of alertness, muscular strength and tone, muscle coordination and movement, tendon reflexes, cranial nerves, pain and temperature sensitivity, and discriminative senses.

neurology *n.* a branch of medicine that studies the nervous system in both healthy and diseased states. —**neurological** *adj.*

neuromodulator *n.* a substance that modulates the effectiveness of neurotransmitters by influencing the release of the transmitters or the RECEPTOR response to the transmitter.

neuromuscular junction the junction between a motor neuron and the muscle fiber it innervates. In skeletal muscle, the muscle-cell plasma membrane (sarcolemma) is greatly folded in the region opposite the terminus of a motor axon, forming a motor END PLATE.

neuron (**neurone**) *n.* the basic cellular unit of the nervous system. Each neuron is composed of a CELL BODY; fine, branching extensions (DENDRITES) that receive incoming nerve signals; and a single, long extension (AXON) that conducts nerve impulses to its branching terminal. The axon terminal transmits impulses to other neurons, or to effector organs (e.g., muscles and glands), via junctions called SYNAPSES or neuromuscular junctions. Neurons can be classified according to their function as MOTOR NEURONS, SENSORY NEURONS, or INTERNEURONS. There are various structural types, including UNIPOLAR NEURONS, BIPOLAR NEURONS, and MULTIPOLAR NEURONS. The axons of vertebrate neurons are often surrounded by a MYELIN SHEATH. Also called **nerve cell**. —**neuronal** *adj.*

neuropeptide *n.* any of several short chains of AMINO ACIDS (peptides) that are released by neurons as NEUROTRANSMITTERS or NEUROHORMONES in both the brain and the peripheral nervous system (e.g., endorphin, SUBSTANCE P, hypothalamic RELEASING HORMONES).

neuropharmacology *n.* the scientific study of the effects of drugs on the nervous system. —**neuropharmacological** *adj.* —**neuropharmacologist** *n.*

neurophysiology *n.* a branch of NEUROSCIENCE that is concerned with the normal and abnormal functioning of the nervous system, including the chemical and electrical activities of individual neurons. —**neurophysiological** *adj.* —**neurophysiologist** *n.*

neuropsychological assessment an evaluation of the presence, nature, and extent of brain damage or dysfunction derived from the results of various NEUROPSYCHOLOGICAL TESTS.

neuropsychological test any of various clinical instruments for assessing cognitive impairment, including those measuring memory, language, learning, attention, and visuospatial and visuoconstructive functioning.

neuropsychology *n.* the branch of science that studies the physiological processes of the nervous system and relates them to behavior and cognition. See also CLINICAL NEUROPSYCHOLOGY. —**neuropsychological** *adj.* —**neuropsychologist** *n.*

neuroscience *n.* the scientific study of the nervous system, including NEUROANATOMY, NEUROCHEMISTRY, NEUROLOGY, NEUROPHYSIOLOGY, and NEUROPHARMACOLOGY, and its applications in psychology and psychiatry. See also BEHAVIORAL NEUROSCIENCE; COGNITIVE NEUROSCIENCE.

neurosis *n.* any one of a variety of mental disorders characterized by significant anxiety or other distressing emotional symptoms, such as persistent and irrational fears, obsessive thoughts, compulsive acts, dissociative states, and somatic and depressive reactions. The symptoms do not involve gross personality disorganization, total lack of insight, or loss of contact with reality (compare PSYCHOSIS). In psychoanalysis, neuroses are generally viewed as exaggerated, unconscious methods of coping with internal conflicts and the anxiety they produce. In DSM–IV-TR, most of what used to be called neuroses are now classified as ANXIETY DISORDERS. —**neurotic** *adj.*, *n.*

neurosurgery *n.* surgical procedures performed on the brain, spinal cord, or peripheral nerves for the purpose of restoring functioning or preventing further impairment. See also PSYCHOSURGERY. —**neurosurgeon** *n.* —**neurosurgical** *adj.*

neurotic anxiety in psychoanalytic theory, anxiety that originates in unconscious conflict and is maladaptive in nature: It has a disturbing effect on emotion and behavior and also intensifies resistance to treatment. Neurotic anxiety contrasts with realistic anxiety, about an external danger or threat, and with moral anxiety, which is guilt posited to originate in the superego.

neuroticism *n.* one of the dimensions of the FIVE-FACTOR PERSONALITY MODEL and the BIG FIVE PERSONALITY MODEL, characterized by a chronic level of emotional instability and proneness to psychological distress.

neurotic need in psychoanalytic theory, an excessive drive or demand that may arise out of the strategies individuals use to defend themselves against BASIC ANXIETY. German-born U.S. psychoanalyst Karen D. Horney (1885–1952) enumerated ten neurotic needs: for

affection and approval, for a partner to take over one's life, for restriction of one's life, for power, for exploitation of others, for prestige, for admiration, for achievement, for self-sufficiency and independence, and for perfection.

neurotransmission *n.* the process by which a signal or other activity in a neuron is transferred to an adjacent neuron or other cell (e.g., a skeletal muscle cell). Synaptic transmission, which occurs between two neurons via a SYNAPSE, is largely chemical, by the release and binding of NEUROTRANSMITTER, but it may also be electrical (see ELECTRICAL SYNAPSE).

neurotransmitter *n.* any of a large number of chemicals that can be released by neurons to mediate transmission or inhibition of nerve signals across the junctions (SYNAPSES) between neurons. When triggered by a nerve impulse, the neurotransmitter is released from the terminal button of the AXON, travels across the SYNAPTIC CLEFT, and binds to and reacts with RECEPTOR molecules in the postsynaptic membrane. Neurotransmitters include amines, such as ACETYLCHOLINE, NOREPINEPHRINE, DOPAMINE, and SEROTONIN; and amino acids, such as GAMMA-AMINOBUTYRIC ACID, GLUTAMATE, and GLYCINE.

neurotrophin *n.* any of various proteins that promote the development and survival of specific populations of neurons. Neurotrophins include NERVE GROWTH FACTOR, deficits in the AXONAL TRANSPORT of which have been linked to Alzheimer's disease, and brain-derived neurotrophic factor, which plays a crucial role in cognition, learning, and memory formation by modulating synaptic PLASTICITY. Also called **neurotrophic factor**.

neurulation *n.* the process of de-

N

velopment of the rudimentary nervous system in early embryonic life, including formation of the NEURAL TUBE from the neural plate.

neutral stimulus in PAVLOVIAN CONDITIONING, a stimulus that does not elicit a response of the sort to be measured as an index of conditioning. For example, the sound of a bell has no effect on salivation, therefore it is a neutral stimulus with respect to salivation and a good candidate for conditioning of that response.

Newman–Keuls test a testing procedure used for making post hoc pairwise comparisons among a set of means.

NGF abbreviation for NERVE GROWTH FACTOR.

nicotine *n.* an alkaloid obtained primarily from the tobacco plant (*Nicotiana tabacum*). One of the most widely used psychoactive drugs, nicotine produces multiple pharmacological effects on the central nervous system by activating NICOTINIC RECEPTORS, facilitating the release of several neurotransmitters, particularly dopamine. —**nicotinic** *adj.*

nicotinic receptor (nAchR) a type of ACETYLCHOLINE RECEPTOR that responds to NICOTINE as well as to acetylcholine. Nicotinic receptors mediate chiefly the excitatory activities of acetylcholine, including those at neuromuscular junctions. Compare MUSCARINIC RECEPTOR.

night blindness a visual impairment marked by partial or complete inability to see objects in a dimly lighted environment. Night blindness can be inherited or due to defective DARK ADAPTATION or dietary deficiency of vitamin A.

nightmare *n.* a frightening or otherwise disturbing dream, in which fear, sadness, despair, disgust, or some combination of these forms

the emotional content. Nightmares contain visual imagery and some degree of narrative structure and typically occur during REM SLEEP. The dreamer tends to waken suddenly from a nightmare and is immediately alert and aware of his or her surroundings. The occurrence of frequent nightmares is classified as **nightmare disorder**. Nightmares are also a symptom of POSTTRAUMATIC STRESS DISORDER. —**nightmarish** *adj.*

night terror see SLEEP TERROR DISORDER.

nitric oxide a compound present in numerous body tissues, where it has a variety of functions: In the brain and other parts of the central nervous system it functions as a neurotransmitter or an agent that influences neurotransmitters. In peripheral tissues it is involved in the relaxation of smooth muscle, and thus acts as a vasodilator, a bronchodilator, and as a relaxant of smooth muscle in the penis and clitoris, being involved in erection and other components of the sexual response.

NMDA receptor see GLUTAMATE RECEPTOR.

nociceptor *n.* a sensory RECEPTOR that responds to stimuli that are generally painful or detrimental to the organism.

nocturnal *adj.* active or occurring during the dark period of the daily cycle. Compare DIURNAL.

node *n.* **1.** a point in a graph, tree diagram, or the like at which lines intersect or branch. **2.** a single point or unit in an associative model of memory. Nodes typically represent a single concept or feature, are connected to other nodes (usually representing semantically related concepts and features) by links in an associative network, and may be activated or inhibited to varying degrees, depending on the conditions. —**nodal** *adj.*

node of Ranvier any of successive regularly spaced gaps in the MYELIN SHEATH surrounding an axon. The gaps permit the exchange of ions across the plasma membrane at those points, allowing the nerve impulse to leap from one node to the next in so-called SALTATION along the axon. [Louis A. **Ranvier** (1835–1922), French pathologist]

noise *n.* any unwanted sound or, more generally, any unwanted disturbance (e.g., electrical noise), particularly as it interferes with, obscures, reduces, or otherwise adversely affects the clarity or precision of an ongoing process, such as the communication of a message or signal.

nomenclature *n.* a systematic classification of technical terms used in an art or science.

nominal data numerical values that represent membership in specific categories. For example, the category male could be labeled 0 and the category female labeled 1, and each person within the population of interest (e.g., a particular town) assigned the number corresponding to their sex. Nominal data are similar to CATEGORICAL DATA, and the two terms are often used interchangeably.

nominal scale a sequence of numbers that do not indicate order, magnitude, or a true zero point but rather identify items as belonging to mutually exclusive categories. For example, a nominal scale for the performance of a specific group of people on a particular test might use the number 1 to denote pass and the number 2 to denote fail. Also called **categorical scale**.

nominal stimulus in stimulus–response experiments, the stimulus as defined and presented by the experi-menter. This may be different from the FUNCTIONAL STIMULUS experienced by the organism.

nomothetic *adj.* relating to the formulation of general laws as opposed to the study of the individual case. A **nomothetic approach** involves the study of groups of people or cases for the purpose of discovering those general and universally valid laws or principles that characterize the average person or case. Compare IDIOGRAPHIC.

nonadherence *n.* failure of an individual to follow a prescribed therapeutic regimen. Although nonadherence has traditionally been ascribed to oppositional behavior, it is more likely due to inadequate communication between the practitioner and the individual, physical or cognitive limitations that prevent the patient from following therapeutic recommendations (e.g., language differences between patient and practitioner, physical disabilities), or adverse effects that are not being adequately addressed. A primary aspect of health psychology involves methods of reducing nonadherence and increasing adherence. Also called **noncompliance**.

nonassociative learning a process in which an organism's behavior toward a specific stimulus changes over time in the absence of any evident link (association) to any consequences that would induce such change. Nonassociative learning is thus based on FREQUENCY, while ASSOCIATIVE LEARNING is based on REINFORCEMENT. There are two major forms of nonassociative learning: HABITUATION and SENSITIZATION.

noncentrality parameter a parameter in many probability distributions used in hypothesis testing that has a value different from zero when a sample is obtained from a population whose parameters have values different from those specified by the NULL HYPOTHESIS under test. This parameter is important in determining the POWER of a statistical procedure.

nonconscious *adj.* describing anything that is not available to conscious report. See UNCONSCIOUS.

noncontingent reinforcement the process or circumstances in which a stimulus known to be effective as a REINFORCER is presented independently of any particular behavior.

nondeclarative memory a collection of various forms of memory that operate automatically and accumulate information that is not accessible to conscious recollection. For instance, one can do something faster if one has done it before, even if one cannot recall the earlier performance. Compare DECLARATIVE MEMORY.

nondirectional hypothesis a prediction that one experimental group will differ from another without specification of the expected form of the effect or relationship. For example, a researcher might hypothesize that college students will perform differently from elementary school students on a memory task. If he or she were to predict which group of students will perform better, the statement would be a DIRECTIONAL HYPOTHESIS instead.

nondirectional test see TWO-TAILED TEST.

nondirective therapy see CLIENT-CENTERED THERAPY.

nonequivalent-groups design a NONRANDOMIZED DESIGN in which the responses of a treatment group and a control group are compared on measures collected at the beginning and end of the research.

nonexperimental research research in which the investigator cannot randomly assign units to conditions, cannot control or manipulate the independent variable, and cannot limit the influence of extraneous variables. Examples of nonexperimental research are studies that deal with the responses of large groups to natural disasters or widespread changes in social policy.

nonfluent aphasia see APHASIA.

noninvasive *adj.* **1.** denoting procedures or tests that do not require puncture or incision of the skin or insertion of an instrument or device into the body for diagnosis or treatment. **2.** not capable of spreading from one tissue to another, as in the case of a benign tumor. Compare INVASIVE.

nonlinear *adj.* describing any relationship between two variables (X and Y) that cannot be expressed in the form $Y = a + bX$, where a and b are numerical constants. The relationship therefore does not appear to be a straight line when depicted graphically.

nonnormative *adj.* not conforming to or following the NORM: deviating from a specific standard of comparison for a person or group of people, particularly one determined by cultural ideals of how things ought to be. This general term is used in a variety of contexts, referring for example to such things as socially deviant or otherwise distinct behavior, ordinary life events happening at unusual times (e.g., a 78-year-old man earning his bachelor's degree), or statistical results that do not reflect the standard of a measured group (i.e., values well above or below the mean or some other measure of CENTRAL TENDENCY).

nonparametric statistics statistical tests that do not make assumptions about the distribution of the attribute (or attributes) in the population being tested, such as normality and homogeneity of variance. Compare PARAMETRIC STATISTICS.

nonrandomized design any of a large number of research designs in which sampling units are not assigned to experimental conditions at random.

nonregulatory drive any generalized state of arousal or motivation that serves functions that are unrelated to preserving physiological HOMEOSTASIS and thus not necessary for the physical survival of the individual organism, for example, sex or achievement. Compare REGULATORY DRIVE.

non-REM sleep see NREM SLEEP.

nonsense syllable any three-letter nonword used in learning and memory research to study learning of items that do not already have meaning or associations with other information in memory.

nonshared environment in behavioral genetics analyses, those aspects of an environment that individuals living together (e.g., in a family household) do not share and that therefore cause them to become dissimilar to each other. Examples of nonshared environmental factors include the different friends or teachers that siblings in the same household might have outside of the home. Compare SHARED ENVIRONMENT.

nonverbal communication the act of conveying information without the use of words. Nonverbal communication occurs through facial expressions, gestures, body language, tone of voice, and other physical indications of mood, attitude, approbation, and so forth, some of which may require knowledge of the culture or subculture to understand. In psychotherapy, clients' nonverbal communication can be as important to note as their verbal communication.

nonverbal learning disorder a LEARNING DISORDER that is characterized by limited skills in critical thinking and deficits in processing nonverbal information. This affects a child's academic progress as well as other areas of functioning, which may include social competencies, visual-spatial abilities, motor coordination, and emotional functioning.

nonzero-sum game in GAME THEORY, a situation in which the rewards and costs experienced by all players do not balance (i.e., they add up to less than or more than zero). In such a situation, unlike a ZERO-SUM GAME, one player's gain is not necessarily another player's loss.

nootropic *n.* any of various drugs that are used to enhance cognitive function, usually in the treatment of progressive dementias, such as Alzheimer's disease, but also of cognitive dysfunction due to traumatic brain injury. They do not reverse the course of the dementia, but are reported to slow its progress in mild to moderate forms of the disease. Many of these drugs work by inhibiting the activity of acetylcholinesterase in the central nervous system, thereby counteracting the disruption of CHOLINERGIC neurotransmission.

noradrenergic *adj.* responding to, releasing, or otherwise involving norepinephrine (noradrenaline). For example, a **noradrenergic neuron** is one that employs norepinephrine as a neurotransmitter.

norepinephrine (**NE**) *n.* a catecholamine NEUROTRANSMITTER and hormone produced mainly by brainstem nuclei and in the adrenal medulla. Also called **noradrenaline**.

norm *n.* **1.** a standard or range of values that represents the typical performance of a group or of an individual (of a certain age, for example)

N

against which comparisons can be made. **2.** a conversion of a raw score into a scaled score that is more easily interpretable, such as percentiles or IQ scores. —**normative** *adj.*

normal *adj.* relating to what is considered standard, average, typical, or healthy. This general meaning is applied in a variety of different contexts, including statistics (referring to scores that are within the usual or expected range), biology (referring to the absence of malformation or other pathology), and development (referring to progression and growth that is comparable to those of similar age). The term, however, is most often applied to behavior that conforms to a culturally accepted norm, especially as an indication that a person is mentally healthy and does not have a psychological disorder.

normal distribution a theoretical continuous PROBABILITY DISTRIBUTION that is a function of two parameters: the expected value, μ, and the VARIANCE, σ^2. It is given by

$$(x) = [\exp(-(x - \mu)^2/2\sigma^2)]/\sigma\sqrt{(2\pi)}$$

The normal distribution is the type of distribution expected when the same measurement is taken several times and the variation about the mean value is random. It has certain convenient properties in statistics, and unknown distributions are often assumed to be normal distributions. Also called **Gaussian distribution**.

normality *n.* a broad concept that is roughly the equivalent of MENTAL HEALTH. Although there are no absolutes and there is considerable cultural variation, some flexible psychological and behavioral criteria can be suggested: (a) freedom from incapacitating internal conflicts; (b) the capacity to think and act in an organized and reasonably effective manner; (c) the ability to cope with the ordinary demands and problems

of life; (d) freedom from extreme emotional distress, such as anxiety, despondency, and persistent upset; and (e) the absence of clear-cut symptoms of mental disorder, such as obsessions, phobias, confusion, and disorientation.

normal science a science at the stage of development when it is characterized by a PARADIGM consisting of universal agreement about the nature of the science, its practices, assumptions, and methods, and satisfaction with its empirical progress.

normative *adj.* relating to a NORM: pertaining to a particular standard of comparison for a person or group of people, often as determined by cultural ideals of how things ought to be regarding behavior, achievements or abilities, and other areas. For example, a **normative life event** such as marriage or the birth of a child is one that is expected to occur during a similar period within the life spans of many individuals, and **normative data** reflect group averages with regard to particular variables or factors, such as the scores of females on a specific test or the language skills of 10-year-olds.

normative influence see SOCIAL PRESSURE.

norm-referenced testing an approach to testing based on a comparison of one person's performance with that of a specifically selected norm group on the same test. Norm-referenced testing differentiates among individuals and ranks them on the basis of their performance. For example, a nationally standardized norm-referenced test will indicate how a given person performs compared to the performance of a national sample. See CRITERION-REFERENCED TESTING.

novelty *n.* the quality of being new and unusual. It is one of the major determining factors directing attention. The attraction to novelty has been shown to begin as early as 1 year of age; for example, when infants are shown pictures of visual patterns, they will stare longer at a new pattern than at a pattern they have already seen.

NREM sleep *n*onrapid-*e*ye-*m*ovement sleep: periods of sleep in which dreaming, as indicated by RAPID EYE MOVEMENTS (REM), usually does not occur. During these periods, which occur most frequently in the first hours of sleep, the electroencephalogram shows only minimal activity, and there is little or no change in pulse, respiration, and blood pressure. Also called **non-REM sleep**. Compare REM SLEEP.

nuclear family a family unit consisting of two parents and their dependent children (whether biological or adopted). With various modifications, the nuclear family has been and remains the norm in developed Western societies. Compare EXTENDED FAMILY.

nucleus *n*. (*pl.* **nuclei**) **1.** a large membrane-bound compartment, found in the cells of nonbacterial organisms, that contains the bulk of the cell's genetic material in the form of chromosomes. **2.** in the central nervous system, a mass of CELL BODIES belonging to neurons with the same or related functions. Examples are the amygdaloid nuclei (see AMYGDALA), the basal nuclei (see BASAL GANGLIA), the thalamic nuclei (see THALAMUS), and the NUCLEUS ACCUMBENS. Compare GANGLION.

nucleus accumbens a large mass of cell bodies in the forebrain that receives dopaminergic innervation from the ventral tegmental area in the midbrain and forms part of the LIMBIC SYSTEM. Dopamine release in this region may mediate the rein-forcing qualities of many activities, including drug abuse.

nucleus basalis magno-cellularis see BASAL FOREBRAIN.

nucleus of the solitary tract see SOLITARY NUCLEUS.

null finding the result of an experiment indicating that there is no relationship, or no significant relationship, between variables. Also called **null result**.

null hypothesis (symbol: H_0) the statement that an experiment will find no difference between the experimental and control conditions, that is, no relationship between variables. Statistical tests are applied to experimental results in an attempt to disprove or reject the null hypothesis at a predetermined SIGNIFICANCE LEVEL. See also ALTERNATIVE HYPOTHESIS.

null hypothesis significance testing computation of a test of significance to evaluate the tenability of the NULL HYPOTHESIS. See SIGNIFICANCE TESTING.

nursing *n*. the health care profession that focuses on the protection and promotion of health through the alleviation and treatment of illness, injury, disease, and physical suffering. **Nurses** practice in a variety of contexts, including hospitals, nursing and independent-living homes, schools, workplaces, and community centers, among others.

nurture *n*. the totality of environmental factors that influence the development and behavior of a person, particularly sociocultural and ecological factors such as family attributes, child-rearing practices, and economic status. Compare NATURE. See also NATURE–NURTURE.

nystagmus *n*. involuntary, rapid movement of the eyeballs. The eyeball motion may be rotatory, horizontal, vertical, or a mixture.

N

Oo

obedience *n.* behavior in compliance with a direct command, often one issued by a person in a position of authority. Examples include a child who cleans his or her room when told to do so by a parent and a soldier who follows the orders of a superior officer. Obedience has the potential to be highly destructive and ethically questionable, however, as demonstrated in the BEHAVIORAL STUDY OF OBEDIENCE. **—obedient** *adj.*

obesity *n.* the condition of having excess body fat resulting in overweight, typically defined in terms of weight–height ratio (see BODY MASS INDEX). Although genetic, environmental, and behavioral factors all contribute, overeating may also have psychological or physiological components as well. The consequences of obesity are a matter for concern: It predisposes to heart disease, diabetes, and other serious medical conditions, and obese individuals may develop emotional and psychological problems relating to BODY IMAGE. **—obese** *adj.*

object *n.* the "other," that is, any person or symbolic representation of a person that is not the self and toward whom behavior, cognitions, or affects are directed. The term is sometimes used to refer to nonpersonal phenomena (e.g., an interest might be considered to be an "object") but the other-person connotation is far more typical and central.

object constancy 1. in OBJECT RELATIONS THEORY, the ability of an infant to maintain an attachment which is relatively independent of gratification or frustration, based on a cognitive capacity to conceive of a mother who exists when she is out of sight and who has positive attributes when she is unsatisfying. Thus an infant becomes attached to the mother herself rather than to her tension-reducing ministrations; she comes to exist continuously for the infant and not only during instances of need satisfaction. This investment by an infant in a specific libidinal object indicates that he or she no longer finds people to be interchangeable. **2.** see PERCEPTUAL CONSTANCY.

objectification *n.* see REIFICATION.

objective 1. *adj.* having actual existence in reality, based on observable phenomena. **2.** *adj.* impartial or uninfluenced by personal feelings, interpretations, or prejudices. Compare SUBJECTIVE.

objective self-awareness a reflective state of self-focused attention in which a person evaluates him- or herself and attempts to attain correctness and consistency in beliefs and behaviors. This involves the viewing of oneself as a separate object, acknowledging limitations and the existing disparity between the ideal self and the actual self. Objective self-awareness is often a necessary part of SELF-REGULATION.

objective test a type of assessment instrument consisting of a set of factual items that have specific correct answers, such that no interpretation or personal judgment is required in scoring. A "true or false" test is an example of an objective test. Compare SUBJECTIVE TEST.

objectivity *n.* a quality of a research study such that its hypotheses, choices of variables studied, measurements, techniques of control, and observations are as free from bias as possible. Judgments and interpretations are based on external data rather than on personal factors, such as feelings, beliefs, and experiences. Compare SUBJECTIVITY.

object loss in psychoanalytic theory, the actual loss of a person who has served as a good OBJECT, which precedes INTROJECTION and is involved in separation anxiety. In this perspective adult GRIEF and MOURNING are related to object loss and separation anxiety in infancy and childhood, which often intensifies and complicates the grief reaction.

object permanence knowledge of the continued existence of objects even when they are not directly perceived. In cognitive development, milestones that indicate the acquisition of object permanence include reaching for and retrieving a covered object (about 8 months), retrieving an object at location B even though it was previously hidden several times at location A (the A-not-B task, about 12 months), and removing a series of covers to retrieve an object, even though the infant only witnessed the object being hidden under the outermost cover (invisible displacement, about 18 months).

object play play that involves the manipulation of items in the environment, such as banging toys together, throwing them around, or arranging them in specific configurations. It is one of three traditionally identified basic types of play (the others being LOCOMOTOR PLAY and SOCIAL PLAY).

object relations theory any psychoanalytically based theory that views the need to relate to OBJECTS as more central to personality organization and motivation than the vicissitudes of the INSTINCTS. These theories developed from and in reaction to classic Freudian theories of psychodynamics. Some theories view the personality as organized in terms of a complex world of internal object representations and their relationships with each other, for example, the approaches of Austrian-born British psychoanalyst Melanie Klein (1882–1960) and British psychoanalyst W. Ronald D. Fairbairn (1889–1964).

oblique rotation see FACTOR ROTATION.

observation *n.* the careful, close examination of an object, process, or other phenomenon for the purpose of collecting data about it or drawing conclusions. —**observational** *adj.*

observational learning the acquisition of information, skills, or behavior through watching the performance of others.

observational method the scientific method in which observers are trained to watch and record behavior, events, or processes as precisely and completely as possible without personal bias or interpretation.

observational study a study in which the experimenter passively observes the behavior of the participants without any attempt at intervention or manipulation of the behaviors being observed. Such studies typically involve observation of cases under naturalistic conditions rather than the random assignment of cases to experimental conditions.

observer bias any expectations, beliefs, or personal preferences of a researcher that unintentionally in-

O

fluence his or her observations during an OBSERVATIONAL STUDY. See EXPERIMENTER EFFECT.

obsession *n.* a persistent thought, idea, image, or impulse that is experienced as intrusive and inappropriate and results in marked anxiety, distress, or discomfort. Common obsessions include repeated thoughts about contamination, a need to have things in a particular order or sequence, repeated doubts, aggressive or horrific impulses, and sexual imagery. Obsessions can be distinguished from excessive worries about everyday occurrences in that they are not concerned with real-life problems. The response to an obsession is often an effort to ignore or suppress the thought or impulse or to neutralize it by a COMPULSION. See OBSESSIVE-COMPULSIVE DISORDER. **—obsessional** *adj.* **—obsessive** *adj.*

obsessive-compulsive disorder (**OCD**) an ANXIETY DISORDER characterized by recurrent intrusive thoughts (OBSESSIONS) that prompt the performance of neutralizing rituals (COMPULSIONS). Typical obsessions involve themes of contamination, dirt, or illness (fearing that one will contract or transmit a disease) and doubts about the performance of certain actions (e.g., an excessive preoccupation that one has neglected to turn off a home appliance). Common compulsive behaviors include repetitive cleaning or washing, checking, ordering, repeating, and hoarding. The obsessions and compulsions—which are recognized by the individual as excessive or unreasonable—are time consuming (more than one hour per day), cause significant distress, or interfere with the individual's functioning.

obsessive-compulsive personality disorder a personality disorder characterized by an extreme need for perfection, an excessive orderliness, an inability to compromise, and an exaggerated sense of responsibility.

obtrusive measure any method of obtaining measurements or observations in which the participants are aware that a measurement is being made. Compare UNOBTRUSIVE MEASURE.

Occam's razor (Ockham's razor) the maxim that, given a choice between two hypotheses, the one involving the fewer assumptions should be preferred. See also LAW OF PARSIMONY. [William of **Occam** or **Ockham** (c. 1285–1347), English Franciscan monk and Scholastic philosopher]

occipital lobe the most posterior (rearward) subdivision of each cerebral hemisphere, roughly shaped like a pyramid and lying under the skull's occipital bone. It is associated with vision, containing the several VISUAL AREAS that receive and process information regarding visual stimuli, being involved in the basic functions (e.g., visual acuity, contrast sensitivity, and perception of color, form, and motion) as well as the higher level ones (e.g., figure-ground segregation based on textural cues).

occlusion *n.* obstruction or closure, for example of an artery. **—occlusive** *adj.*

occupational psychology see INDUSTRIAL AND ORGANIZATIONAL PSYCHOLOGY.

occupational therapy (OT) a rehabilitative process that uses purposeful tasks and activities to improve health; prevent injury or disability; enhance quality of life; and develop, sustain, or restore the highest possible level of independence of individuals who have been injured or who have an illness, impairment, or other mental or

O

physical disability or disorder. OT involves assessment of an individual's ability to perform ACTIVITIES OF DAILY LIVING independently, the development and implementation of a customized treatment program, and recommendations for adaptive modifications in home and work environments as well as training in the use of appropriate assistive devices.

OCD abbreviation for OBSESSIVE-COMPULSIVE DISORDER.

ocular dominance column a vertical slab of STRIATE CORTEX in which the neurons are preferentially responsive to stimulation through one of the two eyes. It is important for binocular vision. Ocular dominance columns for each eye alternate in a regular pattern, so that an electrode inserted tangentially to the cortical surface encounters neurons that are responsive to stimulation through first the IPSILATERAL eye, then the CONTRALATERAL eye, then back to the ipsilateral eye. Compare ORIENTATION COLUMN.

oculomotor nerve the third CRANIAL NERVE, which innervates most of the muscles associated with movement and accommodation of the eye and constriction of the pupil.

Oedipus complex in psychoanalytic theory, the erotic feelings of the son toward the mother, accompanied by rivalry and hostility toward the father, during the PHALLIC STAGE of development. The corresponding relationship between the daughter and father is referred to as the female Oedipus complex. Austrian psychiatrist Sigmund Freud (1856–1939) saw the Oedipus complex as the basis for NEUROSIS when it is not adequately resolved by the boy's fear of castration and gradual IDENTIFICATION with the father. The female Oedipus complex is posited to be resolved by the threat of losing the mother's love and by finding

fulfillment in the feminine role. Contemporary psychoanalytic thought has decentralized the importance of the Oedipus complex and has largely modified the classical theory by emphasizing the earlier, primal relationship between child and mother. See also CASTRATION COMPLEX.

off-label *adj.* denoting or relating to the clinical use of a drug for a purpose that has not been approved by the U.S. Food and Drug Administration.

off response (OFF response) the depolarization of a neuron in the visual system that occurs in response to light decrement. Neurons with off responses in the center of their receptive fields are often called **off cells**. Compare ON RESPONSE.

ogive *n.* the somewhat flattened S-shaped curve typically obtained by graphing a cumulative FREQUENCY DISTRIBUTION.

oldest old see ADULTHOOD.

old-old *adj.* see ADULTHOOD.

olfaction *n.* the sense of smell. Molecules of airborne volatile substances called odorants are absorbed into nasal mucus and carried to the OLFACTORY EPITHELIUM (located in the nasal passages), where they stimulate OLFACTORY RECEPTORS. The olfactory receptors carry impulses in axonal bundles through tiny holes in the cribriform plate, the bony layer separating the base of the skull from the nasal cavity. On the top surface of the cribriform plate rests the OLFACTORY BULB, which receives the impulses and sends them on to a region of the brain called the periamygdaloid cortex. —**olfactory** *adj.*

olfactory bulb a bulblike ending on the olfactory nerve in the anterior region of each cerebral hemisphere. This first synapse in the olfactory system picks up excitation from the nose, specifically from the cilia in the OLFACTORY EPITHELIUM.

olfactory cortex a three-layed area of CEREBRAL CORTEX at the base of the TEMPORAL LOBE that is attached to the OLFACTORY BULB and devoted to the sense of smell. The olfactory cortex receives and interprets information from OLFACTORY RECEPTORS in the nasal cavity and is involved in the identification of odors.

olfactory epithelium an area of OLFACTORY RECEPTORS in the lining of the upper part of the nose. The epithelium is separated from the OLFACTORY BULB by a sievelike layer in the skull called the cribriform plate, through which the receptor cells synapse with cells in the olfactory bulb.

olfactory hallucination a false perception of odors, which are usually unpleasant or repulsive, such as poison gas or decaying flesh.

olfactory nerve the first CRANIAL NERVE, which carries sensory fibers concerned with the sense of smell. It originates in the olfactory lobe and is distributed to OLFACTORY RECEPTORS in the nasal mucous membrane.

olfactory receptor a spindle-shaped receptor cell in the OLFACTORY EPITHELIUM of the nasal cavity that is sensitive to airborne volatile substances (odorants). Cilia at the base of the olfactory receptors contain receptor sites for odorants. The receptors themselves collectively form the OLFACTORY NERVE, which synapses with cells in the OLFACTORY BULB.

olfactory system the primary structures and processes involved in an organism's detection of and responses to airborne volatile substances. The olfactory system includes several million OLFACTORY RECEPTORS in the OLFACTORY EPITHELIUM of the nasal cavity, the process of olfactory TRANSDUCTION, the OLFACTORY BULB and OLFACTORY NERVE, and the OLFACTORY CORTEX and associated brain areas and their functions.

oligodendrocyte *n.* a type of nonneuronal central nervous system cell (GLIA) that forms MYELIN SHEATHS around axons. Also called **oligodendroglia**.

omega squared (symbol: ω^2) a measure of the STRENGTH OF ASSOCIATION based on the proportion of variance of one measure predictable from variance in other measures.

one-tailed test a statistical test of an experimental hypothesis in which the expected direction of an effect or relationship is specified. Also called **directional test**. Compare TWO-TAILED TEST.

one-trial learning the mastery of a skill or an increment of learning on the first practice session or performance.

one-way analysis of variance a statistical test of the probability that the means of three or more samples have been drawn from the same population; that is, an ANALYSIS OF VARIANCE with a single independent variable.

one-word stage the developmental period, between approximately 10 and 18 months, when children use one word at a time when speaking. For example, depending on the context and how the word is spoken, *milk* may mean *That is milk, I want more milk*, or *I spilled the milk*. Also called **holophrastic stage**. See HOLOPHRASE.

on response (ON response) the depolarization of a neuron in the visual system that occurs in response to light increment. Neurons with on responses in the center of their receptive fields are often called **on cells**. Compare OFF RESPONSE.

ontogeny *n.* the biological origin and development of an individual organism from fertilization of the egg cell until death. Compare PHYLOGENY. **—ontogenetic** *adj.*

oogenesis *n.* the process by which germ cells divide and differentiate to produce female gametes (ova). In human females, primary oocytes are formed in the ovary during embryonic development and enter into the first division of MEIOSIS but then remain suspended at this stage of cell division until puberty. Thereafter, roughly once a month until menopause, one primary oocyte resumes meiosis to produce two unequally sized daughter cells: The larger one is the secondary oocyte, while the smaller is a polar body. Following OVULATION, the secondary oocyte undergoes the second meiotic division to produce an ovum and another polar body. These two polar bodies are normally nonfunctional and degenerate.

open-field test a technique for measuring (quantifying) behaviors and physiological reactions (e.g., those indicative of anxiety) in rats and other small animals. The animal is placed in a space divided into squares so that the researcher may observe the number of squares the animal traverses in a specified time period.

operant *n.* a class of responses that produces a common effect on the environment. An operant is defined by its effect rather than by the particular type of behavior producing that effect. For example, all forms of behavior that result in a lever being moved 4 mm downward constitute an operant. Compare RESPONDENT.

operant behavior behavior that produces a particular effect on the environment and whose likelihood

of recurrence is influenced by consequences. Operant behavior is nearly synonymous with voluntary behavior.

operant conditioning the process in which behavioral change (i.e., learning) occurs as a function of the consequences of behavior. Examples are teaching a dog to do tricks and rewarding behavioral change in a misbehaving child (see BEHAVIOR THERAPY). The term is essentially equivalent to INSTRUMENTAL CONDITIONING.

operant conditioning chamber an apparatus used to study behavior. Generally, it provides a relatively small and austere environment that blocks out extraneous stimuli. Included in the environment are devices that can present stimuli (e.g., reinforcers) and measure responses. For example, the apparatus for a rat might consist of a 25-cm^3 space containing a food tray and a small lever that the rat may press to release food from the feeder. The apparatus, initially developed in the 1930s by U.S. psychologist B. F. Skinner (1904–1990), later became known colloquially as the **Skinner box**.

operant response a single instance from an OPERANT class. For example, if lever pressing has been conditioned, each single lever press is an operant response.

operation *n.* in PIAGETIAN THEORY, a type of cognitive SCHEME that requires symbols, derives from action, exists in an organized system in which it is integrated with all other operations, and follows a set of logical rules, most importantly that of REVERSIBILITY.

operational definition a definition of something in terms of the operations (procedures, actions, or processes) by which it could be observed and measured. For example, the operational definition of anxiety could be in terms of a test score, behavioral withdrawal, or activation of the sympathetic nervous system.

operationalism *n.* the position that the meaning of a scientific concept depends upon the procedures used to establish it, so that each concept can be defined by a single observable and measurable operation. This approach is mainly associated with RADICAL BEHAVIORISM. Also called **operationism**.

opiate *n.* any of a variety of natural and semisynthetic compounds derived from OPIUM. They include the alkaloids MORPHINE and CODEINE and their derivatives (e.g., HEROIN [diacetylmorphine]). Opiates, together with synthetic compounds having the pharmacological properties of opiates, are known as OPIOIDS.

opioid *n.* any of a group of compounds that include the naturally occurring OPIATES (e.g., morphine, codeine) and their semisynthetic derivatives (e.g., heroin) as well as both synthetic and ENDOGENOUS compounds with morphinelike effects. The effects of opioids include analgesia, drowsiness, euphoria or other mood changes, slow and shallow breathing, and reduced gastrointestinal motility. Opioids are used clinically as pain relievers, anesthetics, cough suppressants, and antidiarrheal drugs, and many are subject to abuse and dependence.

opioid receptor a RECEPTOR that binds OPIOIDS (including ENDOGENOUS opioids) and mediates their effects via G PROTEINS. Opioid receptors are widely distributed in the brain, spinal cord, and periphery. They are categorized as mu receptors (largely responsible for the analgesic and euphoric effects associated with opioid use), kappa receptors, delta receptors, or N/OFQ receptors.

opium *n.* the dried resin of the unripe seed pods of the opium poppy, *Papaver somniferum*. Opium contains more than 20 alkaloids, the principal one being MORPHINE, which accounts for most of its pharmacological (including addictive) properties. Natural and synthetic derivatives (see OPIATE; OPIOID) induce analgesia and euphoria and produce a deep, dreamless sleep.

opponent process theory of color vision any one of a class of theories describing color vision on the basis of the activity of mechanisms that respond to red–green, blue–yellow, or black–white. The HERING THEORY OF COLOR VISION, the most highly developed opponent process theory, contrasted with the YOUNG–HELMHOLTZ THEORY OF COLOR VISION, which relied on receptors sensitive to specific regions of the spectrum. In the 1950s it was suggested that both theories were correct, the Young–Helmholtz model describing a first stage of processing in the visual system, while the outputs of that system were fed into an opponent process. This combined theory is known as the **dual process theory of color vision**.

opportunistic sampling the selection of participants or other sampling units for an experiment or survey simply because they are readily available.

oppositional defiant disorder a behavior disorder of childhood characterized by recurrent disobedient, negativistic, or hostile behavior toward authority figures that is more pronounced than usually seen in children of similar age and lasts for at least 6 months. It is manifest as temper tantrums, active defiance of rules, dawdling, argumentativeness, stubbornness, or being easily annoyed. The defiant behaviors typically do not involve aggression, destruction, theft, or deceit, which distinguishes this disorder from CONDUCT DISORDER.

optical flow pattern the total field of apparent velocities of visual stimuli that impinge upon a physical or theoretical visual system when objects move relative to the visual system or the visual system moves relative to the objects.

optic ataxia inability to direct the hand to an object under visual guidance, typically caused by damage to the cortex of the PARIETAL LOBE. It is a feature of BÁLINT'S SYNDROME.

optic chiasm the location at the base of the brain at which the optic nerves from the two eyes meet. In humans, the nerve fibers from the nasal half of each retina cross, so that each hemisphere of the brain receives input from both eyes. This partial crossing is called a partial decussation.

optic disk the area of the retina at which the axons of the RETINAL GANGLION CELLS gather before leaving the retina to form the optic nerve. Because this region contains no photoreceptors, it creates a BLIND SPOT in the visual field.

optic nerve the second CRANIAL NERVE, which carries the axons of RETINAL GANGLION CELLS and extends from the retina to the OPTIC CHIASM.

optic radiations nerve fibers that project from the LATERAL GENICULATE NUCLEUS to the VISUAL CORTEX in the occipital lobe and to the pretectum, a structure in the midbrain important for the reflexive contraction of the pupils in the presence of light.

optics *n.* the study of the physics of light, including its relations to the mechanisms of vision.

optic tract the bundle of optic nerve fibers after the partial decussation of the optic nerves at the OPTIC CHIASM. The major targets of the optic tract are the LATERAL GENICULATE NUCLEUS in the thalamus and the superior COLLICULUS in the midbrain.

optimal foraging theory a theory of foraging behavior arguing that NATURAL SELECTION has created optimal strategies for food selection (based on nutritional value and costs of locating, capturing, and processing food) and for deciding when to depart a particular patch to seek resources elsewhere.

optimism *n.* hopefulness: the attitude that good things will happen and that people's wishes or aims will ultimately be fulfilled. **Optimists** are people who anticipate positive outcomes, whether serendipitously or through perseverance and effort, and who are confident of attaining desired goals (compare PESSIMISM). Most individuals lie somewhere on the spectrum between the two polar opposites of pure optimism and pure pessimism but tend to demonstrate sometimes strong, relatively stable or situational tendencies in one direction or the other. **—optimistic** *adj.*

optokinetic reflex the involuntary compensatory eye movements that allow the eyes to maintain fixation on a visual target as it moves by an observer. The optokinetic reflex is driven by signals from neurons in the retina. Compare VESTIBULO-OCULAR REFLEX.

oral stage in psychoanalytic theory, the first stage of PSYCHOSEXUAL DEVELOPMENT, occupying the first year of life, in which the LIBIDO is concentrated on the mouth, which is the principal erotic zone. The stage is divided into the early **oral-sucking phase**, during which gratification is achieved by sucking the nipple during feeding, and the later **oral-biting phase**, when gratification is also achieved by biting. FIXATION during the oral stage is posited to cause an oral personality.

orbitofrontal cortex the CEREBRAL CORTEX of the ventral part of each FRONTAL LOBE, having strong connections to the HYPOTHALAMUS. Lesions of the orbitofrontal cortex can result in loss of inhibitions, forgetfulness, and apathy broken by bouts of euphoria.

orchidectomy *n.* the surgical removal of a testis. An orchidectomy may be performed when a testis is injured or diseased, as when the male reproductive system has been affected by cancer. Also called **orchiectomy**.

order effect in WITHIN-SUBJECTS DESIGNS, the effect of the order in which treatments are administered, that is, the effect of being the first administered treatment (rather than the second, third, and so forth). This is often confused with the SEQUENCE EFFECT.

ordinal data numerical values that represent rankings along a continuum of lowest and highest, as in a judge's assignment of a 1 to denote that a particular athlete's performance was fair and a 2 to denote that a subsequent athlete's performance was better. Ordinal data may be counted (i.e., how many athletes obtained a 1, how many a 2, etc.) and arranged in descending or ascending sequence but may not be manipulated; it is meaningless to add, subtract, divide, or multiply any rank by any other because the actual differential in performance between adjacent values is unspecified and may vary. In other words, one does not know how much better a 2 is than a 1, and the difference between a 1 and a 2 may not be the same as the difference between a 2 and a 3.

ordinal scale a sequence of numbers that do not indicate magnitude or a true zero point but rather reflect a rank ordering of the attribute being measured. For example, an ordinal scale for the performance of a specific group of people on a particular test might use the number 1 to indicate the person who obtained the highest score, the number 2 to indicate the person who obtained the next highest score, and so on. It is important to note, however, that an ordinal scale does not provide any information about the degree of difference between adjacent ranks (e.g., it is not clear what the actual point difference is between the rank 1 and 2 scores).

ordinate *n.* the vertical coordinate in a graph or data plot; that is, the *y*-axis. See also ABSCISSA.

orexin *n.* any of a group of proteins, expressed in the LATERAL HYPOTHALAMUS, that trigger feeding and have also been implicated in NARCOLEPSY.

organic *adj.* denoting a condition or disorder that results from structural alterations of an organ or tissue. In psychology and psychiatry, the term is equivalent to somatic or physical, as contrasted with FUNCTIONAL or PSYCHOGENIC.

organism *n.* an individual living entity, such as an animal, plant, or bacterium, that is capable of reproduction, growth, and maintenance.

organization *n.* structure. This basic meaning is applied to numerous areas of psychology with varying degrees of specificity. For example, in memory research organization refers to the structure discovered in or imposed upon a set of items in order to guide memory performance, whereas in GESTALT PSYCHOLOGY the term denotes an integrated perception composed of various components that appear together as a single whole (e.g., a face). **—organizational** *adj.*

organizational culture a distinctive pattern of thought and behavior shared by members of the same business or service entity and reflected in their language, values, attitudes, beliefs, and customs. This type of culture is in many ways analogous to the personality of an individual.

organizational effect a long-term effect of hormonal action typically occurring in fetal development or the early postnatal period that leads to permanent changes in behavior and neural functioning. The presence of testosterone in young male rats leads to long-term male-typical behavior, and female rats can be masculinized by neonatal exposure to testosterone. Compare ACTIVATIONAL EFFECT.

organizational psychology see INDUSTRIAL AND ORGANIZATIONAL PSYCHOLOGY.

organ of Corti a specialized structure that sits on the BASILAR MEMBRANE within the cochlea in the inner ear. It contains the HAIR CELLS (the sensory receptors for hearing), their nerve endings, and supporting cells (Deiters cells). See also TECTORIAL MEMBRANE. [Alfonso **Corti** (1822–1876), Italian anatomist]

orgasm *n.* the climax of the SEXUAL-RESPONSE CYCLE, when the peak of pleasure is achieved, marked by the release of tension and rhythmic contractions of the perineal muscles, anal sphincter, and pelvic reproductive organs. In men, orgasm is also accompanied by the emission of semen (**ejaculation**); in women, it is accompanied by contractions of the wall of the outer third of the vagina. **—orgasmic** or **orgastic** *adj.*

orientation *n.* **1.** awareness of the self and of the external environment, that is, the ability to identify one's self and to know the time, the place, and other aspects of one's surroundings and activities. **2.** the act of directing the body or of moving toward an external stimulus, such as light, gravity, or some other aspect of the environment. **3.** relative position or alignment. For example, in vision orientation refers to the degree of tilt of the long axis of a visual stimulus (e.g., a vertical bar is oriented at 0°; a horizontal bar is oriented at 90°). Many neurons in the visual system respond most vigorously to a stimulus of a certain orientation: They are said to be **orientation selective**. **—orient** *vb.*

orientation column a vertical slab of STRIATE CORTEX in which all the neurons are maximally responsive to stimuli of the same ORIENTATION. Adjacent columns have slightly different orientation preferences, so that electrode penetration tangential to the cortical surface that passes through many columns would encounter neurons with orientation preferences that shift smoothly around a reference axis. Compare OCULAR DOMINANCE COLUMN.

orienting response a behavioral response to an altered, novel, or sudden stimulus, for example, turning one's head toward an unexpected noise. Various physiological components of the orienting response have subsequently been identified as well, including dilation of pupils and blood vessels and changes in heart rate and electrical resistance of the skin.

orthogonal rotation see FACTOR ROTATION.

osmometric thirst thirst resulting from a loss of intracellular fluids and a relative increase in OSMOTIC PRESSURE. Also called **osmotic thirst**. Compare HYPOVOLEMIC THIRST.

osmoreceptor *n.* a hypothetical re-

O

ceptor in the HYPOTHALAMUS that responds to changes in the concentrations of various substances in the body's extracellular fluid and to cellular dehydration. It also regulates the secretion of VASOPRESSIN and contributes to thirst.

osmosis *n.* the passive movement of solvent molecules through a differentially permeable membrane (e.g., a cell membrane) separating two solutions of different concentrations. The solvent tends to flow from the weaker solution to the stronger solution. —**osmotic** *adj.*

osmotic pressure the pressure required to prevent the passage of water (or other solvent) through a semipermeable membrane (e.g., a cell membrane) from an area of low concentration of solute to an area of higher concentration.

ossicles *pl. n.* any small bones, but particularly the auditory ossicles: the chain of three tiny bones in the middle ear that transmit sound vibrations from the tympanic membrane (eardrum) to the OVAL WINDOW of the inner ear. They are the **malleus** (or hammer), which is attached to the tympanic membrane; the **incus** (or anvil); and the **stapes** (or stirrup), whose footplate nearly fills the oval window. The ossicles allow efficient transmission of sound from air to the fluid-filled cochlea.

osteoporosis *n.* a disorder in which the bones become brittle and break easily, due to loss of calcified bone as a result of disease or aging.

OT abbreviation for OCCUPATIONAL THERAPY.

otolith *n.* any of numerous tiny calcium particles embedded in the gelatinous matrix of the VESTIBULAR SACS of the inner ear. See MACULA.

ought self in analyses of self-concept, a mental representation of a set of attributes that one is obligated to possess according to social norms or one's personal responsibilities.

outcome research a systematic investigation of the effectiveness of a single type or technique of psychotherapy, or of the comparative effectiveness of different types or techniques, when applied to one or more disorders.

outer ear see EXTERNAL EAR.

outer nuclear layer the layer of cell bodies of the rods and cones in the retina.

outer plexiform layer the synaptic layer in the retina in which contacts are made between PHOTORECEPTORS, RETINAL BIPOLAR CELLS, and RETINAL HORIZONTAL CELLS.

outgroup *n.* any group to which one does not belong or with which one does not identify, but particularly a group that is judged to be different from, and inferior to, one's own group (the INGROUP).

outgroup homogeneity bias the tendency to assume that the members of other groups are very similar to each other, particularly in contrast to the assumed diversity of the membership of one's own groups.

outlier *n.* an extreme observation or measurement, that is, one that significantly differs from all others obtained. Outliers can have a high degree of influence on summary statistics and estimates of parametric values and their precision and may distort research findings if they are the result of error.

out-of-body experience a dissociative experience in which the individual imagines that his or her mind, soul, or spirit has left the body and is acting or perceiving independently. Such experiences are sometimes reported by those who have recovered from the point of death (see NEAR-DEATH EXPERI-ENCE); they have also been reported by those using hallucinogens or under hypnosis. Certain occult or spiritualistic practices may also attempt to induce such experiences.

outpatient *n.* a person who obtains diagnosis, treatment, or other service at a hospital, clinic, physician's office, or other health care facility without overnight admission. Compare INPATIENT.

output interference see INTERFERENCE.

oval window a membrane-covered opening in the bony wall of the cochlea in the ear (see SCALA VESTIBULI). Vibration of the stapes (see OSSICLES) is transmitted to the oval window and into the cochlear fluids.

ovariectomy *n.* the surgical removal of an ovary. This procedure may be performed when the ovaries are diseased or injured or in some circumstances, such as when a woman is at very high risk for ovarian cancer, as a preventive measure.

ovary *n.* the female reproductive organ, which produces ova (egg cells) and sex hormones (estrogens and progesterone). In humans the two ovaries are almond-shaped organs, normally located in the lower abdomen on either side of the upper end of the uterus, to which they are linked by the FALLOPIAN TUBES. See also MENSTRUAL CYCLE; OOGENESIS. **—ovarian** *adj.*

overanxious disorder disproportionate and persistent anxiety or worry occurring in childhood or adolescence across a variety of different situations and objects. In some current diagnostic classifications, notably the DSM–IV–TR, overanxious disorder has been subsumed under GENERALIZED ANXIETY DISORDER.

overcompensation *n.* see COMPENSATION. **—overcompensate** *vb.*

overconfidence *n.* an unsupported belief or unrealistically positive expectation that a desired outcome will occur. In a sports setting, for example, overconfidence might involve overestimating one's ability to perform or underestimating the ability of a competitor to perform. **—overconfident** *adj.*

overdetermination *n.* in psychoanalytic theory, the concept that several unconscious factors may combine to produce one symptom, dream, disorder, or aspect of behavior. Because drives and defenses operate simultaneously and derive from different layers of the personality, a dream may express more than one meaning, and a single symptom may serve more than one purpose or fulfill more than one unconscious wish. **—overdetermined** *adj.*

overextension *n.* the tendency of very young children to extend the use of a word beyond the scope of its specific meaning, for example, by referring to all animals as "doggie." Compare UNDEREXTENSION.

overgeneralization *n.* the process of extending something beyond the circumstances to which it actually applies. It is a common linguistic tendency of young children, who generalize standard grammatical rules to apply to irregular words, for example, pluralizing *foot* to *foots*. See also OVEREXTENSION; OVERREGULARIZATION.

overjustification effect a paradoxical effect in which rewarding (or offering to reward) a person for his or her performance can lead to lower, rather than higher, effort and attainment. It occurs when introduction of the reward weakens the strong INTRINSIC MOTIVATION that was the key to the person's original high performance.

overlearning *n.* practice that is continued beyond the point at which the individual knows or performs well. The benefits of overlearning may be seen in increased persistence of the learning over time. **—overlearned** *adj.*

overload *n.* a psychological condition in which situations and experiences are so cognitively, perceptually, and emotionally stimulating that they tax or even exceed the individual's capacity to process incoming information. See COGNITIVE OVERLOAD; INFORMATION OVERLOAD; SENSORY OVERLOAD; STIMULUS OVERLOAD.

overprotection *n.* the process of sheltering a child to such an extent that he or she fails to become independent and may experience later adjustment and other difficulties, including development of a DEPENDENT PERSONALITY DISORDER.

overregularization *n.* a transient error in linguistic development in which the child attempts to make language more grammatically regular than it actually is, for example, by saying *breaked* instead of *broken*. See also OVEREXTENSION; OVERGENERALIZATION.

overt *adj.* **1.** denoting anything that is directly observable, open to view, or publicly known. **2.** not hidden. Compare COVERT.

overweight *adj.* the condition of having more body fat than is considered normal or healthy for an individual of a particular age, body type, or build. Individuals may lie anywhere on a spectrum from mildly overweight to seriously overweight (see OBESITY). One of the most frequently used standards for assessing the degree of body fat is the BODY MASS INDEX.

ovulation *n.* the production of a mature secondary oocyte (see OOGENESIS) and its release from a small pouchlike cavity (graafian follicle) at the surface of the ovary. Rupture of the follicle causes the oocyte to be discharged into a FALLOPIAN TUBE. In humans, the oocyte matures into an OVUM in the strict sense only if it is penetrated by a sperm during its passage along the fallopian tube.

ovum *n.* (*pl.* **ova**) an egg cell: a single female GAMETE that develops from a secondary oocyte following its release from the ovary at OVULATION. See also OOGENESIS.

oxytocin *n.* a hormone produced in the hypothalamus and secreted by the posterior lobe (neurohypophysis) of the PITUITARY GLAND in response to direct neural stimulation. It stimulates smooth muscle, particularly in the mammary glands during lactation and in the wall of the uterus during labor.

Pp

Pacinian corpuscle a type of cutaneous receptor organ that is sensitive to contact and vibration. It consists of a nerve-fiber ending surrounded by concentric layers of connective tissue. Pacinian corpuscles are found in the fingers, the hairy skin, the tendons, and the abdominal membrane. [Filippo **Pacini** (1812–1883), Italian anatomist]

PAG abbreviation for PERIAQUEDUCTAL GRAY.

pain *n.* an unpleasant sensation due to damage to nerve tissue, stimulation of free nerve endings, or excessive stimulation (e.g., extremely loud sounds). It is elicited by stimulation of pain receptors, which occur in groups throughout the body, but also involves various cognitive, affective, and behavioral factors. Pain may also be a feeling of severe distress and suffering resulting from acute anxiety, loss of a loved one, or other psychological factors. Psychologists have made important contributions to understanding pain by demonstrating the psychosocial and behavioral factors in the etiology, severity, exacerbation, maintenance, and treatment of both physical and mental pain. See also GATE-CONTROL THEORY.

pain disorder a SOMATOFORM DISORDER characterized by severe, prolonged pain that significantly interferes with a person's ability to function. The pain cannot be accounted for solely by a medical condition, and it is not feigned or produced intentionally (compare FACTITIOUS DISORDER; MALINGERING).

paired-associates learning a technique used in studying learning in which participants learn syllables, words, or other items in pairs and are later presented with one half of each pair to which they must respond with the matching half.

pairing *n.* in behavioral studies, the juxtaposing of two events in time. For example, if a tone is presented immediately before a puff of air to the eye, the tone and the puff have been paired.

paleocortex *n.* see ALLOCORTEX.

paleopsychology *n.* the study of certain psychological processes in contemporary humans that are believed to have originated in earlier stages of human and, perhaps, nonhuman animal evolution. These include unconscious processes, such as the COLLECTIVE UNCONSCIOUS. —**paleopsychological** *adj.*

palliative care terminal care that focuses on symptom control and comfort instead of aggressive, cure-oriented intervention. This is the basis of the HOSPICE approach. Emphasis is on careful assessment of the patient's condition throughout the end phase of life in order to provide the most effective medications and other procedures to relieve pain.

palsy *n.* an obsolete name for paralysis, still used in such compound names as CEREBRAL PALSY.

panic *n.* a sudden, uncontrollable

fear reaction that may involve terror, confusion, and irrational behavior, precipitated by a perceived threat (e.g., earthquake, fire, or being stuck in an elevator).

panic attack a sudden onset of intense apprehension and fearfulness, in the absence of actual danger, accompanied by the presence of such physical symptoms as palpitations, difficulty in breathing, chest pain or discomfort, choking or smothering sensations, excessive perspiration, and dizziness. The attack occurs in a discrete period of time and often involves fears of going crazy, losing control, or dying.

panic disorder an ANXIETY DISORDER characterized by recurrent, unexpected PANIC ATTACKS that are associated with (a) persistent concern about having another attack, (b) worry about the possible consequences of the attacks, or (c) significant change in behavior related to the attacks (e.g., avoiding situations, not going out alone).

Papez circuit a circular network of nerve centers and fibers in the brain that is associated with emotion and memory. It includes such structures as the HIPPOCAMPUS, FORNIX, anterior THALAMUS, CINGULATE GYRUS, and PARAHIPPOCAMPAL GYRUS. [first described in 1937 by James W. **Papez** (1883–1958), U.S. neuroanatomist]

papilla *n. (pl.* **papillae**) any of the four types of swellings on the tongue. In humans, some 200 fungiform papillae are toward the front of the tongue; 10–14 foliate papillae are on the sides; 7–11 circumvallate papillae are on the back; and filiform papillae, with no taste function, cover most of the tongue's surface.

paradigm *n.* **1.** a model, pattern, or representative example, as of the functions and interrelationships of a process, a behavior under study, or

the like. **2.** a set of assumptions, attitudes, concepts, values, procedures, and techniques that constitutes a generally accepted theoretical framework within, or a general perspective of, a discipline.

paradoxical sleep see REM SLEEP.

parahippocampal gyrus a ridge (gyrus) on the medial (inner) surface of the TEMPORAL LOBE of cerebral cortex, lying over the HIPPOCAMPUS. It is a component of the LIMBIC SYSTEM thought to be involved in spatial or topographic memory.

parakinesis *n.* in parapsychology, the movement of objects in the absence of contact sufficient to explain the motion. The phenomenon is closely related to that of PSYCHOKINESIS, which involves manipulation of objects by thought alone.

paralanguage *n.* the vocal but nonverbal elements of communication by speech, such as tone and stress, volume and speed of delivery, voice quality, hesitations, and nonlinguistic sounds, such as sighs or groans. These **paralinguistic cues** help shape the total meaning of an utterance, for example, by conveying the fact that a speaker is angry when this would not be apparent from the same words written down. In some uses, the term paralanguage is extended to include gestures, facial expressions, and other aspects of BODY LANGUAGE.

parallax *n.* an illusion of movement of objects in the visual field when the head is moved from side to side. Objects beyond a point of visual fixation appear to move in the same direction as the head movement; those closer seem to move in the opposite direction. Parallax provides a monocular cue for DEPTH PERCEPTION.

parallel distributed processing (PDP) any model of cognition based on the idea that the representation of information is distributed as patterns of activation over a richly connected set of hypothetical neural units that function interactively and in parallel with one another.

parallel fiber any of the axons of the small, grainlike neurons that form the outermost layer of the CEREBELLAR CORTEX.

parallel forms see ALTERNATE-FORMS RELIABILITY.

parallel play play in which a child is next to others and using similar objects but still engaged in his or her own activity.

parallel processing INFORMATION PROCESSING in which two or more sequences of operations are carried out simultaneously by independent processors. A capacity for parallel processing in the human mind would account for people's apparent ability to carry on different cognitive functions at the same time, as, for example, when driving a car while also listening to music and having a conversation. The term is usually reserved for processing at a higher, symbolic level, as opposed to the level of individual neural units described in models of PARALLEL DISTRIBUTED PROCESSING. Compare SERIAL PROCESSING.

parameter *n.* **1.** a numerical constant that characterizes a population with respect to some attribute, for example, the location of its central point. **2.** an ARGUMENT of a function. —**parametric** *adj.*

parametric statistics statistical procedures that are based on assumptions about the distribution of the attribute (or attributes) in the population being tested. Compare NONPARAMETRIC STATISTICS.

paramnesia *n.* see FALSE MEMORY.

paranoia *n.* a condition characterized by delusions of persecution or grandiosity that are not as system-

atized and elaborate as in a DELUSIONAL DISORDER nor as disorganized and bizarre as in paranoid schizophrenia. —**paranoiac** *n., adj.*

paranoid personality disorder a personality disorder characterized by pervasive, unwarranted suspiciousness and mistrust, specifically expectation of trickery or harm, guardedness and secretiveness, avoidance of accepting blame, overconcern with hidden motives and meanings, hypersensitivity, and restricted affectivity.

paranoid schizophrenia a subtype of SCHIZOPHRENIA characterized by prominent delusions or auditory hallucinations. Delusions are typically persecutory, grandiose, or both; hallucinations are typically related to the content of the delusional theme. Cognitive functioning and mood are affected to a much lesser degree than in other types of schizophrenia.

paranormal *adj.* denoting any purported phenomenon involving the transfer of information or energy that cannot be explained by existing scientific knowledge. The term is particularly applied to those forms of alleged EXTRASENSORY PERCEPTION that are the province of parapsychological investigation (see PARAPSYCHOLOGY).

paraphilia *n.* a sexual disorder in which unusual or bizarre fantasies or behavior are necessary for sexual excitement, including preference for a nonhuman object, activity involving real or simulated suffering or humiliation, or activity with nonconsenting partners. Paraphilias include such specific types as FETISHISM, FROTTEURISM, PEDOPHILIA, EXHIBITIONISM, VOYEURISM, SEXUAL MASOCHISM, and SEXUAL SADISM. —**paraphiliac** *adj.*

parapraxis *n.* a minor cognitive or behavioral error. Examples of such

P

errors include slips of the pen, SLIPS OF THE TONGUE, forgetting significant events, mislaying objects, and unintentional puns. In psychoanalytic theory, a parapraxis is believed to express unconscious wishes, attitudes, or impulses and is referred to as a FREUDIAN SLIP.

paraprofessional *n.* a trained but not professionally credentialed worker who assists in the treatment of patients in both hospital and community settings.

parapsychology *n.* the systematic study of alleged psychological phenomena involving the transfer of information or energy that cannot be explained in terms of presently known scientific data or laws. Such study has focused largely on the various forms of EXTRASENSORY PERCEPTION, such as TELEPATHY and CLAIRVOYANCE, but also encompasses such phenomena as alleged poltergeist activity and the claims of mediums. Parapsychology is regarded with suspicion by many scientists, including most psychologists. —**parapsychological** *adj.* —**parapsychologist** *n.*

parasomnia *n.* a disorder characterized by abnormal behavior or physiological events occurring during sleep or the transitional state between sleep and waking. Types include NIGHTMARE disorder, SLEEP TERROR DISORDER, and SLEEPWALKING DISORDER. The parasomnias form one of two broad groups of primary sleep disorders, the other being DYSSOMNIAS.

parasuicide *n.* a range of behaviors involving deliberate self-harm that falls short of suicide and may or may not be intended to result in death.

parasympathetic nervous system one of two branches of the AUTONOMIC NERVOUS SYSTEM (ANS, which controls smooth muscle and gland functions), the other being the SYMPATHETIC NERVOUS SYSTEM. It is the system controlling rest, repair, enjoyment, eating, sleeping, sexual activity, and social dominance, among other functions. The parasympathetic nervous system stimulates salivary secretions and digestive secretions in the stomach and produces pupillary constriction, decreases in heart rate, and increased blood flow to the genitalia during sexual excitement. Also called **parasympathetic division**.

paraventricular nucleus a particular collection of neurons in the HYPOTHALAMUS that synthesize numerous hormones, among them OXYTOCIN and VASOPRESSIN.

parental investment theory the proposition that many sex differences in sexually reproducing species (including humans) can be understood in terms of the amount of time, energy, and risk to their own survival that males and females put into parenting versus mating.

parenting *n.* all actions related to the raising of offspring. Researchers have described different human **parenting styles**—ways in which parents interact with their children—with most classifications varying on the dimensions of emotional warmth and control. One of the most influential of these classifications is that of U.S. developmental psychologist Diana Baumrind (1927–), which involves four types of styles: **authoritarian parenting**, in which the parent or caregiver stresses obedience and employs strong forms of punishment; **authoritative parenting**, in which the parent or caregiver encourages a child's autonomy yet still places certain limitations on behavior; **permissive parenting**, in which the parent or caregiver makes few demands and avoids exercising control; and **rejecting–neglecting**

parenting, in which the parent or caregiver is more attentive to his or her needs than those of the child.

paresis *n.* partial or incomplete paralysis.

paresthesia *n.* an abnormal skin sensation, such as tingling, tickling, burning, itching, or pricking, in the absence of external stimulation. Paresthesia may be temporary, as in the "pins and needles" feeling that many people experience (e.g., after having sat with legs crossed too long), or chronic and due to such factors as neurological disorder or drug side effects. **—paresthetic** *adj.*

parietal lobe one of the four main subdivisions of each cerebral hemisphere. It occupies the upper central area of each hemisphere, behind the FRONTAL LOBE, ahead of the OCCIPITAL LOBE, and above the TEMPORAL LOBE. Parts of the parietal lobe participate in somatosensory activities, such as discrimination of size, shape, and texture of objects; visual activities, such as visually guided actions; and auditory activities, such as speech perception.

Parkinson's disease a progressive neurodegenerative disease caused by the death of dopamine-producing neurons in the SUBSTANTIA NIGRA of the brain, which controls balance and coordinates muscle movement. Symptoms typically begin late in life with mild tremors, increasing rigidity of the limbs, and slowness of voluntary movements. Later symptoms include postural instability, impaired balance, and difficulty walking. DEMENTIA occurs in some 20–60% of patients, usually in older patients in whom the disease is far advanced. [first described in 1817 by James **Parkinson** (1755–1824), British physician]

parsimony *n.* see LAW OF PARSIMONY.

part correlation the correlation

between two variables with the influence of a third variable removed from one (but only one) of the two variables. Compare PARTIAL CORRELATION.

partial agonist see AGONIST.

partial correlation the correlation between two variables with the influence of one or more other variables on their intercorrelation statistically removed or held constant. Compare PART CORRELATION.

partial reinforcement see INTERMITTENT REINFORCEMENT.

partial reinforcement effect increased resistance to extinction after intermittent reinforcement rather than after continuous reinforcement.

partial seizure a seizure that begins in a localized area of the brain, although it may subsequently progress to a GENERALIZED SEIZURE. Simple partial seizures produce no alteration of consciousness despite clinical manifestations, which may include sensory, motor, or autonomic activity. Complex partial seizures may produce similar sensory, motor, or autonomic symptoms but are also characterized by some impairment or alteration of consciousness during the event. Also called **focal seizure**.

participant *n.* a person who takes part in an investigation, study, or experiment, for example by performing tasks set by the experimenter or by answering questions set by a researcher. The participant may be further identified as an experimental participant (see EXPERIMENTAL GROUP) or a control participant (see CONTROL GROUP). Participants are also called SUBJECTS, although the former term is now often preferred when referring to humans.

participant modeling a procedure for changing behavior in which effective styles of behavior are modeled (i.e., demonstrated, broken down step by step, and analyzed) by a therapist for an individual. Various aids are introduced to help the individual master the tasks, such as viewing videotaped enactments of effective and ineffective behavioral responses to prototypical situations in a variety of social contexts (e.g., at school or work).

participant observation a type of observational method in which a trained observer enters the group under study as a member, while avoiding a conspicuous role that would alter the group processes and bias the data. For example, cultural anthropologists become **participant observers** when they enter the life of a given culture to study its structure and processes.

part method of learning a learning technique in which the material is divided into sections, each to be mastered separately in a successive order. Compare WHOLE METHOD OF LEARNING.

parvocellular system the part of the visual system that projects to or originates from small neurons in the four dorsal layers (the **parvocellular layers**) of the LATERAL GENICULATE NUCLEUS. It allows the perception of fine details, colors, and large changes in brightness but conducts information relatively slowly because of its small cells and slender axons. Compare MAGNOCELLULAR SYSTEM. See also P-CELL.

passion *n.* an intense, driving, or overwhelming feeling or conviction, particularly a strong sexual desire. Passion is often contrasted with emotion, in that passion affects a person unwillingly. —**passionate** *adj.*

passionate love a type of love in which sexual passion and a high

level of emotional arousal are prominent features; along with COMPANIONATE LOVE, it is one of the two main types of love identified by social psychologists. Passionate lovers typically are greatly preoccupied with the loved person, want their feelings to be reciprocated, and are usually greatly distressed when the relationship seems awry. See also ROMANTIC LOVE; TRIANGULAR THEORY OF LOVE.

passive-aggressive *adj.* characteristic of behavior that is seemingly innocuous, accidental, or neutral but that indirectly displays an unconscious aggressive motive. For example, a child who appears to be compliant but is routinely late for school, misses the bus, or forgets his or her homework may be expressing unconscious resentment at having to attend school.

passive-aggressive personality disorder a personality disorder of long standing in which underlying AMBIVALENCE and NEGATIVISM toward the self and others is expressed by such means as procrastination, dawdling, stubbornness, intentional inefficiency, "forgetting" appointments, or misplacing important materials. The pattern persists even where more adaptive behavior is clearly possible; it frequently interferes with occupational, domestic, and academic success.

passive euthanasia the intentional withholding of treatment that might prolong the life of a person who is approaching death. It is distinguished from ACTIVE EUTHANASIA, in which direct action (e.g., a lethal injection) is taken to end the life.

patch-clamp technique the use of very fine-bore pipette MICROELECTRODES, clamped by suction onto tiny patches of the plasma membrane of a neuron, to record the electrical activity of a single square micrometer of the membrane, including single ION CHANNELS.

paternalism *n.* a policy or attitude in which those having authority over others extend this authority into areas usually left to individual choice or conscience (e.g., smoking or sexual behavior), usually on the grounds that this is necessary for the welfare or protection of the individuals concerned. —**paternalist** *n.* —**paternalistic** *adj.*

path analysis a set of quantitative procedures used to verify the existence of causal relationships among several variables, displayed in graph form showing the various hypothesized routes of causal influence. The causal relationships are theoretically determined, and the path analysis determines both the accuracy and the strength of the hypothesized relationships.

pathogen *n.* any agent (e.g., a bacterium or virus) that contributes to disease or otherwise induces unhealthy structural or functional changes. —**pathogenicity** *n.*

pathological gambling an impulse-control disorder characterized by chronic, maladaptive wagering, leading to significant interpersonal, professional, or financial difficulties.

pathology *n.* **1.** the scientific study of functional and structural changes involved in physical and mental disorders and diseases. **2.** more broadly, any departure from what is considered healthy or adaptive. —**pathological** *adj.* —**pathologist** *n.*

patient *n.* a person receiving health care from a licensed health professional (including the services of most psychologists and psychiatrists). See INPATIENT; OUTPATIENT. See also PATIENT–CLIENT ISSUE.

patient–client issue the dilemma of how to identify the recipient of psychological services or intervention (i.e., the nomenclature used for the recipient). Psychiatrists, many clinical psychologists, and some other mental health providers tend to follow the traditional language of the medical model and refer to the people seeking their services as patients. Counseling psychologists, some clinical psychologists, social workers, and counselors tend to avoid the word "patient," which is associated with illness and dysfunction, using instead the word client to refer to the person seeking their services.

patients' rights any statement, listing, summary, or the like that articulates the rights that health care providers (e.g., physicians, medical facilities) ethically ought to provide to those receiving their services in such basic categories as (a) the provision of adequate information regarding benefits, risks, costs, and alternatives; (b) fair treatment (e.g., respect, responsiveness, timely attention to health issues); (c) autonomy over medical decisions (e.g., obtaining full consent for medical interventions); and (d) CONFIDENTIALITY.

patriarchy *n.* **1.** a society in which descent and inheritance is **patrilineal**, that is, traced through the male only. **2.** more loosely, a family, group, or society in which men are dominant. Compare MATRIARCHY. —**patriarchal** *adj.*

pattern recognition the ability to identify a complex whole composed of, or embedded in, many separate elements. Pattern recognition is not only a visual ability; in audition, it refers to (a) the recognition of temporal patterns of sounds or (b) the recognition of patterns of excitation of the BASILAR MEMBRANE, such as that which occurs during the perception of vowels in speech.

P

pattern theory of taste coding a theory postulating that each taste stimulus evokes a unique pattern of neural activity from the TASTE-CELL population and that this pattern serves as the neural representation of the evoking stimulus. Taste quality is coded in the shape of the evoked pattern, while intensity is represented by the total discharge rate. Compare LABELED-LINE THEORY OF TASTE CODING.

Pavlovian conditioning a type of learning in which an initially neutral stimulus—the CONDITIONED STIMULUS (CS)—when paired with a stimulus that elicits a reflex response—the UNCONDITIONED STIMULUS (US)—results in a learned, or conditioned, response (CR) when the CS is presented. For example, the sound of a tone may be used as a CS, and food in a dog's mouth as a US. After repeated pairings, namely, the tone followed immediately by food, the tone, which initially had no effect on salivation (i.e., was neutral with respect to it), will elicit salivation even if the food is not presented. Also called **classical conditioning; respondent conditioning**. [discovered in the early 20th century by Ivan **Pavlov** (1849–1936), Russian physiologist]

P-cell *n.* any of various small neurons in the four dorsal layers of the six-layered LATERAL GENICULATE NUCLEUS. P-cells are the origin of the PARVOCELLULAR SYSTEM. The RETINAL GANGLION CELLS that provide input to the P-cells of the lateral geniculate nucleus are called **P-ganglion cells**. See also M-CELL.

PCP *n.* 1-(1-*p*henyl*c*yclohexyl)*p*iperidine (phencyclidine): a hallucinogenic drug originally developed for use in surgical anesthesia and later found to produce psychedelic or dissociative effects. PCP has a complex mechanism of action—blocking the reuptake of dopamine, norepinephrine, and serotonin, among other activities—and in high doses may induce stupor or coma. Additionally, PCP can produce symptoms resembling both the positive and negative symptoms of schizophrenia, leading some to consider it a useful drug model of schizophrenia. PCP became common as an illicit drug in the 1970s and remains so, despite speculation about its potential neurotoxicity (ability to damage nerve tissue).

Pcs abbreviation for PRECONSCIOUS.

PDM abbreviation for PSYCHODYNAMIC DIAGNOSTIC MANUAL.

PDP abbreviation for PARALLEL DISTRIBUTED PROCESSING.

peak experience in the HUMANISTIC PSYCHOLOGY of U.S. psychologist Abraham Maslow (1908–1970), a moment of awe, ecstasy, or sudden insight into life as a powerful unity transcending space, time, and the self that may at times be experienced by individuals in their pursuit of SELF-ACTUALIZATION. See also TRANSPERSONAL PSYCHOLOGY.

Pearson product–moment correlation see PRODUCT–MOMENT CORRELATION.

pecking order regular patterns of dominance (pecking, threatening, chasing, fighting, avoiding, crouching, and vocalizing) in chickens and other animals. This term has been extended to denote any (usually linear) sequence of authority, status, and privilege that prevails in some organizations and social groups, although this meaning is more properly referred to as a DOMINANCE HIERARCHY.

pediatric *adj.* pertaining to the health and medical care of children or to child development.

pedophilia *n.* a PARAPHILIA in which sexual acts or fantasies with prepubertal children are the persistently preferred or exclusive method of achieving sexual excitement. Pedophilia is seen almost exclusively in men. **—pedophilic** *adj.*

peer *n.* an individual who shares a feature or function (e.g., age, sex, occupation, social group membership) with one or more other individuals. In developmental psychology, a peer is typically an age mate with whom a child or adolescent interacts.

peer group a group of individuals who share one or more characteristics, such as age, social status, economic status, occupation, or education. Members of a peer group typically interact with each other on a level of equality and exert influence on each other's attitudes, emotions, and behavior (see PEER PRESSURE).

peer pressure the influence exerted by a PEER GROUP on its individual members to fit in with or adapt to group expectations by thinking, feeling, and (most importantly) behaving in a similar or acceptable manner (see CONFORMITY). Peer pressure may have positive SOCIALIZATION value but may also have negative consequences for mental or physical health.

penis *n.* the male organ for urination and intromission, which enters the female's vagina to deliver semen. The urethra runs through the penis, which is composed largely of erectile tissue and has a mushroom-shaped cap (glans penis). **—penile** *adj.*

penis envy in the classic psychoanalytic theory of Austrian psychiatrist Sigmund Freud (1856–1939), the hypothesized desire of girls and women to possess a male genital organ. German-born U.S. psychoanalyst Karen D. Horney (1885–1952), among others, later argued that penis envy is not an envy of the biological organ itself but represents women's envy of men's superior social status. In any sense, the concept has been actively disputed from the beginning and is rarely considered seriously in current psychology. See also CASTRATION COMPLEX.

penology *n.* the scientific study of the management of correctional facilities and the rehabilitation of criminals.

peptide *n.* a short chain of AMINO ACIDS linked by **peptide bonds**. Peptides are usually identified by the number of amino acids in the chain, for example, dipeptides have two, tripeptides three, tetrapeptides four, and so on. See also POLYPEPTIDE; PROTEIN.

peptide hormone any hormone that is classed chemically as a PEPTIDE. Peptide hormones include CORTICOTROPIN, OXYTOCIN, and VASOPRESSIN.

percentile *n.* the location of a score in a distribution coded to reflect the percentage of cases in the batch that have scores equal to or below the score in question. Thus, if a score is said to be at the 90th percentile, the implication is that 90% of the scores in the batch are equal to or lower than that score.

percept *n.* the product of PERCEPTION: the stimulus object or event as experienced by the individual.

perception *n.* the process or result of becoming aware of objects, relationships, and events by means of the senses, which includes such activities as recognizing, observing, and discriminating. These activities enable organisms to organize and interpret the stimuli received into meaningful knowledge.

perceptual constancy the phenomenon in which a perceived object or its properties (e.g., size,

P

shape, color) appears to remain unchanged despite variations in the stimulus itself or in the external conditions of observation, such as object orientation or level of illumination. Examples of perceptual constancy include BRIGHTNESS CONSTANCY, COLOR CONSTANCY, SHAPE CONSTANCY, and SIZE CONSTANCY.

perceptual defense in psychoanalytic theory, a misperception that occurs when anxiety-arousing stimuli are unconsciously distorted. If taboo words are rapidly presented, they may be misinterpreted; for example, if the stimulus word *anal* is presented, participants may report seeing the innocuous *canal*.

perceptual filtering the process of focusing attention on a selected subset of the large number of sensory stimuli that are present at any one time. Perceptual filtering is necessary because the cognitive and physical capacity of an individual to process and respond to multiple sources of information is limited.

perceptual organization the process enabling such properties as structure, pattern, and form to be imposed on the senses to provide conceptual organization. Each of the senses establishes (or learns) such organizational schemata. Recent research has more precisely defined the properties that enable such organized tasks. Also called **perceptualization**.

perceptual set 1. a temporary readiness to perceive certain objects or events rather than others. For example, a person driving a car has a perceptual set to identify anything that might impact his or her safety. **2.** a SCHEMA or FRAME OF REFERENCE that influences the way in which a person perceives objects, events, or people. For example, an on-duty police officer and a painter might regard a crowded street scene with very different perceptual sets.

perfect correlation a relationship between two variables in which the change in value of one variable is proportional to the change in value of the other variable; knowing the value of one variable will exactly predict the value of the other variable. When plotted graphically, a perfect correlation forms a perfectly straight line. If the variables change in the same direction (i.e., they both increase or both decrease), the correlation is perfect positive, whereas if the variables change in opposite directions (i.e., one increases as the other decreases or vice versa), the correlation is perfect negative. See also CORRELATION COEFFICIENT.

perfectionism *n.* the tendency to demand of others or of oneself an extremely high or even flawless level of performance, particularly when this is not required by the situation. It is thought by some to be a risk factor for depression and other disorders. —**perfectionist** *adj., n.*

performance *n.* **1.** any activity or collection of responses that leads to a result or has an effect upon the environment. **2.** in linguistics, see COMPETENCE.

performance anxiety anxiety associated with the apprehension and fear of the consequences of being unable to perform a task or of performing the task at a level that will lead to expectations of higher levels of performance achievement. Fear of taking a test, public speaking, participating in classes or meetings, playing a musical instrument in public, or even eating in public are common examples. If the fear associated with performance anxiety is focused on negative evaluation by others, embarrassment, or humiliation, the anxiety may be classified as a SOCIAL PHOBIA.

performance test any test of ability requiring primarily motor, rather than verbal, responses, such as a test requiring manipulation of a variety of different kinds of objects.

periaqueductal gray (PAG) a region of the brainstem, rich in nerve cell bodies (i.e., gray matter), that surrounds the CEREBRAL AQUEDUCT. A component of the LIMBIC SYSTEM, it plays an important role in organizing defensive behaviors (e.g., freezing). Also called **central gray**.

perilymph *n.* the fluid that fills the space between the membranous LABYRINTH and the walls of the bony labyrinth in the inner ear. —**perilymphatic** *adj.*

period effect any outcome associated with living during a particular time period or era, regardless of how old one was at the time. Period effects may be difficult to distinguish from AGE EFFECTS and COHORT EFFECTS in research.

peripheral dyslexia a form of acquired DYSLEXIA that is characterized by difficulties in processing the visual aspects of words (e.g., difficulties identifying letter forms) and results from damage to the visual analysis system. Compare CENTRAL DYSLEXIA.

peripheral nervous system (PNS) the portion of the nervous system that lies outside the brain and spinal cord, that is, all parts outside the CENTRAL NERVOUS SYSTEM. Afferent fibers of the PNS bring messages from the sense organs to the central nervous system; efferent fibers transmit messages from the central nervous system to the muscles and glands. It includes the CRANIAL NERVES, SPINAL NERVES, and parts of the AUTONOMIC NERVOUS SYSTEM.

peripheral route to persuasion the process by which attitudes are formed or changed as a result of using peripheral cues (factors external to the merits of the argument) rather than carefully scrutinizing

and thinking about the central merits of attitude-relevant information. See also ELABORATION; ELABORATION-LIKELIHOOD MODEL. Compare CENTRAL ROUTE TO PERSUASION.

perirhinal cortex a structure in the medial TEMPORAL LOBE adjacent to the hippocampus that plays an important role as an interface between visual perception and memory.

permastore *n.* very long-term or permanent memory that develops after extensive learning, training, or experience. Details of foreign languages or algebra learned years ago in school, and even the names of classmates, are said to be stored in permastore.

permissiveness *n.* an interpersonal style or approach that involves giving a wide range of freedom and autonomy to those with whom one has dealings or over whom one has authority. For example, regarding child rearing it refers to a particular PARENTING style in which the child is given wide latitude in expressing his or her feelings and opinions and in which artificial restrictions and punishment are avoided as much as possible. —**permissive** *adj.*

permissive parenting see PARENTING.

permutation *n.* an ordered sequence of elements from a set. A permutation is similar to a COMBINATION but distinguished by its emphasis on order.

perseverance effect the phenomenon in which people's beliefs about themselves and others persist despite a lack of supporting evidence or even a contradiction of supporting evidence.

perseveration *n.* **1.** an inability to interrupt a task or to shift from one strategy or procedure to another. Perseveration may be observed, for

P

example, in workers under extreme task demands or environmental conditions (mainly heat stress); in the abnormal or inappropriate repetition of a sound, word, or phrase, as occurs in stuttering; or in the inappropriate repetition of behavior in individuals with damage to the FRONTAL LOBE. **2.** according to the PERSEVERATION–CONSOLIDATION HYPOTHESIS, the repetition, after a learning experience, of neural processes that are responsible for memory formation, which is necessary for the consolidation of LONG-TERM MEMORY. **—perseverate** *vb.*

perseveration–consolidation hypothesis the hypothesis that information passes through two stages in memory formation. During the first stage the memory is held by perseveration (repetition) of neural activity and is easily disrupted. During the second stage the memory becomes fixed, or consolidated, and is no longer easily disrupted. The perseveration–consolidation hypothesis guides much contemporary research on the biological basis of long-term learning and memory. Also called **consolidation hypothesis**; **consolidation–perseveration hypothesis**. See also DUAL TRACE HYPOTHESIS.

persistence *n.* **1.** continuance or repetition of a particular behavior, process, or activity despite cessation of the initiating stimulus. **2.** the quality or state of maintaining a course of action or keeping at a task and finishing it despite the obstacles (such as opposition or discouragement) or the effort involved. **—persistent** *adj.*

persistent vegetative state (**PVS**) a prolonged biomedical condition in which rudimentary brain function and, usually, spontaneous respiration continue but there is no awareness of self or environment, no communication, and no voluntary response to stimuli.

persona *n.* in the approach of Swiss psychoanalyst Carl Jung (1875–1961), the public face an individual presents to the outside world, in contrast to more deeply rooted and authentic personality characteristics. This sense has now passed into popular usage.

personal attribution see DISPOSITIONAL ATTRIBUTION.

personal construct one of the concepts by which an individual perceives, understands, predicts, and attempts to control the world. Understanding a client's personal constructs is a central way of beginning to help that person change rigid or negative beliefs. See REPERTORY GRID.

personal disposition in the personality theory of U.S. psychologist Gordon W. Allport (1897–1967), any of a number of enduring characteristics that describe or determine an individual's behavior across a variety of situations and that are peculiar to and uniquely expressed by that individual. Personal dispositions are divided into three categories: cardinal dispositions are the most pervasive and influence virtually every behavior of that person; central dispositions are less pervasive but nonetheless generally influential; and secondary dispositions are much more narrowly expressed and situation specific.

personal fable a belief in one's uniqueness and invulnerability, which is an expression of adolescent EGOCENTRISM and may extend further into the lifespan.

personal identity see IDENTITY.

personalism *n.* **1.** the philosophical position that human personality is the sole means through which reality can be understood or interpreted. At the core of this approach is the concept of the person as a unique living whole irreducible in value or worth, who is striving toward goals and is simultaneously self-contained yet open to the world around him or her. Personalism thus reorients the material of psychology around an experiencing individual as a systematic focal point. In other words, the findings of psychology can be organized only by reference to such a unique, living individual as the originator, carrier, and regulator of all psychological states and processes. This school of psychology stressing individual personality is more properly termed **personalistic psychology. 2.** a tendency to believe that another person's actions are directed at oneself rather than being an expression of that individual's characteristics.

personality *n.* the configuration of characteristics and behavior that comprises an individual's unique adjustment to life, including major traits, interests, drives, values, self-concept, abilities, and emotional patterns. Personality is generally viewed as a complex, dynamic integration or totality, shaped by many forces, including: hereditary and constitutional tendencies; physical maturation; early training; identification with significant individuals and groups; culturally conditioned values and roles; and critical experiences and relationships. Various theories explain the structure and development of personality in different ways but all agree that personality helps determine behavior.

personality assessment the evaluation of such factors as intelligence, skills, interests, aptitudes, creative abilities, attitudes, and facets of psychological development by a variety of techniques. These include (a) observational methods that use behavior sampling, interviews, and rating scales; (b) personality inventories, such as the MINNESOTA MULTIPHASIC PERSONALITY INVENTORY; and (c) projective techniques, such as the RORSCHACH INKBLOT TEST and THEMATIC APPERCEPTION TEST. The uses of personality assessment are manifold, for example, in clinical evaluation of children and adults; in educational and vocational counseling; in industry and other organizational settings; and in rehabilitation.

personality disorder any of a group of disorders involving pervasive patterns of perceiving, relating to, and thinking about the environment and the self that interfere with long-term functioning of the individual and are not limited to isolated episodes. Among the specific types are paranoid, schizoid, schizotypal, histrionic, narcissistic, antisocial, borderline, avoidant, dependent, and obsessive-compulsive—each of which has its own entry in the dictionary.

personality inventory a personality assessment device that usually consists of a series of statements covering various characteristics and behavioral patterns to which the participant responds by fixed answers, such as True, False, Always, Often, Seldom, or Never, as applied to himself or herself. The scoring of such tests is objective, and the results are interpreted according to standardized norms. An example is the MINNESOTA MULTIPHASIC PERSONALITY INVENTORY.

personality profile a presentation of the results of psychological testing in graphic form so as to provide a summary of a person's TRAITS or other unique attributes and tendencies. Personality profiles are used to summarize the characteristics of groups of individuals as well (e.g., people with a particular disorder, people employed in a particular profession).

personality psychology the systematic study of the human personality, with the aim of synthesizing cognitive, emotional, motivational, developmental, and social aspects of human individuality into integrative frameworks for making sense of the individual human life. Personality psychologists tend to study more-or-less enduring and stable individual differences in adults and have traditionally assigned a central role to human motivation and the internal dynamics of human behavior. The major families of personality theories include the psychodynamic, behavioral, and humanistic families.

personality test any instrument used to help evaluate personality or measure PERSONALITY TRAITS. Personality tests may collect self-report data, in which participants answer questions about their personality or select items that describe themselves, or they may take the form of projective tests (see PROJECTIVE TECHNIQUE), which claim to measure unconscious aspects of a participant's personality.

personality trait a relatively stable, consistent, and enduring internal characteristic that is inferred from a pattern of behaviors, attitudes, feelings, and habits in the individual. Personality traits can be useful in summarizing, predicting, and explaining an individual's conduct, and a variety of **personality trait theories** exist.

personal space an area of defended space around an individual. Personal space differs from other types of defended space (e.g., territory) by being a surrounding "bubble" that moves with the individual. Because human use of personal space varies among cul-

tures, at least part of it must represent a learned behavior. See PROXEMICS.

personal unconscious in the ANALYTIC PSYCHOLOGY of Swiss psychiatrist Carl Jung (1875–1961), the portion of each individual's unconscious that contains the elements of his or her own experience as opposed to the COLLECTIVE UNCONSCIOUS, which contains the ARCHETYPES universal to humankind. The personal unconscious consists of everything subliminal, forgotten, and repressed in an individual's life.

person-centered therapy see CLIENT-CENTERED THERAPY.

personnel psychology the branch of INDUSTRIAL AND ORGANIZATIONAL PSYCHOLOGY that deals with the selection, placement, training, promotion, evaluation, and counseling of employees.

person perception the processes by which people think about, appraise, and evaluate other people. An important aspect of person perception is the attribution of motives for action (see ATTRIBUTION THEORY).

persuasion *n.* an active attempt by one person to change another person's attitudes, beliefs, or emotions associated with some issue, person, concept, or object. **—persuasive** *adj.*

pervasive developmental disorder any one of a class of disorders characterized by severe and widespread impairment in social interaction and verbal or nonverbal communication or the presence of stereotyped behavior, interests, and activities. These disorders are frequently apparent from an early age; they include ASPERGER'S DISORDER, AUTISTIC DISORDER, CHILDHOOD DISINTEGRATIVE DISORDER, and RETT SYNDROME. This term is synon-

ymous with AUTISTIC SPECTRUM DIS-
ORDER.

pessimism *n.* the attitude that
things will go wrong and that people's wishes or aims are unlikely to
be fulfilled. **Pessimists** are people
who expect unpleasant or bad
things to happen to them and to
others or who are otherwise doubt-
ful or hesitant about positive
outcomes of behavior. Pessimism
can be defined in terms of expectancy: lack of confidence of
attaining desired goals (compare OP-
TIMISM). Most individuals lie
somewhere on the spectrum between the two polar opposites of
pure optimism and pure pessimism
but tend to demonstrate sometimes
strong, relatively stable or situational tendencies in one direction or
the other. **—pessimistic** *adj.*

PET acronym for POSITRON EMIS-
SION TOMOGRAPHY.

petit mal see ABSENCE SEIZURE.

phallic stage in the classic psychoanalytic theory of Austrian
psychiatrist Sigmund Freud (1856–
1939), the third stage of PSYCHO-
SEXUAL DEVELOPMENT beginning
around age 3, when the LIBIDO is focused on the genital area (penis or
clitoris) and discovery and manipulation of the body become a major
source of pleasure. During this period boys are posited to experience
CASTRATION ANXIETY, girls to experience PENIS ENVY, and both to
experience the OEDIPUS COMPLEX.

phallus *n.* (*pl.* **phalli**) the PENIS or
an object that resembles the form of
the penis (the latter often referred to
as a **phallic symbol**). As a symbolic
object, it often represents fertility or
potency.

phantasy *n.* in the OBJECT RELA-
TIONS THEORY of Austrian-born
British psychoanalyst Melanie Klein
(1882–1960), one of the unconscious constructions, wishes, or

impulses that are presumed to underlie all thought and feeling. The
ph spelling is used to distinguish this
from the everyday form of FANTASY,
which can include conscious daydreaming.

phantom limb the feeling that an
amputated limb is still present,
often manifested as a tingling or, occasionally, painful sensation in the
area of the missing limb (**phantom
limb pain**). It is thought that the
brain's representation of the limb remains intact and, in the absence of
normal somesthetic stimulation, becomes active spontaneously or as a
result of stimulation from other
brain tissue.

pharmacological antagonism
see ANTAGONIST.

pharmacology *n.* the branch of
science that involves the study of
substances that interact with living
organisms to alter some biological
process affecting the HOMEOSTASIS
of the organism. **—pharmacological** or **pharmacologic** *adj.*

pharmacotherapy *n.* the
treatment of a disorder by the administration of drugs, as opposed
to such means as surgery, psychotherapy, or complementary and
alternative methods. Also called
drug therapy. See PSYCHO-
PHARMACOTHERAPY.

phase locking the tendency for a
neural ACTION POTENTIAL to occur
at the same point or phase of a pure-
tone (single-frequency) auditory
stimulus. Phase locking underlies
the ability to localize sounds based
on interaural phase differences or
interaural time differences (see BIN-
AURAL CUE) and has been proposed
as a mechanism for the coding of
pitch.

phencyclidine *n.* see PCP.

phenomenal self the SELF as experienced by the individual at a given

time. Only a small portion of self-knowledge is active in working memory or consciousness at any time, with the remainder lying dormant or inactive. The same person might have a very different phenomenal self at different times, without any change in actual self-knowledge, simply because different views are brought into awareness by events.

phenomenal space the environment as experienced by a given individual at a given time. The term refers not to objective reality but to personal and subjective reality, including everything within one's field of awareness. In the phenomenological personality theory of U.S. psychologist Carl Rogers (1902–1987), it is also known as the **phenomenological field**. Also called **phenomenal field**.

phenomenology n. a movement in modern European philosophy initiated by German philosopher Edmund Husserl (1859–1938). Husserl argued for a new approach to human knowledge in which mental events should be studied and described in their own terms, rather than in terms of their relationship to events in the body or in the external world. However, phenomenology should be distinguished from introspection as it is concerned with the relationship between acts of consciousness and the objects of such acts. Husserl's approach proved widely influential in psychology—especially GESTALT PSYCHOLOGY and EXISTENTIAL PSYCHOLOGY. —**phenomenological** adj. —**phenomenologist** n.

phenomenon n. (pl. **phenomena**) an observable event or physical occurrence. In Greek philosophy, most notably that of Plato (c. 427–c. 347 BCE), phenomena are the sensible things that constitute the world of experience, as contrasted with the

transcendent realities that are known only through reason. German philosopher Immanuel Kant (1724–1804) used the term *phenomena* to refer to things as they appear to the senses and are interpreted by the categories of the human understanding. For Kant, knowledge of phenomena is the kind of knowledge available to human beings, as knowledge of "noumena," or things in themselves, remains beyond human experience or reason. —**phenomenal** adj.

phenothiazine n. any of a group of chemically related compounds most of which are used as ANTIPSYCHOTIC drugs, originally developed as such in the 1950s. It is commonly assumed that their therapeutic effects are produced by blockade of a particular type of dopamine RECEPTOR. They also block acetylcholine, histamine, and norepinephrine receptors, actions that are associated with many of their adverse effects, which include EXTRAPYRAMIDAL SYMPTOMS, TARDIVE DYSKINESIA, and sedation.

phenotype n. the observable characteristics of an individual, such as morphological or biochemical features and the presence or absence of a particular disease or condition. Phenotype is determined by the expression of the individual's GENOTYPE coupled with the effects of environmental factors (e.g., nutritional status or climate). —**phenotypic** adj.

phenylketonuria n. an inherited metabolic disease marked by a deficiency of an enzyme (phenylalanine hydroxylase) needed to utilize the amino acid phenylalanine. Unless it is diagnosed in early infancy and treated by a restricted dietary intake of phenylalanine, phenylketonuria leads to severe mental retardation and other nervous-system disorders.

pheromone n. a chemical signal

that is released outside the body by members of a species and that influences the behavior of other members of the same species. For example, it may serve to attract the opposite sex or to act as an alarm. The existence of true pheromones in humans is controversial. Compare ALLOMONE.

phi coefficient (symbol: ϕ) a measure of association for two dichotomous RANDOM VARIABLES. The phi coefficient is the PRODUCT–MOMENT CORRELATION when both variables are coded (0,1).

philosophy *n.* the intellectual discipline that uses careful reasoned argument to elucidate fundamental questions, notably those concerning the nature of reality (metaphysics), the nature of knowledge (EPISTEMOLOGY), and the nature of moral judgments (ETHICS). As such, it provides an intellectual foundation for many other disciplines, including psychology. Psychology as a scientific discipline has its roots in the epistemological preoccupations of 18th- and 19th-century philosophy and continues to be influenced by philosophical ideas. **—philosopher** *n.* **—philosophical** *adj.*

phi phenomenon an illusion seen when two lights flash on and off about 150 m apart. The light appears to move from one location to the other. The phi phenomenon is a form of beta movement (see APPARENT MOVEMENT).

phobia *n.* a persistent and irrational fear of a specific situation, object, or activity (e.g., heights, dogs, water, blood, driving, flying), which is consequently either strenuously avoided or endured with marked distress. The many types of individual phobia are classified as SPECIFIC PHOBIAS. See also SOCIAL PHOBIA. **—phobic** *adj.*

phoneme *n.* a speech sound that

plays a meaningful role in a language and cannot be analyzed into smaller meaningful sounds, conventionally indicated by slash symbols: /b/. A speech sound is held to be meaningful in a given language if its contrast with other sounds is used to mark distinctions of meaning: In English, for example, /p/ and /b/ are phonemes because they distinguish between [pan] and [ban] and other such pairs. **—phonemic** *adj.*

phonemics *n.* the branch of linguistics concerned with the classification and analysis of the PHONEMES in a language. While PHONETICS tries to characterize all possible sounds represented in human language, phonemics identifies which of the phonetic distinctions are considered meaningful by a given language.

phonetics *n.* the branch of linguistics that studies the physical properties of speech sounds and the physiological means by which these are produced and perceived (placing the tongue or lip in contact with the teeth, directing the airstream against the hard palate, etc.).

phonological disorder a communication disorder characterized by failure to develop and consistently use speech sounds that are appropriate for the child's age. It most commonly involves misarticulation of the later acquired speech sounds, such as [l], [r], [s], [z], [ch], [sh], or [th], but may also include substitution of sounds (e.g., [t] for [k]) or omission of sounds (e.g., final consonants).

phonological dyslexia a form of acquired DYSLEXIA characterized primarily by difficulties in reading pronounceable nonwords. Semantic errors are not seen in this type of dyslexia, a feature that distinguishes it from DEEP DYSLEXIA. See also SURFACE DYSLEXIA.

P

phonological loop see WORKING MEMORY.

phonology *n.* the branch of linguistics that studies the system of speech sounds in a language or in language generally. The term is less specific than either PHONEMICS or PHONETICS. **—phonological** *adj.*

phosphene *n.* a sensation of a light flash in the absence of actual light stimulation to the eye. It can be caused by mechanical stimulation of the retina, by rubbing the eyes when closed, or by direct electrical stimulation of the visual cortex.

photographic memory exceptionally detailed and highly accurate recollection of information or visual experiences. Photographic memory is widely but mistakenly considered synonymous with an EIDETIC IMAGE.

photopigment *n.* a substance in a RETINAL ROD or RETINAL CONE that interacts with light to initiate a chemical cascade resulting in the conversion of light energy into an electrical signal. All rods contain the photopigment **rhodopsin**, while cones have one of three different photopigments (**iodopsins**), each with a different wavelength sensitivity. Photopigment is located in disks of membrane in the outer segment of a rod or cone.

photoreceptor *n.* a visual receptor, especially a RETINAL ROD or a RETINAL CONE.

phototherapy *n.* therapy involving exposure to ultraviolet or infrared light, which is used for treating not only certain skin conditions or disorders (e.g., jaundice, psoriasis) but also depression, particularly for patients with SEASONAL AFFECTIVE DISORDER (SAD). Also called **light therapy**.

phrase-structure grammar a type of GENERATIVE GRAMMAR in which a system of **phrase-structure rules** is used to describe a sentence in terms of the grammatical structures that generate its form and define it as grammatical. The phrase-structure rules are usually set out in the form X → Y + Z, in which the arrow is an instruction to reformulate ("rewrite") X in terms of its immediate constituents (Y + Z). Formal phrase-structure analysis of this kind was developed by U.S. linguist Noam Chomsky (1928–). His TRANSFORMATIONAL GENERATIVE GRAMMAR added an important new dimension by proposing that sentences have a DEEP STRUCTURE as well as the linear SURFACE STRUCTURE described in phrase-structure grammar, and that the relationship between the two levels can be described through a system of transformational rules.

phrenology *n.* a theory of personality formulated in the 18th and 19th centuries by German physician Franz Josef Gall (1757–1828) and Austrian philosopher and anatomist Johann Kaspar Spurzheim (1776–1832). It stated that specific abilities or personality traits are represented by specific areas of the brain: The size of these brain areas, and hence the degree of the corresponding skill or trait, could be indicated by bumps and hollows on the skull surface. See also PHYSIOGNOMY. **—phrenological** *adj.* **—phrenologist** *n.*

phylogeny *n.* **1.** the evolutionary origin and development of a particular group (species) of organisms. Compare ONTOGENY. **2.** a diagram that shows genetic linkages between ancestors and descendants. Also called **phylogenetic tree**. **—phylogenetic** *adj.*

physical abuse deliberately aggressive or violent behavior by one person toward another that results in bodily injury. Physical abuse may

P

involve such actions as punching, kicking, biting, choking, burning, shaking, and beating, which may at times be severe enough to result in permanent damage (e.g., TRAU-MATIC BRAIN INJURY) or death. It is most frequently observed in relationships of trust, particularly between parents and children or between intimate partners (e.g., in a marriage); indeed, violence against women and children is recognized as a major public health problem. Individuals who experience physical abuse often feel helpless and isolated, and are prone to the subsequent development of numerous pathological conditions, including depression, eating disorders, posttraumatic stress disorder, anxiety disorders, and substance use problems. See also BATTERED-CHILD SYNDROME; BATTERED-WOMAN SYNDROME.

physical dependence the state of an individual who has repeatedly taken a drug and will experience unpleasant physiological symptoms (see SUBSTANCE WITHDRAWAL) if he or she stops taking the drug. Compare PSYCHOLOGICAL DEPENDENCE.

physician-assisted suicide see ASSISTED DEATH.

physiognomy *n.* **1.** the form of a person's physical features, especially the face. **2.** the attempt to read personality from the facial features and expression, assuming, for example, that a person with a receding chin is weak or one with a high forehead is bright. The idea dates back to Greek philosopher Aristotle (383–322 BCE) and was later developed into a pseudoscientific system by Swiss pastor Johann Lavater (1741–1801) and Italian psychiatrist Cesare Lombroso (1835–1909). See also PHRENOLOGY.

physiological antagonism see ANTAGONIST.

physiological arousal aspects of AROUSAL shown by physiological responses, such as increases in blood pressure and rate of respiration and decreased activity of the gastrointestinal system. Such primary arousal responses are largely governed by the SYMPATHETIC NERVOUS SYSTEM, but responses of the PARASYMPA-THETIC NERVOUS SYSTEM may compensate or even overcompensate for the sympathetic activity. See also AUTONOMIC NERVOUS SYSTEM.

physiological correlate an association between a physiological measure and a behavioral measure. The existence of a physiological correlate may suggest a causal relation, but it does not establish a cause.

physiological need any of the requirements for survival, such as food, water, oxygen, and sleep. Physiological needs make up the lowest level of MASLOW'S MOTIVA-TIONAL HIERARCHY. Also called **basic need.**

physiological psychology a term used interchangeably with PSYCHOPHYSIOLOGY or, less commonly, BIOLOGICAL PSYCHOLOGY.

physiology *n.* the science of the functions of living organisms, including the chemical and physical processes involved and the activities of the cells, tissues, and organs, as opposed to static anatomical or structural factors. —**physiological** *adj.* —**physiologist** *n.*

Piagetian theory the theory of cognitive development proposed by Swiss child psychologist Jean Piaget (1896–1980), according to which intelligence develops through four major stages: (a) the sensorimotor stage (roughly 0–2 years), (b) the preoperational stage (roughly 2–7 years), (c) the concrete operational stage (roughly 7–12 years), and (d) the formal operational stage (roughly 12 years and beyond). According to this theory, each stage builds upon the preceding one. Passage through the stages is facilitated by a balance of two processes: ASSIMILATION, in which new information is incorporated into already existing cognitive structures; and ACCOMMODATION, in which new information that does not fit into already existing cognitive structures is used to create new cognitive structures.

pia mater see MENINGES.

piblokto *n.* a CULTURE-BOUND SYNDROME observed primarily in female Inuit and other arctic populations. Individuals experience a sudden dissociative period of extreme excitement in which they often tear off clothes, run naked through the snow, scream, throw things, and perform other wild behaviors. This typically ends with convulsive seizures, followed by an acute coma and amnesia for the event.

Pick's disease a form of DEMENTIA characterized by progressive degeneration of the frontal and temporal areas of the brain with the presence of particles called **Pick bodies** in the cytoplasm of the neurons. The disease is characterized by personality changes and deterioration of social skills and complex thinking; symptoms include problems with new situations and abstractions, difficulty in thinking or concentrating, loss of memory, lack of spontaneity, gradual emotional dullness, loss of moral judgment, and disturbances of speech. [described in 1892 by Arnold **Pick** (1851–1924), Czech psychiatrist and neuroanatomist]

pidgin *n.* an improvised contact language incorporating elements of two or more languages, often devised for purposes of trading. Pidgins are characterized by simple rules and limited vocabulary. Compare CREOLE.

pie chart a graphic display in which a circle is cut into pielike wedges, the area of the wedge being proportional to the percentage of cases in the category represented by that wedge.

piloerection *n.* a temporary raising of the hairs covering the surface of the skin caused by contraction of the piloerector muscles, which are attached to the individual FOLLICLES from which each hair arises. Piloerection is involuntary, being directed by the SYMPATHETIC NERVOUS SYSTEM, and elicited by cold, fear, or a startling stimulus. In mammals with a thick, visible covering of hair (e.g., cats), piloerection serves a protective function: the resulting "fluffed up" appearance makes the animal seem larger and may deter attack by others. In humans, whose skin has only a sparse covering of hair, piloerection creates a temporary roughness as the muscles pucker the surrounding skin, giving rise to such colloquial names for the effect as **goose bumps, goose flesh,** and **goose pimples.** Also called **pilomotor response** (or **effect**).

pilot study a small, preliminary research project designed to evaluate procedures in preparation for a subsequent and more detailed research project. Although pilot studies are conducted to reveal information about the viability of a proposed experiment and implement necessary modifications, they may also provide useful initial data on the topic of study and suggest avenues or offer implications for future research.

pineal gland a small, cone-shaped gland attached by a stalk to the posterior wall of the third VENTRICLE of the brain; it is part of the EPITHALAMUS. In amphibians and reptiles, the gland appears to function as a part of the visual system. In mammals it secretes the hormone

MELATONIN and is an important component of the circadian system regulating BIOLOGICAL RHYTHMS. Also called **pineal body**.

pinna *n.* (*pl.* **pinnae**) the funnel-shaped part of the external ear that projects beyond the head. Consisting of cartilage, it collects and focuses sounds toward the EXTERNAL AUDITORY MEATUS (auditory canal).

pitch *n.* the subjective attribute that permits sounds to be ordered on a musical scale. It is determined primarily by frequency but other physical parameters, such as intensity and duration, can affect pitch. The unit of pitch is the mel.

pituitary gland a gland, pea-sized in humans, that lies at the base of the brain, connected by a stalk (the infundibulum) to the HYPOTHALAMUS. The anterior lobe produces and secretes seven hormones—thyroid-stimulating hormone, follicle-stimulating hormone, corticotropin, growth hormone, luteinizing hormone, prolactin, and melanocyte-stimulating hormone—in response to RELEASING HORMONES from the hypothalamus. The posterior lobe secretes two hormones, vasopressin and oxytocin, which are synthesized in the hypothalamus and transported down axons in the infundibulum. The pituitary's role of secreting such tropic hormones, which regulate the production of other hormones, has resulted in its designation as the "master gland of the endocrine system."

PK abbreviation for PSYCHOKINESIS.

placebo *n.* (*pl.* **placebos**) a pharmacologically inert substance, such as a sugar pill, that is often administered as a control in testing new drugs. Placebos are generally used in double-BLIND trials and may be dummies, which appear identical in all aspects (e.g., dosage form,

method of administration) to the active drug under investigation but have no pharmacological activity, or active placebos, which have no therapeutic effect but may produce side effects characteristic of the drug under investigation. See PLACEBO EFFECT.

placebo control group a group of participants in a study who receive an inert substance (placebo) instead of the active drug under investigation, thus functioning as a neutral condition against which to make comparisons regarding the actual pharmacological effects of the active drug.

placebo effect a clinically significant response to a therapeutically inert substance or nonspecific treatment, based on the recipient's expectations or beliefs regarding the intervention. It is now recognized that placebo effects accompany the administration of any drug (active or inert) and contribute to the therapeutic effectiveness of a specific treatment. See PLACEBO.

place cell any of various neurons in the HIPPOCAMPUS that fire selectively when an animal is in a particular spatial location or moving toward that location.

placenta *n.* the specialized organ produced by the mammalian embryo that attaches to the wall of the uterus to permit removal of waste products and to provide nutrients, energy, and gas exchange for the fetus via the maternal circulation. —**placental** *adj.*

place theory the theory that (a) different frequencies stimulate different places along the BASILAR MEMBRANE and (b) pitch is coded by the place of maximal stimulation. The first proposition is strongly supported by experimental evidence and stems from the fact that the mammalian auditory system shows

P

TONOTOPIC ORGANIZATION. The second hypothesis remains controversial.

planned comparison a comparison among two or more means in ANALYSIS OF VARIANCE or REGRESSION ANALYSIS that has been specified prior to the observation of the data. Also called **planned contrast**. Compare POST HOC COMPARISON.

plantar reflex the involuntary flexing of the toes of a healthy infant when the sole of the foot is stroked. The plantar reflex appears around age 2 and replaces the earlier BABINSKI REFLEX.

planum temporale a region of the superior temporal cortex of the brain, adjacent to the primary AUDITORY CORTEX, that includes part of WERNICKE'S AREA. In most people it is larger in the left cerebral hemisphere than in the right hemisphere.

plaque *n.* a small patch of abnormal tissue on or within a bodily structure, formed as the result of an accumulation of substances or as the result of localized damage. Examples of the former type include the SENILE PLAQUES of Alzheimer's disease, arising from clumps of beta-amyloid protein, and the atheromatous plaques of ATHEROSCLEROSIS, consisting of lipid deposits on the lining of arterial walls. Examples of the latter type include the demyelination plaques on the protective nerve sheaths of individuals with MULTIPLE SCLEROSIS.

plasticity *n.* flexibility and adaptability. Plasticity of the nervous or hormonal systems makes it possible to learn and register new experiences. Early experiences can also modify and shape gene expression to induce long-lasting changes in neurons or endocrine organs. See also NEURAL PLASTICITY.

platykurtic *adj.* describing a distribution of scores flatter than a normal distribution, that is, having more scores at the extremes and fewer in the center than in a normal distribution. See also MESOKURTIC; LEPTOKURTIC.

play *n.* activities that appear to be freely sought and pursued solely for the sake of individual or group enjoyment. Although play is typically regarded as serving no immediate purpose beyond enjoyment, studies indicate that it contributes significantly to development. Various types of play have been described, ranging from locomotor play to social play to cognitive play, and numerous theories about play have been proposed. Swiss psychologist Jean Piaget (1895–1980), for example, regarded it as advancing children's cognitive development through mastery play, playing games with defined rules (such as hide-and-seek), and symbolic play. Advocates of the practice theory of play propose that play prepares children for activities or roles they will encounter as adults, whereas others suggest that it serves a more immediate function, such as exercise, establishing social relations among peers, or using up excess energy. Although the preponderance of research on play focuses on the activities of children, the play behavior of nonhuman animals is also actively studied.

play therapy the use of play activities and materials (e.g., clay, water, blocks, dolls, puppets, drawing, and finger paint) in child psychotherapy. Play-therapy techniques are based on the theory that such activities mirror the child's emotional life and fantasies, enabling the child to "play out" his or her feelings and problems and to test out new approaches and understand relationships in action rather than words.

P

pleasure center any of various areas of the brain (including areas of the hypothalamus and limbic system) that, upon intracranial self-stimulation, have been implicated in producing pleasure. The existence of pure pleasure centers has not been definitively established, particularly because the self-stimulation response rate varies according to such factors as the duration and strength of the electrical stimulation.

pleasure principle the view that human beings are governed by the desire for instinctual gratification, or pleasure, and for the discharge of tension that builds up as pain or "unpleasure" when gratification is lacking. According to psychoanalytic theory, the pleasure principle is the psychic force that motivates people to seek immediate gratification of instinctual, or libidinal, impulses, such as sex, hunger, thirst, and elimination. It dominates the ID and operates most strongly during childhood. Later, in adulthood, it is opposed by the REALITY PRINCIPLE of the EGO. Also called **pleasure–pain principle**.

plethysmography *n.* the process of measuring and recording volume or volume changes in organs or body tissues, such as the blood supply flowing through an organ.

pluralistic ignorance the state of affairs in which virtually every member of a group privately rejects what are held to be the prevailing attitudes and beliefs of the group. Each member falsely believes that these standards are accepted by everyone else in the group.

PMS abbreviation for PREMENSTRUAL SYNDROME.

PNS abbreviation for PERIPHERAL NERVOUS SYSTEM.

point biserial correlation coefficient a numerical index reflecting the degree of relationship between two random variables, one continuous and one dichotomous.

point estimate a single estimated numerical value of a given population parameter. Compare INTERVAL ESTIMATE.

point of subjective equality the value of a comparison stimulus that, for a given observer, is equally likely to be judged as higher or lower than that of a standard stimulus.

polarization *n.* a difference in electric potential between two surfaces or two sides of one surface because of chemical activity. Polarization occurs normally in living cells, such as neurons and muscle cells, which maintain a positive charge on one side of the plasma membrane and a negative charge on the other.

polyandry *n.* an animal mating system in which a female mates with more than one male but a male mates with only one female. Compare MONOGAMY; POLYGYNANDRY; POLYGYNY. —**polyandrous** *adj.*

polygamy *n.* marriage to more than one spouse at the same time, which is an accepted custom in certain cultures. See also POLYANDRY; POLYGYNY. Compare MONOGAMY. —**polygamous** *adj.* —**polygamist** *n.*

polygenic *adj.* relating to two or more genes, as in polygenic inheritance (see MULTIFACTORIAL INHERITANCE).

polygenic inheritance see MULTIFACTORIAL INHERITANCE.

polygenic trait an attribute that is determined by numerous genes rather than only one. An example is a person's height. Also called **polygenetic trait**. See MULTIFACTORIAL INHERITANCE.

polygraph *n.* a device that mea-

P

sures and records several physiological indicators of anxiety or emotion, such as heart rate, blood pressure, and SKIN CONDUCTANCE or GALVANIC SKIN RESPONSE. The instrument has been widely used in the interrogation of criminal suspects and in employee screening to measure marked physiological reactions to questions about such issues as theft, sexual deviation, or untruthfulness. It has been colloquially referred to as a **lie detector**, although no one has ever documented a close relation between physiological patterns and deceptive behavior.

polygynandry *n.* an animal mating system in which females mate with multiple males and males mate with multiple females. Compare MONOGAMY; POLYANDRY; POLYGYNY.

polygyny *n.* an animal mating system in which a male mates with more than one female but a female mates with only one male. Compare MONOGAMY; POLYANDRY; POLYGAMY. —**polygynous** *adj.*

polymorphism *n.* **1.** in biology, the condition of having multiple behavioral or physical types within a species or population. In some fish species, for example, there are two distinct sizes of males. **2.** in genetics, the presence in a population of two or more variants of a gene (i.e., ALLELES) at a given genetic locus. For example, the variety of human blood groups is due to polymorphism of particular genes governing the characteristics of red blood cells. —**polymorphic** *adj.*

polymorphous perversity in the classic psychoanalytic theory of Austrian psychiatrist Sigmund Freud (1856–1939), the response of the human infant to many kinds of normal, daily activities posited to provide sexual excitation, such as

touching, smelling, sucking, rocking, defecating, and urinating.

polynomial regression a class of linear regression models (see LINEAR MODEL) in which one or more of the terms is raised to a power greater than 1 (e.g., $Y_i = \beta_0 + \beta_1 X_i + \beta_2 X_i^2 + \beta_3 X_i^3 + ...$).

polypeptide *n.* a molecule consisting of numerous (usually more than 10–20) AMINO ACIDS linked by PEPTIDE bonds. Polypeptides are assembled by the cell into PROTEINS.

polysomnography *n.* the recording of various physiological processes (e.g., eye movements, brain waves, heart rate, respiration) throughout the night, for the diagnosis of sleep-related disorders. —**polysomnograph** *n.*

pons *n.* a swelling on the ventral surface of the brainstem between the MIDBRAIN and the MEDULLA OBLONGATA. It serves primarily as a bridge, or transmission structure, between different areas of the nervous system. It also works with the CEREBELLUM in controlling equilibrium, and with the CEREBRAL CORTEX in smoothing and coordinating voluntary movements. —**pontine** *adj.*

Ponzo illusion a visual illusion in which the upper of two parallel horizontal lines of equal length appears to be longer than the bottom of the two lines when the horizontal lines are flanked by oblique lines that are closer together at the top than they are at the bottom. [Mario **Ponzo** (1882–1960), Italian psychologist]

pooled variance the estimate of a single common variance achieved by combining several independent estimates of that variance.

pop-out *n.* in visual search tasks, a target that is different from the distractors. One or more basic features will mark the pop-out as distinct from the other stimuli, hence allowing the target to be easily detected and identified regardless of the number of distractors.

population *n.* in statistics, a theoretically defined, complete group of objects (people, animals, institutions) from which a sample is drawn in order to obtain empirical observations and to which results can be generalized.

population psychology a relatively new subfield of psychology that studies the relationships between the characteristics and dynamics of human populations and the attitudes and behavior of individuals and groups. Representing an interface between psychology and DEMOGRAPHY, population psychology is particularly concerned with family planning and fertility regulation (i.e., reproductive behavior), high population density, and public policy development. Additional research topics include family formation and structure, migration, urbanization, mortality, and population education. Population psychology also encompasses the conceptualization of specific theoretical frameworks and methodological approaches for the study of population.

population vector the mechanism used in the MOTOR CORTEX to encode the direction of an intended movement. The activity in each neuron increases when the intended movement is close to its preferred direction. The direction of the intended movement is derived from the activity across the population of neurons.

positive affect the internal feeling state (AFFECT) that occurs when a goal has been attained, a source of threat has been avoided, or the individual is satisfied with the present state of affairs. The tendency to experience such states is called **positive affectivity**.

positive correlation a relationship between two variables in which as the value of one variable increases or decreases the value of the other variable does as well. For example, people with more years of education tend to have higher incomes. See also CORRELATION COEFFICIENT.

positive feedback 1. an arrangement whereby some of the output of a system, whether mechanical or biological, is fed back to increase the effect of input signals. Positive feedback is rare in biological systems. **2.** acceptance, approval, affirmation, or praise received by a person in response to his or her performance. Compare NEGATIVE FEEDBACK.

positive psychology a field of psychological theory and research that focuses on the psychological states (e.g., contentment, joy), individual traits or character strengths (e.g., intimacy, integrity, altruism, wisdom), and social institutions that enhance SUBJECTIVE WELL-BEING and make life most worth living. A manual, *Character Strengths and Virtues: A Handbook and Classification*, serves this perspective in a manner parallel to the DSM–IV–TR for the categorization of mental illness.

positive punishment punishment that results because some stimulus or circumstance is presented as a consequence of a response. For example, if a response results in presentation of a loud noise and the response becomes less likely as a result of this experience, then positive punishment has occurred. Compare NEGATIVE PUNISHMENT.

positive regard feelings of warmth, caring, acceptance, and importance expressed by someone toward another. Positive regard is considered necessary for psychological health and the development of a consistent sense of self-worth and is

P

also a cornerstone of certain therapeutic approaches, particularly that of U.S. psychologist Carl Rogers (1902–1987). See also CONDITIONAL POSITIVE REGARD; UNCONDITIONAL POSITIVE REGARD.

positive reinforcement an increase in the probability of occurrence of some activity because that activity results in the presentation of a desired stimulus or of some desired circumstance. Compare NEGATIVE REINFORCEMENT.

positive schizophrenia a form of schizophrenia in which POSITIVE SYMPTOMS predominate, as evidenced in the person's bizarre behavior, illogical speech or writing, or expression of hallucinations and delusions. Although more dramatically evident than NEGATIVE SCHIZOPHRENIA, the positive aspect is usually less challenging to treat.

positive skew see SKEWNESS.

positive symptom a symptom of schizophrenia that represents an excess or distortion of normal function, as distinct from a deficiency in or lack of normal function (compare NEGATIVE SYMPTOM). Positive symptoms include delusions or hallucinations, disorganized behavior, and manifest conceptual disorganization. Positive symptoms are more dramatic than negative symptoms and are less distinctive of schizophrenia. See POSITIVE SCHIZO-PHRENIA.

positive transfer the improvement or enhancement of present learning by previous learning. For instance, learning to program a digital video recorder could facilitate learning to program a digital telephone. See also TRANSFER OF TRAINING. Compare NEGATIVE TRANSFER.

positivism *n.* a family of philosophical positions holding that all meaningful propositions must be re-

ducible to sensory experience and observation, and thus that all genuine knowledge is to be built on strict adherence to empirical methods of verification. Its effect is to establish science as the model for all forms of valid inquiry and to dismiss the truth claims of religion, metaphysics, and speculative philosophy. Positivism was extremely influential in the early development of psychology and continues to be a major force in contemporary psychology. —**positivist** *adj.*

positron emission tomography (PET) a technique used to evaluate cerebral metabolism using radio-labeled tracers, such as 2-deoxy-glucose labeled with fluorine-18, which emit positrons as they are metabolized. This technique enables documentation of functional changes that occur during the performance of mental activities.

possible self in models of self-concept, a mental representation of what one could become. Possible selves are cognitive manifestations of enduring goals, aspirations, fears, and threats that provide plans and strategies for the future. They may be positive, providing an image of something to strive for, or negative, providing an image of something to be avoided.

postcentral gyrus a ridge in the PARIETAL LOBE of the brain, just behind the CENTRAL SULCUS, that is the site of the PRIMARY SOMATO-SENSORY AREA.

postconventional level in KOHLBERG'S THEORY OF MORAL DE-VELOPMENT, the third and highest level of moral reasoning, characterized by an individual's commitment to moral principles sustained independently of any identification with family, group, or country. This level is divided into two stages: the earlier social contract orientation, in which moral behavior is that which balances general individual rights with public welfare and democratically agreed upon societal rights; and the later ethical principle orientation, in which moral behavior is based upon self-chosen, abstract ethical standards. Also called **postconventional morality**. See also conventional level; PRECONVENTIONAL LEVEL.

posterior *adj.* in back of or toward the back. In reference to two-legged upright animals, this term sometimes is used interchangeably with DORSAL to mean toward the back surface of the body. Compare ANTERIOR.

posterior commissure see COMMISSURE.

postformal thought adult cognition that includes an understanding of the relative, nonabsolute nature of knowledge; an acceptance of contradiction as a basic aspect of reality; the ability to synthesize contradictory thoughts, feelings, and experiences into more coherent, all-encompassing wholes; and the ability to resolve both ill- and well-defined problems. It is an extension of the FORMAL OPERATIONAL STAGE beyond adolescence.

post hoc comparison a comparison among two or more means in ANALYSIS OF VARIANCE or MULTIPLE REGRESSION analysis that is formulated after the data have been examined. Also called **post hoc contrast**. Compare PLANNED COMPARISON.

posthypnotic amnesia an individual's incapacity to remember what transpired during a period of hypnosis, typically by instruction of the hypnotist. However, highly susceptible individuals may show spontaneous posthypnotic amnesia.

posthypnotic suggestion a suggestion made to a person under hypnosis and acted upon after awakening from the hypnotic trance. Usually, the act is carried out in response to a prearranged cue from the hypnotist, and the participant does not know why he or she is performing the act.

postmodernism *n.* a number of related philosophical tendencies that developed in reaction to classical MODERNISM during the late 20th century. They see the ideal of objective truth that has been a guiding principle in the sciences and most other disciplines since the 17th century as basically flawed: There can be no such truth, only a plurality of "narratives" and "perspectives." Postmodernism emphasizes the construction of knowledge and truth through discourse and lived experience, the similar construction of the self, and RELATIVISM in all questions of value. See also POSTSTRUCTURALISM. —**postmodern** *adj.*

postpartum depression a MAJOR DEPRESSIVE EPISODE that affects women within 4 weeks after childbirth.

poststructuralism *n.* a broad intellectual movement that developed from French STRUCTURALISM in the late 1960s and 1970s and is rooted in the structuralist account of language given by Swiss linguist Ferdinand de Saussure (1857–1913), which holds that linguistic SIGNS acquire meaning only through structural relationships with other signs in the same language system. Poststructuralism endorses the arbitrariness of the sign, but from this basis proceeds to question the whole idea of fixed and determinate meaning, and ultimately the idea of personal identity itself. In psychology, poststructuralism is mainly significant because of its influence on the radical psychoanalytical theories of the 1960s and 1970s. For example, Jacques Lacan (1901–1981), who trained and practiced as

P

a psychiatrist, rejected the idea of a stable autonomous EGO and reinterpreted the Freudian UNCONSCIOUS in terms of Saussure's structural linguistics. —**poststructuralist** *adj.*

postsynaptic potential (**PSP**) the electric potential at a dendrite or other surface of a neuron after an impulse has reached it across a SYNAPSE. Postsynaptic potentials may be either EXCITATORY POSTSYNAPTIC POTENTIALS or INHIBITORY POSTSYNAPTIC POTENTIALS.

posttest *n.* **1.** a test administered after completion of the principal test or instruction program. It may be given in conjunction with a PRETEST to assess comprehension of the content and nature of the main test as well as its effectiveness as an assessment instrument. **2.** a test administered after the application of an intervention or control condition.

posttraumatic amnesia a disturbance of memory following a a physical injury (e.g., a concussion) or a psychologically upsetting experience (e.g., sexual abuse). The traumatic event itself may be forgotten or events following the trauma may be forgotten. The period of forgetting may be continuous, or the person may experience vague, incomplete recollections of the traumatic event.

posttraumatic stress disorder (**PTSD**) a disorder that results when an individual lives through or witnesses an event in which there is a threat to life or physical integrity and safety and experiences fear, terror, or helplessness. The symptoms are characterized by (a) reexperiencing the trauma in painful recollections, flashbacks, or recurrent nightmares; (b) emotional anesthesia or numbing, with disinterest in or active avoidance of activities and with feelings of detachment and estrangement from

others; and (c) chronic physiological arousal, leading to such symptoms as exaggerated startle response, disturbed sleep, and difficulty in concentrating or remembering. When the symptoms do not last longer than 4 weeks a diagnosis of ACUTE STRESS DISORDER is given instead.

posture *n.* the position or bearing of the body. Movements typically involve coordinated changes in posture (e.g., to maintain balance or distribute forces). —**postural** *adj.*

potency *n.* **1.** the ability of a male to perform sexual intercourse, that is, to maintain an erection and achieve ejaculation. Compare IMPOTENCE. **2.** in pharmacology, see DOSE–RESPONSE RELATIONSHIP. —**potent** *adj.*

potential *n.* **1.** the capacity to develop or come into existence. **2.** electric potential, measured in volts: a property of an electric field equal to the energy needed to bring unit electric charge from infinity to a given point. The potential difference between two points is the driving force that causes a current to flow. Because messages in the nervous system are conveyed by electrochemical potentials, many kinds of potential are of importance in neuroscience and biological psychology, including the ACTION POTENTIAL, GRADED POTENTIAL, MEMBRANE POTENTIAL, POSTSYNAPTIC POTENTIAL, and RESTING POTENTIAL.

power *n.* **1.** the capacity to influence others, even when they try to resist this influence. Social power derives from a number of sources: control over rewards and punishments; a right to require and demand obedience; others' identification with, attraction to, or respect for the powerholder; others' belief that the powerholder possesses superior skills and abilities; and the powerholder's access to and use of informational resources. **2.** in hypothesis testing, the probability that the NULL HYPOTHESIS will be rejected when it is in fact false and the ALTERNATIVE HYPOTHESIS is true.

power law see STEVENS LAW.

power test a type of test intended to calculate the participant's level of mastery of a particular topic under conditions of little or no time pressure. The test is designed so that items become progressively more difficult. Compare SPEED TEST.

practical intelligence the ability to apply one's intelligence in practical, everyday situations. In the TRIARCHIC THEORY OF INTELLIGENCE it is the aspect of intelligence that requires adaptation to, shaping of, and selection of new environments. Compare ANALYTICAL INTELLIGENCE; CREATIVE INTELLIGENCE.

practice effect any change or improvement that results from practice or repetition of task items or activities. The practice effect is of particular concern in experimentation, as the performance of participants on the variable of interest may improve simply from repeating the activity rather than from any manipulation or intervention imposed by the researcher.

pragmatics *n.* the analysis of language in terms of its functional communicative properties (rather than its formal and structural properties, as in PHONOLOGY, SEMANTICS, and GRAMMAR) and in terms of the intentions and perspectives of its users.

pragmatism *n.* a philosophical position holding that the truth value of a proposition or a theory is to be found in its practical consequences: If, for example, the hypothesis of God makes people virtuous and happy, then it may be considered true. Although some forms of prag-

matism emphasize only the material consequences of an idea, more sophisticated positions recognize conceptual and moral consequences. See also INSTRUMENTALISM. —**pragmatist** *adj., n.*

Prägnanz *n.* one of the GESTALT PRINCIPLES OF ORGANIZATION. It states that people tend to perceive forms as the simplest and most meaningful, stable, and complete structures that conditions permit. Also called **law of Prägnanz; principle of Prägnanz.** [German: "terseness"]

praxis *n.* **1.** a medical name for motor planning, or the brain's ability to conceive, organize, and carry out a sequence of actions. Inadequate praxis is APRAXIA. **2.** practice, as opposed to theory. The term is sometimes used to denote knowledge derived from and expressed chiefly in practical or productive activity, as opposed to theoretical or conceptual knowledge.

preattentive processing unconscious mental processing of a stimulus that occurs before attention has focused on this particular stimulus from among the array of those present in a given environment. An example of this is the disambiguation of the meaning of a particular word from among an array of words present in a given visual stimulus before conscious perception of the word.

precentral gyrus a ridge in the FRONTAL LOBE of the brain, just in front of the CENTRAL SULCUS, that is crucial for motor control, being the site of the primary MOTOR CORTEX.

precipitating cause the particular factor, sometimes a traumatic or stressful experience, that is the immediate cause of a mental or physical disorder. Compare PREDISPOSING CAUSE.

precision *n.* a measure of accuracy.

In statistics, an estimate with a small STANDARD ERROR is regarded as having a high degree of precision. **—precise** *adj.*

precognition *n.* in parapsychology, the purported ability to see or experience future events through some form of EXTRASENSORY PERCEPTION. In a test of precognition, the participant would be asked to predict the outcome of a future set of trials involving ZENER CARDS or similar stimulus materials. **—precognitive** *adj.*

preconscious 1. *n.* (**Pcs**) in the classical psychoanalytic theory of Austrian psychiatrist Sigmund Freud (1856–1939), the level of the psyche that contains thoughts, feelings, and impulses not presently in awareness, but which can be more or less readily called into consciousness. Examples are the face of a friend, a verbal cliché, or the memory of a recent event. Compare CONSCIOUS; UNCONSCIOUS. **2.** *adj.* denoting or relating to thoughts, feelings, and impulses at this level of the psyche.

preconventional level in KOHLBERG'S THEORY OF MORAL DEVELOPMENT, the first level of moral reasoning, characterized by the child's evaluation of actions in terms of material consequences. This level is divided into two stages: the earlier punishment and obedience orientation, in which moral behavior is that which avoids punishment; and the later naive hedonism (or instrumental relativist) orientation, in which moral behavior is that which obtains reward or serves one's needs. Also called **preconventional morality**. See also CONVENTIONAL LEVEL; POSTCONVENTIONAL LEVEL.

prediction *n.* an attempt to foretell what will happen in a particular case, generally on the basis of past instances or accepted principles. In science, the use of prediction and observation to test hypotheses is a cornerstone of the empirical method (see FALSIFIABILITY). However, by their very nature, the theories, constructs, and explanatory models current in psychology are not always open to direct validation or falsification in this way. **—predict** *vb.* **—predictable** *adj.* **—predictive** *adj.*

predictive validity an index of how well a test correlates with a variable that is measured in the future, at some point after the test has been administered. For example, the predictive validity of a test designed to predict the onset of a disease would be calculated by the extent to which it was successful at identifying those individuals who did, in fact, later develop that disease.

predictor *n.* a variable or other information used to estimate future events or circumstances. In personnel selection, for example, obvious predictors used to estimate an applicant's future job performance include qualifications, relevant work experience, and job-specific skills such as the ability to type or speak a particular language.

predictor variable see INDEPENDENT VARIABLE.

predisposing cause a factor that increases the probability that a mental or physical disorder or hereditary characteristic will develop but is not the immediate cause of it. Compare PRECIPITATING CAUSE.

predisposition *n.* a susceptibility to developing a disorder or disease, the actual development of which is initiated by the interaction of certain biological, psychological, or environmental factors.

preferential looking technique a method for assessing the perceptual capabilities of nonverbal human infants and animals. Infants will preferentially fixate a "more interesting" stimulus when it is presented at the same time as a "less interesting" stimulus, but only if the stimuli can be distinguished from one another. To minimize bias, on each trial the investigator is positioned so that he or she can observe the infant and make a judgment about which stimulus the infant fixates, but the stimuli themselves are visible only to the infant.

prefrontal cortex the most anterior (forward) part of the cerebral cortex of each FRONTAL LOBE in the brain. It functions in attention, planning, working memory, and the expression of emotions and appropriate social behavior and is divided into a dorsolateral region and an orbitofrontal region (see ORBITOFRONTAL CORTEX).

prefrontal lobe the furthest forward area of each CEREBRAL HEMISPHERE of the brain, which is concerned with such functions as memory and learning, emotion, and social behavior. See also FRONTAL LOBE.

prefrontal lobotomy see LOBOTOMY.

prejudice *n.* **1.** a negative attitude toward another person or group formed in advance of any experience with that person or group. Prejudices include an affective component (emotions that range from mild nervousness to hatred), a cognitive component (assumptions and beliefs about groups, including STEREOTYPES), and a behavioral component (negative behaviors, including DISCRIMINATION and violence). They tend to be resistant to change because they distort the prejudiced individual's perception of information pertaining to the group. Prejudice based on racial grouping is RACISM; prejudice based on sex is SEXISM. **2.** any preconceived attitude or view, whether favorable or unfavorable.

prelinguistic *adj.* denoting or relating to the period of an infant's life before it has acquired the power of speech. The **prelinguistic period** includes the earliest infant vocalizations as well as the babbling stage typical of the second half of the first year. HOLOPHRASES usually emerge around the time of the child's first birthday.

Premack's principle the view that the opportunity to engage in behavior with a relatively high baseline probability will reinforce behavior of lower baseline probability. For example, a hungry rat may have a high probability of eating but a lower probability of pressing a lever. Making the opportunity to eat depend on pressing the lever will result in reinforcement of lever pressing. Also called **Premack's rule**. [David **Premack** (1925–), U.S. psychologist]

premature ejaculation a sexual dysfunction in which male ORGASM occurs with minimal sexual stimulation, before, on, or shortly after penetration or simply earlier than desired. The diagnosis takes into account such factors as age, novelty of the sexual partner, and the frequency and duration of intercourse.

prematurity *n.* a state of underdevelopment, particularly the birth of a baby before it has completed the full gestational period of a normal pregnancy.

premenstrual dysphoric disorder a MOOD DISORDER in women that begins in the week prior to the onset of menstruation and subsides within the first few days of menstruation. Women experience markedly depressed mood, anxiety, feelings of helplessness, and decreased interest in activities. In contrast to PREMENSTRUAL SYNDROME, the symptoms must be severe enough to impair functioning in social activities, work, and relationships.

P

premenstrual syndrome (PMS) a collection of psychological and physical symptoms experienced by women during the week prior to the onset of menstruation and subsiding within the first few days of menstruation. Symptoms can include mood swings, irritability, fatigue, headache, bloating, abdominal discomfort, and breast tenderness. In contrast to the more severe PREMENSTRUAL DYSPHORIC DISORDER, premenstrual syndrome has a less distinctive pattern of symptoms and does not involve major impairment in social and occupational functioning.

premise *n.* a proposition forming part of a larger argument: a statement from which a further statement is to be deduced, especially as one of a series of such steps leading to a conclusion.

premoral stage in the theory of moral development proposed by Swiss child psychologist Jean Piaget (1896–1980), the stage at which young children (under the age of 5) are unaware of rules as cooperative agreements, that is, they are unable to distinguish right from wrong. Compare AUTONOMOUS STAGE; HETERONOMOUS STAGE.

premorbid *adj.* characterizing an individual's condition before the onset of a disease or disorder. —**premorbidity** *n.*

premotor area an area of the MOTOR CORTEX concerned with motor planning, or the ability to conceive, organize, and carry out a sequence of actions. In contrast to the SUPPLEMENTARY MOTOR AREA, input to the premotor area is primarily visual, and its activity is usually triggered by external events. Also called **premotor cortex**.

prenatal *adj.* prior to birth: pertaining to that which exists or occurs between conception and birth.

preoccupation *n.* a state of being self-absorbed and "lost in thought."

preoccupied attachment an adult attachment style that combines a negative INTERNAL WORKING MODEL OF ATTACHMENT of oneself, characterized by doubt in one's own competence and efficacy, and a positive internal working model of attachment of others, characterized by one's trust in the ability and dependability of others. Compare DISMISSIVE ATTACHMENT; FEARFUL ATTACHMENT; SECURE ATTACHMENT.

preoperational stage the second major period in the PIAGETIAN THEORY of cognitive development, approximately between the ages of 2 and 7, when the child becomes able to record experience in a symbolic fashion and to represent an object, event, or feeling in speech, movement, drawing, and the like. During the later 2 years of the preoperational stage, egocentrism diminishes noticeably with the emerging ability to adopt the point of view of others.

preoptic area a region of the HYPOTHALAMUS lying above and slightly anterior to the OPTIC CHIASM. Nuclei here are involved in temperature regulation and in the release of hypothalamic HORMONES.

prepared learning a species-specific and innate tendency to quickly learn a certain type of knowledge. Some associations between stimuli, responses, and reinforcers may be more easily formed due to biological PREPAREDNESS. For example, animals readily associate foods with illness, and it has been suggested that humans learn certain phobias more readily due to preparedness.

preparedness *n.* a genetically influenced predisposition for certain stimuli to be more effective than others in eliciting particular responses. For example, flavors may be more effective as stimuli in establishing a CONDITIONED TASTE AVERSION than are colors of lights.

presbycusis *n.* the gradual diminution of hearing acuity associated with aging.

presbyopia *n.* a normal, age-related change in vision due to decreased lens elasticity and accommodative ability, resulting in reduced ability to focus vision on near tasks (e.g., reading).

presenile dementia see DEMENTIA.

presenting symptom a symptom or problem (e.g., anxiety, insomnia) that is offered by a client or a patient as the reason for seeking treatment. In psychotherapy, such symptoms may become the focus of treatment or may represent a different, underlying problem that is not recognized or regarded by the client as requiring help.

pressure *n.* excessive or stressful demands made on an individual to think, feel, or act in particular ways. The experience of pressure is often the source of cognitive and affective discomfort or disorder, as well as of maladaptive coping strategies, the correction of which may be a mediate or end goal in psychotherapy.

prestriate cortex visually responsive regions in the cerebral cortex outside the STRIATE CORTEX. On the basis of function and connectivity, the prestriate cortex has been divided into multiple VISUAL AREAS. Also called **extrastriate cortex**; **prestriate area**.

pretest *n.* **1.** a preliminary test or trial run to familiarize the person or group tested with the content and nature of a particular test. It may be given in conjunction with a POSTTEST. **2.** a trial run adminis-

tered before the application of an intervention or control condition.

prevalence *n.* the total number of cases (e.g., of a disease or disorder) existing in a given population at a given time (point prevalence) or during a specified period (period prevalence). See also INCIDENCE.

prevention *n.* behavioral, biological, or social interventions intended to reduce the risk of disorders, diseases, or social problems for both individuals and entire populations. See PRIMARY PREVENTION; SECONDARY PREVENTION; TERTIARY PREVENTION.

pride *n.* a SELF-CONSCIOUS EMOTION that occurs when a goal has been attained and one's achievement has been recognized and approved by others. It differs from JOY and HAPPINESS in that these emotions do not require the approval of others for their existence. Pride can become antisocial if the sense of accomplishment is not deserved or the reaction is excessive. —**proud** *adj.*

primacy effect the tendency for facts, impressions, or items that are presented first to be better learned or remembered than material presented later in the sequence. This can occur in both formal learning situations and social contexts. For example, it can result in a **first-impression bias**, in which the first information gained about a person has an inordinate influence on later impressions and evaluations of that person. Compare RECENCY EFFECT.

primal scene in psychoanalytic theory, the child's first observation of parental intercourse.

primary ability any of the seven unitary factors proposed in the early 20th century to be essential components of intelligence: verbal ability, word fluency, numerical ability, spatial intelligence, memory, perceptual

P

speed, and reasoning. Also called **primary mental ability.**

primary aging changes associated with normal aging that are inevitable and caused by intrinsic biological or genetic factors. Examples include the appearance of gray hair and skin wrinkles. However, some age-related diseases have genetic influences, making the distinction between primary aging and SECONDARY AGING imprecise.

primary auditory cortex (A1) the first region of the cerebral cortex that receives auditory (sound) input, analyzing and processing information from the MEDIAL GENICULATE NUCLEUS in the thalamus. Located on the upper side of the TEMPORAL LOBE, the primary auditory cortex is equivalent to BRODMANN'S AREA 41 and encompasses HESCHL'S GYRUS. It displays both FREQUENCY SELECTIVITY and TONOTOPIC ORGANIZATION, and is critical to the discrimination and localization of sounds. Neurons in the primary auditory cortex predominantly project to WERNICKE'S AREA.

primary care the basic or general health care a patient receives when he or she first seeks assistance from a health care system. General practitioners, family practitioners, internists, obstetricians, and pediatricians are known as **primary care providers (PCPs)**. Compare SECONDARY CARE; TERTIARY CARE.

primary circular reaction in PIAGETIAN THEORY, a type of repetitive action that represents the earliest nonreflexive infantile behavior. For example, in the first months of life, a hungry baby may repeatedly attempt to put a hand in the mouth. Primary circular reactions develop in the SENSORIMOTOR STAGE, following the activation of such reflexes as sucking, swallowing, crying, and moving the arms and legs. See also SECONDARY CIRCULAR REACTION; TERTIARY CIRCULAR REACTION.

primary cortex any of the regions of the CEREBRAL CORTEX that receive the main input from sensory receptors or send the main output to muscles. Examples are primary MOTOR CORTEX, primary visual cortex (see STRIATE CORTEX), PRIMARY TASTE CORTEX, and the PRIMARY SOMATOSENSORY AREA. Most neurons in primary sensory regions have more direct sensory input than do neurons in adjacent sensory cortical regions.

primary drive an innate DRIVE, which may be universal or species-specific, that is created by deprivation of a needed substance (e.g., food) or the need to engage in a specific activity (e.g., nest building in birds). Compare SECONDARY DRIVE.

primary gain in psychoanalytic theory, any of various basic psychological benefits derived from possessing neurotic symptoms, essentially relief from anxiety generated by conflicting impulses or threatening experiences. Compare SECONDARY GAIN.

primary group any of the small, long-term groups characterized by face-to-face interaction and high levels of COHESION, solidarity, and group IDENTIFICATION. These groups are primary in the sense that they are the initial socializers of the individual members, providing them with the foundation for attitudes, values, and a social orientation. Families, partnerships, and long-term psychotherapy groups are examples of such groups. Compare SECONDARY GROUP.

primary gustatory cortex see PRIMARY TASTE CORTEX.

primary mental ability see PRIMARY ABILITY.

primary motor cortex see
MOTOR CORTEX.

primary prevention research and
programs, designed for and directed
to nonclinical populations or populations at risk, that seek to promote
and lay a firm foundation for mental, behavioral, or physical health so
that psychological disorders, illness,
or disease will not develop. Compare SECONDARY PREVENTION;
TERTIARY PREVENTION.

primary process in psychoanalytic theory, unconscious mental
activity in which there is free, unin-
hibited flow of PSYCHIC ENERGY
from one idea to another. Such
thinking operates without regard for
logic or reality, is dominated by the
PLEASURE PRINCIPLE, and provides
hallucinatory fulfillment of wishes.
Examples are the dreams, fantasies,
and magical thinking of young children. These processes are posited to
predominate in the ID.

primary reinforcement 1. in
OPERANT CONDITIONING, the
process in which presentation of
a stimulus or circumstance following a response increases the future
probability of that response, without the need for special experience
with the stimulus or circumstance.
That is, the stimulus or circumstance functions as effective REIN-
FORCEMENT without any special
experience or training. **2.** the contingent occurrence of such a
stimulus or circumstance after a
response. Also called **unconditioned reinforcement**. Compare
SECONDARY REINFORCEMENT.

primary sensory area any area
within the NEOCORTEX of the brain
that acts to receive sensory input—
for most senses, from the thalamus.
The primary sensory area for hearing
is in the temporal lobe, for vision in
the occipital lobe (see STRIATE COR-
TEX), and for touch and taste in
the parietal lobe (see PRIMARY

SOMATOSENSORY AREA; PRIMARY
TASTE CORTEX). Compare SECOND-
ARY SENSORY AREA.

primary sex characteristic see
SEX CHARACTERISTIC.

**primary somatosensory area
(S1)** an area of the cerebral cortex,
located in a ridge of the anterior PA-
RIETAL LOBE just posterior to the
CENTRAL SULCUS, where the first
stage of cortical processing of tactile
information takes place (see
SOMATOSENSORY AREA). It receives
input from the ventroposterior nuclear complex of the thalamus and
projects to other areas of the parietal
cortex. See also SECONDARY
SOMATOSENSORY AREA.

primary taste cortex the area of
cerebral cortex that is the first cortical relay for taste. Located along the
sharp bend that includes the frontal
operculum laterally and the anterior
INSULA medially, it receives taste,
touch, visceral, and other sensory
inputs from the thalamus and permits an integrated evaluation of a
chemical. Its output goes to regions
that control oral and visceral reflexes in response to foods. Also
called **primary gustatory cortex**.
See SECONDARY TASTE CORTEX.

primary visual cortex (V1) see
STRIATE CORTEX.

primate *n.* a member of the Primates, an order of mammals that
includes the lemurs, monkeys, apes,
and humans. Characteristics of the
order include an opposable thumb
(i.e., a thumb capable of touching
other digits), a relatively large brain,
and binocular vision. The young are
usually born singly and mature over
an extended period.

priming *n.* the effect in which recent experience of a stimulus
facilitates or inhibits later processing
of the same or a similar stimulus. In
REPETITION PRIMING, presentation
of a particular sensory stimulus

increases the likelihood that participants will identify the same or a similar stimulus later in the test. In SEMANTIC PRIMING, presentation of a word or sign influences the way in which participants interpret a subsequent word or sign. —**prime** *vb.*

principal component analysis a statistical technique in which the interrelationship among many correlated variables can be completely reproduced by a smaller number of new variables (called principal components) that are mutually orthogonal and ordered in terms of the percentage of the total system variance for which they account. Often, most of the total variance can be captured in the first few principal components. This technique is similar in its aims to FACTOR ANALYSIS but has different technical features.

principle of closure see CLOSURE.

principle of common fate see COMMON FATE.

principle of continuity see GOOD CONTINUATION.

principle of good continuation see GOOD CONTINUATION.

principle of parsimony see LAW OF PARSIMONY.

principle of Prägnanz see PRÄGNANZ.

principle of proximity see PROXIMITY.

principle of similarity see SIMILARITY.

prisoner's dilemma in GAME THEORY investigations of competition and cooperation, a situation in which each participant must choose between a self-beneficial course of action that could be costly for the other players and an action that would bring a smaller individual payoff but would lead to some benefits for all the players. The name derives from a police tactic, used when incriminating evidence is lacking, in which two suspects are separated and told that the one who confesses will go free or receive a light sentence. The prisoner's dilemma has implications for SOCIAL EXCHANGE THEORY and the study of SOCIAL DILEMMAS.

privacy *n.* **1.** the right to control (psychologically and physically) others' access to one's personal world, for example by regulating others' input through use of physical or other barriers (e.g., doors, partitions) and by regulating one's own output in the form of communication with others. **2.** the right of patients and other consumers to control the amount and disposition of the information they divulge about themselves. See PRIVILEGED COMMUNICATION. —**private** *adj.*

private acceptance see CONVERSION.

private speech spontaneous self-directed talk in which a person "thinks aloud," particularly as a means of regulating cognitive processes and guiding behavior. In the theorizing of Russian psychologist Lev Semenovich Vygotsky (1896–1934), private speech is considered equivalent to EGOCENTRIC SPEECH.

privation *n.* absence of something needed or desired, particularly something required to satisfy essential physiological needs, such as those for food and sleep. Privation is distinct from DEPRIVATION, which involves the initial presence and then removal of such requirements or wants.

privileged communication confidential information, especially as provided by an individual to a professional in the course of their relationship, that may not be divulged to a third party without the knowledge and consent of that individual. This protection applies to communications not only between patients and physicians, clinical psychologists, psychiatrists, or other health care professionals, but also between clients and attorneys, confessors and priests, and spouses.

proactive aggression see AGGRESSION.

proactive interference see INTERFERENCE.

probability (symbol: *p*) *n.* the degree to which an event is likely to occur. —**probabilistic** *adj.*

probability distribution a curve that specifies, by the areas below it, the probability that a random variable occurs at a particular point. The best known example is the bell-shaped NORMAL DISTRIBUTION.

probability level the *p*-value for a particular statistical test in SIGNIFICANCE TESTING. It indicates the likelihood of obtaining the observed effect if there is indeed no real effect in nature (i.e., of falsely rejecting the NULL HYPOTHESIS and thus committing a TYPE I ERROR). Small *p*-values suggest that the chance of experimental results mistakenly being attributed to the independent variables present in the study (instead of the actual random factors responsible) is small. See SIGNIFICANCE LEVEL.

proband *n.* the family member whose possible genetic disease or disorder forms the center of the investigation into the extent of the illness in the family. Also called **index case**.

probe *n.* a follow-up question in an interview, survey, or other type of research that is designed to ascertain additional information or explore in depth a topic previously introduced.

probit analysis a form of REGRESSION ANALYSIS for a dichotomous dependent variable. In this model

an observable independent variable is thought to affect a latent continuous variable that determines the probability that a dichotomous event will occur.

problem checklist a type of self-report scale listing various personal, social, educational, or vocational problems. The participant indicates the items that apply to his or her situation.

problem drinking see ALCOHOL DEPENDENCE.

problem-focused coping a type of COPING STRATEGY that is directed toward decreasing or eliminating stressors, for example, by generating possible solutions to a problem. Compare EMOTION-FOCUSED COPING.

problem solving the process by which individuals attempt to overcome difficulties, achieve plans that move them from a starting situation to a desired goal, or reach conclusions through the use of higher mental functions, such as reasoning and creative thinking. In laboratory studies, many animals display problem-solving strategies, such as the win–stay, lose–shift strategy, which allows an animal to solve a new problem quickly, based on whether the first response was successful or unsuccessful.

problem space the set of all possible paths to the solution of a given problem.

procedural memory long-term memory for the skills involved in particular tasks. Procedural memory is demonstrated by skilled performance and is often separate from the ability to verbalize this knowledge (see DECLARATIVE MEMORY). Knowing how to type or skate, for example, requires procedural memory.

procedure *n.* a sequence of steps or

actions delineating the manner in which a study is to be conducted or has been conducted.

proceptivity *n.* the period during mating behavior when females actively solicit males for copulation. Proceptivity is distinguished from the more passive RECEPTIVITY to indicate the female's active role in mating.

process loss in the social psychology of groups, any action, operation, or dynamic that prevents the group from reaching its full potential, such as reduced effort (SOCIAL LOAFING), inadequate coordination of effort, poor communication, or ineffective leadership.

process schizophrenia a form of schizophrenia that begins early in life, develops gradually, is believed to be due to endogenous (biological or physiological) rather than environmental factors, and has a poor prognosis. Psychosocial development before the onset of the disorder is poor; individuals are withdrawn, socially inadequate, and indulge in excessive fantasies. Compare REACTIVE SCHIZOPHRENIA.

prodigy *n.* an individual, typically a child, who displays unusual or exceptional talent or intelligence, quite often in a discrete area of expertise, such as mathematics, music, or chess. Prodigies do not always develop into accomplished adults: There appears to be an important transition between the two, and only a proportion of prodigies successfully negotiate this transition. See also GIFTEDNESS.

prodrome *n.* an early symptom or symptoms of a mental or physical disorder. A prodrome frequently serves as a warning or premonitory sign that may, in some cases, enable preventive measures to be taken. Examples are the auras that often precede epileptic seizures or mi-graine headaches and the headache, fatigue, dizziness, and insidious impairment of ability that often precede a stroke. —**prodromic** *adj.* —**prodromal** *adj.*

production deficiency in problem solving, failure to find the right or best strategy for completing a task (even, sometimes, after successful instruction), as opposed to failure in implementing it. Compare MEDIATIONAL DEFICIENCY; UTILIZATION DEFICIENCY.

productivity *n.* the capacity to produce goods and services having exchange value. Vocational REHABILITATION programs often use the productivity of people with disabilities as a major measure of the effectiveness of the programs.

product–moment correlation a statistic that indexes the degree of linear relationship between two variables. Invented by British statistician Karl Pearson (1857–1936), it is often known as the **Pearson product–moment correlation (Pearson's *r*)**.

progesterone *n.* a hormone that stimulates proliferation of the endometrium (lining) of the uterus required for implantation of an embryo. If implantation occurs, progesterone continues to be secreted, maintaining the pregnant uterus and preventing further release of egg cells from the ovary. It also stimulates development of milk-secreting cells in the breasts.

prognosis *n.* a prediction of the future course, duration, severity, and outcome of a condition, disease, or disorder. —**prognostic** *adj.*

programmed cell death the orderly death and disposal of surplus tissue cells, which occurs as part of tissue remodeling during development, or of worn-out and infected cells, which occurs throughout life. Also called **apoptosis**.

P

programmed instruction a learning technique, used for self-instruction and in academic and some applied settings, in which the material is presented in a series of sequential, graduated steps, or frames. The learner is required to make a response at each step: If the response is correct, it leads to the next step; if it is incorrect, it leads to further review. Also called **programmed learning**.

progressive relaxation a technique in which the individual is trained to relax the entire body by becoming aware of tensions in various muscle groups and then relaxing one muscle group at a time. In some cases, the individual consciously tenses specific muscles or muscle groups and then releases tension to achieve relaxation throughout the body.

projection *n.* the process by which one attributes one's own individual positive or negative characteristics, affects, and impulses to another person or group. This is often a DEFENSE MECHANISM in which unpleasant or unacceptable impulses, stressors, ideas, affects, or responsibilities are attributed to others. For example, the defense mechanism of projection enables a person conflicted over expressing anger to change "I hate him" to "He hates me." —**project** *vb.*

projective technique any personality assessment procedure that consists of a fixed series of relatively ambiguous stimuli designed to elicit unique, sometimes highly idiosyncratic, responses. Examples of this type of procedure are the ROR-SCHACH INKBLOT TEST, the THEMATIC APPERCEPTION TEST, and various sentence completion and word association tests. Projective techniques are quite controversial, with opinions ranging from the belief that personality assessment is

incomplete without data from at least one or more of these procedures to the view that such techniques lack reliability and validity and that interpretations of personality organization and functioning derived from them are hypothetical and unscientific.

proliferation *n.* rapid reproduction or multiplication, particularly of new or diseased cells. Both benign and malignant tumors, for instance, experience a high rate of cell division and growth.

promiscuity *n.* transient, casual sexual relations with a variety of partners. In humans, this type of behavior is generally regarded unfavorably; however, in many other animal species females appear to display promiscuity to prevent certainty of paternity but often mate with the most dominant or successful male at the time when conception is most likely. —**promiscuous** *adj.*

prompt *n.* see RETRIEVAL CUE.

propinquity *n.* the geographic nearness of two or more people to each other, an element in the formation of close relationships. See also PROXEMICS.

proportionality *n.* in statistics, a relationship between two variables in which one changes in constant ratio to another. Two variables are directly proportional (written $x \propto y$) if $x = ay$, where a is a constant. They are inversely proportional ($x \propto 1/y$) if $x = a/y$.

proprioception *n.* the sense of body movement and position, resulting from stimulation of specialized receptors called **proprioceptors** located in the muscles, tendons, and joints and of specialized vestibular receptors in the labyrinth of the inner ear (see VESTIBULAR SENSE). Proprioception enables the body to determine its spatial orientation without visual clues and to maintain postural stability. —**proprioceptive** *adj.*

prosencephalon *n.* see FOREBRAIN.

prosocial *adj.* denoting or exhibiting behavior that benefits one or more other people, such as providing assistance to an older adult crossing the street. Compare ANTISOCIAL.

prosody *n.* the pattern of stress, rate, intonation, or rhythm of speech. See PARALANGUAGE; SUPRASEGMENTAL.

prosopagnosia *n.* see VISUAL AGNOSIA.

prospective memory remembering to do something in the future, such as taking one's medicine later. Prospective memory contrasts with **retrospective memory**, or remembering past events.

prospective research research that is planned before the data have been collected; that is, research that starts with the present and follows subjects forward in time, as in randomized experiments and in longitudinal research. Compare RETROSPECTIVE RESEARCH.

prospective sampling a method for determining which subjects or cases to include in experiments or other research that selects cases on the basis of their exposure to a risk factor. Participants are then followed in order to see if the condition of interest develops. A study design using this method is referred to as a **prospective study**. See RETROSPECTIVE SAMPLING.

protective factor a variable or clearly defined behavior that promotes relative healthiness and well-being because it is associated with a decreased probability that a particular disease or disorder will develop or because it reduces the severity of an existing pathological condition.

For example, exercising regularly can serve as a protective factor by decreasing the likelihood or severity of coronary heart disease, hypertension, and depression. Likewise, supportive social networks and positive coping skills are examples of protective factors that help alleviate depression and anxiety and enhance mental health generally.

protein *n.* a molecule that consists of a long-chain polymer of AMINO ACIDS. Proteins are involved in virtually every function performed by a cell; they are the principal building blocks of living organisms and, in the form of ENZYMES, the basic tools for construction, repair, and maintenance. See also PEPTIDE.

protein hormone any of a class of substances secreted into the bloodstream that regulates processes in distant target organs and tissues and that consists of a long-chain polymer of AMINO ACIDS. Examples are growth hormone and INSULIN.

protocol *n.* the original notes of a study or experiment recorded during or immediately after a particular session or trial, particularly as recorded from participant's verbalizations during the process.

protocol analysis a methodology in which people are encouraged to think out loud as they perform some task. Transcripts of these sessions (protocols) are then analyzed to investigate the cognitive processes underlying performance of the task.

prototype *n.* in the formation of concepts, the best or average exemplar of a category. For example, the prototypical bird is some kind of mental average of all the different kinds of birds of which a person has knowledge or with which a person has had experience. —**prototypal**, **prototypical**, or **prototypic** *adj.*

proxemics *n.* the study of interpersonal spatial behavior. Proxemics is concerned with territoriality, interpersonal distance, spatial arrangements, crowding, and other aspects of the physical environment that affect behavior.

proximal *adj.* **1.** situated near or directed toward the trunk or center of an organism. **2.** near, or mostly closely related, to the point of reference or origin. Compare DISTAL. —**proximally** *adv.*

proximal stimulus the physical energy from a stimulus as it directly stimulates a sense organ or receptor, in contrast to the DISTAL STIMULUS in the actual environment. In reading, for example, the distal stimulus is the print on the page of a book, whereas the proximal stimulus is the light energy reflected by the print that stimulates the photoreceptors of the retina.

proximate cause the most direct or immediate cause of an event. In a sequence of occurrences, it is the one that directly produces the effect. For example the proximate cause of Smith's aggression may be an insult, but the REMOTE CAUSE may be Smith's early childhood experiences.

proximate explanation an explanation for behavior in terms of physiological mechanisms or developmental experiences, rather than in terms of the adaptive value of the behavior (see ULTIMATE EXPLANATION).

proximity *n.* one of the GESTALT PRINCIPLES OF ORGANIZATION. It states that people tend to organize objects close to each other into a perceptual group and interpret them as a single entity. Also called **law of proximity**; **principle of proximity**.

proximodistal *adj.* from the central to the peripheral. The term typically is used in the context of maturation to refer to the tendency to acquire motor skills from the cen-

ter outward, as when children learn to move their heads, trunks, arms, and legs before learning to move their hands and feet. Compare CEPHALOCAUDAL.

Prozac *n.* a trade name for FLUOXETINE.

pseudodementia *n.* deterioration or impairment of cognitive functions in the absence of neurological disorder or disease (compare DEMENTIA). The condition may occur, reversibly, in a MAJOR DEPRESSIVE EPISODE—particularly among older adults—or as a psychological symptom of FACTITIOUS DISORDER.

pseudopsychology *n.* an approach to understanding or analyzing the mind or behavior that utilizes unscientific or fraudulent methods. Examples include palmistry, PHRENOLOGY, and PHYSIOGNOMY. See also PARAPSYCHOLOGY. —**pseudopsychological** *adj.*

psi *n.* **1.** the Greek letter ψ, often used to symbolize psychology. **2.** the phenomena or alleged phenomena studied by PARAPSYCHOLOGY, including EXTRASENSORY PERCEPTION, PRECOGNITION, and PSYCHOKINESIS.

psilocin *n.* an indolealkylamine HALLUCINOGEN that is the principal psychoactive compound in "magic mushrooms" of the genus *Psilocybe*. **Psilocybin**, first isolated in 1958, differs from psilocin only in having an additional phosphate group; it is rapidly metabolized in the body and converted to psilocin.

PSP abbreviation for POSTSYNAPTIC POTENTIAL.

psyche *n.* in psychology, the mind in its totality, as distinguished from the physical organism. The term had earlier been used to refer to the soul or the very essence of life.

psychedelic drug see HALLUCINOGEN.

psychiatric hospital a public or private institution providing a wide range of diagnostic techniques and treatment to individuals with mental disorders on an inpatient basis. Also called **mental hospital**.

psychiatrist *n.* a physician who specializes in the diagnosis, treatment, prevention, and study of mental and emotional disorders. In the United States, education for this profession consists of 4 years of premedical training in college; a 4-year course in medical school, the final 2 years of which are spent in clerkships studying with physicians in at least five specialty areas; and a 4-year residency in a hospital or agency approved by the American Medical Association.

psychiatry *n.* the medical specialty concerned with the study, diagnosis, treatment, and prevention of personality, behavioral, and mental disorders, based on the premise that biological causes are at the root of mental and emotional problems. Training for psychiatry includes the study of psychopathology, biochemistry, psychopharmacology, neurology, neuropathology, psychology, psychoanalysis, genetics, social science, and community mental health, as well as the many theories and approaches advanced in the field itself. —**psychiatric** *adj.*

psychic 1. *adj.* denoting phenomena associated with the mind. **2.** *adj.* denoting a class of phenomena, such as TELEPATHY and CLAIRVOYANCE, that appear to defy scientific explanation. The term is also applied to any putative powers, forces, or faculties associated with such phenomena. See PSI. **3.** *n.* a medium, sensitive, or other person with alleged paranormal abilities.

psychic determinism the position, associated particularly with Austrian psychiatrist Sigmund Freud (1856–1939), that mental (psychic) events do not occur by chance but always have an underlying cause that can be uncovered by analysis.

psychic energy in psychoanalytic theory, the dynamic force behind all mental processes. According to Austrian psychiatrist Sigmund Freud (1856–1939), the basic sources of this energy are the INSTINCTS or drives that are located in the ID and seek immediate gratification according to the PLEASURE PRINCIPLE. Swiss psychoanalyst Carl Jung (1875–1961) also believed that there is a reservoir of psychic energy, but objected to Freud's emphasis on the pleasurable gratification of biological instincts and emphasized the means by which this energy is channeled into the development of the personality and the expression of cultural and spiritual values. See also LIBIDO.

psychoactive drug any of a group of drugs that have significant effects on psychological processes, such as thinking, perception, and emotion. Psychoactive drugs include those taken recreationally to produce an altered state of consciousness (e.g., HALLUCINOGENS) and therapeutic agents designed to ameliorate a mental condition (e.g., ANTIDEPRESSANTS, ANTIPSYCHOTICS). Psychoactive drugs are often referred to as **psychotropic drugs** (or **psychotropics**) in clinical contexts.

psychoanalysis *n.* an approach to the mind, psychological disorders, and psychological treatment originally developed by Austrian psychiatrist Sigmund Freud (1856–1939) at the beginning of the 20th century. The hallmark of psychoanalysis is the assumption that much of mental activity is unconscious and, consequently, that understanding people requires interpreting the unconscious meaning underlying their overt, or manifest, behavior. Psychoanalysis (often shortened to **analysis**) focuses primarily, then, on the influence of such unconscious forces as repressed impulses, internal conflicts, and childhood traumas on the mental life and adjustment of the individual. The foundations on which classic psychoanalysis rests are: (a) the concept of INFANTILE SEXUALITY; (b) the OEDIPUS COMPLEX; (c) the theory of INSTINCTS; (d) the PLEASURE PRINCIPLE and the REALITY PRINCIPLE; (e) the threefold division of the psyche into ID, EGO, and SUPEREGO; and (f) the central importance of anxiety and DEFENSE MECHANISMS in neurotic reactions. Psychoanalysis as a form of therapy is directed primarily to psychoneuroses, which it seeks to eliminate by bringing about basic modifications in the personality. This is done by establishing a constructive therapeutic relationship, or TRANSFERENCE, with the analyst, which enables him or her to elicit and interpret the unconscious conflicts that have produced the neurosis. The specific methods used to achieve this goal are FREE ASSOCIATION, DREAM ANALYSIS, analysis of RESISTANCES and defenses, and WORKING THROUGH the feelings revealed in the transference process. **—psychoanalytic** *adj.*

psychoanalyst *n.* a therapist who has undergone special training in psychoanalytic theory and practice and who applies the techniques developed by Austrian psychiatrist Sigmund Freud (1856–1939) to the treatment of mental disorders. This involves a thorough study of the works of Freud and others in the field, supervised clinical training, a TRAINING ANALYSIS, and a personal program of psychoanalysis. See also ANALYST.

psychoanalytic theory the diverse complex of assumptions and constructs underlying the approach known as PSYCHOANALYSIS. Classically—and properly—the term focuses specifically on the formulations of Austrian psychiatrist Sigmund Freud (1856-1939), but it may also be taken to include such subsequent offshoots and counter-approaches as ANALYTIC PSYCHOLOGY, INDIVIDUAL PSYCHOLOGY, OBJECT RELATIONS THEORY, and others that are based on PSYCHODYNAMIC THEORY.

psychobiology *n.* **1.** a school of thought in the mental health professions in which the individual is viewed as a holistic unit and both normal and abnormal behavior are explained in terms of the interaction of biological, sociological, and psychological determinants. **2.** a rare synonym for BIOLOGICAL PSYCHOLOGY. **—psychobiological** *adj.*

psychodrama *n.* a technique of psychotherapy in which clients achieve new insight and alter undesired patterns of behavior through acting out roles or incidents. The process involves: (a) a protagonist, or client, who presents and acts out his or her emotional problems and interpersonal relationships; (b) trained auxiliary egos, who play supportive roles representing significant individuals in the dramatized situations; and (c) a director, or therapist, who guides this process and leads an interpretive session when it is completed.

Psychodynamic Diagnostic Manual (**PDM**) a handbook for the diagnosis and treatment of mental health disorders that attempts to characterize an individual's personality and the full range of his or her emotional, social, and interpersonal functioning. Published in 2006, by a task force of various major psychoanalytical organizations, the *PDM* is meant to serve as a complement to the *Diagnostic and Statistical Manual*

P

of Mental Disorders (see DSM–IV–TR) and the *ICD* (see INTERNATIONAL CLASSIFICATION OF DISEASES).

psychodynamic psychotherapy those forms of psychotherapy, falling within or deriving from the psychoanalytic tradition, that view individuals as reacting to unconscious forces (e.g., motivation, drive), that focus on processes of change and development, and that place a premium on self-understanding and making meaning of what is unconscious. Most psychodynamic approaches share common features, such as emphasis on dealing with the unconscious in treatment, emphasis on the role of analyzing TRANSFERENCE, and the use of dream analysis and INTERPRETATION. Also called **dynamic psychotherapy**.

psychodynamic theory a constellation of theories of human functioning that are based on the interplay of drives and other forces within the person, especially (and originating in) the psychoanalytic theories developed by Austrian psychiatrist Sigmund Freud (1856–1939) and his colleagues and successors, such as Anna Freud (1895–1982), Carl Jung (1875–1961), and Melanie Klein (1882–1960). Later psychodynamic theories, while retaining concepts of the interworking of drives and motives to varying degrees, moved toward the contemporary approach, which emphasizes the process of change and incorporates interpersonal and transactional perspectives of personality development.

psychogenic *adj.* resulting from mental factors. The term is used particularly to denote or refer to a disorder that cannot be accounted for by any identifiable organic dysfunction and is believed to be due to psychological factors (e.g., a conversion disorder). In psychology and psychiatry, psychogenic disorders are improperly considered equivalent to FUNCTIONAL disorders.

psychohistory *n.* the application of psychoanalytic theory to the study of historical figures, events, and movements.

psychokinesis *n.* (**PK**) the alleged ability to control external events and move or change the shape of objects through the power of thought. Examples include the supposed ability of certain psychics to influence the roll of dice or to bend a piece of metal by exerting "mind over matter." Also called **telekinesis**. —**psychokinetic** *adj.*

psycholinguistics *n.* a branch of psychology that employs formal linguistic models to investigate language use and the cognitive processes that accompany it. In particular, the models of GENERATIVE GRAMMAR proposed by U.S. linguist Noam Chomsky (1928–) and others have been used to explain and predict LANGUAGE ACQUISITION in children and the production and comprehension of speech by adults. To this extent psycholinguistics is a specific discipline that can be distinguished from the more general area of psychology of language, which encompasses many other fields and approaches. —**psycholinguistic** *adj.*

psychological abuse see EMOTIONAL ABUSE.

psychological acculturation see ACCULTURATION.

psychological assessment the gathering and integration of data in order to evaluate a person's behavior, abilities, and other characteristics, particularly for the purposes of making a diagnosis or treatment recommendation. Psychologists assess diverse psychiatric problems (e.g., anxiety, substance abuse) and nonpsychiatric concerns (e.g., intelligence, career interests) across a range of areas, including clinical, educational, organizational, health, and forensic settings. Assessment data may be gathered through various methods, such as interviews, observation, PROJECTIVE TECHNIQUES, standardized tests, physiological or psychophysiological measurement devices, or other specialized procedures and apparatuses.

psychological autopsy an analysis that is conducted following a person's death in order to determine his or her mental state prior to death. Psychological autopsies are often performed when a death occurs in a complex or ambiguous manner and are frequently used to determine if a death was the result of suicide.

psychological dependence reliance on a psychoactive substance for the reinforcement it provides, such as relief from tension. It has been suggested that reinforcement is the driving force behind drug addiction, and that TOLERANCE and PHYSICAL DEPENDENCE are co-occuring but not essential related phenomena.

psychological determinism see DETERMINISM.

psychological disorder see MENTAL DISORDER.

psychological field in the social psychology of German-born U.S. psychologist Kurt Lewin (1890–1947), the individual's LIFE SPACE or environment as he or she perceives it at any given moment. See also FIELD THEORY.

psychological model 1. a theory, usually including a mechanism for predicting psychological outcomes, intended to explain specific psychological processes. See also CONSTRUCT. **2.** a representation of human cognitive and response char-

acteristics used to approximate and evaluate the performance of an actual individual in a complex situation, such as a novel aircraft cockpit.

psychological need any need that is essential to mental health or that is otherwise not a biological necessity. It may be generated entirely internally, as in the need for pleasure, or it may be generated by interactions between the individual and the environment, as in the need for social approval, justice, or job satisfaction. Psychological needs comprise the four higher levels of MASLOW'S MOTIVATIONAL HIERARCHY. Compare PHYSIOLOGICAL NEED.

psychological test any standardized instrument, including scales and self-report inventories, used in measuring behavior, emotional functioning, intelligence and cognitive abilities (reasoning, comprehension, abstract thinking, etc.), aptitudes, attitudes, values, interests, personality characteristics, or other attributes of interest to psychologists.

psychological warfare a broad class of activities designed to influence the attitudes, beliefs, and behavior of soldiers and civilians with regard to military operations. Such activities include attempts to bolster the attitudes and morale of one's own people as well as to change or undermine the attitudes and morale of an opposing army or civilian population.

psychologism *n.* any position or theoretical perspective that holds one or more of the following: (a) that the rules of logic are reflective of the way the mind works, so that logic is persuasive only because it "fits" the working of the mind; (b) that truth is established by verifying the correspondence of external facts to ideas in the mind; (c) that epistemological questions can be answered by an understanding of the laws by which the mind works; and (d) that the meanings of words are established by the ideas corresponding to them. The term is generally employed as a criticism of particular approaches or theories on the grounds that such positions make psychological processes that are accidental and contingent the foundation of knowledge.

psychologist *n.* an individual who is professionally trained in the research, practice, or teaching (or all three) of one or more branches or subfields of PSYCHOLOGY. Training is obtained at a university or a school of professional psychology, leading to a doctoral degree in philosophy (PhD), psychology (PsyD), or education (EdD). Psychologists work in a variety of settings, including laboratories, schools, colleges, universities, social agencies, hospitals, clinics, the military, industry and business, prisons, the government, and private practice. The professional activities of psychologists are also varied but can include psychological counseling, health care services, educational testing and assessment, research, teaching, and business and organizational consulting.

psychology *n.* **1.** the study of the mind and behavior. Historically, psychology was an area of PHILOSOPHY. It is now a diverse scientific discipline comprising several major branches of research (e.g., experimental psychology, biological psychology, cognitive psychology, developmental psychology, personality, and social psychology), as well as several subareas of research and applied psychology (e.g., clinical psychology, industrial and organizational psychology, school and educational psychology, human factors, health psychology, neuro-

psychology, cross-cultural psychology). Research in psychology involves observation, experimentation, testing, and analysis to explore the biological, cognitive, emotional, personal, and social processes or stimuli underlying human and animal behavior. The practice of psychology involves the use of psychological knowledge for any of several purposes: to understand and treat mental, emotional, physical, and social dysfunction; to understand and enhance behavior in various settings of human activity (e.g., school, workplace, courtroom, sports arena, battlefield, etc.); and to improve machine and building design for human use. **2.** the supposed collection of behaviors, traits, attitudes, and so forth that characterize an individual or a group (e.g., the psychology of women). —**psychological** *adj.*

psychometric *adj.* **1.** of or relating to PSYCHOMETRICS. **2.** of or relating to PSYCHOPHYSICS.

psychometric function see PSYCHOPHYSICAL FUNCTION.

psychometrics *n.* the psychological theory and technique (e.g., the science and process) of mental measurement. Also called **psychometry**.

psychomotor *adj.* relating to movements or motor effects that result from mental activity.

psychomotor agitation restless physical and mental activity that is inappropriate for its context. It includes pacing, hand wringing, and pulling or rubbing clothing and other objects and is a common symptom of both MAJOR DEPRESSIVE EPISODES and MANIC EPISODES. Also called **psychomotor excitement**.

psychomotor retardation a slowing down or inhibition of mental and physical activity, manifest as slow speech with long pauses before answers, slowness in thinking, and slow body movements. Psychomotor retardation is a common symptom of MAJOR DEPRESSIVE EPISODES.

psychoneuroimmunology *n.* the study of how the brain and behavior affect immune responses. **—psychoneuroimmunological** *adj.*

psychonomic *adj.* of or relating to **psychonomics**, the science that seeks to identify laws governing the mind through an emphasis on quantitative measurement, experimental control, and OPERATIONAL DEFINITIONS.

psychopathic personality see ANTISOCIAL PERSONALITY DISORDER.

psychopathology *n.* **1.** the scientific study of mental disorders, including theory, etiology, progression, symptomatology, diagnosis, and treatment. The term in this sense is sometimes used synonymously with ABNORMAL PSYCHOLOGY. **2.** the behavioral or cognitive manifestations of such disorders. The term in this sense is sometimes considered synonymous with MENTAL DISORDER itself. **—psychopathological** *adj.* **—psychopathologist** *n.*

psychopathy *n.* a former term for a personality trait marked by egocentricity, impulsivity, and lack of such emotions as guilt and remorse.

psychopharmacology *n.* the study of the influence of drugs on mental, emotional, and behavioral processes. Psychopharmacology is concerned primarily with the mode of action of various substances that affect different areas of the brain and nervous system, including drugs of abuse. **—psychopharmacological** *adj.* **—psychopharmacologist** *n.*

psychopharmacotherapy *n.* the use of pharmacological agents in the treatment of mental disorders. For example, acute or chronic schizophrenia is treated by administration of antipsychotic drugs or other agents. Although such drugs do not cure mental disorders, they may—when used appropriately—produce significant relief from symptoms.

psychophysical *adj.* of or relating to the relationship between physical stimuli and mental events.

psychophysical function a relationship between a stimulus and judgments about the stimulus, as expressed in a mathematical formula. In the METHOD OF CONSTANT STIMULI, for example, it is the proportion of "yes" responses (i.e., that the stimulus was perceived) as a function of physical magnitude of the stimuli. Also called **psychometric function**.

psychophysical method any of the standard techniques used in investigating psychophysical problems, such as the METHOD OF ADJUSTMENT and the METHOD OF LIMITS.

psychophysical scaling any of the procedures used to construct scales relating physical stimulus properties to perceived magnitude. Methods are often classified as direct or indirect, based on whether the observer directly judges magnitude.

psychophysics *n.* a branch of psychology that studies the relationship between the objective physical characteristics of a stimulus (e.g., its measured intensity) and the subjective perception of that stimulus (e.g., its apparent brightness).

psychophysiology *n.* the study of the relation between the chemical and physical functions of organisms (physiology) and cognitive processes, emotions, and behavior (psychology). Also called **physio-**

P

logical psychology. —psycho-physiological *adj.* **—psycho-physiologist** *n.*

psychosexual development in the classic psychoanalytic theory of Austrian psychiatrist Sigmund Freud (1856–1939), the step-by-step growth of sexual life from infancy through adulthood as it affects personality development. Freud posited that the impetus for psychosexual development stems from a single energy source, the LIBIDO, which is concentrated in different organs throughout the process and produces the various **psychosexual stages**: the ORAL STAGE, ANAL STAGE, PHALLIC STAGE, LATENCY STAGE, and GENITAL STAGE. Each stage gives rise to its own characteristic erotic activities (e.g., sucking and biting in the oral stage), which may persist in characteristic tendencies if sexual development is arrested in a FIXATION at one particular stage.

psychosis *n.* **1.** an abnormal mental state involving significant problems with REALITY TESTING and characterized by serious impairments or disruptions in the most fundamental higher brain functions—perception, cognition and cognitive processing, and emotions or affect—as manifested in behavioral phenomena, such as delusions, hallucinations, and significantly disorganized speech. See PSYCHOTIC DISORDER. **2.** historically, any severe mental disorder that significantly interferes with functioning and ability to perform activities essential to daily living.

psychosocial *adj.* describing the intersection and interaction of social and cultural influences on mental health, personality development, and behavior.

psychosocial development 1. according to the theory of German-born U.S. psychologist Erik Erikson (1902–1994), personality develop-ment as a process influenced by social and cultural factors throughout the life span. See ERIKSON'S EIGHT STAGES OF DEVELOPMENT. **2.** the development of normal social behavior, both prosocial behavior (e.g., cooperation) and negative (e.g., aggressive) behavior. Psychosocial development involves changes not only in children's overt behavior but also in their SOCIAL COGNITION. For example, they become able to take the perspective of others and to understand that other people's behavior is based on their knowledge and desires.

psychosomatic *adj.* characterizing an approach based on the belief that the mind (psyche) plays a role in all the diseases affecting the various bodily systems (soma).

psychosomatic disorder a type of disorder in which psychological factors are believed to play an important role in the origin or course (or both) of the disease.

psychosurgery *n.* the treatment of a mental disorder by surgical removal or destruction of selective brain areas. The most well-known example of psychosurgery is prefrontal LOBOTOMY, historically used particularly for schizophrenia but also a variety of other disorders. Psychosurgery was most popular from 1935 to 1960 and is among the most controversial of all psychiatric treatments ever introduced. Contemporary psychosurgery approaches are far more precisely targeted and confined in extent than the early techniques, employing high-tech imaging and a variety of highly controllable methods of producing minute lesions. Additionally, they are used only as a last resort and only for a handful of specific psychiatric disorders—MAJOR DEPRESSIVE DISORDER, BIPOLAR DISORDER, OBSESSIVE-COMPULSIVE DISORDER, and GENERALIZED ANXI-

ETY DISORDER—that have been resistant to other available therapies.

psychotherapy *n.* any psychological service provided by a trained professional that primarily uses forms of communication and interaction to assess, diagnose, and treat dsyfunctional emotional reactions, ways of thinking, and behavior patterns of an individual, family, or group. There are many types of psychotherapy, but generally they fall into four major categories: PSYCHODYNAMIC PSYCHOTHERAPY, COGNITIVE THERAPY or BEHAVIOR THERAPY, HUMANISTIC THERAPY, and INTEGRATIVE PSYCHOTHERAPY. The **psychotherapist** is an individual who has been professionally trained and licensed (in the United States by a state board) to treat mental, emotional, and behavioral disorders by psychological means. **—psychotherapeutic** *adj.*

psychotic *adj.* of, relating to, or affected by PSYCHOSIS or a PSYCHOTIC DISORDER.

psychotic disorder any one of a number of severe mental disorders, regardless of etiology, characterized by gross impairment in REALITY TESTING. The accuracy of perceptions and thoughts is incorrectly evaluated, and incorrect inferences are made about external reality, even in the face of contrary evidence. Specific symptoms indicative of psychotic disorders are delusions, hallucinations, and markedly disorganized speech, thought, or behavior; individuals may have little or no insight into their symptoms.

psychoticism *n.* a dimension of personality in the TYPOLOGY developed by German-born British psychologist Hans Eysenck (1916–1997), characterized by aggression, impulsivity, aloofness, and antisocial behavior.

psychotropic drug see PSYCHO-ACTIVE DRUG.

PTSD abbreviation for POST-TRAUMATIC STRESS DISORDER.

puberty *n.* the stage of development when the genital organs reach maturity and secondary SEX CHARACTERISTICS begin to appear, signaling the start of ADOLESCENCE. It is marked by ejaculation of sperm in the male, onset of menstruation and development of breasts in the female, and, in both males and females, growth of pubic hair and increasing sexual interest. **—pubertal** *adj.*

pubescence *n.* the period or process of reaching puberty. **—pubescent** *adj.*

Publication Manual of the American Psychological Association a large reference book that contains hundreds of guidelines on how to present written material in the behavioral and social sciences clearly and effectively. Based on the special requirements of psychology but applicable to sociology, business, economics, nursing, social work, criminology, and other disciplines as well, the *Publication Manual* describes the editorial style established by the American Psychological Association (APA) and used in all of the books and journals that it publishes (i.e., APA STYLE). In addition to guidance on the content and organization of a manuscript, the *Publication Manual* offers direction in such areas as grammar and the mechanics of writing, the uniform use of punctuation and abbreviations, the construction of tables and figures, the selection of headings, the citation and formatting of references, and the presentation of statistics. The forerunner of the *Publication Manual* was a brief article published in the February 1929 issue of the APA journal *Psychological Bulletin* that discussed instructions for

P

the preparation of journal manuscripts. A revised and expanded version of these instructions was published as a first edition of the *Publication Manual* in 1952, as a supplement to an article in the *Psychological Bulletin*. The second edition was published in 1974, the third edition in 1983, and the fourth in 1994; APA released the current fifth edition in 2001.

punctuated equilibrium a theory of EVOLUTION proposing that periods of rapid change, resulting in the development of new species, are separated by longer periods of little or no change.

punishment *n.* in OPERANT CONDITIONING, the process in which the relationship, or CONTINGENCY, between a response and some stimulus or circumstance results in the response becoming less probable. For example, a pigeon's pecks on a key may at first occasionally be followed by presentation of food; this will establish some probability of pecking. Next, each peck produces a brief electric shock (while the other conditions remain as before). If pecking declines as a result, then punishment is said to have occurred, and the shock is called a **punisher**. **—punish** *vb.*

pupil *n.* the aperture through which light passes on entering the eye. It is located immediately in front of the LENS. The size of the opening is controlled by a circle of muscle (the IRIS) innervated by fibers of the autonomic nervous system.

pupillary reflex the automatic change in size of the pupil in response to light changes. The pupil constricts in response to bright light and dilates in dim light. See also ACCOMMODATION.

pure alexia see ALEXIA.

pure word deafness a type of AU-DITORY AGNOSIA in which an individual is unable to understand spoken language but can comprehend nonverbal sounds and read, write, and speak in a relatively normal manner. The syndrome is considered "pure" in the sense that it is relatively free of the language difficulties encountered in the APHASIAS.

purging *n.* the activity of expelling food that has just been ingested, usually by vomiting or the use of laxatives. Purging often occurs in conjunction with an eating binge in ANOREXIA NERVOSA or BULIMIA NERVOSA; its purpose is to eliminate or reduce real or imagined weight gain.

Purkinje cell a type of large, highly branched cell in the CEREBELLAR CORTEX of the brain that receives incoming signals about the position of the body and transmits signals to spinal nerves for coordinated muscle actions. [Johannes Evangelista **Purkinje** (1787–1869), Czech physiologist and physician]

putamen *n.* a part of the lenticular nucleus in the BASAL GANGLIA of the brain. It receives input from the motor cortex and is involved in control of movements.

p-value *n.* see SIGNIFICANCE LEVEL.

PVS abbreviation for PERSISTENT VEGETATIVE STATE.

Pygmalion effect a consequence or reaction in which the expectations of a leader or superior lead to behavior on the part of followers or subordinates that is consistent with these expectations: a form of SELF-FULFILLING PROPHECY or EXPECTANCY EFFECT. For example, raising manager expectations regarding the performance of subordinate employees has been found to enhance the performance of those employees.

pyramidal cell a type of large neuron that has a roughly pyramid-shaped CELL BODY and is found in the cerebral cortex.

pyramidal tract the primary pathway followed by motor neurons that originate in the motor area of the cortex, the premotor area, and the somatosensory area. Fibers of the pyramidal tract cross in the pyramid of the medulla oblongata and communicate with fibers supplying the peripheral muscles. The pyramidal tract includes the corticospinal tract (see VENTROMEDIAL PATHWAY), and the two terms are occasionally used synonymously.

pyriform area (piriform area) a pear-shaped region of the RHIN-ENCEPHALON, at the base of the medial temporal lobe of the brain, that forms part of the OLFACTORY CORTEX.

pyromania *n.* an impulse-control disorder characterized by (a) repeated failure to resist impulses to set fires and watch them burn, without monetary, social, political, or other motivations; (b) an extreme interest in fire and things associated with fire; and (c) a sense of increased tension before starting the fire and intense pleasure, gratification, or release while committing the act.

P

Qq

QALYs acronym for QUALITY ADJUSTED LIFE YEARS.

Q sort a data-collection procedure, often used in personality measurement, in which a participant or independent rater sorts a set of stimuli (short descriptive statements printed on cards commonly are used) into various categories according to their relevance to or representativeness of the participant, under a restriction that a predetermined number of stimuli must be placed in each category.

quadrantanopia *n.* loss of vision in one fourth, or one quadrant, of the visual field.

qualitative research a type of research methodology that produces descriptive (non-numerical) data, such as observations of behavior or personal accounts of experiences. The goal of gathering this **qualitative data** is to examine how things look from different vantage points. A variety of techniques are subsumed under qualitative research, including interviews, PARTICIPANT OBSERVATION, and CASE STUDIES.

quality adjusted life years (QALYs) a measure that combines the quantity of life, expressed in terms of survival or life expectancy, with the quality of life. The value of a year of perfect health is taken as 1; a year of ill health is worth less than 1; death is taken as 0. The measure provides a method to assess the benefits to be gained from medical procedures and interventions.

quality of life the extent to which a person obtains satisfaction from life. The following are important for a good quality of life: emotional, material, and physical well-being; engagement in interpersonal relations; opportunities for personal (e.g., skill) development; exercising rights and making self-determining lifestyle choices; and participation in society. Enhancing quality of life is a particular concern for those with chronic disease or developmental and other disabilities and for those undergoing medical or psychological treatment.

quantal hypothesis (quantal theory) see NEURAL QUANTUM THEORY.

quantification *n.* introduction of the dimension of quantity (amount): the process of expressing a concept in numerical form, which may aid in analysis and understanding.

quantitative research a type of research methodology that produces numerical data, such as test scores or measurements of reaction time. The goal of gathering this **quantitative data** is to understand the nature of a phenomenon, particularly through the development of models and theories. Quantitative research techniques include experiments and surveys.

quartile *n.* one of the three values within a statistical distribution that divide it into equal-sized fourths. For example, the first (or lower) quartile of a distribution would be the data value below which are the lowest 25% of scores, the second quartile would be the data value below which are 26% to 50% of scores, and the third (or upper) quartile would be the data value below which are 51% to 75% of scores (or, conversely, above which are 25% of scores).

quasi-experimental research research in which the investigator cannot assign participants to experimental or control groups at random but can still manipulate the independent variable and limit the influence of extraneous variables to some degree. An example of such a study, called a **quasi experiment**, is provided by a researcher assessing the memory performance of individuals with and without hearing loss: while the investigator cannot choose which people have hearing loss and which do not, he or she can decide upon the types of memory tasks to present and how to present them. Quasi-experimental research is similar to NONEXPERIMENTAL RESEARCH but distinguished by its retention of influence over the independent variable.

questionnaire *n.* a set of questions asked to obtain information from a respondent about a topic of interest, such as his or her attitudes, behaviors, or other characteristics.

quota sampling a method of selecting participants for a study in which a prespecified number of individuals with specific background characteristics, such as a particular age, race, sex, or education, is selected in order to obtain a sample with the same proportional representation of these characteristics as the target population.

Q

Rr

r symbol for CORRELATION COEFFICIENT.

r² symbol for COEFFICIENT OF DETERMINATION.

R symbol for MULTIPLE CORRELATION COEFFICIENT.

R² symbol for COEFFICIENT OF MULTIPLE DETERMINATION.

race *n.* a socially defined concept sometimes used to designate a portion, or "subdivision," of the human population with common physical characteristics, ancestry, or language. The term is also loosely applied to geographic, cultural, religious, or national groups. The significance often accorded to racial categories might suggest that such groups are objectively defined and homogeneous; however, there is much heterogeneity within categories, and the categories themselves differ across cultures. Moreover, self-reported race frequently varies owing to changing social contexts and an individual's identification with more than one race. —**racial** *adj.*

racism *n.* a form of PREJUDICE that assumes that the members of racial categories have distinctive charac-eristics and that these differences result in some racial groups being inferior to others. Racism generally includes negative emotional reactions to members of the group, acceptance of negative STEREOTYPES, and DISCRIMINATION against individuals; in some cases it leads to violence. —**racist** *adj., n.*

radial glia a type of nonneuronal cell (GLIA) that forms early in development, spanning the width of the emerging cerebral hemispheres to guide migrating neurons.

radial maze a type of maze that has a central starting point with several arms (typically six to eight) extending from the center. A non-human animal might be required to learn to find food in only certain of the arms or to search systematically through each arm without entering the same arm twice. Radial mazes have been used extensively to study spatial memory and learning.

radical behaviorism the view that behavior, rather than consciousness and its contents, should be the proper topic for study in psychological science. This term is often used to distinguish classical BEHAVIORISM, as originally formulated in 1913 by U.S. psychologist John B. Watson (1878–1958), from more moderate forms of NEOBEHAVIORISM. However, it has evolved to denote as well the descriptive behaviorism later proposed by U.S. psychologist B. F. Skinner (1904–1990), which emphasized the importance of reinforcement and its relationship to behavior (i.e., the environmental determinants of behavior).

rage *n.* intense, typically uncontrolled anger. It is usually differentiated from hostility in that it is not necessarily accompanied by destructive actions but rather by excessive expressions.

random *adj.* without order or predictability.

random assignment see RANDOMIZE.

random-interval schedule (RI schedule) in conditioning, an arrangement in which the first response after an interval has elapsed is reinforced, the duration of the interval varies randomly from reinforcement to reinforcement, and a fixed probability of reinforcement over time is used to reinforce a response. For example, if every second the probability that reinforcement would be arranged for the next response was .1, then the random-interval schedule value would be 10 s (i.e., RI 10 s).

randomize *vb.* to assign participants or other sampling units to the conditions of an experiment at random, that is, in such a way that each participant or sampling unit has an equal chance of being assigned to any particular condition. **—randomization** *n.*

randomized block design a research design in which participants are first classified into groups (blocks), on the basis of a variable for which the experimenter wishes to control. Individuals within each block are then randomly assigned to one of several treatment groups.

randomized-group design an experimental design in which the participants are assigned at random to either experimental or control groups without matching on one or more background variables. Compare MATCHED-GROUP DESIGN.

random mating mating behavior without mate selection. Many early behavioral ECOLOGY theories were based on the idea of random mating, but it is now recognized that most animals select specific mates and often show ASSORTATIVE MATING.

random-ratio schedule (RR schedule) in conditioning, an arrangement in which the number of responses required for each reinforcement varies randomly from reinforcement to reinforcement. It is usually arranged by having the same probability of reinforcement for each response regardless of the history of reinforcement for prior responses. For example, a random-ratio 100 schedule would result from a reinforcement probability of .01 for any given response.

random sampling a process for selecting individuals for a study from a larger potential group of individuals in such a way that each is selected with a fixed (equal) probability of inclusion. This selected group of individuals is called a **random sample**.

random selection the procedure used for random sampling.

random variable a variable whose value depends upon the outcome of chance.

range *n.* in statistics, a measure of DISPERSION, obtained by subtracting the lowest score from the highest score in a distribution.

rank *n.* a particular position along an ordered continuum.

rank correlation coefficient a numerical index reflecting the degree of relationship between two variables that have each been arranged in ascending or descending order of magnitude (i.e., ranked). It is an assessment not of the association between the actual values of the variables but rather of the association between their rankings. Among the most commonly used is the **Spearman rank correlation coefficient** (**Spearman's rho**, symbolized by ρ), appropriate when the variables being compared do not follow the NORMAL DISTRIBUTION. Also called **rank order correlation coefficient**.

rank order the arrangement of a series of items (e.g., scores or individuals) in order of magnitude.

rape *n.* the nonconsensual oral, anal, or vaginal penetration of an individual by another person with a part of the body or an object, using force or threats of bodily harm, or by taking advantage of someone incapable of giving consent.

raphe nucleus a group of SEROTO-NERGIC neurons in the midline of the brainstem that project widely to the spinal cord, thalamus, basal ganglia, and cerebral cortex.

rapid cycling mood disturbance that fluctuates over a short period, most commonly between manic and depressive symptoms. A rapid-cycling BIPOLAR DISORDER, for example, is characterized by four or more mood episodes over a 12-month period.

rapid eye movement (REM) the rapid, jerky, but coordinated movement of the eyes behind closed lids, observed during dreaming sleep. See REM SLEEP.

rapport *n.* a warm, relaxed relationship of mutual understanding, acceptance, and sympathetic compatibility between or among individuals. The establishment of rapport with the client in psychotherapy is frequently a significant mediate goal for the therapist in order to facilitate and deepen the therapeutic experience and promote optimal progress and improvement in the client.

RAS abbreviation for RETICULAR ACTIVATING SYSTEM.

Rasch model the simplest model for ITEM RESPONSE THEORY, in which only a single parameter, item difficulty, is specified. [proposed in 1960 by Georg **Rasch** (1901–1980), Danish statistician]

rate 1. *n.* relative frequency. **2.** *vb.* to evaluate or judge subjectively, especially by assigning a numerical value. For example, a supervisor could assess an employee's quality of work by choosing a number from 1 (excellent) to 10 (poor). Any instrument used in this process is called a **rating scale**.

rate coding a type of neural plotting of the frequency at which ACTION POTENTIALS occur. Compare TEMPORAL CODING.

ratio *n.* the quotient of two numbers, that is, one number divided by the other number.

ratio data numerical values that indicate magnitude and have a true, meaningful zero point. Ratio data represent exact quantities of the variables under consideration, and when arranged consecutively have equal differences among adjacent values (regardless of the specific values selected) that correspond to genuine differences between the physical quantities being measured. Income provides an example: the difference between an income of $40,000 and $50,000 is the same as the difference between $110,000 and $120,000, and an income of $0 indicates a complete and genuine absence of earnings. Ratio data are continuous in nature (i.e., able to take on any of an infinite variety of amounts) and of the highest MEASUREMENT LEVEL, surpassing NOMINAL DATA, ORDINAL DATA, and INTERVAL DATA in precision and complexity.

ratio IQ see IQ.

rational *adj.* pertaining to REASONING or, more broadly, to higher thought processes: influenced by thought rather than by emotion. **—rationally** *adv.*

rational emotive behavior therapy (**REBT**) a form of COGNITIVE BEHAVIOR THERAPY based on the concept that an individual's irrational or self-defeating beliefs and feelings influence and cause his or her undesirable behaviors and damaging self-concept. REBT teaches the individual to modify and replace self-defeating thoughts to achieve new and more effective ways of feeling and behaving.

rationalism *n.* any philosophical position holding that (a) it is possible to obtain knowledge of reality by reason alone, unsupported by experience, and (b) all human knowledge can be brought within a single deductive system. However, the term "rationalist" is chiefly applied to thinkers in the Continental philosophical tradition initiated by French philosopher René Descartes (1596–1650), most notably Dutch Jewish philosopher Baruch Spinoza (1632–1677) and German philosopher Gottfried Wilhelm Leibniz (1646–1716). Rationalism is usually contrasted with EMPIRICISM, which holds that knowledge comes from or must be validated by sensory experience. In psychology, psychoanalytical approaches, humanistic psychology, and some strains of cognitive theory are heavily influenced by rationalism. —**rationalist** *adj., n.*

rationalization *n.* an explanation, or presentation, in which apparently logical reasons are given to justify unacceptable behavior. In psychoanalytic theory, rationalization is considered to be a DEFENSE MECHANISM used to defend against feelings of guilt, to maintain self-respect, and to protect from criticism. In psychotherapy, rationalization is considered counterproductive to deep exploration and confrontation of the client's thoughts and feelings and of how they affect behavior. —**rationalize** *vb.*

ratio reinforcement in OPERANT CONDITIONING, reinforcement presented after a prearranged number of responses, in contrast to reinforcement delivered on the basis of a time schedule only. In such schedules, the rate of reinforcement is a direct function of the rate of responding. Compare INTERVAL REINFORCEMENT.

ratio scale a measurement scale having a true zero (i.e., zero on the scale indicates an absence of the measured attribute) and a constant ratio of values. Thus, on a ratio scale an increase from 3 to 4 (for example) is the same as an increase from 7 to 8. The existence of a true zero point is what distinguishes a ratio scale from an INTERVAL SCALE.

Raven's Progressive Matrices a nonverbal test of mental ability consisting of abstract designs, each of which is missing one part. The participant chooses the missing component from several alternatives in order to complete the design. The test comprises 60 designs arranged in five groups of 12; the items within each group become progressively more difficult. The test, introduced in 1938, is often viewed as the prototypical measure of general intelligence. [John C. **Raven** (1902–1970), British psychologist]

raw score an original score before it is converted to other units or another form through statistical analysis.

RBC theory abbreviation for RECOGNITION BY COMPONENTS THEORY.

reactance theory a model stating that in response to a perceived threat to or loss of a behavioral freedom a person will experience psychological reactance (or, more simply, reactance), a motivational state characterized by distress, anxiety, resistance, and the desire to restore that freedom. According to

R

this model, when people feel coerced or forced into a certain behavior, they will react against the coercion, often by demonstrating an increased preference for the behavior that is restrained, and may perform the opposite behavior to that desired.

reaction formation in psychoanalytic theory, a DEFENSE MECHANISM in which unacceptable or threatening unconscious impulses are denied and are replaced in consciousness with their opposite. For example, to conceal an unconscious prejudice an individual may preach tolerance; to deny feelings of rejection, a mother may be overindulgent toward her child. Through the symbolic relationship between the unconscious wish and its opposite, the outward behavior provides a disguised outlet for the tendencies it seems to oppose.

reaction time (RT) the time that elapses between onset or presentation of a stimulus and occurrence of a response to that stimulus. There are several specific types, including SIMPLE REACTION TIME and CHOICE REACTION TIME.

reactive *adj.* associated with or originating in response to a given stimulus or situation. For example, a psychotic episode that is secondary to a traumatic or otherwise stressful event in the life of the individual would be considered reactive and generally associated with a more favorable prognosis than an ENDOGENOUS episode unrelated to a specific happening.

reactive aggression see AGGRESSION.

reactive depression a MAJOR DEPRESSIVE EPISODE that is apparently precipitated by a distressing event or situation, such as a career or relationship setback. Also called

exogenous depression. Compare ENDOGENOUS DEPRESSION.

reactive schizophrenia an acute form of schizophrenia that clearly develops in response to predisposing or precipitating environmental factors, such as extreme stress. The prognosis is generally more favorable than for PROCESS SCHIZOPHRENIA.

reading disorder a LEARNING DISORDER that is characterized by a level of reading ability substantially below that expected for a child of a given age, intellectual ability, and educational experience. The reading difficulty involves faulty oral reading, slow oral and silent reading, and often reduced comprehension.

realism *n.* the philosophical doctrine that objects have an existence independent of the observer. **—realist** *adj., n.*

realistic anxiety anxiety in response to an identifiable threat or danger. This type of anxiety is considered a normal response to danger in the real world and serves to mobilize resources in order to protect the individual from harm.

realistic group-conflict theory a conceptual framework predicated on the assumption that intergroup tensions will occur whenever social groups must compete for scarce resources (e.g., food, territory, jobs, wealth, power, and natural resources) and that this competition fuels prejudice and other antagonistic attitudes that lead to conflicts such as rivalries and warfare. Also called **realistic conflict theory**.

reality monitoring see SOURCE MONITORING.

reality principle in psychoanalytic theory, the regulatory mechanism that represents the demands of the external world and requires the individual to forgo or modify instinctual gratification or to postpone it to a more appropriate time. In contrast to the PLEASURE PRINCIPLE, which is posited to dominate the life of the infant and child and govern the ID, or instinctual impulses, the reality principle is posited to govern the EGO, which controls impulses and enables people to deal rationally and effectively with the situations of life.

reality testing any means by which an individual determines and assesses his or her limitations in the face of biological, physiological, social, or environmental actualities or exigencies. It enables the individual to distinguish between self and nonself and between fantasy and real life. Defective reality testing is the major criterion of PSYCHOSIS.

real self the individual's true wishes and feelings and his or her potential for further growth and development.

reasonable accommodations adjustments made within an employment or educational setting that allow an individual with a physical, cognitive, or psychiatric disability to perform required tasks and essential functions. This might include installing ramps in an office cafeteria for wheelchair accessibility, altering the format of a test for a person with learning disabilities, or providing a sign language interpreter for a person with hearing loss.

reasoning *n.* thinking in which logical processes of an inductive or deductive character are used to draw conclusions from facts or premises. —**reason** *vb.*

REBT abbreviation for RATIONAL EMOTIVE BEHAVIOR THERAPY.

recall 1. *vb.* to transfer prior learning or past experience to current consciousness: that is, to retrieve and reproduce information. **2.** *n.* the process by which this occurs.

receiver-operating characteristic curve (**ROC curve**) in a detection, discrimination, or recognition task, the relationship between the hit rate (the proportion of correct "yes" responses) and the false-alarm rate (the proportion of incorrect "yes" responses). This is plotted as a curve to determine what effect the observer's response criterion is having on the results.

recency effect a memory phenomenon in which the most recently presented facts, impressions, or items are learned or remembered better than material presented earlier. This can occur in both formal learning situations and social contexts. For example, it can result in inaccurate ratings or impressions of a person's abilities or other characteristics due to the inordinate influence of the most recent information received about that person. Compare PRIMACY EFFECT.

receptive field the spatially discrete region and the features associated with it that can be stimulated to cause the maximal response of a sensory cell. In vision, for example, the receptive field of a retinal ganglion cell is the area on the retina (containing a particular number of photoreceptors) that evokes a neural response.

receptivity *n.* the period of time when a female is responsive to sexual overtures from a male, typically (but not exclusively) around the time of ovulation. Receptivity has a connotation of passive female acceptance or tolerance of male sexual overtures. In contrast, PROCEPTIVITY conveys active solicitation of males by females. —**receptive** *adj.*

receptor *n.* **1.** the cell in a sensory system that is responsible for stimulus TRANSDUCTION. Receptor cells are specialized to detect and respond to specific stimuli in the external or internal environment. Examples in-

R

clude the RETINAL RODS and RETINAL CONES in the eye and the HAIR CELLS in the cochlea of the ear. **2.** a molecule in a cell membrane that specifically binds a particular molecular messenger (e.g., a neurotransmitter, hormone, or drug) and elicits a response in the cell.

receptor potential the electric potential produced by stimulation of a receptor cell, which is roughly proportional to the intensity of the sensory stimulus and may be sufficient to trigger an ACTION POTENTIAL in a neuron that is postsynaptic to the receptor.

receptor site a region of specialized membrane on the surface of a cell (e.g., a neuron) that contains RECEPTOR molecules, which receive and react with particular messenger molecules (e.g., neurotransmitters).

recessive allele the version of a gene (see ALLELE) whose effects are manifest only if it is carried on both members of a HOMOLOGOUS pair of chromosomes. Hence, the trait determined by a recessive allele (the **recessive trait**) is apparent only in the absence of another version of that same gene (the DOMINANT ALLELE).

recidivism *n.* relapse. The term typically denotes the repetition of delinquent or criminal behavior. **—recidivist** *n., adj.* **—recidivistic** *adj.*

reciprocal altruism see ALTRUISM.

reciprocal determinism a concept that opposes the radical or exclusive emphasis on environmental determination of responses and instead maintains that the environment influences behavior, behavior influences the environment, and both influence the individual, who also influences them. This concept is associated with SOCIAL LEARNING THEORY.

reciprocal inhibition a technique in BEHAVIOR THERAPY that aims to replace an undesired response with a desired one by COUNTERCONDITIONING. It relies on the gradual substitution of a response that is incompatible with the original one and is potent enough to neutralize the anxiety-evoking power of the stimulus. See also SYSTEMATIC DESENSITIZATION.

reciprocity *n.* the quality of an act, process, or relation in which one person receives benefits from another and, in return, provides the giver with an equivalent benefit. **—reciprocal** *adj.*

reciprocity norm the social standard (NORM) that people who help others will receive equivalent benefits from these others in return. Compare SOCIAL JUSTICE NORM; SOCIAL RESPONSIBILITY NORM.

recognition *n.* a sense of awareness and familiarity experienced when one encounters people, events, or objects that have been encountered before or when one comes upon material that has been learned in the past.

recognition by components theory (**RBC theory**) the theory that perception of objects entails their decomposition into a set of simple three-dimensional elements called **geons**, together with the skeletal structure connecting them.

recollection *n.* remembrance, particularly vivid and detailed memory for past events or information pertaining to a specific time or place.

recombination *n.* the exchange of genetic material between paired chromosomes during the formation of sperm and egg cells. It involves the breaking and rejoining of chromatids (filament-like subunits) of homologous chromosomes in a process called **crossing over**. It results in offspring having combinations of genes that are different from those of either parent.

reconstruction *n.* **1.** in psychoanalysis, the revival and analytic interpretation of past experiences that have been instrumental in producing present emotional disturbance. **2.** see RECONSTRUCTIVE MEMORY. —**reconstruct** *vb.*

reconstructive memory a form of remembering marked by the logical recreation of an experience or event that has been only partially stored in memory. It draws on general knowledge and SCHEMAS or on memory for what typically happens in order to reconstruct the experience or event.

recovered memory the subjective experience of recalling details of a prior traumatic event, such as sexual or physical abuse, that has previously been unavailable to conscious recollection. Before recovering the memory, the person may be unaware that the traumatic event has occurred. The phenomenon is controversial: Because such recoveries often occur while the person is undergoing therapy, there is debate about their veracity vis-à-vis the role that the therapist may have played in suggesting or otherwise arousing them. Also called **repressed memory**.

recovery *n.* the period during which an individual exhibits consistent progress in terms of measurable return of abilities, skills, and functions following illness or injury.

recreational drug any substance that is used in a nontherapeutic manner for its effects on motor, sensory, or cognitive activities.

recurrent *adj.* occurring repeatedly or reappearing after an interval of time or a period of remission: often applied to disorders marked by chronicity, relapse, or repeated episodes (e.g., depressive symptoms).

redintegration *n.* restoration to completeness, particularly the process of recollecting memories from partial cues or reminders, as in recalling an entire song when a few notes are played. —**redintegrative** *adj.*

red nucleus see RUBROSPINAL TRACT.

reductionism *n.* the strategy of explaining or accounting for some phenomenon or construct A by claiming that, when properly understood, it can be shown to be some other phenomenon or construct B, where B is seen to be simpler, more basic, or more fundamental. The term is mainly applied to those positions that attempt to understand human culture, society, or psychology in terms of animal behavior or physical laws. In psychology, a common form of reductionism is that in which psychological phenomena are reduced to biological phenomena, so that mental life is shown to be merely a function of biological processes. See also EPIPHENOMENON; MATERIALISM.

redundancy *n.* in linguistics and information theory, the condition of those parts of a communication that could be deleted without loss of essential content. Redundancy includes not only repetitions, tautologies, and polite formulas, but also the multiple markings of a given meaning required by conventions of grammar and syntax. For example, in the sentence *All three men were running*, the plurality of the subject is signaled four times: by *all*, *three*, and the plural forms *men* and *were*. —**redundant** *adj.*

reeducation *n.* a form of psychological treatment in which the client learns effective ways of handling and coping with problems and relationships through a form of nonreconstructive therapy, such as

R

RELATIONSHIP THERAPY, BEHAVIOR THERAPY, or HYPNOTHERAPY.

reference group a group or social aggregate that individuals use as a standard or frame of reference when selecting and appraising their own abilities, attitudes, or beliefs. According to the general conceptual framework known as **reference-group theory**, individuals' attitudes, values, and self-appraisals are shaped, in part, by their identification with, and comparison to, reference groups. For example, a reference-group theory of values suggests that individuals adopt, as their own, the values expressed by the majority of the members of their reference group.

referral *n.* the act of directing a patient to a therapist, physician, agency, or institution for evaluation, consultation, or treatment. —**refer** *vb.*

referred sensation a sensation that is localized (i.e., experienced) at a point different from the area stimulated. For example, when struck on the elbow, the mechanical stimulation of the nerve may cause one to feel tingling of the fingers.

reflection *n.* see MEDITATION. —**reflect** *vb.*

reflection of feeling a statement made by a therapist or counselor that is intended to highlight the feelings or attitudes implicitly expressed in a client's communication. The statement reflects and communicates the essence of the client's experience from the client's point of view so that hidden or obscured feelings can be exposed for clarification.

reflective *adj.* describing or displaying behavior characterized by significant forethought and slow, deliberate examination of available options. Compare IMPULSIVE. —**reflectivity** *n.*

reflex *n.* any of a number of automatic, unlearned, relatively fixed responses to stimuli that do not require conscious effort and that often involve a faster response than might be possible if a conscious evaluation of the input was required. Reflexes are innate in that they do not arise as a result of any special experience. An example is the PUPILLARY REFLEX.

reflex arc a specific arrangement of neurons involved in a reflex. In its simplest form it consists of an afferent, or sensory, neuron that conducts nerve impulses from a receptor to the spinal cord, where it connects directly or via an INTERNEURON to an efferent, or motor, neuron that carries the impulses to a muscle or gland.

reflexive behavior responses to stimuli that are involuntary or free from conscious control (e.g., the salivation that occurs with the presentation of food) and therefore serve as the basis for PAVLOVIAN CONDITIONING.

reflexivity *n.* the quality of a relationship among elements such that they are continuously referential to one another. For example, in the context of an arbitrary matching to sample procedure, if a stimulus is chosen when it also appears as the sample, reflexivity has been shown.

refraction *n.* in vision, the bending of light as it passes through the cornea and lens of the eye so that it is focused on the retina.

refractory period a period of inactivity after a neuron or muscle cell has undergone excitation. As the cell is being repolarized, it will not respond to any stimulus during the early part of the refractory period, called the **absolute refractory period**. In the subsequent **relative refractory period**, it responds only to a stronger than normal stimulus.

reframing *n.* a process of reconceptualizing an idea for the purpose of changing an attitude by seeing it from a different perspective. In changing the conceptual or emotional context of a problem, and placing it in a different frame that fits the given facts equally well but changes its entire meaning, perceptions of weakness or difficulty in handling the problem may be changed to strength and opportunity. In psychotherapy, the manner in which a client frames behavior may be part of the problem. Part of the therapist's response might be to reframe thoughts or feelings so as to provide alternative ways to evaluate the situation or respond to others. Compare RESTATEMENT.

register *n.* a form of a language associated with specific social functions and situations or with particular subject matter. Examples include the different types of language considered appropriate for a scientific meeting, a kindergarten class, or a barroom story. Register differs from DIALECT in that it varies with social context rather than with the sociological characteristics of the user. See ELABORATED CODE.

regression *n.* a return to a prior, lower state of cognitive, emotional, or behavioral functioning. This term is associated particularly with psychoanalytic theory, denoting a DEFENSE MECHANISM in which the individual reverts to immature behavior or to an earlier stage of PSYCHOSEXUAL DEVELOPMENT when threatened with anxiety caused by overwhelming external problems or internal conflicts. —**regress** *vb.* —**regressive** *adj.*

regression analysis any of several statistical techniques that are designed to allow the prediction of the score on one variable, the DEPENDENT VARIABLE, from the scores on one or more other variables, the IN-DEPENDENT VARIABLES. Regression analysis is a subset of the GENERAL LINEAR MODEL.

regression equation the mathematical expression of the relationship between the dependent variable and one or more independent variables that results from conducting a REGRESSION ANALYSIS. It usually takes the form $y = a + bx + e$, in which y is the dependent variable, x is the independent variable, a is the intercept, b is the **regression coefficient** (a specific WEIGHT associated with x), and e is the error term.

regression line a straight or curved line fitting a set of data points, usually obtained by a least squares method. It is a geometric representation of the REGRESSION EQUATION for the variables.

regression toward the mean a phenomenon in which earlier measurements that were extremely deviant from a sample mean will tend, on retesting, to result in a value closer to the sample mean than the original value.

regulatory drive any generalized state of arousal or motivation that helps preserve physiological HOMEO-STASIS and thus is necessary for the survival of the individual organism, such as hunger and thirst. Compare NONREGULATORY DRIVE.

R

rehabilitation *n.* the process of bringing an individual to a condition of health or useful and constructive activity, restoring to the fullest possible degree their independence, well-being, and level of functioning following injury, disability, or disorder. It involves providing appropriate resources, such as treatment or training, to enable such a person (e.g., one who has had a stroke) to redevelop skills and abilities he or she had acquired previously or to compensate for their loss. Compare HABILITATION.

rehearsal *n.* **1.** preparation for a forthcoming event or confrontation that is anticipated to induce some level of discomfort or anxiety. By practicing what is to be said or done in a future encounter, the event itself may be less stressful. Rehearsal may be carried out in psychotherapy with the therapist coaching or role-playing to help the client practice the coming event. **2.** the repetition of information in an attempt to maintain it longer in memory. According to the DUAL-STORE MODEL OF MEMORY, rehearsal occurs in SHORT-TERM MEMORY and may allow a stronger trace to be then stored in LONG-TERM MEMORY. Although rehearsal implies a verbal process, it is hypothesized to occur also in other modalities.

reification *n.* treating an abstraction, concept, or formulation as though it were a real object or static structure. Also called **objectification**.

reinforcement *n.* in OPERANT CONDITIONING, a process in which the frequency or probability of a response is increased by a dependent relationship, or contingency, with a stimulus or circumstance (the REINFORCER).

reinforcement contingency the contingency (relationship) between a response and a REINFORCER. The contingency may be positive (if the occurrence of the reinforcer is more probable after the response) or negative (if it is less probable given the response). Reinforcement contingencies can be arranged by establishing dependencies between a particular type of response and a reinforcer (as when an experimenter arranges that a rat's lever presses are followed by presentation of food), or they can occur as natural consequences of a response (as when a door opens when pushed), or they can occur by accident.

reinforcement schedule see SCHEDULE OF REINFORCEMENT.

reinforcer *n.* a stimulus or circumstance that acts effectively to produce REINFORCEMENT when it occurs in a dependent relationship, or contingency, with a response.

Reissner's membrane a thin layer of tissue within the auditory LABYRINTH that separates the SCALA VESTIBULI from the SCALA MEDIA inside the cochlea. [Ernst **Reissner** (1824–1878), German anatomist]

rejecting–neglecting parenting see PARENTING.

rejection *n.* denial of love, attention, interest, or approval.

relapse *n.* the recurrence of symptoms of a disorder or disease after a period of improvement or apparent cure.

relapse prevention procedures that are used after successful treatment of a condition, disease, or disorder in order to reduce relapse rates. These often include a combination of cognitive and behavioral skills that are taught to clients before therapy is terminated. Such procedures are often used with disorders (e.g., addictions and depression) that have unusually high relapse rates. See also TERTIARY PREVENTION.

relational aggression behavior that manipulates or damages relationships between individuals or groups, such as bullying, gossiping, and humiliation.

relational research research investigating the strength of the relationships between two or more variables.

relationship *n.* a connection between objects, events, variables, or other phenomena, particularly a continuing and usually binding association between two or more people, as in a family, friendship, marriage, partnership, or other interpersonal link in which the participants have some degree of influence on each other's thoughts, feelings, and even actions. In psychotherapy, the therapist–patient relationship is thought to be an essential aspect of patient improvement.

relationship therapy 1. any form of psychotherapy that emphasizes the nature of the relationship between client and therapist and views it as the primary therapeutic tool and agent of positive change. Relationship therapy is based on the idea of providing emotional support and creating an accepting atmosphere that fosters personality growth and elicits attitudes and past experiences for examination and analysis during sessions. **2.** any form of psychotherapy focused on improving the RELATIONSHIP between individuals, particularly those in a marriage or other committed partnership, by helping them to resolve interpersonal issues and modify maladaptive patterns of interactions, which in turn fosters the healthy psychosocial growth of all parties. It is an umbrella term encompassing COUPLES THERAPY and FAMILY THERAPY.

relative deprivation the perception by an individual that the amount of a desired resource (e.g., money, social status) he or she has is less than some comparison standard. This standard can be the amount that was expected or the amount possessed by others with whom the person compares him- or herself.

relative efficiency for two tests (A and B) of the same hypothesis operating at the same SIGNIFICANCE LEVEL, the ratio of the number of cases needed by test A to the number of cases needed by test B in order for the two tests to have the same POWER.

relative refractory period see REFRACTORY PERIOD.

relativism *n.* in EPISTEMOLOGY, the assertion that there exist no absolute grounds for truth or knowledge claims. Thus, what is considered true will depend on individual judgments and local conditions of culture, reflecting individual and collective experience. Such relativism challenges the validity of science except as a catalog of experience and a basis for ad hoc empirical prediction. —**relativist** *adj.*

relaxation *n.* **1.** abatement of intensity, vigor, energy, or tension, resulting in calmness of mind, body, or both. **2.** the return of a muscle to its resting condition after a period of contraction. —**relax** *vb.*

relaxation training see PROGRESSIVE RELAXATION.

relearning method the learning again of material that was once known but is now forgotten, a technique for measuring knowledge that may be present even if unrecallable. Savings in time or trials over the original learning indicate the amount of retention.

releaser *n.* in ethology, a stimulus that, when presented under the proper conditions, initiates a FIXED ACTION PATTERN (see also MODAL ACTION PATTERN). For example, a red belly on a male stickleback fish elicits aggressive behavior from other male sticklebacks but is attractive to gravid female sticklebacks. Also called **sign stimulus**. See also INNATE RELEASING MECHANISM.

releasing hormone any of a class of HORMONES secreted by the hypothalamus that control the release of hormones by the anterior pituitary

R

gland. GONADOTROPIN-RELEASING HORMONE is an example.

reliability *n.* the ability of a measurement instrument (e.g., a test) to measure an attribute consistently, yielding the same results across multiple applications to the same sample. —**reliable** *adj.*

REM abbreviation for RAPID EYE MOVEMENT.

REM behavior disorder a sleep disorder involving motor activity during REM SLEEP, which typically includes an actual physical enactment of dream sequences. Because the dreams that are acted out are generally unpleasant or combative, this behavior is usually disruptive and can result in violence.

remembering *n.* the process of consciously reviving or bringing to awareness previous events, experiences, or information, or the process of retaining such material.

remission *n.* a reduction or significant abatement in symptoms of a disease or disorder, or the period during which this occurs. Remission of symptoms does not necessarily indicate that a disease or disorder is fully cured. See also SPONTANEOUS REMISSION.

remote cause a cause that is removed from its effect in time or space but is nevertheless the ultimate or overriding cause. In a sequence of occurrences, it may be considered to be the precipitating event without which the chain would not have begun (the original cause). For example, the PROXIMATE CAUSE of Smith's aggression may be a trivial snub, but the remote cause may be Smith's early childhood experiences.

REM rebound the increased recurrence of REM SLEEP, the stage of sleep in which dreaming is associated with mild involuntary eye movements, following a period in which it was inhibited.

REM sleep *r*apid-*e*ye-*m*ovement sleep: the stage of sleep in which dreaming occurs and the electroencephalogram shows activity characteristic of wakefulness (hence it is also known as **paradoxical sleep**) except for inhibition of motor expression other than coordinated movements of the eyes. It accounts for one quarter to one fifth of total sleep time. Compare NREM SLEEP.

repeated measures design see WITHIN-SUBJECTS DESIGN.

repertory grid a technique used to analyze an individual's PERSONAL CONSTRUCTS. A number of significant concepts are selected, each of which is rated by the participant on a number of dimensions using a numerical scale. The findings are displayed in matrix form and can be subjected to statistical analysis to reveal correlations.

repetition compulsion in psychoanalytic theory, an unconscious need to reenact early traumas in the attempt to overcome or master them. In repetition compulsion the early painful experience is repeated in a new situation symbolic of the repressed prototype. Repetition compulsion acts as a RESISTANCE to therapeutic change, since the goal of therapy is not to repeat but to remember the trauma and to see its relation to present behavior.

repetition priming a change in the processing of a stimulus (e.g., speed of response, number of errors) due to previous exposure to the same or a related stimulus.

repetitive transcranial magnetic stimulation (rTMS) see TRANSCRANIAL MAGNETIC STIMULATION.

replication *n.* the repetition of an original experiment to bolster confidence in its results, based on the assumption that correct hypotheses and procedures consistently will be supported. In **direct (exact) replication**, procedures are identical to the original experiment or duplicated as closely as possible. In **conceptual replication**, different techniques and manipulations are introduced to gain theoretical information.

representation *n.* that which stands for or signifies something else. For example, in cognitive psychology the term denotes a MENTAL REPRESENTATION whereas in psychoanalytic theory it refers to the use of a SYMBOL to stand for a threatening object or a repressed impulse. **—represent** *vb.* **—representational** *adj.* **—representative** *adj.*

representativeness heuristic a strategy for making categorical judgments about a given person or target based on how closely the exemplar matches the typical or average member of the category. For example, given a choice of the two categories "poet" and "accountant," judges are likely to assign a person in unconventional clothes reading a poetry book to the former category; however, the much greater frequency of accountants in the population means that such a person is more likely to be an accountant. The representativeness heuristic is thus a form of the BASE-RATE FALLACY. Compare AVAILABILITY HEURISTIC.

representative sampling the selection of individuals for a study from a larger group (population) in such a way that the sample obtained accurately reflects the total population.

repressed memory see RECOVERED MEMORY.

repression *n.* **1.** in classic psychoanalytic theory and other forms of DEPTH PSYCHOLOGY, the basic DEFENSE MECHANISM that consists of excluding painful experiences and unacceptable impulses from consciousness. Repression operates on an unconscious level as a protection against anxiety produced by objectionable sexual wishes, feelings of hostility, and ego-threatening experiences of all kinds. **2.** the suppression or exclusion of individuals or groups within the social context, through limitations on personal rights and liberties. Compare SUPPRESSION. **—repress** *vb.*

reproduction *n.* **1.** in biology, the production of new individuals from parent organisms, which perpetuates the species. Sexual reproduction involves the fusion of male and female GAMETES in the process of FERTILIZATION; asexual reproduction does not. **2.** the process of replicating information from memory. It potentially is subject to numerous errors of distortion, as demonstrated via SERIAL REPRODUCTION and other techniques.

reproductive success the degree to which an individual is successful in producing progeny that in turn are able to produce progeny of their own. Individuals vary in their success in finding mates and reproducing successfully. NATURAL SELECTION is based on this differential reproductive success. The genetic and behavioral traits that lead to greatest reproductive success survive in a population over generations, while traits producing low reproductive success eventually become extinct within a population. See also INCLUSIVE FITNESS.

research *n.* the systematic effort to discover or confirm facts or to investigate a problem or topic, most often by scientific methods of observation and experiment.

research design an outline or plan of the procedures to be followed during a study in order to reach valid conclusions, with particular consideration given to data collection and analysis. Research designs may take a variety of forms, including not only experiments but also quasi-experiments (see QUASI-EXPERIMENTAL RESEARCH), OBSERVATIONAL STUDIES, surveys, focus groups, and other nonexperimental methods.

research method a system for the formulation and evaluation of hypotheses that is intended to reveal relationships between variables and provide an understanding of the phenomenon under investigation. Generally in psychology this involves empirical testing and takes the form of the SCIENTIFIC METHOD.

reserve capacity the difference between performance on a psychological task and the individual's maximum capability to perform that task. Training, intervention, and practice can be used to minimize reserve capacity on a given task.

residual *n.* in statistics, the difference between the value of an empirical observation and the value of that observation predicted by a model.

residual schizophrenia a subtype of schizophrenia diagnosed when there has been at least one schizophrenic episode but positive symptoms (e.g., delusions, hallucinations, disorganized speech or behavior) are no longer present and only negative symptoms (e.g., flat affect, poverty of speech, or avolition) or mild behavioral and cognitive disturbances (e.g., eccentricities, odd beliefs) occur.

resilience *n.* the process and outcome of successfully adapting to difficult or challenging life experiences, especially through mental, emotional, and behavioral flexibility and adjustment to external and internal demands. A number of factors contribute to how well people adapt

to adversities, predominant among them (a) the ways in which individuals view and engage with the world, (b) the availability and quality of social resources, and (c) specific COPING STRATEGIES. —**resilient** *adj.*

resistance *n.* in psychotherapy and analysis, unconscious obstruction, through the client's words or behavior, of the therapist's or analyst's methods of eliciting or interpreting psychic material brought forth in therapy. —**resist** *vb.* —**resistant** *adj.*

resistance stage see GENERAL ADAPTATION SYNDROME.

resistance to extinction the endurance or persistence of a conditioned response in the absence of reinforcement.

resistant attachment another name for ambivalent attachment (see INSECURE ATTACHMENT).

resolution *n.* in optics, a measure of the ability of the eye to detect two distinct objects when these are close together.

respect *n.* an attitude of, or behavior demonstrating, esteem, honor, regard, concern, or other such positive qualities on the part of one individual or entity for another individual or entity. Respect can serve an important purpose in interpersonal and intergroup relations by aiding in communication, for example. It is considered to play a crucial role as a bidirectional process in psychotherapy according to many theorists and practitioners.

respiration *n.* **1.** the series of chemical reactions that enables organisms to convert the chemical energy stored in food into energy that can be used by cells. **2.** the process by which an animal takes up oxygen from its environment and discharges carbon dioxide into it.

respite care assistance, supervision, and recreational or social activities provided for a person who is unable to care for him- or herself (e.g., because of a disability or chronic illness) for a limited period in order to temporarily relieve family members from caregiving responsibilities or enable them to conduct necessary personal or household affairs. These services may be provided either in the home or at another location.

respondent *n.* any REFLEX that can be conditioned by PAVLOVIAN CONDITIONING procedures. Compare OPERANT.

respondent behavior behavior that is evoked by a specific stimulus and will consistently and predictably occur if the stimulus is presented. Compare EMITTED BEHAVIOR.

respondent conditioning see PAVLOVIAN CONDITIONING.

response *n.* any glandular, muscular, neural, or other reaction to a stimulus. A response is a clearly defined, measurable unit of behavior discussed in terms of its result (e.g., pressing a lever) or its physical characteristics (e.g., raising an arm).

response acquiescence see YEA-SAYING.

response bias a tendency to give one response more than others, regardless of the stimulus condition. In SIGNAL DETECTION THEORY, for example, response bias is the overall willingness to say "yes" (signal present) or "no" (signal not present), regardless of the actual presence or absence of the signal.

response generalization see INDUCTION.

response rate the number of responses that occur within a specified time interval.

response selection an intermediate stage of human information processing in which a response to an identified stimulus is chosen. Response selection is typically studied by varying relationships between the stimuli and their assigned responses.

response set a tendency to answer questions in a systematic manner that is unrelated to their content. Examples include the ACQUIESCENT RESPONSE SET and SOCIAL DESIRABILITY RESPONSE SET.

response variable the DEPENDENT VARIABLE in a study.

restatement *n.* in psychotherapy and counseling, the verbatim repetition or rephrasing by the therapist or counselor of a client's statement. The purpose is not only to confirm that the client's remarks have been understood, but also to provide a "mirror" in which the client can see his or her feelings and ideas more clearly. Compare REFRAMING.

resting potential the electric potential across the plasma membrane of a neuron when it is in the nonexcited, or resting, state. It is usually in the range –50 to –100 mV for vertebrate neurons, representing an excess of negatively charged ions on the inside of the membrane. See also ACTION POTENTIAL.

restricted code see ELABORATED CODE.

restriction of range the limitation by a researcher—via sampling, measurement procedures, or other aspects of experimental design—of the full range of total possible scores that may be obtained to only a narrow, limited portion of that total. For example, in a study of the grade-point averages of university students, restriction of range would occur if only students from the dean's list were included. Range restriction on a particular variable may lead to a failure to observe, or the improper characterization of, a relationship between the variables of interest.

retardation *n.* a slowing down of or delay in an activity or process, as in PSYCHOMOTOR RETARDATION or MENTAL RETARDATION.

retention *n.* the storage and maintenance of a memory. Retention is the second stage of memory, after ENCODING and before RETRIEVAL. —**retentive** *adj.*

retest reliability an estimate of the ability of an assessment instrument (e.g., a test) to measure an attribute consistently: It is obtained as the correlation between scores on two administrations of the test to the same individual. Also called **test–retest reliability**.

reticular activating system (**RAS**) a part of the RETICULAR FORMATION thought to be particularly involved in the regulation of arousal, alertness, and sleep–wake cycles.

reticular formation an extensive network of nerve cell bodies and fibers within the brainstem, extending from the medulla oblongata to the upper part of the midbrain, that is widely connected to the spinal cord, cerebellum, thalamus, and cerebral cortex. It is most prominently involved in arousal, alertness, and sleep–wake cycles, but also functions to control some aspects of action and posture.

reticulospinal tract see VENTROMEDIAL PATHWAY.

retina *n.* the innermost, light-sensitive layer of the eye. A layer of neurons lines the inner surface of the back of the eye and provides the sensory signals required for vision. The retina contains the photoreceptors, that is, the RETINAL RODS and RETINAL CONES, as well as addi-tional neurons that process the signals of the photoreceptors and convey an output signal to the brain by way of the OPTIC NERVE.

retinal bipolar cell any of various neurons in the INNER NUCLEAR LAYER of the retina that receive input from the photoreceptors (RETINAL RODS and RETINAL CONES) and transmit signals to RETINAL GAN-GLION CELLS and AMACRINE CELLS. Rods and cones are served by differ-ent populations of retinal bipolar cells, called **rod bipolars** and **cone bipolars**, respectively.

retinal cone any of various photoreceptors in the retina that re-quire moderate to bright light for activation, as opposed to RETINAL RODS, which require very little light for activation. In primates retinal cones are concentrated in the FOVEA CENTRALIS of the retina, where their high spatial density and the pattern of connections within the cone pathway are critical for high-acuity vision. The cone pathways also pro-vide information about the color of stimuli. This is achieved by the pres-ence of three different populations of cones, each having their maxi-mum sensitivity to light in the short, middle, or long wavelengths of the spectrum, respectively. Other animals may have additional popu-lations of cones; for example, some fish have cones that are sensitive to ultraviolet wavelengths. See also PHOTOPIGMENT.

retinal disparity see BINOCULAR DISPARITY.

retinal ganglion cell the only type of neuron in the retina that sends signals to the brain resulting from visual stimulation. Retinal ganglion cells receive input from RETINAL BIPOLAR CELLS and AMACRINE CELLS, the axons of reti-nal ganglion cells forming the OPTIC NERVE.

R

retinal horizontal cell any of various neurons in the retina that make lateral connections between photoreceptors, RETINAL BIPOLAR CELLS, and one another. Their cell bodies are located in the INNER NUCLEAR LAYER of the retina.

retinal image the inverted picture of an external object formed on the retina of the eye.

retinal rivalry see BINOCULAR RIVALRY.

retinal rod any of various photoreceptors in the retina that respond to low light levels, as opposed to RETINAL CONES, which require moderate to bright light for activation. In primates, which have both rods and cones, the rods are excluded from the center of the retina, the FOVEA CENTRALIS. All rods contain the same PHOTOPIGMENT, rhodopsin; therefore the rod pathways do not provide color information to the visual system. The connections of the rod pathway enhance retinal sensitivity to light, while acuity is relatively poor.

retinex theory a theory suggesting that various wavelengths register on the color-sensitive components of the retina as a large number of color-separated "photos." The visual mechanisms in the brain then average together and compare long-wave photos with the average of the shorter-wave photos, assigning different colors to them according to the ratios between them.

retrieval *n.* the process of recovering or locating information stored in memory. Retrieval is the final stage of memory, after ENCODING and RETENTION.

retrieval cue a prompt or stimulus used to guide memory recall.

retroactive interference see INTERFERENCE.

retrograde amnesia see AMNESIA.

retrograde memory the ability to recall events that occurred or information that was acquired prior to a particular point in time, often the onset of illness or physical damage such as brain injury. For example, an individual with deficits of retrograde memory (retrograde AMNESIA) might not remember the name of a close childhood friend but would remember the name of a new person just introduced to him or her. Compare ANTEROGRADE MEMORY.

retrospection *n.* the process of reviewing or reflecting upon an experience from the past, either directed (as in learning and memory research) or spontaneous (as in evaluating one's behavior in a given situation).

retrospective memory see PROSPECTIVE MEMORY.

retrospective research observational, nonexperimental research that tries to explain the present in terms of past events; that is, research that starts with the present and follows subjects backward in time. For example, a **retrospective study** may be undertaken in which individuals are selected on the basis of whether they exhibit a particular problematic symptom and are then studied to determine if they had been exposed to a risk factor of interest. Compare PROSPECTIVE RESEARCH.

retrospective sampling a technique for determining which subjects or cases to include in experiments or other research that selects cases on the basis of their previous exposure to a risk factor or the completion of some particular process. Participants are then examined in the present to see if a particular condition or state exists, often in comparison to others who were not exposed to the risk or did not complete the particular process. See also PROSPECTIVE SAMPLING.

R

Rett syndrome a PERVASIVE DE-VELOPMENTAL DISORDER that occurs almost exclusively in female children who develop normally early in life but then, between 6 and 18 months, undergo rapid regression in motor, cognitive, and social skills; these skills subsequently stabilize at a level that leaves the child with mental retardation. Symptoms generally include loss of language skills, hand motion abnormalities (e.g., hand wringing and other repetitive, purposeless movements), learning difficulties, gait disturbances, breathing problems, seizures, and pronounced deceleration of head growth. [first described in 1966 by Andreas **Rett** (1924–1997), Austrian pediatrician]

reuptake *n.* the process by which neurotransmitter molecules that have been released at a SYNAPSE are taken up by the presynaptic neuron that released them. Reuptake is performed by TRANSPORTER proteins in the presynaptic membrane.

reversal design an experimental design that attempts to counteract the confounding effects (see CON-FOUND) of sequence, order, and treatment in LATIN SQUARES by alternating baseline conditions (A) with treatment conditions (B), for example by employing two sets of three observations (A then B then A; B then A then B) to yield counterbalanced estimates of A versus B.

reversal learning in DISCRIMINA-TIONS involving two alternatives, the effects of reversing the contingencies associated with the two alternatives. For example, a monkey could be trained under conditions in which lever presses when a red light is present result in food presentation and lever presses when a green light is on are without effect. The contingencies are then reversed, so that presses when the red light is on are ineffective and presses when the

green light is on result in food presentation. If the monkey's behavior adapts to the new contingencies (i.e., it presses the lever only when the green light is present), reversal learning has occurred.

reversibility *n.* in PIAGETIAN THE-ORY, a mental operation that reverses a sequence of events or restores a changed state of affairs to the original condition. It is exemplified by the ability to realize that a glass of milk poured into a bottle can be poured back into the glass and remain unchanged. See also CONSERVATION.

reversible figure an AMBIGUOUS FIGURE in which the perspective easily shifts between FIGURE–GROUND, such that at certain times specific elements appear to comprise a distinct figure while at others those same elements appear as an indistinct background. Examples include the NECKER CUBE and RUBIN'S FIGURE.

ReVia *n.* a trade name for NALTREXONE.

revolving-door phenomenon the repeated readmission of patients to hospitals or other institutions, often because they were discharged before they had adequately recovered.

reward *n.* a lay word that is nearly synonymous with REINFORCEMENT. Sometimes it is used to describe the intent of someone providing consequences for behavior, rather than the effectiveness of a consequence (as is required in the definition of reinforcement) in influencing the frequency or probability of occurrence of a particular behavior.

Rhine cards see ZENER CARDS. [Joseph B. **Rhine** (1895–1980), U.S. psychologist]

rhinencephalon *n.* the portion of the brain that includes the limbic system; olfactory nerves, bulbs, and tracts; and related structures.

rhodopsin *n.* see PHOTOPIGMENT.

rhombencephalon *n.* see HINDBRAIN.

ribonucleic acid see RNA.

ribosome *n.* a specialized, membrane-bound structure (organelle), consisting of RNA and proteins, found in large numbers in all cells and responsible for the translation of genetic information (in the form of messenger RNA) and the assembly of proteins. **—ribosomal** *adj.*

right hemisphere the right half of the CEREBRUM, the part of the brain concerned with sensation and perception, motor control, and higher level cognitive processes. The two CEREBRAL HEMISPHERES differ somewhat in function; for example, in most people the right hemisphere has greater responsibility for spatial attention. Some have proposed the hypothesis of **right-hemisphere consciousness**, specifying that the right hemisphere is conscious, like the LEFT HEMISPHERE, even though it has no control of spoken communication. See HEMISPHERIC LATERALIZATION.

right to refuse treatment the right of patients with mental illness to refuse treatment that may be potentially hazardous or intrusive (e.g., ELECTROCONVULSIVE THERAPY or PSYCHOACTIVE DRUGS), particularly when such treatment does not appear to be in the best interests of the patient. In the United States, various state laws and court rulings support the rights of patients to receive or reject certain treatments, but there is a lack of uniformity in such regulations.

right to treatment a statutory right, established at varying governmental levels, stipulating that people with disabilities or disorders,

usually persistent or chronic in nature, have the right to receive care and treatment suited to their needs. Such statutory rights may apply nationally or to certain state or provincial areas, or they may be limited to certain conditions and disabilities.

right to withdraw the right of participants in research to remove themselves from the study or procedure at any point. Ethically speaking, this prerogative would follow naturally from voluntary participation and from the guarantee that refusal to continue will not result in penalty or loss of any benefits that a participant might have independent of the study. See also INFORMED CONSENT.

rigidity *n.* stiffness or inflexibility. The term typically denotes muscular rigidity or a personality trait characterized by strong resistance to changing one's behavior, opinions, or attitudes. **—rigid** *adj.*

risk *n.* **1.** the probability or likelihood that an event will occur, such as the risk that a disease or disorder will develop. **2.** the probability of experiencing loss or harm that is associated with an action or behavior. See also AT RISK; RISK FACTOR. **—risky** *adj.*

risk-as-feelings theory a model stating that decision making in situations involving a degree of risk is often driven by emotional reactions, such as worry, fear, or anxiety, rather than by a rational assessment of (a) the desirability and (b) the likelihood of the various possible outcomes.

risk assessment the process of determining the threat an individual would be likely to pose if released from the confinement in which he or she is held as a result of mental illness or criminal acts. It may be a clinician-based prediction of danger-

R

ous or violent behavior (clinical risk assessment) or it may be based on a specific formula or weighting system using empirically derived predictors (actuarial risk assessment).

risk aversion the tendency, when choosing between alternatives, to avoid options that entail a risk of loss, even if that risk is relatively small.

risk factor a clearly defined behavior or constitutional (e.g., genetic), environmental, or other characteristic that is associated with an increased possibility or likelihood that a disease or disorder will subsequently develop in an individual.

risk taking a pattern of engaging in activities or behaviors that are highly subject to chance, particularly those that are physically dangerous (e.g., river rafting, driving while intoxicated) or that simultaneously involve potential for failure as well as for accomplishment or personal benefit (e.g., starting a business, gambling). In the workplace or in educational settings, risk taking tends to be associated with a degree of creativity necessary for success and thus viewed positively, whereas in other contexts it is often seen as unnecessary or the result of poor decision making and thus evaluated negatively. Historically, risk taking has been considered a personality trait, more common in men than women, but recent research suggests biological, cognitive, and social factors are involved in this pattern of behavior as well. For example, current theories include those proposing an evolutionary advantage conveyed by successful risk taking; those proposing a physiological propensity for arousal as governed by levels of the neurotransmitters dopamine, serotonin, and norepinephrine; those focusing on obtaining a sense of personal control over events; and those focusing on fostering comraderie with others.

risky shift see CAUTIOUS SHIFT.

Ritalin *n.* a trade name for METHYLPHENIDATE.

rite of passage a ritual that marks a specific life transition, such as birth, marriage, or death, or a developmental milestone, such as a bar mitzvah, graduation, or puberty rite. In many societies such rites are considered essential if the individual is to make a successful transition from one status to another.

ritual *n.* a ceremonial act or rite, usually involving a fixed order of actions or gestures and the saying of certain prescribed words. Anthropologists distinguish between several major categories of ritual: magic rituals, which involve an attempt to manipulate natural forces; calendrical rituals, which mark the passing of time; liturgical rituals, which involve the reenactment of a sacred story or myth; RITES OF PASSAGE; and formal procedures that have the effect of emphasizing both the importance and the impersonal quality of certain social behaviors, as in a court of law. —**ritualism** *n.* —**ritualistic** *adj.*

ritualization *n.* the process by which a normal behavioral or physiological action becomes a communication signal representing the behavior or its physiological consequence. For example, the flushed face associated with anger and the pale face associated with fear initially derive from actions of the sympathetic nervous system related to vasodilation and vasoconstriction, respectively.

RNA *ribonucleic acid*: a nucleic acid that directs the synthesis of protein molecules in living cells. There are three main types of RNA. MESSENGER RNA carries the GENETIC CODE from the cell nucleus to the cytoplasm. Ribosomal RNA is found in ribosomes, small particles where proteins are assembled from amino acids. Transfer RNA carries specific amino acids for protein synthesis. RNA is similar to DNA in structure except that it consists of a single strand of nucleotides (compared with the double strands of DNA), the base uracil occurs instead of thymine, and the sugar unit is ribose, rather than deoxyribose.

robustness *n.* the ability of a hypothesis-testing or estimation procedure to produce valid results in spite of violations of the assumptions upon which the methodology is based.

ROC curve abbreviation for RECEIVER-OPERATING CHARACTERISTIC CURVE.

rod *n.* see RETINAL ROD.

role *n.* a coherent set of behaviors expected of an individual in a specific position within a group or social setting. Since the term is derived from the dramaturgical concept of role (the dialogue and actions assigned to each performer in a play), there is a suggestion that individuals' actions are regulated by the part they play in the social setting rather than by their personal predilections or inclinations. See also SOCIAL ROLE.

role confusion a state of uncertainty about a given social or group role.

role play a technique used in human relations training and psychotherapy in which participants act out various social roles in dramatic situations. Originally developed in PSYCHODRAMA, role play is now widely used in industrial, educational, and clinical settings for such purposes as training employees to handle sales problems, testing out different attitudes and relationships in group and family psychotherapy, and rehearsing different ways of coping with stresses and conflicts.

role taking awareness or adoption of the viewpoint of another person, typically for the purpose of understanding his or her thoughts and actions.

romantic love a type of love in which intimacy and passion are prominent features. In some taxonomies of love, romantic love is identified with PASSIONATE LOVE and distinguished from COMPANIONATE LOVE; in others, it is seen as involving elements of both. See also TRIANGULAR THEORY OF LOVE.

rooting reflex an automatic, unlearned response of a newborn to a gentle stimulus (e.g., the touch of a finger) applied to the corner of the mouth or to the cheek, in which the infant turns his or her head and makes sucking motions.

root-mean-square the square root of the sum of the squares of a set of values divided by the number of values. For a set of values $x_1, x_2, \ldots x_n$ the root-mean-square value is $\sqrt{[(x_1{}^2 + x_2{}^2 + \ldots x_n{}^2)/n]}$. In the physical sciences the term is used as a synonym for STANDARD DEVIATION under certain circumstances.

Rorschach Inkblot Test a projective test in which the participant is presented with ten unstructured inkblots and is asked "What might this be?" or "What do you see in this?" The examiner classifies the responses according to various structural and thematic (content) factors and attempts to interpret the participant's personality structure in terms of such factors as emotionality, cognitive style, creativity, impulse control, and various defensive patterns. Perhaps the best known, and certainly one of the most controversial, assessment instruments in all of psychology—it is almost considered "representative" by the general public—the Rorschach is widely used and has been extensively researched, with results ranging from those that claim strong support for its clinical utility (e.g., for selecting treatment modalities or monitoring patient change or improvement over time) to those that demonstrate little evidence of robust or consistent validity and that criticize the instrument as invalid and useless. [Hermann **Rorschach** (1884–1922), Swiss psychiatrist]

Rosenthal effect an effect in which the expectancy an experimenter has about the outcome of an experiment unwittingly affects the outcome of the experiment in the direction of the expectancy. [Robert **Rosenthal** (1933–   ), U.S. psychologist]

rostral *adj.* **1.** pertaining to a beak or snout. **2.** situated or occurring toward the nose, or beak, of an organism. Compare CAUDAL. —**rostrally** *adv.*

rote learning the type of learning in which acquisition occurs through drill and repetition, sometimes in the absence of comprehension. Rote learning may lead to the production of correct answers, but without awareness of the reasoning behind

or the logical implications of the response.

round window a membrane-covered opening in the cochlea where it borders the middle ear (see SCALA TYMPANI). Pressure changes in the cochlea produced by vibration of the OVAL WINDOW are ultimately transmitted to the round window. This permits displacement of the BASILAR MEMBRANE and stimulation of the sensory receptors.

RT abbreviation for REACTION TIME.

rTMS abbreviation for repetitive TRANSCRANIAL MAGNETIC STIMULATION.

Rubin's figure an ambiguous figure that may be perceived either as one goblet or as two facing profiles. [Edgar **Rubin** (1886–1951), Danish philosopher]

rubrospinal tract a motor pathway that arises from the **red nucleus** (a collection of cell bodies that receives input from the cerebellum) in the brainstem and descends laterally in the spinal cord, where it stimulates flexor motor neurons and inhibits extensor motor neurons.

rumination *n.* excessive, repetitive thoughts or themes that interfere with other forms of mental activity. —**ruminate** *vb.*

R

Ss

SA abbreviation for SOCIAL AGE.

saccade *n.* a rapid movement of the eyes that allows visual fixation to jump from one location to another in the visual field. Once initiated, a saccade cannot change course. Compare SMOOTH-PURSUIT MOVEMENT. **—saccadic** *adj.*

saccule *n.* the smaller of the two VESTIBULAR SACS of the inner ear, the other being the UTRICLE. Like the utricle, it contains a sensory structure called a MACULA. Movements of the head relative to gravity exert a momentum pressure on hair cells within the macula, which then fire impulses indicating a change in body position in space. **—saccular** *adj.*

SAD abbreviation for SEASONAL AFFECTIVE DISORDER.

sadism *n.* the derivation of pleasure through cruelty and inflicting pain, humiliation, and other forms of suffering on individuals. The term generally denotes SEXUAL SADISM. [Donatien Alphonse François, Comte (Marquis) de **Sade** (1740–1814), French soldier and writer] **—sadist** *n.* **—sadistic** *adj.*

sadness *n.* an emotional state of unhappiness, ranging in intensity from mild to extreme and usually aroused by the loss of something that is highly valued, for example, by the rupture or loss of a relationship. Persistent sadness is one of the two defining symptoms of a MAJOR DEPRESSIVE EPISODE, the other being ANHEDONIA. **—sad** *adj.*

sadomasochism *n.* sexual activity

between consenting partners in which one partner enjoys inflicting pain (see SEXUAL SADISM) and the other enjoys experiencing pain (see SEXUAL MASOCHISM). **—sadomasochist** *n.* **—sadomasochistic** *adj.*

safety need a desire for freedom from illness or danger and for a secure, familiar, predictable environment. Safety needs comprise the second level of MASLOW'S MOTIVATIONAL HIERARCHY, after basic PHYSIOLOGICAL NEEDS.

sagittal *adj.* describing or relating to a plane that divides the body or an organ into left and right portions. A midsagittal plane divides the body centrally into halves, whereas a parasagittal plane lies parallel but to one side of the center. **—sagittally** *adv.*

salient *adj.* distinctive or prominent. A salient stimulus in a multielement array will tend to be easily detected and identified. See POP-OUT. **—salience** *n.*

saltation *n.* a type of conduction of nerve impulses that occurs in myelinated fibers (see MYELIN), in which the impulses skip from one NODE OF RANVIER to the next. This permits much faster conduction velocities compared with unmyelinated fibers. Also called **saltatory conduction**.

sample *n.* a subset of a POPULATION of interest that is selected for study. It is important to ensure that a sample is representative of the population as a whole.

sampling *n.* the process of selecting a limited number of subjects or cases for participation in experiments, surveys, or other research. There are a number of different types (e.g., SIMPLE RANDOM SAMPLING, STRATIFIED SAMPLING, OPPORTUNISTIC SAMPLING, QUOTA SAMPLING), each having a different potential of obtaining a sample appropriately representative of the POPULATION under study.

sampling bias any flaw in SAMPLING processes that makes the resulting sample unrepresentative of the population, hence possibly distorting research results.

sampling error the predictable margin of error that occurs in studies employing sampling, as reflected in the variation in the estimate of a parameter from its true value in the population.

sampling frame a complete listing of all of the elements in a POPULATION from which a sample is to be drawn.

sampling with replacement a SAMPLING technique in which a selected unit is returned to the pool and may subsequently be redrawn in another sample. In **sampling without replacement** the sampling unit is not returned to the pool.

sanction *n.* a punishment or other coercive measure, usually administered by a recognized authority, that is used to penalize and deter inappropriate or unauthorized actions.

Sapir–Whorf hypothesis see LINGUISTIC DETERMINISM. [Edward Sapir (1884–1939) and Benjamin Lee Whorf (1897–1941), U.S. linguists]

SAS abbreviation for SUPERVISORY ATTENTIONAL SYSTEM.

SAT acronym for SCHOLASTIC ASSESSMENT TEST.

satiation *n.* **1.** the full and complete satisfaction of a desire or need, such as hunger or thirst. **2.** the temporary loss of effectiveness of a REINFORCER due to its repeated presentation. —**satiate** *vb.*

saturation *n.* the purity of a color and the degree to which it departs from white. Highly saturated colors are intense and brilliant, whereas colors of low saturation are diluted and dull.

savant *n.* a person with mental retardation or an AUTISTIC SPECTRUM DISORDER (autistic savant) who demonstrates exceptional, usually isolated, cognitive abilities, such as rapid calculation, identifying the day of the week for any given date, or musical talent. The term **idiot savant** initially was used to denote such a person but has been discarded because of its colloquial, pejorative connotation.

SB abbreviation for STANFORD–BINET INTELLIGENCE SCALE.

scaffolding *n.* a teaching style that supports and facilitates the student as he or she learns a new skill or concept, with the ultimate goal of the student becoming self-reliant. Derived from the theories of Russian psychologist Lev Vygotsky (1896–1934), in practice it involves teaching material just beyond the level at which the student could learn alone.

scala media one of the three canals that run the length of the COCHLEA in the inner ear. Located between the scala vestibuli and scala tympani, it is filled with fluid (ENDOLYMPH) and is delimited by REISSNER'S MEMBRANE, the highly vascular **stria vascularis**, and the BASILAR MEMBRANE, which supports the ORGAN OF CORTI.

scala tympani one of the three canals within the COCHLEA in the inner ear. It is located below the scala media, from which it is separated by the BASILAR MEMBRANE, and contains PERILYMPH. At its basal end is the ROUND WINDOW.

scala vestibuli one of the three canals within the COCHLEA in the inner ear. It is located above the scala media, from which it is separated by REISSNER'S MEMBRANE, and contains PERILYMPH. At its basal end is the OVAL WINDOW.

scale *n.* a system for arranging items in a progressive series, for example, according to their magnitude or value. The characteristic of an item that allows it to fit into such a progression is called **scalability**.

scaling *n.* the process of constructing a SCALE to measure or assess some quantity or characteristic (e.g., height, weight, happiness, empathy).

scapegoating *n.* blaming: the process of directing one's anger, frustration, and aggression onto other, usually less powerful, groups or individuals and targeting them as the source of one's problems and misfortunes. —**scapegoat** *n.*, *vb.*

scapegoat theory an analysis of PREJUDICE that assumes that intergroup conflict is caused, in part, by the tendency of individuals to blame their negative experiences on other groups.

scatterplot *n.* a graphical representation of the relationship between two variables, in which the X-AXIS represents one variable and the Y-AXIS the other. A dot or other symbol is placed at each point where the values of the variables intersect, and the overall pattern of symbols provides an indication of the CORRELATION between the two variables. Also called **scattergram.**

Schachter–Singer theory the theory that experiencing emotional states is a function not only of physiological AROUSAL but also cognitive interpretations of the physical state.

Also called **two-factor theory of emotion**. [Stanley **Schachter** (1922–1997) and Jerome E. **Singer** (1924–   ), U.S. psychologists]

schedule of reinforcement in conditioning, a rule that determines which instances of a response will be reinforced. There are numerous types of schedules of reinforcement, among them FIXED-INTERVAL SCHEDULES, FIXED-RATIO SCHEDULES, VARIABLE-INTERVAL SCHEDULES, and VARIABLE-RATIO SCHEDULES. Also called **reinforcement schedule**.

Scheffé test a post hoc statistical test that allows for the testing of all possible contrasts (weighted comparisons of any number of means) while controlling the probability of a TYPE I ERROR for the set of contrasts at a prespecified level. [Henry **Scheffé** (1907–1977), U.S. mathematician]

schema *n.* (*pl.* **schemata**) **1.** a collection of basic knowledge about a concept or entity that serves as a guide to perception, interpretation, imagination, or problem solving. For example, the schema "dorm room" suggests that a bed and a desk are probably part of the scene, that a microwave oven might be, and that expensive Persian rugs probably will not be. **2.** an outlook or assumption that an individual has of the self, others, or the world that endures despite objective reality. For example, "I am a damaged person" and "Anyone I trust will eventually hurt me" are negative schemas that may result from negative experiences in early childhood. A goal of treatment, particularly stressed in COGNITIVE THERAPY, is to help the client to develop more realistic, present-oriented schemas to replace those developed during childhood or through traumatic experiences. See also SELF-IMAGE. —**schematic** *adj.*

S

scheme *n.* a cognitive structure that contains an organized plan for an activity, thus representing generalized knowledge about an entity and serving to guide behavior. For example, there is a simple sucking scheme of infancy, applied first to a nipple or teat and later to a thumb, soft toy, and so forth. This term is often used as a synonym of SCHEMA.

schizoaffective disorder an uninterrupted illness featuring at some time a MAJOR DEPRESSIVE EPISODE, MANIC EPISODE, or MIXED EPISODE concurrently with characteristic symptoms of schizophrenia (e.g., delusions, hallucinations, disorganized speech, catatonic behavior).

schizoid *adj.* denoting characteristics resembling SCHIZOPHRENIA but in a milder form: characterized by lack of affect, social passivity, and minimal introspection.

schizoid personality disorder a personality disorder characterized by long-term emotional coldness, indifference to praise or criticism and to the feelings of others, and inability to form close friendships with others. The eccentricities of speech, behavior, or thought that are characteristic of SCHIZOTYPAL PERSONALITY DISORDER are absent in those with schizoid personality disorder.

schizophrenia *n.* a psychotic disorder characterized by disturbances in thinking (cognition), emotional responsiveness, and behavior. Originally named DEMENTIA PRAECOX, schizophrenia includes POSITIVE SYMPTOMS, such as delusions, hallucinations, and disorganized speech, and NEGATIVE SYMPTOMS, such as lack of emotional responsiveness and extreme apathy. These signs and symptoms are associated with marked social or occupational dysfunction. There are five distinct subtypes: CATATONIC SCHIZOPHRENIA, DISORGANIZED SCHIZOPHRENIA, PARANOID SCHIZOPHRENIA, RESIDUAL SCHIZOPHRENIA, and UNDIFFERENTIATED SCHIZOPHRENIA. —**schizophrenic** *adj.*

schizophreniform disorder a disorder whose essential features are identical to those of SCHIZOPHRENIA except that the total duration is between 1 and 6 months and social or occupational functioning need not be impaired.

schizophrenogenic *adj.* denoting a factor or influence viewed as causing or contributing to the onset or development of schizophrenia. For example, **schizophrenogenic parents** are those whose harmful influences are presumed to cause schizophrenia in their offspring; this concept—the subject of much debate in the 1940s especially—is now considered an oversimplification.

schizotypal personality disorder a personality disorder characterized by various oddities of thought, perception, speech, and behavior that are not severe enough to warrant a diagnosis of schizophrenia. Symptoms may include perceptual distortions, MAGICAL THINKING, social isolation, vague speech without incoherence, and inadequate rapport with others due to aloofness or lack of feeling.

Scholastic Assessment Test (**SAT**) a test used in selecting candidates for college admission, formerly called the **Scholastic Aptitude Test**. It tests ability to understand and analyze what is read and to recognize relationships between parts of a sentence; ability to solve problems involving arithmetic, algebra, and geometry; and ability to organize thoughts, develop and express ideas, use language, and adhere to grammatical rules.

school refusal persistent reluctance to go to school, which is often a symptom of an educational, social, or emotional problem. School refusal may be a feature of SEPARATION ANXIETY DISORDER or it may be triggered by a stressor (e.g., loss of a pet or loved one, a change of school). School refusal is often associated with physical symptoms (e.g., nausea, dizziness, headache) and anxiety at the start of the day along with complaints that the child is too sick to go to school. Also called **school phobia**.

Schwann cell a type of non-neuronal peripheral nervous system cell (GLIA) that forms the MYELIN SHEATH around axons. [Theodor Schwann (1810–1882), German histologist]

scientific method a group of procedures, guidelines, assumptions, and attitudes required for the organized and systematic collection, interpretation, and verification of data and the discovery of reproducible evidence, enabling laws and principles to be stated or modified.

sclera *n.* the tough, white outer coat of the eyeball, which is continuous with the cornea at the front and the sheath of the optic nerve at the back of the eyeball.

score *n.* a quantitative value assigned to test results or other measurable responses.

scotoma *n.* an area of partial or complete loss of vision either in the central visual field (central scotoma) or in the periphery (paracentral scotoma).

screening *n.* **1.** a procedure or program to detect early signs of a disease in an individual or population. **2.** the process of determining, through a preliminary test, whether an individual is suitable for some purpose or task. For example, the initial evaluation of a patient to determine his or her suitability for medical or psychological treatment generally, a specific treatment approach, or referral to a treatment facility would constitute a screening.

script *n.* a cognitive schematic structure—a mental road map—containing the basic actions (and their temporal and causal relations) that comprise a complex action. For example, the script for cooking pasta might be: Open pan cupboard, choose pan, fill pan with water, put pan on stove, get out pasta, weigh correct amount of pasta, add pasta to boiling water, decide when cooked, remove from heat, strain, place in bowl.

SD abbreviation for STANDARD DEVIATION.

SDT abbreviation for SIGNAL DETECTION THEORY.

seasonal affective disorder (SAD) a MOOD DISORDER in which there is a predictable occurrence of MAJOR DEPRESSIVE EPISODES during the fall or winter months.

secondary aging changes due to biological AGING, but accelerated by disabilities resulting from disease or produced by extrinsic factors, such as stress, trauma, lifestyle, and environment. Secondary aging is often distinguished from PRIMARY AGING, which is governed by inborn and age-related processes, but the distinction is not a precise one.

secondary care health care services provided by medical specialists (e.g., cardiologists, urologists, dermatologists), to whom, typically, patients are referred by the PRIMARY CARE provider. Compare TERTIARY CARE.

secondary circular reaction in PIAGETIAN THEORY, a repetitive action emerging at around 4 to 5 months, such as rattling the crib, that has yielded results in the past but that the infant does not modify to meet the requirements of a new situation. See also PRIMARY CIRCU-

LAR REACTION; TERTIARY CIRCULAR REACTION.

secondary drive an acquired drive; that is, a drive that is developed through association with or generalization from a PRIMARY DRIVE. For example, in an AVOIDANCE CONDITIONING experiment in which a rat must go from one compartment into another to escape from an electric shock, the secondary drive is fear of the shock and the primary drive with which it is associated is avoidance of pain.

secondary gain in psychoanalytic theory, any advantage derived from a NEUROSIS in addition to the PRIMARY GAINS of relief from anxiety or internal conflict. Examples are extra attention, sympathy, avoidance of work, and domination of others. Such gains are secondary in that they are derived from others' reactions to the illness instead of causal factors.

secondary group one of the larger, less intimate, more goal-focused groups typical of more complex societies, such as work groups, clubs, congregations, associations, and so on. These social groups influence members' attitudes, beliefs, and actions, but as a supplement to the influence of small, more interpersonally intensive PRIMARY GROUPS.

secondary gustatory cortex see SECONDARY TASTE CORTEX.

secondary motor cortex see MOTOR CORTEX.

secondary prevention intervention for individuals or groups that demonstrate early psychological or physical symptoms, difficulties, or conditions (i.e., subclinical-level problems), which is intended to prevent the development of more serious dysfunction or illness. Compare PRIMARY PREVENTION; TERTIARY PREVENTION.

secondary process in psychoanalytic theory, conscious, rational mental activities under the control of the EGO and the REALITY PRINCIPLE. These thought processes, which include problem-solving, judgment, and systematic thinking, enable individuals to meet both the external demands of the environment and the internal demands of their instincts in rational, effective ways. Compare PRIMARY PROCESS.

secondary reinforcement 1. in OPERANT CONDITIONING, the process in which a neutral stimulus acquires the ability to influence the future probability of a particular response by virtue of being paired with another stimulus that naturally enhances such probability. That is, the initially neutral stimulus or circumstance functions as effective REINFORCEMENT only after special experience or training. For example, a person teaching a dog to understand the command "sit" might provide a treat and a simultaneous popping noise from a clicker tool each time the dog successfully performs the behavior. Eventually, the clicker noise itself can be used alone to maintain the desired behavior, with no treat reward being necessary. **2.** the contingent occurrence of such a stimulus or circumstance after a response. Also called **conditioned reinforcement**. Compare PRIMARY REINFORCEMENT.

secondary sensory area any of the regions of the cerebral cortex that receive direct projections from the PRIMARY SENSORY AREA for any given sense modality. An example is the SECONDARY SOMATOSENSORY AREA.

secondary sex characteristic see SEX CHARACTERISTIC.

secondary somatosensory area (**S2**) an area of the cerebral cortex, located in the PARIETAL LOBE on the upper bank of the LATERAL SULCUS, that receives direct projections from the PRIMARY SOMATOSENSORY AREA and other regions of the anterior parietal cortex and has outputs to other parts of the lateral parietal cortex and to motor and premotor areas.

secondary taste cortex the area of cerebral cortex, located in the ORBITOFRONTAL CORTEX, that is the second cortical relay for taste (see also PRIMARY TASTE CORTEX). It identifies gustatory stimuli as either pleasant and rewarding or unpleasant and undesirable. This information from the secondary taste cortex interacts with analyses from visual, touch, and olfactory cells to permit an integrated appreciation of flavor. Also called **secondary gustatory cortex**.

secondary visual cortex (V2) the area immediately surrounding the primary visual cortex (see STRIATE CORTEX) in the OCCIPITAL LOBES, receiving signals from it secondarily for analysis and further discrimination of visual input in terms of motion, shape (particularly complex shapes), and position.

second-generation antipsychotic see ANTIPSYCHOTIC.

second messenger an ion or molecule inside a cell whose concentration increases or decreases in response to stimulation of a cell RECEPTOR by a neurotransmitter, hormone, or drug. The second messenger acts to relay and amplify the signal from the receptor (the "first messenger") by triggering a range of cellular activities.

second-order conditioning in PAVLOVIAN CONDITIONING, the establishment of a conditioned response as a result of pairing a neutral stimulus with a conditioned stimulus that gained its effectiveness by being paired with an uncondi-

tioned stimulus. See HIGHER ORDER CONDITIONING.

second-order schedule a SCHEDULE OF REINFORCEMENT in which the units counted are not single responses but completions of a particular reinforcement schedule. For example, in a second-order fixed-ratio 5 of fixed-interval 30-s schedule [FR 5 (FI 30 s)], reinforcement is delivered only after five successive FI 30-s schedules have been completed. Often, a brief stimulus of some sort is presented on completion of each unit schedule.

secular trend the main trend or long-term direction of a TIME SERIES, as distinguished from temporary variations.

secure attachment 1. in the STRANGE SITUATION, the positive parent–child relationship, in which the child displays confidence when the parent is present, shows mild distress when the parent leaves, and quickly reestablishes contact when the parent returns. **2.** an adult ATTACHMENT STYLE that combines a positive view of oneself as worthy of love, and a positive view that others are generally accepting and responsive. Compare DISMISSIVE ATTACHMENT; FEARFUL ATTACHMENT; PREOCCUPIED ATTACHMENT.

secure base phenomenon the observation that infants use a place of safety, represented by an attachment figure (e.g., a parent), as a base from which to explore a novel environment. The infant often returns or looks back to the parent before continuing to explore.

sedative *n.* a drug that has a calming effect, and therefore relieves anxiety, agitation, or behavioral excitement, by depressing the central nervous system. The degree of sedation depends on the agent and the size of the dose: A drug that sedates in small doses may induce sleep in

S

larger doses and may be used as a HYPNOTIC; such drugs are commonly known as **sedative–hypnotics**.

segregation *n.* the separation or isolation of people (e.g., ethnic groups) or other entities (e.g., mental processes) so that there is a minimum of interaction between them.

seizure *n.* a discrete episode of uncontrolled, excessive electrical discharge of neurons in the brain. The resulting clinical symptoms vary based on the type and location of the seizure. See EPILEPSY.

selection *n.* in animal behavior, the differential survival of some individuals and their offspring compared with others, causing certain physical or behavioral traits to be favored in subsequent generations. The general process is known as NATURAL SELECTION.

selection bias a systematic and directional error in the choosing of participants or other units for research, such as selecting specially motivated participants. Selection bias is associated with nonrandom sampling and with nonrandom assignment to conditions.

selective adaptation the observation that perceptual adaptation can occur in response to certain stimulus qualities while being unaffected by others. For example, color adaptation can take place independently of motion adaptation.

selective attention concentration on certain stimuli in the environment and not others, enabling important stimuli to be distinguished from peripheral or incidental ones. Selective attention is typically measured by instructing participants to attend to some sources of information while ignoring others and then determining their effectiveness in doing this.

selective mutism a rare disorder, most commonly but not exclusively found in young children, characterized by a persistent failure to speak in certain social situations (e.g., at school) despite the ability to speak and to understand spoken language. Currently, selective mutism is thought to be related to severe anxiety and SOCIAL PHOBIA, but the exact cause is unknown.

selective optimization with compensation a process used to adapt to biological and psychological deficits associated with aging. The process involves emphasizing and enhancing those capacities affected only minimally by aging (optimization) and developing new means of maintaining functioning in those areas that are significantly affected (compensation).

selective serotonin reuptake inhibitor see SSRI.

self *n.* the totality of the individual, consisting of all characteristic attributes, conscious and unconscious, mental and physical. Apart from its basic reference to personal identity, being, and experience, the term's use in psychology is extremely wide-ranging and lacks uniformity, including, for example, the following perspectives: the person as the target of self-appraisal or as having the power and capability to produce an effect or exert influence; the person as he or she gradually develops by a process of INDIVIDUATION; the individual identified with a LIFESTYLE; and the essence of the individual, consisting of a gradually developing body sense, IDENTITY, self-estimate, and set of personal values, attitudes, and intentions.

self-acceptance *n.* a relatively objective sense or recognition of one's abilities and achievements, together with acknowledgment and acceptance of one's limitations. Self-acceptance is often viewed as a major component of mental health.

self-actualization *n.* the complete realization of that of which one is capable, involving maximum development of abilities and full involvement in and appreciation for life, particularly as manifest in PEAK EXPERIENCES. The term is associated particularly with the HUMANISTIC PSYCHOLOGY of U.S. psychologist Abraham Maslow (1908–1970), who viewed the process of striving toward full potential as fundamental yet obtainable only after the basic needs of physical survival, safety, love and belongingness, and esteem are fulfilled.

self-affirmation *n.* any behavior by which a person expresses a positive attitude toward his or her self, often by a positive assertion of his or her values, attributes, or group memberships. **Self-affirmation theory** assumes that the desire for self-affirmation is basic and pervasive and that many different behaviors reflect this motive. According to the theory, people are motivated to maintain views of themselves as well-adapted, moral, and competent. When some aspect of this self-view is challenged, people experience psychological discomfort which they attempt to reduce by directly resolving the inconsistency or by affirming some other aspect of the self.

self-awareness *n.* self-focused attention or knowledge. There has been a continuing controversy over whether nonhuman animals have self-awareness. Evidence of this in animals most often is determined by whether an individual can use a mirror to groom an otherwise unseen spot on its own forehead.

self-awareness theory any hypothetical construct that attempts to describe how self-focused attention occurs and what purpose it serves.

Distinctions are sometimes made between subjective self-awareness, arising directly from the observation and experience of oneself as the source of perception and behavior, and objective self-awareness, arising from comparison between the self and (a) the behaviors, attitudes, and traits of others or (b) some perceived standard for social correctness in any one of these areas.

self-complexity *n.* the degree to which different aspects of the SELF-CONCEPT are disconnected from one another. Low self-complexity entails considerable integration; high self-complexity results from compartmentalization, so that what affects one part of the self may not affect other parts.

self-concept *n.* one's description and evaluation of oneself, including psychological and physical characteristics, qualities, and skills. A self-concept contributes to the individual's sense of identity over time and is dependent in part on unconscious schematization of the self (see SCHEMA).

self-conscious emotion an emotion that celebrates or condemns the self and its actions, generated when the self is known to be the object of another person's evaluation. Self-conscious emotions include SHAME, PRIDE, GUILT, and EMBARRASSMENT. Recently, the term **other-conscious emotions** has been suggested as a better name for these emotions, to emphasize the importance of the appraisal of other human beings in generating them.

self-consciousness *n.* **1.** a personality trait associated with the tendency to reflect on or think about oneself. Some researchers have distinguished between two varieties of self-consciousness: (a) private self-consciousness, or the degree to which people think about private, internal aspects of them-

S

selves (e.g., their own thoughts, motives, and feelings) that are not directly open to observation by others; and (b) public self-consciousness, or the degree to which people think about public, external aspects of themselves (e.g., their physical appearance, mannerisms, and overt behavior) that can be observed by others. **2.** extreme sensitivity about one's own behavior, appearance, or other attributes and excessive concern about the impression one makes on others, which leads to embarrassment or awkwardness in the presence of others. —**self-conscious** *adj.*

self-criticism *n.* the examination and evaluation of one's behavior, with recognition of one's weaknesses, errors, and shortcomings. Self-criticism can have both positive and negative effects; for example, a tendency toward harsh self-criticism is thought by some to be a risk factor for depression. —**self-critical** *adj.*

self-deception *n.* the process or result of convincing oneself of the truth of something that is false or invalid, particularly the overestimation of one's abilities and concurrent failure to recognize one's own limitations.

self-defeating behavior actions by an individual that invite failure or misfortune and thus prevent him or her from attaining goals or fulfilling desires. An example is a college student procrastinating about studying and subsequently getting a poor grade on an important exam.

self-determination *n.* the process or result of engaging in behaviors without interference or undue influence from other people or external demands. Self-determination refers particularly to behaviors that improve one's circumstances, including choice making, problem solving,

self-management, self-instruction, and self-advocacy.

self-disclosure *n.* the act of revealing highly private information about one's self to other people. In psychotherapy, the revelation and expression by the client of personal, innermost feelings, fantasies, experiences, and aspirations is believed by many to be a requisite for therapeutic change and personal growth.

self-discrepancy *n.* an incongruence between different aspects of one's self-concept, particularly between one's actual self and either the IDEAL SELF or the OUGHT SELF.

self-efficacy *n.* an individual's capacity to act effectively to bring about desired results, especially as perceived by the individual.

self-enhancement *n.* any strategic behavior designed to increase esteem, either SELF-ESTEEM or the esteem of others. Self-enhancement can take the form of pursuing success or merely distorting events to make them seem to reflect better on the self. Compare SELF-PROTECTION.

self-enhancement motive the desire to think well of oneself and to be well regarded by others. This motive causes people to prefer favorable, flattering feedback rather than accurate but possibly unfavorable information. Compare APPRAISAL MOTIVE; CONSISTENCY MOTIVE.

self-esteem *n.* the degree to which the qualities and characteristics contained in one's SELF-CONCEPT are perceived to be positive. It reflects a person's physical self-image, view of his or her accomplishments and capabilities, and values and perceived success in living up to them, as well as the ways in which others view and respond to that person. The more positive the cumulative perception of these qualities and characteristics, the higher one's self-esteem. A high or reasonable degree

S

of self-esteem is considered an important ingredient of mental health, whereas low self-esteem and feelings of worthlessness are common depressive symptoms.

self-evaluation maintenance model a conceptual analysis of group affiliations that assumes that an individual maintains and enhances self-esteem by (a) associating with high-achieving individuals who excel in areas with low relevance to his or her sense of self-worth and (b) avoiding association with high-achieving individuals who excel in areas that are personally important to him or her.

self-fulfilling prophecy a belief or expectation that helps to bring about its own fulfillment, as, for example, when a person expects nervousness to impair his or her performance in a job interview or when a teacher's preconceptions about a student's ability influence the child's achievement. See PYGMALION EFFECT.

self-handicapping *n.* a strategy of creating obstacles to one's performance, so that future anticipated failure can be blamed on the obstacle rather than on one's own lack of ability. If one succeeds despite the handicap, it brings extra credit or glory to the self. The theory originally was proposed to explain alcohol and drug abuse among seemingly successful individuals. —**self-handicap** *vb.*

self-help group a group composed of individuals who meet on a regular basis to help one another cope with a common life problem. Unlike therapy groups, self-help groups are not led by professionals, do not charge a fee for service, and do not place a limit on the number of members. They provide many benefits that professionals cannot provide, including friendship, emotional support, experiential knowledge,

identity, meaningful roles, and a sense of belonging. Examples of self-help groups are Alcoholics Anonymous, Compassionate Friends, and Recovery, Inc.

self-hypnosis *n.* the process of putting oneself into a trance or trancelike state, sometimes spontaneously but typically through AUTOSUGGESTION. Also called **autohypnosis**.

self-identity *n.* see IDENTITY.

self-image *n.* one's own view or concept of oneself. Self-image is a crucial aspect of an individual's personality that can determine the success of relationships and a sense of general well-being. A negative self-image is often a cause of dysfunctions and of self-abusive, self-defeating, or destructive behavior. See also SCHEMA.

self-instructional training a form of COGNITIVE BEHAVIOR THERAPY that aims to modify maladaptive beliefs and cognitions and develop new skills in an individual. In therapy, the therapist identifies the client's maladaptive thoughts (e.g., "Everybody hates me") and models appropriate behavior while giving spoken constructive **self-instructions** (or **self-statements**). The client then copies the behavior while repeating these instructions aloud.

self-management *n.* an individual's control of his or her own behavior, particularly regarding the pursuit of a specific objective (e.g., weight loss). Self-management is usually considered a desirable aspect for the individual personally and within the social setting, but some forms of self-management may be detrimental to mental and physical health. Psychotherapy and counseling often seek to provide methods of identifying the latter and modifying them into the former.

S

self-monitoring *n.* **1.** a method used in behavioral management in which individuals keep a record of their behavior (e.g., time spent, place of occurrence, form of the behavior, feelings during performance), especially in connection with efforts to change or regulate the self (see SELF-REGULATION). **2.** a personality trait reflecting an ability to modify one's behavior in response to situational pressures, opportunities, and norms. High self-monitors are typically more in tune with the demands of the situation, whereas low self-monitors tend to be more in tune with their internal feelings.

self-perception theory a theory postulating that people often have only limited access to their attitudes, beliefs, traits, or psychological states. In such cases, people must attempt to infer the nature of these internal cues in a manner similar to the inference processes they use when making judgments about other people (i.e., by considering past behaviors).

self-presentation *n.* any behaviors designed to convey a particular image of, or particular information about, the self to other people. Some common strategies of self-presentation include exemplification (inducing others to regard one as a highly moral, virtuous person), self-promotion (highlighting or exaggerating one's competence and abilities), and supplication (depicting oneself as weak, needy, or dependent). See also IMPRESSION MANAGEMENT. —**self-presentational** *adj.*

self-protection *n.* any strategic behavior that is designed to avoid losing esteem, either SELF-ESTEEM or the esteem of others. Self-protection fosters a risk-avoidant orientation and is often contrasted with SELF-ENHANCEMENT.

self-reference effect the widespread tendency for individuals to have a superior or enhanced memory for stimuli that relate to the SELF or SELF-CONCEPT.

self-regulation *n.* the control of one's own behavior through the use of self-monitoring (keeping a record of behavior), self-evaluation (assessing the information obtained during self-monitoring), and self-reinforcement (rewarding oneself for appropriate behavior or for attaining a goal). Self-regulatory processes are stressed in BEHAVIOR THERAPY.

self-reinforcement *n.* the rewarding of oneself for appropriate behavior or the achievement of a desired goal. The self-reward may be, for example, buying a treat after studying for an exam.

self-report *n.* a statement or series of answers to questions provided by an individual as to his or her state, feelings, beliefs, and so forth. **Self-report methods** rely on the honesty and self-awareness of the participant and are used especially to measure behaviors or traits that cannot easily be directly observed.

self-schema *n.* a cognitive framework comprising organized information and beliefs about the self that guides a person's perception of the world, influencing what information draws the individual's attention as well as how that information is evaluated and retained.

self-serving bias the tendency to interpret events in a way that assigns credit to the self for any success but denies the self's responsibility for any failure, which is blamed on external factors. The self-serving bias is regarded as a form of self-deception designed to maintain high SELF-ESTEEM. Compare GROUP-SERVING BIAS.

self-understanding *n.* the attainment of knowledge about and insight into one's characteristics, including attitudes, motives, behavioral tendencies, strengths, and weaknesses. The achievement of self-understanding is one of the major goals of certain forms of psychotherapy.

self-worth *n.* an individual's evaluation of himself or herself as a valuable, capable human being deserving of respect and consideration. Positive feelings of self-worth tend to be associated with a high degree of SELF-ACCEPTANCE and SELF-ESTEEM.

SEM abbreviation for STRUCTURAL EQUATION MODELING.

semantic dementia a selective, progressive impairment in SEMANTIC MEMORY, leading to difficulties in naming, comprehension of words and their appropriate use in conversation, and appreciation and use of objects. The syndrome results from focal degeneration of specific regions of the temporal lobes.

semantic differential a technique used to explore the connotative meaning that certain words or concepts have for the individuals being questioned. Participants are asked to rate the word or concept on a seven-point scale with reference to pairs of opposites, such as *good–bad*, *beautiful–ugly*, *hot–cold*, *big–small*, and so on. Responses are then averaged or summed to arrive at a final index of attitudes. This procedure is one of the most widely used methods of assessing attitudes.

semantic encoding cognitive ENCODING of new information that focuses on the meaningful aspects of the material as opposed to its perceptual characteristics. This will usually involve some form of ELABORATION. See also DEEP PROCESSING.

semanticity *n.* the property of language that allows it to represent events, ideas, actions, and objects

symbolically, thereby endowing it with the capacity to communicate meaning.

semantic memory memory for general knowledge or meanings, of the kind that allows people to name and categorize the things they see. According to some theories, semantic memory is a form of DECLARATIVE MEMORY, that is, information that can be consciously recalled and related.

semantic network a data structure used to capture conceptual relationships. Created by the artificial intelligence research community, this system has been used in an attempt to model human information storage (particularly the means by which words are connected to meanings and associations in long-term memory), with latencies in retrieval times supposedly reflecting the length of the path of the network searched for the required response.

semantic priming an effect in which the processing of a stimulus is found to be more efficient after the earlier processing of a meaningfully related stimulus, as opposed to an unrelated or perceptually related stimulus. For example, responses to the word *nurse* would be faster following *doctor* than following *purse*.

semantics *n.* **1.** the study of meaning in language, as opposed to the study of formal relationships (GRAMMAR) or sound systems (PHONOLOGY). **2.** aspects of language that have to do with meaning, as distinguished from SYNTACTICS. See also SEMIOTICS.

semicircular canals a set of three looped tubular channels in the inner ear that detect movements of the head and provide the sense of dynamic equilibrium that is essential for maintaining balance. They form part of the vestibular apparatus (see VESTIBULAR SACS). The channels are filled with fluid (endolymph) and are oriented roughly at right angles to each other. Hence they can monitor movements in each of three different planes. Each canal has an enlarged portion, the ampulla, inside which is a sensory structure called a CRISTA. This consists of HAIR CELLS whose processes are embedded in a gelatinous cap (the cupula). When the head moves in a certain plane, endolymph flows through the corresponding canal, displacing the cupula and causing the hairs to bend. This triggers the hair cells to fire nerve impulses, thus sending messages to the brain about the direction and rate of movement.

semi-interquartile range the INTERQUARTILE RANGE divided by 2.

semiotics *n.* the study of verbal and nonverbal SIGNS and of the ways in which they communicate meaning within particular sign systems. Unlike SEMANTICS, which restricts itself to the meanings expressed in language, semiotics is concerned with human symbolic activity generally and premised on the view that signs can only generate meanings within a pattern of relationships to other signs. Also called **semiology**.

senescence *n.* the biological process of growing old, or the period during which this process occurs. **—senescent** *adj.*

senile *adj.* associated with advanced age, particularly referring to dementia or any other cognitive or behavioral deterioration relating to old age.

senile dementia see DEMENTIA.

senile plaque a clump of beta-amyloid protein surrounded by degenerated dendrites that is particularly associated with symptoms of Alzheimer's disease. Increased concentration of senile plaques in the cerebral cortex of the brain is correlated with the severity of dementia. Also called **amyloid plaque**; **neuritic plaque**.

sensate focus an approach to problems of sexual dysfunction in which people are trained to focus attention on their own natural, biological sensual cues and gradually achieve the freedom to enjoy sensory stimuli. The procedures involve prescribed body-massage exercises designed to give and receive pleasure, first not involving breasts and genitals, and then moving to these areas. This eliminates performance anxiety about arousal and allows the clients to relax and enjoy the sensual experience of body caressing without the need to achieve erection or orgasm.

sensation *n.* an irreducible unit of experience produced by stimulation of a sensory RECEPTOR and the resultant activation of a specific brain center, producing basic awareness of a sound, odor, color, shape, or taste or of temperature, pressure, pain, muscular tension, position of the body, or change in the internal organs associated with such processes as hunger, thirst, nausea, and sexual excitement. **—sensational** *adj.*

sensation seeking the tendency to search out and engage in thrilling activities as a method of increasing stimulation and arousal. Limited to human populations, it typically takes the form of engaging in highly stimulating activities accompanied by a perception of danger, such as skydiving or race-car driving.

sense *n.* any of the media through which one gathers information about the external environment or about the state of one's body in relation to this. They include the five primary senses—vision, hearing, taste, touch, and smell— as well as the senses of pressure, pain, temperature, kinesthesis,

S

and equilibrium. Each sense has its own receptors, responds to characteristic stimuli, and has its own pathways to a specific part of the brain.

sensitive period a stage in development when an organism can most advantageously acquire necessary skills or characteristics. For example, in humans the 1st year of life is considered significant for the development of a secure attachment bond. It is important to note, however, that lack of appropriate growth-dependent experiences during a sensitive period does not permanently and irreversibly impact development, as it would during a CRITICAL PERIOD, but rather makes the acquisition process outside the period more difficult.

sensitivity *n.* **1.** the capacity to detect and discriminate. More specifically, the ability of a cell, tissue, or organism to respond to changes in its external or internal environment: a fundamental property of all living organisms. **2.** the probability that a test gives a positive diagnosis given that the individual actually has the condition for which he or she is being tested. Compare SPECIFICITY.

sensitivity training a group process employed in human relations training that is focused on the development of self-awareness, productive interpersonal relations, and sensitivity to the feelings, attitudes, and needs of others. The primary method used in sensitivity training is free, unstructured discussion with a leader functioning as an observer and facilitator, although other techniques, such as ROLE PLAY, may be used. See also T-GROUP.

sensitization *n.* the increased effectiveness of an eliciting stimulus as a function of its repeated presentation. Water torture, in which water is dripped incessantly onto a person's forehead, is a good example.

sensorimotor stage in PIAGETIAN THEORY, the first major stage of cognitive development, extending from birth through the first 2 years of life. The sensorimotor stage is characterized by the development of sensory and motor processes and by the infant's first knowledge of the world acquired by interacting with the environment.

sensorineural deafness see DEAFNESS.

sensory *adj.* relating to the SENSES, to SENSATION, or to a part or all of the neural apparatus and its supporting structures that are involved in any of these.

sensory adaptation see ADAPTATION.

sensory area any area of the cerebral cortex that receives input from sensory neurons, usually via the thalamus. There are specific sensory areas for the different senses, and they are functionally differentiated into PRIMARY SENSORY AREAS and SECONDARY SENSORY AREAS. Also called **sensory cortex**.

sensory ataxia see ATAXIA.

sensory deprivation the reduction of sensory stimulation to a minimum in the absence of normal contact with the environment. Sensory deprivation may be experimentally induced (e.g., via the use of a **sensory deprivation chamber**) for research purposes or it may occur in a real-life situation (e.g., in deep-sea diving). Although short periods of sensory deprivation can be beneficial, extended sensory deprivation has detrimental effects, causing (among other things) hallucinations, delusions, hypersuggestibility, or panic.

sensory interaction the integration of sensory processes in performing a task, as in maintaining balance using sensory input from both vision and PROPRIOCEPTION. See also INTERSENSORY PERCEPTION.

sensory memory brief storage of information from each of the senses in a relatively unprocessed form beyond the duration of a stimulus, for recoding into another memory (such as SHORT-TERM MEMORY) or for comprehension. For instance, sensory memory for visual stimuli, called ICONIC MEMORY, holds a visual image for less than a second, whereas that for auditory stimuli, called ECHOIC MEMORY, retains sounds for a little longer. Also called **sensory-information store (SIS)**.

sensory neuron a neuron that receives information from the environment, via specialized RECEPTOR cells, and transmits this—in the form of nerve impulses—through SYNAPSES with other neurons to the central nervous system.

sensory overload a state in which the senses are overwhelmed with stimuli, to the point that the person is unable to process or respond to all of them.

sensory system the total structure involved in SENSATION, including the sense organs and their RECEPTORS, afferent sensory neurons, and SENSORY AREAS in the cerebral cortex at which these tracts terminate. There are separate systems for each of the senses. See AUDITORY SYSTEM; GUSTATORY SYSTEM; OLFACTORY SYSTEM; SOMATOSENSORY SYSTEM; VISUAL SYSTEM; VESTIBULAR SYSTEM.

sentence-completion test a language ability test in which the participant must complete an unfinished sentence by filling in the specific missing word or phrase. However, the test is used more often to evaluate personality, in which case the participant is presented with an introductory phrase to which he or she may respond in any way. An example might be "Today I am in a __ mood."

separation anxiety disorder an anxiety disorder occurring in childhood or adolescence that is characterized by developmentally inappropriate, persistent, and excessive anxiety about separation from the home or from major attachment figures. Other features may include worry about harm coming to attachment figures, SCHOOL REFUSAL, fear of being alone, nightmares, and repeated complaints of physical symptoms (e.g., headaches, stomachaches) associated with anticipated separation.

separation–individuation *n.* the developmental phase in which the infant gradually differentiates himself or herself from the mother, develops awareness of his or her separate identity, and attains relatively autonomous status.

sequela *n.* (*pl.* **sequelae**) a residual effect of an illness or injury, or of an unhealthy or unstable mental condition, often (but not necessarily) in the form of persistent or permanent impairment. For example, flashbacks may be the sequelae of traumatic stress.

sequence effect in WITHIN-SUBJECTS DESIGNS, the effect of the treatments being administered in a particular sequence (e.g., the sequence ABC versus ACB, versus BCA, and so forth). This is often confused with the ORDER EFFECT.

sequential analysis a class of statistical procedures in which a decision as to whether to continue collecting data is made as the experiment progresses. This approach is contrasted with studies in which the sample size is determined in advance and data are not analyzed until the entire sample is collected.

sequential design any QUASI-

EXPERIMENTAL RESEARCH in which participants of different ages are compared repeatedly over time to elucidate or untangle causes of developmental change. Sequential designs thus combine aspects of CROSS-SECTIONAL DESIGNS, LONGITUDINAL DESIGNS, and potentially TIME-LAG DESIGNS into a single study so as to maximize the benefits of each approach while minimizing the weaknesses. A CROSS-SEQUENTIAL DESIGN provides an example of this type of research scheme.

sequential processing see SERIAL PROCESSING.

serial learning the learning of a sequence of items or responses in the precise order of their presentation. For example, actors must learn their lines in sequence.

serial position curve a graphic representation of the number of items that can be remembered as a function of the order in which they were presented. Items at the beginning and end of the list are usually remembered best, thus producing a U-shaped memory curve.

serial position effect the effect of an item's position in a list of items to be learned on how well it is remembered. The classic serial position effect shows best recall of the first items from a list (see PRIMACY EFFECT) and good recall of the last items (see RECENCY EFFECT), while the middle items are less well recalled.

serial processing INFORMATION PROCESSING in which only one sequence of processing operations is carried on at a time. Those who hold that the human information-processing system operates in this way argue that the mind's apparent ability to carry on different cognitive functions simultaneously is explained by rapid shifts between different information sources. Also

called **sequential processing**. Compare PARALLEL PROCESSING.

serial reproduction a memory research technique in which one person reads a set of information before reproducing it for another person, who then reproduces it for a third person, who does the same for a fourth, and so on. Serial reproduction is widely regarded as a model for the social communication of retained information, and as such is an important experimental tool in the analysis of rumor and gossip transmission, stereotype formation, and similar phenomena.

seriation *n.* the process of arranging a collection of items into a specific order (series) on the basis of a particular dimension (e.g., size). According to PIAGETIAN THEORY, this ability is necessary for understanding the concepts of number, time, and measurement and is acquired by children during the CONCRETE OPERATIONAL STAGE.

serotonergic *adj.* responding to, releasing, or otherwise involving serotonin. For example, a **serotonergic neuron** is one that employs serotonin as a neurotransmitter.

serotonin *n.* a common monoamine neurotransmitter in the brain and other parts of the central nervous system, also found in the gastrointestinal tract, in smooth muscles of the cardiovascular and bronchial systems, and in blood platelets. It is synthesized from the dietary amino acid L-tryptophan, and in the pineal gland it is converted to MELATONIN. Serotonin has roles in numerous bioregulatory processes, including mood, appetite, pain, and sleep, and is implicated in many psychopathological conditions. Also called **5-hydroxytryptamine (5-HT)**.

serotonin reuptake inhibitor (SRI) see SSRI.

S

SES

SES abbreviation for SOCIOECO-NOMIC STATUS.

set *n.* a temporary readiness to re-spond in a certain way to a specific situation or stimulus. For example, a sprinter gets set to run when the starting gun fires (a motor set); a parent is set to hear his or her baby cry from the next room (a PERCEP-TUAL SET); a poker player is set to use a tactic that has been successful in other games (a MENTAL SET).

set point as applied to physiologi-cal and behavioral systems, the preferred level of functioning of an organism or of a system within an organism. When a set point is ex-ceeded (i.e., when physiological responses become higher than the set point), compensatory events take place to reduce functioning; when a set point is not reached, compensa-tory processes take place to help the organism or system reach the set point.

sex *n.* **1.** the traits that distinguish between males and females. Sex re-fers especially to physical and biological traits, whereas GENDER re-fers especially to social or cultural traits, although the distinction be-tween the two terms is not regularly observed. **2.** the physiological and psychological processes related to procreation and erotic pleasure.

sex characteristic any of the traits associated with sex identity. **Primary sex characteristics** (e.g., tes-tes in males, ovaries in females) are directly involved in reproduction of the species. **Secondary sex charac-teristics** are features not directly concerned with reproduction, such as voice quality, facial hair, and breast size.

sex chromosome a chromosome that determines the sex of an indi-vidual. Humans and other mammals have two sex chromosomes: the X CHROMOSOME, which carries genes

for certain sexual traits and occurs in both females and males; and the smaller Y CHROMOSOME, which is normally found only in males. Dis-ease genes that are carried only on a sex chromosome (usually the X chromosome) are responsible for SEX-LINKED inherited conditions.

sex differences the differences in physical features between males and females. These include differences in brain structures as well as differences in primary and secondary SEX CHAR-ACTERISTICS. The term is also used to denote what are more properly called GENDER DIFFERENCES, the dif-ferences between males and females in the way they behave and think.

sex hormone any of the hormones that stimulate various reproductive functions. Primary sources of sex hormones are the male and female gonads (i.e., testis and ovary), which are stimulated to produce sex hor-mones by the pituitary hormones FOLLICLE-STIMULATING HORMONE and LUTEINIZING HORMONE. The principal male sex hormones (AN-DROGENS) include testosterone; female sex hormones include the ESTROGENS and PROGESTERONE.

sexism *n.* discriminatory and preju-dicial beliefs and practices directed against one of the two sexes, usually women. Sexism is associated with acceptance of sex-role STEREOTYPES and can occur at multiple levels: individual, organizational, institu-tional, and cultural. It may be overt, involving the open endorsement of sexist beliefs or attitudes; covert, in-volving the tendency to hide sexist beliefs or attitudes and reveal them only when it is believed that one will not suffer publicly for them; or subtle, involving unequal treatment that may not be noticed because it is part of everyday behavior or per-ceived to be of low importance. See also PREJUDICE. —**sexist** *adj.*

sex-linked *adj.* describing a gene

that is located on one of the SEX CHROMOSOMES, usually the X CHROMOSOME (**X-linked**), or a trait determined by such a gene. Sex-linked diseases, such as hemophilia, generally affect only males, because the defective gene is usually a RECESSIVE ALLELE. In females, who have two X chromosomes, it would be masked by the normal, dominant allele on the other X chromosome. In males, with just a single X chromosome, any sex-linked defective allele is expressed.

sex role the behavior and attitudinal patterns characteristically associated with being male or female as defined in a given society. Sex roles thus reflect the interaction between biological heritage and the pressures of socialization, and individuals differ greatly in the extent to which they manifest typical sex-role behavior.

sexual abuse violation or exploitation by sexual means. Although the term typically is used with reference to any sexual contact between adults and children, sexual abuse can also occur in other relationships of trust.

sexual aversion disorder negative emotional reactions (e.g., anxiety, fear, or disgust) to sexual activity, leading to active avoidance of it and causing distress in the individual or his or her partner.

sexual dimorphism the existence within a species of males and females that differ distinctly from each other in form. See SEX CHARACTERISTIC; SEX DIFFERENCES.

sexual disorder any impairment of sexual function or behavior. Sexual disorders include SEXUAL DYSFUNCTION and PARAPHILIAS.

sexual dysfunction a category of sexual disorders characterized by problems in one or more phases of the SEXUAL-RESPONSE CYCLE. Sexual

dysfunctions include HYPOACTIVE SEXUAL DESIRE DISORDER, SEXUAL AVERSION DISORDER, FEMALE SEXUAL AROUSAL DISORDER, male erectile disorder (see IMPOTENCE), PREMATURE EJACULATION, MALE ORGASMIC DISORDER, FEMALE ORGASMIC DISORDER, DYSPAREUNIA, and VAGINISMUS.

sexual harassment conduct of a sexual nature that is unwelcome or considered offensive, particularly in the workplace. According to the U.S. Equal Employment Opportunity Commission (EEOC), there are two forms of sexual harassment: quid pro quo, compliance with sexual demands in return for positive employment consequences, and behavior that makes for a hostile work environment.

sexual identity the individual's internal identification with heterosexual, homosexual, or bisexual preference, that is, with his or her SEXUAL ORIENTATION.

sexual instinct in psychoanalytic theory, the instinct comprising all the erotic drives and sublimations of such drives. It includes not only genital sex, but also anal and oral manifestations and the channeling of erotic energy into artistic, scientific, and other pursuits. In his later formulations, Austrian psychiatrist Sigmund Freud (1856–1939) saw the sexual instinct as part of a wider LIFE INSTINCT that also included the self-preservative impulses of hunger, thirst, and elimination. See also LIBIDO.

sexuality *n.* **1.** all aspects of sexual behavior, including gender identity, orientation, attitudes, and activity as well as interest in and the capacity to derive pleasure from such behavior. **2.** in psychoanalytic theory, see INFANTILE SEXUALITY.

sexually dimorphic nucleus a nucleus (mass of cell bodies) of the

S

central nervous system that differs in size between males and females. In humans, for example, a nucleus in the medial PREOPTIC AREA of the hypothalamus that synthesizes GO-NADOTROPIN-RELEASING HORMONE tends to be larger and more active in males than in females because gonadotropin release is continuous (it is cyclical in females).

sexually transmitted disease (**STD**) an infection transmitted by sexual activity. Numerous STDs have been identified, including those caused by viruses (e.g., hepatitis B, herpes, and HIV) and those caused by bacteria (e.g., chlamydia, gonorrhea, and syphilis).

sexual masochism a PARAPHILIA in which sexual interest and arousal is repeatedly or exclusively achieved through being humiliated, bound, beaten, or otherwise made to suffer physical harm or threat to life.

sexual orientation one's enduring sexual attraction to male partners, female partners, or both. Sexual orientation may be heterosexual, same-sex (gay or lesbian), or bisexual.

sexual-response cycle a four-stage cycle of sexual response that is exhibited by both men and women, differing only in aspects determined by male or female anatomy. The stages include the arousal (or excitement) phase; the plateau phase, marked by penile erection in men and vaginal lubrication in women; the orgasmic phase, marked by EJACULATION in men and ORGASM in women; and the resolution phase.

sexual sadism a PARAPHILIA in which sexual excitement is achieved by intentional infliction of physical or psychological suffering on another person. When practiced with nonconsenting partners, the severity of the acts often increases over time.

sexual selection a theoretical

mechanism for the evolution of anatomical and behavioral differences between males and females, based on the selection of mates.

shadowing *n.* in cognitive testing, a task in which a participant repeats aloud a message word for word at the same time that the message is being presented, often with other stimuli being presented in the background. It is mainly used in studies of ATTENTION.

shaken baby syndrome the neurological consequences of a form of child abuse in which a small child or infant is repeatedly shaken. The shaking causes diffuse, widespread damage to the brain; in severe cases it may cause death.

shallow affect significant reduction in appropriate emotional responses to situations and events. See also FLAT AFFECT.

shallow processing cognitive processing of a stimulus that focuses on its superficial, perceptual characteristics rather than its meaning. It is considered that processing at this shallow level produces weaker, shorter-lasting memories than DEEP PROCESSING. See also BOTTOM-UP PROCESSING.

shame *n.* a highly unpleasant SELF-CONSCIOUS EMOTION arising from the sense of there being something dishonorable, ridiculous, immodest, or indecorous in one's conduct or circumstances. It is typically characterized by withdrawal from social intercourse but may also motivate defensive, retaliative anger. Psychological research consistently reports a relationship between proneness to shame and a whole host of psychological symptoms, including depression, anxiety, eating disorders, subclinical sociopathy, and low self-esteem. —**shameful** *adj.*

sham rage sudden aggressive behavior and motor activity occurring disproportionally in response to a weak or relatively innocuous stimulus. Sham rage initially was observed by researchers in the 1920s: following surgical DECORTICATION, cats responded to the touch of a hand by growling, spitting, lashing the tail, arching the back, protracting the claws, erecting the hairs, jerking the limbs, rapidly moving the head from side to side, and attempting to bite. It subsequently has been demonstrated to occur with direct electrical stimulation of the LIMBIC SYSTEM as well. Additionally, sham rage has been seen in some pathological human conditions involving similar damage to the cerebral cortex that removes its inhibitory influence over the activities of the HYPOTHALAMUS and other deeper, more primitive structures.

sham surgery in experiments using surgical interventions, surgery that functions as a CONTROL because it mimics the features of the experimental surgery but does not result in the alteration or removal of any bodily structures, that is, it does not have the systemic effects of the experimental procedure. Also called **sham operation**.

shape constancy a type of PERCEPTUAL CONSTANCY in which an object is perceived as having the same shape when viewed at different angles. For example, a plate is still perceived as circular despite changes in its appearance when viewed from above, below, the side, and so forth.

shaping *n.* the production of new forms of OPERANT BEHAVIOR by reinforcement of successive approximations to the behavior. Also called **behavior shaping**.

shared environment in behavioral genetics analyses, those aspects of an environment that individuals living together (e.g., biologically related individuals in a family

household) share and that therefore cause them to become more similar to each other than would be expected on the basis of genetic influences alone. Examples of shared environmental factors include parental child-rearing style, divorce, or family income and related variables. Compare NON-SHARED ENVIRONMENT.

shared psychotic disorder a rare disorder in which the essential feature is an identical or similar delusion that develops in an individual who is involved with another individual who already has a psychotic disorder with prominent delusions. Shared psychotic disorder can involve many people (e.g., an entire family), but is most commonly seen in relationships of only two, in which case it is known as **folie à deux**.

sheltered workshop a work-oriented rehabilitation facility for individuals with disabilities that provides a controlled, noncompetitive, supportive working environment and individually designed work settings, using work experience and related services to assist individuals with disabilities to achieve specific vocational goals.

shock therapy see ELECTRO-CONVULSIVE THERAPY.

short-term memory (**STM**) a temporary information storage system, enabling one to retain, reproduce, recognize, or recall a limited amount of material after a period of about 10–30 s. STM is often theorized to be separate from LONG-TERM MEMORY, and the two are the components of the DUAL-STORE MODEL OF MEMORY.

short-term psychodynamic psychotherapy see BRIEF PSYCHO-DYNAMIC PSYCHOTHERAPY.

short-term psychotherapy see BRIEF PSYCHOTHERAPY.

S

sibling rivalry competition among two or more children in a family for the attention, approval, or affection of one or both parents or for other recognition or rewards, for example, in sports or school grades.

sick role the behavior expected of a person who is physically ill, mentally ill, or injured. Such expectations can be the individual's own or those of the family, the community, or society in general. They influence both how the person behaves and how others will react to him or her. For instance, people with a sick role are expected to cooperate with caregivers and to want to get well but are also provided with an exemption from normal obligations. See also FACTITIOUS DISORDER.

side effect any reaction secondary to the intended therapeutic effect that may occur following administration of a drug or other treatment. Often these are undesirable but tolerable (e.g., headache or fatigue), although more serious effects (e.g., liver failure, seizures) may also occur.

SIDS acronym for SUDDEN INFANT DEATH SYNDROME.

sign *n.* **1.** an objective, observable indication of a disorder or disease. **2.** in linguistics and SEMIOTICS, anything that conveys meaning; a sign may be either verbal (e.g., a spoken or written word) or nonverbal (e.g., a hairstyle). The term is now mainly associated with approaches deriving from the theory of Swiss linguist Ferdinand de Saussure (1857–1913), who emphasized the arbitrary nature of linguistic signs (i.e., the lack of any necessary relationship between the material signifier and the idea signified). The application of this idea to nonlinguistic sign systems provided the basic method of STRUCTURALISM in the social sciences.

signal detection theory (SDT) a body of concepts and techniques from communication theory, electrical engineering, and decision theory that were applied to auditory and visual psychophysics in the late 1950s and are now widely used in many areas of psychology. SDT has provided a valuable theoretical framework for describing perceptual and other aspects of cognition and for quantitatively relating psychophysical phenomena to findings from sensory physiology. A key notion of SDT is that human performance in many tasks is limited by variability in the internal representation of stimuli due to internal or external NOISE. See D PRIME; RECEIVER-OPERATING CHARACTERISTIC CURVE.

signal-to-noise ratio the ratio of signal power (intensity) to noise power, usually expressed in DECIBELS. When the signal is speech, it is called the **speech-to-noise ratio**.

significance *n.* the degree or extent to which something is meaningful or of consequence. In mathematics and related fields, the term denotes STATISTICAL SIGNIFICANCE.

significance level in null hypothesis SIGNIFICANCE TESTING, the probability of rejecting the null hypothesis when it is in fact true (i.e., of making a Type I error). It is set at some criterion, α, usually .01 or .05, and the actual value for a particular test is denoted *p*. Thus when the *p*-value is less than α, the null hypothesis is rejected. Also called **alpha level**.

significance testing a set of procedures that are used to differentiate between two models. In the most common form of significance testing, one model (the NULL HY-

POTHESIS) specifies a condition in which the treatment being studied has no effect and the other model (the ALTERNATIVE HYPOTHESIS) specifies that the treatment has some effect.

significant difference the situation in which a SIGNIFICANCE TESTING procedure indicates that the two models being compared are legitimately different and do not reflect chance variation.

significant other any individual who has a profound influence on a person, particularly his or her self-image and SOCIALIZATION. Although the term most often denotes a spouse or other person with whom one has a committed sexual relationship, it is also used to refer to parents, peers, and others.

sign language any system of communication in which signs formed by hand configuration and movement are used instead of spoken language. The term refers particularly to the system used by people who are deaf or have severe hearing loss, which has its own syntax and methods of conveying nuances of feeling and emotion and is now accepted by most linguists as exhibiting the full set of defining characteristics of human oral–aural language.

sign stimulus see RELEASER.

sign test a nonparametric test of a hypothesis concerning the median of a distribution. It is commonly used to test the hypothesis that the median difference in matched pairs is zero.

similarity *n.* one of the GESTALT PRINCIPLES OF ORGANIZATION. It states that people tend to organize objects with similar qualities into a perceptual group and interpret them as a whole. Also called **law of similarity**; **principle of similarity**.

simple cell a neuron in the STRIATE CORTEX that has a receptive field consisting of an elongated center region and two elongated flanking regions. The response of a simple cell to stimulation in the center of the receptive field is the opposite of its response to stimulation in the flanking zones. This means that a simple cell responds best to an edge or a bar of a particular width and with a particular direction and location in the visual field. Compare COMPLEX CELL.

simple effect in an experimental design involving multiple independent variables, the consistent total effect on a dependent variable of a particular level (quantity, magnitude, or category) of one independent variable at a particular level of another independent variable.

simple phobia see SPECIFIC PHOBIA.

simple random sampling the most basic form of RANDOM SAMPLING, in which the participants are selected individually by the use of a table of random digits or a random number generator.

simple reaction time the total time that elapses between the presentation of a stimulus and the occurrence of a response in a task that requires a participant to make an elementary response (e.g., pressing a key) whenever a stimulus (such as a light or tone) is presented. The individual makes just a single response whenever the only possible stimulus is presented. Compare CHOICE REACTION TIME.

simulation *n.* **1.** an experimental method used to investigate the behavior and psychological processes and functioning of individuals in social and other environments, often those to which investigators cannot easily gain access, by reproducing those environments in a realistic way. **2.** the artificial creation of experiment-like data through the use of a mathematical or computer model of behavior or data. **3.** resemblance or imitation, particularly the mimicking of symptoms of one disorder by another or the faking of an illness.

simultanagnosia *n.* see VISUAL AGNOSIA.

simultaneous conditioning a PAVLOVIAN CONDITIONING technique in which the conditioned stimulus and the unconditioned stimulus are presented at the same time. Compare DELAY CONDITIONING.

single blind see BLIND.

single-case design an experimental design involving only a single participant or other sampling unit. The individual serves as his or her own CONTROL, and typically a number of observations are obtained at different times over the course of treatment.

situational attribution the ascription of one's own or another's behavior, an event, or an outcome to causes outside the person concerned, such as luck, pressure from other people, or external circumstances. Also called **external attribution**. Compare DISPOSITIONAL ATTRIBUTION.

situationism *n.* the view that an organism's interaction with the environment and situational factors, rather than personal characteristics and other internal factors, are the primary determinants of behavior. Also called **situationalism**.

situation test a test that places an individual in a natural setting, or in an experimental setting that approximates a natural one, to assess either the individual's ability to solve a problem that requires adaptive behavior under stressful conditions or

the individual's reactions to what is believed to be a stressful experience.

size constancy the ability to perceive an object as being the same size despite the fact that the size of its retinal image changes depending on its distance from the observer. It is a type of PERCEPTUAL CONSTANCY.

size–distance paradox an illusion that an object is bigger or smaller than is actually the case caused by a false perception of its distance from the viewer. For example, in the so-called **moon illusion** the moon appears to be larger on the horizon, where DEPTH CUES make it appear to be farther away, than at its zenith, where there are no depth cues.

skeletal muscle a muscle that provides the force to move a part of the skeleton, typically under voluntary control of the central nervous system. Skeletal muscles are attached to the bones by tendons and usually span a joint, so that one end of the muscle is attached via a tendon to one bone and the other end is attached to another bone. Skeletal muscle is composed of numerous slender, tapering MUSCLE FIBERS, within which are longitudinal contractile fibrils (myofibrils), organized into arrays (sarcomeres) that give a striped appearance when viewed microscopically. Also called **striated muscle**. Compare CARDIAC MUSCLE; SMOOTH MUSCLE.

skewness *n.* a measure of the degree or extent to which a batch of scores lack symmetry in their distribution around their measure of CENTRAL TENDENCY. **Positive skew** occurs when the MEAN is greater than the MEDIAN; that is, when there are more right tail (higher values) in the distribution. **Negative skew** occurs when the MEDIAN is greater than the MEAN; that is, when there are more left tail (lower values) in the distribution.

skill *n.* an ability or proficiency acquired through training and practice. For example, motor skills are characterized by the ability to perform a complex movement or sequence of behaviors quickly, smoothly, and precisely, whereas SOCIAL SKILLS enable a person to interact competently and appropriately in a given social context.

skin *n.* the external covering of the body, consisting of an outer layer (epidermis) and a deeper layer (dermis) resting on a layer of fatty subcutaneous tissue. The skin prevents injury to underlying tissues, prevents the entry of foreign substances and pathogens, reduces water loss from the body, and forms part of the body's temperature-regulation mechanism through the evaporation of sweat secreted from sweat glands. Various types of sensory nerve ending provide touch and pressure sensitivity, as well as sensations of pain and temperature.

skin conductance the degree of resistance of the skin to the passage of a small electric current between two electrodes, changes in which are typically used to measure a person's level of AROUSAL or energy mobilization (see GALVANIC SKIN RESPONSE).

Skinner box see OPERANT CONDITIONING CHAMBER. [Burrhus Frederic **Skinner** (1904–1990), U.S. psychologist]

sleep *n.* a state of the brain characterized by partial or total suspension of consciousness, muscular relaxation and inactivity, reduced metabolism, and relative insensitivity to stimulation. Other mental and physical characteristics that distinguish sleep from wakefulness include amnesia for events occurring during the loss of consciousness and unique sleep-related electroencephalogram and brain-imaging patterns (see SLEEP STAGES). These

characteristics also help distinguish normal sleep from a loss of consciousness due to injury, disease, or drugs. See also NREM SLEEP; REM SLEEP.

sleep apnea the temporary cessation of breathing while asleep, which occurs when the upper airway briefly becomes blocked (obstructive sleep apnea) or when the respiratory centers in the brain fail to stimulate respiration (central sleep apnea).

sleep cycle a recurring pattern of SLEEP STAGES in which a period of SLOW-WAVE SLEEP is followed by a period of REM SLEEP. In humans, a sleep cycle lasts approximately 90 min.

sleep deprivation deliberate prevention of sleep, particularly for experimental purposes. Studies show that the loss of one night's sleep has a substantial effect on physical or mental functioning; participants score significantly lower on tests of judgment and SIMPLE REACTION TIME and show impairments in daytime alertness and memory. Sleep loss also may be detrimental to the immune and endocrine systems.

sleeper effect the finding that the impact of a persuasive message increases over time.

sleep paralysis brief inability to move or speak just before falling asleep or on awakening, often accompanied by terrifying hallucinations.

sleep spindles characteristic spindle-shaped patterns recorded on an electroencephalogram (EEG) during stage 2 sleep. They are short bursts of waves with a frequency of about 15 Hz that progressively increase then decrease in amplitude and they indicate a state of light sleep. Sleep spindles are often accompanied by K COMPLEXES.

sleep stages the four-cycle progression in electrical activity of the brain during a normal night's sleep, as recorded on an electroencephalogram (EEG). The regular pattern of ALPHA WAVES characteristic of the relaxed state of the individual just before sleep becomes intermittent and attenuated in **stage 1 sleep**, which is marked by drowsiness with rolling eyeball movements. This progresses to **stage 2 sleep** (light sleep), which is characterized by SLEEP SPINDLES and K COMPLEXES. In **stage 3** and **stage 4 sleep** (deep sleep), DELTA WAVES predominate (see SLOW-WAVE SLEEP). These stages comprise NREM SLEEP and are interspersed with periods of dreaming associated with REM SLEEP.

sleep terror disorder a PARASOMNIA characterized by repeated episodes of abrupt awakening from NREM SLEEP accompanied by disorientation and extreme panic. More intense than NIGHTMARES and occurring during the first few hours of sleep, these episodes involve screaming and symptoms of autonomic arousal, such as profuse perspiration, rapid breathing, and a rapid heart rate.

sleepwalking disorder a PARASOMNIA characterized by persistent incidents of complex motor activity during slow-wave NREM SLEEP. These episodes typically occur during the first hours of sleep and involve getting out of bed and walking or performing more complicated tasks. While in this state, the individual stares blankly, is essentially unresponsive, and can be awakened only with great difficulty; he or she does not remember the episode upon waking. Also called **somnambulism**.

slip of the tongue a minor error in speech, such as a SPOONERISM. Psychoanalysts have long been interested in the significance of such slips, referring to them as FREUDIAN SLIPS and believing them to reveal unconscious associations, motivations, or wishes.

slope *n.* in mathematics and statistics, the change in vertical distance on a graph divided by the horizontal distance. It is represented by the slant of a line. See also ACCELERATION.

slow-wave sleep deep sleep that is characterized by DELTA WAVES on the electroencephalogram, corresponding to stages 3 and 4 of sleep. See also SLEEP STAGES.

smoothing *n.* a collection of techniques used to reduce the irregularities in a batch of data or in a plot (curve) of that data, particularly in TIME SERIES analyses.

smooth muscle any muscle that is not striated and is under the control of the AUTONOMIC NERVOUS SYSTEM (i.e., it is not under voluntary control). Smooth muscles are able to remain in a contracted state for long periods of time or maintain a pattern of rhythmic contractions indefinitely without fatigue. Smooth muscle is found, for example, in the digestive organs and blood vessels. Compare CARDIAC MUSCLE; SKELETAL MUSCLE.

smooth-pursuit movement a slow, steady eye movement that is responsive to feedback provided by brain regions involved in processing visual information, thus enabling continuous fixation on an object as it moves. Compare SACCADE.

sociability *n.* the tendency to seek out companionship, engage in interpersonal relations, and participate in social activities. —**sociable** *adj.*

social *adj.* **1.** relating to human society. **2.** relating to the interactions of individuals, particularly as members of a group or a community. In this sense, the term is not restricted

S

to people but rather applies to all animals.

social adaptation see ADAPTATION.

social age (SA) a numerical scale unit expressing how mature a person is in terms of his or her interpersonal skills and ability to fulfill the norms and expectations associated with particular SOCIAL ROLES, as compared to others of the same CHRONOLOGICAL AGE. SA is similar to MENTAL AGE and is derived from ratings gathered from the individual or, in the case of young children, from parents or caregivers using instruments such as the Vineland Adaptive Behavior Scales.

social anxiety fear of social situations (e.g., making conversation, meeting strangers) in which embarrassment may occur or there is a risk of being negatively evaluated by others. When the anxiety causes an individual significant distress or impairment in functioning, a diagnosis of SOCIAL PHOBIA may be warranted.

social anxiety disorder see SOCIAL PHOBIA.

social class a major group or division of society having a common level of power and prestige on the basis of a common SOCIOECONOMIC STATUS. Often the members of a particular social class share values and have similar religious and social patterns. A popularly used classification divides individuals into an upper class, middle class, and working class.

social clock in a given culture, the set of norms governing the ages at which particular life events, such as beginning school, leaving home, getting married, having children, and retiring, are expected to occur.

social cognition the ways in which people perceive, think about, interpret, categorize, and judge their own social behaviors and those of others. The study of social cognition involves aspects of both cognitive psychology and social psychology. Major areas of interest include ATTRIBUTION THEORY, PERSON PERCEPTION, SOCIAL INFLUENCE, and the cognitive processes involved in moral judgments.

social-cognitive theory a theoretical framework in which the functioning of personality is explained in terms of cognitive contents and processes acquired through interaction with the sociocultural environment.

social comparison theory the proposition that people evaluate their abilities and attitudes in relation to those of others (i.e., through a process of comparison) when objective standards for the assessment of these abilities and attitudes are lacking. Some also hold that those chosen as the comparison group are generally those whose abilities or attitudes are relatively similar to the person's own abilities or views.

social competence effectiveness or skill in interpersonal relations and social situations, increasingly considered an important component of mental health. Social competence involves the ability to evaluate social situations and determine what is expected or required; to recognize the feelings and intentions of others; and to select social behaviors that are most appropriate for that given context. It is important to note, however, that what is required and appropriate for effective social functioning is likely to vary across settings.

social constructivism the school of thought that recognizes knowledge as embedded in social context and sees human thoughts, feelings, language, and behavior as the result of interchanges with the external world. Social constructivism argues

S

that there is no separation between subjectivity and objectivity and that the dichotomy between the person and the situation is false: the person is intimately and intricately bound within social, cultural, and historical forces and cannot be understood fully without consideration of these social forces. According to social constructivism, not only knowledge but reality itself is created in an interactive process and thus people are solely what their society shapes them to be.

social-decision scheme a strategy or rule used in a group to select a single alternative from among the various alternatives proposed and discussed during the group's deliberations. These schemes or rules are sometimes explicitly acknowledged by the group, as when a formal tally of those favoring the alternative is taken and the proposal is accepted only when a certain proportion of those present favor it, but are sometimes implicit and informal, as when a group accepts the alternative that its most powerful members seem to favor.

social deprivation 1. limited access to society's resources due to poverty, discrimination, or other disadvantage. **2.** lack of adequate opportunity for social experience.

social desirability the extent to which someone or something is admired or considered valuable within a social group, particularly when this prompts individuals to present themselves in ways that are likely to be seen as positive by the majority of other people.

social desirability response set the tendency of a respondent or participant to give answers that elicit a favorable evaluation rather than answers that genuinely represent their views. This often reduces the validity of interviews, questionnaires, and other self-reports.

social determinism the theory or doctrine that individual behaviors are determined by societal events and other interpersonal experiences. See also CULTURAL DETERMINISM; DETERMINISM.

social development the gradual acquisition of certain skills (e.g., language, interpersonal skills), attitudes, relationships, and behavior that enable the individual to interact with others and to function as a member of society.

social dilemma an interpersonal situation that tempts individuals to seek personal, selfish gain by putting at risk the interests of the larger collective to which they belong. Such mixed-motive situations have reward structures that favor individuals who act selfishly rather than in ways that benefit the larger social collective; however, if a substantial number of individuals seek maximum personal gain, their outcomes will be lower than if they had sought collective outcomes. See also SOCIAL TRAP.

social distance the degree to which, psychologically speaking, a person or group wants to remain separate from members of different social groups. This reflects the extent to which individuals or groups accept others of a different ethnic, racial, national, or other social background.

social distance scale a measure of intergroup attitudes that asks respondents to indicate their willingness to accept members of other ethnic, national, or social groups in situations that range from relatively distant ("would allow to live in my country") to relatively close ("would admit to close kinship by marriage").

social exchange theory a theory envisioning social interactions as an exchange in which the participants seek to maximize their benefits within the limits of what is regarded as fair or just. Intrinsic to this hypothesis is the RECIPROCITY NORM: People are expected to reciprocate for the benefits they have received. Social exchange theory is similar to EQUITY THEORY, which also maintains that people seek fairness in social relationships.

social facilitation the improvement in an individual's performance of a task that often occurs when others are present. This effect tends to occur with tasks that are uncomplicated or have been previously mastered through practice. There is some disagreement as to whether the improvement is due to a heightened state of arousal, a greater self-awareness, or a reduced attention to unimportant and distracting peripheral stimuli. See also AUDIENCE EFFECT.

social identity the personal qualities that one claims and displays to others so consistently that they are considered to be part of one's essential, stable self. This public persona may be an accurate indicator of the private, personal self, but it may also be a deliberately contrived image.

social identity theory a conceptual perspective on group processes and intergroup relations that assumes that groups influence their members' self-concepts and self-esteem, particularly when individuals categorize themselves as group members and identify strongly with the group. According to this theory, people tend to favor their INGROUP over an OUTGROUP because the former is part of their self-identity.

social impact theory a theory of social influence postulating that the amount of influence exerted by a source on a target depends on (a) the strength of the source compared to that of the target (e.g., the social status of the source versus that of

the target); (b) the immediacy of the source to the target (e.g., the physical or psychological distance between them); and (c) the number of sources and targets (e.g., several sources influencing a single target).

social influence any change in an individual's thoughts, feelings, or behaviors caused by other people. See SOCIAL PRESSURE.

social inhibition the restraint placed on an individual's expression of her or his feelings, attitudes, motives, and so forth by the belief that others could learn of this behavior and disapprove of it.

social intelligence the ability to understand people and effectively relate to them.

social interaction any process that involves reciprocal stimulation or response between two or more individuals. Social interaction includes the development of cooperation and competition, the influence of status and social roles, and the dynamics of group behavior, leadership, and conformity. Persistent social interaction between specific individuals leads to the formation of social RELATIONSHIPS.

sociality *n.* the tendency to live as part of a group with clear organization of social interactions and the ability to cooperate with and adapt to the demands of the group.

socialization *n.* the process by which individuals acquire social skills, beliefs, values, and behaviors necessary to function effectively in society or in a particular group. It involves becoming aware of the social or group value-system behavior pattern and what is considered normal or desirable for the social environment in which they will be members. —**socialize** *vb.*

social justice norm the social standard (NORM) stating that people should be helped by others only if they deserve to be helped. Compare RECIPROCITY NORM; SOCIAL RESPONSIBILITY NORM.

social learning learning that is facilitated through social interactions with other individuals. Several forms of social learning have been identified, including SOCIAL FACILITATION and IMITATION.

social learning theory the general view that learning is largely or wholly due to imitation, modeling, and other social interactions. Behavior is assumed to be developed and regulated (a) by external stimulus events, such as the influence of other individuals; (b) by external reinforcement, such as praise, blame, and reward; and (c) by the effects of cognitive processes, such as thinking and judgment, on the individual's behavior and on the environment that influences him or her.

social loafing the reduction of individual effort that occurs when people work in groups compared to when they work alone.

social need see LOVE NEED.

social neuroscience an emerging discipline that aims to integrate the social and biological approaches to human behavior that have often been seen as mutually exclusive. Social neuroscientists use a range of methodologies to elucidate the reciprocal interactions of the brain's biological mechanisms (especially the nervous, immune, and endocrine systems) with the social and cultural contexts in which human beings operate.

social norm any of the socially determined consensual standards that indicate (a) what behaviors are considered typical in a given context (**descriptive norms**) and (b) what behaviors are considered proper in the context (**injunctive norms**). Unlike statistical norms, social norms of both types include an evaluative quality such that those who do not comply and cannot provide an acceptable explanation for their violation are evaluated negatively. Social norms apply across groups and social settings, whereas **group norms** are specific to a particular group.

social penetration theory a model stating that close relationships grow closer with increasingly intimate SELF-DISCLOSURES.

social perception the processes by which a person uses the behavior of others to form opinions or make inferences about those individuals, particularly as regards their motives, attitudes, or values.

social phobia an anxiety disorder that is characterized by extreme and persistent SOCIAL ANXIETY or PERFORMANCE ANXIETY that causes significant distress or prevents participation in everyday activities. The feared situation is most often avoided altogether or else it is endured with marked discomfort. Also called **social anxiety disorder**.

social play play that involves interacting with others for fun or sport. It is one of three basic types of play traditionally identified, the others being OBJECT PLAY and LOCOMOTOR PLAY.

social pressure the exertion of influence on a person or group by another person or group. Social pressure includes rational argument and persuasion (**informational influence**), calls for conformity (**normative influence**), and direct forms of influence, such as demands, threats, or personal attacks on the one hand and promises of rewards or social approval on the other (**interpersonal influence**). See also SOCIAL INFLUENCE.

social psychology the study of how an individual's thoughts, feelings, and actions are affected by the actual, imagined, or symbolically represented presence of other people. Psychological social psychology differs from sociological social psychology in that the former tends to give greater emphasis to internal psychological processes, whereas the latter focuses on factors that affect social life, such as status, role, and class.

social reality the consensus of attitudes, opinions, and beliefs held by members of a group or society.

social referencing evaluating one's own modes of thinking, expression, or behavior by comparing them with those of other people so as to understand how to react in a particular situation and to adapt ones actions and reactions in some manner and to some degree that are perceived to be appropriate. This ability has been demonstrated to emerge at a very early age: young infants use caregivers' emotional expressions to guide their behavior in novel, ambiguous situations.

social representation a system, model, or code for unambiguously naming and organizing values, ideas, and conduct, which enables communication and social exchange (i.e., at the levels of language and behavior) among members of a particular group or community.

social responsibility norm the social standard or NORM that, when possible, one should assist those in need. Compare RECIPROCITY NORM; SOCIAL JUSTICE NORM.

social role the functional role played by an individual who holds a formal position in a social group, such as the role of squadron leader, teacher, or vice president of an organization. Positions of this kind are termed role categories, and the attitudes and behavior associated with

each category are termed role expectations.

social role theory a model contending that behavioral differences between men and women can be attributed to cultural standards and expectations about GENDER, rather than to biological factors.

social schema a cognitive structure of organized information, or representations, about social norms and collective patterns of behavior within society. Whereas a SELF-SCHEMA involves a person's conception of herself or himself as an individual and in terms of a particular personal role (or roles) in life, social schemata often underlie behavior of the person acting within group—particularly large group, or societal—contexts.

social science any of a number of disciplines concerned with the social interactions of individuals, studied from a scientific and research perspective. These disciplines traditionally have included anthropology, economics, geography, history, linguistics, political science, psychiatry, psychology, and sociology, as well as associated areas of mathematics and biology. The focus of analysis ranges from the individual to institutions and entire social systems. The general goal is to understand social interactions and to propose solutions to social problems.

social self the aspects of the SELF that are important to or influenced by social relations. See also SOCIAL IDENTITY.

social skills a set of learned abilities that enable an individual to interact competently and appropriately in a given social context. The most commonly identified social skills include assertiveness, coping, communication and friendship-making skills, interpersonal problem

S

solving, and the ability to regulate one's cognitions, feelings, and behavior. See also SOCIAL COMPETENCE.

social skills training a form of individual or group therapy for those who need to overcome social inhibition or ineffectiveness. It uses many techniques for teaching effective social interaction in specific situations (e.g., job interviews, dating), including ASSERTIVENESS TRAINING and behavioral and cognitive REHEARSAL.

social status the relative prestige, authority, and privilege of an individual or group. Social status can be determined by any number of factors—including occupation, level of education, ethnicity, religion, age, rank, achievements, wealth, reputation, authority, and ancestry—with different groups and societies stressing some qualities more than others when allocating status to members.

social stratification the existence or emergence of separate socioeconomic levels in a society. See SOCIAL CLASS; SOCIOECONOMIC STATUS.

social support the provision of assistance or comfort to others, typically in order to help them cope with a variety of biological, psychological, and social stressors. Support may arise from any interpersonal relationship in an individual's social network, involving family members, friends, neighbors, religious institutions, colleagues, caregivers, or support groups. It may take the form of practical help with chores or money, informational assistance (e.g., advice or guidance), and, at the most basic level, emotional support that allows the individual to feel valued, accepted, and understood.

social trap a SOCIAL DILEMMA over a public good in which individuals can maximize their resources by seeking personal goals rather than collective goals, but if too many individuals act selfishly, all members of the collective will experience substantial long-term losses. The "tragedy of the commons" is an example: A grazing area will be destroyed if too many of the farmers who share it increase the size of their herds.

social work a profession devoted to helping individuals, families, and other groups deal with personal and practical problems within the larger community context of which they are a part. **Social workers** address a variety of problems, including those related to mental or physical disorder, poverty, living arrangements, child care, occupational stress, and unemployment, especially through involvement in the provision of services through various government and nongovernment agencies and organizations.

society *n.* **1.** an enduring social group living in a particular place whose members are mutually interdependent and share political and other institutions, laws and mores, and a common culture. **2.** any well-established group of individuals (human or animal) that typically obtains new members at least in part through sexual reproduction and has relatively self-sufficient systems of action. —**societal** *adj.*

sociobiology *n.* the systematic study of the biological basis for social behavior, particularly in the context of the Darwinian principle of NATURAL SELECTION. —**sociobiological** *adj.*

sociocentrism *n.* **1.** the tendency to put the needs, concerns, and perspective of the social unit or group before one's individual, egocentric concerns. See also ALLOCENTRIC. **2.** the tendency to judge one's own group as superior to other groups across a variety of domains. Whereas

ETHNOCENTRISM refers to the selective favoring of one's ethnic, religious, racial, or national groups, sociocentrism usually means the favoring of smaller groups characterized by face-to-face interaction among members. Compare EGO-CENTRISM. **—sociocentric** *adj.*

sociocultural perspective any viewpoint or approach to health, mental health, history, politics, economics, or any other area of human experience that emphasizes the environmental factors of society, culture, and social interaction. In developmental psychology, for example, the term refers to the view that cognitive development is guided by adults interacting with children, with the cultural context determining to a large extent how, where, and when these interactions take place. See also GUIDED PARTICIPATION.

socioeconomic status (SES) the position of an individual or group on the socioeconomic scale, which is determined by a combination or interaction of social and economic factors, such as income, amount and kind of education, type and prestige of occupation, place of residence, and (in some societies or parts of society) ethnic origin or religious background. See SOCIAL CLASS.

sociogenic *adj.* resulting from social factors. For example, a **sociogenic hypothesis** of schizophrenia posits that social conditions, such as living in impoverished circumstances, are major contributors to and causal agents of the disorder.

sociolinguistics *n.* the study of the relationship between language and society and of the social circumstances of language usage, especially as related to such characteristics as gender, social class, and ethnicity.

sociology *n.* the scientific study of the origin, development, organiza-

tion, forms, and functioning of human society, including the analysis of the relationships between individuals and groups, institutions, and society itself. **—sociological** *adj.* **—sociologist** *n.*

sociometry *n.* a field of research in which various techniques are used to analyze the patterns of intermember relations within groups and to summarize these findings in mathematical and graphic form. In most cases the group members' responses to questions about their fellow members are displayed in a **sociogram**, which places those individuals who are most frequently chosen in the center of the diagram and others about the periphery. **—sociometric** *adj.*

sociopathic personality see ANTISOCIAL PERSONALITY DISORDER.

sociopathy *n.* a former name for ANTISOCIAL PERSONALITY DISORDER.

sodium pump a membrane protein that uses energy to actively transport sodium ions out of a cell against their concentration gradient. The main sodium pump responsible for maintaining the RESTING POTENTIAL of animal cells, and hence the excitability of neurons and muscle cells, is called an **Na⁺/K⁺ ATPase**. In each cycle, this moves three sodium ions out of the cell, across the plasma membrane, in exchange for two potassium ions entering the cell, using energy derived from ATP.

soft determinism the position that all events, including human actions and choices, have causes, but that free will and responsibility are compatible with such DETERMINISM. Compare HARD DETERMINISM.

solipsism *n.* the philosophical position that one can be sure of the existence of nothing outside the self, as other people and things may be mere figments of one's own consciousness. The question posed by

S

solipsism has been put in various ways, but all arise from the fact that one's experience of one's own consciousness and identity is direct and unique, such that one is cut off from the same kind of experience of other minds and the things of the world. —**solipsist** *n.* —**solipsistic** *adj.*

solitary nucleus a collection of neural cell bodies in the medulla oblongata of the brainstem that relays information from the intermediate nerve (the sensory component of the FACIAL NERVE), GLOSSOPHARYNGEAL NERVE, and VAGUS NERVE. Gustatory neurons project from the solitary nucleus to control reflexes of acceptance or rejection, to anticipate digestive processes, and to activate higher levels of the taste system. Also called **nucleus of the solitary tract (NST)**.

soma *n.* see CELL BODY.

somatic *adj.* **1.** describing, relating to, or arising in the body as distinguished from the mind. For example, a **somatic disorder** is one involving a demonstrable abnormality in the structure or biochemistry of body tissues or organs. **2.** describing, relating to, or arising in cells of the body other than the sex cells or their precursors (i.e., germ-line cells). Hence, a **somatic mutation** cannot be transmitted to the offspring of the affected individual.

somatic hallucination the false perception of a physical occurrence within the body, such as feeling electric currents.

somatic nervous system the part of the nervous system comprising the sensory and motor neurons that innervate the sense organs and the skeletal muscles, as opposed to the AUTONOMIC NERVOUS SYSTEM.

somatic therapy the treatment of mental disorders by physical methods that directly influence the body,

such as the administration of drugs (PHARMACOTHERAPY) or the application of a controlled, low-dose electric current (ELECTROCONVULSIVE THERAPY). Also called **somatotherapy**.

somatization *n.* the expression of psychological disturbance in physical (bodily) symptoms.

somatization disorder a SOMATOFORM DISORDER involving a history of multiple physical symptoms of several years' duration, for which medical attention has been sought but which are apparently not due to any physical disorder or injury. The complaints often involve abdominal and other pain, nausea, diarrhea, sexual indifference and other difficulties, shortness of breath, palpitations, and apparent neurological symptoms (such as blurred vision).

somatoform disorder any of a group of disorders marked by physical symptoms suggesting a specific medical condition for which there is no demonstrable organic evidence and for which there is positive evidence or a strong probability that they are linked to psychological factors. The symptoms must cause marked distress or significantly impair normal social or occupational functioning. Somatoform disorders include BODY DYSMORPHIC DISORDER, CONVERSION DISORDER, HYPOCHONDRIASIS, PAIN DISORDER, and SOMATIZATION DISORDER.

somatosense *n.* any of the senses related to touch and position, including KINESTHESIS, the visceral sense (see VISCERA), and the CUTANEOUS senses. Also called **somatic sense**.

somatosensory area either of two main areas of the CEREBRAL CORTEX that respond to stimulation associated with touch, vibration, pain, temperature, and position (see

SOMATOSENSE). The PRIMARY
SOMATOSENSORY AREA is located
in the POSTCENTRAL GYRUS of the
anterior parietal lobe, and the SEC-
ONDARY SOMATOSENSORY AREA is
on the lateral surface of the parietal
lobe just dorsal to the LATERAL
SULCUS. Also called **somatosensory cortex**.

somatosensory system the parts
of the nervous system that serve perception of touch, vibration, pain,
temperature, and position (see
SOMATOSENSE). Nerve fibers from receptors for these senses enter the
dorsal roots of the spinal cord and
ascend to the thalamus, from which
they are relayed (directly or indirectly) to the SOMATOSENSORY
AREAS of the parietal cortex.

somatostatin *n.* a hormone that is
secreted by the hypothalamus and
inhibits the release of the growth
hormone (somatotropin) by the anterior pituitary gland. It is also
secreted by cells in the ISLETS OF
LANGERHANS in the pancreas, where
it inhibits the secretion of insulin
and glucagon.

somatotopic organization the
topographic distribution of areas of
the MOTOR CORTEX relating to specific activities of skeletal muscles, as
mapped by electrically stimulating a
point in the cortex and observing
associated movement of a skeletal
muscle in the face, the trunk, or a
limb.

somatotype *n.* the body build or
physique of a person, particularly as
it relates to his or her temperament
or behavioral characteristics. Numerous categories of somatotypes have
been proposed by various investigators since ancient times. The
classification of individuals in this
way is called **somatotypology**.

somnambulism *n.* see SLEEPWALK-
ING DISORDER.

S–O–R psychology stimulus–

organism–response psychology: an
extension of the S–R PSYCHOLOGY of
behaviorists incorporating the notion that biological or psychological
factors within the organism help determine what stimuli the organism
is sensitive to and which responses
may occur.

sound *n.* variations in pressure that
occur over time in an elastic medium, such as air or water. Sound
does not necessarily elicit an auditory sensation—infrasound and
ultrasound are respectively below
and above the audible range of humans—but in psychology sound
usually denotes a stimulus capable
of being heard by an organism.

sound localization see AUDITORY
LOCALIZATION.

source amnesia impaired memory
for how, when, or where information was learned despite good
memory for the information itself.
Source amnesia is often linked to
frontal lobe pathology.

source memory remembering the
origin of a memory or of knowledge,
that is, memory of where or how
one came to know what one now re-
members. More recently, this
construct has been expanded to encompass any aspects of context
associated with an event, including
spatial-temporal, perceptual, or affective attributes. Although the
PREFRONTAL CORTEX is known to be
involved in source memory, its
exact contribution remains uncertain. Additionally, evidence suggests
that processes used by young and
older adults may differ.

source monitoring determining
the origins of one's memories,
knowledge, or beliefs, for example,
whether an event was personally experienced, witnessed on television,
or overheard. Also called **reality
monitoring**.

spaced practice see DISTRIBUTED PRACTICE.

spasm *n.* a sudden, involuntary muscle contraction. It may be continuous or sustained (TONIC) or it may alternate between contraction and relaxation (CLONIC). A spasm may be restricted to a particular body part; for example, a vasospasm involves a blood vessel, and a bronchial spasm involves the bronchi. —**spasmodic** *adj.*

spastic *adj.* **1.** relating to SPASM. **2.** relating to increased muscle tension (see SPASTICITY).

spasticity *n.* a state of increased tension of resting muscles resulting in resistance to passive stretching. It is caused by damage to upper MOTOR NEURONS and is marked by muscular stiffness or inflexibility.

spatial attention the manner in which an individual distributes attention over the visual scene. Spatial attention is usually directed at the part of the scene on which a person fixates.

spatial memory the capacity to remember the position and location of objects or places, which may include orientation, direction, and distance. Spatial memory is essential for route learning and navigation.

spatial neglect a disorder in which individuals are unaware of a portion of their surrounding physical, personal, or extrapersonal space, usually on the left side. For example, if approached on the left side, an individual with spatial neglect may not notice the approaching person but would respond normally when approached on the right side.

spatial summation a neural mechanism in which an impulse is propagated by two or more POST-SYNAPTIC POTENTIALS occurring simultaneously at different synapses on the same neuron, when the discharge of a single synapse would not be sufficient to activate the neuron. Compare TEMPORAL SUMMATION.

spatial-temporal reasoning the ability to conceptualize the three-dimensional relationships of objects in space and to mentally manipulate them as a succession of transformations over a period of time. Spatial-temporal reasoning is a cognitive ability that plays an important role in such fields as architecture, engineering, and mathematics, among others, and in such basic tasks as everyday movement of the body through space.

speaking in tongues see GLOSSO-LALIA.

Spearman rank correlation coefficient (symbol: ρ) see RANK CORRELATION COEFFICIENT. [Charles Edward **Spearman** (1863–1945), British psychologist and psychometrician)]

special needs the requirements of individuals with physical, mental, or emotional disabilities or financial, community-related, or resource disadvantages. Special needs may include special education, training, or therapy.

speciesism *n.* discriminatory, prejudicial, or exploitative practices against nonhuman animals, often on the basis of an assumption of human superiority. —**speciesist** *n.*, *adj.*

species-specific behavior spontaneously developed behavior that is common to nearly all members of a particular species and expressed in essentially the same way. Human language is a prominent example.

specific factor (symbol: *s*) a specialized ability that is postulated to come into play in particular kinds of cognitive tasks. Specific factors, such as mathematical ability, are contrasted with the GENERAL FACTOR (*g*), which underlies every cognitive performance. Also called **special factor**.

specificity *n.* **1.** the quality of being unique, of a particular kind, or limited to a single phenomenon. For example, a stimulus that elicits a particular response or a symptom localized in a particular organ (e.g., the stomach) is said to have specificity. **2.** the probability that a test yields a negative diagnosis given that the individual does not have the condition for which he or she is being tested. Compare SENSITIVITY.

specific learning disability a substantial deficit in scholastic or academic skills that does not pervade all areas of learning but rather is limited to a particular aspect, for example, reading or arithmetic difficulty.

specific phobia an ANXIETY DISORDER, formerly called **simple phobia**, characterized by a marked and persistent fear of a specific object, activity, or situation (e.g., dogs, blood, flying, heights). The fear is excessive or unreasonable and is invariably triggered by the presence or anticipation of the feared object or situation; consequently, this is either avoided or endured with marked anxiety or distress.

spectrogram *n.* a quasi-three-dimensional representation of sound produced by analyzing a sound source (typically human speech) in terms of its variations in frequency and intensity over time.

spectrum *n.* (*pl.* **spectra**) a distribution of electromagnetic energy displayed by decreasing wavelength. In the case of the **visible spectrum**, it is the series of visible colors (with wavelengths in the range 400–700 nm) produced when white light is refracted through a prism. —**spectral** *adj.*

speech *n.* the product of oral–motor movement resulting in articulation of language expression: the utterance of sounds and words.

speech act an instance of the use of speech considered as an action, especially with regard to the speaker's intentions and the effect on a listener. A single utterance usually involves several simultaneous speech acts. The study of speech acts is part of the general field of PRAGMATICS.

speech and language disorder any disorder that affects verbal or written communication. A **speech disorder** is one that affects the production of speech, potentially including such problems as poor audibility or intelligibility; unpleasant tonal quality; unusual, distorted, or abnormally effortful sound production; lack of conventional rhythm and stress; and inappropriateness in terms of age or physical or mental development. A **language disorder** is one that affects the expression or reception (comprehension) of ideas and feelings, potentially including such problems as reduced vocabulary, omissions of articles and modifiers, understanding of nouns but not verbs, difficulties following oral instructions, and syntactical errors. While speech disorders and language disorders are two distinct entities, they often occur together and thus generally are referred to together.

speech and language therapy the application of remedies, treatment, and counseling for the improvement of verbal or written communication.

speech area any of the areas of the cerebral cortex that are associated with verbal (oral, rather than written) communication. The speech areas are located in the left hemisphere in most individuals; they include BROCA'S AREA in the third convolution of the frontal lobe and

S

WERNICKE'S AREA in the temporal lobe.

speech perception the process in which a listener decodes, combines, and converts into a meaningful sequence and phonological representation an incoming stream of otherwise meaningless sound.

speed test a type of test intended to calculate the number of problems or tasks the participant can solve or perform in a predesignated block of time. The participant is often, but not always, made aware of the time limit. Compare POWER TEST.

spelling dyslexia see WORD-FORM DYSLEXIA.

spermatogenesis *n.* the process of production of spermatozoa in the seminiferous tubules of the TESTIS. Male germ cells (spermatogonia) lining the seminiferous tubules mature into primary spermatocytes, which undergo MEIOSIS. In the first meiotic division, each primary spermatocyte gives rise to two HAPLOID secondary spermatocytes, each of which then undergoes a further division to form two spermatids. The latter, attached to protective, nourishing Sertoli cells, mature into spermatozoa. —**spermatogenetic** *adj.*

spermatozoon *n.* (*pl.* **spermatozoa**) a single male GAMETE that develops from a secondary spermatocyte following its development from spermatogonia of the seminiferous tubules. A spermatozoon fuses with a female gamete (see OVUM) in the process of fertilization. Also called **sperm**. See also SPERMATOGENESIS.

spherical aberration see ABERRATION.

sphericity *n.* an assumption encountered in the analysis of data obtained when individuals are measured on two or more occasions that requires the correlation among the

time points to be constant for all time points. See WITHIN-SUBJECTS DESIGN.

spinal column the backbone, consisting of a series of bones (vertebrae) connected by disks of cartilage (intervertebral disks) and held together by muscles and tendons. It extends from the cranium to the coccyx, encloses the spinal cord, and forms the main axis of the body. Also called **spine**.

spinal cord the part of the CENTRAL NERVOUS SYSTEM that extends from the lower end of the MEDULLA OBLONGATA, at the base of the brain, through a canal in the center of the spine as far as the lumbar region. In transverse section, the cord consists of an H-shaped core of gray matter surrounded by white matter consisting of tracts of long ascending and descending nerve fibers on either side of the cord that are linked by a bundle of myelinated fibers called the **white commissure**. The spinal cord is enveloped by the MENINGES and is the origin of the 31 pairs of SPINAL NERVES. See also SPINAL ROOT.

spinal nerve any of the 31 pairs of nerves that originate in the gray matter of the SPINAL CORD and emerge through openings between the vertebrae of the spine to extend into the body's dermatomes (skin areas) and skeletal muscles. The spinal nerves comprise 8 cervical nerves, 12 thoracic nerves, 5 lumbar nerves, 5 sacral nerves, and 1 coccygeal nerve. Each attaches to the spinal cord via two short branches, a DORSAL ROOT and a VENTRAL ROOT. See also SPINAL ROOT.

spinal root the junction of a SPINAL NERVE and the SPINAL CORD. Near the cord, each spinal nerve divides into a DORSAL ROOT, carrying sensory fibers, and a VENTRAL ROOT, carrying motor fibers, as stated by the BELL–MAGENDIE LAW.

spiral ganglion the mass of cell bodies on the inner wall of the CO-CHLEA, near the organ of Corti, whose axons form the AUDITORY NERVE.

splanchnic nerve any of certain nerves that serve the abdominal VIS-CERA. They originate in the ganglia of the SYMPATHETIC CHAIN.

split brain a brain in which the cerebral hemispheres have been separated by severence of the corpus callosum (see COMMISSUROTOMY). Surgical transection of the corpus callosum is used to create split-brain animals for experimental purposes and is also occasionally performed on humans to alleviate some forms of severe epilepsy.

split-half reliability a measure of the ability of a test to measure an attribute consistently, obtained by correlating scores on one half of the test with scores on the other half.

split personality a lay term for an individual with DISSOCIATIVE IDEN-TITY DISORDER. It is sometimes confused with SCHIZOPHRENIA, which means literally "splitting of the mind" but does not involve the formation of a second personality.

split-span test a test in which brief auditory messages in the form of two different lists of digits or words are presented rapidly and simultaneously, one list to each ear. Participants are required to report as many digits or words as possible in any order. Typically, participants report first the stimuli presented to one ear, then those presented to the other.

spontaneous abortion see ABOR-TION.

spontaneous recovery the reappearance of a conditioned response, after either operant or Pavlovian conditioning, after it has been ex-

perimentally extinguished (see EX-TINCTION).

spontaneous remission a reduction or disappearance of symptoms without any therapeutic intervention, which may be temporary or permanent. It most commonly refers to medical, rather than psychological, conditions.

spoonerism *n.* a SLIP OF THE TONGUE in which two sound elements (usually initial consonants) are unintentionally transposed, resulting in an utterance with a different and often amusing sense, for example, *sons of toil* for *tons of soil*. [W. A. **Spooner** (1844–1930), British academic noted for slips of this kind]

sport and exercise psychology the application and development of psychological theory for the understanding and modification or enhancement of human behavior in the sport and physical exercise environment. This discipline evolved from an exclusive focus on sport performance and historically has been called **sport psychology**. However, health and well-being through regular participation in vigorous physical activity programs have become of increasing interest to consumers, researchers, and practitioners to such an extent that the field is progressively becoming two separate disciplines as **exercise psychology** merges with HEALTH PSYCHOLOGY.

spread *n.* see DISPERSION.

spreading activation 1. in neuroscience, a hypothetical process in which the activation of one neuron is presumed to spread to connected neurons, making it more likely that they will fire. **2.** in cognitive psychology, an analogous model for the association of ideas, memories, and the like, based on the notion that activation of one item stored in

S

memory travels through associated links to activate another item. Spreading activation is a feature of some CONNECTIONIST MODELS of memory.

SQ3R one of a variety of study methods developed on the basis of research in cognitive psychology. The formula represents a method for enhanced learning of reading material. It consists of five steps: *s*urvey, *q*uestion, *r*ead, *r*ecite, and *r*eview.

SRI abbreviation for serotonin reuptake inhibitor. See SSRI.

S–R psychology an approach to psychology that conceptualizes behavior in terms of *s*timulus and *r*esponse. The fundamental goal is therefore describing functional relationships between stimulus and response, that is, manipulating a stimulus and observing the response. **S–R theories** are sometimes contrasted with cognitive theories of learning.

SSRI *s*elective *s*erotonin *r*euptake *i*nhibitor: any of a class of antidepressants that act by blocking the reuptake of serotonin into serotonin-containing presynaptic neurons in the central nervous system. SSRIs have less adverse side effects than the TRICYCLIC ANTIDEPRESSANTS and the MONOAMINE OXIDASE INHIBITORS; common side effects include nausea, headache, anxiety, and tremor. SSRIs include FLUOXETINE, paroxetine, sertraline, citalopram, and fluvoxamine. Also called **SRI** (**serotonin reuptake inhibitor**).

stability *n.* the absence of variation, as applied, for example, to personality (few emotional or mood changes) or testing (invariance of measurements).

stabilized image an image on the retina that does not move when the eye is moved. A stabilized image will fade rapidly since neurons in the visual system are sensitive to change rather than to maintained stimulation. Even during visual FIXATION images are normally not truly stabilized, because very small eye movements (microsaccades) continually refresh the stimulation of the retina by moving the eyes relative to a target.

stage *n.* a relatively discrete period of time in which functioning is qualitatively different from functioning at other periods.

stages of grief a hypothetical model depicting psychological states, moods, or coping strategies that occur during the dying process or during periods of BEREAVEMENT, great loss, or TRAUMA. These begin with the **denial stage**, followed by the **anger stage**, **bargaining stage**, **depression stage**, and **acceptance stage**. The stages do not necessarily occur for a set period of time; moreover, they can recur and overlap before some degree of psychological and emotional resolution occurs.

stage theory any hypothetical construct that attempts to describe phases, or steps, in a process that occurs over time. Examples in psychology abound, including Sigmund Freud's stages of PSYCHOSEXUAL DEVELOPMENT and Jean Piaget's stages of cognitive development (see PIAGETIAN THEORY). See also STAGES OF GRIEF.

staircase method a variation of the METHOD OF LIMITS in which stimuli are presented in ascending and descending order. When the observer's response changes, the direction of the stimulus sequence is reversed. This method is efficient because it does not present stimuli that are well above or below threshold.

stalking *n.* a repeated pattern of following or observing a person in an obsessional, intrusive, or harassing manner. Often associated with a failed relationship with the one pursued, stalking may involve direct threats, the intent to cause distress or bodily harm, and interpersonal violence.

standard *n.* any positive idea about how things might be, such as an ideal, norm, value, expectation, or previous performance, that is used to measure and judge the way things are. Evaluation of the self is often based on comparing the current reality (or perceptions of the current reality) against one or more standards.

standard deviation (symbol: *SD*) a measure of the dispersion of a set of scores, indicating how narrowly or broadly they are distributed around the MEAN. It is equal to the square root of the VARIANCE.

standard error a measure of the potential for error inherent to calculating a particular value using a subset of a population. It is equal to the standard deviation of the distribution of values within the sample divided by the size of a sample. For example, the **standard error of the mean** is equal to $\sigma/\sqrt{n}$, where σ is the standard deviation from the mean for the values within the sample and *n* is the sample size.

standard error of estimate a measure of the degree to which a REGRESSION LINE fits a set of data. If y' is an estimated value from a regression line and y is the actual value, then the standard error of estimate is $\sqrt{[\Sigma(y - y')^2/n]}$, where *n* is the number of points.

standard error of measurement (symbol: *SEM*) in measurement theory, the error in estimating true scores from observed scores.

standardization *n.* the process of establishing NORMS or uniform procedures for a test.

standardized test a test whose VALIDITY and RELIABILITY have been established by thorough empirical investigation and analysis and which has clearly defined norms.

standard score a score obtained from an original score by subtracting the mean value of all scores in the batch and dividing by the standard deviation of the batch. This conversion from raw scores to standard scores allows comparisons to be made between measurements on different scales. A standard score is often given the symbol *z* and is sometimes referred to as a **z score**.

standard stimulus a stimulus used as the basis of comparison for other stimuli in an experiment, for example, in comparing loud sounds to a sound of a given intensity.

Stanford–Binet Intelligence Scale (**SB**) a standardized assessment of intelligence and cognitive abilities, particularly fluid reasoning, knowledge, quantitative reasoning, visual-spatial processing, and working memory. The Stanford–Binet test was so named because it was brought to the United States by U.S. psychologist Lewis M. Terman (1877–1956), a professor at Stanford University, in 1916, as a revision and extension of the original **Binet–Simon Scale** (the first modern intelligence test) developed in 1905 by French psychologist Alfred Binet (1857–1911) and French physician Théodore Simon (1873–1961) to assess the intellectual ability of French children.

Stanford prison experiment a highly controversial 1971 study of the psychological effects of becoming a prisoner or a prison guard, conducted by a research team under the direction of U.S. psychologist Philip G. Zimbardo (1933–). The paid-volunteer participants—both "prisoners" and "guards"—were 24 mostly white male and middle-class

S

undergraduate students. Prisoners were "arrested" and "incarcerated" in a simulated jail in the basement of the building housing the psychology department at Stanford University. A variety of methods and situations were used to depersonalize participants, diminish their sense of identity, and increase a sense of power on the one hand (guards) and powerlessness on the other (prisoners). The experiment was terminated after only 6 days of the originally scheduled 14, because of Zimbardo's realization that it had far exceeded the extent of behavior that was predicted and had led to emotionally and psychologically damaging outcomes; several of the guards were seen to exhibit sadistic tendencies in their treatment of prisoners, and several of the prisoners showed physical manifestations of stress and psychological trauma. Apart from ethical considerations, the study was criticized as methodologically flawed and invalid from multiple perspectives, including the small size of the sample, lack of ECOLOGICAL VALIDITY, and lack of sufficient controls. Nonetheless, the Stanford prison experiment is often cited as a demonstration of the way in which social contexts can influence, alter, shape, and transform human behavior.

stapes *n.* (*pl.* **stapedes**) see OSSI-CLES.

startle response an unlearned, involuntary response to unexpected, intense stimuli (loud noises, flashing lights, etc.). This response includes behaviors that serve a protective function, such as closing the eyes, lowering the head, and hunching the shoulders.

state *n.* the condition or status of an entity or person at a particular time.

state-dependent learning learning that occurs in a particular

biological or psychological state and is better recalled when the individual is subsequently in the same state. For example, an animal trained to run a maze while under the influence of a psychoactive drug (e.g., pentobarbital) may not run it successfully without the drug.

state-dependent memory a condition in which memory for a past event is improved when the person is in the same biological or psychological state as when the memory was initially formed. Thus, alcohol may improve recall of events experienced when previously under the influence of alcohol. See also MOOD-DEPENDENT MEMORY.

statistic *n.* any function of the observations in a set of data. Statistics may be used to describe a batch of data, to estimate parameters in optimal ways, or to test hypotheses.

statistical analysis examination of data through the use of probabilistic models in order to make inferences and draw conclusions.

statistical significance the degree to which a result cannot reasonably be attributed to the operation of chance or random factors alone.

statistical test a specific mathematical technique used to test the correctness of an empirical hypothesis. See HYPOTHESIS TESTING.

statistics *n.* the branch of mathematics that uses data descriptively or inferentially to find or support answers for scientific and other quantifiable questions. —**statistical** *adj.* —**statistician** *n.*

status *n.* **1.** the standing or position of an individual or group relative to others, for example, an individual's SOCIAL STATUS. **2.** a persistent condition, as in **status epilepticus**, a continuous series of seizures.

STD abbreviation for SEXUALLY TRANSMITTED DISEASE.

steady state a condition of stability or equilibrium. For example, in behavioral studies it is a state in which behavior is practically the same over repeated observations in a particular context. In pharmacology, it refers to a state in the body in which the amount of a drug administered is equal to that excreted.

stem-and-leaf plot a graphical method for the display of data that resembles a HISTOGRAM but carries more detailed information about the values of the data points.

stem cell a cell that is itself undifferentiated but can divide to produce one or more types of specialized tissue cells (e.g., blood cells, nerve cells). Stem cells are found in embryos (embryonic stem cells) but also occur in adults as tissue stem cells. Adult and embryonic stem cell research have the potential for changing treatment of disease through use of the cells to repair specific tissues; however, the ethics of the latter are the subject of intense debate.

stenosis *n.* the abnormal narrowing of a body conduit or passage. For example, **carotid stenosis** is narrowing of a carotid artery (e.g., by atherosclerosis) in the neck, which limits blood flow to the brain. —**stenotic** *adj.*

stepfamily *n.* a family unit formed by the union of parents one or both of whom brings a child or children from a previous union (or unions) into the new household. Also called **blended family**.

stepwise regression a group of regression techniques that enter predictor (independent) variables into (or delete them from) the REGRESSION EQUATION one variable (or block of variables) at a time according to some predefined criterion.

stereocilia *pl. n.* see HAIR CELL.

stereogram *n.* a picture perceived to have depth because it is produced by the binocular summation of two separate images of the same scene, each image slightly offset from the other in the horizontal plane. Although a **stereoscope** is commonly used to view the images, some observers can fuse the two images by simply crossing or uncrossing their eyes.

stereopsis *n.* DEPTH PERCEPTION provided by means of the BINOCULAR DISPARITY of the images in the two eyes.

stereotaxy *n.* determination of the exact location of a specific structure within the brain by means of three-dimensional measurements. Stereotaxy is used for positioning MICROELECTRODES, cannulas (small tubes), or other devices in the brain for diagnostic, experimental, or therapeutic purposes and for locating an area of the brain prior to surgery. —**stereotactic** or **stereotaxic** *adj.*

stereotype *n.* a set of cognitive generalizations (e.g., beliefs, expectations) about the qualities and characteristics of the members of a particular group or social category. Stereotypes simplify and expedite perceptions and judgments, but they are often exaggerated, negative rather than positive, and resistant to revision even when perceivers encounter individuals with qualities that are not congruent with the stereotype (see PREJUDICE). —**stereotypic** *adj.*

stereotype threat an individual's expectation that negative stereotypes about his or her member group will adversely influence others' judgments of his or her performance. This expectation may in turn undermine the individual's actual ability to perform well.

S

stereotypy *n.* persistent repetition of the same words, movements, or other behavior, particularly as a symptom of disorder (e.g., autism, obsessive-compulsive disorder, schizophrenia).

steroid hormone any of a class of hormones whose molecular structure is based on the steroid nucleus of four interconnected rings of carbon atoms. Examples include the SEX HORMONES and CORTICO-STEROIDS.

Stevens law a psychophysical relationship stating that the psychological magnitude of a sensation is proportional to a power of the stimulus producing it. This can be expressed as $\psi = ks^n$, where ψ is the sensation, k is a constant of proportionality, s is the stimulus magnitude, and n is a function of the particular stimulus. Also called **Stevens power law**. See also FECHNER'S LAW; WEBER'S LAW. [Stanley Smith **Stevens** (1906–1973), U.S. psychophysicist]

stigma *n.* the negative social attitude attached to a characteristic of an individual that may be regarded as a mental, physical, or social deficiency. A stigma implies social disapproval and can lead unfairly to discrimination against and exclusion of the individual.

stimulant *n.* any of various agents that excite functional activity in an organism or in a part of an organism. Stimulants are usually classified according to the body system or function excited (e.g., cardiac stimulants, respiratory stimulants). In psychology, the term usually refers to the central nervous system stimulants (or psychostimulants).

stimulation *n.* the act or process of increasing the level of activity of an organism, particularly that of evoking heightened activity in (eliciting

a response from) a sensory receptor, neuron, or other bodily tissue.

stimulus *n.* (*pl.* **stimuli**) **1.** any agent, event, or situation—internal or external—that elicits a response from an organism. See CONDITIONED STIMULUS; UNCONDITIONED STIMULUS. **2.** any change in physical energy that activates a sensory RECEPTOR. See DISTAL STIMULUS; PROXIMAL STIMULUS.

stimulus control the extent to which behavior is influenced by different stimulus conditions. It can refer to different responses occurring in the presence of different stimuli or to differences in the rate, temporal organization, or physical characteristics of a single response in the presence of different stimuli.

stimulus discrimination the ability to distinguish among different stimuli (e.g., to distinguish a circle from an ellipse) and to respond differently in the presence of such.

stimulus generalization the spread of effects of conditioning (either operant or Pavlovian) to stimuli that differ in certain aspects from the stimulus present during original conditioning. For example, a dog conditioned to bark when a particular bell sounds tends to bark to bells of any pitch.

stimulus onset asynchrony the time between the onset of one stimulus and the onset of the following stimulus. The term is used mainly in experiments with MASKING.

stimulus overload the condition in which the environment presents too many stimuli to be comfortably processed, resulting in stress and behavior designed to restore equilibrium.

STM abbreviation for SHORT-TERM MEMORY.

stop-signal task a procedure used

in choice-reaction tasks in which a signal instructing the participant to withhold the response is presented on some trials at varying intervals after presentation of the stimulus. This is done to determine at what point in processing a response can no longer be inhibited.

storage *n.* the state of an item that is retained in memory, after ENCODING and before RETRIEVAL. See also RETENTION.

storytelling *n.* **1.** the recounting by a client of the events, concerns, and problems that led him or her to seek treatment. Therapists can learn much about the motives and origins of conflicts by attending carefully (see ACTIVE LISTENING) to the stories that clients bring to the session. **2.** the use of symbolic talk and allegorical stories by the therapist to aid the client's understanding of issues. Also called **therapeutic storytelling**.

strabismus *n.* any chronic abnormal alignment of the eyes. Because strabismic eyes look in different directions, they give the brain conflicting messages, which may result in double vision or the suppression by the brain of one eye's view altogether. The most common form of strabismus occurs horizontally: One or both eyes deviate inward (convergent strabismus) or outward (divergent strabismus). **—strabismic** *adj.*

stranger anxiety the distress and apprehension experienced by young children when they are around individuals who are unfamiliar to them. Stranger anxiety is a normal part of cognitive development: Babies differentiate caregivers from other people and display a strong preference for familiar faces. Stranger anxiety usually begins around 8 or 9 months of age and typically lasts into the 2nd year.

Strange Situation an experimental technique used to assess quality of ATTACHMENT in infants and young children (up to the age of 2). The procedure subjects the child to increasing amounts of stress induced by a strange setting, the entrance of an unfamiliar person, and two brief separations from the parent. The reaction of the child to each of these situations is used to evaluate the security or insecurity of his or her attachment to the parent.

stratification *n.* arrangement into a layered configuration, as for example in SOCIAL STRATIFICATION. **—stratify** *vb.*

stratified sampling a technique in which a population is divided into subdivisions (strata) and individuals or cases are selected for study from each strata. The sample obtained (called a **stratified sample**) thus includes a number of individuals representing each stratum (e.g., young and old or men and women), the goal being to reproduce as accurately as possible their proportional representation in the population of interest. Typically, RANDOM SAMPLING is used to select the cases from each stratum, in which case the technique is referred to as **stratified random sampling**.

stream of consciousness the concept of consciousness as a continuous, dynamic flow of ideas and images rather than a static series of discrete components. It emphasizes the subjective quality of conscious experience as a never-ending and never-repeating stream.

strength of association in statistics, the degree of relationship between two or more variables. Common measures are OMEGA SQUARED and the CORRELATION COEFFICIENT.

stress *n.* a state of physiological or psychological response to internal

S

or external forces or events, involving changes affecting nearly every system of the body. For example, it may be manifested by palpitations, sweating, dry mouth, shortness of breath, fidgeting, faster speech, augmentation of negative emotions (if already being experienced), and longer duration of fatigue. Severe stress is manifested by the GENERAL ADAPTATION SYNDROME. By causing these mind–body changes, stress contributes directly to psychological and physiological disorder and disease and affects mental and physical health, reducing the quality of life.

stress-inoculation training a four-phase training program for stress management often used in COGNITIVE BEHAVIOR THERAPY. Phase 1 entails the identification of reactions to stress and their effects on functioning and psychological well-being; phase 2 involves learning relaxation and self-regulation techniques; phase 3 consists of learning coping self-statements; phase 4 involves assisted progression through a series of increasingly stressful situations using imagery, video, role playing, and real-life situations until the individual is eventually able to cope with the original stress-inducing situation or event.

stress management the use of specific techniques, strategies, or programs—such as relaxation training, anticipation of stress reactions, and breathing techniques—for dealing with stress-inducing situations and the state of being stressed.

stressor *n.* any event, force, or condition that results in physical or emotional stress. Stressors may be internal or external forces that require adjustment or COPING STRATEGIES on the part of the affected individual.

stretch reflex the contraction of a muscle in response to stretching of that muscle. Stretch reflexes support the body against the pull of gravity.

striate cortex (**V1**) the first region of the cerebral cortex that receives visual input from the thalamus, particularly from the LATERAL GENICULATE NUCLEUS. The striate cortex is located in the occipital lobe and contains a dense band of myelinated fibers that appears as a white stripe (stripe of Gennari). Neurons in the striate cortex project to visual areas in the PRESTRIATE CORTEX and to subcortical visual nuclei. Also called **primary visual cortex**.

striated muscle see SKELETAL MUSCLE.

striatum *n.* see BASAL GANGLIA.

stroboscopic illusion 1. the apparent motion of a series of separate stimuli occurring in close consecutive order, as in motion pictures. **2.** the apparent lack of motion or reverse motion of a moving object, such as a rotating fan, produced by illuminating it with a series of intermittent light flashes. Also called **stroboscopic effect**.

stroke *n.* disruption of blood flow to the brain, which deprives the tissue of oxygen and nutrients, causing tissue damage and loss of normal function and, potentially, tissue death. A stroke may result from massive bleeding into brain tissue (hemorrhagic stroke); an embolism (obstructing material) or thrombus (blood clot) blocking an artery in the brain (embolic stroke or thrombotic stroke); or multiple small areas of brain tissue death from occlusion of small branches of the cerebral arteries (lacunar stroke). This term is often used interchangeably with CEREBROVASCULAR ACCIDENT. See also TRANSIENT ISCHEMIC ATTACK.

Stroop Color–Word Interference Test a three-part test in which (a) color names are read as fast as possible; (b) the colors of bars or other shapes are rapidly named; and, most importantly, (c) color hues are named quickly when used to print the names of other colors (such as the word *green* printed in the color red). The degree to which the participants are subject to interference by the printed words is a measure of their cognitive flexibility and selective attention. Also called **Stroop test**. [John Ridley **Stroop** (1897–1973), U.S. psychologist]

Stroop effect the finding that the time it takes a participant to name the color of ink in which a word is printed is longer for words that denote incongruent color names than for neutral words or for words that denote a congruent color. For example, if the word *blue* is written in red ink (incongruent), participants take longer to say "red" than if the word *glue* is written in red ink (neutral) or if the word *red* is written in red ink (congruent). See STROOP COLOR–WORD INTERFERENCE TEST. [John Stroop]

structural equation modeling (**SEM**) a statistical modeling technique that includes LATENT VARIABLES as causal elements. SEM is an advanced statistical method for testing causal models involving constructs that cannot be directly measured but are, rather, approximated through several measures presumed to assess part of the given construct.

structural family therapy a type of FAMILY THERAPY that assesses the subsystems, boundaries, hierarchies, and coalitions within a family (its structure) and focuses upon direct interactions between the family members (enactment) as the primary method of inducing positive change. Structural family therapy assumes the competence and uniqueness of families with problems, stressing that when ap-

propriately induced to do so families will discover their own alternatives to their ineffective patterns of relating to one another and that this process of discovery cannot proceed in a specific predetermined form but instead can only be directed toward a fairly well-defined area of functioning. For example, a structural family therapist working with a family whose daughter is anorexic would examine such family issues as the framework of authority, the rules that govern the assumption of roles, the various functions members perform, and the coalitions created by the bonding of certain family members, and then encourage the mother, daughter, and father to use this information to develop more productive patterns of functioning.

structuralism *n.* **1.** a movement considered to be the first school of psychology as a science, independent of philosophy. Usually attributed to German psychologist and physiologist Wilhelm Wundt (1832–1920), but probably more directly influenced by British-born U.S. psychologist Edward Bradford Titchener (1867–1927), structuralism defined psychology as the study of mental experience and sought to investigate the structure of such experience through a systematic program of experiments based on trained INTROSPECTION. **2.** a movement in various disciplines that study human behavior and culture that took its impetus from the radically new approach to linguistic analysis pioneered by Swiss linguist Ferdinand de Saussure (1857–1913). He maintained that linguistic SIGNS acquire meaning not through their relationships to external referents but through their structural relationships to other signs in the same system. The structuralist model of language was extended to cover essentially all social and cultural

S

phenomena, including human thought and action, in the work of French anthropologist Claude Lévi-Strauss (1908–). Structuralist explanations play down individual autonomy and agency, positivistic science, and linear-time causation in favor of explanations in terms of structural and systemic influences operating in the present to produce rule-governed behavior, the true nature of which can be revealed as the underlying structures are revealed. See also POSTSTRUCTURALISM.

structural model see STRUCTURAL EQUATION MODELING.

structured interview an interview consisting of a predetermined set of questions or topics. Structured interviews are popular in marketing research, personnel selection, and other fields. Compare UNSTRUCTURED INTERVIEW.

structured observation any of various methods for measuring overt behaviors and interpersonal processes that require that each observed unit of action be classified into an objectively defined category. INTERACTION-PROCESS ANALYSIS is an example.

Student's t distribution see T DISTRIBUTION. [**Student**, pseudonym of William S. Gosset (1876–1937), British statistician]

study *n.* **1.** any research investigation, but particularly a project, such as a survey or systematic observation, that is less rigorously controlled than a true EXPERIMENT. **2.** any attempt to acquire and remember information.

stupor *n.* a state of lethargy and impaired consciousness, in which an individual is unresponsive and immobile and experiences DISORIENTATION.

stuttering *n.* a disturbance in the normal fluency and time patterning of speech. It is characterized by frequent repetition or prolongation of sounds, syllables, or words, with hesitations and pauses that disrupt speech, particularly in situations where communication is important or stressful. —**stutter** *vb.*, *n.*

style *n.* a typically stable characteristic mode or manner of expressing oneself or acting. Various psychological researchers have examined particular areas of human activity to identify and classify modal differences, as for example in COGNITIVE STYLE and LEADERSHIP STYLE.

subconscious 1. *adj.* denoting mental processes that occur outside consciousness but can easily be brought into awareness. **2.** *n.* in the conceptualization of Austrian psychiatrist Sigmund Freud (1856–1939), the concept of the mind beneath the level of consciousness, comprising the PRECONSCIOUS.

subcortical *adj.* relating to structures or processes in the brain that are located or take place beneath the CEREBRAL CORTEX. For example, a **subcortical center** is any region of the brain at a level below the cerebral cortex that has a particular function or functions (e.g., the THALAMUS, HYPOTHALAMUS, and BASAL GANGLIA).

subculture *n.* a group that maintains a characteristic set of customs, interests, or beliefs that serve to distinguish it from the larger culture in which the members live. See also COUNTERCULTURE. —**subcultural** *adj.*

subfornical organ a structure in the brain that is responsive to ANGIOTENSIN II and contributes to thirst and drinking behavior. It is located below the FORNIX.

subitize *vb.* to perceive at a glance how many objects are presented, without counting. [from Latin *subito*, "at once"]

subject *n.* the individual human or nonhuman animal that takes part in an experiment or research study and whose responses or performance are reported or evaluated. PARTICIPANT is now often the preferred term for human subjects, because the word "subject" is depersonalizing and implies passivity and submissiveness on the part of the experimentee.

subjective *adj.* **1.** taking place or existing only within the mind and thus intrinsically inaccessible to the experience or observation of others. **2.** based on or influenced by personal feelings, interpretations, or prejudices. Compare OBJECTIVE.

subjective contour an edge or border perceived in an image as a result of the inference of the observer. A common example is the Kanizsa triangle, which is induced by three black circles—each with a 60° wedge removed—placed as the apexes of a triangle.

subjective test an assessment tool that is scored according to personal judgment or to standards that are less systematic than those used in OBJECTIVE TESTS, as in an essay examination.

subjective well-being a judgment that people make about the overall quality of their lives by summing emotional ups and downs to determine how well their actual life circumstances match their wishes or expectations concerning how they should or might feel.

subjectivity *n.* in empirical research, the failure to attain proper standards of OBJECTIVITY, such that data are interpreted or judgments are made in the light of personal feelings, beliefs, or experiences.

subject variable a variable of individual differences in a study (e.g., the participant's sex or occupation). A variable of this type is neither manipulated by the experimenter, as an INDEPENDENT VARIABLE might be, nor is it usually changed in the course of the experiment, as a DEPENDENT VARIABLE might be.

sublimation *n.* in psychoanalytic theory, a DEFENSE MECHANISM in which unacceptable sexual or aggressive drives are unconsciously channeled into socially acceptable modes of expression. For example, an exhibitionistic impulse may gain a new outlet in choreography. As well as allowing for substitute satisfactions, such outlets are posited to protect individuals from the anxiety induced by the original drive. —**sublimate** *vb.*

subliminal *adj.* denoting or relating to stimuli that are below the threshold of awareness. —**subliminally** *adv.*

subliminal perception the registration of stimuli below the level of awareness, particularly stimuli that are too weak (or too rapid) to affect the individual on a conscious level. It is questionable whether responses to subliminal stimuli actually occur and whether it is possible for subliminal commands or advertising messages to influence behavior.

subscale *n.* a SCALE that taps some specific constituent or otherwise differentiated category of information as part of a larger, overall scheme. For example, the WECHSLER ADULT INTELLIGENCE SCALE consists of 14 subscales (or subtests) assessing various verbal and performance dimensions, which in combination yield a verbal IQ score, a performance IQ score, and an overall IQ score.

substance *n.* **1.** in psychopathology, a drug or a toxin that is capable of producing intoxicating or harmful effects when ingested or otherwise taken into the body. **2.** in philosophy, that which has an independent, self-sufficient existence and remains unalterably itself even though its attributes or properties may change. Philosophers have differed over what qualifies as a substance and whether reality consists of a single substance (see MONISM) or more (see DUALISM).

substance abuse a pattern of compulsive substance use manifested by recurrent significant social, occupational, legal, or interpersonal adverse consequences, such as repeated absences from work or school, arrests, and marital difficulties. DSM–IV–TR identifies nine drug classes associated with abuse: alcohol, amphetamines, cannabis, cocaine, hallucinogens, inhalants, opioids, phencyclidines, and sedatives, hypnotics, or anxiolytics. This diagnosis is preempted by the diagnosis of SUBSTANCE DEPENDENCE: If the criteria for substance abuse and substance dependence are both met, only the latter diagnosis is given.

substance dependence a cluster of cognitive, behavioral, and physiological symptoms indicating continued use of a substance despite significant substance-related problems. There is a pattern of repeated substance ingestion resulting in tolerance, withdrawal symptoms if use is suspended, and an uncontrollable drive to continue use. DSM–IV–TR identifies 10 drug classes associated with dependence: alcohol, amphetamines, cannabis, cocaine, hallucinogens, inhalants, nicotine, opioids, phencyclidines, and sedatives, hypnotics, or anxiolytics. This term currently is preferred over the equivalent ADDICTION. See also SUBSTANCE ABUSE.

substance intoxication a reversible syndrome due to the recent ingestion of a specific substance, including clinically significant behavioral or psychological changes, as well as one or more signs of physiological involvement. Although

symptoms vary by substance there are some common manifestations, for example, perceptual disturbances; mood changes; impairments of judgment, attention and memory; alterations of heartbeat and vision; and speech and coordination difficulties.

substance P a NEUROPEPTIDE found in the DORSAL HORN of the spinal cord, where it plays a role in the modulation of pain, and in peripheral nervous system tissues, where it acts as a vasodilator. Substance P also has a role in sexual behavior and has been implicated in the regulation of mood.

substance-related disorder any of various disorders caused by the effects of a drug or a toxin. This DSM–IV–TR category encompasses the substance use disorders (substance abuse and substance dependence) and the substance-induced disorders (e.g., intoxication).

substance withdrawal a syndrome that develops after cessation of prolonged, heavy consumption of a substance. Symptoms vary by substance but generally include physiological, behavioral, and cognitive manifestations, such as nausea and vomiting, insomnia, mood alterations, and anxiety. DSM–IV–TR identifies six drug classes associated with withdrawal: alcohol, amphetamines, cocaine, nicotine, opioids, and sedatives, hypnotics, or anxiolytics.

substantia gelatinosa a gelatinous-appearing mass of extensively interconnected small neurons at the tip of the DORSAL HORN of the spinal cord. Some cells in the substantia gelatinosa contain ENDORPHINS and are involved in regulation of pain.

substantia nigra a region of gray matter in the midbrain, named for its dark pigmentation, that sends

DOPAMINERGIC neurons to the BASAL GANGLIA. Depletion of dopaminergic neurons in this region is implicated in PARKINSON'S DISEASE.

substitution *n.* in psychoanalytic theory, the replacement of unacceptable emotions or unattainable goals with alternative satisfactions or feelings. Substitution may be viewed as a positive adaptation or solution (e.g., adoption when one cannot have a child of one's own) or as a negative, maladaptive response (e.g., emotional eating after a frustrating day at the office). See also DEFENSE MECHANISM.

subthalamic nucleus a part of the subthalamus that receives fibers from the GLOBUS PALLIDUS as a part of the descending pathway from the BASAL GANGLIA.

subthalamus *n.* a part of the DIENCEPHALON of the brain, wedged between the THALAMUS and the HYPOTHALAMUS. It contains the subthalamic nucleus and functions in the regulation of movements controlled by skeletal muscles, together with the BASAL GANGLIA and the SUBSTANTIA NIGRA. **—subthalamic** *adj.*

successive approximations see SHAPING.

sudden infant death syndrome (**SIDS**) the sudden and unexpected death of a seemingly healthy infant during sleep for no apparent reason. The risk of SIDS is greatest between 2 and 6 months of age and is a common cause of death in babies less than 1 year old.

suffering *n.* the experience of pain or acute distress, either psychological or physical, in response to a significant event, particularly one that is threatening or involves loss (e.g., the death of a loved one) or a physical trauma.

suggestibility *n.* a state in which the ideas, beliefs, attitudes, or actions of others are readily and uncritically adopted.

suicidal ideation suicidal thoughts or a preoccupation with suicide, often as a symptom of a MAJOR DEPRESSIVE EPISODE.

suicide *n.* the act of killing oneself. Frequently, suicide occurs in the context of a MAJOR DEPRESSIVE EPISODE, but it may also occur as a result of a substance-use or other disorder. It sometimes occurs in the absence of any psychiatric disorder, especially in untenable situations, such as bereavement or declining health. **—suicidal** *adj.*

suicidology *n.* a multiprofessional discipline devoted to the study of suicidal phenomena and their prevention.

sulcus *n.* (*pl.* **sulci**) a groove, especially one on the surface of the cerebral cortex. The term is often used synonymously with FISSURE. **—sulcal** *adj.*

summation *n.* **1.** the process in which a neural impulse is propagated by the cumulative effects of two or more stimuli that alone would not be sufficient to activate the neuron. See SPATIAL SUMMATION; TEMPORAL SUMMATION. **2.** (symbol: Σ) a mathematical operation involving the addition of numbers, quantities, or the like.

sum of squares the total obtained by adding together the squares of each deviation score in a sample (i.e., each score minus the sample mean squared, and then added together).

superego *n.* in psychoanalytic theory, the moral component of the personality that represents society's standards and determines personal standards of right and wrong, or conscience, as well as aims and aspirations (see EGO-IDEAL). In the classic Freudian tripartite structure of the psyche, the EGO, which controls personal impulses and directs actions, operates by the rules and principles of the superego, which basically stem from parental demands and prohibitions. The formation of the superego occurs on an unconscious level, beginning in the first 5 years of life and continuing throughout childhood and adolescence and into adulthood, largely through identification with the parents and later with admired models of behavior.

superior *adj.* in anatomy, higher, above, or toward the head. Compare INFERIOR.

superior colliculus see COLLICULUS.

superiority complex in the INDIVIDUAL PSYCHOLOGY of Austrian psychiatrist Alfred Adler (1870–1937), an exaggerated opinion of one's abilities and accomplishments that derives from an overcompensation (see COMPENSATION) for feelings of inferiority. See also INFERIORITY COMPLEX.

superior olivary complex a collection of brain nuclei located in the PONS. The cells receive excitatory input from the contralateral COCHLEAR NUCLEI in the brainstem and inhibitory input from the ipsilateral cochlear nuclei. The contralateral input comes through the **trapezoid body**, a concentration of transverse nerve fibers in the pons. Also called **superior olive**.

superordinate goal a goal that can be attained only if the members of two or more groups work together by pooling their skills, efforts, and resources. For example, in the Robbers' Cave experiment studying intergroup conflict reduction, superordinate goals were introduced by creating emergencies and prob-

lems that could only be resolved through the joint efforts of both groups.

supervision *n.* oversight: critical evaluation and guidance provided by a qualified and experienced person—the supervisor—to another individual—the trainee—during the learning of a task or process. In psychotherapy and counseling, supervision by a senior therapist or counselor is required while the trainee learns therapeutic techniques. A prescribed number of hours of supervision is required by state licensing boards as part of the requirements for obtaining a license in a mental health field.

supervisory attentional system (SAS) a theoretical higher level cognitive mechanism active in nonroutine or novel situations, responsible for troubleshooting and decision making when habitual responses or automatic processes are ineffective or otherwise unsatisfactory. Thought to be involved in carrying out a variety of other EXECUTIVE FUNCTIONS as well, it is considered a network for the coordination and control of cognitive activity and intentional behavior.

supplementary motor area an area of the MOTOR CORTEX with SOMATOTOPIC ORGANIZATION involved in planning and learning new movements that have coordinated sequences. In contrast to the PREMOTOR AREA, neuronal input to the supplementary motor area is triggered more by internal representations than by external events.

suppression *n.* a conscious effort to put disturbing thoughts and experiences out of mind, or to control and inhibit the expression of unacceptable impulses and feelings. It is distinct from the unconscious DEFENSE MECHANISM of REPRESSION in psychoanalytic theory. —**suppress** *vb.*

suprachiasmatic nucleus a small region of the HYPOTHALAMUS in the brain, above the OPTIC CHIASM, that is the location of the circadian oscillator, which controls daily BIOLOGICAL RHYTHMS (i.e., circadian rhythms). It receives direct input from the retina. See also BIOLOGICAL CLOCK.

supraliminal *adj.* describing stimulation that is above the threshold of awareness.

supraoptic nucleus a particular collection of neurons in the HYPOTHALAMUS that lies above the OPTIC CHIASM. Neurons in this nucleus project to the posterior lobe of the PITUITARY GLAND and secrete the hormones OXYTOCIN and VASOPRESSIN.

suprasegmental *adj.* in linguistics, denoting those phonological features of speech that extend over a series of consonantal or vowel phonemes (segments) rather than forming individual phonemes. In English the principal suprasegmental features are TONE (pitch) and STRESS. See also PARALANGUAGE; PROSODY.

surface dyslexia a form of acquired dyslexia in which a person is overly reliant on spelling-to-sound correspondence and therefore has difficulty reading irregularly spelled words.

surface structure in the TRANSFORMATIONAL GENERATIVE GRAMMAR of U.S. linguist Noam Chomsky (1928–), the structure of a grammatical sentence as it actually occurs in speech or writing, as opposed to its underlying DEEP STRUCTURE or abstract logical form. In Chomsky's theory, the surface structure of a sentence is generated from the deep structure by a series of transformational rules involving the addition, deletion, or reordering of sentence elements. Psycholinguists have investigated whether and to what extent this may serve as a model for the cognitive processes involved in forming and interpreting sentences.

surface therapy psychotherapy directed toward relieving the client's symptoms and emotional stress through such measures as reassurance, suggestion, and direct attempts to modify attitudes and behavior patterns, rather than through exploration and analysis of unconscious motivation and underlying dynamics. Compare DEPTH THERAPY.

surrogate *n.* a person or object that substitutes for the role of an individual who has a significant position in a family or group. For example, young children may use stuffed toys as surrogate companions.

survey *n.* a study in which a group of participants is selected from a population and some selected characteristics or opinions of those participants are collected, measured, and analyzed. See also SURVEY RESEARCH.

survey research a research method in which the investigator attempts to determine the current state of a population with regard to one or more attributes. Survey research does not involve any intervention imposed by the investigator.

survival analysis a set of statistical procedures used to build models calculating the time until some event occurs (e.g., the death of a patient, the failure of a piece of equipment).

survival value the degree to which a behavioral, physiological, or physical trait will contribute to reproductive success. A trait that can be shown to increase the probability of reproductive success in a given

S

environment has high survival value.

survivor guilt remorse or guilt for having survived a catastrophic situation when others did not. It is a common reaction stemming in part from a feeling of having failed to do enough to prevent the tragedy or to save those who did not survive.

susceptibility *n.* vulnerability: readily affected by or at increased risk of acquiring a particular condition, such as an infection, injury, or disorder.

sustained attention attentional focus on a task for an extended length of time.

susto *n.* a CULTURE-BOUND SYNDROME occurring among Latinos in the United States and populations in Mexico, Central America, and South America. After experiencing a frightening event, individuals fear that their soul has left their body. Symptoms include troubled sleep, lack of motivation, and low self-esteem.

Sylvian fissure see LATERAL SULCUS.

symbiosis *n.* **1.** any relationship in which two species live together in close association, especially one in which both species benefit. For example, in tropical Amazonia, a species of ant lives on a particular tree species that it uses for food and shelter, at the same time removing lichen and other parasites that might harm the tree. **2.** by extension, any mutually reinforcing, interdependent relationship between individuals (e.g., between a mother and infant), but particularly one in which one person is overdependent on another to satisfy needs. —**symbiotic** *adj.*

symbol *n.* any object, figure, or image that represents something else. For example, in psychoanalytic theory, a symbol is a disguised repre-

sentation of a repressed idea, impulse, or wish. See SYMBOLISM. —**symbolic** *adj.*

symbolic function in PIAGETIAN THEORY, the cognitive ability to mentally represent objects that are not in sight. For example, a child playing with a toy can mentally picture and experience the toy even after it has been taken away and he or she can no longer see it. Symbolic function emerges early in the PREOPERATIONAL STAGE and is expressed through DEFERRED IMITATION, language, play, and mental IMAGERY.

symbolic interactionism a sociological theory that assumes that self-concept is created through interpretation of symbolic gestures, words, actions, and appearances exhibited by others during social interaction. In contrast to Freudian and other approaches that postulate extensive inner dispositions and regard social interaction as resulting from them, symbolic interactionists believe that inner structures result from social interactions. See GENERALIZED OTHER; LOOKING-GLASS SELF.

symbolism *n.* in psychoanalytic theory, the substitution of a SYMBOL for a repressed impulse or threatening object in order to avoid censorship by the superego (e.g., dreaming of a steeple or other phallic symbol instead of a penis).

symmetry *n.* **1.** one of the GESTALT PRINCIPLES OF ORGANIZATION. It states that people tend to perceive objects as coherent wholes organized around a center point; this is particularly evident when the objects involve unconnected regions bounded by borders. Also called **law of symmetry**; **principle of symmetry**. **2.** in mathematics and statistics, equality relative to some axis. —**symmetrical** *adj.*

sympathetic chain either of two

beadlike chains of GANGLIA of the SYMPATHETIC NERVOUS SYSTEM, one chain lying on each side of the spinal column.

sympathetic nervous system one of the two divisions of the AUTONOMIC NERVOUS SYSTEM (ANS, which controls smooth muscle and gland functions), the other being the PARASYMPATHETIC NERVOUS SYSTEM. It innervates organs ranging from the eye to the reproductive organs and acts as an integrated whole in affecting a large number of smooth muscle systems simultaneously, usually in the service of enhancing "fight or flight" (see FIGHT-OR-FLIGHT RESPONSE). Typical sympathetic changes include dilation of the pupils to facilitate vision, constriction of the peripheral arteries to supply more blood to the muscles and the brain, secretion of epinephrine to raise the blood-sugar level and increase metabolism, and reduction of stomach and intestinal activities so that energy can be directed elsewhere. Also called **sympathetic division**.

sympathy *n.* **1.** feelings of concern or compassion resulting from an awareness of the suffering or sorrow of another. **2.** more generally, a capacity to share in and respond to the concerns or feelings of others. —**sympathetic** *adj.* —**sympathize** *vb.*

symptom *n.* any deviation from normal functioning that is considered indicative of physical or mental disorder. A recognized pattern of symptoms constitutes a SYNDROME. —**symptomatic** *adj.*

symptom substitution in the classic psychoanalytic theory of Austrian psychiatrist Sigmund Freud (1856–1939), the development of a symptom to replace one that has cleared up as a result of treatment. It is said to occur if the unconscious impulses and conflicts responsible for the original symptom are not dealt with.

synapse *n.* the specialized junction through which neural signals are transmitted from one neuron (the presynaptic neuron) to another (the postsynaptic neuron). In most synapses the knoblike ending (terminal button) of the axon of a presynaptic neuron faces the dendrite or cell body of the postsynaptic neuron across a narrow gap, the synaptic cleft. The arrival of a neural signal triggers the release of NEUROTRANSMITTER from SYNAPTIC VESICLES in the terminal button into the synaptic cleft. Here the molecules of neurotransmitter activate receptors in the postsynaptic membrane and cause the opening of ION CHANNELS in the postsynaptic cell. This may lead to excitation or inhibition of the postsynaptic cell, depending on which ion channels are affected. See also ELECTRICAL SYNAPSE. —**synaptic** *adj.*

synaptic cleft the gap within a synapse between the knoblike ending of the axon of one neuron and the dendrite or cell body of a neighboring neuron. The synaptic cleft is typically 20–30 nm wide.

synaptic transmission see NEUROTRANSMISSION.

synaptic vesicle any of numerous small spherical sacs in the cytoplasm of the knoblike ending of the axon of a presynaptic neuron that contain molecules of NEUROTRANSMITTER. The transmitter is released into the SYNAPTIC CLEFT when a nerve impulse arrives at the axon ending.

synaptogenesis *n.* the formation of synapses between neurons as axons and dendrites grow. See also EXPERIENCE-DEPENDENT SYNAPTOGENESIS; EXPERIENCE-EXPECTANT SYNAPTOGENESIS.

synchronicity *n.* in the ANALYTIC PSYCHOLOGY of Swiss psychiatrist

S

Carl Jung (1875–1961), the simultaneous occurrence of events that appear to have a meaningful connection when there is no explicable causal relationship between these events, as in extraordinary coincidences or purported examples of telepathy. Jung suggested that some simultaneous occurrences possess significance through their very coincidence in time.

syncope *n.* fainting: a transient loss of consciousness resulting from sudden reduction in the blood supply to the brain. **—syncopal** *adj.*

syndrome *n.* a set of symptoms and signs that are usually due to a single cause (or set of related causes) and together indicate a particular physical or mental disease or disorder.

synergism *n.* the joint action of different elements such that their combined effect is greater than the sum of their individual effects, as in drug synergism. **—synergistic** *adj.*

synesthesia *n.* a condition in which stimulation of one sensory system arouses sensations in another. For example, sounds may be experienced as colors while they are being heard, and specific sounds (e.g., different musical notes) may yield specific colors. Research suggests that about one in 2,000 people regularly experience synesthesia.

syntactics *n.* the structural and grammatical aspects of language, as distinguished from SEMANTICS.

syntax *n.* the set of rules that describes how words and phrases in a language are arranged into grammatical sentences, or the branch of linguistics that studies such rules. With MORPHOLOGY, syntax is one of the two traditional subdivisions of grammar. **—syntactic** or **syntactical** *adj.*

synthesis *n.* **1.** the bringing together of disparate parts or elements—whether they be physical or conceptual—into a whole. For example, biosynthesis is the process by which chemical or biochemical compounds are formed from their constituents, and mental synthesis involves combining ideas and images into meaningful objects of thought. **2.** in philosophy, the final stage of a dialectical process: a third proposition that resolves the opposition between THESIS and ANTITHESIS. The synthesis then serves as the thesis in the next phase of the ongoing dialectic. **—synthetic** *adj.*

system *n.* **1.** any collective entity consisting of a set of interrelated or interacting elements that have been organized together to perform a function. For example, a living organism or one of its major bodily structures constitutes a system. **2.** a structured set of facts, concepts, and hypotheses that provide a framework of thought or belief, as in a philosophical system. **—systematic** *adj.*

systematic desensitization a form of BEHAVIOR THERAPY in which COUNTERCONDITIONING is used to reduce anxiety associated with a particular stimulus. It involves the following stages: (a) The client is trained in deep-muscle relaxation; (b) various anxiety-provoking situations related to a particular problem, such as fear of death or a specific phobia, are listed in order from weakest to strongest; and (c) each of these situations is presented in imagination or in reality, beginning with the weakest, while the client practices muscle relaxation. Since the muscle relaxation is incompatible with the anxiety, the client gradually responds less to the anxiety-provoking situations. See also IN VIVO DESENSITIZATION; RECIPROCAL INHIBITION.

systematic error an error in data or in a conclusion drawn from the data that is regular and repeatable as a result of improper collection methods or statistical treatment of the data.

systematic observation an objective, well-ordered method for close examination of some phenomenon or aspect of behavior so as to obtain reliable data unbiased by observer interpretation. Systematic observation typically involves specification of the exact actions, attributes, or other variables that are to be recorded and precisely how they are to be recorded.

systematic processing see HEU-RISTIC-SYSTEMATIC MODEL.

systematic sampling a type of SAMPLING in which all the members of a population are listed and then some objective, orderly procedure is applied to select specific cases. For example, the population might be listed alphabetically and every seventh case selected.

systems analysis the process—and the specialty area itself—of studying any SYSTEM (e.g., the circulatory system, an organization, a family) so as to comprehend or clarify its internal workings and its purposes, often with a view to improving interrelations among constituent elements or to achieving a desired end more effectively. —**systems analyst** *n.*

systems theory see GENERAL SYSTEMS THEORY.

S

Tt

TA abbreviation for TRANSACTIONAL ANALYSIS.

table *n.* a presentation of data in the form of an ordered arrangement of overlaid vertical columns and horizontal rows. As with a GRAPH, the purpose of a table is to communicate information (either in words or numerical values) in a concise, space-efficient manner that can be assessed at a glance and interpreted easily. The columns have headings (the leftmost column is referred to as the **stub column**). The intersection of a column and row is called a CELL. Tables are often accompanied by explanatory notes. —**tabular** *adj.*

taboo (tabu) *n.* a religious, moral, or social convention prohibiting a particular behavior, object, or person.

tachycardia *n.* see ARRHYTHMIA.

tacit knowledge knowledge that is informally acquired rather than explicitly taught (e.g., knowledge of social rules) and allows a person to succeed in certain environments and pursuits. It is stored without self-reflective awareness and therefore not easily articulated. PRACTICAL INTELLIGENCE requires a facility for acquiring tacit knowledge.

tactile agnosia loss or impairment of the ability to recognize and understand the nature of objects through touch. Several distinct subtypes have been identified, including amorphagnosia, impaired recognition of the size and shape of objects; ahylognosia, impaired recognition of such object qualities as weight and texture; and finger agnosia, impaired recognition of one's own or another person's fingers.

tactile hallucination a false perception involving the sense of touch. These sensations occur in the absence of any external stimulus and may include itching, feeling electric shocks, and feeling insects biting or crawling under the skin.

tactile perception the ability to perceive objects or judge sensations through the sense of touch. The term often refers to judgments of spatial stimulation of the skin and patterns imposed on the skin. Tactile perception may also involve judging sensory events involving stimulation of the skin, for example, the thermal properties of a liquid.

talent *n.* an innate skill or ability, or an aptitude to excel in one or more specific activities or subject areas, that cannot be accounted for by normal development patterns. —**talented** *adj.*

tapering *n.* a gradual reduction in the dose of a drug in order to avoid undesirable effects that may occur with rapid cessation. Such effects may be extreme (e.g., convulsions) or relatively mild (e.g., head pain, mild gastrointestinal distress). Drugs that produce physiological dependence (e.g., opiates, benzodiazepines) must be tapered to prevent a withdrawal syndrome.

Tarasoff decision the 1976 California Supreme Court decision in

Tarasoff v. Regents of the University of California, which placed limits on a client's right to confidentiality by ruling that mental health practitioners who know or reasonably believe that a client poses a threat to another person are obligated to protect the potential victim from danger. Depending on the circumstances, that protection may involve such actions as warning the potential victim, notifying the police of the potential threat posed by the client, or both.

tardive dyskinesia a movement disorder associated with the use of ANTIPSYCHOTICS, particularly conventional antipsychotics that act primarily as dopamine-receptor ANTAGONISTS. Symptoms include tremor and spasticity of muscle groups, especially those of the face. Onset is insidious and may be masked by continued use of the antipsychotic, only appearing when the drug is discontinued or the dose lowered. It is more common with prolonged use and no effective treatment is known.

task analysis the breakdown of a complex task into component tasks to identify the different skills needed to correctly complete the task. For example, in organizational settings, a job may be broken down into the skills, knowledge, and specific operations required.

taste *n.* the sense devoted to the detection of molecules dissolved in liquids (also called **gustation**), or the sensory experience resulting from perception of gustatory qualities (e.g., sweetness, saltiness, sourness, bitterness). Dissolved molecules are delivered to the taste receptors—TASTE CELLS—on the tongue, soft palate, larynx, and pharynx. Taste combines with smell, texture, and appearance to generate a sense of flavor.

taste-aversion learning see CONDITIONED TASTE AVERSION.

taste bud a goblet-shaped structure, 30×50 μm, about 6,000 of which occur in the human mouth. Each bud is a collection of about 50 TASTE CELLS arranged like sections of an orange. At its apex is a taste pore through which each taste cell sends a slender, hairlike extention (microvillus) studded with receptor proteins to sample the environment.

taste cell a receptor cell for gustatory stimuli. Each has a slender, hairlike extension (microvillus) that protrudes from the opening in the TASTE BUD. Humans have about 300,000 taste cells, though the number can vary across individuals, and there are about 50 cells per taste bud. Taste cells can be divided into four anatomical types: Type I cells comprise 60% of the total, Type II cells 20%, Type III cells 15%, and Type IV cells 5%. All but Type IV cells may be involved in taste TRANSDUCTION.

TAT abbreviation for THEMATIC APPERCEPTION TEST.

taxonomy *n.* the science of classification—for example the biological taxonomy that groups organisms into a hierarchical system of ranks (in ascending order: species, genus, family, order, class, phylum, and kingdom)—or any scheme of classification itself. —**taxonomic** *adj.* —**taxonomist** *n.*

Tay–Sachs disease (**TSD**) a disorder due to a deficiency of the enzyme hexosaminidase A, resulting in the accumulation of G_{M2} gangliosides in all tissues. This process gradually destroys the brain and nerve cells by altering the shape of neurons. Development is normal until the 6th month of infancy, after which there is a deterioration of motor, visual, and cognitive abili-

T

ties. Death usually occurs between 3 and 5 years of age.

TBI abbreviation for TRAUMATIC BRAIN INJURY.

TCA abbreviation for TRICYCLIC ANTIDEPRESSANT.

T cell see LYMPHOCYTE.

t distribution a theoretical PROBABILITY DISTRIBUTION that plays a central role in testing hypotheses about population means among other parameters. It is the sampling distribution of the statistic $(M - \mu_0)/s$, where μ_0 is the population mean of the population from which the sample is drawn, M is the data estimate of the mean of the population, and s is the standard deviation of the batch of scores. Also called **Student's t distribution**.

tectorial membrane part of the ORGAN OF CORTI in the cochlea. It consists of a semigelatinous membrane in which the stereocilia of the outer HAIR CELLS are embedded.

tectospinal tract see VENTROMEDIAL PATHWAY.

tectum *n.* (*pl.* **tecta**) the roof of the MIDBRAIN, dorsal to the CEREBRAL AQUEDUCT. The tectum contains the superior COLLICULI, which act as relay and reflex centers for the visual system, and the inferior colliculi, which are sensory centers for the auditory system. —**tectal** *adj.*

tegmentum *n.* (*pl.* **tegmenta**) the central core of the MIDBRAIN and PONS. It contains sensory and motor tracts passing through the midbrain, the SUBTHALAMIC NUCLEUS, and several other nuclei. —**tegmental** *adj.*

telegraphic speech condensed or abbreviated speech in which only the most central words, carrying the highest level of information, are spoken. Nouns and verbs are typically featured, while adjectives, adverbs, articles, and connective parts of speech are omitted. It is typical of children roughly between the ages of 18 and 30 months, usually in the form of two-word expressions up to the age of about 24 months (see TWO-WORD STAGE) and short but multiword expressions (e.g., *dog eat bone*) thereafter.

telekinesis *n.* see PSYCHOKINESIS.

telemetry *n.* the process of measuring and transmitting quantitative information to a remote location, where it can be recorded and interpreted. For example, a small radio transmitter may be implanted inside an animal to measure general activity level as well as a variety of physiological variables, including body temperature, heart rate, and blood pressure. This transmitter sends signals to a receiver located outside the animal. —**telemetric** *adj.*

telencephalon *n.* see CEREBRUM.

teleology *n.* the position that certain phenomena are best understood and explained in terms of their purposes rather than their causes. In psychology, its proponents hold that mental processes are purposive, that is, directed toward a goal. The view that behavior is to be explained in terms of ends and purposes is frequently contrasted with explanations in terms of causes, such as INSTINCTS and CONDITIONED RESPONSES. —**teleologic** or **teleological** *adj.*

telepathy *n.* the alleged direct communication of information from one mind to another, in the absence of any known sensory means of transmission. It is a form of EXTRASENSORY PERCEPTION. —**telepath** *n.* —**telepathic** *adj.*

temperament *n.* the basic foundation of personality, usually assumed to be biologically determined and

T

present early in life, including such characteristics as energy level, emotional responsiveness, demeanor, mood, response tempo, and willingness to explore.

temporal *adj.* **1.** of or pertaining to time or its role in some process. **2.** relating or proximal to the temple, as in TEMPORAL LOBE. —**temporally** *adv.*

temporal coding a type of neural plotting of the precise timing of the points of maximum intensity ("spikes") between ACTION POTENTIALS. It can provide valuable additional detail to information obtained through simple RATE CODING.

temporal conditioning a procedure in PAVLOVIAN CONDITIONING in which the unconditioned stimulus is presented at regular intervals but in the absence of an accompanying conditioned stimulus. Compare TRACE CONDITIONING.

temporal lobe one of the four main lobes of each CEREBRAL HEMISPHERE in the brain, lying immediately below the LATERAL SULCUS on the lower lateral surface of each hemisphere. It contains the auditory projection and auditory association areas and also areas for higher order visual processing and for memory formation.

temporal lobe amnesia a memory disorder, secondary to injury of the temporal lobe (particularly medial structures, such as the hippocampus), that prevents the formation of new memories.

temporal summation a neural mechanism in which an impulse is propagated by two successive POSTSYNAPTIC POTENTIALS (PSPs), neither of which alone is of sufficient intensity to cause a response. The partial DEPOLARIZATION caused by the first PSP continues for a few milliseconds and is able, with the additive effect of the second PSP, to produce an above-threshold depolarization sufficient to elicit an ACTION POTENTIAL. Compare SPATIAL SUMMATION.

tend-and-befriend response a proposed physiological and behavioral stress regulatory system in females, in which tending involves nurturant activities designed to protect the self and offspring, to promote a sense of safety, and to reduce distress, and befriending is expressed in the creation and maintenance of social networks that aid in this process. This model has been characterized as a human stress response in females that is secondary to the classic FIGHT-OR-FLIGHT RESPONSE. Neuroendocrinal evidence from animal and human research suggests an underlying physiological mechanism mediated by OXYTOCIN and moderated by female sex hormones and opioid peptide mechanisms.

tender-mindedness *n.* a personality trait characterized by intellectualism, idealism, optimism, dogmatism, religiousness, and monism. Compare TOUGH-MINDEDNESS. —**tender-minded** *adj.*

tension *n.* **1.** a feeling of physical and psychological strain accompanied by discomfort, uneasiness, and pressure to seek relief through talk or action. **2.** the force resulting from contraction or stretching of a muscle or tendon.

teratogen *n.* an agent that induces developmental abnormalities in a fetus. The process that results in such abnormal developments is called **teratogenesis**; a **teratomorph** is a fetus or offspring with developmental abnormalities.

terminal button see AXON.

terminal drop a rapid decline in cognitive abilities immediately before death. The cognitive abilities that appear to be most prone to terminal drop are those least affected by normal aging.

territoriality *n.* the defense by an animal of a specific geographic area (its **territory**) against intrusion from other members of the same species. Territoriality is observed in a wide range of animals and is found most often where there are specific defensible resources, such as a concentration of food or shelter. Territoriality is also extended to humans, denoting behavior associated with the need or ability to control and regulate access to a space, which reflects feelings of identity derived from use of and attachment to a familiar place.

terrorism *n.* systematic intimidation or coercion to attain political or religious objectives using unlawful and unpredictable force or violence against property, persons, or governments. —**terrorist** *adj., n.*

terror management theory a theory proposing that control of death-related anxiety is the primary function of society and the main motivation in human behavior. Individual SELF-ESTEEM and a sense of being integrated into a powerful human culture are regarded as the most effective ways for human beings to defend themselves against the frightening recognition of their own mortality.

tertiary care highly specialized care given to patients who are in danger of disability or death. Tertiary care often requires sophisticated technologies provided by highly specialized practitioners and facilities, for example, neurologists, neurosurgeons, thoracic surgeons, and intensive care units. Compare PRIMARY CARE; SECONDARY CARE.

tertiary circular reaction in the PIAGETIAN THEORY of cognitive development, an infant's action that creatively alters former SCHEMES to fit the requirements of new situations. Tertiary circular reactions emerge toward the end of the SENSORIMOTOR STAGE, at about the beginning of the 2nd year; they differ from earlier behaviors in that the child can, for the first time, develop new schemes to achieve a desired goal. See also PRIMARY CIRCULAR REACTION; SECONDARY CIRCULAR REACTION.

tertiary prevention intervention and treatment for individuals or groups with already established psychological or physical conditions, disorders, or diseases. Tertiary interventions include attempts to minimize negative effects, prevent further disease or disorder related to complications, prevent relapse, and restore the highest physical or psychological functioning possible. Compare PRIMARY PREVENTION; SECONDARY PREVENTION.

test *n.* **1.** a standardized set of questions or other items designed to assess knowledge, skills, interests, or other characteristics of an examinee. See PSYCHOLOGICAL TEST. **2.** a set of operations, usually statistical in nature, designed to determine the VALIDITY of a hypothesis.

testability *n.* the degree to which a hypothesis or theory is capable of being evaluated empirically.

test battery a group or series of related tests administered at one time to obtain a comprehensive assessment of a particular factor or phenomenon (e.g., intelligence, language skill). Scores may be recorded separately or combined to yield a single score.

testicular feminization syndrome see ANDROGEN-INSENSITIVITY SYNDROME.

testing effect in studies of recognition memory, the phenomenon whereby taking an initial test improves subsequent memory performance in a later recall test.

testis *n.* (*pl.* **testes**) the principal reproductive organ in males, a pair of which is normally located in the scrotum. The testes produce sperm in the seminiferous tubules (see SPERMATOGENESIS) and male sex hormones (ANDROGENS) in interstitial cells.

testosterone *n.* a male sex hormone and the most potent of the ANDROGENS produced by the testes. It stimulates the development of male reproductive organs, including the prostate gland, and secondary SEX CHARACTERISTICS, such as beard, bone, and muscle growth. Women normally secrete small amounts of testosterone from the adrenal cortex and ovary.

test–retest reliability see RETEST RELIABILITY.

test statistic the numerical result of a STATISTICAL TEST, which is used to evaluate the viability of a hypothesis. Common examples are the value of *t* in the T TEST and the value of *z* in the Z TEST.

test-wise *adj.* describing individuals who have taken a number of tests and are therefore more adept at taking them than those who are relatively new to the testing process.

tetrahydrocannabinol (THC) *n.* one of a number of CANNABINOIDS occurring in the CANNABIS plant that is the agent principally responsible for the psychoactive properties of cannabis.

texture gradient the progressively finer appearance of textures and surface grains of objects as the viewer moves away from them.

T-group *n.* *t*raining group: a type of experiential group, usually of up to a dozen or so people, concerned with fostering the development of "basic skills," such as effective leadership and communication, and attitude change. Although the term is sometimes used synonymously with ENCOUNTER GROUP, in a T-group less emphasis is placed on personal growth and more on SENSITIVITY TRAINING and practical interpersonal skills.

thalamus *n.* (*pl.* **thalami**) a mass of gray matter, forming part of the DIENCEPHALON of the brain, whose two lobes form the walls of the third VENTRICLE. It consists of a collection of sensory, motor, autonomic, and associational nuclei, serving as a relay for nerve impulses traveling between the spinal cord and brainstem and the cerebral cortex. **—thalamic** *adj.*

thanatology *n.* the study of death and death-related behaviors, thoughts, feelings, and phenomena. Death was mostly the province of theology until the 1960s, when existential thinkers and a broad spectrum of care providers, educators, and social and behavioral scientists became interested in death-related issues. **—thanatologist** *n.*

Thanatos *n.* the personification of death and the brother of Hypnos (sleep) in Greek mythology, whose name was chosen by Austrian psychiatrist Sigmund Freud (1856–1939) to designate a theoretical set of strivings oriented toward the reduction of tension and life activity (see DEATH INSTINCT). In Freud's dual instinct theory, Thanatos is seen as involved in a dialectic process with EROS (love), the striving toward sexuality, continued development, and heightened experience (see LIFE INSTINCT).

that's-not-all technique a two-step procedure for enhancing compliance that consists of presenting an initial, large request and then, before the person can respond, im-

T

mediately reducing it to a more modest target request that is made more attractive by offering some additional benefit. Compliance with the target request is greater following the initial request than would have been the case if the target request had been presented on its own. See also DOOR-IN-THE-FACE TECHNIQUE; FOOT-IN-THE-DOOR TECHNIQUE; LOW-BALL TECHNIQUE.

THC abbreviation for TETRAHYDRO-CANNABINOL.

Thematic Apperception Test (TAT) a projective test in which participants are held to reveal their attitudes, feelings, conflicts, and personality characteristics in the oral or written stories they make up about a series of relatively ambiguous black-and-white pictures. Systematic coding schemes have been developed to assess different aspects of personality functioning derived from TAT stories, including motivation for achievement, power, affiliation, and intimacy; gender identity; DEFENSE MECHANISMS; and mental processes influencing interpersonal relations. The TAT is one of the most frequently used and researched tests in psychology, particularly in clinical settings for diagnosis, personality description, and assessment of strengths and weakness in personality functioning.

theory *n.* **1.** a principle or body of interrelated principles that purports to explain or predict a number of interrelated phenomena. See CONSTRUCT; MODEL. **2.** in the philosophy of science, a set of logically related explanatory hypotheses that are consistent with a body of empirical facts and that may suggest more empirical relationships. —**theoretical** *adj.*

theory of mind the ability to imagine or make deductions about the mental states of other individuals: What does the other individual know? What actions is that individual likely to take? Theory of mind is an essential component of attributing beliefs, intentions, and desires to others, specifically in order to predict their behavior.

theory of planned behavior a theory that resembles the THEORY OF REASONED ACTION but also incorporates the construct of perceived behavioral control. That is, the extent to which a person believes behavior is under his or her active control is added to attitude toward behavior and subjective norms (perceived expectations) as the antecedents influencing both the intention to perform a behavior and the performance of the behavior itself.

theory of reasoned action the theory that attitudes toward a behavior and subjective norms (perceived expectations) regarding a behavior determine a person's intention to perform that behavior. Intentions are in turn assumed to cause the actual behavior. See also THEORY OF PLANNED BEHAVIOR.

theory theory any model of cognitive development that combines NEONATIVISM and CONSTRUCTIVISM, proposing that cognitive development progresses by children generating, testing, and changing theories about the physical and social world.

therapeutic *adj.* **1.** pertaining to **therapeutics**, the branch of medical science concerned with the treatment of diseases and disorders and the discovery and application of remedial agents or methods. **2.** having beneficial or curative effects.

therapeutic alliance a cooperative working relationship between client and therapist, considered by many to be an essential aspect of successful therapy. Derived from the concept of the psychoanalytic work-

T

ing alliance, the therapeutic alliance comprises bonds, goals, and tasks. Bonds are constituted by the core conditions of therapy, the client's attitude toward the therapist, and the therapist's style of relating to the client; goals are the mutually negotiated, understood, agreed upon, and regularly reviewed aims of the therapy; and tasks are the activities carried out by both client and therapist.

therapeutic community a setting for individuals requiring therapy for a range of psychosocial problems and disorders that is based on an interpersonal, socially interactive approach to treatment, both among residents and among residents and staff (i.e., "community as method or therapy"). The term covers a variety of short- and long-term residential programs as well as day treatment and ambulatory programs. See MILIEU THERAPY.

therapist *n.* an individual who has been trained in and practices one or more types of therapy to treat mental or physical disorders or diseases: often used synonymously with psychotherapist (see PSYCHOTHERAPY).

therapy *n.* remediation of physical, mental, or behavioral disorders or disease. See also PSYCHOTHERAPY.

thermoreceptor *n.* a receptor or sense organ that is activated by temperature stimuli (e.g., cold or warm stimuli).

thesis *n.* (*pl.* **theses**) in philosophy, the first stage of a dialectical process: a proposition that is opposed by an ANTITHESIS, thereby generating a new proposition referred to as a SYNTHESIS. The synthesis serves as thesis for the next phase of the ongoing process.

theta wave in electroencephalography, a type of BRAIN WAVE with a frequency of 4–7 Hz. Theta waves are observed in the REM SLEEP of an-

imals, stage 2 sleep in humans, and in the drowsiness state of newborn infants, adolescents, and young adults. Theta waves are also recorded in TRANCES, HYPNOSIS, and deep DAYDREAMS. Also called **theta rhythm**.

thinking *n.* cognitive behavior in which ideas, images, MENTAL REPRESENTATIONS, or other hypothetical elements of thought are experienced or manipulated. In this sense thinking includes imagining, remembering, problem solving, daydreaming, FREE ASSOCIATION, concept formation, and many other processes. Thinking may be said to have two defining characteristics: (a) It is covert, that is, it is not directly observable but must be inferred from behavior or self-reports; and (b) it is symbolic, that is, it seems to involve operations on mental symbols or representations, the nature of which remains obscure and controversial.

third-person effect a tendency for a person to expect that others are more strongly influenced by (i.e., respond to and take action as a result of) a persuasive communication in the mass media than himself or herself. The third-person effect has been studied extensively and is of particular interest in politics, social policy, and health psychology. It generally is explained in terms of a desire for self-enhancement: people are motivated to reinforce their positive self-images and thus are unrealistically optimistic in comparing themselves to others. Negative attitudes toward the media generally may also play a role. Also called **third-person perception**.

third-variable problem the fact that an observed correlation between two variables may be due to the common correlation between each of the variables and a third variable rather than because the two

T

variables have any underlying relationship (in a causal sense) with each other.

third ventricle see VENTRICLE.

Thorazine *n.* a trade name for CHLORPROMAZINE.

thought disorder a disturbance in the cognitive processes that affects communication, language, or thought content. A thought disorder is considered by some to be the most important mark of schizophrenia, but thought disorders are also associated with mood disorders, dementia, mania, and neurological diseases (among others).

thought stopping the skill of using a physical or cognitive cue to stop negative thoughts and redirect them to a neutral or positive orientation. This skill is taught in some behavior therapies, when the therapist shouts "Stop!" to interrupt a trend toward undesirable thoughts and trains clients to apply this technique to themselves.

thought suppression the attempt to control the content of one's mental processes and specifically to rid oneself of undesired thoughts or images.

threat *n.* a condition that is appraised as a danger to one's self or well-being or to a group. **—threaten** *vb.* **—threatening** *adj.*

threat display any of various ritualized animal communication signals used to indicate that attack or aggression might follow. Examples are fluffed-out fur or feathers, certain facial expressions or body postures, and low-frequency vocalizations (e.g., growls). The use of ritualized threat displays can minimize direct physical aggression to the benefit of both individuals.

three-stratum model of intelligence a psychometric model of intelligence based on a factorial reanalysis of several hundred data sets available in the literature. The three strata correspond to (a) minor group factors at the first (lowest) level, (b) major group factors at the second level (fluid intelligence, crystallized intelligence, general memory and learning, broad visual perception, broad auditory perception, broad retrieval ability, broad cognitive speediness, and processing speed), and (c) the general factor at the third (highest) level.

threshold *n.* **1.** in psychophysics, the magnitude of a stimulus that will lead to its detection 50% of the time. **2.** the minimum intensity of a stimulus that is necessary to evoke a response. For example, an auditory threshold is the slightest perceptible sound and an excitatory threshold is the minimum stimulus that triggers an ACTION POTENTIAL in a neuron. Also called **limen.** See also ABSOLUTE THRESHOLD; DIFFERENCE THRESHOLD.

thrombosis *n.* the presence or formation of a blood clot (thrombus) in a blood vessel. Thrombosis is likely to develop where blood flow is impeded by disease, injury, or a foreign substance. **—thrombotic** *adj.*

thyroid gland an endocrine gland forming a shieldlike structure on the front and sides of the throat, just below the thyroid cartilage. It produces the iodine-containing thyroid HORMONES (thyroxine and triiodothyronine) in response to thyroid-stimulating hormone from the anterior pituitary gland. C cells (parafollicular cells) in the thyroid produce the hormone calcitonin, which controls levels of calcium and phosphate in the blood.

TIA abbreviation for TRANSIENT ISCHEMIC ATTACK.

tic *n.* a sudden, involuntary contraction of a small group of muscles (motor tic) or vocalization (vocal tic) that is recurrent, nonrhythmic, and stereotyped. Tics may be psychogenic in origin; alternatively, they may occur as an adverse effect of a medication or other substance or result from a head injury, neurological disorder, or general medical condition.

timbre *n.* the perceptual attribute relating to the quality of a sound. Two perceptually different sounds with the same pitch and loudness differ in their timbre. Timbre is determined primarily by the sound SPECTRUM but also is affected by temporal and intensive characteristics. —**timbral** *adj.*

time and motion study an analysis of industrial operations or other complex tasks into their component steps, observing the time required for each. Such studies may serve a number of different purposes, enabling an employer to set performance targets, increase productivity, rationalize pay rates and pricing policy, reduce employee fatigue, and prevent accidents.

time-lag design a type of QUASI-EXPERIMENTAL RESEARCH in which participants of the same age are compared at different time periods. For example, a time-lag study of intelligence might compare a group of people who were 20 years old in 2005 with groups who were 20 years old in 2006, 2007, and 2008. Used in examining human developmental processes, time-lag designs have the benefit of controlling for time of testing effects but the drawbacks of low INTERNAL VALIDITY and the difficulty in separating COHORT EFFECTS from AGE EFFECTS.

time out a technique, originating in BEHAVIOR THERAPY, in which undesirable behavior is weakened and its occurrence decreased by moving the individual away from the area that is reinforcing the behavior. For example, a child may be temporarily removed from an area when misbehaving. The technique is used in schools and by parents to decrease the undesirable behavior by isolating the misbehaver for a period.

time sampling a strategy commonly used in direct observation that involves noting and recording the occurrence of a target behavior whenever it is seen during a stated time interval. The process may involve fixed time periods (e.g., every 5 min) or random time intervals. For example, a researcher may observe a group of children for 10 s every 5 min for a specific 30 min period each day, noting the occurrence or nonoccurrence of particular behaviors. Observations taken during these periods are known as **time samples**.

time series a set of measures on a single attribute measured repeatedly over time.

time-series design an experimental design that involves the observation of units (e.g., people or countries) over a defined time period.

timing-of-events model a theoretical paradigm that describes adult psychosocial development as occurring relatively flexibly (often unexpectedly) in response to particular life events. A MIDLIFE CRISIS, for example, might be triggered at any time within a broad age-spectrum between 35 and 65 years as a response to a particular event in a person's life (e.g., the death of a parent or spouse; a forced retirement) rather than occur invariably during a more specified period (e.g., 40-45 years).

tinnitus *n.* noises in one or both ears, including ringing, buzzing, or clicking sounds.

tip-of-the-tongue phenomenon (TOT phenomenon) the experience of attempting to retrieve from memory a specific name or word but not being able to do so: The fact is ordinarily accessible and seems to hover tantalizingly on the rim of consciousness.

titration *n.* a technique used in determining the optimum dose of a drug needed to produce a desired effect in a particular individual. The dosage may be either gradually increased until a noticeable improvement is observed in the patient or adjusted downward from a level that is obviously excessive because of unwanted adverse effects.

T maze a maze shaped like the letter T and consisting of a start box and stem leading to a choice between left and right arms, one being incorrect while the other leads to the goal box. More complicated mazes can be formed by joining several T mazes in sequence.

TMS abbreviation for TRANS- CRANIAL MAGNETIC STIMULATION.

token economy in BEHAVIOR THERAPY, a program, sometimes conducted in an institutional setting (e.g., a hospital or classroom), in which desired behavior is reinforced by offering tokens that can be exchanged for special foods, television time, passes, or other rewards.

tolerance *n.* **1.** a condition, resulting from persistent use of a drug, characterized by a markedly diminished effect with regular use of the same dose of the drug or by a need to increase the dose markedly over time to achieve the same desired effect. Tolerance is one of the two prime indications of physical dependence on a drug, the other being a characteristic withdrawal syndrome. See SUBSTANCE DEPENDENCE. **2.** acceptance of others whose actions, beliefs, physical capabilities, religion, customs, ethnicity, nation-

ality, and so on differ from one's own. —**tolerant** *adj.*

tomography *n.* a technique for revealing the detailed structure of a tissue or organ through a particular plane that involves the compilation of a series of images taken from multiple perspectives. Examples include COMPUTED TOMOGRAPHY and POSI- TRON EMISSION TOMOGRAPHY. —**tomographic** *adj.*

tone *n.* in linguistics, a phonetic variable along the dimension of pitch. In a **tonal language**, such as Mandarin or Thai, differences in tone are sufficient to mark a distinction between words that are otherwise pronounced identically. In English, different patterns of intonation distinguish between different types of utterance, such as statements and questions. —**tonal** *adj.*

tonic *adj.* of or relating to muscle tone, especially a state of continuous muscle tension or contraction, which may be normal (**tonus**) or abnormal. For example, a tonic phase of facial muscles prevents the lower jaw from falling open, a normal function. Abnormally, in the tonic phase of a TONIC–CLONIC SEIZURE, the muscles controlling respiration may undergo tonic SPASM, resulting in a temporary suspension of breathing.

tonic–clonic seizure a seizure characterized by both TONIC and CLONIC motor movements (it was formerly known as a **grand mal seizure**). In the tonic phase the muscles go into spasm and the individual falls to the ground unconscious; breathing may be suspended. This is followed by the clonic phase, marked by rapidly alternating contraction and relaxation of the muscles, resulting in jaw movements (the tongue may be bitten) and urinary incontinence.

T

tonotopic organization the fundamental principle that different frequencies stimulate different places within structures of the mammalian auditory system. This organization begins in the COCHLEA, where different frequencies tend to cause maximal vibration at different places along the BASILAR MEMBRANE and thus stimulate different HAIR CELLS. The hair cells are discretely innervated, and thus different auditory nerve fibers respond to a relatively limited range of frequencies. This frequency-to-place mapping is preserved in the AUDITORY CORTEX.

top-down processing information processing that proceeds from a hypothesis about what a stimulus might be: a person's higher level knowledge, concepts, or expectations influence the processing of lower level information. Typically, perceptual or cognitive mechanisms use top-down processing when information is familiar and not especially complex. Compare BOTTOM-UP PROCESSING. See also DEEP PROCESSING.

totem *n.* a revered animal, plant, natural force, or inanimate object that is conceived as the ancestor, symbol, protector, or tutelary spirit of a people, clan, or community. It is usually made the focus of certain ritual activities and TABOOS, typically against killing or eating it. —**totemic** *adj.* —**totemism** *n.*

TOTE model see FEEDBACK LOOP.

TOT phenomenon abbreviation for TIP-OF-THE-TONGUE PHENOMENON.

tough-mindedness *n.* a personality trait characterized by empiricism, materialism, skepticism, and fatalism. Compare TENDER-MINDEDNESS. —**tough-minded** *adj.*

Tourette's disorder a disorder characterized by many motor tics and one or more vocal tics, such as grunts, yelps, barks, sniffs, and in a few cases an irresistible urge to utter obscenities (see COPROLALIA). The tics occur many times a day for more than a year, and the age of onset for the disorder is before 18 years.

toxicity *n.* the capacity of a substance to produce toxic (poisonous) effects in an organism. Toxicity generally is related to the size of the dose per body weight of the individual, expressed in terms of milligrams of chemical per kilogram of body weight. It also may be expressed in terms of the median lethal dose (LD_{50}).

trace conditioning a procedure in PAVLOVIAN CONDITIONING in which a conditioned stimulus and an unconditioned stimulus are separated by a constant interval, with the conditioned stimulus presented first. Compare TEMPORAL CONDITIONING.

trace-decay theory see DECAY THEORY.

tracking *n.* the process of following a moving object with the eyes or using eye movements to follow a path of some kind. —**track** *vb.*

tract *n.* **1.** a bundle or group of nerve fibers within the central nervous system. The name of a tract typically indicates its site of origin followed by its site of termination; for example, the reticulospinal tract runs from the reticular formation of the brainstem to the spinal cord. Compare NERVE. **2.** a series of organs that as a whole accomplishes a specific function (e.g., the digestive tract).

training analysis PSYCHOANALYSIS of a trainee analyst. Its purpose is not only to provide training in the concepts and techniques of psychoanalysis, but also to increase insight into personal sensitivities or other emotional reactions that might in-

T

terfere with the process of analyzing patients in the form of a COUNTER-TRANSFERENCE.

trait *n.* **1.** an enduring personality characteristic that describes or determines an individual's behavior across a range of situations. **2.** in genetics, an attribute resulting from a hereditary predisposition (e.g., hair color or facial features).

trait theory approaches that explain personality in terms of TRAITS, that is, internal characteristics that are presumed to determine behavior. An example is the FIVE-FACTOR PERSONALITY MODEL.

trance *n.* an ALTERED STATE OF CONSCIOUSNESS involving markedly reduced awareness of and responsiveness to stimuli. It may be induced by HYPNOSIS or AUTOSUGGESTION and characterized by openness to suggestion.

tranquilizer *n.* a drug that is used to reduce physiological and subjective symptoms of anxiety. In the past, distinctions were made between so-called major tranquilizers (ANTIPSYCHOTICS) and minor tranquilizers (ANXIOLYTICS, e.g., benzodiazepines).

transaction *n.* any interaction between the individual and the social or physical environment, especially during encounters between two or more people.

transactional analysis (TA) a theory of personality and a form of dynamic group or individual psychotherapy focusing on characteristic interactions that reveal internal "ego states" and the games people play in social situations. Specifically, the approach involves: (a) a study of three primary ego states (parent, child, adult) and determination of which one is dominant in the transaction in question; (b) identification of the tricks and expedients, or games, habitually used in the client's transactions; and (c) analysis of the total SCRIPT, or unconscious plan, of the client's life, in order to uncover the sources of his or her emotional problems.

transactionalism *n.* an approach to perception that emphasizes the interaction of people and their environment. Rather than being mere passive observers, people draw on past experiences in order to form perceptions of present situations and even of novel stimuli.
—**transactionalist** *adj., n.*

transactional leadership a style of leadership in which the emphasis is on ensuring followers accomplish tasks. Transactional leaders influence others through exchange relationships in which benefits are promised in return for compliance. Compare TRANSFORMATIONAL LEADERSHIP.

transactive memory system a system in which information to be remembered is distributed among various members of a group, who can then each be relied on to provide that information when it is needed.

transcendental meditation a technique of concentrative MEDITATION for achieving a **transcendental state** of consciousness involving ultimate self-awareness and restful alertness. It consists of six steps that culminate in sitting with one's eyes closed, while repeating a mantra, for two 20-minute periods a day. Repetition of the mantra serves to block distracting thoughts and to induce a state of relaxation and tranquillity in which images and ideas can arise from deeper levels of the mind and from the cosmic source of all thought and being.

transcranial magnetic stimulation (TMS) localized electrical stimulation of the brain through the skull caused by changes in the magnetic field in coils of wire placed around the head. The technique was originally devised and is primarily used as an investigatory tool to assess the effects of electrical stimulation of the motor cortex. It is also being investigated as a possible therapy for some types of movement disorders and psychological conditions, such as depression, obsessive-compulsive disorder, and Tourette's disorder. **Repetitive transcranial magnetic stimulation** (**rTMS**) consists of a series of TMS pulses.

transcription *n.* in genetics, the process whereby the genetic information contained in DNA is transferred to a molecule of MESSENGER RNA (mRNA), which subsequently directs protein synthesis. The base sequence of the mRNA is complementary to that of the coding DNA strand and faithfully represents the instructions for assembling the component amino acids of the protein encoded by the gene (see GENETIC CODE).

transcultural psychotherapy any form of PSYCHODYNAMIC PSYCHOTHERAPY that emphasizes cultural sensitivity and awareness, including culturally defined concepts of emotion, psychodynamics, and behavior. In the psychiatric community the term is used somewhat more often in a sense similar to MULTICULTURAL THERAPY in clinical psychology.

transducer *n.* a device or system that converts energy from one form to another. Sensory RECEPTOR cells are an example.

transduction *n.* the process by which one form of energy is converted into another, especially **sensory transduction**: the transformation of the energy of a stimulus into a change in the electric potential across the membrane of a RECEPTOR cell.

transfer-appropriate processing a concept of mental processing based on the idea that memory performance is better when a person processes material during study in the same way as the material will be processed during testing. For example, test performance should be relatively good if both study and test conditions emphasize either semantic processing on the one hand or perceptual processing on the other; but test performance will not be as good if study conditions emphasize one (e.g., semantic) and test conditions emphasize another (e.g., perceptual).

transference *n.* in psychoanalysis, the DISPLACEMENT or PROJECTION onto the analyst of unconscious feelings and wishes originally directed toward important individuals, such as parents, in the patient's childhood. This process, which is at the core of the psychoanalytic method, brings repressed material to the surface where it can be reexperienced, studied, and worked through. In the course of this process, it is posited that the sources of neurotic difficulties are frequently discovered and their harmful effects alleviated. Although quite specific to psychoanalysis, the term's meaning has had an impact far beyond its narrow confines, and transference—as unconscious repetition of earlier behaviors and projection onto new subjects—is acknowledged as ubiquitous in human interactions. The role of transference in counseling and short-term dynamic psychotherapy is well recognized, and ongoing attempts to study its role in a range of therapeutic encounters promise to expand and elucidate its meanings. See also COUNTERTRANSFERENCE.

transfer of training the influence of prior learning on new learning, either to enhance it (see POSITIVE TRANSFER) or to hamper it

T

(see NEGATIVE TRANSFER). The general principles of mathematics, for example, transfer to computer programming, but a knowledge of Spanish may have both positive and negative effects in learning Italian.

transformation *n.* any change in appearance, form, function, or structure. In mathematics, for example, it is the conversion of data to a different form through a rule-based process, whereas in psychoanalytic theory it is the process by which unconscious wishes or impulses are disguised in order that they can gain admittance to CONSCIOUSNESS. —**transform** *vb.* —**transformational** *adj.*

transformational generative grammar in linguistics, a type of GENERATIVE GRAMMAR based on the idea that sentences have an underlying DEEP STRUCTURE as well as the SURFACE STRUCTURE observable in speech or writing, and that the former gives rise to the latter through the operation of a small number of **transformational rules** involving the movement, addition, and deletion of constituents. This approach to syntactic structures was pioneered by U.S. linguist Noam Chomsky (1928–) in the late 1950s as a means of supplementing the more limited analysis made possible by PHRASE-STRUCTURE GRAMMAR. Also called **transformational grammar**.

transformational leadership a charismatic, inspiring style of leading others that usually involves heightening followers' motivation, confidence, and satisfaction, uniting them in the pursuit of shared, challenging goals, and changing their beliefs, values, and needs. Compare TRANSACTIONAL LEADERSHIP.

transgender *adj.* having or relating to gender identities that differ from culturally determined gender roles and biological sex. Transgender

states include transsexualism and intersexuality. —**transgenderism** *n.*

transience *n.* impermanence that implies ending and may invoke anticipation of loss. In classical psychoanalytic theory, the idea that everything is transient may interfere with enjoyment and preclude the establishment of deep or lasting relationships. —**transient** *adj.*

transient ischemic attack (**TIA**) an episode during which an area of the brain is suddenly deprived of oxygen because its blood supply is temporarily interrupted, for example by thrombosis, embolism, or vascular spasm. Symptoms are the same as those of STROKE but disappear completely, typically within 24 hours.

transitivity *n.* the quality of a relationship among elements such that the relationship transfers across elements. For example, a transitive relationship would be: Given that $a > b$, and $b > c$, it must be the case that $a > c$. —**transitive** *adj.*

translation and back-translation a method of ensuring that the translation of an assessment instrument into another language is adequate, used primarily in cross-cultural research. A bilingual person translates items from the source language to the target language, and a different bilingual person then independently translates the items back into the source language. The researcher can then compare the original with the back-translated version to see if anything important was changed in the translation.

transorbital lobotomy see LOBOTOMY.

transpersonal psychology an area in HUMANISTIC PSYCHOLOGY concerned with the exploration of the nature, varieties, causes, and effects of "higher" states of consciousness and other experiences that transcend personal identity and individual, immediate desires. See also PEAK EXPERIENCE.

transporter *n.* a protein complex that spans a cell membrane and conveys ions, neurotransmitters, or other substances between the exterior and interior of the cell. For example, at SYNAPSES between neurons, transporters in the presynaptic membrane recognize and bind to neurotransmitter molecules and return them to the presynaptic neuron for reuse (see REUPTAKE).

transsexualism *n.* a GENDER IDENTITY DISORDER consisting of a persistent sense of discomfort and inappropriateness relating to one's anatomical sex, with a persistent wish to be rid of one's genitals and to live as a member of the other sex. Many transsexuals feel that they belong to the opposite sex and are somehow trapped in the wrong body. They therefore seek to change their sex through surgical and hormonal means. —**transsexual** *adj., n.*

transtheoretical model a theory to explain changes in people's health behavior in terms of five stages: precontemplation, contemplation, preparation, action, and maintenance. It suggests that change takes time, that different interventions are effective at different stages, and that there are multiple outcomes occurring across the stages (e.g., belief structure, self-efficacy).

transvestic fetishism a PARA-PHILIA consisting of the persistent wearing by a heterosexual male of female clothes with the purpose of achieving sexual excitement and arousal. It typically begins in childhood or adolescence and should not be confused with transvestism, the nonpathological cross-dressing by men or women of any sexual preference.

transvestism *n.* the process or habit of wearing the clothes of the opposite sex. Transvestism, or cross-dressing, is distinct from TRANSVESTIC FETISHISM. —**transvestic** *adj.* —**transvestite** *n.*

trauma *n.* **1.** any disturbing experience that results in significant fear, helplessness, DISSOCIATION, confusion, or other disruptive feelings intense enough to have a long-lasting negative impact on a person's attitudes, behavior, and other aspects of functioning. Traumatic events include those caused by human behavior (e.g., rape, toxic accidents) as well as by nature (e.g., earthquakes) and often challenge an individual's view of the world as a just, safe, and predictable place. **2.** any serious physical injury, such as a widespread burn or a blow to the head. —**traumatic** *adj.*

traumatic brain injury (**TBI**) damage to brain tissue caused by external mechanical forces, as evidenced by objective neurological findings, posttraumatic amnesia, skull fracture, or loss of consciousness.

treatment *n.* **1.** the administration of appropriate measures (e.g., drugs, surgery, therapy) that are designed to relieve a pathological condition. **2.** the level of an INDEPENDENT VARIABLE in an experiment, or the independent variable itself. See TREATMENT LEVEL.

treatment effect the magnitude of the effect of a treatment (i.e., the INDEPENDENT VARIABLE) upon the response variable (i.e., the DEPENDENT VARIABLE) in a study. It is usually measured as the difference between the level of response under a control condition and the level of response under the treatment condition in standardized units.

treatment level the specific condition to which a group or participant is exposed in a study or experiment. For example, in a design employing four groups, each of which is exposed to a different dosage of a particular drug, each dosage amount represents a level of the treatment factor.

tremor *n.* any involuntary trembling of the body or a part of the body (e.g., the hands) due to neurological or psychological causes. A coarse tremor involves a large muscle group in slow movements, whereas a fine tremor is caused by a small bundle of muscle fibers that move rapidly. Some tremors occur only during voluntary movements (action tremor); others occur in the absence of voluntary movement (resting tremor).

trend analysis any of several analytic techniques designed to uncover systematic changes (trends) in a set of variables, such as linear growth over time or quadratic increases in response with increased dosage levels.

trephination *n.* a surgical procedure in which a disk of bone is removed from the skull with a circular instrument (a **trephine**) having a sawlike edge. On the basis of evidence found in skulls of Neolithic humans, trephining is believed to be one of the oldest types of surgery. Among the numerous conjectural reasons given for the practice is the possibility that it was a treatment for headaches, infections, skull fractures, convulsions, mental disorders, or supposed demonic possession. Also called **trepanation**. —**trephine** *vb.*

trial *n.* **1.** in testing, conditioning, or other experimentation, one performance of a given task (e.g., one run through a maze) or one presentation of a stimulus (e.g., an ordered list of three-letter words). **2.** a clinical trial: a research study design to compare a new treatment or drug with an existing standard of care.

trial-and-error learning a type of learning in which the organism successively tries various responses in a situation, seemingly at random, until one is successful in producing the goal. In successive trials, the successful response appears earlier and earlier. Maze learning, with its eventual elimination of blind-alley entrances, is an example of trial-and-error learning.

triangular theory of love the proposition that the various kinds of love can be characterized in terms of the degree to which they possess the three basic components of love relationships: passion, intimacy, and commitment. See COMPANIONATE LOVE; PASSIONATE LOVE; ROMANTIC LOVE.

triangulation *n.* **1.** the process of confirming a hypothesis by collecting evidence from multiple sources or experiments or using multiple procedures. The data from each source, experiment, or procedure support the hypothesis from a somewhat different perspective. **2.** in FAMILY THERAPY, a situation in which two members of a family in conflict each attempt to draw another member onto their side. Triangulation can occur, for example, when two parents are in conflict and their child is caught in the middle. —**triangulate** *vb.*

triarchic theory of intelligence a theory of intelligence proposing three key abilities—analytical, creative, and practical—which are viewed as largely although not entirely distinct. According to the theory, intelligence comprises a number of information-processing components, which are applied to experience (especially novel experiences) in order to adapt to, shape, and select environments. The theory contains three subtheories: one

T

specifying the components of intelligence (componential subtheory), another specifying the kinds of experience to which the components are applied (experiential subtheory), and a third specifying how the components are applied to experience to be used in various kinds of environmental contexts (contextual subtheory).

trichromatic theory one of several concepts of the physiological basis of color vision based on a mixture of three primary colors. The YOUNG–HELMHOLTZ THEORY OF COLOR VISION is the best known trichromatic theory. Subsequent studies determined that there are three different retinal cone PHOTO-PIGMENTS with peak sensitivities roughly corresponding to the three primary colors of trichromatic theory: blue, green, and red. See also OPPONENT PROCESS THEORY OF COLOR VISION.

trichromatism *n.* normal color vision: the capacity to distinguish the three primary color systems of light–dark, red–green, and blue–yellow, attributable to the presence of all three types of PHOTOPIGMENT. See also ACHROMATISM; DICHROMATISM; MONOCHROMATISM.

tricyclic antidepressant (TCA) any of a group of drugs, developed in the 1950s, that were the original first-line medications for depression and represented the mainstay of antidepressant treatment until fluoxetine (Prozac)—the first SSRI—was introduced in 1987. They are presumed to act by blocking the REUPTAKE of monoamine neurotransmitters (serotonin, dopamine, and norepinephrine), thereby increasing the amount of neurotransmitter available. Side effects of TCAs include significant anticholinergic effects (e.g., dry mouth, blurred vision, constipation, urinary retention), drowsiness or insomnia,

confusion, anxiety, nausea, weight gain, and impotence. They can also cause cardiovascular complications (particularly disturbances in heart rhythm). Although they are effective as antidepressants, their adverse side effects and their lethality in overdose have led to a profound decline in their use.

trigeminal nerve the fifth and largest CRANIAL NERVE, which carries both sensory and motor fibers. The motor fibers are primarily involved with the muscles used in chewing, tongue movements, and swallowing. The sensory fibers innervate the same areas, including the teeth and most of the tongue in addition to the jaws. Some fibers of the trigeminal nerve innervate the cornea, face, scalp, and the dura mater membrane of the brain.

trigram *n.* any three-letter combination, particularly a NONSENSE SYLLABLE.

trimming *n.* the exclusion of a fixed percentage of cases at each end of a distribution before calculating a statistic on the batch of data. This is done to eliminate the influence of extreme scores on the estimate.

triple blind see BLIND.

trochlear nerve the fourth CRANIAL NERVE, which contains motor fibers supplying the superior oblique muscle of the eyeball.

truncated distribution a set of scores lacking values beyond a specific maximum point, below a specific minimum point, or both.

trust *n.* reliance on or confidence in the worth, truth, or value of someone or something. Trust is considered by most psychological researchers to be a primary component in mature relationships with others, whether intimate, social, or therapeutic. See also BASIC TRUST VERSUS MISTRUST.

trust versus mistrust see BASIC TRUST VERSUS MISTRUST.

T score any of a set of scores scaled so that they have a MEAN equal to 50 and STANDARD DEVIATION equal to 10.

TSD abbreviation for TAY–SACHS DISEASE.

t test any of a class of statistical tests based on the fact that the test statistic follows the T DISTRIBUTION when the null hypothesis is true. Most *t* tests deal with hypotheses about the mean of a population or about differences between means of different populations.

Tukey's Honestly Significant Difference Test (Tukey's HSD Test) a post hoc testing procedure that allows for the comparison of all pairs of groups while maintaining the overall SIGNIFICANCE LEVEL of the set of tests at a prescribed level. [John Wilder **Tukey** (1915–2000), U.S. statistician]

Turner's syndrome a chromosomal disorder, specific to women, marked by the absence of all or a part of one of the two X (female) chromosomes. The effects include underdevelopment or absence of primary and secondary SEX CHARACTERISTICS, infertility, and various physical abnormalities (e.g., short stature, lack of menstruation). [reported in 1938 by Henry H. **Turner** (1892–1970), U.S. endocrinologist]

twelve-step program a distinctive approach to overcoming addictive, compulsive, or behavioral problems that was developed initially in Alcoholics Anonymous (AA) to guide recovery from alcoholism and is now used, often in an adapted form, by a number of other SELF-HELP GROUPS. In the context of alcoholism, for instance, the twelve-step program in AA asks each member to (a) admit that he or she cannot control his or her drinking; (b) recognize a supreme spiritual power, which can give the member strength; (c) examine past errors, a process that is carried out with another member who serves as sponsor; (d) make amends for these errors; (e) develop a new code and style of life; and (f) help other alcoholics who are in need of support.

twins *pl. n.* see DIZYGOTIC TWINS; MONOZYGOTIC TWINS.

twin study any research design utilizing twins. The purpose of such research is usually to assess the relative contributions of heredity and environment to some attribute (e.g., intelligence). Specifically, twin studies often involve comparing the characteristics of identical and fraternal twins and comparing twins of both types who have been reared together or reared apart. The assumptions made in these studies are, however, never completely fulfilled, making the estimations of heritability of any attribute open to some doubts.

two-by-two factorial design an experimental design in which there are two INDEPENDENT VARIABLES each having two levels. When this design is depicted as a matrix, two rows represent one of the independent variables and two columns represent the other independent variable. See FACTORIAL DESIGN.

two-factor theory of emotion see SCHACHTER–SINGER THEORY.

two-factor theory of work motivation a theory holding that the factors causing worker satisfaction (those addressing higher-order psychological needs such as achievement, recognition, and advancement; see MOTIVATORS) and the factors causing worker dissatisfaction (those addressing basic needs and interpersonal processes, including salary,

T

work conditions, and supervision; see HYGIENE FACTORS) are not opposites of one another but are, in fact, independent factors. Thus, to improve job attitudes and productivity—that is, work motivation—employers and administrators must evaluate and address both sets of factors separately.

two-point threshold the point of stimulus separation, that is, the smallest distance between two points of stimulation on the skin at which the two stimuli are perceived as two stimuli rather than as a single stimulus.

two-tailed test a statistical test of an experimental hypothesis that does not specify the expected direction of an effect or a relationship. Also called **nondirectional test**. Compare ONE-TAILED TEST.

two-way analysis of variance a statistical test analyzing the joint and separate influences of two INDEPENDENT VARIABLES on a DEPENDENT VARIABLE.

two-word stage the developmental period, between approximately 18 and 24 months of age, when children use two words at a time when speaking (e.g., *dog bone*, *mama cup*). See TELEGRAPHIC SPEECH.

tympanic membrane a conically shaped membrane that separates the external ear from the middle ear and serves to transform the pressure waves of sounds into mechanical vibration of the OSSICLES. The first ossicle (malleus) is attached to the inner surface of the tympanic membrane. Also called **eardrum**.

Type A personality a personality pattern characterized by chronic competitiveness, high levels of ACHIEVEMENT MOTIVATION, and hostility. The lifestyles of Type A individuals are said to predispose

them to coronary heart disease. Compare TYPE B PERSONALITY.

Type B personality a personality pattern characterized by low levels of competitiveness and frustration and a relaxed, easy-going approach. Type B individuals typically do not feel the need to prove their superiority or abilities. Compare TYPE A PERSONALITY.

type D personality a "distressed" personality pattern, characterized by a high degree of negative affectivity (i.e., a tendency to experience negative emotions) in combination with a conscious tendency to suppress self-expression in social interaction (see SOCIAL INHIBITION). Accumulating evidence suggests that type D individuals are at increased risk of developing CORONARY HEART DISEASE and other chronic medical conditions.

Type I error the error of rejecting the NULL HYPOTHESIS when it is in fact true. Investigators make this error when they believe they have detected an effect or a relationship that does not actually exist.

Type II error the error of failing to reject the NULL HYPOTHESIS when it is in fact not true. Investigators make this error if they conclude that a particular effect or relationship does not exist when in fact it does.

Type III error an error in direction (positive/negative, higher/lower) when two groups are shown empirically to be different. Researchers frequently investigate the direction rather than the size of a relationship (e.g., investigating "Which is more?" or "Which is better?"), and they make a Type III error when they use a nondirectional TWO-TAILED TEST to make a directional decision: After conducting the test and finding STATISTICAL SIGNIFICANCE, the researcher inspects data

T

visually to decide (incorrectly) upon the direction of the observed relationship.

type theory any hypothetical proposition or principle for the grouping of people by kind of personality or by personality characteristics. An example of such a theoretical system of personality classification is that of Swiss psychoanalyst Carl Jung (1875–1961), who divided individuals into types according to (a) attitudes of INTROVERSION and EXTRAVERSION and (b) the dominant functions of the psyche.

typology *n.* any analysis of a particular category of phenomena (e.g., individuals, things) into classes based on common characteristics, for example, a typology of personality. —**typological** *adj.*

Uu

UCR abbreviation for UNCONDITIONED RESPONSE.

Ucs abbreviation for UNCONSCIOUS.

UCS abbreviation for UNCONDITIONED STIMULUS.

ultimate attribution error see GROUP-SERVING BIAS.

ultimate cause see REMOTE CAUSE.

ultimate explanation an account or explanation for a particular behavior in terms of its adaptive value. Compare PROXIMATE EXPLANATION.

ultradian rhythm any periodic variation in physiological or psychological function recurring in a cycle of more than 24 hours, such as the human menstrual cycle. Compare INFRADIAN RHYTHM.

ultrasound *n.* sound whose frequency exceeds the human audibility range, often used to measure and record structures and structural change within the body in the imaging technique called **ultrasonography.** Echoes from ultrasound waves reflected from tissue surfaces are recorded to form structural images for diagnostic purposes, for example, to examine a growing fetus during pregnancy or to examine internal organs, such as the heart, liver, kidneys, and gallbladder, for signs of health or disease. Compare INFRASOUND.

unbiased *adj.* impartial or without net error. For example, in unbiased procedures, studies, and the like any errors that do occur are random and therefore self-cancelling in the long run.

unbiased estimator a statistic whose expected value is the value of the parameter being estimated. Thus if G is used to estimate the parameter Θ, G is said to be unbiased if and only if $E(G) = \Theta$.

uncertainty *n.* **1.** the state or condition in which something (e.g., the probability of a particular outcome) is not accurately or precisely known. **2.** lack of confidence or clarity in one's ideas, decisions, or intentions. **—uncertain** *adj.*

unconditional positive regard an attitude of caring, acceptance, and prizing expressed by others irrespective of an individual's behavior and without regard to the other's personal standards, which is considered conducive to self-awareness, self-worth, and personality growth. Posited by U.S. psychologist Carl Rogers (1902–1987) to be a universal human need essential to healthy development, unconditional positive regard is the centerpiece of his CLIENT-CENTERED THERAPY and is also emphasized in many other therapeutic approaches. Compare CONDITIONAL POSITIVE REGARD.

unconditioned reinforcement see PRIMARY REINFORCEMENT.

unconditioned response (**UCR; UR**) the unlearned response to a stimulus: any original response that occurs naturally and in the absence of conditioning (e.g., salivation in response to the presentation of food). The unconditioned response is a REFLEX that serves as the basis for establishment of the CONDI-

TIONED RESPONSE in PAVLOVIAN CONDITIONING.

unconditioned stimulus (UCS; US) a stimulus that elicits an UNCONDITIONED RESPONSE, as in withdrawal from a hot radiator, contraction of the pupil on exposure to light, or salivation when food is in the mouth. Compare CONDITIONED STIMULUS.

unconscious 1. (Ucs) *n.* in the classical psychoanalytic theory of Austrian psychiatrist Sigmund Freud (1856–1939), the region of the psyche that contains memories, emotional conflicts, wishes, and repressed impulses that are not directly accessible to awareness but that have dynamic effects on thought and behavior. Compare CONSCIOUS; PRECONSCIOUS. See also COGNITIVE UNCONSCIOUS; COLLECTIVE UNCONSCIOUS; PERSONAL UNCONSCIOUS. **2.** *adj.* relating to or marked by absence of awareness or lack of consciousness.

unconscious motivation in psychoanalytic theory, wishes, impulses, aims, and drives of which the self is not aware. Examples of behavior produced by unconscious motivation are purposive accidents, slips of the tongue, and dreams that express unfulfilled wishes. See also PARAPRAXIS.

underextension *n.* the incorrect restriction of the use of a word, which is a mistake commonly made by young children acquiring language. For example, a child may believe that the label *dog* applies only to Fido, the family pet. Compare OVEREXTENSION.

understanding *n.* the process of gaining insight about oneself or others or of comprehending the meaning or significance of something. In many forms of counseling and psychotherapy understanding the network of relationships between a client's behavior and such things as his or her environment, experiences, and feelings is considered essential to success. **—understand** *vb.*

undifferentiated schizophrenia a subtype of SCHIZOPHRENIA in which the individual exhibits prominent psychotic features, such as delusions, hallucinations, disorganized thinking, or grossly disorganized behavior, but does not meet the criteria for any of the other subtypes of the disorder.

unidimensional *adj.* having a single dimension or composed of a single or a pure factor. Compare MULTIDIMENSIONAL.

unilateral *adj.* denoting or relating to one side of the body or an organ or to one of two or more parties. For example, a unilateral cerebral lesion involves one cerebral hemisphere, left or right, and unilateral couple counseling is the counseling of one partner on his or her relationship with the other. **—unilaterally** *adv.*

unimodal distribution a set of scores that has one mode (represented by one peak in their graphical distribution), reflecting a tendency for scores to cluster around a specific value. See also BIMODAL DISTRIBUTION.

unipolar depression any DEPRESSIVE DISORDER, that is, any mood disorder marked by one or more MAJOR DEPRESSIVE EPISODES or a prolonged period of depressive symptoms with no history of manic or hypomanic symptoms or MIXED EPISODES.

unipolar disorder persistent or pervasive DEPRESSION that does not involve a MANIC EPISODE, a HYPOMANIC EPISODE, or a MIXED EPISODE. As such, it contrasts with BIPOLAR DISORDER. The term is sometimes used synonymously with MAJOR DEPRESSIVE DISORDER.

U

unipolar neuron a neuron that has only a single extension of the CELL BODY. This extension divides into two branches, oriented in opposite directions and representing the axon. One end is the receptive pole, and the other is the output zone. Compare BIPOLAR NEURON; MULTIPOLAR NEURON.

uniqueness *n.* in FACTOR ANALYSIS, the part of the variance of a variable that it does not share with any other variable in the system.

unit of analysis in experimental design and research, the group of people, things, or entities that are being investigated or studied.

univariate *adj.* characterized by a single variable. Compare MULTIVARIATE. See also BIVARIATE.

universal grammar a theoretical linguistic construct positing the existence of a set of rules or grammatical principles that are innate in human beings and underlie most natural languages. The concept is of considerable interest to psycholinguists who study LANGUAGE ACQUISITION and the formation of valid sentences.

universalism *n.* the position that certain aspects of the human mind, human behavior, and human morality are universal and essential and are therefore to be found in all cultures and historical periods. Universalism is thus a form of ESSENTIALISM and is opposed to RELATIVISM. —**universalist** *adj.*

universality *n.* **1.** the tendency to assume that one's personal qualities and characteristics, including attitudes and values, are common in the general social group or culture. See also FALSE-CONSENSUS EFFECT. **2.** in self-help and psychotherapy groups, a curative factor fostered by members' recognition that their problems and difficulties are not unique to them, but instead are experienced by many of the group members.

unobtrusive measure a measure obtained without disturbing the participant or alerting him or her that a measurement is being made. The behavior or responses of such participants are thus assumed to be unaffected by the investigative process or the surrounding environment. Compare OBTRUSIVE MEASURE.

unstructured interview an interview that imposes minimal structure by asking open-ended (rather than set) questions and allowing the interviewee to steer the discussion into areas of his or her choosing. Unstructured interviews are used in a variety of contexts but are particularly popular in personnel selection, where the idea is that such an approach will reveal more of the applicant's traits, interests, priorities, and interpersonal and verbal skills than a STRUCTURED INTERVIEW.

upper motor neuron see MOTOR NEURON.

UR abbreviation for UNCONDITIONED RESPONSE.

US abbreviation for UNCONDITIONED STIMULUS.

U test see MANN–WHITNEY U TEST.

utilitarianism *n.* an ethical theory based on the premise that the good is to be defined as that which brings the greatest amount or degree of happiness; thus, an act is considered moral if, compared to possible alternatives, it provides the greatest good for the greatest number of people. The doctrine is often reduced to the single maxim: The greatest good for the greatest number. —**utilitarian** *adj.*

utilization deficiency the inability of individuals to improve task performance by using strategies that they have already acquired and

U

demonstrated the ability to use because they are not spurred to do so by memory. Although historically most frequently studied in children, current research suggests that such deficiencies are not developmental per se but may occur at any age as a by-product of diminished WORKING MEMORY capacity. Compare MEDIATIONAL DEFICIENCY; PRODUCTION DEFICIENCY.

utricle *n.* the larger of the two VESTIBULAR SACS in the inner ear, the other being the SACCULE. Like the saccule, the utricle senses not only the position of the head with respect to gravity but also acceleration and deceleration. This is achieved by a special patch of epithelium—the MACULA—inside both the utricle and saccule. **—utricular** *adj.*

utterance *n.* a unit of spoken language, which may be of any length but can usually be identified by conversational turn taking or by clear breaks in the stream of speech. MEAN LENGTH OF UTTERANCE is considered an important index of language development in young children.

Vv

vagina *n.* a tubelike structure in female mammals that leads from the cervix (neck) of the uterus to the exterior. The muscular walls of the vagina are lined with mucous membrane, and two pairs of vestibular glands around the vaginal opening secrete a fluid that facilitates penetration by the penis during coitus. —**vaginal** *adj.*

vaginismus *n.* a sexual dysfunction in which spasmic contractions of the muscles around the vagina occur during or immediately preceding sexual intercourse, causing the latter to be painful or impossible. Vaginismus is not diagnosed if the dysfunction is due solely to the effects of a medical condition.

vagus nerve the tenth CRANIAL NERVE, a mixed nerve with both sensory and motor fibers that serves many functions. The sensory fibers innervate the external ear, vocal organs, and thoracic and abdominal VISCERA. The motor nerves innervate the tongue, vocal organs, and—through many ganglia of the PARASYMPATHETIC NERVOUS SYSTEM—the thoracic and abdominal viscera.

validity *n.* the degree to which a test or measurement accurately measures or reflects what it purports to measure. There are various types of validity, including CONCURRENT VALIDITY, CONSTRUCT VALIDITY, and ECOLOGICAL VALIDITY. —**valid** *adj.*

value *n.* **1.** the mathematical magnitude or quantity of a variable. **2.** a moral, social, or aesthetic principle accepted by an individual or society as a guide to what is good, desirable, or important. **3.** the worth, usefulness, or importance attached to something.

value judgment an assessment of individuals, objects, or events in terms of the values held by the observer rather than in terms of their intrinsic characteristics objectively considered. In some areas, such as aesthetics or morality, value judgments are common, but in hard and social sciences they are frequently considered undesirable.

variability *n.* in statistics and experimental design, the degree to which members of a group or population differ from each other.

variable *n.* a quantity in an experiment or test that varies, that is, takes on different values (such as test scores, ratings assigned by judges, and other personal, social, or physiological indicators) that can be quantified (measured).

variable-interval schedule (**VI schedule**) in free-operant conditioning, a type of INTERVAL REINFORCEMENT in which the reinforcement or reward is presented for the first response after a variable period has elapsed since the previous reinforcement. Reinforcement does not depend on the number of responses during the intervals. The value of the schedule is given by the average interval length; for example, "VI 3" indicates that the average length of the intervals between potential reinforcements is 3 min.

variable-ratio schedule (**VR**

schedule) in free-operant conditioning, a type of INTERMITTENT REINFORCEMENT in which a response is reinforced after a variable number of responses. The value of the schedule is given by the average number of responses per reinforcer; for example, "VR 10" indicates that the average number of responses before reinforcement is 10.

variance (symbol: σ^2) *n.* a measure of the spread, or DISPERSION, of scores within a sample, whereby a small variance indicates highly similar scores, all close to the sample mean, and a large variance indicates more scores at a greater distance from the mean and possibly spread over a larger range.

variation *n.* the existence of qualitative differences in form, structure, behavior, and physiology among the individuals of a population, whether due to heredity or to environment. Both ARTIFICIAL SELECTION and NATURAL SELECTION operate on variations among organisms, but only genetic variation is transmitted to the offspring.

vascular dementia severe loss of cognitive functioning as a result of cerebrovascular disease. It is often due to repeated strokes. Also called **multi-infarct dementia**.

vasoconstriction *n.* narrowing of blood vessels, which is controlled by VASOMOTOR nerves of the sympathetic nervous system or by such agents as VASOPRESSIN or drugs. It has the effect of increasing blood pressure.

vasodilation *n.* widening of blood vessels, as by the action of a VASOMOTOR nerve or a drug, which has the effect of lowering blood pressure.

vasomotor *adj.* describing or relating to nerve fibers, drugs, or other agents that can affect the diameter of blood vessels, especially small arteries, by causing contraction or relaxation of the smooth muscle of their walls. Fibers of the sympathetic and parasympathetic divisions of the AUTONOMIC NERVOUS SYSTEM have a vasomotor effect.

vasopressin *n.* a peptide hormone synthesized in the hypothalamus and released by the posterior pituitary gland. It plays an important role in the retention of water in the body (by signaling the kidneys to reabsorb water instead of excreting it in urine) and in regulation of blood pressure (by constricting small blood vessels, which raises blood pressure). Vasopressin secretion may also activate the HYPOTHALAMIC–PITUITARY–ADRENOCORTICAL SYSTEM and may be associated with mechanisms of learning and memory. Also called **antidiuretic hormone (ADH)**.

vegetative *adj.* **1.** pertaining to basic physiological functions, such as those involved in growth, respiration, sleep, digestion, excretion, and homeostasis, which are governed primarily by the AUTONOMIC NERVOUS SYSTEM. **2.** living without apparent cognitive neurological function or responsiveness, as in PERSISTENT VEGETATIVE STATE.

ventral *adj.* denoting the abdomen or the front surface of the body. In reference to the latter, this term sometimes is used interchangeably with ANTERIOR. Compare DORSAL. **—ventrally** *adv.*

ventral horn either of the bottom regions of the H-shaped pattern formed by the GRAY MATTER in the central portion of the spinal cord. The ventral horns contain large motor neurons whose axons form the ventral roots. Compare DORSAL HORN.

ventral root any of the SPINAL ROOTS that carry motor nerve fibers and arise from the spinal cord on the front surface of each side. Compare DORSAL ROOT.

ventral stream a series of specialized visual regions in the cerebral cortex of the brain that originate in the STRIATE CORTEX (primary visual cortex) of the occipital lobe and project forward and downward into the lower temporal lobe. It is known informally as the "what" pathway of perception. Compare DORSAL STREAM.

ventricle *n.* an anatomical cavity in the body, such as any of the ventricles of the heart but particularly any of the four interconnected cavities inside the brain, which serve as reservoirs of CEREBROSPINAL FLUID. Each of the two **lateral ventricles** communicates with the third ventricle via an opening called the interventricular foramen; the third and fourth ventricles communicate with each other, via the CEREBRAL AQUEDUCT, and with the central canal of the spinal cord. **—ventricular** *adj.*

ventriloquism effect the tendency for sounds to appear to emanate from plausible visual objects, regardless of the actual source of the sound. For example, the voices of actors in a movie are localized to the images on the screen, rather than to the speakers that produce the sound. The ventriloquism effect stems from VISUAL CAPTURE.

ventrodorsal *adj.* oriented or directed from the front (ventral) region of the body to the back (dorsal) region. Compare DORSOVENTRAL. **—ventrodorsally** *adv.*

ventromedial hypothalamic syndrome a set of symptoms caused by experimental lesions in the VENTROMEDIAL NUCLEUS of the hypothalamus in the brain. The syndrome consists of two stages. The first is characterized by HYPERPHAGIA (overeating) and subsequent weight

gain, resulting in obesity. The second includes stabilization of body weight and willingness to eat only easily obtainable and palatable foods. Compare LATERAL HYPOTHALAMIC SYNDROME.

ventromedial nucleus an area of the hypothalamus in the brain that receives input from the AMYGDALA and is associated particularly with eating and sexual behavior. The ventromedial nucleus traditionally has been referred to as the **satiety center** because of its presumed dominance over the cessation of eating, but it is now known that other neural areas are involved in this function as well. See also VENTROMEDIAL HYPOTHALAMIC SYNDROME.

ventromedial pathway any of four major descending groups of nerve fibers within the MOTOR SYSTEM, conveying information from diffuse areas of the cerebral cortex, midbrain, and cerebellum. These pathways include the anterior **corticospinal tract**, which descends directly from motor cortex to the anterior horn of the spinal cord; the **vestibulospinal tract**, which carries information from the VESTIBULAR NUCLEI for control of equilibratory responses; the **tectospinal tract**, for control of head and eye movements; and the **reticulospinal tract**, for maintaining posture.

verbal communication see COMMUNICATION.

verbal learning the process of learning about verbal stimuli and responses, such as letters, digits, nonsense syllables, or words.

V

verbal memory the capacity to remember something written or spoken (e.g., a poem).

verbal test any test or scale in which performance depends upon one's ability to comprehend, use, or otherwise manipulate words.

vergence *n.* a turning movement of the eyes. If they turn inward, the movement is CONVERGENCE; if outward, it is DIVERGENCE.

vertical décalage in PIAGETIAN THEORY, the invariable sequence in which the different stages of development (sensorimotor, preoperational, concrete operational, formal operational) are attained. Compare HORIZONTAL DÉCALAGE.

vertical–horizontal illusion see HORIZONTAL–VERTICAL ILLUSION.

vertigo *n.* an unpleasant, illusory sensation of movement or spinning of oneself or one's surroundings due to neurological disorders, psychological stress (e.g., anxiety), or activities that disturb the labyrinth (which contains the organs of balance) in the inner ear (as in a roller-coaster ride).

vesicle *n.* a fluid-filled saclike structure, such as any of the SYNAPTIC VESICLES in axon terminals that contain neurotransmitter molecules. —**vesicular** *adj.*

vestibular nucleus any of four masses of CELL BODIES in the dorsolateral part of the PONS and the MEDULLA OBLONGATA in the brain that receives input from the VESTIBULAR SYSTEM in the inner ear and serves the sense of balance and orientation in space. It sends fibers to the cerebellum, reticular formation, thalamus, and the vestibulospinal tract (see VENTROMEDIAL PATHWAY).

vestibular sacs two sacs in the inner ear—the UTRICLE and SACCULE—that, together with the SEMICIRCULAR CANALS, comprise the **vestibular apparatus.** The vestibular sacs respond to gravity and encode information about the head's orientation.

vestibular sense the sense of equilibrium: the sense that enables the maintenance of balance while sitting, standing, walking, or otherwise maneuvering the body. A subset of PROPRIOCEPTION, it is in part controlled by the VESTIBULAR SYSTEM in the INNER EAR, which contains specialized **vestibular receptors** that detect motions of the head.

vestibular system a system in the body that is responsible for maintaining balance, posture, and the body's orientation in space and plays an important role in regulating locomotion and other movements. It consists of the VESTIBULAR SACS and the SEMICIRCULAR CANALS in the inner ear, the vestibular nerve (a division of the VESTIBULOCOCHLEAR NERVE), and the various cortical regions associated with the processing of vestibular (balance) information.

vestibulocochlear nerve the eighth CRANIAL NERVE: a sensory nerve containing tracts that innervate both the sense of balance and the sense of hearing. It has two divisions: the **vestibular nerve**, originating in the VESTIBULAR SACS and the semicircular canals, and the AUDITORY NERVE, originating in the cochlea. The vestibulocochlear nerve transmits impulses from the inner ear to the medulla oblongata and pons and has fibers that continue into the cerebrum and cerebellum.

vestibulo-ocular reflex the involuntary compensatory movement of the eyes that occurs to maintain fixation on a visual target during small, brief head movements. It is triggered by vestibular signals. Compare OPTOKINETIC REFLEX.

vestibulospinal tract see VENTROMEDIAL PATHWAY.

vicarious reinforcement secondary or indirect REINFORCEMENT: the process whereby a person becomes more likely to engage in a particular behavior (response) by observing the consequences of that behavior for another individual. An important concept in SOCIAL LEARNING THEORY, vicarious reinforcement is often indicated by imitation: for example, a student who hears the teacher praise a classmate for neat penmanship on an assignment and who then carefully handwrites his or her own assignment is considered to have received vicarious reinforcement. See also OBSERVATIONAL LEARNING.

vicarious traumatization the impact on a therapist of repeated emotionally intimate contact with trauma survivors. More than COUNTERTRANSFERENCE, vicarious traumatization affects the therapist across clients and situations. It results in a change in the therapist's own worldview and sense of the justness and safety of the world.

vigilance *n.* a state of extreme awareness and watchfulness directed by one or more members of a group toward the environment, often toward potential threats (e.g., predators, intruders, enemy forces in combat). It demands maximum physiological and psychological attention and an ability to attend and respond to stimulus changes for uninterrupted periods of time, which can produce significant cognitive stress and occasional physiological stress reactions. —**vigilant** *adj.*

violation-of-expectation method a technique, based on habituation and dishabituation procedures, in which increases in an infant's looking time are interpreted as evidence that the outcome expected by the infant has not occurred.

violence *n.* the expression of hostility and rage with the intent to injure or damage people or property through physical force. See also DOMESTIC VIOLENCE. —**violent** *adj.*

virilism *n.* the presence in a female of secondary sexual characteristics that are peculiar to men, such as muscle bulk and hirsutism. The condition is due to overactivity of the adrenal cortex, with excessive secretion of androgen.

virtual reality therapy a form of IN VIVO EXPOSURE in which clients are active participants immersed in a three-dimensional computer-generated interactive environment that allows them a sense of actual presence in scenarios related to their presenting problems. This treatment is currently used primarily for anxiety-related disorders, such as fear of flying.

viscera *pl. n.* (*sing.* **viscus**) the organs in any major body cavity, especially the abdominal organs (stomach, intestines, kidneys, etc.). —**visceral** *adj.*

visible spectrum see SPECTRUM.

vision *n.* the sense of sight, in which the eye is the receptor and the stimulus is radiant energy in the visible SPECTRUM. See also VISUAL SYSTEM. —**visual** *adj.*

visual agnosia loss or impairment of the ability to recognize and understand the nature of visual stimuli. Various subtypes exist, based on the type of visual stimulus the person has difficulty recognizing, such as objects (**visual object agnosia** or **visual form agnosia**), multiple objects or pictures (**simultanagnosia**), or faces (**prosopagnosia**).

visual area any of many regions of the cerebral cortex in which the neurons are primarily sensitive to visual stimulation. Together, all the visual areas comprise the VISUAL CORTEX. Most visual areas can be distinguished from one another on the basis of their anatomical connections (i.e., their CYTOARCHITECTURE) and their specific visual sensitivities. Individual areas are designated by

V

"V" and a number (e.g., V1, V2...V5), which indicates roughly how distant the area is from STRIATE CORTEX.

visual capture the tendency for vision to override the other senses. It is responsible for the VENTRILO-QUISM EFFECT.

visual cliff an apparatus to investigate the development of DEPTH PERCEPTION in nonverbal human infants and animals, in particular, whether depth perception is an innate ability or learned through visuomotor experience. The apparatus consists of a table with a checkerboard pattern, dropping steeply down a "cliff" to a surface with the same pattern some distance below the tabletop. The apparatus is covered with a transparent surface, and the participant is positioned on this at the border between the tabletop and the cliff. Reluctance to crawl onto the surface covering the cliff is taken as an indication that the participant can discriminate the apparent difference in depth between the two sides of the apparatus. Most infants as young as 6 months of age will not cross over to the side over the cliff.

visual cortex the cerebral cortex of the occipital lobe, specifically the STRIATE CORTEX (primary visual cortex). In humans this occupies a small region on the lateral surface of the occipital pole of the brain, but most is buried in the banks of the calcarine fissure on the medial surface of the brain. The visual cortex receives input directly from the LATERAL GENICULATE NUCLEUS via the OPTIC TRACT and sends output to the multiple visual areas that make up the visual ASSOCIATION CORTEX.

visual field the extent of visual space over which vision is possible with the eyes held in a fixed position. The outer limit of vision for each eye extends approximately 60° nasally, 90° temporally, 50° superiorly, and 70° inferiorly. The extent varies with age: Very young children and older people have a smaller visual field.

visual form agnosia see VISUAL AGNOSIA.

visual hallucination visual perception in the absence of any external stimulus. Visual hallucinations may be unformed (e.g., shapes, colors) or complex (e.g., figures, faces, scenes). They may be associated with psychotic disorders or with pathological states of the visual system.

visual illusion a misperception of external visual stimuli that occurs as a result of a misinterpretation of the stimuli, such as a GEOMETRIC ILLUSION. Visual illusions are among the most common type of illusion.

visual imagery mental imagery that involves the sense of having "pictures" in the mind. Such images may be memories of earlier visual experiences or syntheses produced by the imagination (as, for example, in visualizing a pink kangaroo). Visual imagery can be used for such purposes as dealing with traumatic events, establishing DESENSITIZATION hierarchies, or improving physical performance.

visual masking see MASKING.

visual object agnosia see VISUAL AGNOSIA.

visual perception the awareness of visual sensations that arises from the interplay between the physiology of the VISUAL SYSTEM and the internal and external environments of the observer.

visual search the process of detecting a target visual stimulus among distractor stimuli. In experimental studies, the characteristics of the target and distractors are manipulated to explore the mental operations that underlie visual attention. See also FEATURE-INTEGRATION THEORY.

visual system the components of the nervous system and the nonneural apparatus of the eye that contribute to the perception of visual stimulation. The anterior structures of the eye, such as the CORNEA and LENS, focus light on the RETINA, which transduces photons into neural signals. These are transmitted via the OPTIC NERVE and OPTIC TRACT to nuclei in the thalamus and brainstem. These in turn transmit the signals either to the VISUAL AREAS of the cerebral cortex for conscious analysis or directly to motor centers in the brainstem and spinal cord to produce eye movements.

visuospatial scratchpad see WORKING MEMORY.

vital capacity the capacity of the lungs to hold air, measured as the maximum volume of air that can be exhaled after maximum inspiration.

vitality *n.* physical or intellectual vigor or energy: the state of being full of zest and enthusiastic about ongoing activities. See also FITNESS.

vitreous humor see EYE.

vocalization *n.* the production of sounds by means of vibrations of the vocal cords, as in speaking, babbling, singing, screaming, and so forth. —**vocalize** *vb.*

voice-onset time in phonetics, the brief instant that elapses between the initial movement of the speech organs as one begins to articulate a speech sound and the vibration of the vocal cords. Voice-onset time has been the subject of intense research in adult and infant speech perception because of evidence that this continuous acoustic dimension is perceived categorically (see CATEGORICAL PERCEPTION).

volley theory the principle that

individual fibers in an auditory nerve respond to one or another stimulus in a rapid succession of rhythmic sound stimuli, whereas other fibers in the nerve respond to the second, third, or *n*th stimulus. The result is that successive volleys of impulses are fired to match the inputs of stimuli, yet no single fiber is required to respond to every stimulus. Thus a nerve can reflect a more rapid frequency of stimulation (e.g., 1000 Hz) than any individual fiber could follow.

volumetric thirst see HYPO-VOLEMIC THIRST.

voluntary *adj.* describing activity, movement, behavior, or other processes produced by choice or intention and under cortical control, in contrast to automatic movements (e.g., reflexes) or action that is not intended (**ideomotor activity**). Compare INVOLUNTARY.

volunteer bias any systematic difference between participants who volunteer to be in a study versus those who do not.

vomeronasal system a set of specialized receptor cells that in nonhuman mammals is sensitive to PHEROMONES and thus plays an important role in the sexual behavior and reproductive physiology of these animals. In humans this system responds physiologically to chemical stimulation and, in turn, excites brain centers, but its role in human olfaction is not known.

voodoo death a CULTURE-BOUND SYNDROME observed in Haiti, Africa, Australia, and islands of the Pacific and the Caribbean. An individual who has disobeyed a ritual or taboo is hexed or cursed by a medicine man or sorcerer and dies within a few days. The individual's strong belief in the curse is posited to be the

V

cause of physiological reactions in the body resulting in death.

voyeurism *n.* a PARAPHILIA in which preferred or exclusive sexual interest and arousal is focused on observing unsuspecting people who are nude or in the act of undressing or engaging in sexual activity. Although the **voyeur** seeks no sexual activity with the person observed, orgasm is usually produced through masturbation during the act of "peeping" or later, while visualizing and remembering the event. **—voyeuristic** *adj.*

vulnerability *n.* susceptibility to developing a condition, disorder, or disease when exposed to specific agents or conditions. **—vulnerable** *adj.*

Ww

Wada test a presurgical and diagnostic technique for determining hemispheric functions, typically memory and language, by injecting a small dose of a barbiturate into an internal carotid artery. While each hemisphere is separately anesthetized, various cognitive tasks are administered; impairments on these tasks suggest that these functions are represented in the anesthetized hemisphere. [Juhn Atsushi **Wada** (1924–), Japanese-born Canadian neurosurgeon]

WAIS abbreviation for WECHSLER ADULT INTELLIGENCE SCALE.

waiting-list control group a group of research participants that will receive the same intervention given to the EXPERIMENTAL GROUPS but at a later time, thus functioning as a CONTROL GROUP in the interim.

Wason selection task a reasoning task involving four cards, each with a letter on one side and a number on the other, and a rule that is supposed to govern their correlation (e.g., if the letter is a vowel, then the number should be even). One side of each card is shown (e.g., the cards might show E D 3 8), and the solver is asked which cards must be turned over to determine if the rule has been followed. Also called **four-card problem**. [developed in 1966 by Peter Cathcart **Wason** (1924–2003), British psychologist]

waterfall illusion see MOTION AFTEREFFECT.

wavelength *n.* the distance between successive peaks in a wave motion of a given FREQUENCY, such as a sound wave or a wave of electromagnetic radiation. The wavelength is equal to the speed of propagation of the wave motion divided by its frequency.

WCST abbreviation for WISCONSIN CARD SORTING TEST.

weapons effect increased hostility or a heightened inclination to aggression produced by the mere sight of a weapon. If provoked, individuals who have previously been exposed to the sight of a weapon will behave more aggressively than those who have not. Subsequent research has shown that this aggressive behavior is primed by the sight of weapons (see PRIMING) and that any other object associated with aggression can have the same effect.

wear-and-tear theory of aging a theory of biological aging suggesting that aging results from an accumulation of damage to cells, tissues, and organs in the body caused by toxins in our diet and by environmental agents. This leads to the weakening and eventual death of the cells, tissues, and organs.

Weber's law a mathematical model of the DIFFERENCE THRESHOLD, stating that the magnitude needed to detect physical change in a stimulus is proportional to the absolute magnitude of that stimulus. Thus the more intense the stimulus, the greater the change that must be made in it to be noticed. This can be expressed as $\Delta I/I = k$, where ΔI is the difference threshold, I is the original stimulus magnitude, and *k* is a constant called **Weber's fraction**. See also FECHNER'S LAW. [proposed in 1834 by Ernst **Weber** (1795–1878), German physiologist and psychophysicist]

Wechsler Adult Intelligence Scale (**WAIS**) an intelligence test originally published in 1955. A modification and replacement of the **Wechsler–Bellevue Intelligence Scale**, the WAIS currently includes seven verbal subtests (Information, Comprehension, Arithmetic, Similarities, Digit Span, Vocabulary, Letter–Number Sequencing) and seven performance subtests (Digit Symbol, Picture Completion, Block Design, Picture Arrangement, Object Assembly, Matrix Reasoning, Symbol Search). The most recent version is the **WAIS-III**, published in 1997. [David **Wechsler** (1896–1981), Romanian-born U.S. psychologist]

Wechsler Intelligence Scale for Children (**WISC**) a children's intelligence test developed initially in 1949. It currently includes 10 core subtests (Similarities, Vocabulary, Comprehension, Block Design, Picture Concepts, Matrix Reasoning, Digit Span, Letter–Number Sequencing, Coding, Symbol Search) and 5 supplemental subtests (Word Reasoning, Information, Picture Completion, Arithmetic, Cancellation) that measure verbal comprehension, perceptual reasoning, processing speed, and working memory capabilities. The most recent version of the test is the **WISC–IV**, published in 2003. [David **Wechsler**]

Wechsler Preschool and Primary Scale of Intelligence (**WPPSI**) an intelligence test for young children that currently includes seven verbal subtests (Information, Vocabulary, Receptive Vocabulary, Word Reasoning, Similarities, Comprehension,

Picture Naming) and seven performance subtests (Picture Completion, Picture Concepts, Block Design, Object Assembly, Matrix Reasoning, Symbol Search, Coding). The WPPSI was originally published in 1967; the most recent version is the **WPPSI–III**, published in 2002. [David **Wechsler**]

weight *n.* a coefficient or multiplier used in an equation or statistical investigation and applied to a particular variable to reflect the contribution to the data. The process of doing this is called **weighting**.

well-being *n.* a state of happiness, contentment, low levels of distress, overall good physical and mental health and outlook, or good quality of life.

wellness *n.* a dynamic state of physical, mental, and social WELL-BEING. Some researchers and clinicians have viewed wellness as the result of four key factors over which an individual has some control: biology (i.e., body condition and fitness), environment, lifestyle, and health care management. The **wellness concept** is the notion that individual health care and health care programs should actively involve the promotion of good mental and physical health rather than merely being concerned with the prevention and treatment of illness and disease.

Wernicke's aphasia a loss of the ability to comprehend sounds or speech (auditory amnesia), and in particular to understand or repeat spoken language and to name objects or qualities (anomia). The condition is a result of brain damage and may be associated with other disorders of communication, including ALEXIA, ACALCULIA, or AGRAPHIA. [Karl **Wernicke** (1848–1904), German neurologist]

Wernicke's area a region in the

W

posterior temporal gyrus of the left hemisphere of the cerebrum in the brain, containing nerve tissue associated with the interpretation of sounds. See also SPEECH AREA. [Karl **Wernicke**, who reported, in 1874, a lack of comprehension of speech in patients who had suffered a brain lesion in that area]

Wernicke's encephalopathy a neurological disorder caused by a deficiency of vitamin B_1 (thiamine). The principal symptoms are confusion, oculomotor abnormalities, and ATAXIA. The disorder is most frequently associated with chronic alcoholism and is likely to resolve with thiamine treatment, although most individuals then develop severe retrograde and anterograde amnesia as well as impairment in other areas of cognitive functioning, including executive functions (see KORSAKOFF'S SYNDROME). [first described in 1881 by Karl **Wernicke**]

what pathway see VENTRAL STREAM.

where pathway see DORSAL STREAM.

white matter parts of the nervous system composed of nerve fibers that are enclosed in a MYELIN SHEATH, which gives a white coloration to otherwise grayish neural structures. The sheaths cover only the fibers, so regions containing mainly CELL BODIES are gray. Compare GRAY MATTER.

whole-language approach a top-down approach to teaching reading that emphasizes the reader's active construction of meaning and often excludes the use of phonics.

whole method of learning a learning technique in which the entire block of material is memorized, as opposed to learning the material in parts. Compare PART METHOD OF LEARNING.

Wilcoxon test a nonparametric test of the difference in distribution for matched sets of research participants or for repeatedly observed participants. [Frank **Wilcoxon** (1892–1965), Irish mathematician and statistician]

Williams syndrome (Williams–Barratt syndrome; Williams–Beuren syndrome) a rare disorder caused by deletion of a segment of chromosome 7. In addition to mental retardation, it is characterized by FAILURE TO THRIVE, high concentrations of calcium in the blood, narrowing of blood vessels (particularly the aorta, which restricts blood flow from the heart), and unusual facial features (e.g., short nose with a broad tip, wide mouth, small chin). Additionally, individuals with Williams syndrome are highly sociable and have superior verbal (compared to nonverbal) skills. [described in the 1960s by J. C. P. **Williams**, 20th-century New Zealand cardiologist; Brian Gerald **Barratt–Boyes** (1924–), British cardiologist; and Alois J. **Beuren** (1919–1984), German cardiologist]

windigo *n.* a severe CULTURE-BOUND SYNDROME occurring among northern Algonquin Indians living in Canada and the northeastern United States. The syndrome is characterized by delusions of becoming possessed by a flesh-eating monster (the windigo) and is manifested in symptoms including depression, violence, a compulsive desire for human flesh, and sometimes actual cannibalism.

WISC abbreviation for WECHSLER INTELLIGENCE SCALE FOR CHILDREN.

Wisconsin Card Sorting Test (WCST) a test that requires participants to deduce from feedback (right vs. wrong) how to sort a series of cards depicting different geometric shapes in various colors and quantities. Once the participant has

W

identified the underlying sorting principle (e.g., by color) and correctly sorts 10 consecutive cards, the principle is changed without notification. Although the task involves many aspects of brain function, it is primarily considered a test of EXECUTIVE FUNCTIONS.

wisdom *n.* the ability of an individual to make sound decisions, to find the right—or at least good—answers to difficult and important life questions, and to give advice about the complex problems of everyday life and interpersonal relationships. The role of knowledge and life experience and the importance of applying knowledge toward a common good through balancing of one's own, others', and institutional interests are two perspectives that have received significant psychological study.

wish-fulfillment *n.* in psychoanalytic theory, the gratification, in fantasy or in a dream, of a wish associated with a biological INSTINCT.

withdrawal *n.* see SUBSTANCE WITHDRAWAL.

within-group variance variation in experimental scores among identically treated individuals within the same group who experienced the same experimental conditions. It is determined through an ANALYSIS OF VARIANCE and compared with BETWEEN-GROUPS VARIANCE to obtain an F RATIO.

within-subjects design an experimental design in which the effects of treatments are seen through the comparison of scores of the same participant observed under all the treatment conditions. Also called **repeated measures design**. Compare BETWEEN-SUBJECTS DESIGN.

Wolffian duct a rudimentary duct system in the embryo that develops into structures of the male reproductive system (the epididymis, vas deferens, and seminal vesicles). In the female, the Wolffian duct does not develop. Compare MÜLLERIAN DUCT. [Kaspar F. **Wolff** (1734–1794), German embryologist]

word-association test a projective test in which the participant responds to a stimulus word with the first word that comes to mind.

word-form dyslexia a type of acquired DYSLEXIA characterized by the inability to recognize and read whole words, which can be read only by spelling them out letter by letter. Also called **spelling dyslexia**.

word salad an extreme form of thought disorder, manifest in severely disorganized and virtually incomprehensible speech or writing; the person's associations appear to have little or no logical connection. It is strongly suggestive of schizophrenia.

word-superiority effect the finding that, when presented briefly, individual letters are more easily identified in the context of a word than when presented alone. A similar but weaker effect is obtained when letters are presented as part of a pronounceable but meaningless vowel-consonant combination, such as *deet* or *pling*.

working memory a multicomponent model of SHORT-TERM MEMORY that has a **phonological** (or **articulatory**) **loop** to retain verbal information, a **visuospatial scratchpad** to retain visual information, and a **central executive** to deploy attention between them.

working through 1. in psychotherapy, the process by which clients identify, explore, and deal with psychological issues, on both an intellectual and emotional level, through the presentation of such

W

material to, and in discussion with, the therapist. **2.** in psychoanalysis, the process by which patients gradually overcome their RESISTANCE to the disclosure of unconscious material and are repeatedly brought face to face with the repressed feelings, threatening impulses, and internal conflicts at the root of their difficulties.

work psychology see INDUSTRIAL AND ORGANIZATIONAL PSYCHOLOGY.

WPPSI abbreviation for WECHSLER PRESCHOOL AND PRIMARY SCALE OF INTELLIGENCE.

W

Xx

$\bar{x}$ abbreviation for MEAN.

x-axis *n.* the horizontal axis on a graph. See ABSCISSA.

X chromosome the SEX CHROMOSOME that is responsible for determining femaleness in humans and other mammals. The body cells of normal females possess two X chromosomes (XX), whereas males have one X chromosome and one Y CHROMOSOME (XY). In humans, various authorities estimate that the X chromosome carries between 1,000 and about 2,000 genes, including many responsible for hereditary diseases (see SEX-LINKED). Abnormal numbers of X chromosomes lead to genetic imbalance and a range of disorders and syndromes.

xenophobia *n.* a strong and irrational, sometimes pathological, fear of strangers. Xenophobia may manifest as hostile attitudes or aggressive behavior toward people of other nationalities, ethnic groups, or even different regions or neighborhoods. **—xenophobic** *adj.*

X-linked *adj.* see SEX-LINKED.

XX see X CHROMOSOME.

XXY syndrome see KLINEFELTER'S SYNDROME.

XY see Y CHROMOSOME.

XYY syndrome a chromosomal anomaly discovered in 1961 and associated with males who were aggressive or violent in institutions for criminals. It was originally assumed that the extra Y chromosome predisposes males to such behavior, but the theory was modified when XYY anomalies were later found among normal males.

Yy

y-axis *n.* the vertical axis on a graph. See ORDINATE.

Y chromosome the SEX CHROMOSOME that is responsible for determining maleness in humans and other mammals. The body cells of normal males possess one Y chromosome and one X CHROMOSOME (XY). The Y chromosome is much smaller than the X chromosome and is thought to carry just a handful of functioning genes. Hence, males are far more susceptible to SEX-LINKED diseases than females, because the Y chromosome cannot counteract any defective genes carried on the X chromosome.

yea-saying *n.* answering questions positively regardless of their content, which can distort the results of surveys, questionnaires, and similar instruments. Also called **response acquiescence**. Compare NAY-SAYING.

Yerkes–Dodson law a law stating that the relation between motivation (AROUSAL) and performance can be represented by an inverted U-curve (see INVERTED-U HYPOTHESIS). [Robert M. **Yerkes** (1876–1956) and John Dillingham **Dodson** (1879–1955), U.S. psychologists]

yoked control a procedure to ensure experimental control (e.g., baseline measures) in OPERANT CONDITIONING in which the rate of responding of an experimental subject is yoked—and, thus, compared—with that of a control subject. The subject and the control receive reinforcers or punishers on the same schedule, but the subject's receipt is dependent on behavior, whereas the control's is independent of behavior. For example, in one condition a nonhuman animal might press a lever so as to avoid electric shocks. In a yoked-control condition, the same temporal pattern of shocks received in the first case would be presented to the control animal independently of its behavior.

Young–Helmholtz theory of color vision a theory to explain color vision in terms of components or processes sensitive to three different parts of the spectrum corresponding to the colors red, green, and blue. According to this theory, other colors are perceived by stimulation of two of the three processes, while light that stimulates all three processes equally is perceived as white. The components are now thought to be RETINAL CONES, although the original theory was not tied to a particular (or indeed to any) cell type. See TRICHROMATIC THEORY. Compare HERING THEORY OF COLOR VISION; OPPONENT PROCESS THEORY OF COLOR VISION. [Thomas **Young** (1773–1829), British physician and physicist; Hermann Ludwig Ferdinand von **Helmholtz** (1821–1894), German physiologist and physicist]

young-old *adj.* see ADULTHOOD.

Zz

Zeigarnik effect the tendency for interrupted, uncompleted tasks to be better remembered than completed tasks. Some theorists relate this phenomenon to certain GESTALT PRINCIPLES OF ORGANIZATION but at the level of higher mental processing (e.g., memory), rather than at the level of pure perception. [described in 1927 by Bluma **Zeigarnik** (1900–1988), Russian psychologist]

Zeitgeber *n.* a cue, such as day length, used to activate or time a BIOLOGICAL RHYTHM. See ENTRAINMENT. [German, "time giver"]

Zeitgeist *n.* the spirit of the times (German, "time spirit"). The term was used by German philosopher Georg Wilhelm Friedrich Hegel (1770–1831) to refer to a type of supraindividual mind at work in the world and manifest in the cultural worldview that pervades the ideas, attitudes, and feelings of a particular society in a specific historical period.

Zener cards a standardized set of stimulus materials, similar to a deck of playing cards, designed for use in experiments on EXTRASENSORY PERCEPTION and other parapsychological phenomena. The set consists of 25 cards, each of which bears one of five printed symbols (star, wavy lines, cross, circle, or square). In a typical test of TELEPATHY, the cards are shuffled and a designated "sender" turns the cards over one at a time to inspect the symbol, while a "receiver" attempts to guess the symbol by reading the thoughts of

the sender. Also called **Rhine cards**. [named in honor of Karl E. **Zener** (1903–1964), U.S. perceptual psychologist who designed the symbols, by his colleague U.S. psychologist Joseph B. **Rhine** (1895–1980), who devised the deck]

zero-sum game in GAME THEORY, a type of game in which the players' gains and losses add up to zero. The total amount of resources available to the participants is fixed, and therefore one player's gain necessarily entails the others' loss. The term is used particularly in analyses of bargaining and economic behavior but is sometimes also used in other sociocultural contexts (e.g., politics).

Zöllner illusion a visual illusion in which parallel lines appear to diverge when one of the lines is intersected by short diagonal lines slanting in one direction, and the other by lines slanting in the other direction. [Johann Karl Friedrich **Zöllner** (1834–1882), German astrophysicist]

zone of proximal development in the sociocultural theory of Russian psychologist Lev Vygotsky (1896–1934), the difference between a child's actual level of ability and the level of ability that he or she can achieve when working under the guidance of an instructor. See SOCIOCULTURAL PERSPECTIVE.

zoomorphism *n.* **1.** the attribution of animal traits to human beings, deities, or inanimate objects. **2.** the use of animal psychology or physiology to explain human behavior. Compare ANTHROPOMORPHISM.

zoophilia *n.* a PARAPHILIA in which animals are repeatedly preferred or exclusively used to achieve sexual excitement and gratification. The animal, which is usually a household pet or farm animal, is either used as the object of intercourse or is trained to lick or rub the human partner, referred to as a **zoophile**.

z score see STANDARD SCORE.

z test a type of statistical test that compares the MEANS of two different groups to determine whether there is a SIGNIFICANT DIFFERENCE between them (i.e., one not likely to have occurred by chance). Generally, this involves comparing the mean from a SAMPLE of a POPULATION to the mean for the whole population but may also involve comparing the means of two different populations. The z test is based on the NORMAL DISTRIBUTION and is used when the STANDARD DEVIATION is known or the sample is large (greater than 30). The equivalent T TEST is used with unknown standard deviations or smaller samples.

Z transformation see FISHER'S R TO Z TRANSFORMATION.

zygote *n.* a fertilized egg, or ovum, with a DIPLOID set of chromosomes, half contributed by the mother and half by the father. The zygote divides to become an EMBRYO, which continues to divide as it develops and differentiates—in humans eventually forming a FETUS. —**zygotic** *adj.*

Z

Appendix

Significant Historical Figures
in Psychology

Adler, Alfred (1870–1937) Austrian psychiatrist: the first disciple of Sigmund Freud to break away to found his own school, INDIVIDUAL PSYCHOLOGY, which evolved such concepts as the INFERIORITY COMPLEX and COMPENSATION.

Ainsworth, Mary Dinsmore Salter (1913–1999) U.S. developmental psychologist: assisted John Bowlby in formulating the highly influential ATTACHMENT THEORY; later devised the STRANGE SITUATION.

Allport, Floyd Henry (1890–1971) U.S. psychologist: a founder of experimental social psychology; his approach emphasized individuals over the group, established a behaviorist framework, and advanced experimental methodology; brother of Gordon W. Allport.

Allport, Gordon Willard (1897–1967) U.S. psychologist: a major figure in social psychology; originator of Allport's personality trait theory and coauthor of two personality inventories—the **Allport–Vernon–Lindzey Study of Values** and the **Allport AS Reaction Study**; brother of Floyd H. Allport.

Anastasi, Anne (1908–2001) U.S. psychologist: an important contributor to the discussion of the NATURE–NURTURE controversy and, especially, to psychological testing.

Angell, James Rowland (1869–1949) U.S. psychologist: a major spokesperson for the development of psychology as a science in the United States and a leading exponent of FUNCTIONALISM.

Asch, Solomon E. (1907–1996) Polish-born U.S. psychologist: best known for his contributions to social psychology, especially in showing how social context influences fundamental processes, such as perception (his studies of CONFORMITY influenced the research of Stanley Milgram).

Baldwin, James Mark (1861–1934) U.S. psychologist: an influential figure in the early development of experimental and professional psychology in the United States; a proponent of FUNCTIONALISM and early contributor in developmental psychology.

Bandura, Albert (1925–) Canadian-born U.S. psychologist: best known for his work on SOCIAL LEARNING THEORY; especially influential were his studies of OBSERVATIONAL LEARNING and, in the field of SOCIAL-COGNITIVE THEORY, of self-regulatory processes and their role in motivation and behavior.

Baltes, Paul (1939–2006) German developmental psychologist: helped to define the perspective upon which LIFE-SPAN DEVELOPMENTAL PSYCHOLOGY is based; with his wife, psychologist Margaret Baltes, described SELECTIVE OPTIMIZATION WITH COMPENSATION and introduced a method to study adult age differences in cognition that makes use of the concept of RESERVE CAPACITY.

Bayley, Nancy (1899–1994) U.S. developmental psychologist: best known as the developer of the BAYLEY SCALES OF INFANT AND TODDLER DEVELOPMENT.

Beach, Frank A. (1911–1988) U.S. psychologist: a founder of BEHAVIORAL ENDOCRINOLOGY and an important comparative psychologist, known especially for research on patterns of sexual behavior.

Beers, Clifford (1876–1943) U.S. philanthropist: founder of the MENTAL HYGIENE movement, which helped establish psychology as a discipline in the United States through encouraging the use of mental tests and contributing to the rise of clinical and industrial and organizational psychology.

Békésy, Georg von (1899–1972) Hungarian-born U.S. physicist: groundbreaking researcher in auditory science, especially his studies of mammalian hearing and on the pattern of movement in the BASILAR MEMBRANE of the inner ear known as the **traveling wave**.

Bekhterev, Vladimir Mikhailovich (1857–1927) Russian neuropathologist: founder of Russia's first psychophysiological laboratory and first institute for brain research on mental diseases; now credited with playing a greater role than Ivan Pavlov in the introduction of CONDITIONING to psychology.

Benussi, Vittorio (1878–1927) Italian psychologist: His research on optical illusions and time perception contributed to GESTALT PSYCHOLOGY; later research on posthypnotic states (e.g., POSTHYPNOTIC SUGGESTION) sought to provide evidence for Freud's concept of REPRESSION.

Binet, Alfred (1857–1911) French psychologist: often considered the initiator of the modern approach to intelligence testing, especially as the developer of the Binet–Simon Scale (see STANFORD–BINET INTELLIGENCE SCALE).

Bingham, Walter Van Dyke (1880–1952) U.S. psychologist: the founder of industrial and organizational psychology and a key figure in the development of the U.S. Army mental testing program in World War I.

Bleuler, Eugen (1857–1939) Swiss psychiatrist: best known for naming SCHIZOPHRENIA and for his theory of its basic underlying symptomatology; advocated psychosocial treatments for people with severe mental illness and introduced OCCUPATIONAL THERAPY.

Boring, Edwin Garrigues (1886–1968) U.S. psychologist: perhaps the most influential definer of the field of experimental psychology from the 1930s through the 1960s.

Bowlby, Edward John Mostyn (1907–1990) British psychiatrist and psychoanalyst: best known as the developer of ATTACHMENT THEORY; his most important early work centered on the deleterious effects of maternal deprivation.

Brentano, Franz (1838–1917) German philosopher and psychologist: His research on the intentionality of mental acts later developed into the field of **act psychology** and contributed to the debate in artificial intelligence about whether mechanical processes can assume the intentionality of genuine mental acts.

Breuer, Josef (1842–1925) Austrian physician and physiologist: called by Freud the "father of psychoanalysis," best remembered for his treatment of Austrian social worker and feminist Bertha Pappenheim (known as "Anna

O."), whom he identified as having HYSTERIA; Freud's technique of FREE ASSOCIATION evolved from the concepts behind Breuer's methods.

Broadbent, Donald E. (1926–1993) British psychologist: best known for his application of communications engineering and mathematical DECISION THEORY to psychology.

Broca, Paul (1824–1880) French physician and anthropologist: proved that motor aphasia (later known as BROCA'S APHASIA) was associated with the third frontal convolution of the cerebral cortex (now called BROCA'S AREA) and that fluent speech depends on this area; among the first to recognize the phenomenon of CEREBRAL DOMINANCE.

Bronfenbrenner, Urie (1917–2005) Russian-born developmental psychologist: originator of the watershed ECOLOGICAL SYSTEMS THEORY; later developed this approach into the BIOECOLOGICAL MODEL.

Brown, Roger (1925–1997) U.S. social psychologist: a classic contributor in the field of PSYCHOLINGUISTICS (particularly to the first stages of LANGUAGE ACQUISITION); coined the term FLASHBULB MEMORY.

Brunswik, Egon (1903–1955) Austrian-born U.S. psychologist: recognized for his research on visual DISCRIMINATION and categorization and for the **Brunswik ratio**, a mathematical expression of PERCEPTUAL CONSTANCY.

Calkins, Mary Whiton (1863–1930) U.S. psychologist: her best known empirical contribution was the development of the technique of PAIRED-ASSOCIATES LEARNING for studying memory; the first woman president of the American Psychological Association.

Campbell, Donald Thomas (1916–1996) U.S. social psychologist: known for developing methods for determining the CONSTRUCT VALIDITY of psychological measures and contributions to the philosophy of science.

Cannon, Walter Bradford (1871–1945) U.S. physician and physiologist: known particularly for his investigations of emotion, in which he identified the biological mechanisms associated with the FIGHT-OR-FLIGHT RESPONSE and proposed the CANNON–BARD THEORY.

Carr, Harvey A. (1873–1954) U.S. psychologist: His contributions focused on adaptive human behavior as a manifestation of mental processes, on MAZE learning in rats, and on visual and spatial perception.

Cattell, James McKeen (1860–1944) U.S. psychologist: a founder of psychology in the United States and an influential journal editor; devised the first battery of psychological tests of special abilities; cofounded the Psychological Corporation.

Cattell, Raymond Bernard (1905–1998) British psychologist: developed, with colleagues, the **Sixteen Personality Factor Questionnaire**, one of the most frequently used self-report personality inventories.

Charcot, Jean-Martin (1825–1893) French neurologist: sometimes called the "father of neurology" for his pioneering research on such disorders as locomotor ataxia, multiple sclerosis, and Parkinson's disease; his research on hysteria had great influence on the early careers of his students Sigmund Freud and Alfred Binet.

Chomsky, Noam (1928–) U.S. linguist: known for his revolutionary TRANSFORMATIONAL GENERATIVE GRAMMAR, which had major and controversial influence in the field of PSYCHOLINGUISTICS.

Claparède, Edouard (1873–1940) Swiss psychologist: a key figure in the child study and progressive education movements; demonstrated the importance of intelligence testing in the educational context; also contributed significant research on the biology of sleep.

Clark, Kenneth Bancroft (1914–2005) U.S. psychologist: the first African American president of the American Psychological Association; his work was influential in the U.S. Supreme Court's 1954 ruling *Brown v. the Board of Education,* which banned racial segregation in U.S. public schools.

Cronbach, Lee J. (1916–2001) U.S. psychologist: an influential contributor to the topic of test VALIDITY and the developer of CRONBACH'S ALPHA.

Darwin, Charles R. (1809–1882) British naturalist: His theory of NATURAL SELECTION has had significant and ongoing influence in various approaches to psychology, including EVOLUTIONARY PSYCHOLOGY and SOCIOBIOLOGY.

Dewey, John (1859–1952) U.S. philosopher, educator, and psychologist: a founder of FUNCTIONALISM, who strongly influenced the field of education.

Doll, Edgar Arnold (1889–1968) U.S. psychologist: best known for the development of the Vineland Social Maturity Scale, the antecedent of the now widely used **Vineland Adaptive Behavior Scales** for assessing a person's communication, daily living, socialization, and motor skills.

Dollard, John (1900–1980) U.S. social scientist: developer of the FRUSTRATION–AGGRESSION HYPOTHESIS; also known for his work (with Neal E. Miller) on the importance of IMITATION in social behavior and learning.

Durkheim, Emile (1858–1917) French sociologist: known especially for his theories of suicide and schematic categorization encompassing four types—egoistic (resulting from abject loneliness), altruistic (self-sacrifice to save others), anomic (resulting from social adversity), and fatalistic (resulting from excessive social regulation).

Ebbinghaus, Hermann (1850–1909) German psychologist: a pioneer in the application of quantitative methods of psychophysics to the study of higher mental processes and in establishing experimental psychology as a scientific discipline.

Erickson, Milton Hyland (1901–1980) U.S. psychiatrist: developed the hypnosis- and metaphor-based system known as **Ericksonian psychotherapy**; devised a "strategic therapy," in which the therapist directly influences clients by initiating what happens during sessions.

Erikson, Erik H. (1902–1994) German-born U.S. psychologist: preeminent personality theorist and contributor to the field of EGO PSYCHOLOGY; known for his theory of life stages—ERIKSON'S EIGHT STAGES OF DEVELOPMENT—and as coiner of the term IDENTITY CRISIS.

Estes, William Kaye (1919–) U.S. psychologist: a founding figure of mathematical psychology and a pioneer (with B. F. Skinner) in the use of CONDITIONED RESPONSES involving negative emotions (e.g., fear or anxiety).

Eysenck, Hans Jurgen (1916–1997) German-born British psychologist: founder of the Institute of Psychiatry at the Maudsley Hospital at the University of London; popularized the terms "introvert" and "extravert" and developed the EYSENCK PERSONALITY INVENTORY.

Fechner, Gustav Theodor (1801–1887) German physician and philosopher: developer of still-used methods to study sensations, including the METHOD OF ADJUSTMENT and the METHOD OF CONSTANT STIMULI; developed the mathematical formula called FECHNER'S LAW.

Ferenczi, Sandor (1873–1933) Hungarian psychoanalyst: an early associate of Sigmund Freud who articulated an "active" therapy as an alternative to Freud's psychoanalytic approach; later (with Otto Rank) advanced the concept of BRIEF PSYCHODYNAMIC PSYCHOTHERAPY.

Festinger, Leon (1919–1989) U.S. social psychologist: best known for his theory of COGNITIVE DISSONANCE and for his investigations into such group dynamics as COHESION, CONFORMITY, and SOCIAL COMPARISON THEORY.

Frankel, Viktor Emil (1905–1997) Austrian psychiatrist: a chief exponent of EXISTENTIAL PSYCHOLOGY; his approach, **logotherapy**, focuses on crises of meaning and is often referred to as the "third Viennese school of psychotherapy" (after Freud's psychoanalysis and Adler's individual psychology).

Freud, Anna (1895–1982) Austrian-born British psychoanalyst: Her studies on DEFENSE MECHANISMS and pioneering work in child analysis were original contributions to theory and practice in psychoanalysis; youngest daughter of Sigmund Freud.

Freud, Sigmund (1856–1939) Austrian neurologist and psychiatrist: inventor of the technique of PSYCHOANALYSIS and developer of many of its central theoretical concepts (e.g., DEFENSE MECHANISMS, PSYCHOSEXUAL DEVELOPMENT, TRANSFERENCE, etc.) and methods of practice, such as FREE ASSOCIATION and DREAM ANALYSIS.

Fromm, Erich (1900–1980) German-born U.S. psychoanalyst: developer of a broad cultural, yet personal, approach in analysis that focused on the search for meaning and the development of socially productive relationships, individuality, and the need to belong.

Galton, Francis (1822–1911) British scientist: developed theories about the HERITABILITY and selective breeding of human intelligence, from which emerged the idea of intelligence tests and the movement he later called EUGENICS; also introduced techniques of statistical CORRELATION; cousin of Charles Darwin.

Gemelli, Agostino (1878–1959) Italian psychologist: promoter of practical, applied psychology; cofounded an influential European academic journal on psychology, neurology, and psychiatry.

Gesell, Arnold L. (1880–1961) U.S. psychologist and physician: the first school psychologist in the United States; established special education classrooms, pioneered the co-twin technique to study the impact of learning and heredity, and advanced the concept of school readiness programs to prepare children for formal classroom instruction.

Gibson, Eleanor Jack (1910–2002) U.S. experimental psychologist: best known for her research on perceptual learning, especially on the VISUAL CLIFF; married to James J. Gibson.

Gibson, James Jerome (1904–1979) U.S. experimental psychologist: a highly influential researcher in the area of visual (and other sense) perception, known especially for developing the theory of ECOLOGICAL PERCEPTION; married to Eleanor J. Gibson.

Gilbreth, Lillian (1878–1972) U.S. psychologist: best known, with her husband Frank (an engineer), for developing TIME AND MOTION STUDIES.

Goddard, Henry Herbert (1866–1957) U.S. psychologist: a founder of intelligence testing in the United States; produced influential research in the fields of special education, mental retardation, and army testing.

Goldstein, Kurt (1875–1965) German neurologist: his investigations of neurological impairments resulted in an influential proposal that manifestations of brain damage (e.g., regression to concrete thinking) are often an individual's adaptive response to an impaired ability to form a whole perception of the outside world.

Goodenough, Florence (1886–1959) U.S. psychologist: developer of widely used tests of intelligence and verbal intelligence in children and adapter of the Stanford–Binet scale for use with preschoolers (called the Minnesota Preschool Scale); formulated the method now known as TIME SAMPLING.

Griffith, Coleman Roberts (1893–1960) U.S. psychologist: known as the "father of sport psychology"; established the first laboratory in the United States to investigate psychological and physiological problems associated with sports and athletic performance.

Guilford, Joy Paul (1897–1987) U.S. psychologist: best known for his contributions to psychometrics and his use of FACTOR ANALYSIS in personality and intelligence research.

Gulliksen, Harold (1903–1996) U.S. psychologist: a founder of the Psychometric Society; known for his applications of mathematical methods to PSYCHOPHYSICS, LEARNING THEORY, and attitude measurement, which contributed advancements in paired comparison scaling and MULTIDIMENSIONAL SCALING.

Guthrie, Edwin Ray (1886–1959) U.S. psychologist: best known for developing a variation in behaviorist theory termed **contiguity learning theory** and for pioneering use of teaching evaluations for college faculties.

Hall, Granville Stanley (1844–1924) U.S. psychologist: chief founder and organizer of psychology in the United States and first president of the American Psychological Association.

Harlow, Harry Frederick (1905–1981) U.S. psychologist: best known for investigations on LEARNING SETS and on mothering that disproved the idea that nonhuman animals were incapable of higher levels of information processing or METACOGNITION; also known for studying social development in rhesus monkeys.

Hathaway, Starke Rosencrans (1903–1984) U.S. psychologist: developer, in collaboration with psychiatrist John C. McKinley, of the MINNESOTA MULTIPHASIC PERSONALITY INVENTORY.

Head, Henry (1861–1940) British neurologist: remembered chiefly for his taxonomy of APHASIA and for his theory characterizing all types of aphasia as cognitive disturbances of symbolic formation and expression; coined the term "semantic aphasia."

Hebb, Donald Olding (1904–1985) Canadian psychobiologist: an important contributor to the understanding of the brain–behavior relationship; his proposal of CELL ASSEMBLIES remains influential in biological theories of memory.

Heider, Fritz (1896–1988) Austrian-born U.S. psychologist: a preeminent theorist on interpersonal relations; established the conceptual foundations for much of social psychology research (e.g., ATTRIBUTION THEORY, BALANCE THEORY).

Helmholtz, Herman von (1821–1894) German physiologist and physicist: a founder of psychosensory physiology, whose research laid the foundations of modern visual and auditory science (see YOUNG–HELMHOLTZ THEORY OF COLOR VISION).

Helson, Harold (1898–1977) U.S. psychologist: developed ADAPTATION-LEVEL theory to describe the effects of context on subjective judgment.

Hering, Evald (1834–1918) German physiologist: His sensory perception research (see HERING THEORY OF COLOR VISION) influenced the development of German psychology and the school of PHENOMENOLOGY.

Hilgard, Ernest R. (1904–2001) U.S. psychologist: an influential researcher and synthesizer in the fields of CONDITIONING, LEARNING THEORY, and HYPNOTHERAPY.

Hollingworth, Harry L. (1880–1956) U.S. psychologist: a pioneer in applied psychology and coauthor of the first textbook in that field; particularly known for his work in advertising psychology; married to Leta S. Hollingworth.

Hollingworth, Leta Stetter (1886–1939) U.S. psychologist: a major contributor in educational psychology, clinical psychology, and the psychology of women; her work in education focused on both children with mental retardation and gifted children; married to Harry L. Hollingworth.

Hooker, Evelyn (1907–1996) U.S. psychologist: performed the first major controlled study in which groups of gay and heterosexual men were compared on psychological measures of adjustment; her findings influenced the American Psychiatric Association to remove homosexuality from the *Diagnostic and Statistical Manual of Mental Disorders*.

Horney, Karen D. (1885–1952) German-born U.S. psychoanalyst: the first great psychoanalytic feminist and a member of the NEO-FREUDIAN school; stressed culture and disturbed interpersonal relationships as the causes of neuroses and emphasized the importance of current defenses and inner conflicts over early experience; recognized as one of the founders of HUMANISTIC PSYCHOLOGY.

Hovland, Carl Ivor (1912–1961) U.S. psychologist: contributor to the development of NEOBEHAVIORISM—through his research on the generalization of conditioning—and a pioneer in computer studies simulating human concept formation and thinking; studied the processes by which persuasive messages change attitudes.

Hull, Clark Leonard (1884–1952) U.S. psychologist: originator of the influential DRIVE-REDUCTION THEORY and one of the founders of NEOBEHAVIORISM.

Hunt, Joseph McVicker (1906–1991) U.S. psychologist: known for his "feeding frustration" studies on rats, demonstrating a link between early food deprivation and adult hoarding behavior, and for his A/S ratio (the ratio of association to sensory areas in the brain), highlighting the importance of INTRINSIC MOTIVATION; laid the conceptual foundations for programs (e.g., Project Head Start) emphasizing the value of early childhood education in cognitive development.

Hunter, Walter S. (1889–1954) U.S. psychologist: known especially for his studies of animal cognition, particularly the DELAYED-RESPONSE phenomenon; later contributed to the study of MAZE learning in animals.

James, William (1842–1910) U.S. psychologist and philosopher: one of the principal founders of psychology in the United States and, arguably, the most influential of the first generation of American psychologists; his promotion of FUNCTIONALISM in psychology and his pioneering contributions to the psychology of religion had enduring effects.

Janet, Pierre (1859–1947) French psychologist and neurologist: His analysis emphasizing observable behavior and the continuity of subconscious and conscious events, largely dismissed by psychoanalysts of his day, has since been seen as a forerunner in the study of traumatic stress and DISSOCIATION and a precursor of INTEGRATIVE PSYCHOTHERAPY.

Janis, Irving Lester (1918–1990) U.S. social and health psychologist: noted for introducing the concept of GROUPTHINK; researched stress and decision making, especially in the contexts of individual personal health and group dynamics.

Jastrow, Joseph (1863–1944). U.S. psychologist: early U.S. contributor in psychophysics, particularly on how subliminal factors influence psychophysical judgments; influential in introducing the new scientific psychology to the American public.

Jones, Mary Cover (1896–1987) U.S. developmental psychologist: best known for her observational study of the development of infant behavior patterns, such as smiling, eye coordination, visual pursuit, and reaching.

Jung, Carl Gustav (1875–1961) Swiss psychiatrist and psychoanalyst: originator of ANALYTIC PSYCHOLOGY, which laid emphasis on personality dynamics, such as conscious versus unconscious, introversive versus extroversive tendencies, and rational versus irrational processes; originated such theoretical constructs as ARCHETYPES, the COLLECTIVE UNCONSCIOUS, and SYNCHRONICITY.

Kelley, Harold Harding (1921–2003) U.S. social psychologist: known for his formulation of ATTRIBUTION THEORY; conducted pioneering research on communication, persuasion, the social psychology of groups, and interpersonal relations.

Kinsey, Alfred (1894–1956) U.S. zoologist and sex researcher: an influential researcher on human sexual behavior; presented the first statistical data on a large range of sexual behaviors in both sexes; his **Kinsey (Six) Scale** offered an index on a continuum from *pure homosexual* to *pure heterosexual* orientation.

Klein, Melanie (1882–1960) Austrian-born British psychoanalyst: a pioneer in child analysis and the first to use PLAY THERAPY as an analytic and treatment tool; her approach emphasized primal conflicts and the primary object relationship with the mother (see OBJECT RELATIONS THEORY).

Klineberg, Otto (1899–1992) Canadian-born U.S. social psychologist: a seminal figure through his research on race, which challenged racial superiority theories and contributed to the U.S. Supreme Court's 1954 ruling in *Brown v. Board of Education*; focused on cross-cultural studies and international affairs.

Koch, Sigmund (1917–1996) U.S. psychologist: author of a six-volume comprehensive survey outlining the parameters of psychology in the mid-20th century; promoted empirically grounded, rationally defensible investigation in a field he claimed could never become a single, coherent discipline.

Koffka, Kurt (1886–1941) German experimental psychologist: one of the founders of and chief spokesperson for GESTALT PSYCHOLOGY; contributed significantly to the study of visual perception (e.g., the study of APPARENT MOVEMENT).

Kohlberg, Lawrence (1927–1987) U.S. psychologist: originator of the groundbreaking KOHLBERG'S THEORY OF MORAL DEVELOPMENT; his use of INTERVIEW format was also influential.

Köhler, Wolfgang (1887–1967) German experimental psychologist: one of the founders of GESTALT PSYCHOLOGY; his contributions in primate learning (see INSIGHT LEARNING) and to the concept of goodness of configuration (the significance of simplicity, regularity, or symmetry in a shape or form) remain influential.

Kraepelin, Emil (1856–1926) German psychiatrist: a founding father of modern psychiatry and pioneer theorist and researcher on serious mental disease; his development of the concept of DEMENTIA PRAECOX was the forerunner of the modern concept of schizophrenia.

Krech, David (1909–1977) Belarus-born U.S. psychologist: a major contributor in physiological psychology (e.g., on the brain–behavior relationship) and social psychology (e.g., on racial prejudice, international conflict).

Ladd-Franklin, Christine (1847–1930) U.S. psychologist and mathematician: an early authority on vision and color theory.

Lashley, Karl Spencer (1890–1958) U.S. psychologist: an influential contributor in animal learning, comparative psychology, and neurophysiology; asserted that the brain could recover some disrupted functions in specific damaged areas (see EQUIPOTENTIALITY; MASS ACTION).

Lewin, Kurt (1890–1947) German-born U.S. social psychologist: developer of FIELD THEORY; particularly known for experiments on styles of LEADERSHIP, group COHESION, and GROUP DYNAMICS (a term he coined); promoted ACTION RESEARCH.

Lorenz, Konrad (1903–1989) Austrian zoologist: Nobel Prize-winning cofounder of ETHOLOGY; discovered several major concepts still useful for behavior study, including the FIXED ACTION PATTERN, the RELEASER, and IMPRINTING.

Luria, Alexander R. (1902–1977) Russian neuropsychologist: a major contributor to research on brain function and brain trauma; collaborated early in his career with Lev Vygotsky on a sociocultural theory of language.

Maslow, Abraham Harold (1908–1970) U.S. psychologist: a founder of HUMANISTIC PSYCHOLOGY and originator of MASLOW'S MOTIVATIONAL HIERARCHY.

May, Rollo (1909–1994) U.S. psychologist and psychoanalyst: a central proponent and spokesperson for HUMANISTIC PSYCHOLOGY and

EXISTENTIAL PSYCHOLOGY; emphasized the adaptive and curative qualities of positive human values, such as love, free will, and self-awareness.

McClelland, David (1917–1998) U.S. psychologist: best known for theoretical and empirical contributions to the study of personality and motivation; developed the highly popular THEMATIC APPERCEPTION TEST to assess ACHIEVEMENT MOTIVATION.

Meehl, Paul Everett (1920–2003) U.S. psychologist: a significant contributor to research in clinical psychology and clinicometrics (the use of mathematical statistics to analyze client historical data); his work on diagnosis and classification of mental disorders was revolutionary in its development of computerized scoring of psychology tests.

Michotte, Albert Edouard (1881–1965) Belgian psychologist: remembered for experimental-phenomenological studies of mechanical causality (see MECHANISTIC THEORY) that clarify commonly experienced adaptive situations.

Milgram, Stanley (1933–1984) U.S. social psychologist: best known for his BEHAVIORAL STUDY OF OBEDIENCE; pioneered the field of urban psychology, working on STIMULUS OVERLOAD and INFORMATION OVERLOAD.

Miller, Neal Elgar (1909–2002) U.S. psychologist: considered the founder of BEHAVIORAL MEDICINE; his work significantly affected the fields of learning, motivation, and clinical psychology.

Montessori, Maria (1870–1952) Italian educator: one of the first women to attend medical school in Italy; developed a psychologically based educational system called the **Montessori method.**

Mowrer, O. Hobart (1907–1982) U.S. psychologist: best known for his contributions to the fields of learning and LANGUAGE ACQUISITION, which he explained using elementary principles of conditioning.

Münsterberg, Hugo (1863–1916) German-born U.S. psychologist: a founder in the field of industrial and organizational psychology; made early contributions in the fields of educational, abnormal, and FORENSIC PSYCHOLOGY (e.g., his studies of eyewitness testimony and lie detection).

Murphy, Gardner (1895–1979) U.S. psychologist: encouraged psychological research on and the use of biofeedback; greatly influenced the field through his texts, particularly that on experimental social psychology; recognized for his guidance of U.S. psychologist Rensis Likert (1903–1981) in the development of the LIKERT SCALE.

Murray, Henry Alexander (1893–1988) U.S. psychologist: His work ushered in a new era of personality psychology in the United States; noteworthy for establishing numerous professional opportunities for women in psychology and for collaborating in the creation of the THEMATIC APPERCEPTION TEST.

Neugarten, Bernice Levin (1916–2001) U.S. developmental psychologist: known for significantly advancing the study of adult development and aging; saw later adulthood as a period of increased activity and self-enhancement and proposed the distinctions of young-old and old-old (see ADULTHOOD).

Newcomb, Theodore Mead (1903–1984) U.S. social psychologist: a major contributor in the field, emphasizing its interdisciplinary nature (e.g., the integration of behavioral concepts from psychology, anthropology, and sociology); his attitudes and value research focused on real-setting social relations and placed attitude change in the context of norms, group membership, leadership, and friendship.

Nissen, Henry Wieghorst (1901–1958) U.S. comparative psychologist: a leading expert on the biology and behavior of chimpanzees (e.g., in the acquisition of resources, emotional expression, and social interaction); viewed behavioral sequences as clusters of independent acts, each with its own motivation.

Orne, Martin Theodore (1927–2000) Austrian-born U.S. psychiatrist: originator of the concept of **trance logic**, the presumed tendency of hypnotized individuals to engage simultaneously in contradictory trains of thought; applied the notion of DEMAND CHARACTERISTICS in his hypnosis research.

Osgood, Charles Egerton (1916–1991) U.S. psychologist: a significant theorist and researcher in PSYCHOLINGUISTICS and CROSS-CULTURAL PSYCHOLOGY; developed the SEMANTIC DIFFERENTIAL model of determining word meanings.

Pavlov, Ivan Petrovich (1849–1936) Russian physiologist: best known for experimentation on the physiology of the digestive system and its control by the nervous system, which yielded the concepts of the UNCONDITIONED RESPONSE, the CONDITIONED STIMULUS, DISCRIMINATION of stimuli, and EXTINCTION of response.

Payton, Carolyn R. (1925–2001) U.S. psychologist: a powerful advocate of the mental health needs of African Americans; her highly successful Counseling Services program at Howard University was one of the few programs at any African American institution to offer accredited training for Black therapists and counselors.

Piaget, Jean (1896–1980) Swiss child psychologist and epistemologist: His theoretical and research work on the stages of cognitive development in children was enormously influential (see PIAGETIAN THEORY); a central proponent of the theoretical perspective known as CONSTRUCTIVISM.

Rhine, Joseph Banks (1895–1980) U.S. parapsychologist: coiner of the term EXTRASENSORY PERCEPTION and the first researcher to investigate a psychical topic scientifically—using ZENER CARDS (also called **Rhine cards**).

Ribot, Théodule Armand (1839–1916) French philosopher and psychologist: a founder of experimental psychology in France; proposed what is now called **Ribot's law**, the principle that the most recently acquired memories are the most vulnerable to disruption from brain damage.

Rogers, Carl (1902–1987) U.S. psychologist: originator of CLIENT-CENTERED THERAPY; created such concepts as UNCONDITIONAL POSITIVE REGARD and **uncriticalness** (a nonjudgmental attitude) on the part of the therapist as central to the psychotherapeutic endeavor.

Rorschach, Hermann (1884–1922) Swiss psychiatrist: originator of the RORSCHACH INKBLOT TEST of personality, which, although still widely used, has not demonstrated robust or consistent validity.

Sanford, Edmund Clark (1859–1924) U.S. experimental psychologist: author of the first English-language laboratory manual in experimental psychology; the first psychologist to promote the subsequently common study of MAZE learning in rats.

Schachter, Stanley (1922–1997) U.S. psychologist: an influential theorist and researcher in social and health psychology, focusing on such issues as SOCIAL PRESSURE, ATTRIBUTION THEORY, and addiction (see also SCHACHTER–SINGER THEORY).

Schneirla, Theodore Christian (1902–1968) U.S. comparative psychologist: one of the foremost 20th-century animal psychologists; elaborated the APPROACH–AVOIDANCE CONFLICT into **biphasic A–W theory**, which viewed approach and withdrawal as essential in all behavior— mainly governed by stimulus intensity yet subject to the organism's internal conditions as well as to environmental conditions.

Scott, Walter Dill (1869–1955) U.S. psychologist: a key figure in the development of applied psychology and, especially, advertising psychology and personnel selection.

Scripture, Edward Wheeler (1864–1945) U.S. psychologist and speech therapist: known for his research on localization of sound and other perceptual phenomena; studied speech and language pathology and conducted innovative speech therapy, combining psychoanalytic techniques (to address underlying emotional origins) with exercises (to correct faulty speech patterns).

Sears, Pauline Kirkpatrick (1908–1993) U.S. psychologist: known for rigorous and creative use of quantitative research methods, such as systematic TIME SAMPLING, to study socialization, family processes, and child rearing; her research focused on schoolchildren and the psychological factors affecting academic achievement and performance; married to Robert R. Sears.

Sears, Robert Richardson (1908–1989) U.S. psychologist: best known for research on the influence of parental discipline and other child-rearing practices on children's behavior, especially their levels of aggression and dependency; widely recognized for research on empirical evidence for psychoanalytic theory; married to Pauline K. Sears.

Seashore, Carl Emil (1866–1949) Swedish-born U.S. psychologist: a prolific designer and builder of research equipment, including the **Seashore audiometer** (which generated standardized stimulus tones to measure threshold sound intensity) and the **Seashore Measures of Musical Talent** (phonographically recorded tests of tonal memory, of time, rhythm, and timbre awareness, and of pitch and loudness discrimination).

Sechenov, Ivan Mikhailovich (1829–1905) Russian physiologist: He saw psychology as the physiological study of brain reflexes; described reflexes as tripartite units consisting of a sensory nerve, a central connection, and a motor nerve and proposed that they are modifiable by association from infancy.

Shakow, David (1901–1981) U.S. psychologist: best known for helping the American Psychological Association professionalize the field of clinical psychology and for helping develop the **scientist-practitioner model** for training clinical psychologists both to provide services and to conduct research on mental health problems.

Sherif, Muzafer (1906–1988) Turkish social psychologist: known particularly for his work on group norms (see SOCIAL NORM); articulated the notion that perception and behavior are determined in bipolar fashion by external and internal factors, the combined totality of which he termed FRAME OF REFERENCE; this view inspired the development of such novel theories as ADAPTATION LEVEL.

Sherrington, Charles Scott (1857–1952) British physiologist: His research on the mechanics of muscular activation revolutionized neurophysiology; introduced many basic terms and concepts in neuroscience, among them PROPRIOCEPTION, NEURON, SYNAPSE, SPATIAL SUMMATION, and TEMPORAL SUMMATION.

Simon, Herbert Alexander (1916–2001) U.S. economist, political scientist, and psychologist: generally regarded as the founder of artificial intelligence and cognitive science; one of the first to use computers to model human decision making and problem solving.

Skinner, Burrhus Frederic (1904–1990) U.S. psychologist: originator of OPERANT CONDITIONING, a form of RADICAL BEHAVIORISM; also initiated the field of **applied behavioral analysis** by extending the principles of operant conditioning to practical settings.

Spearman, Charles Edward (1863–1945) British psychologist and psychometrician: formulator of the two-factor theory of intelligence proposing an underlying GENERAL FACTOR and multiple SPECIFIC FACTORS; renowned for his mathematical work, including the development of the SPEARMAN RANK CORRELATION COEFFICIENT and of the technique of FACTOR ANALYSIS.

Spence, Kenneth Wartenbee (1907–1967) U.S. experimental psychologist: developer, with Clark L. Hull, of an influential version of NEOBEHAVIORISM—the **Hull–Spence model**—which offered a theoretical system to explain animal learning and motivation on the basis of Pavlovian conditioning.

Sperry, Roger Wolcott (1913–1994) U.S. psychologist: best known for his nerve-regeneration theory and his research into the functions of the two hemispheres of the brain using the split-brain technique (see COMMISSUROTOMY).

Stern, Louis William (1871–1938) German psychologist: best known for developing the concept of the intelligence quotient (see IQ); also a pioneer in developmental psychology, applied psychology, and DIFFERENTIAL PSYCHOLOGY.

Stone, Calvin Perry (1892–1954) U.S. psychologist: the first comparative psychologist in the United States to focus on the scientific investigation of sexual behavior; particularly studied neural and hormonal influences and discovered evidence for the importance of SUBCORTICAL brain regions.

Strong, Edward Kellogg, Jr. (1884–1963) U.S. psychologist: a founder of applied psychology—especially in the areas of personnel selection and occupational analysis—and best known as a co-creator of the **Strong Interest Inventory**, a widely used assessment of an individual's suitability for different types of work.

Stumpf, Carl (1848–1936) German experimental psychologist: best known for investigating the psychological factors involved in acoustic perception; his institute produced many famous psychologists, including Koffka, Köhler, Lewin, and Wertheimer; his pioneering research on emotions proposed a cognitively based theory in which judgments are crucial.

Sullivan, Harry Stack (1892–1949) U.S. psychiatrist: a major contributor to personality theory through his INTERPERSONAL THEORY, which eventually gave rise to INTERPERSONAL PSYCHOTHERAPY; his approach derived from Freud's psychoanalysis but emphasized social elements over biological instincts and focused on how key relationships develop and change over time.

Sumner, Francis Cecil (1895–1954) U.S. psychologist: the first African American to receive a doctorate in psychology in the United States; became head of the psychology department at Howard University and had great influence in creating programs to train Black psychologists in the era of desegregation; his own department trained more Black psychologists than all other U.S. colleges and universities at this time.

Terman, Lewis Madison (1877–1956) U.S. psychologist: responsible for the validation of the Binet scales (see STANFORD–BINET INTELLIGENCE SCALE) and for the construction of the Army intelligence tests of World War I; also known for initiating (in the 1920s) a longitudinal study of some 1,500 gifted children.

Thibaut, John W. (1917–1986) U.S. social psychologist: developer of SOCIAL EXCHANGE THEORY; proposed that the benefits derived from taking account of the broader context of behavior underlie the existence of such values as altruism, competitiveness, and fairness.

Thorndike, Edward Lee (1874–1949) U.S. psychologist: an important early contributor to the field of animal intelligence; developed the concept of TRIAL-AND-ERROR LEARNING and the theory of CONNECTIONISM.

Thurstone, Louis Leon (1887–1955) U.S. psychologist: a pioneer in psychometrics; developed and maintained the examination that was the forerunner of the SCHOLASTIC ASSESSMENT TEST; further developed the statistical technique of FACTOR ANALYSIS to tease out PRIMARY ABILITIES.

Tinbergen, Nikolaas (1907–1988) Dutch-born British behavioral biologist: Nobel Prize-winning cofounder of ETHOLOGY; advanced the practice of FIELD RESEARCH in the study of nonhuman animals.

Titchener, Edward Bradford (1867–1927) British-born U.S. psychologist: a chief exponent of STRUCTURALISM, which emphasized the use of systematic introspection in laboratory settings to uncover the elements of experience (sensations, images, and feelings).

Tolman, Edward Chace (1886–1959) U.S. psychologist: a founder of NEOBEHAVIORISM and proposer of the theory of **purposive behaviorism** postulating that behavioral acts have a goal that selects and guides the behavioral sequence; emphasized such mentalist concepts as purpose and COGNITIVE MAPS.

Troland, Leonard T. (1889–1932) U.S. scientist and psychologist: a significant contributor to visual science; the **troland** (a unit of retinal illumination) was named in his honor; his promotion of a comprehensive motivational psychology that accommodated feelings as a causal element in behavior anticipated later emphases on the cognitive–emotional factors in behavior regulation.

Tryon, Robert Choate (1901–1967) U.S. psychologist: widely known for his investigations of INDIVIDUAL DIFFERENCES in learning; his breeding of generations of rats based on performance in a standardized MAZE problem demonstrated the genetic substrate of learning ability; also developed computerized CLUSTER ANALYSIS.

Tversky, Amos (1937–1996) Israeli-born U.S. psychologist: known for his studies with Israeli-born U.S. psychologist Daniel Kahneman of similarity, judgment under uncertainty, and decision making.

Tyler, Leona Elizabeth (1906–1993) U.S. counseling psychologist: author of one of the first and seminally influential textbooks on INDIVIDUAL DIFFERENCES and of the leading textbook in the mid-20th century on counseling psychology.

Underwood, Benton J. (1915–1994) U.S. psychologist and methodologist: author of the textbook that played the leading role in defining experimental psychology throughout the mid-20th century.

Upham, Thomas Cogswell (1799–1872) U.S. mental philosopher: author of the first U.S. textbook in psychology, which appeared in 1827 and remained in use through much of the 19th century.

Vygotsky, Lev Semenovich (or **Vigotsky**; 1896–1934) Russian psychologist: known for his sociocultural theory of cognitive development emphasizing the interaction of children's natural abilities with the cultural mediators of written and oral language; held that developmental stages were partially driven by education and that education should take place in the ZONE OF PROXIMAL DEVELOPMENT.

Washburn, Margaret Floy (1871–1939) U.S. psychologist: author of the first U.S. textbook of comparative psychology; served as the second woman president of the American Psychological Association and only the second woman scientist to be elected to the National Academy of Sciences.

Watson, John Broadus (1878–1958) U.S. psychologist: an important figure in the early history of comparative psychology, best known as the founder of BEHAVIORISM; introduced PAVLOVIAN CONDITIONING in the United States.

Weber, Ernst Heinrich (1795–1878) German physiologist: a founder of psychophysics and formulator of WEBER'S LAW; also known for his work on two-point DISCRIMINATION, which led to the formulation of the concept of the DIFFERENCE THRESHOLD.

Wechsler, David (1896–1981) Romanian-born U.S. psychologist: developer of the **Wechsler–Bellevue Intelligence Scale,** which eventually was standardized as the WECHSLER ADULT INTELLIGENCE SCALE; this latter and the WECHSLER INTELLIGENCE SCALE FOR CHILDREN remain the dominant psychological tests for measuring cognitive abilities.

Wertheimer, Max (1880–1943) German-born U.S. psychologist: a founder of GESTALT PSYCHOLOGY, whose research added greatly to theories of perception (see PHI PHENOMENON); also known for his GESTALT PRINCIPLES OF ORGANIZATION.

White, Robert W. (1904–2001) U.S. psychologist: best known for his holistic approach to the study of personality; argued the case of INTRINSIC MOTIVATION at a time dominated by DRIVE-REDUCTION THEORY; also advocated the CASE STUDY method rather than the statistical method of analyzing aggregated data.

Witmer, Lightner (1867–1956) U.S. psychologist: founder of clinical psychology in the United States; also considered a primary pioneer of school psychology and a major figure in the development of special education.

Wolpe, Joseph (1915–1997) South African-born U.S. psychiatrist: father of BEHAVIOR THERAPY, best known for his development of SYSTEMATIC DESENSITIZATION.

Woodworth, Robert Sessions (1869–1962) U.S. psychologist: best known for textbooks that shaped the field of experimental psychology; also known for his research on motivation, which led to his most important conceptual contribution, S–O–R PSYCHOLOGY.

Woolley, Helen Bradford Thompson (1874–1947) U.S. psychologist: a powerful advocate of child welfare, whose studies of young employed children were instrumental in reforming child labor and compulsory education laws in the United States; among the first to study psychological likenesses and differences of the sexes.

Wundt, Wilhelm Maximilian (1832–1920) German psychologist and physiologist: the founder of experimental psychology, establishing the first official psychology laboratory in 1879; his application of introspective and psychophysical methods to such subjects as reaction time, attention, judgment, and emotions had international influence.

Yerkes, Robert Mearns (1876–1956) U.S. psychobiologist: recognized as a preeminent comparative psychologist of his time through his research in animal behavior; also instrumental in the development of Army intelligence tests during World War I.